THE

THEORY OF

COMPUTATION

THE

THEORY OF

COMPUTATION

BERNARD M. MORET

University of New Mexico

 **ADDISON-WESLEY**

Addison-Wesley is an imprint
of Addison Wesley Longman, Inc.

Reading, Massachusetts • Harlow, England • Menlo Park, California
Berkeley, California • Don Mills, Ontario • Sydney
Bonn • Amsterdam • Tokyo • Mexico City

Associate Editor: Deborah Lafferty
Production Editor: Amy Willcutt
Cover Designer: Diana Coe

Library of Congress Cataloging-in-Publication Data

Moret, B. M. E. (Bernard M. E.)
    The theory of computation / Bernard M. Moret.
        p.   cm.
    Includes bibliographical references (p.   –   ) and index.
    ISBN 0-201-25828-5
    1. Machine theory.   I. Title.
QA267.M67   1998
511.3–dc21   97-27356
                                     CIP

Access the latest information about Addison-Wesley titles from our World Wide
Web site: http://www.awl.com/cseng

Reproduced by Addison-Wesley from camera-ready copy supplied by the author.

Cover image courtesy of the National Museum of American Art,
Washington DC/Art Resource, NY

0 1 2 3 4 5 6 7 8 9 10-MA-0100999897

Theoretical computer science covers a wide range of topics, but none is as fundamental and as useful as the theory of computation. Given that computing is our field of endeavor, the most basic question that we can ask is surely "What can be achieved through computing?"

In order to answer such a question, we must begin by defining computation, a task that was started last century by mathematicians and remains very much a work in progress at this date. Most theoreticians would at least agree that computation means solving problems through the mechanical, preprogrammed execution of a series of small, unambiguous steps. From basic philosophical ideas about computing, we must progress to the definition of a model of computation, formalizing these basic ideas and providing a framework in which to reason about computation. The model must be both reasonably realistic (it cannot depart too far from what is perceived as a computer nowadays) and as universal and powerful as possible. With a reasonable model in hand, we may proceed to posing and resolving fundamental questions such as "What can and cannot be computed?" and "How efficiently can something be computed?" The first question is at the heart of the theory of computability and the second is at the heart of the theory of complexity.

In this text, I have chosen to give pride of place to the theory of complexity. My basic reason is very simple: complexity is what really defines the limits of computation. Computability establishes some absolute limits, but limits that do not take into account any resource usage are hardly limits in a practical sense. Many of today's important practical questions in computing are based on resource problems. For instance, encryption of transactions for transmission over a network can never be entirely proof against snoopers, because an encrypted transaction must be decrypted by some means and thus can always be deciphered by someone determined to do so, given sufficient resources. However, the real goal of encryption is to make it sufficiently "hard"—that is, sufficiently resource-intensive—to decipher the message that snoopers will be discouraged or that even determined spies will take too long to complete the decryption. In other words, a good encryption scheme does not make it impossible to decode the message, just very difficult—the problem is not one of computability but one of complexity. As another example, many tasks carried out by computers today involve some type of optimization: routing of planes in the sky or of packets through a network so as to get planes or packets to their destination as efficiently as possible; allocation of manufactured products to warehouses in a retail chain so as to minimize waste and further shipping; processing of raw materials into component parts (e.g., cutting cloth into patterns pieces or cracking crude oil into a range of oils and distillates) so as to minimize wastes; designing new products to minimize production costs for a given level of performance; and so forth. All of these problems are certainly computable: that is, each such problem has a well-defined optimal solution that could be found through sufficient computation (even if this computation is nothing more than an exhaustive search through all possible solutions). Yet these problems are so complex that they cannot be solved optimally within a reasonable amount of time; indeed, even deriving good approximate solutions for these problems remains resource-intensive. Thus the complexity of solving (exactly or approximately) problems is what determines the usefulness of computation in practice. It is no accident that complexity theory is the most active area of research in theoretical computer science today.

Yet this text is not just a text on the theory of complexity. I have two reasons for covering additional material: one is to provide a graduated approach to the often challenging results of complexity theory and the other is to paint a suitable backdrop for the unfolding of these results. The backdrop is mostly computability theory—clearly, there is little use in asking what is the complexity of a problem that cannot be solved at all! The graduated approach is provided by a review chapter and a chapter on finite automata. Finite automata should already be somewhat familiar to the reader; they provide an ideal testing ground for ideas and methods needed in working with complexity models. On the other hand, I have deliberately omitted theoretical topics (such as formal grammars, the Chomsky hierarchy, formal semantics, and formal specifications) that, while interesting in their own right, have limited impact on everyday computing—some because they are not concerned with resources, some because the models used are not well accepted, and grammars because their use in compilers is quite different from their theoretical expression in the Chomsky hierarchy. Finite automata and regular expressions (the lowest level of the Chomsky hierarchy) are covered here but only by way of an introduction to (and contrast with) the universal models of computation used in computability and complexity.

Of course, not all results in the theory of complexity have the same impact on computing. Like any rich body of theory, complexity theory has applied aspects and very abstract ones. I have focused on the applied aspects: for instance, I devote an entire chapter on how to prove that a problem is hard but less than a section on the entire topic of structure theory (the part of complexity theory that addresses the internal logic of the field). Abstract results found in this text are mostly in support of fundamental results that are later exploited for practical reasons.

Since theoretical computer science is often the most challenging topic studied in the course of a degree program in computing, I have avoided the dense presentation often favored by theoreticians (definitions, theorems, proofs, with as little text in between as possible). Instead, I provide intuitive as well as formal support for further derivations and present the idea behind any line of reasoning before formalizing said reasoning. I have included large numbers of examples and illustrated many abstract ideas through diagrams; the reader will also find useful synopses of methods (such as steps in an NP-completeness proof) for quick reference. Moreover, this text offers strong support through the Web for both students and instructors. Instructors will find solutions for most of the 250 problems in the text, along with many more solved problems; students will find interactive solutions for chosen problems, testing and validating their reasoning process along the way rather than delivering a complete solution at once. In addition, I will also accumulate on the Web site addenda, errata, comments from students and instructors, and pointers to useful resources, as well as feedback mechanisms—I want to hear from all users of this text suggestions on how to improve it. The URL for the Website is `http://www.cs.unm.edu/~moret/computation/`; my email address is `moret@cs.unm.edu`.

Using This Text in the Classroom

I wrote this text for well prepared seniors and for first-year graduate students. There is no specific prerequisite for this material, other than the elusive "mathematical maturity" that instructors expect of students at this level: exposure to proofs, some calculus (limits and series), and some basic discrete mathematics, much of which is briefly reviewed in Chapter 2. However, an undergraduate course in algorithm design and analysis would be very helpful, particularly in enabling the student to appreciate the other side of the complexity issues—what problems do we know that *can* be solved efficiently? Familiarity with basic concepts of graph theory is also

useful, inasmuch as a majority of the examples in the complexity sections
are graph problems. Much of what an undergraduate in computer science
absorbs as part of the culture (and jargon) of the field is also helpful: for
instance, the notion of state should be familiar to any computer scientist,
as should be the notion of membership in a language.

The size of the text alone will indicate that there is more material here
than can be comfortably covered in a one-semester course. I have mostly
used this material in such a setting, by covering certain chapters lightly and
others quickly, but I have also used it as the basis for a two-course sequence
by moving the class to the current literature early in the second semester,
with the text used in a supporting role throughout. Chapter 9, in particular,
serves as a tutorial introduction to a number of current research areas. If
this text is used for a two-course sequence, I would strongly recommend
covering all of the material not already known to the students before moving
to the current literature for further reading. If it is used in a one-semester,
first course in the theory of computation, the instructor has a number of
options, depending on preparation and personal preferences. The instructor
should keep in mind that the most challenging topic for most students
is computability theory (Chapter 5); in my experience, students find it
deceptively easy at first, then very hard as soon as arithmetization and
programming systems come into play. It has also been my experience that
finite automata, while interesting and a fair taste of things to come, are
not really sufficient preparation: most problems about finite automata are
just too simple or too easily conceptualized to prepare students for the
challenges of computability or complexity theory. With these cautions in
mind, I propose the following traversals for this text.

Seniors: A good coverage starts with Chapter 1 (one week), Chapter 2 (one
to two weeks), and the Appendix (assigned reading or up to two weeks,
depending on the level of mathematical preparation). Then move to Chapter
3 (two to three weeks—Section 3.4.3 can be skipped entirely) and Chapter 4
(one to two weeks, depending on prior acquaintance with abstract models).
Spend three weeks or less on Sections 5.1 through 5.5 (some parts can be
skipped, such as 5.1.2 and some of the harder results in 5.5). Cover Sections
6.1 and 6.2 in one to two weeks (the proofs of the hierarchy theorems can
be skipped along with the technical details preceding them) and Sections
6.3.1 and 6.3.3 in two weeks, possibly skipping the P-completeness and
PSPACE-completeness proofs. Finally spend two to three weeks on Section
7.1, a week on Section 7.3.1, and one to two weeks on Section 8.1. The
course may then conclude with a choice of material from Sections 8.3 and
8.4 and from Chapter 9.

If the students have little mathematical background, then most of the proofs can be skipped to devote more time to a few key proofs, such as reductions from the halting problem (5.5), the proof of Cook's theorem (6.3.1), and some NP-completeness proofs (7.1). In my experience, this approach is preferable to spending several weeks on finite automata (Chapter 3), because finite automata do not provide sufficient challenge. Sections 9.2, 9.4, 9.5, and 9.6 can all be covered at a non-technical level (with some help from the instructor in Sections 9.2 and 9.5) to provide motivation for further study without placing difficult demands on the students.

Beginning Graduate Students: Graduate students can be assumed to be acquainted with finite automata, regular expressions, and even Turing machines. On the other hand, their mathematical preparation may be more disparate than that of undergraduate students, so that the main difference between a course addressed to this group and one addressed to seniors is a shift in focus over the first few weeks, with less time spent on finite automata and Turing machines and more on proof techniques and preliminaries. Graduate students also take fewer courses and so can be expected to move at a faster pace or to do more problems.

In my graduate class I typically expect students to turn in 20 to 30 complete proofs of various types (reductions for the most part, but also some less stereotyped proofs, such as translational arguments). I spend one lecture on Chapter 1, three lectures reviewing the material in Chapter 2, assign the Appendix as reading material, then cover Chapter 3 quickly, moving through Sections 3.1, 3.2, and 3.3 in a couple of lectures, but slowing down for Kleene's construction of regular expressions from finite automata. I assign a number of problems on the regularity of languages, to be solved through applications of the pumping lemma, of closure properties, or through sheer ingenuity! Section 4.1 is a review of models, but the translations are worth covering in some detail to set the stage for later arguments about complexity classes. I then spend three to four weeks on Chapter 5, focusing on Section 5.5 (recursive and r.e. sets) with a large number of exercises. The second half of the semester is devoted to complexity theory, with a thorough coverage of Chapter 6, and Sections 7.1, 7.3, 8.1, 8.2, and 8.4. Depending on progress at that time, I may cover some parts of Section 8.3 or return to 7.2 and couple it with 9.4 to give an overview of parallel complexity theory. In the last few lectures, I give highlights from Chapter 9, typically from Sections 9.5 and 9.6.

Second-Year Graduate Students: A course on the theory of computation given later in a graduate program typically has stronger prerequisites than one given in the first year of studies. The course may in fact be on complexity theory alone, in which case Chapters 4 (which may just be a review), 6, 7, 8, and 9 should be covered thoroughly, with some material from Chapter 5 used as needed. With well-prepared students, the instructor needs only ten weeks for this material and should then supplement the text with a selection of current articles.

Exercises

This text has over 250 exercises. Most are collected into exercise sections at the end of each chapter, wherein they are ordered roughly according to the order of presentation of the relevant material within the chapter. Some are part of the main text of the chapters themselves; these exercises are an integral part of the presentation of the material, but often cover details that would unduly clutter the presentation.

I have attempted to classify the exercises into three categories, flagged by the number of asterisks carried by the exercise number (zero, one or two). *Simple exercises* bear no asterisk; they should be within the reach of any student and, while some may take a fair amount of time to complete, none should require more than 10 to 15 minutes of critical thought. Exercises within the main body of the chapters are invariably simple exercises. *Advanced exercises* bear one asterisk; some may require additional background, others special skills, but most simply require more creativity than the simple exercises. It would be unreasonable to expect a student to solve every such exercise; when I assign starred exercises, I usually give the students a choice of several from which to pick. A student does well in the class who can reliably solve two out of three of these exercises. The rare *challenge problems* bear two asterisks; most of these were the subject of recent research articles. Accordingly, I have included them more for the results they state than as reasonable assignments; in a few cases, I have turned what would have been a challenge problem into an advanced exercise by giving a series of detailed hints.

I have deliberately refrained from including really easy exercises—what are often termed "finger exercises." The reason is that such exercises have to be assigned in large numbers by the instructor, who can generate new ones in little more time than it would take to read them in the text. A sampling of such exercises can be found on the Web site.

I would remind the reader that solutions to almost all of the exercises can be found on the Web site; in addition, the Web site stores many additional exercises, in particular a large number of NP-complete problems with simple completeness proofs. Some of the exercises are given extremely detailed solutions and thus may serve as first examples of certain techniques (particularly NP-completeness reductions); others are given incremental solutions, so that the student may use them as tutors in developing proofs.

Acknowledgments

As I acknowledge the many people who have helped me in writing this text, two individuals deserve a special mention. In 1988, my colleague and friend Henry Shapiro and I started work on a text on the design and analysis of algorithms, a text that was to include some material on NP-completeness. I took the notes and various handouts that I had developed in teaching computability and complexity classes and wrote a draft, which we then proceeded to rewrite many times. Eventually, we did not include this material in our text (*Algorithms from P to NP, Volume I* at Benjamin-Cummings, 1991); instead, with Henry Shapiro's gracious consent, this material became the core of Sections 6.3.1 and 7.1 and the nucleus around which this text grew. Carol Fryer, my wife, not only put up with my long work hours but somehow found time in her even busier schedule as a psychiatrist to proofread most of this text. The text is much the better for it, not just in terms of readability, but also in terms of correctness: in spite of her minimal acquaintance with these topics, she uncovered some technical errors.

The faculty of the Department of Computer Science at the University of New Mexico, and, in particular, the department chairman, James Hollan, have been very supportive. The department has allowed me to teach a constantly-changing complexity class year after year for over 15 years, as well as advanced seminars in complexity and computability theory, thereby enabling me to refine my vision of the theory of computation and of its role within theoretical computer science.

The wonderful staff at Addison-Wesley proved a delight to work with: Lynne Doran Cote, the Editor-in-Chief, who signed me on after a short conversation and a couple of email exchanges (authors are always encouraged by having such confidence placed in them!); Deborah Lafferty, the Associate Editor, with whom I worked very closely in defining the scope and level of the text and through the review process; and Amy Willcutt, the Production Editor, who handled with complete cheerfulness the hundreds of questions that I sent her way all through the last nine months of work. These must be three of the most efficient and pleasant professionals with whom I have had a chance to work: my heartfelt thanks go to all three. Paul C. Anagnostopoulos, the Technical Advisor, took my initial rough design and turned it into what you see, in the process commiserating with me on the limitations of typesetting tools and helping me to work around each such limitation in turn.

The reviewers, in addition to making very encouraging comments that helped sustain me through the process of completing, editing, and typesetting the text, had many helpful suggestions, several of which resulted in entirely new sections in the text. At least two of the reviewers gave me extremely detailed reviews, closer to what I would expect of referees on a 10-page journal submission than reviewers on a 400-page text. My thanks to all of them: Carl Eckberg (San Diego State University), James Foster (University of Idaho), Desh Ranjan (New Mexico State University), Roy Rubinstein, William A. Ward, Jr. (University of South Alabama), and Jie Wang (University of North Carolina, Greensboro).

Last but not least, the several hundred students who have taken my courses in the area have helped me immensely. An instructor learns more from his students than from any other source. Those students who took to theory like ducks to water challenged me to keep them interested by devising new problems and by introducing ever newer material. Those who suffered through the course challenged me to present the material in the most accessible manner, particularly to distill from each topic its guiding principles and main results. Through the years, every student contributed stimulating work: elegant proofs, streamlined reductions, curious gadgets, new problems, as well as enlightening errors. (I have placed a few flawed proofs as exercises in this text, but look for more on the Web site.)

Since I typeset the entire text myself, any errors that remain (typesetting or technical) are entirely my responsibility. The text was typeset in Sabon at 10.5 pt, using the MathTime package for mathematics and Adobe's Mathematical Pi fonts for script and other symbols. I used LaTeX2e, wrote a lot of custom macros, and formatted everything on my laptop under Linux, using gv to check the results. In addition to saving a lot of paper, using a laptop certainly eased my task: typesetting this text was a very comfortable experience compared to doing the same for the text that Henry Shapiro and I published in 1991. I even occasionally found time to go climbing and skiing!

Bernard M.E. Moret
Albuquerque, New Mexico

NOTATION

S, T, U	sets
E	the set of edges of a graph
V	the set of vertices of a graph
$G = (V, E)$	a graph
K_n	the complete graph on n vertices
K	the diagonal (halting) set
Q	the set of states of an automaton
q, q_i	states of an automaton
M	an automaton or Turing machine
$\mathbb{N}$	the set of natural numbers
$\mathbb{Z}$	the set of integer numbers
$\mathbb{Q}$	the set of rational numbers
$\mathbb{R}$	the set of real numbers
$|S|$	the cardinality of set S
$\aleph_0$	aleph nought, the cardinality of countably infinite sets
$O(\ )$	"big Oh," the asymptotic upper bound
$o(\ )$	"little Oh," the asymptotic unreachable upper bound
$\Omega(\ )$	"big Omega," the asymptotic lower bound
$\omega(\ )$	"little Omega," the asymptotic unreachable lower bound
$\Theta(\ )$	"big Theta," the asymptotic characterization
f, g, h	functions (total)
$p(\ )$	a polynomial
δ	the transition function of an automaton
$\mu(x)$	a probability distribution
χ_S	the characteristic function of set S
$A(\ )$	Ackermann's function (also F in Chapter 5)
$s(k, i)$	an s-1-1 function
$K(x)$	the descriptional complexity of string x
$IC(x|\Pi)$	the instance complexity of x with respect to problem Π
ϕ, ψ	functions (partial or total)
ϕ_i	the ith partial recursive function in a programming system
$dom\phi$	the domain of the partial function ϕ
$ran\phi$	the range of the partial function ϕ

$\phi(x)\uparrow$	$\phi(x)$ converges (is defined)
$\phi(x)\downarrow$	$\phi(x)$ diverges (is not defined)
$-$	subtraction, but also set difference
$+$	addition, but also union of regular expressions
S^*	"S star," the Kleene closure of set S
S^+	"S plus," S^* without the empty string
Σ	the reference alphabet
a, b, c	characters in an alphabet
Σ^*	the set of all strings over the alphabet Σ
w, x, y	strings in a language
ε	the empty string
$|x|$	the length of string x
$\cup$	set union
$\cap$	set intersection
$\vee$	logical OR
$\wedge$	logical AND
$\overline{x}$	the logical complement of x
Zero	the zero function, a basic primitive recursive function
Succ	the successor function, a basic primitive recursive function
P_i^k	the choice function, a basic primitive recursive function
$x \# y$	the "guard" function, a primitive recursive function
$x \mid y$	"x is a factor of y," a primitive recursive predicate
$\mu x[\ ]$	μ-recursion (minimization), a partial recursive scheme
$\langle x, y \rangle$	the pairing of x and y
$\Pi_1(z), \Pi_2(z)$	the projection functions that reverse pairing
$\langle x_1, \ldots, x_k \rangle_k$	the general pairing of the k elements $x_1, \ldots, x_k$
$\Pi_i^k(z)$	the general projection functions that reverse pairing
$\mathscr{C}, \mathscr{D}$	generic classes of programs or problems
Π_i^p	a co-nondeterministic class in the polynomial hierarchy
Σ_i^p	a nondeterministic class in the polynomial hierarchy
Δ_i^p	a deterministic class in the polynomial hierarchy
#P	"sharp P" or "number P," a complexity class
$\leqslant_T$	a Turing reduction
$\leqslant_m$	a many-one reduction
$\mathscr{A}$	an algorithm
$R_{\mathscr{A}}$	the approximation ratio guaranteed by $\mathscr{A}$

COMPLEXITY CLASSES

CONTENTS

CHAPTER 1

Introduction

1.1   Motivation and Overview

Why do we study the theory of computation? Apart from the interest in studying any rich mathematical theory (something that has sustained research in mathematics over centuries), we study computation to learn more about the fundamental principles that underlie practical applications of computing. To a large extent, the theory of computation is about bounds. The types of questions that we have so far been most successful at answering are: "What cannot be computed at all (that is, what cannot be solved with *any* computing tool)?" and "What cannot be computed efficiently?" While these questions and their answers are mostly negative, they contribute in a practical sense by preventing us from seeking unattainable goals. Moreover, in the process of deriving these negative results, we also obtain better characterizations of what *can* be solved and even, sometimes, better methods of solution.

For example, every student and professional has longed for a compiler that would not just detect syntax errors, but would also perform some "simple" checks on the code, such as detecting the presence of infinite loops. Yet no such tool exists to date; in fact, as we shall see, theory tells us that no such tool can exist: whether or not a program halts under all inputs is an unsolvable problem. Another tool that faculty and professionals would dearly love to use would check whether or not two programs compute the same function—it would make grading programs much easier and would allow professionals to deal efficiently with the growing problem of "old" code. Again, no such tool exists and, again, theory tells us that deciding whether or not two programs compute the same function is an unsolvable problem. As a third example, consider the problem of determining the

1

shortest C program that will do a certain task—not that we recommend conciseness in programs as a goal, since ultimate conciseness often equates with ultimate obfuscation! Since we cannot determine whether or not two programs compute the same function, we would expect that we cannot determine the shortest program that computes a given function; after all, we would need to verify that the alleged shortest program does compute the desired function. While this intuition does not constitute a proof, theory does indeed tell us that determining the shortest program to compute a given function is an unsolvable problem.

All of us have worked at some point at designing some computing tool—be it a data structure, an algorithm, a user interface, or an interrupt handler. When we have completed the design and perhaps implemented it, how can we assess the quality of our work? From a commercial point of view, we may want to measure it in profits from sales; from a historical point of view, we may judge it in 10 or 20 or 100 years by the impact it may have had in the world. We can devise other measures of quality, but few are such that they can be applied immediately after completion of the design, or even during the design process. Yet such a measure would give us extremely useful feedback and most likely enable us to improve the design. If we are designing an algorithm or data structure, we can analyze its performance; if it is an interrupt handler, we can measure its running time and overhead; if it is a user interface, we can verify its robustness and flexibility and conduct some simple experiments with a few colleagues to check its "friendliness." Yet none of these measures tells us if the design is excellent, good, merely adequate, or even poor, because all lack some basis for comparison.

For instance, assume you are tasked to design a sorting algorithm and, because you have never opened an algorithms text and are, in fact, unaware of the existence of such a field, you come up with a type of bubble sort. You can verify experimentally that your algorithm works on all data sets you test it on and that its running time appears bounded by some quadratic function of the size of the array to be sorted; you may even be able to prove formally both correctness and running time, by which time you might feel quite proud of your achievement. Yet someone more familiar with sorting than you would immediately tell you that you have, in fact, come up with a very poor sorting algorithm, because there exist equally simple algorithms that will run very much faster than yours. At this point, though, you could attempt to reverse the attack and ask the knowledgeable person if such faster algorithms are themselves good? Granted that they are better than yours, might they still not be pretty poor? And, in any case, how do you verify that they are better than your algorithm? After all, they may run faster on one platform, but slower on another; faster for certain data, but slower for others; faster for certain amounts of data, but slower for others; and so forth. Even judging relative merit is difficult and may require the establishment of some common measuring system.

We want to distinguish relative measures of quality (you have or have not improved what was already known) and absolute measures of quality (your design is simply good; in particular, there is no longer any need to look for major improvements, because none is possible). The theory of computation attempts to establish the latter—*absolute* measures. Questions such as "What can be computed?" and "What can be computed efficiently?" and "What can be computed simply?" are all absolute questions. To return to our sorting example, the question you might have asked the knowledgeable person can be answered through a fundamental result: a lower bound on the number of comparisons needed in the worst case to sort n items by any comparison-based sorting method (the famous $n \log n$ lower bound for comparison-based sorting). Since the equally simple—but very much more efficient—methods mentioned (which include mergesort and quicksort) run in asymptotic $n \log n$ time, they are as good as any comparison-based sorting method can ever be and thus can be said without further argument to be *good*. Such lower bounds are fairly rare and typically difficult to derive, yet very useful. In this text, we derive more fundamental lower bounds: we develop tools to show that certain problems cannot be solved at all and to show that other problems, while solvable, cannot be solved efficiently.

Whether we want relative or absolute measures of quality, we shall need some type of common assumptions about the environment. We may need to know about data distributions, about sizes of data sets, and such. Most of all, however, we need to know about the platform that will support the computing activities, since it would appear that the choice of platform strongly affects the performance (the running time on a 70s vintage, 16-bit minicomputer will definitely be different from that on a state-of-the-art workstation) and perhaps the outcome (because of arithmetic precision, for instance). Yet, if each platform is different, how can we derive measures of quality? We may not want to compare code designed for a massively parallel supercomputer and for a single-processor home computer, but we surely would want some universality in any measure. Thus are we led to a major concern of the theory of computation: what is a *useful* model of computation? By useful we mean that any realistic computation is supported in the model, that results derived in the model apply to actual platforms, and that, in fact, results derived in the model apply to as large a range of platforms as possible. Yet even this ambitious agenda is not quite enough: platforms will change very rapidly, yet the model should not;

indeed, the model should still apply to future platforms, no matter how sophisticated. So we need to devise a model that is as universal as possible, not just with respect to existing computation platforms, but with respect to an abstract notion of computation that will apply to future platforms as well.

Thus we can identify two major tasks for a useful "theory of computation":

- to devise a universal model of computation that is credible in terms of both current platforms and philosophical ideas about the nature of computation; and
- to use such models to characterize problems by determining if a problem is solvable, efficiently solvable, simply solvable, and so on.

As we shall see, scientists and engineers pretty much agree on a universal model of computation, but agreement is harder to obtain on how close such a model is to actual platforms and on how much importance to attach to theoretical results about bounds on the quality of possible solutions.

In order to develop a universal model and to figure out how to work with it, it pays to start with less ambitious models. After all, by their very nature, universal models must have many complex characteristics and may prove too big a bite to chew at first. So, we shall proceed in three steps in this text:

1. We shall present a very *restricted model of computation* and work with it to the point of deriving a number of powerful characterizations and tools. The point of this part is twofold: to hone useful skills (logical, analytical, deductive, etc.) and to obtain a model useful for certain limited tasks.

   We shall look at the model known as a finite automaton. Because a finite automaton (as its name indicates) has only a fixed-size, finite memory, it is very limited in what it can do—for instance, it cannot even count! This simplicity, however, enables us to derive powerful characterizations and to get a taste of what could be done with a model.

2. We shall develop a *universal model of computation*. We shall need to justify the claims that it can compute anything computable and that it remains close enough to modern computing platforms so as not to distort the theory built around it.

   We shall present the Turing machine for such a model. However, Turing machines are not really anywhere close to a modern computer, so we shall also look at a much closer model, the register-addressed machine (RAM). We shall prove that Turing machines and RAMs have equivalent modeling power, in terms of both ultimate capabilities and efficiency.

3. We shall use the tool (Turing machines) to develop a *theory of computability* (what can be solved by a machine if we disregard any resource bounds) and *a theory of complexity* (what can be solved by a machine in the presence of resource bounds, typically, as in the analysis of algorithms, time or space).

We shall see that, unfortunately, most problems of any interest are provably unsolvable and that, of the few solvable problems, most are provably intractable (that is, they cannot be solved efficiently). In the process, however, we shall learn a great deal about the nature of computational problems and, in particular, about relationships among computational problems.

1.2   History

Questions about the nature of computing first arose in the context of pure mathematics. Most of us may not realize that mathematical rigor and formal notation are recent developments in mathematics. It is only in the late nineteenth century that mathematicians started to insist on a uniform standard of rigor in mathematical arguments and a corresponding standard of clarity and formalism in mathematical exposition. The German mathematician Gottlob Frege (1848–1925) was instrumental in developing a precise system of notation to formalize mathematical proofs, but his work quickly led to the conclusion that the mathematical system of the times contained a contradiction, apparently making the entire enterprise worthless. Since mathematicians were convinced in those days that any theorem (that is, any true assertion in a mathematical system) could be proved if one was ingenious and persevering enough, they began to study the formalisms themselves—they began to ask questions such as "What is a proof?" or "What is a mathematical system?" The great German mathematician David Hilbert (1862–1943) was the prime mover behind these studies; he insisted that each proof be written in an explicit and unambiguous notation and that it be checkable in a finite series of elementary, mechanical steps; in today's language we would say that Hilbert wanted all proofs to be checkable by an algorithm. Hilbert and most mathematicians of that period took it for granted that such a proof-checking algorithm existed.

Much of the problem resided in the notion of completed infinities—objects that, if they really exist, are truly infinite, such as the set of all natural numbers or the set of all points on a segment—and how to treat them. The French Augustin Cauchy (1789–1857) and the German Karl Weierstrass (1815–1897) had shown how to handle the problem of infinitely small values in calculus by formalizing limits and continuity through the notorious δ and ϵ, thereby reducing reasoning about infinitesimal values to reasoning about the finite values δ and ϵ. The German mathematician Georg Cantor (1845–1918) showed in 1873 that one could discern different "grades" of infinity. He went on to build an elegant mathematical theory about infinities (the transfinite numbers) in the 1890s, but any formal basis for reasoning about such infinities seemed to lead to paradoxes. As late as 1925, Hilbert, in an address to the Westphalian Mathematical Society in honor of Weierstrass, discussed the problems associated with the treatment of the infinite and wrote ". . . deductive methods based on the infinite [must] be replaced by finite procedures that yield exactly the same results." He famously pledged that "no one shall drive us out of the paradise that Cantor has created for us" and restated his commitment to "establish throughout mathematics the same certitude for our deductions as exists in elementary number theory, which no one doubts and where contradictions and paradoxes arise only through our own carelessness." In order to do this, he stated that the first step would be to show that the arithmetic of natural numbers, a modest subset of mathematics, could be placed on such a firm, unambiguous, consistent basis.

In 1931, the Austrian-American logician Kurt Gödel (1906–1978) put an end to Hilbert's hopes by proving the incompleteness theorem: any formal theory at least as rich as integer arithmetic is incomplete (there are statements in the theory that cannot be proved either true or false) or inconsistent (the theory contains contradictions). The second condition is intolerable, since anything can be proved from a contradiction; the first condition is at least very disappointing—in the 1925 address we just mentioned, Hilbert had said "If mathematical thinking is defective, where are we to find truth and certitude?" In spite of the fact that Hilbert's program as he first enounced it in 1900 had already been questioned, Gödel's result was so sweeping that many mathematicians found it very hard to accept (indeed, a few mathematicians are still trying to find flaws in his reasoning). However, his result proved to be just the forerunner of a host of similarly negative results about the nature of computation and problem solving.

The 1930s and 1940s saw a blossoming of work on the nature of computation, including the development of several utterly different and unrelated models, each purported to be universal. No fewer than four important models were proposed in 1936:

- Gödel and the American mathematician Stephen Kleene (1909–1994) proposed what has since become the standard tool for studying computability, the theory of *partial recursive functions*, based on an inductive mechanism for the definition of functions.
- The same two authors, along with the French logician Jacques Herbrand (1908–1931) proposed general recursive functions, defined through an equational mechanism. In his Ph.D. thesis, Herbrand proved a number of results about quantification in logic, results that validate the equational approach to the definition of computable functions.
- The American logician Alonzo Church (1903–1995) proposed his *lambda calculus*, based on a particularly constrained type of inductive definitions. Lambda calculus later became the inspiration for the programming language Lisp.
- The British mathematician Alan Turing (1912–1954) proposed his *Turing machine*, based on a mechanistic model of problem solving by mathematicians; Turing machines have since become the standard tool for studying complexity.

A few years later, in 1943, the Polish-American logician Emil Post (1897–1954) proposed his *Post systems*, based on deductive mechanisms; he had already worked on the same lines in the 1920s, but had not published his work at that time. In 1954, the Russian logician A.A. Markov published his *Theory of Algorithms*, in which he proposed a model very similar to today's formal grammars. (Most of the pioneering papers are reprinted in *The Undecidable*, edited by M. Davis, and are well worth the reading: the clarity of the authors' thoughts and writing is admirable, as is their foresight in terms of computation.) Finally, in 1963, the American computer scientists Shepherdson and Sturgis proposed a model explicitly intended to reflect the structure of modern computers, the *universal register machines*; nowadays, many variants of that model have been devised and go by the generic name of *register-addressable machines*—or sometimes *random access machines*—or RAMs.

The remarkable result about these varied models is that all of them define exactly the same class of computable functions: whatever one model can compute, all of the others can too! This equivalence among the models (which we shall examine in some detail in Chapter 4) justifies the claim that all of these models are indeed *universal models of computation* (or problem solving). This claim has become known as the *Church-Turing thesis*. Even as Church enounced it in 1936, this thesis (Church called it a definition, and Kleene a working hypothesis, but Post viewed it as a natural law) was controversial: much depended on whether it was viewed as a statement about *human* problem-solving or about mathematics in general. As we shall see, Turing's model (and, independently, Church's and Post's models as well) was explicitly aimed at capturing the essence of human problem-solving. Nowadays, the Church-Turing thesis is widely accepted among computer scientists.[1] Building on the work done in the 1930s, researchers in computability theory have been able to characterize quite precisely what is computable. The answer, alas, is devastating: as we shall shortly see, *most* functions are not computable.

As actual computers became available in the 1950s, researchers turned their attention from computability to complexity: assuming that a problem was indeed solvable, how efficiently could it be solved? Work with ballistics and encryption done during World War II had made it very clear that computability alone was insufficient: to be of any use, the solution had to be computed within a reasonable amount of time. Computing pioneers at the time included Turing in Great Britain and John von Neumann (1903–1957) in the United States; the latter defined a general model of computing (von Neumann machines) that, to this day, characterizes all computers ever produced.[2] A von Neumann machine consists of a computing unit (the CPU), a memory unit, and a communication channel between the two (a bus, for instance, but also a network connection).

In the 1960s, Juris Hartmanis, Richard Stearns, and others began to define and characterize classes of problems defined through the resources used in solving them; they proved the hierarchy theorems (see Section 6.2.1) that established the existence of problems of increasing difficulty. In 1965 Alan Cobham and Jack Edmonds independently observed that a number of problems were apparently hard to solve, yet had solutions that were clearly easy to verify. Although they did not define it as such, their work prefaced the introduction of the class NP. (Indeed, the class NP was defined much earlier by Gödel in a letter to von Neumann!) In 1971, Stephen Cook (and, at the same time, Leonid Levin in the Soviet Union) proved the existence of NP-complete problems, thereby formalizing the insights of Cobham and Edmonds. A year later, Richard Karp showed the importance of this concept by proving that over 20 common optimization problems (that had resisted

---

[1]Somewhat ironically, however, several prominent mathematicians and physicists have called into question its applicability to humans, while accepting its application to machines.

[2]Parallel machines, tree machines, and data flow machines may appear to diverge from the von Neumann model, but are built from CPUs, memory units, and busses; in that sense, they still follow the von Neumann model closely.

all attempts at efficient solutions—some for more than 20 years) are NP-complete and thus all equivalent in difficulty. Since then, a rich theory of complexity has evolved and again its main finding is pessimistic: most solvable problems are *intractable*—that is, they cannot be solved efficiently.

In recent years, theoreticians have turned to related fields of enquiry, including cryptography, randomized computing, alternate (and perhaps more efficient) models of computation (parallel computing, quantum computing, DNA computing), approximation, and, in a return to sources, proof theory. The last is most interesting in that it signals a clear shift in what is regarded to be a proof. In Hilbert's day, a proof was considered absolute (mathematical truth), whereas all recent results have been based on a model where proofs are provided by one individual or process and checked by another—that is, a proof is a communication tool designed to convince someone else of the correctness of a statement. This new view fits in better with the experience of most scientists and mathematicians, reflects Gödel's results, and has enabled researchers to derive extremely impressive results. The most celebrated of these shows that a large class of "concise" (i.e., polynomially long) proofs, when suitably encoded, can be checked with high probability of success with the help of a few random bits by reading only a fixed number (currently, a bound of 11 can be shown) of characters selected at random from the text of the proof. Most of the proof remains unread, yet the verifier can assert with high probability that the proof is correct! It is hard to say whether Hilbert would have loved or hated this result.

CHAPTER 2

Preliminaries

2.1 Numbers and Their Representation

The set of numbers most commonly used in computer science is the set of natural numbers, denoted $\mathbb{N}$. This set will sometimes be taken to include 0, while at other times it will be viewed as starting with the number 1; the context will make clear which definition is used. Other useful sets are $\mathbb{Z}$, the set of all integers (positive and negative); $\mathbb{Q}$, the set of rational numbers; and $\mathbb{R}$, the set of real numbers. The last is used only in an idealistic sense: irrational numbers cannot be specified as a parameter, since their description in almost any encoding would take an infinite number of bits.

Indeed, we must remember that the native instruction set of real computers can represent and manipulate only a finite set of numbers; in order to manipulate an arbitrary range of numbers, we must resort to representations that use an unbounded number of basic units and thus become quite expensive for large ranges. The basic, finite set can be defined in any number of ways: we can choose to consider certain elements to have certain values, including irrational or complex values. However, in order to perform arithmetic efficiently, we are more or less forced to adopt some simple number representation and to limit ourselves to a finite subset of the integers and another finite subset of the rationals (the so-called floating-point numbers).

Number representation depends on the choice of base, along with some secondary considerations. The choice of base is important for a real architecture (binary is easy to implement in hardware, as quinary would probably not be, for instance), but, from a theoretical standpoint, the only critical issue is whether the base is 1 or larger.

In base 1 (in unary, that is), the value n requires n digits—basically, unary notation simply represents each object to be counted by a mark (a digit) with no other abstraction. In contrast, the value n expressed in binary requires only $\lfloor \log_2 n \rfloor + 1$ digits; in quinary, $\lfloor \log_5 n \rfloor + 1$ digits; and so on. Since we have $\log_a n = \log_a b \cdot \log_b n$, using a different base only contributes a constant factor of $\log_a b$ (unless, of course, either a or b is 1, in which case this factor is either 0 or infinity). Thus number representations in bases larger than 1 are all closely related (within a constant factor in length) and are all exponentially more concise than representation in base 1. Unless otherwise specified, we shall assume throughout that numbers are represented in some base larger than 1; typically, computer scientists use base 2. We shall use $\log n$ to denote the logarithm of n in some arbitrary (and unspecified) base larger than one; when specifically using natural logarithms, we shall use $\ln n$.

2.2   Problems, Instances, and Solutions

Since much of this text is concerned with problems and their solutions, it behooves us to examine in some detail what is meant by these terms. A *problem* is defined by a finite set of (finite) parameters and a question; the question typically includes a fair amount of contextual information, so as to avoid defining everything *de novo*. The parameters, once instantiated, define an *instance* of the problem.

A simple example is the problem of deciding membership in a set S_0: the single parameter is the unknown element x, while the question asks if the input element belongs to S_0, where S_0 is defined through some suitable mechanism. This problem ("membership in S_0") is entirely different from the problem of membership of x in S, where *both* x and S are parameters. The former ("membership in S_0") is a special case of the latter, formed from the latter by *fixing* the parameter S to the specific set S_0; we call such special cases *restrictions* of the more general problem. We would expect that the more general problem is at least as hard as, and more likely much harder than, its restriction. After all, an algorithm to decide membership for the latter problem automatically decides membership for the former problem as well, whereas the reverse need not be true.

We consider a few more elaborate examples. The first is one of the most studied problems in computer science and remains a useful model for a host of applications, even though its original motivation and gender specificity have long been obsolete: the *Traveling Salesman Problem (TSP)* asks us to find the least expensive way to visit each city in a given set exactly once and return to the starting point. Since each possible tour corresponds to a distinct permutation of the indices of the cities, we can define this problem formally as follows:

> *Instance*: a number $n > 1$ of cities and a distance matrix (or cost function), (d_{ij}), where d_{ij} is the cost of traveling from city i to city j.
>
> *Question*: what is the permutation π of the index set $\{1, 2, \ldots, n\}$ that minimizes the cost of the tour, $\sum_{i=1}^{n-1} d_{\pi(i)\pi(i+1)} + d_{\pi(n)\pi(1)}$?

A sample instance of the problem for 9 eastern cities is illustrated in Figure 2.1; the optimal tour for this instance has a length of 1790 miles and moves from Washington to Baltimore, Philadelphia, New York, Buffalo, Detroit, Cincinnati, Cleveland, and Pittsburgh, before returning to its starting point.

The second problem is known as *Subset Sum* and generalizes the problem of making change:

> *Instance*: a set S of items, each associated with a natural number (its value) $v: S \to \mathbb{N}$, and a target value $B \in \mathbb{N}$.
>
> *Question*: does there exist a subset $S' \subseteq S$ of items such that the sum of the values of the items in the subset exactly equals the target value, i.e., obeying $\sum_{x \in S'} v(x) = B$?

We can think of this problem as asking whether or not, given the collection S of coins in our pocket, we can make change for the amount B.

Perhaps surprisingly, the following is also a well-defined (and extremely famous) problem:

> *Question*: is it the case that, for any natural number $k \geqslant 3$, there cannot exist a triple of natural numbers (a, b, c) obeying $a^k + b^k = c^k$?

This problem has no parameters whatsoever and thus has a single instance; you will have recognized it as Fermat's conjecture, finally proved correct nearly 350 years after the French mathematician Pierre de Fermat (1601–1665) posed it.

While two of the last three problems ask for yes/no answers, there is a fundamental difference between the two: Fermat's conjecture requires only one answer because it has only one instance, whereas *Subset Sum*, like *Traveling Salesman*, requires an answer that will vary from instance to instance. Thus we can speak of the *answer* to a particular instance, but we must distinguish that from a *solution* to the entire problem, except in the cases (rare in computer science, but common in mathematics) where the

Baltimore	0	345	514	355	522	189	97	230	39
Buffalo	345	0	430	186	252	445	365	217	384
Cincinnati	514	430	0	244	265	670	589	284	492
Cleveland	355	186	244	0	167	507	430	125	356
Detroit	522	252	265	167	0	674	597	292	523
New York	189	445	670	507	674	0	92	386	228
Philadelphia	97	365	589	430	597	92	0	305	136
Pittsburgh	230	217	284	125	292	386	305	0	231
Washington	39	384	492	356	523	228	136	231	0

(a) the distance matrix

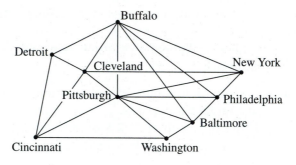

(b) the graph, showing only direct connections

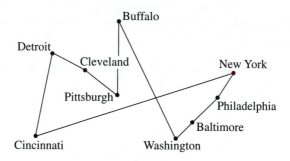

(c) a sample tour of 2056 miles

Figure 2.1   An instance of the symmetric traveling salesman problem with triangle inequality.

problem is made of a single instance. Clearly, knowing that the answer to the instance of *Subset Sum* composed of three quarters, one dime, three nickels, and four pennies and asking to make change for 66 cents is "yes" does not entitle us to conclude that we have solved the problem of *Subset Sum*. Knowing a few more such answers will not really improve the situation: the trouble arises from the fact that *Subset Sum* has an infinite number of instances! In such a case, a solution cannot be anything as simple as a list of answers, since such a list could never be completed nor stored; instead, the solution must be an *algorithm*, which, when given any instance, prints the corresponding answer.

This discussion leads us to an alternate, if somewhat informal, view of a problem: a problem is a (possibly infinite) list of pairs, where the first member is an instance and the second the answer for that instance. A solution is then an algorithm that, when given the first member of a pair, prints the second. This informal view makes it clear that any problem with a finite number of instances has a simple solution: search the list of pairs until the given instance is found and print the matching answer. We may not have the table handy and so may not be able to run the algorithm, but we do know that such an algorithm exists; in that sense, the problem is known to be solvable efficiently. For a problem with a single instance such as Fermat's conjecture the algorithm is trivial: it is a one-line program that prints the answer. In the case of Fermat's conjecture, until the mid-1990s, the solution could have been the program "`print yes`" or the program "`print no`," but we now know that it is the former. From the point of view of computer science, only problems with an infinite (in practice, a very large) number of instances are of interest, since all others can be solved very efficiently by prior tabulation of the instance/answer pairs and by writing a trivial program to search the table.

The answer to an instance of a problem can be a single bit (yes or no), but it can also be a very elaborate structure. For instance, we could ask for a list of all possible legal colorings of a graph or of all shortest paths from one point to another in a three-dimensional space with obstacles. In practice, we shall distinguish several basic varieties of answers, in turn defining corresponding varieties of problems. When the answers are simply "yes" or "no," they can be regarded as a simple decision to accept (yes) or reject (no) the instance; we call problems with such answers *decision problems*. When the answer is a single structure (e.g., a path from A to B or a truth assignment that causes a proposition to assume the logical value "true" or a subset of tools that will enable us to tackle all of the required jobs), we call the corresponding problems *search problems*, signaling the fact that a solution algorithm must search for the correct structure to return. When the answer is a structure that not only meets certain requirements, but also optimizes some objective function (e.g., the shortest path from A to B rather than just any path or the least expensive subset of tools that enable us to tackle all of the required jobs rather than just any sufficient subset), we call the associated problems *optimization problems*. When the answer is a list of all satisfactory structures (e.g., return all paths from A to B or return all shortest paths from A to B), we have an *enumeration problem*. Finally, when the answer is a count of such structures rather than a list (e.g., return the number of distinct paths from A to B), we have a *counting problem*. The same basic problem can appear in all guises: in the case of paths from A to B, for instance, we can ask if there exists a path from A to B (decision) and we have just seen search, optimization, enumeration, and counting versions of that problem. Among four of these five fundamental types of problems, we have a natural progression: the simplest version is decision; search comes next, since a solution to the search version automatically solves the decision version; next comes optimization (the best structure is certainly an acceptable structure); and hardest is enumeration (if we can list all structures, we can easily determine which is best). The counting version is somewhat apart: if we can count suitable structures, we can certainly answer the decision problem (which is equivalent to asking if the count is nonzero) and we can easily count suitable structures if we can enumerate them.

Given a problem, we can *restrict* its set of instances to obtain a new *subproblem*. For instance, given a graph problem, we can restrict instances to planar graphs or to acyclic graphs; given a set problem, we can restrict it to finite sets or to sets with an even number of elements; given a geometric problem based on line segments, we can restrict it to rectilinear segments (where all segments are aligned with the axes) or restrict it to one dimension. In our first example, we restricted the problem of set membership (Does input element x belong to input set S?) to the problem of membership in a fixed set S_0 (Does input element x belong to S_0?). Be sure to realize that a restriction alters *the set of instances*, but not *the question*; altering the question, however minutely, completely changes the problem.

Clearly, if we know how to solve the general problem, we can solve the subproblem obtained by restriction. The converse, however, need not hold: the subproblem may be much easier to solve than the general problem. For instance, devising an efficient algorithm to find the farthest-neighbor pair among a collection of points in the plane is a difficult task, but the subproblem obtained by restricting the points to have the same ordinate (effectively turning the problem into a one-dimensional version) is easy to solve in linear time, since it then suffices to find the two points with the smallest and largest abscissae.

2.3   Asymptotic Notation

In analyzing an algorithm, whether through a worst-case or an average-case (or an amortized) analysis, algorithm designers use asymptotic notation to describe the behavior of the algorithm on large instances of the problem. Asymptotic analysis ignores start-up costs (constant and lower-order overhead for setting up data structures, for instance) and concentrates instead on the growth rate of the running time (or space) of the algorithm. While asymptotic analysis has its drawbacks (what if the asymptotic behavior appears only for extremely large instances that would never arise in practice? and what if the constant factors and lower-order terms are extremely large for reasonable instance sizes?), it does provide a clean characterization of at least one essential facet of the behavior of the algorithm. Now that we are working at a higher level of abstraction, concentrating on the structure of problems rather than on the behavior of algorithmic solutions, asymptotic characterizations become even more important. We shall see, for instance, that classes of complexity used in characterizing problems are defined in terms of asymptotic worst-case running time or space. Thus we briefly review some terminology.

Asymptotic analysis aims at providing lower bounds and upper bounds on the rate of growth of functions; it accomplishes this by grouping functions with "similar" growth rate into families, thereby providing a framework within which a new function can be located and thus characterized. In working with asymptotics, we should distinguish two types of analysis: that which focuses on behavior exhibited *almost everywhere* (or *a.e.*) and that which focuses on behavior exhibited *infinitely often* (or *i.o.*). For functions of interest to us, which are mostly functions from $\mathbb{N}$ to $\mathbb{N}$, a.e. behavior is behavior that is observed on all but a finite number of function arguments; in consequence, there must exist some number $N \in \mathbb{N}$ such that the function exhibits that behavior for all arguments $n \geq N$. In contrast, i.o. behavior is observable on an infinite number of arguments (for instance, on all perfect squares); in the same spirit, we can only state that, for each number $N \in \mathbb{N}$, there exists some larger number $N' \geq N$ such that the function exhibits the desired behavior on argument N'.

Traditional asymptotic analysis uses a.e. behavior, as does calculus in defining the limit of a function when its argument grows unbounded. Recall that $\lim_{n\to\infty} f(n) = a$ is defined by

$$\forall \varepsilon > 0, \exists N > 0, \forall n \geq N, |f(n) - a| \leq \varepsilon$$

In other words, for all $\varepsilon > 0$, the value $|f(n) - a|$ is almost everywhere no larger than ε. While a.e. analysis is justified for upper bounds, a good case can be made that i.o. analysis is a better choice for lower bounds. Since most of complexity theory (where we shall make the most use of asymptotic analysis and notation) is based on a.e. analysis of worst-case behavior and since it mostly concerns upper bounds (where a.e. analysis is best), we do not pursue the issue any further and instead adopt the convention that all asymptotic analysis, unless explicitly stated otherwise, is done in terms of a.e. behavior.

Let f and g be two functions mapping the natural numbers to themselves:

- f is $O(g)$ (pronounced "big Oh" of g) if and only if there exist natural numbers N and c such that, for all $n \geqslant N$, we have $f(n) \leqslant c \cdot g(n)$.
- f is $\Omega(g)$ (pronounced "big Omega" of g) if and only if g is $O(f)$.
- f is $\Theta(g)$ (pronounced "big Theta" of g) if and only if f is both $O(g)$ and $\Omega(g)$.

Both $O(\ )$ and $\Omega(\ )$ define partial orders (reflexive, antisymmetric, and transitive), while $\Theta(\ )$ is an equivalence relation. Since $O(g)$ is really an entire class of functions, many authors write "$f \in O(g)$" (read "f is *in* big Oh of g") rather than "f is $O(g)$." All three notations carry information about the growth rate of a function: big Oh gives us a (potentially reachable) upper bound, big Omega a (potentially reachable) lower bound, and big Theta an exact asymptotic characterization. In order to be useful, such characterizations keep the representative function g as simple as possible. For instance, a polynomial is represented only by its leading (highest-degree) term stripped of its coefficient. Thus writing "$2n^2 + 3n - 10$ is $O(n^2)$" expresses the fact that our polynomial grows asymptotically no faster than n^2, while writing "$3n^2 - 2n + 22$ is $\Omega(n^2)$" expresses the fact that our polynomial grows at least as fast as n^2. Naturally the bounds need not be tight; we can correctly write "$2n + 1$ is $O(2^n)$," but such a bound is so loose as to be useless. When we use the big Theta notation, however, we have managed to bring our upper bounds and lower bounds together, so that the characterization is tight. For instance, we can write "$3n^2 - 2n + 15$ is $\Theta(n^2)$."

Many authors and students abuse the big Oh notation and use it as both an upper bound and an exact characterization; it pays to remember that the latter is to be represented by the big Theta notation. However, note that our focus on a.e. lower bounds may prevent us from deriving a big Theta characterization of a function, even when we understand all there is to understand about this function. Consider, for instance, the running time of an algorithm that decides if a number is prime by trying as potential

```
divisor := 1
loop
    divisor := divisor + 1
    if (n mod divisor == 0) exit("no")
    if (divisor * divisor >= n) exit("yes")
endloop
```

Figure 2.2 A naïve program to test for primality.

divisors all numbers from 2 to the (ceiling of the) square root of the given number; pseudocode for this algorithm is given in Figure 2.2. On half of the possible instances (i.e., on the even integers), this algorithm terminates with an answer of "no" after one trial; on a third of the remaining instances, it terminates with an answer of "no" after two trials; and so forth. Yet every now and then (and infinitely often), the algorithm encounters a prime and takes on the order of $\sqrt{n}$ trials to identify it as such. Ignoring the cost of arithmetic, we see that the algorithm runs in $O(\sqrt{n})$ time, but we cannot state that it takes $\Omega(\sqrt{n})$ time, since there is no natural number N beyond which it will always require on the order of $\sqrt{n}$ trials. Indeed, the best we can say is that the algorithm runs in $\Omega(1)$ time, which is clearly a poor lower bound. (An i.o. lower bound would have allowed us to state a bound of $\sqrt{n}$, since there is an infinite number of primes.)

When designing algorithms, we need more than just analyses: we also need goals. If we set out to improve on an existing algorithm, we want that improvement to show in the subsequent asymptotic analysis, hence our goal is to design an algorithm with a running time or space that grows asymptotically more slowly than that of the best existing algorithm. To define these goals (and also occasionally to characterize a problem), we need notation that does not accept equality:

- f is $o(g)$ (pronounced "little Oh" of g) if and only if we have

$$\lim_{n \to \infty} \frac{f(n)}{g(n)} = 0$$

- f is $\omega(g)$ (pronounced "little Omega" of g) if and only if g is $o(f)$.

If f is $o(g)$, then its growth rate is strictly less than that of g. If the best algorithm known for our problem runs in $\Theta(g)$ time, we may want to set ourselves the goal of designing a new algorithm that will run in $o(g)$ time, that is, asymptotically faster than the best algorithm known.

When we define complexity classes so as to be independent of the chosen model of computation, we group together an entire range of growth rates;

a typical example is polynomial time, which groups under one name the classes $O(n^a)$ for each $a \in \mathbb{N}$. In such a case, we can use asymptotic notation again, but this time to denote the fact that the exponent is an arbitrary positive constant. Since an arbitrary positive constant is any member of the class $O(1)$, polynomial time can also be defined as $O(n^{O(1)})$ time. Similarly we can define exponential growth as $O(2^{O(n)})$ and polylogarithmic growth (that is, growth bounded by $\log^a n$ for some positive constant a) as $O(\log^{O(1)} n)$.

2.4   Graphs

Graphs were devised in 1736 by the Swiss mathematician Leonhard Euler (1707–1783) as a model for path problems. Euler solved the celebrated "Bridges of Königsberg" problem. The city of Königsberg had some parks on the shores of a river and on islands, with a total of seven bridges joining the various parks, as illustrated in Figure 2.3. Ladies of the court allegedly asked Euler whether one could cross every bridge exactly once and return to one's starting point. Euler modeled the four parks with vertices, the seven bridges with edges, and thereby defined a (multi)graph.

A (finite) *graph* is a set of *vertices* together with a set of pairs of distinct vertices. If the pairs are ordered, the graph is said to be *directed* and a pair of vertices (u, v) is called an *arc*, with u the *tail* and v the *head* of the arc. A directed graph is then given by the pair $G = (V, A)$, where V is the set of vertices and A the set of arcs. If the pairs are unordered, the graph is said to be *undirected* and a pair of vertices $\{u, v\}$ is called an *edge*, with u and v the *endpoints* of the edge. An undirected graph is then given by the pair $G = (V, E)$, where V is the set of vertices and E the set of edges. Two vertices connected by an edge or arc are said to be *adjacent*; an arc is said

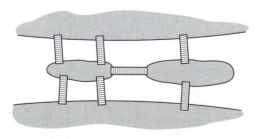

Figure 2.3   The bridges of Königsberg.

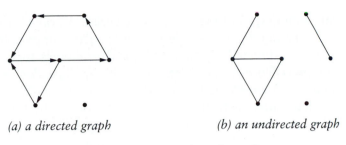

(a) a directed graph   (b) an undirected graph

Figure 2.4   Examples of graphs.

to be *incident upon* its head vertex, while an edge is incident upon both its endpoints. An *isolated vertex* is not adjacent to any other vertex; a subset of vertices of the graph such that no vertex in the subset is adjacent to any other vertex in the subset is known as an *independent set*. Note that our definition of graphs allows at most one edge (or two arcs) between any two vertices, whereas Euler's model for the bridges of Königsberg had multiple edges: when multiple edges are allowed, the collection of edges is no longer a set, but a bag, and the graph is termed a *multigraph*.

Graphically, we represent vertices by points in the plane and edges or arcs by line (or curve) segments connecting the two points; if the graph is directed, an arc (u, v) also includes an arrowhead pointing at and touching the second vertex, v. Figure 2.4 shows examples of directed and undirected graphs. In an undirected graph, each vertex has a *degree*, which is the number of edges that have the vertex as one endpoint; in a directed graph, we distinguish between the *outdegree* of a vertex (the number of arcs, the tail of which is the given vertex) and its *indegree* (the number of arcs pointing to the given vertex). In the graph of Figure 2.4(a), the leftmost vertex has indegree 2 and outdegree 1, while, in the graph of Figure 2.4(b), the leftmost vertex has degree 3. An isolated vertex has degree (indegree and outdegree) equal to zero; each example in Figure 2.4 has one isolated vertex. An undirected graph is said to be *regular of degree k* if every vertex in the graph has degree k. If an undirected graph is regular of degree $n - 1$ (one less than the number of vertices), then this graph includes every possible edge between its vertices and is said to be the *complete graph on n vertices*, denoted K_n.

A *walk* (or *path*) in a graph is a list of vertices of the graph such that there exists an arc (or edge) from each vertex in the list to the next vertex in the list. A walk may pass through the same vertex many times and may use the same arc or edge many times. A *cycle* (or *circuit*) is a walk that returns to its starting point—the first and last vertices in the list are identical. Both graphs of Figure 2.4 have cycles. A graph without any cycle is said to be *acyclic*; this property is particularly important among directed graphs. A *directed acyclic graph* (or *dag*) models such common structures as precedence ordering among tasks or dependencies among program modules. A *simple path* is a path that does not include the same vertex more than once—with the allowed exception of the first and last vertices: if these two are the same, then the simple path is a *simple cycle*. A cycle that goes through each arc or edge of the graph exactly once is known as an *Eulerian circuit*—such a cycle was the answer sought in the problem of the bridges of Königsberg; a graph with such a cycle is an *Eulerian graph*. A simple cycle that includes all vertices of the graph is known as a *Hamiltonian circuit*; a graph with such a cycle is a *Hamiltonian graph*. Trivially, every complete graph is Hamiltonian.

An undirected graph in which there exists a path between any two vertices is said to be *connected*. The first theorem of graph theory was stated by Euler in solving the problem of the bridges of Königsberg: a connected undirected graph has an Eulerian cycle if and only if each vertex has even degree. The undirected graph of Figure 2.4(b) is not connected but can be partitioned into three (maximal) *connected components*. The same property applied to a directed graph defines a *strongly connected* graph. The requirements are now stronger, since the undirected graph can use the same path in either direction between two vertices, whereas the directed graph may have two entirely distinct paths for the two directions. The directed graph of Figure 2.4(a) is not strongly connected but can be partitioned into two strongly connected components, one composed of the isolated vertex and the other of the remaining six vertices. A *tree* is a connected acyclic graph; an immediate consequence of this definition is that a tree on n vertices has exactly $n - 1$ edges.

Exercise 2.1 Prove this last statement.   □

It also follows that a tree is a minimally connected graph: removing any edge breaks the tree into two connected components. Given a connected graph, a *spanning tree* for the graph is a subset of edges of the graph that forms a tree on the vertices of the graph. Figure 2.5 shows a graph and one of its spanning trees.

Many questions about graphs revolve around the relationship between edges and their endpoints. A *vertex cover* for a graph is a subset of vertices such that every edge has one endpoint in the cover; similarly, an *edge cover* is a subset of edges such that every vertex of the graph is the endpoint of an edge in the cover. A legal *vertex coloring* of a graph is an assignment of

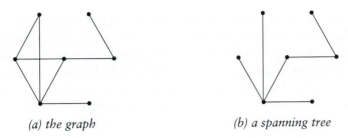

(a) the graph   (b) a spanning tree

Figure 2.5   A graph and one of its spanning trees.

colors to the vertices of the graph such that no edge has identically colored endpoints; the smallest number of colors needed to produce a legal vertex coloring is known as the *chromatic number* of a graph.

Exercise 2.2   Prove that the chromatic number of K_n equals n and that the chromatic number of any tree with at least two vertices is 2.   □

Similarly, a legal *edge coloring* is an assignment of colors to edges such that no vertex is the endpoint of two identically colored edges; the smallest number of colors needed to produce a legal edge coloring is known as the *chromatic index* of the graph. In a legal vertex coloring, each subset of vertices of the same color forms an independent set. In particular, if a graph has a chromatic number of two or less, it is said to be *bipartite*: its set of vertices can be partitioned into two subsets (corresponding to the two colors), each of which is an independent set. (Viewed differently, all edges of a bipartite graph have one endpoint in one subset of the partition and the other endpoint in the other subset.) A bipartite graph with $2n$ vertices that can be partitioned into two subsets of n vertices each and that has a maximum number (n^2) of edges is known as a *complete bipartite graph on 2n vertices* and denoted $K_{n,n}$. A bipartite graph is often given explicitly by the partition of its vertices, say $\{U, V\}$, and its set of edges and is thus written $G = (\{U, V\}, E)$.

   A *matching* in an undirected graph is a subset of edges of the graph such that no two edges of the subset share an endpoint; a *maximum matching* is a matching of the largest possible size (such a matching need not be unique). If the matching includes every vertex of the graph (which must then have an even number of vertices), it is called a *perfect matching*. In the *minimum-cost matching* problem, edges are assigned costs; we then seek the maximum matching that minimizes the sum of the costs of the selected edges. When the graph is bipartite, we can view the vertices on one side as men, the vertices on the other side as women, and the edges as defining the compatibility relationship "this man and this woman are willing to marry each other." The maximum matching problem is then generally called the *marriage* problem, since each selected edge can be viewed as a couple to be married. A different interpretation has the vertices on one side representing individuals and those on the other side representing committees formed from these individuals; an edge denotes the relation "this individual sits on that committee." A matching can then be viewed as a selection of a distinct individual to represent each committee. (While an individual may sit on several committees, the matching requires that an individual may represent at most one committee.) In this interpretation, the problem is known as finding a *Set of Distinct Representatives*. If costs are assigned to the edges of the bipartite graph, the problem is often interpreted as being made of a set of tasks (the vertices on one side) and a set of workers (the vertices on the other side), with the edges denoting the relation "this task can be accomplished by that worker." The minimum-cost matching in this setting is called the *Assignment* problem. Exercises at the end of this chapter address some basic properties of these various types of matching.

Two graphs are *isomorphic* if there exists a bijection between their vertices that maps an edge of one graph onto an edge of the other. Figure 2.6 shows three graphs; the first two are isomorphic (find a suitable mapping of vertices), but neither is isomorphic to the third. Isomorphism defines an equivalence relation on the set of all graphs. A graph G' is a *homeomorphic subgraph* of a graph G if it can be obtained from a subgraph of G by successive removals of vertices of degree 2, where each pair of edges leading to the two neighbors of each deleted vertex is replaced by a single edge in G' connecting the two neighbors directly (unless that edge already exists). Entire chains of vertices may be removed, with the obvious cascading of the edge-replacement mechanism. Figure 2.7 shows a graph and one of its homeomorphic subgraphs. The subgraph was obtained by removing a

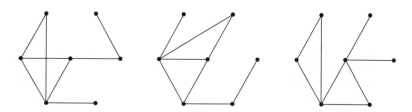

Figure 2.6 Isomorphic and nonisomorphic graphs.

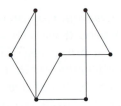 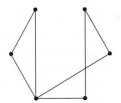

Figure 2.7   A graph and a homeomorphic subgraph.

single vertex; the resulting edge was not part of the original graph and so was added to the homeomorphic subgraph.

A graph is said to be *planar* if it can be drawn in the plane without any crossing of its edges. An algorithm due to Hopcroft and Tarjan [1974] can test a graph for planarity in linear time and produce a planar drawing if one exists. A famous theorem due to Kuratowski [1930] states that every non-planar graph contains a homeomorphic copy of either the complete graph on five vertices, K_5, or the complete bipartite graph on six vertices, $K_{3,3}$.

2.5   Alphabets, Strings, and Languages

An *alphabet* is a finite set of *symbols* (or *characters*). We shall typically denote an alphabet by Σ and its symbols by lowercase English letters towards the beginning of the alphabet, e.g., $\Sigma = \{a, b, c, d\}$. Of special interest to us is the binary alphabet, $\Sigma = \{0, 1\}$. A *string* is defined over an alphabet as a finite ordered list of symbols drawn from the alphabet. For example, the following are strings over the alphabet $\{0, 1\}$: 001010, 00, 1, and so on. We often denote a string by a lowercase English character, usually one at the end of the alphabet; for instance, we may write $x = 001001$ or $y = aabca$. The *length* of a string x is denoted $|x|$; for instance, we have $|x| = |001001| = 6$ and $|y| = |aabca| = 5$. The special *empty string*, which has zero symbols and zero length, is denoted ε. The universe of all strings over the alphabet Σ is denoted Σ^*. For specific alphabets, we use the star operator directly on the alphabet set; for instance, $\{0, 1\}^*$ is the set of all binary strings, $\{0, 1\}^* = \{\varepsilon, 0, 1, 00, 01, 10, 11, 000, \dots\}$. To denote the set of all strings of length k over Σ, we use the notation Σ^k; for instance, $\{0, 1\}^2$ is the set $\{00, 01, 10, 11\}$ and, for any alphabet Σ, we have $\Sigma^0 = \{\varepsilon\}$. In particular, we can also write $\Sigma^* = \bigcup_{k \in \mathbb{N}} \Sigma^k$. We define Σ^+ to be the set of all non-null strings over Σ; we can write $\Sigma^+ = \Sigma^* - \{\varepsilon\} = \bigcup_{k \in \mathbb{N}, k \neq 0} \Sigma^k$.

The main operation on strings is *concatenation*. Concatenating string x and string y yields a new string $z = xy$ where, if we let $x = a_1 a_2 \ldots a_n$ and $y = b_1 b_2 \ldots b_m$, then we get $z = a_1 a_2 \ldots a_n b_1 b_2 \ldots b_m$. The length of the resulting string, $|xy|$, is the sum of the lengths of the two operand strings, $|x| + |y|$. Concatenation with the empty string does not alter a string: for any string x, we have $x\varepsilon = \varepsilon x = x$. If some string w can be written as the concatenation of two strings x and y, $w = xy$, then we say that x is a *prefix* of w and y is a *suffix* of w. More generally, if some string w can be written as the concatenation of three strings, $w = xyz$, then we say that y (and also x and z) is a *substring* of w. Any of the substrings involved in the concatenation can be empty; thus, in particular, any string is a substring of itself, is a prefix of itself, and is a suffix of itself. If we have a string $x = a_1 a_2 \ldots a_n$, then any string of the form $a_{i_1} a_{i_2} \ldots a_{i_k}$, where we have $k \leqslant n$ and $i_j < i_{j+1}$, is a *subsequence* of x. Unlike a substring, which is a consecutive run of symbols occurring with the original string, a subsequence is just a sampling of symbols from the string as that string is read from left to right. For instance, if we have $x = aabbacbbabacc$, then $aaaaa$ and abc are both subsequences of x, but neither is a substring of x. Finally, if $x = a_1 a_2 \ldots a_n$ is a string, then we denote its reverse, $a_n \ldots a_2 a_1$, by x^R; a string that is its own reverse, $x = x^R$, is a *palindrome*.

A *language* L over the alphabet Σ is a subset of Σ^*, $L \subseteq \Sigma^*$; that is, a language is a set of strings over the given alphabet. A language may be empty: $L = \emptyset$. Do not confuse the empty language, which contains no strings whatsoever, with the language that consists only of the empty string, $L = \{\varepsilon\}$; the latter is not an empty set. The key question we may ask concerning languages is the same as that concerning sets, namely membership: given some string x, we may want to know whether x belongs to L. To settle this question for large numbers of strings, we need an algorithm that computes the *characteristic function* of the set L—i.e., that returns 1 when the string is in the set and 0 otherwise. Formally, we write c_L for the characteristic function of the set L, with $c_L : L \to \{0, 1\}$ such that $c_L(x) = 1$ holds if and only if x is an element of L. Other questions of interest about languages concern the result of simple set operations (such as union and intersection) on one or more languages.

These questions are trivially settled when the language is finite and specified by a list of its members. Asking whether some string w belongs to some language L is then a simple matter of scanning the list of the members of L for an occurrence of w. However, most languages with which we work are defined implicitly, through some logical predicate, by a statement of the form $\{x \mid x$ has property P$\}$. The predicate mechanism allows us to define infinite sets (which clearly cannot be explicitly listed!), such as the language

$$L = \{x \in \{0, 1\}^* \mid x \text{ ends with a single } 0\}$$

It also allows us to provide concise definitions for large, complex, yet finite sets—which could be listed only at great expense, such as the language

$$L = \{x \in \{0, 1\}^* \mid x = x^R \text{ and } |x| \leq 10{,}000\}$$

When a language is defined by a predicate, deciding membership in that language can be difficult, or at least very time-consuming. Consider, for instance, the language

$$L = \{x \mid \text{considered as a binary-coded natural number, } x \text{ is a prime}\}$$

The obvious test for membership in L (attempt to divide by successive values up to the square root, as illustrated in Figure 2.2) would run in time proportional to $2^{|x|}$ whenever the number is prime.

2.6 Functions and Infinite Sets

A *function* is a mapping that associates with each element of one set, the *domain*, an element of another set, the *co-domain*. A function f with domain A and co-domain B is written $f : A \rightarrow B$. The set of all elements of B that are associated with some element of A is the *range* of the function, denoted $f(A)$. If the range of a function equals its co-domain, $f(A) = B$, the function is said to be *surjective* (also *onto*). If the function maps distinct elements of its domain to distinct elements in its range, $(x \neq y) \Rightarrow (f(x) \neq f(y))$, the function is said to be *injective* (also *one-to-one*). A function that is both injective and surjective is said to be *bijective*, sometimes called a *one-to-one correspondence*. Generally, the inverse of a function is not well defined, since several elements in the domain can be mapped to the same element in the range. An injective function has a well-defined inverse, since, for each element in the range, there is a unique element in the domain with which it was associated. However, that inverse is a function from the range to the domain, not from the co-domain to the domain, since it may not be defined on all elements of the co-domain. A bijection, on the other hand, has a well-defined inverse from its co-domain to its domain, $f^{-1} : B \rightarrow A$ (see Exercise 2.33).

How do we compare the sizes of sets? For finite sets, we can simply count the number of elements in each set and compare the values. If two finite sets have the same size, say n, then there exists a simple bijection between the two (actually, there exist $n!$ bijections, but one suffices): just map the first element of one set onto the first element of the other and, in general, the ith element of one onto the ith element of the other. Unfortunately, the counting idea fails with infinite sets: we cannot directly "count" how many elements they have. However, the notion that two sets are of the same size whenever there exists a bijection between the two remains applicable. As a simple example, consider the two sets $\mathbb{N} = \{1, 2, 3, 4, \ldots\}$ (the set of the natural numbers) and $\mathbb{E} = \{2, 4, 6, 8, \ldots\}$ (the set of the even numbers). There is a very natural bijection that puts the number $n \in \mathbb{N}$ into correspondence with the even number $2n \in \mathbb{E}$. Hence these two infinite sets are of the same size, even though one (the natural numbers) appears to be twice as large as the other (the even numbers).

Example 2.1 We can illustrate this correspondence through the following tale. A Swiss hotelier runs the *Infinite Hotel* at a famous resort and boasts that the hotel can accommodate an infinite number of guests. The hotel has an infinite number of rooms, numbered starting from 1. On a busy day in the holiday season, the hotel is full (each of the infinite number of rooms is occupied), but the manager states that any new guest is welcome: all current guests will be asked to move down by one room (from room i to room $i + 1$), then the new guest will be assigned room 1. In fact, the manager accommodates that night an infinite number of new guests: all current guests are asked to move from their current room (say room i) to a room with twice the number (room $2i$), after which the (infinite number of) new guests are assigned the (infinite number of) odd-numbered rooms.

□

We say that the natural numbers form a *countably infinite* set—after all, these are the very numbers that we use for counting! Thus a set is *countable* if it is finite or if it is countably infinite. We denote the cardinality of $\mathbb{N}$ by $\aleph_0$ (aleph, $\aleph$, is the first letter of the Hebrew alphabet[1]; $\aleph_0$ is usually pronounced as "aleph nought"). In view of our example, we have $\aleph_0 + \aleph_0 = \aleph_0$. If we let $\mathbb{O}$ denote the set of odd integers, then we have shown that $\mathbb{N}$, $\mathbb{E}$, and $\mathbb{O}$ all have cardinality $\aleph_0$; yet we also have $\mathbb{N} = \mathbb{E} \cup \mathbb{O}$, with

---

[1] A major problem of theoreticians everywhere is notation. Mathematicians in particular are forever running out of symbols. Thus having exhausted the lower- and upper-case letters (with and without subscripts and superscripts) of the Roman and Greek alphabets, they turned to alphabets a bit farther afield. However, Cantor, a deeply religious man, used the Hebrew alphabet to represent infinities for religious reasons.

$\mathbb{E} \cap \mathbb{O} = \emptyset$ (that is, $\mathbb{E}$ and $\mathbb{O}$ form a partition of $\mathbb{N}$) and thus $|\mathbb{N}| = |\mathbb{E}| + |\mathbb{O}|$, yielding the desired result.

More interesting yet is to consider the set of all (positive) rational numbers—that is, all numbers that can be expressed as a fraction. We claim that this set is also countably infinite—even though it appears to be much "larger" than the set of natural numbers. We arrange the rational numbers in a table where the ith row of the table lists all fractions with a numerator of i and the jth column lists all fractions with a denominator of j. This arrangement is illustrated in Figure 2.8. Strictly speaking, the same rational number appears infinitely often in the table; for instance, all diagonal elements equal one. This redundancy does not impair our following argument, since we show that, even with all these repetitions, the rational numbers can be placed in a one-to-one correspondence with the natural numbers. (Furthermore, these repetitions can be removed if so desired: see Exercise 2.35.)

The idea is very simple: since we cannot enumerate one row or one column at a time (we would immediately "use up" all our natural numbers in enumerating one row or one column—or, if you prefer to view it that way, such an enumeration would never terminate, so that we would never get around to enumerating the next row or column), we shall use a process known as *dovetailing*, which consists of enumerating the first element of the first row, followed by the second element of the first row and the first of the second row, followed by the third element of the first row, the second of the second row, and the first of the third row, and so on. Graphically, we use the backwards diagonals in the table, one after the other; each successive diagonal starts enumerating a new row while enumerating the next element

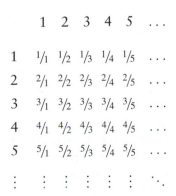

Figure 2.8   Placing rational numbers into one-to-one correspondence with natural numbers.

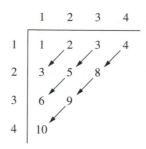

Figure 2.9   A graphical view of dovetailing.

of all rows started so far, thereby never getting trapped in a single row or column, yet eventually covering all elements in all rows. This process is illustrated in Figure 2.9.

We can define the induced bijection in strict terms. Consider the fraction in the ith row and jth column of the table. It sits in the $(i + j - 1)$st back diagonal, so that all back diagonals before it must have already been listed— a total of $\sum_{l=1}^{i+j-2} l = (i + j - 1)(i + j - 2)/2$ elements. Moreover, it is the ith element enumerated in the $(i + j - 1)$st back diagonal, so that its index is $f(i, j) = (i + j - 1)(i + j - 2)/2 + i$. In other words, our bijection maps the pair (i, j) to the value $(i^2 + j^2 + 2ij - i - 3j + 2)/2$. Conversely, if we know that the index of an element is k, we can determine what fraction defines this element as follows. We have $k = i + (i + j - 1)(i + j - 2)/2$, or $2k - 2 = (i + j)(i + j - 1) - 2j$. Let l be the least integer with $l(l - 1) > 2k - 2$; then we have $l = i + j$ and $2j = l(l - 1) - (2k - 2)$, which gives us i and j.

Exercise 2.3   Use this bijection to propose a solution to a new problem that just arose at the *Infinite Hotel*: the hotel is full, yet an infinite number of tour buses just pulled up, *each* loaded with an infinite number of tourists, all asking for rooms. How will our Swiss manager accommodate all of these new guests and keep all the current ones?   □

Since our table effectively defines $\mathbb{Q}$ (the rational numbers) to be $\mathbb{Q} = \mathbb{N} \times \mathbb{N}$, it follows that we have $\aleph_0 \cdot \aleph_0 = \aleph_0$. Basically, the cardinality of the natural numbers acts in the arithmetic of infinite cardinals much like 0 and 1 in the arithmetic of finite numbers.

Exercise 2.4   Verify that the function defined below is a bijection between the positive, nonzero rational numbers and the nonzero natural numbers, and define a procedure to reverse it:

$$\begin{cases} f(1) = 1 \\ f(2n) = f(n) + 1 \\ f(2n + 1) = 1/f(2n) \end{cases}$$

□

2.7   Pairing Functions

A *pairing function* is a bijection between $\mathbb{N} \times \mathbb{N}$ and $\mathbb{N}$ that is also strictly monotone in each of its arguments. If we let $p: \mathbb{N} \times \mathbb{N} \to \mathbb{N}$ be a pairing function, then we require:

- p is a bijection: it is both one-to-one (injective) and onto (surjective).
- p is strictly monotone in each argument: for all x, $y \in \mathbb{N}$, we have both $p(x, y) < p(x + 1, y)$ and $p(x, y) < p(x, y + 1)$.

We shall denote an arbitrary pairing function $p(x, y)$ with pointed brackets as $\langle x, y \rangle$. Given some pairing function, we need a way to reverse it and to recover x and y from $\langle x, y \rangle$; we thus need two functions, one to recover each argument. We call these two functions *projections* and write them as $\Pi_1(z)$ and $\Pi_2(z)$. Thus, by definition, if we have $z = \langle x, y \rangle$, then we also have $\Pi_1(z) = x$ and $\Pi_2(z) = y$.

At this point, we should stop and ask ourselves whether pairing and projection functions actually exist! In fact, we have seen the answer to that question. Our dovetailing process to enumerate the positive rationals was a bijection between $\mathbb{N} \times \mathbb{N}$ and $\mathbb{N}$. Moreover, the item in row i, column j of our infinite table was enumerated before the item in row $i + 1$, column j and before the item in row i, column $j + 1$, so that the bijection was monotone in each argument. Finally, we had seen how to reverse the enumeration. Thus our dovetailing process defined a pairing function.

Perhaps a more interesting pairing function is as follows: $z = \langle x, y \rangle = 2^x(2y + 1) - 1$. We can easily verify that this function is bijective and monotone in each argument; it is reversed simply by factoring $z + 1$ into a power of two and an odd factor.

Exercise 2.5 Consider the new pairing function given by

$$\langle x, y \rangle = x + (y + \lfloor \frac{(x + 1)}{2} \rfloor)^2$$

Verify that it is a pairing function and can be reversed with $\Pi_1(z) = z - \lfloor \sqrt{z} \rfloor^2$ and $\Pi_2(z) = \lfloor \sqrt{z} \rfloor - \lfloor \frac{(\Pi_1(z)+1)}{2} \rfloor$.   □

So pairing functions abound! However, not every bijection is a valid pairing function; for instance, the bijection of Exercise 2.4 is not monotonic in each argument and hence not a pairing function.

As we just saw, a pairing function is at the heart of a dovetailing process. In computability and complexity theory, we are often forced to resort to dovetailing along 3, 4, or even more "dimensions," not just 2 as we used before. For the purpose of dovetailing along two dimensions, a pairing function works well. For three or more dimensions, we need pairing functions that pair 3, 4, or more natural numbers together. Fortunately, a moment of thought reveals that we can define such "higher" pairing functions recursively, by using two-dimensional pairing functions as a base case. Formally, we define the function $\langle -, -, \ldots, - \rangle_n$, which pairs n natural numbers (and thus is a bijection between $\mathbb{N}^n$ and $\mathbb{N}$ that is strictly monotone in each argument) recursively as follows:

$$
\begin{cases}
\langle \, \rangle_0 = 0 \text{ and } \langle x \rangle_1 = x & \text{trivial cases} \\
\langle x, y \rangle_2 = \langle x, y \rangle & \text{normal base case} \\
\langle x_1, \ldots, x_{n-1}, x_n \rangle_n = \langle x_1, \ldots, \langle x_{n-1}, x_n \rangle \rangle_{n-1} & \text{inductive step}
\end{cases}
$$

where we have used our two-dimensional pairing function to reduce the number of arguments in the inductive step. For these general pairing functions, we need matching general projections; we would like to define a function $\Pi(i, n, z)$, which basically takes z to be the result of a pairing of n natural numbers and then returns the ith of these. We need the n as argument, since we now have pairing functions of various arity, so that, when given just z, we cannot tell if it is the result of pairing 2, 3, 4, or more items. Perhaps even more intriguing is the fact that we can always project back from z as if it had been the pairing of n items even when it was produced differently (by pairing $m < n$ or $k > n$ items).

We define $\Pi(i, n, z)$, which we shall normally write as $\Pi_i^n(z)$, recursively as follows:

$$
\begin{cases}
\Pi_i^0(z) = 0 \text{ and } \Pi_i^1(z) = z, \ \forall i & \text{trivial cases} \\[4pt]
\Pi_i^2(z) = \begin{cases} \Pi_1(z) & i \leq 1 \\ \Pi_2(z) & i > 1 \end{cases} & \text{normal base cases} \\[12pt]
\Pi_i^{n+1}(z) = \begin{cases} \Pi_i^n(z) & i < n \\ \Pi_1(\Pi_n^n(z)) & i = n \\ \Pi_2(\Pi_n^n(z)) & i > n \end{cases} & \text{inductive step}
\end{cases}
$$

Exercise 2.6 Verify that our definition of the projection functions is correct. Keep in mind that the notation $\Pi_i^n(z)$ allows argument triples that do not correspond to any valid pairing, such as $\Pi_{10}^5(z)$, in which case we are at liberty to define the result in any convenient way.   □

Exercise 2.7 Prove the following simple properties of our pairing and projection functions:

1. $\langle 0, \ldots, 0 \rangle_n = 0$ and $\langle x, 0 \rangle = \langle x, 0, \ldots, 0 \rangle_n$ for any $n > 2$ and any x.
2. $\Pi_0^n(z) = \Pi_1^n(z)$ and $\Pi_i^n(z) = \Pi_n^n(z)$ for all n, all z, and all $i \geq n$.
3. $\Pi_1^n(z) \leq z$ for all n and all z.   □

When we need to enumerate all possible k-tuples of natural numbers (or arguments from countably infinite sets), we simply enumerate the natural numbers, $1, 2, 3, \ldots, i, \ldots$, and consider i to be the pairing of k natural numbers, $i = \langle x_1, x_2, \ldots, x_k \rangle_k$; hence the ith number gives us the k arguments, $x_1 = \Pi_1^k(i), \ldots, x_k = \Pi_k^k(i)$, allowing us to dovetail. Conversely, whenever we need to handle a finite number k of arguments, each taken from a countably infinite set, we can just pair the k arguments together to form a single argument. In particular, this k-tuple pairing will allow us to define theories based on one- or two-argument functions and then extend them to arbitrary numbers of arguments by considering one argument to be the pairing of $k > 1$ "actual" arguments. If we do not know in advance the arity of the tuple (the value of k), we can encode it as part of the pairing: if we need to pair together k values, $x_1, \ldots, x_k$, where k may vary, we begin by pairing the k values together, $\langle x_1, \ldots, x_k \rangle_k$, then pair the result with k itself, to obtain finally $z = \langle k, \langle x_1, \ldots, x_k \rangle_k \rangle$; then we have $k = \Pi_1(z)$ and $x_i = \Pi_i^{\Pi_1(z)}(\Pi_2(z))$.

2.8 Cantor's Proof: The Technique of Diagonalization

We now show that no bijection can exist between the natural numbers and the real numbers. Specifically, we will show the somewhat stronger result that no bijection can exist between the natural numbers and the real numbers whose integer part is 0—i.e., those in the semi-open interval $[0, 1)$. This result was first proved in 1873 by Cantor—and provoked quite a furor in the world of mathematics. The proof technique is known as diagonalization, for reasons that will become obvious as we develop the proof. Essentially, such a proof is a proof by contradiction, but with a built-in enumeration/construction process in the middle.

$$\begin{array}{ll} 1 & 0.d_{11}d_{12}d_{13}d_{14}d_{15} \ldots \\ 2 & 0.d_{21}d_{22}d_{23}d_{24}d_{25} \ldots \\ 3 & 0.d_{31}d_{32}d_{33}d_{34}d_{35} \ldots \\ 4 & 0.d_{41}d_{42}d_{43}d_{44}d_{45} \ldots \\ 5 & 0.d_{51}d_{52}d_{53}d_{54}d_{55} \ldots \\ \vdots & \qquad\qquad\qquad \ddots \end{array}$$

Figure 2.10   The hypothetical list of reals in the range $[0, 1)$.

Let us then assume that a bijection exists and attempt to derive a contradiction. If a bijection exists, we can use it to list in order $(1, 2, 3, \ldots)$ all the real numbers in the interval $[0, 1)$. All such real numbers are of the form $0.wxyz\ldots$; that is, they have a zero integer part followed by an infinite decimal expansion. Our list can be written in tabular form as shown in Figure 2.10, where d_{ij} is the jth decimal in the expansion of the ith real number in the list. Now we shall construct a new real number, $0 \leqslant x < 1$, which cannot, by construction, be in the list—yielding the desired contradiction, since then our claimed bijection is not between the natural numbers and $[0, 1)$, but only between the natural numbers and some subset of $[0, 1)$, a subset that does not include x. Our new number x will be the number $0.d_1d_2d_3d_4d_5 \ldots$, where we set $d_i = (d_{ii} + 1 \bmod 10)$, so that d_i is a valid digit and we have ensured $d_i \neq d_{ii}$. Thus x differs from the first number in the list in its first decimal, from the second number in its second decimal, and, in general, from the ith number in the list in its ith decimal—and so cannot be in the list. Yet it should be, because it belongs to the interval $[0, 1)$; hence we have the desired contradiction. We have constructed x by moving down the diagonal of the hypothetical table, hence the name of the technique.

A minor technical problem could arise if we obtained $x = 0.\overline{9} = 0.9999\ldots$, because then we actually would have $x = 1$ and x would not be in the interval $[0, 1)$, escaping the contradiction. However, obtaining such an x would require that each d_{ii} equal 8, which is absurd, because the interval $[0, 1)$ clearly contains numbers that have no decimal equal to 8, such as the number $0.\overline{1}$. In fact, this problem is due to the ambiguity of decimal notation and is not limited to $0.\overline{9}$: any number with a finite decimal expansion (or, alternatively viewed, with a decimal period of 0) has an "identical twin," where the last decimal is decreased by one and, in compensation, a repeating period of 9 is added after this changed decimal. Thus $x = 0.1$ is the same as $y = 0.0\overline{9}$. This ambiguity gives rise to another minor technical problem with our diagonalization: what if the number x

constructed through diagonalization, while not in the table, had its "identical twin" in the table? There would then be no contradiction, since the table would indeed list the number x, even if not in the particular form in which we generated it. However, note that, in order to generate such a number (either member of the twin pair), all diagonal elements in the table beyond some fixed index must equal 8 (or all must equal 9, depending on the chosen twin); but our table would then contain only a finite number of entries that do not use the digit 8 (or the digit 9), which is clearly false, since there clearly exist infinitely many real numbers in $[0, 1)$ that contain neither digit (8 or 9) in their decimal expansion.

A good exercise is to consider why we could not have used exactly the same technique to "prove" that no bijection is possible between the natural numbers and the rational numbers in the interval $[0, 1)$. The reasoning can proceed as above until we get to the construction of x. The problem is that we have no proof that the x as constructed is a *bona fide* rational number: not all numbers that can be written with an infinite decimal expansion are rational—the rational numbers share the feature that their decimal expansion has a repeating period, while any number with a nonrepeating expansion is irrational. This defect provides a way to escape the contradiction: the existence of x does not cause a contradiction because it need not be in the enumeration, not being rational itself. A proof by diagonalization thus relies on two key pieces: (i) the element constructed must be in the set; and yet (ii) it cannot be in the enumeration.

So the real numbers form an *uncountable* set; the cardinality of the real numbers is larger than that of the natural numbers—it is sometimes called the cardinality of the continuum.

2.9   Implications for Computability

The set of all programs is countable: it is effectively the set of all strings over, say, the ASCII alphabet. (This set includes illegal strings that do not obey the syntax of the language, but this has only the effect of making our claim stronger.) However, the set of all functions from $\mathbb{N}$ to $\{0, 1\}$—which is simply a way to view $2^{\mathbb{N}}$, the set of all subsets of $\mathbb{N}$, since 0/1-valued functions can be regarded as characteristic functions of sets, and which can also be viewed as the set of all decision problems—is easily shown to be uncountable by repeating Cantor's argument.[2] This time, we write on each

---

[2] Actually, Cantor had proved the stronger result $|S| < 2^{|S|}$ for any nonempty set S, a result that directly implies that 0/1-valued functions are uncountable.

$$
\begin{array}{cccccc}
 & 1 & 2 & 3 & 4 & 5 & \ldots \\
f_1 & f_1(1) & f_1(2) & f_1(3) & f_1(4) & f_1(5) & \ldots \\
f_2 & f_2(1) & f_2(2) & f_2(3) & f_2(4) & f_2(5) & \ldots \\
f_3 & f_3(1) & f_3(2) & f_3(3) & f_3(4) & f_3(5) & \ldots \\
f_4 & f_4(1) & f_4(2) & f_4(3) & f_4(4) & f_4(5) & \ldots \\
f_5 & f_5(1) & f_5(2) & f_5(3) & f_5(4) & f_5(5) & \ldots
\end{array}
$$

Figure 2.11   Cantor's argument applied to functions.

successive line the next function in the claimed enumeration; each function can be written as an infinite list of 0s and 1s—the ith element in the list for f is just $f(i)$. Denoting the jth function in the list by f_j, we obtain the scheme of Figure 2.11. Now we use the diagonal to construct a new function that cannot be in the enumeration: recalling that $f_j(i)$ is either 0 or 1, we define our new function as $f'(n) = 1 - f_n(n)$. (In other words, we switch the values along the diagonal.) The same line of reasoning as in Cantor's argument now applies, allowing us to conclude that the set of 0/1-valued functions (or the set of subsets of $\mathbb{N}$) is uncountable.

Since the number of programs is countable and the number of 0/1-valued functions (and, *a fortiori*, the number of integer-valued functions) is uncountable, there are many functions (a "large" infinity of them, in fact) for which no solution program can exist. Hence most functions are not computable! This result, if nothing else, motivates our study of computability and computation models. Among the questions we may want to ask are:

- Do we care that most problems are unsolvable? After all, it may well be that none of the unsolvable problems is of any interest to us.
- We shall see that unsolvable problems actually arise in practice. (The prototype of the unsolvable problem is the "halting problem": is there an algorithm that, given any input program and any input data, determines whether the input program eventually halts when run on the input data? This is surely the most basic property that we may want to test about programs, a prerequisite to any correctness proof.) That being the case, what can we say about unsolvable problems? Are they characterizable in some general way?
- How hard to solve are specific instances of unsolvable problems? This question may seem strange, but many of us regularly solve instances

of unsolvable problems—for instance, many of us regularly determine whether or not some specific program halts under some specific input.
- Are all solvable problems easy to solve? Of course not, so what can we say about their difficulty? (Not surprisingly, it will turn out that most solvable problems are intractable, that is, cannot be solved efficiently.)

2.10   Exercises

Exercise 2.8 Give a formal definition (question and instance description) for each of the following problems:

1. *Binpacking*: minimize the number of bins (all of the same size) used in packing a collection of items (each with its own size); sizes are simply natural numbers (that is, the problem is one-dimensional).
2. *Satisfiability*: find a way, if any, to satisfy a Boolean formula—that is, find a truth assignment to the variables of the formula that makes the formula evaluate to the logical value "true."
3. *Ascending Subsequence*: find the longest ascending subsequence in a string of numbers—a sequence is ascending if each element of the subsequence is strictly larger than the previous.

Exercise 2.9 Consider the following variations of the problem known as *Set Cover*, in which you are given a set and a collection of subsets of the set and asked to find a *cover* (a subcollection that includes all elements of the set) for the set with certain properties.

1. Find the smallest cover (i.e., one with the smallest number of subsets) for the set.
2. Find the smallest cover for the set, given that all subsets have exactly three elements each.
3. Find the smallest cover for the set, subject to all subsets in the cover being disjoint.
4. Find a cover of size n for the set, given that the set has $3n$ elements and that all subsets have exactly three elements each.

Which variation is a subproblem of another?

Exercise 2.10 The *Minimum Test Set* problem is given by a collection of classes $\mathscr{C} = \{C_1, \ldots, C_n\}$ and a collection of binary-valued tests $\mathscr{T} = \{T_1, \ldots, T_k\}$. Each test can be viewed as a subset of the collection of classes, $T_i \subseteq \mathscr{C}$—those classes where the test returns a positive answer. (A typical application is in the microbiology laboratory of a hospital, where a battery of tests must be designed to identify cultures.) The problem is to return a minimum subcollection $\mathcal{T}' \subseteq \mathcal{T}$ of tests that provides the same discrimination as the original collection—i.e., such that any pair separated by some test in the original collection is also separated by some test in the subcollection.

Rephrase this problem as a set cover problem—refer to Exercise 2.9.

Exercise 2.11 Prove that, if f is $O(g)$ and g is $O(h)$, then f is $O(h)$.

Exercise 2.12 Verify that 3^n is not $O(2^n)$ but that it is $O(2^{\alpha n})$ for some suitable constant $\alpha > 1$. Do these results hold if we replace n by n^k for some fixed natural number $k > 1$?

Exercise 2.13 Verify that n^n is not $O(n!)$ but that $\log(n^n)$ is $O(\log(n!))$; similarly verify that $n^{\alpha \log n}$ is not $O(n^{\log n})$ for any $\alpha > 1$ but that $\log(n^{\alpha \log n})$ is $O(\log(n^{\log n}))$ for all $\alpha > 1$.

Exercise 2.14 Derive identities for the $O(\ )$ behavior of the sum and the product of functions; that is, knowing the $O(\ )$ behavior of functions f and g, what can you state about the $O(\ )$ behaviors of $h_1(x) = f(x) + g(x)$ and $h_2(x) = f(x) \cdot g(x)$?

Exercise 2.15 Asymptotic behavior can also be characterized by ratios. An alternate definition of $\Theta(\ )$ is given as follows: f is $\Theta(g)$ whenever

$$\lim_{n \to \infty} \frac{f(n)}{g(n)} = c$$

holds for some constant $c > 0$. Is this definition equivalent to ours?

Exercise 2.16 Prove that the number of nodes of odd degree in an undirected graph is always even.

Exercise 2.17* Prove Euler's result. One direction is trivial: if a vertex has odd degree, no Eulerian circuit can exist. To prove the other direction, consider moving along some arbitrary circuit that does not reuse edges, then remove its edges from the graph and use induction.

Exercise 2.18 Verify that a strongly connected graph has a single circuit (not necessarily simple) that includes every vertex.

Exercise 2.19 The *complement* of an undirected graph $G = (V, E)$ is the graph $\overline{G} = (V, \overline{E})$ in which two vertices are connected by an edge if and only if they are no so connected in G. A graph is *self-complementary* if it is isomorphic to its complement.

Prove that the number of vertices of a self-complementary graph must be a multiple of 4 or a multiple of 4 plus 1.

Exercise 2.20* A celebrated theorem of Euler's can be stated as follows in two-dimensional geometry: if $G = (V, E)$ is a connected planar graph, then the number of *regions* in any planar embedding of G is $|E| - |V| + 2$. (Any planar graph partitions the plane into regions, or faces; a region is a contiguous area of the plane bordered by a cycle of the graph and not containing any other region.)

Prove this result by using induction on the number of edges of G.

Exercise 2.21 Use the result of Exercise 2.20 to prove that the number of edges in a connected planar graph of at least three vertices cannot exceed $3|V| - 6$.

Exercise 2.22 Use the result of Exercise 2.21 to prove that the complement of a planar graph with a least eleven vertices must be nonplanar. Is eleven the smallest value with that property?

Exercise 2.23 Prove that a tree is a critically connected acyclic graph in the sense that (i) adding any edge to a tree causes a cycle and (ii) removing any edge from a tree disconnects the graph.

Exercise 2.24 Verify that, if $G = (V, E)$ is a tree, then the sum of the degrees of its vertices is $\sum_{i=1}^{|V|} d_i = 2(|V| - 1)$. Now prove that the converse is true; namely that, given n natural numbers, $\{d_i \mid i = 1, \ldots, n\}$, with $d_i \geq 1$ for all i and $\sum_{i=1}^{n} d_i = 2(n - 1)$, there exists a tree of n vertices where the ith vertex has degree d_i.

Exercise 2.25 A collection of trees is called (what else?) a *forest*. Prove that every tree has at least one vertex, the removal of which creates a forest where no single tree includes more than half of the vertices of the original tree.

Exercise 2.26 Devise a linear-time algorithm to find a maximum matching in a (free) tree.

Exercise 2.27* The problem of the *Set of Distinct Representatives (SDR)* is given by a bipartite graph, $G = (\{U, V\}, E)$, where U is the set of individuals and V the set of committees, with $|V| < |U|$; we desire a matching of size $|V|$. A celebrated result known as *Hall's theorem* states that such a matching (an SDR) exists if and only if, for each collection, $X \subseteq V$, of committees, the number of distinct individuals making up these committees is at least as large as the number of committees in the collection—that is, if and only if the following inequality holds for all collections X:

$$|\{u \in U \mid \exists v \in X, \ \{u, v\} \in E\}| \geq |X|$$

Prove this result—only the sufficiency part needs a proof, since the necessity of the condition is obvious; use induction on the size of X. (In the formulation in which we just gave it, this theorem may be more properly ascribed to König and Hall.)

Exercise 2.28* A *vertex cover* for an undirected graph is a subset of vertices such that every edge of the graph has at least one endpoint in the subset. Prove the *König-Egerváry theorem*: in a bipartite graph, the size of a maximum matching equals the size of a minimum cover.

Exercise 2.29 The *term rank* of a matrix is the maximum number of nonzero entries, no two in the same row or column. Verify that the following is an alternate formulation of the König-Egerváry theorem (see Exercise 2.28): the term rank of a matrix equals the minimum number of rows and columns that contain all of the nonzero entries of the matrix.

Exercise 2.30 A string of parentheses is *balanced* if and only if each left parenthesis has a matching right parenthesis and the substring of parentheses enclosed by the pair is itself balanced. Assign the value 1 to each left parenthesis and the value -1 to each right parenthesis. Now replace each value by the sum of all the values to its left, including itself—an operation known as *prefix sum*. Prove that a string of parentheses is balanced if and only if every value in the prefix sum is nonnegative and the last value is zero.

Exercise 2.31 How many distinct surjective (onto) functions are there from a set of m elements to a set of n elements (assuming $m \geq n$)? How many injective functions (assuming now $m \leq n$)?

Exercise 2.32 A *derangement* of the set $\{1, \ldots, n\}$ is a permutation π of the set such that, for any i in the set, we have $\pi(i) \neq i$. How many derangements are there for a set of size n? (Hint: write a recurrence relation.)

Exercise 2.33 Given a function $f \colon S \to T$, an inverse for f is a function $g \colon T \to S$ such that $f \cdot g$ is the identity on T and $g \cdot f$ is the identity on S. We denote the inverse of f by f^{-1}. Verify the following assertions:

1. If f has an inverse, it is unique.
2. A function has an inverse if and only if it is a bijection.
3. If f and g are two bijections and $h = f \cdot g$ is their composition, then the inverse of h is given by $h^{-1} = (f \cdot g)^{-1} = g^{-1} \cdot f^{-1}$.

Exercise 2.34 Prove that, at any party with at least two people, there must be two individuals who know the same number of people present at the party. (It is assumed that the relation "a knows b" is symmetric.)

Exercise 2.35 Design a bijection between the rational numbers and the natural numbers that avoids the repetitions of the mapping of Figure 2.8.

Exercise 2.36 How would you pair rational numbers; that is, how would you define a pairing function $p\colon \mathbb{Q} \times \mathbb{Q} \to \mathbb{Q}$?

Exercise 2.37 Compare the three pairing functions defined in the text in terms of their computational complexity. How efficiently can each pairing function and its associated projection functions be computed? Give a formal asymptotic analysis.

Exercise 2.38* Devise a new (a fourth) pairing function of your own with its associated projection functions.

Exercise 2.39 Consider again the bijection of Exercise 2.4. Although it is not a pairing function, show that it can be used for dovetailing.

Exercise 2.40 Would diagonalization work with a finite set? Describe how or discuss why not.

Exercise 2.41 Prove Cantor's original result: for any nonempty set S (whether finite or infinite), the cardinality of S is strictly less than that of its power set, $2^{|S|}$. You need to show that there exists an injective map from S to its power set, but that no such map exists from the power set to S—the latter through diagonalization. (A proof appears in Section A.3.4.)

Exercise 2.42 Verify that the union, intersection, and Cartesian product of two countable sets are themselves countable.

Exercise 2.43 Let S be a finite set and T a countable set. Is the set of all functions from S to T countable?

Exercise 2.44 Show that the set of all polynomials in the single variable x with integer coefficients is countable. Such polynomials are of the form $\sum_{i=0}^{n} a_i x^i$, for some natural number n and integers a_i, $i = 1, \ldots, n$. (Hint: use induction on the degree of the polynomials. Polynomials of degree zero are just the set $\mathbb{Z}$; each higher degree can be handled by one more application of dovetailing.)

Exercise 2.45 (Refer to the previous exercise.) Is the set of all polynomials in the two variables x and y with integer coefficients countable? Is the set of all polynomials (with *any* finite number of variables) with integer coefficients countable?

2.11   Bibliography

A large number of texts on discrete mathematics for computer science have appeared over the last fifteen years; any of them will cover most of the material in this chapter. Examples include Rosen [1988], Gersting [1993], and Epp [1995]. A more complete coverage may be found in the outstanding text of Sahni [1981]. Many texts on algorithms include a discussion of the nature of problems; Moret and Shapiro [1991] devote their first chapter to such a discussion, with numerous examples. Graphs are the subject of many texts and monographs; the text of Bondy and Murty [1976] is a particularly good introduction to graph theory, while that of Gibbons [1985] offers a more algorithmic perspective. While not required for an understanding of complexity theory, a solid grounding in the design and analysis of algorithms will help the reader appreciate the results; Moret and Shapiro [1991] and Brassard and Bratley [1996] are good references on the topic. Dovetailing and pairing functions were introduced early in this century by mathematicians interested in computability theory; we use them throughout this text, so that the reader will see many more examples. Diagonalization is a fundamental proof technique in all areas of theory, particularly in computer science; the reader will see many uses throughout this text, beginning with Chapter 5.

CHAPTER 3

Finite Automata and Regular Languages

3.1 Introduction

3.1.1 States and Automata

A *finite-state machine* or *finite automaton* (the noun comes from the Greek; the singular is "automaton," the Greek-derived plural is "automata," although "automatons" is considered acceptable in modern English) is a limited, mechanistic model of computation. Its main focus is the notion of *state*. This is a notion with which we are all familiar from interaction with many different controllers, such as elevators, ovens, stereo systems, and so on. All of these systems (but most obviously one like the elevator) can be in one of a fixed number of states. For instance, the elevator can be on any one of the floors, with doors open or closed, or it can be moving between floors; in addition, it may have pending requests to move to certain floors, generated from inside (by passengers) or from outside (by would-be passengers). The current state of the system entirely dictates what the system does next—something we can easily observe on very simple systems such as single elevators or microwave ovens. To a degree, of course, every machine ever made by man is a finite-state system; however, when the number of states grows large, the finite-state model ceases to be appropriate, simply because it defies comprehension by its users—namely humans. In particular, while a computer is certainly a finite-state system (its memory and registers can store either a 1 or a 0 in each of the bits, giving rise to a fixed number of states), the number of states is so large (a machine with 32 Mbytes of memory has on the order of $10^{81,000,000}$ states—a mathematician from the intuitionist school would flatly deny that this is a "finite" number!) that it is altogether unreasonable to consider it to be a finite-state machine. However, the finite-state model works well for logic circuit design (arithmetic and logic units, buffers, I/O handlers, etc.) and for certain programming utilities (such well-known Unix tools as `lex`, `grep`, `awk`, and others, including the pattern-matching tools of editors, are directly based on finite automata), where the number of states remains small.

Informally, a finite automaton is characterized by a finite set of states and a *transition function* that dictates how the automaton moves from one state to another. At this level of characterization, we can introduce a graphical representation of the finite automaton, in which states are represented as disks and transitions between states as arcs between the disks. The starting state (the state in which the automaton begins processing) is identified by a tail-less arc pointing to it; in Figure 3.1(a), this state is q_1. The input can be regarded as a string that is processed symbol by symbol from left to right, each symbol inducing a transition before being discarded. Graphically, we label each transition with the symbol or symbols that cause it to happen. Figure 3.1(b) shows an automaton with input alphabet $\{0, 1\}$. The automaton stops when the input string has been completely processed; thus on an input string of n symbols, the automaton goes through exactly n transitions before stopping.

More formally, a finite automaton is a four-tuple, made of an alphabet, a set of states, a distinguished starting state, and a transition function. In the example of Figure 3.1(b), the alphabet is $\Sigma = \{0, 1\}$; the set of states is $Q = \{q_1, q_2, q_3\}$; the start state is q_1; and the transition function δ, which uses the current state and current input symbol to determine the next state, is given by the table of Figure 3.2. Note that δ is not defined for every possible input pair: if the machine is in state q_2 and the current input symbol is 1, then the machine stops in error.

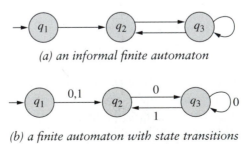

(a) an informal finite automaton

(b) a finite automaton with state transitions

Figure 3.1   Informal finite automata.

δ	0	1
q_1	q_2	q_2
q_2	q_3	
q_3	q_3	q_2

Figure 3.2   The transition function for the automaton of Figure 3.1(b).

As defined, a finite automaton processes an input string but does not produce anything. We could define an automaton that produces a symbol from some output alphabet at each transition or in each state, thus producing a transducer, an automaton that transforms an input string on the input alphabet into an output string on the output alphabet. Such transducers are called *sequential machines* by computer engineers (or, more specifically, *Moore machines* when the output is produced in each state and *Mealy machines* when the output is produced at each transition) and are used extensively in designing logic circuits. In software, similar transducers are implemented in software for various string handling tasks (`lex`, `grep`, and `sed`, to name but a few, are all utilities based on finite-state transducers). We shall instead remain at the simpler level of language membership, where the transducers compute maps from Σ^* to $\{0, 1\}$ rather than to Δ^* for some output alphabet Δ. The results we shall obtain in this simpler framework are easier to derive yet extend easily to the more general framework.

3.1.2   Finite Automata as Language Acceptors

Finite automata can be used to recognize languages, i.e., to implement functions $f : \Sigma^* \to \{0, 1\}$. The finite automaton decides whether the string is in the language with the help of a label (the value of the function) assigned to each of its states: when the finite automaton stops in some state q, the label of q gives the value of the function. In the case of language acceptance, there are only two labels: 0 and 1, or "reject" and "accept." Thus we can view the set of states of a finite automaton used for language recognition as partitioned into two subsets, the *rejecting* states and the *accepting* states. Graphically, we distinguish the accepting states by double circles, as shown in Figure 3.3. This finite automaton has two states, one accepting and one rejecting; its input alphabet is $\{0, 1\}$; it can easily be seen to accept every string with an even (possibly zero) number of 1s. Since the initial state is accepting, this automaton accepts the empty string. As further examples, the automaton of Figure 3.4(a) accepts *only* the empty string,

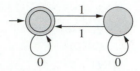

Figure 3.3   An automaton that accepts strings with an even number of 1s.

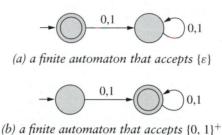

(a) a finite automaton that accepts {ε}

(b) a finite automaton that accepts {0, 1}⁺

Figure 3.4   Some simple finite automata.

while that of Figure 3.4(b) accepts everything *except* the empty string. This last construction may suggest that, in order to accept the complement of a language, it suffices to "flip" the labels assigned to states, turning rejecting states into accepting ones and vice versa.

Exercise 3.1   Decide whether this idea works in all cases.   □

A more complex example of finite automaton is illustrated in Figure 3.5. It accepts all strings with an equal number of 0s and 1s such that, in any prefix of an accepted string, the number of 0s and the number of 1s differ by at most one. The bottom right-hand state is a *trap*: once the automaton

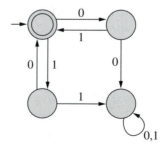

Figure 3.5   A more complex finite automaton.

has entered this state, it cannot leave it. This particular trap is a rejecting state; the automaton of Figure 3.4(b) had an accepting trap.

We are now ready to give a formal definition of a finite automaton.

Definition 3.1 A *deterministic finite automaton* is a five-tuple, $(\Sigma, Q, q_0, F, \delta)$, where Σ is the input alphabet, Q the set of states, $q_0 \in Q$ the start state, $F \subseteq Q$ the final states, and $\delta: Q \times \Sigma \to Q$ the transition function.   □

Our choice of the formalism for the transition function actually makes the automaton *deterministic*, conforming to the examples seen so far. Nondeterministic automata can also be defined—we shall look at this distinction shortly.

Moving from a finite automaton to a description of the language that it accepts is not always easy, but it is always possible. The reverse direction is more complex because there are many languages that a finite automaton cannot recognize. Later we shall see a formal proof of the fact, along with an exact characterization of those languages that can be accepted by a finite automaton; for now, let us just look at some simple examples.

Consider first the language of all strings that end with 0. In designing this automaton, we can think of its having two states: when it starts or after it has seen a 1, it has made no progress towards acceptance; on the other hand, after seeing a 0 it is ready to accept. The result is depicted in Figure 3.6.

Consider now the set of all strings that, viewed as natural numbers in unsigned binary notation, represent numbers divisible by 5. The key here is to realize that division in binary is a very simple operation with only two possible results (1 or 0); our automaton will mimic the longhand division by 5 (101 in binary), using its states to denote the current value of the remainder. Leading 0s are irrelevant and eliminated in the start state (call it A); since this state corresponds to a remainder of 0 (i.e., an exact division by 5), it is an accepting state. Then consider the next bit, a 1 by assumption. If the input stopped at this point, we would have an input value and thus also a remainder of 1; call the state corresponding to a remainder of 1 state B—a rejecting state. Now, if the next bit is a 1, the input (and also remainder)

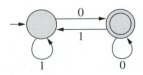

Figure 3.6 An automaton that accepts all strings ending with a 0.

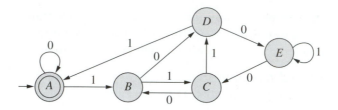

Figure 3.7   An automaton that accepts multiples of 5.

so far is 11, so we move to a state (call it C) corresponding to a remainder of 3; if the next bit is a 0, the input (and also remainder) is 10, so we move to a state (call it D) corresponding to a remainder of 2. From state D, an input of 0 gives us a current remainder of 100, so we move to a state (call it E) corresponding to a remainder of 4; an input of 1, on the other hand, gives us a remainder of 101, which is the same as no remainder at all, so we move back to state A. Moves from states C and E are handled similarly. The resulting finite automaton is depicted in Figure 3.7.

3.1.3   Determinism and Nondeterminism

In all of the fully worked examples of finite automata given earlier, there was exactly one transition out of each state for each possible input symbol. That such must be the case is implied in our formal definition: the transition function δ is well defined. However, in our first example of transitions (Figure 3.2), we looked at an automaton where the transition function remained undefined for one combination of current state and current input, that is, where the transition function δ did not map every element of its domain. Such transition functions are occasionally useful; when the automaton reaches a configuration in which no transition is defined, the standard convention is to assume that the automaton "aborts" its operation and rejects its input string. (In particular, a rejecting trap has no defined transitions at all.) In a more confusing vein, what if, in some state, there had been two or more different transitions for the same input symbol? Again, our formal definition precludes this possibility, since $\delta(q_i, a)$ can have only one value in Q; however, once again, such an extension to our mechanism often proves useful. The presence of multiple valid transitions leads to a certain amount of uncertainty as to what the finite automaton will do and thus, potentially, as to what it will accept. We define a finite automaton to be *deterministic* if and only if, for each combination of state and input symbol, it has at most one transition. A finite automaton that allows multiple transitions for the same combination of state and input symbol will be termed *nondeterministic*.

Nondeterminism is a common occurrence in the worlds of particle physics and of computers. It is a standard consequence of concurrency: when multiple systems interact, the timing vagaries at each site create an inherent unpredictability regarding the interactions among these systems. While the operating system designer regards such nondeterminism as both a boon (extra flexibility) and a bane (it cannot be allowed to lead to different outcomes, a catastrophe known in computer science as indeterminacy, and so must be suitably controlled), the theoretician is simply concerned with suitably defining under what circumstances a nondeterministic machine can be termed to have accepted its input. The key to understanding the convention adopted by theoreticians regarding nondeterministic finite automata (and other nondeterministic machines) is to realize that nondeterminism induces a *tree* of possible computations for each input string, rather than the single line of computation observed in a deterministic machine. The branching of the tree corresponds to the several possible transitions available to the machine at that stage of computation. Each of the possible computations eventually terminates (after exactly n transitions, as observed earlier) at a leaf of the computation tree. A stylized computation tree is illustrated in Figure 3.8. In some of these computations, the machine may accept its input; in others, it may reject it—even though it is the same input. We can easily dispose of computation trees where all leaves correspond to accepting states: the input can be defined as accepted; we can equally easily dispose of computation trees where all leaves correspond to rejecting states: the input can be defined as rejected. What we need to address is those computation trees where some computation paths lead to acceptance and others to rejection; the convention adopted by the

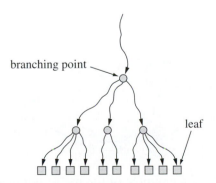

Figure 3.8   A stylized computation tree.

(evidently optimistic) theory community is that such mixed trees also result in acceptance of the input. This convention leads us to define a general finite automaton.

Definition 3.2 A *nondeterministic finite automaton* is a five-tuple, $(\Sigma, Q, q_0, F, \delta)$, where Σ is the input alphabet, Q the set of states, $q_0 \in Q$ the start state, $F \subseteq Q$ the final states, and $\delta: Q \times \Sigma \to 2^Q$ the transition function.   □

Note the change from our definition of a deterministic finite automaton: the transition function now maps $Q \times \Sigma$ to 2^Q, the set of all subsets of Q, rather than just into Q itself. This change allows transition functions that map state/character pairs to zero, one, or more next states. We say that a finite automaton is deterministic whenever we have $|\delta(q, a)| \leq 1$ for all $q \in Q$ and $a \in \Sigma$.

Using our new definition, we say that a nondeterministic machine accepts its input whenever there is a sequence of choices in its transitions that will allow it to do so. We can also think of there being a separate *deterministic* machine for each path in the computation tree—in which case there need be only one deterministic machine that accepts a string for the nondeterministic machine to accept that string. Finally, we can also view a nondeterministic machine as a perfect guesser: whenever faced with a choice of transitions, it always chooses one that will allow it to accept the input, assuming any such transition is available—if such is not the case, it chooses any of the transitions, since all will lead to rejection.

Consider the nondeterministic finite automaton of Figure 3.9, which accepts all strings that contain one of three possible substrings: 000, 111, or 1100. The computation tree on the input string 01011000 is depicted in Figure 3.10. (The paths marked with an asterisk denote paths where the automaton is stuck in a state because it had no transition available.) There are two accepting paths out of ten, corresponding to the detection of the substrings 000 and 1100. The nondeterministic finite automaton thus accepts 01011000 because there is at least one way (here two) for it to do

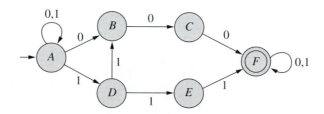

Figure 3.9   An example of the use of nondeterminism.

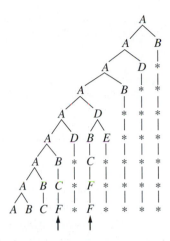

Figure 3.10   The computation tree for the automaton of Figure 3.9 on input string 01011000.

so. For instance, it can decide to stay in state A when reading the first three symbols, then guess that the next 1 is the start of a substring 1100 or 111 and thus move to state D. In that state, it guesses that the next 1 indicates the substring 1100 rather than 111 and thus moves to state B rather than E. From state B, it has no choice left to make and correctly ends in accepting state F when all of the input has been processed. We can view its behavior as checking the sequence of guesses (*left, left, left, right, left, –, –, –*) in the computation tree. (That the tree nodes have at most two children each is peculiar to this automaton; in general, a node in the tree can have up to $|Q|$ children, one for each possible choice of next state.)

When exploiting nondeterminism, we should consider the idea of *choice*. The strength of a nondeterministic finite automaton resides in its ability to choose with perfect accuracy under the rules of nondeterminism. For example, consider the set of all strings that end in either 100 or in 001. The deterministic automaton has to consider both types of strings and so uses states to keep track of the possibilities that arise from either suffix or various substrings thereof. The nondeterministic automaton can simply guess which ending the string will have and proceed to verify the guess—since there are two possible guesses, there are two verification paths. The nondeterministic automaton just "gobbles up" symbols until it guesses that there are only three symbols left, at which point it also guesses which ending the string will have and proceeds to verify that guess, as shown in Figure 3.11. Of course, with all these choices, there are many guesses that

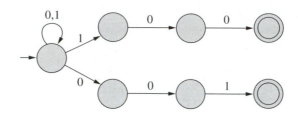

Figure 3.11   Checking guesses with nondeterminism.

lead to a rejecting state (guess that there are three remaining symbols when there are more, or fewer, left, or guess the wrong ending), but the string will be accepted as long as there is one accepting path for it.

However, this accurate guessing must obey the rules of nondeterminism: the machine cannot simply guess that it should accept the string or guess that it should reject it—something that would lead to the automaton illustrated in Figure 3.12. In fact, this automaton accepts Σ^*, because it is possible for it to accept any string and thus, in view of the rules of nondeterminism, it must then do so.

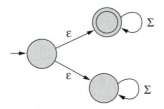

Figure 3.12   A nondeterministic finite automaton that simply guesses whether to accept or reject.

3.1.4   Checking vs. Computing

A better way to view nondeterminism is to realize that the nondeterministic automaton need only *verify* a simple guess to establish that the string is in the language, whereas the deterministic automaton must painstakingly process the string, keeping information about the various pieces that contribute to membership. This guessing model makes it clear that nondeterminism allows a machine to make efficient decisions whenever a series of guesses leads rapidly to a conclusion. As we shall see later (when talking about complexity), this aspect is very important. Consider the simple example of deciding whether a string has a specific character occurring 10 positions from the end. A nondeterministic automaton can simply guess which is the tenth position from the end of the string and check that (i) the desired character occurs there and (ii) there are indeed exactly 9 more characters left in the string. In contrast, a deterministic automaton must keep track in its finite-state control of a "window" of 9 consecutive input characters— a requirement that leads to a very large number of states and a complex transition function. The simple guess of a position within the input string changes the scope of the task drastically: verifying the guess is quite easy, whereas a direct computation of the answer is quite tedious.

In other words, nondeterminism is about *guessing and checking*: the machine guesses both the answer and the path that will lead to it, then follows that path, verifying its guess in the process. In contrast, determinism is just straightforward computing—no shortcut is available, so the machine simply crunches through whatever has to be done to derive an answer. Hence the question (which we tackle for finite automata in the next section) of whether or not nondeterministic machines are more powerful than deterministic ones is really a question of whether verifying answers is easier than computing them. In the context of mathematics, the (correct) guess is the *proof* itself! We thus gain a new perspective on Hilbert's program: we can indeed write a proof-checking machine, but any such machine will efficiently verify certain types of proofs and not others. Many problems have easily verifiable proofs (for instance, it is easy to check a proof that a Boolean formula is satisfiable if the proof is a purported satisfying truth assignment), but many others do not appear to have any concise or easily checkable proof. Consider for instance the question of whether or not White, at chess, has a forced win (a question for which we do not know the answer). What would it take for someone to convince you that the answer is "yes"? Basically, it would appear that verifying the answer, in this case, is just as hard as deriving it.

Thus, depending on the context (such as the type of machines involved or the resource bounds specified), verifying may be easier than or just as hard as solving—often, we do not know which is the correct statement. The most famous (and arguably the most important) open question in computer science, "Is P equal to NP?" (about which we shall have a great deal to say in Chapters 6 and beyond), is one such question. We shall soon see that nondeterminism does not add power to finite automata—whatever a nondeterministic automaton can do can also be done by a (generally much larger) deterministic finite automaton; the attraction of nondeterministic finite automata resides in their relative simplicity.

3.2   Properties of Finite Automata

3.2.1   Equivalence of Finite Automata

We see from their definition that nondeterministic finite automata include deterministic ones as a special case—the case where the number of transitions defined for each pair of current state and current input symbol never exceeds one. Thus any language that can be accepted by a deterministic finite automaton can be accepted by a nondeterministic one—the same machine. What about the converse? Are nondeterministic finite automata more powerful than deterministic ones? Clearly there are problems for which a nondeterministic automaton will require fewer states than a deterministic one, but that is a question of resources, not an absolute question of potential.

We settle the question in the negative: nondeterministic finite automata are no more powerful than deterministic ones. Our proof is a simulation: given an arbitrary nondeterministic finite automaton, we construct a deterministic one that mimics the behavior of the nondeterministic machine. In particular, the deterministic machine uses its state to keep track of all of the possible states in which the nondeterministic machine could find itself after reading the same string.

Theorem 3.1 For every nondeterministic finite automaton, there exists an equivalent deterministic finite automaton (i.e., one that accepts the same language). ☐

Proof. Let the nondeterministic finite automaton be given by the five-tuple $(\Sigma, Q, F, q_0, \delta)$. We construct an equivalent deterministic automaton $(\Sigma', Q', F', q_0', \delta')$ as follows:

- $\Sigma' = \Sigma$
- $Q' = 2^Q$
- $F' = \{s \in Q' \mid s \cap F \neq \emptyset\}$
- $q_0' = \{q_0\}$

The key idea is to define one state of the deterministic machine for each possible combination of states of the nondeterministic one—hence the $2^{|Q|}$ possible states of the equivalent deterministic machine. In that way, there is a unique state for the deterministic machine, no matter how many computation paths exist at the same step for the nondeterministic machine. In order to define δ', we recall that the purpose of the simulation is to keep track, in the state of the deterministic machine, of all computation paths of the nondeterministic one. Let the machines be at some step in their computation where the next input symbol is a. If the nondeterministic machine can be in any of states $q_{i_1}, q_{i_2}, \ldots, q_{i_k}$ at that step—so that the corresponding deterministic machine is then in state $\{q_{i_1}, q_{i_2}, \ldots, q_{i_k}\}$—then it can move to any of the states contained in the sets $\delta(q_{i_1}, a), \delta(q_{i_2}, a), \ldots, \delta(q_{i_k}, a)$—so that the corresponding deterministic machine moves to state

$$\delta'(\{q_{i_1}, q_{i_2}, \ldots, q_{i_k}\}, a) = \bigcup_{j=1}^{k} \delta(q_{i_j}, a)$$

Since the nondeterministic machine accepts if any computation path leads to acceptance, the deterministic machine must accept if it ends in a state that includes any of the final states of the nondeterministic machine—hence our definition of F'. It is clear that our constructed deterministic finite automaton accepts exactly the same strings as those accepted by the given nondeterministic finite automaton.   Q.E.D.

Example 3.1 Consider the nondeterministic finite automaton given by

$\Sigma = \{0, 1\}$, $Q = \{a, b\}$, $F = \{a\}$, $q_0 = a$,

$\delta:$
$$\delta(a, 0) = \{a, b\} \quad \delta(a, 1) = \{b\}$$
$$\delta(b, 0) = \{b\} \quad\quad \delta(b, 1) = \{a\}$$

and illustrated in Figure 3.13(a). The corresponding deterministic finite automaton is given by

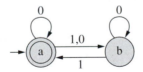

(a) the nondeterministic finite automaton

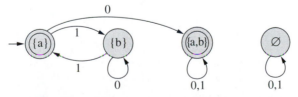

(b) the equivalent deterministic finite automaton

Figure 3.13 A nondeterministic automaton and an equivalent deterministic finite automaton.

$\Sigma = \{0, 1\}$, $Q' = \{\emptyset, \{a\}, \{b\}, \{a, b\}\}$, $F' = \{\{a\}, \{a, b\}\}$, $q_0' = \{a\}$,

δ':
$$\delta'(\emptyset, 0) = \emptyset \qquad\qquad \delta'(\emptyset, 1) = \emptyset$$
$$\delta'(\{a\}, 0) = \{a, b\} \qquad \delta'(\{a\}, 1) = \{b\}$$
$$\delta'(\{b\}, 0) = \{b\} \qquad\quad\; \delta'(\{b\}, 1) = \{a\}$$
$$\delta'(\{a, b\}, 0) = \{a, b\} \quad \delta'(\{a, b\}, 1) = \{a, b\}$$

and illustrated in Figure 3.13(b) (note that state $\emptyset$ is unreachable).   □

Thus the conversion of a nondeterministic automaton to a determin-istic one creates a machine, the states of which are all the subsets of the set of states of the nondeterministic automaton. The conversion takes a nondeterministic automaton with n states and creates a deterministic au-tomaton with 2^n states, an exponential increase. However, as we saw briefly, many of these states may be useless, because they are unreachable from the start state; in particular, the empty state is always unreachable. In general, the conversion may create any number of unreachable states, as shown in Figure 3.14, where five of the eight states are unreachable. When generat-ing a deterministic automaton from a given nondeterministic one, we can avoid generating unreachable states by using an iterative approach based on reachability: begin with the initial state of the nondeterministic automa-ton and proceed outward to those states reachable by the nondeterministic automaton. This process will generate only useful states—states reachable from the start state—and so may be considerably more efficient than the brute-force generation of all subsets.

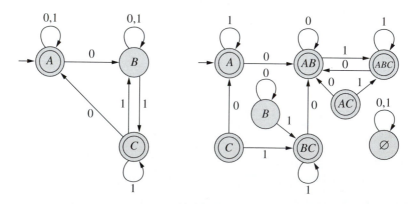

Figure 3.14   A conversion that creates many unreachable states.

3.2.2   ε Transitions

An ε transition is a transition that does not use any input—a "spontaneous" transition: the automaton simply "decides" to change states without reading any symbol.

Such a transition makes sense only in a nondeterministic automaton: in a deterministic automaton, an ε transition from state A to state B would have to be the single transition out of A (any other transition would induce a nondeterministic choice), so that we could merge state A and state B, simply redirecting all transitions into A to go to B, and thus eliminating the ε transition. Thus an ε transition is essentially nondeterministic.

Example 3.2 Given two finite automata, M_1 and M_2, design a new finite automaton that accepts all strings accepted by either machine. The new machine "guesses" which machine will accept the current string, then sends the whole string to that machine through an ε transition.   □

The obvious question at this point is: "Do ε transitions add power to finite automata?" As in the case of nondeterminism, our answer will be "no."

Assume that we are given a finite automaton with ε transitions; let its transition function be δ. Let us define $\delta'(q, a)$ to be the set of all states that can be reached by

1. zero or more ε transitions; followed by
2. one transition on a; followed by
3. zero or more ε transitions.

This is the set of all states reachable from state q in our machine while reading the single input symbol a; we call δ' the *ε-closure* of δ.

In Figure 3.15, for instance, the states reachable from state q through the three steps are:

1. {q, 1, 2, 3}
2. {4, 6, 8}
3. {4, 5, 6, 7, 8, 9, 10}

so that we get $\delta'(q, a) = \{4, 5, 6, 7, 8, 9, 10\}$

Theorem 3.2 For every finite automaton with ε transitions, there exists an equivalent finite automaton without ε transitions.   □

We do not specify whether the finite automaton is deterministic or nondeterministic, since we have already proved that the two have equivalent power.

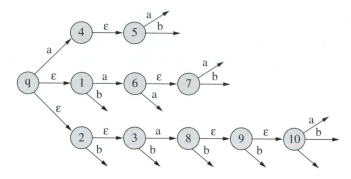

Figure 3.15   Moving through ε transitions.

Proof. Assume that we have been given a finite automaton with ε transitions and with transition function δ. We construct δ' as defined earlier. Our new automaton has the same set of states, the same alphabet, the same starting state, and (with one possible exception) the same set of accepting states, but its transition function is now δ' rather than δ and so does not include any ε moves. Finally, if the original automaton had any (chain of) ε transitions from its start state to an accepting state, we make that start state in our new automaton an accepting state. We claim that the two machines recognize the same language; more specifically, we claim that the set of states reachable under some input string $x \neq \varepsilon$ in the original machine is the same as the set of states reachable under the same input string in our ε-free machine and that the two machines both accept or both reject the empty string. The latter is ensured by our correction for the start state. For the former, our proof proceeds by induction on the length of strings. The two machines can reach exactly the same states from any given state (in particular from the start state) on an input string of length 1, by construction of δ'. Assume that, after processing i input characters, the two machines have the same reachable set of states. From each of the states that could have been reached after i input characters, the two machines can reach the same set of states by reading one more character, by construction of δ'. Thus the set of all states reachable after reading $i + 1$ characters is the union of identical sets over an identical index and thus the two machines can reach the same set of states after $i + 1$ steps. Hence one machine can accept whatever string the other can.   Q.E.D.

Thus a finite automaton is well defined in terms of its power to recognize languages—we do not need to be more specific about its characteristics, since all versions (deterministic or not, with or without ε transitions) have equivalent power. We call the set of all languages recognized by finite automata the *regular languages*.

Not every language is regular: some languages cannot be accepted by any finite automaton. These include all languages that can be accepted only through some unbounded count, such as $\{1, 101, 101001, 1010010001, \dots\}$ or $\{\varepsilon, 01, 0011, 000111, \dots\}$. A finite automaton has no dynamic memory: its only "memory" is its set of states, through which it can count only to a fixed constant—so that counting to arbitrary values, as is required in the two languages just given, is impossible. We shall prove this statement and obtain an exact characterization later.

3.3 Regular Expressions

3.3.1 Definitions and Examples

Regular expressions were designed by mathematicians to denote regular languages with a mathematical tool, a tool built from a set of primitives (generators in mathematical parlance) and operations.

For instance, arithmetic (on nonnegative integers) is a language built from one generator (zero, the one fundamental number), one basic operation (successor, which generates the "next" number—it is simply an incrementation), and optional operations (such as addition, multiplication, etc.), each defined inductively (recursively) from existing operations. Compare the ease with which we can prove statements about nonnegative integers with the incredible lengths to which we have to go to prove even a small piece of code to be correct. The mechanical models—automata, programs, etc.—all suffer from their basic premise, namely the notion of state. States make formal proofs extremely cumbersome, mostly because they offer no natural mechanism for induction.

Another problem of finite automata is their nonlinear format: they are best represented graphically (not a convenient data entry mechanism), since they otherwise require elaborate conventions for encoding the transition table. No one would long tolerate having to define finite automata for pattern-matching tasks in searching and editing text. Regular expressions, on the other hand, are simple strings much like arithmetic expressions, with a simple and familiar syntax; they are well suited for use by humans in describing patterns for string processing. Indeed, they form the basis for the pattern-matching commands of editors and text processors.

Definition 3.3 A regular expression on some alphabet Σ is defined inductively as follows:

- $\emptyset$, ε, and a (for any $a \in \Sigma$) are regular expressions.
- If P and Q are regular expressions, $P + Q$ is a regular expression (union).
- If P and Q are regular expressions, PQ is a regular expression (concatenation).
- If P is a regular expression, P^* is a regular expression (Kleene closure).
- Nothing else is a regular expression.   □

The three operations are chosen to produce larger sets from smaller ones—which is why we picked union but not intersection. For the sake of avoiding large numbers of parentheses, we let Kleene closure have highest precedence, concatenation intermediate precedence, and union lowest precedence.

This definition sets up an abstract universe of expressions, much like arithmetic expressions. Examples of regular expressions on the alphabet $\{0, 1\}$ include ε, 0, 1, $\varepsilon + 1$, 1^*, $(0 + 1)^*$, $10^*(\varepsilon + 1)1^*$, etc. However, these expressions are not as yet associated with languages: we have defined the syntax of the regular expressions but not their semantics. We now rectify this omission:

- $\emptyset$ is a regular expression denoting the empty set.
- ε is a regular expression denoting the set $\{\varepsilon\}$.
- $a \in \Sigma$ is a regular expression denoting the set $\{a\}$.
- If P and Q are regular expressions, PQ is a regular expression denoting the set $\{xy \mid x \in P \text{ and } y \in Q\}$.
- If P and Q are regular expressions, $P + Q$ is a regular expression denoting the set $\{x \mid x \in P \text{ or } x \in Q\}$.
- If P is a regular expression, P^* is a regular expression denoting the set $\{\varepsilon\} \cup \{xw \mid x \in P \text{ and } w \in P^*\}$.

This last definition is recursive: we define P^* in terms of itself. Put in English, the *Kleene closure* of a set S is the infinite union of the sets obtained by concatenating zero or more copies of S. For instance, the Kleene closure of $\{1\}$ is simply the set of all strings composed of zero or more 1s, i.e., $1^* = \{\varepsilon, 1, 11, 111, 1111, \dots\}$; the Kleene closure of the set $\{0, 11\}$ is the set $\{\varepsilon, 0, 11, 00, 011, 110, 1111, \dots\}$; and the Kleene closure of the set Σ (the alphabet) is Σ^* (yes, that is the same notation!), the set of all possible strings over the alphabet. For convenience, we shall define $P^+ = PP^*$; that is, P^+ differs from P^* in that it must contain at least one copy of an element of P.

Let us go through some further examples of regular expressions. Assume the alphabet $\Sigma = \{0, 1\}$; then the following are regular expressions over Σ:

- ∅ representing the empty set
- 0 representing the set $\{0\}$
- 1 representing the set $\{1\}$
- 11 representing the set $\{11\}$
- $0 + 1$, representing the set $\{0, 1\}$
- $(0 + 1)1$, representing the set $\{01, 11\}$
- $(0 + 1)1^*$, representing the infinite set $\{1, 11, 111, 1111, \ldots, 0, 01, 011, 0111, \ldots\}$
- $(0 + 1)^* = \varepsilon + (0 + 1) + (0 + 1)(0 + 1) + \ldots = \Sigma^*$
- $(0 + 1)^+ = (0 + 1)(0 + 1)^* = \Sigma^+ = \Sigma^* - \{\varepsilon\}$

The same set can be denoted by a variety of regular expressions; indeed, when given a complex regular expression, it often pays to simplify it before attempting to understand the language it defines. Consider, for instance, the regular expression $((0 + 1)10^*(0 + 1^*))^*$. The subexpression $10^*(0 + 1^*)$ can be expanded to $10^*0 + 10^*1^*$, which, using the $^+$ notation, can be rewritten as $10^+ + 10^*1^*$. We see that the second term includes all strings denoted by the first term, so that the first term can be dropped. (In set union, if A contains B, then we have $A \cup B = A$.) Thus our expression can be written in the simpler form $((0 + 1)10^*1^*)^*$ and means in English: zero or more repetitions of strings chosen from the set of strings made up of a 0 or a 1 followed by a 1 followed by zero or more 0s followed by zero or more 1s.

3.3.2   Regular Expressions and Finite Automata

Regular expressions, being a mathematical tool (as opposed to a mechanical tool like finite automata), lend themselves to formal manipulations of the type used in proofs and so provide an attractive alternative to finite automata when reasoning about regular languages. But we must first prove that regular expressions and finite automata are equivalent, i.e., that they denote the same set of languages.

Our proof consists of showing that (i) for every regular expression, there is a (nondeterministic) finite automaton with ε transitions and (ii) for every deterministic finite automaton, there is a regular expression. We have previously seen how to construct a deterministic finite automaton from a nondeterministic one and how to remove ε transitions. Hence, once the proof has been made, it will be possible to go from any form of finite automaton to a regular expression and vice versa. We use a deterministic finite automaton in part (i) because it is an easier machine to simulate with regular expressions; conversely, we use nondeterministic finite automata with ε transitions for part (ii) because they are a more expressive (though not more powerful) model in which to translate regular expressions.

Theorem 3.3 For every regular expression there is an equivalent finite automaton.

□

Proof. The proof hinges on the fact that regular expressions are defined recursively, so that, once the basic steps are shown for constructing finite automata for the primitive elements of regular expressions, finite automata for regular expressions of arbitrary complexity can be constructed by showing how to combine component finite automata to simulate the basic operations. For convenience, we shall construct finite automata with a unique accepting state. (Any nondeterministic finite automaton with ε moves can easily be transformed into one with a unique accepting state by adding such a state, setting up an ε transition to this new state from every original accepting state, and then turning all original accepting states into rejecting ones.)

For the regular expression $\emptyset$ denoting the empty set, the corresponding finite automaton is

For the regular expression ε denoting the set $\{\varepsilon\}$, the corresponding finite automaton is

For the regular expression a denoting the set $\{a\}$, the corresponding finite automaton is

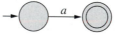

If P and Q are regular expressions with corresponding finite automata M_P and M_Q, then we can construct a finite automaton denoting $P + Q$ in the following manner:

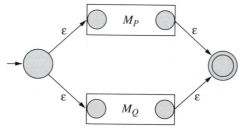

The ε transitions at the end are needed to maintain a unique accepting state.

If P and Q are regular expressions with corresponding finite automata M_P and M_Q, then we can construct a finite automaton denoting PQ in the following manner:

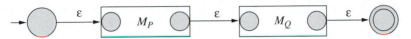

Finally, if P is a regular expression with corresponding finite automaton M_P, then we can construct a finite automaton denoting P^* in the following manner:

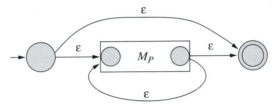

Again, the extra ε transitions are here to maintain a unique accepting state.

It is clear that each finite automaton described above accepts exactly the set of strings described by the corresponding regular expression (assuming inductively that the submachines used in the construction accept exactly the set of strings described by their corresponding regular expressions). Since, for each constructor of regular expressions, we have a corresponding constructor of finite automata, the induction step is proved and our proof is complete.   *Q.E.D.*

We have proved that for every regular expression, there exists an equivalent nondeterministic finite automaton with ε transitions. In the proof, we chose the type of finite automaton with which it is easiest to proceed— the nondeterministic finite automaton. The proof was by constructive induction. The finite automata for the basic pieces of regular expressions ($\emptyset$, ε, and individual symbols) were used as the basis of the proof. By converting the legal operations that can be performed on these basic pieces into finite automata, we showed that these pieces can be inductively built into larger and larger finite automata that correspond to the larger and larger pieces of the regular expression as it is built up. Our construction made no attempt to be efficient: it typically produces cumbersome and redundant machines. For an "efficient" conversion of regular expressions to finite automata, it is generally better to understand what the expression is conveying, and then design an *ad hoc* finite automaton that accomplishes the same thing. However, the mechanical construction used in the proof was needed to prove that *any* regular expression can be converted to a finite automaton.

3.3.3   Regular Expressions from Deterministic Finite Automata

In order to show the equivalence of finite automata to regular expressions, it is necessary to show both that there is a finite automaton for every regular expression and that there is a regular expression for every finite automaton. The first part has just been proved. We shall now demonstrate the second part: given a finite automaton, we can always construct a regular expression that denotes the same language. As before, we are free to choose the type of automaton that is easiest to work with, since all finite automata are equivalent. In this case the most restricted finite automaton, the deterministic finite automaton, best serves our purpose. Our proof is again an inductive, mechanical construction, which generally produces an unnecessarily cumbersome, though infallibly correct, regular expression.

In finding an approach to this proof, we need a general way to talk about and to build up paths, with the aim of describing all accepting paths through the automaton with a regular expression. However, due to the presence of loops, paths can be arbitrarily large; thus most machines have an infinite number of accepting paths. Inducting on the length or number of paths, therefore, is not feasible. The number of states in the machine, however, is a constant; no matter how long a path is, it cannot pass through more distinct states than are contained in the machine. Therefore we should be able to induct on some ordering related to the number of distinct states present in a path. The length of the path is unrelated to the number of distinct states seen on the path and so remains (correctly) unaffected by the inductive ordering.

For a deterministic finite automaton with n states, which are numbered from 1 to n, consider the paths from node (state) i to node j. In building up an expression for these paths, we proceed inductively on the index of the highest-numbered intermediate state used in getting from i to j. Define R_{ij}^k as the set of all paths from state i to state j that do not pass through any intermediate state numbered higher than k. We will develop the capability to talk about the universe of all paths through the machine by inducting on k from 0 to n (the number of states in the machine), for all pairs of nodes i and j in the machine.

On these paths, the intermediate states (those states numbered no higher than k through which the paths can pass), can be used repeatedly; in contrast, states i and j (unless they are also numbered no higher than k) can be only left (i) or entered (j). Put another way, "passing through" a node means both entering and leaving the node; simply entering or leaving the node, as happens with nodes i and j, does not matter in figuring k.

This approach, due to Kleene, is in effect a dynamic programming technique, identical to Floyd's algorithm for generating all shortest paths in a graph. The construction is entirely artificial and meant only to yield an ordering for induction. In particular, the specific ordering of the states (which state is labeled 1, which is labeled 2, and so forth) is irrelevant: for each possible labeling, the construction proceeds in the same way.

The Base Case

The base case for the proof is the set of paths described by R_{ij}^0 for all pairs of nodes i and j in the deterministic finite automaton. For a specific pair of nodes i and j, these are the paths that go directly from node i to node j without passing through any intermediate states. These paths are described by the following regular expressions:

- ε if we have $i = j$ (ε is the path of length 0); and/or
- a if we have $\delta(q_i, a) = q_j$ (including the case $i = j$ with a self-loop).

Consider for example the deterministic finite automaton of Figure 3.16. Some of the base cases for a few pairs of nodes are given in Figure 3.17.

The Inductive Step

We now devise an inductive step and then proceed to build up regular expressions inductively from the base cases.

The inductive step must define R_{ij}^k in terms of lower values of k (in terms of $k - 1$, for instance). In other words, we want to be able to talk about how to get from i to j without going through states higher than k in terms of what is already known about how to get from i to j without going through states higher than $k - 1$. The set R_{ij}^k can be thought of as the union of two sets: paths that do pass through state k (but no higher) and paths that do not pass through state k (or any other state higher than k).

The second set can easily be recursively described by R_{ij}^{k-1}. The first set presents a bit of a problem because we must talk about paths that pass

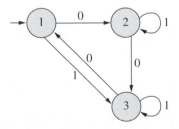

Figure 3.16   A simple deterministic finite automaton.

Path Sets	Regular Expression
$R_{11}^0 = \{\varepsilon\}$	ε
$R_{12}^0 = \{0\}$	0
$R_{13}^0 = \{1\}$	1
$R_{21}^0 = \{\ \}$	$\emptyset$
$R_{22}^0 = \{\varepsilon, 1\}$	$\varepsilon + 1$
. . .	. . .
$R_{33}^0 = \{\varepsilon, 1\}$	$\varepsilon + 1$

Figure 3.17   Some base cases in constructing a regular expression for the automaton of Figure 3.16.

through state k without passing through any state higher than $k - 1$, even though k is higher than $k - 1$. We can circumvent this difficulty by breaking any path through state k every time it reaches state k, effectively splitting the set of paths from i to j through k into three separate components, none of which passes through any state higher than $k - 1$. These components are:

- R_{ik}^{k-1}, the paths that go from i to k without passing through a state higher than $k - 1$ (remember that entering the state at the end of the path does not count as passing through the state);
- R_{kk}^{k-1}, one iteration of any loop from k to k, without passing through a state higher than $k - 1$ (the paths exit k at the beginning and enter k at the end, but never pass *through* k); and
- R_{kj}^{k-1}, the paths that go from state k to state j without passing through a state higher than $k - 1$.

The expression R_{kk}^{k-1} describes one iteration of a loop, but this loop could occur any number of times, including none, in any of the paths in R_{ij}^k. The expression corresponding to any number of iterations of this loop therefore must be $(R_{kk}^{k-1})^*$. We now have all the pieces we need to build up the inductive step from $k - 1$ to k:

$$R_{ij}^k = R_{ij}^{k-1} + R_{ik}^{k-1}(R_{kk}^{k-1})^* R_{kj}^{k-1}$$

Figure 3.18 illustrates the second term, $R_{ik}^{k-1}(R_{kk}^{k-1})^* R_{kj}^{k-1}$.

With this inductive step, we can proceed to build all possible paths in the machine (i.e., all the paths between every pair of nodes i and j for each

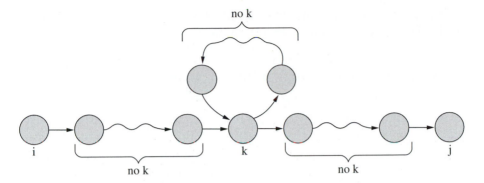

Figure 3.18   Adding node k to paths from i to j.

k from 1 to n) from the expressions for the base cases. Since the R^ks are built from the regular expressions for the various R^{k-1}s using only operations that are closed for regular expressions (union, concatenation, and Kleene closure—note that we need all three operations!), the R^ks are also regular expressions. Thus we can state that R_{ij}^k is a regular expression for any value of i, j, and k, with $1 \leqslant i, j, k \leqslant n$, and that this expression denotes all paths (or, equivalently, strings that cause the automaton to follow these paths) that lead from state i to state j while not passing through any state numbered higher than k.

Completing the Proof

The language of the deterministic finite automaton is precisely the set of all paths through the machine that go from the start state to an accepting state. These paths are denoted by the regular expressions R_{1j}^n, where j is some accepting state. (Note that, in the final expressions, we have $k = n$; that is, the paths are allowed to pass through *any* state in the machine.) The language of the whole machine is then described by the union of these expressions, the regular expression $\sum_{j \in F} R_{1j}^n$. Our proof is now complete: we have shown that, for any deterministic finite automaton, we can construct a regular expression that defines the same language. As before, the technique is mechanical and results in cumbersome and redundant expressions: it is not an efficient procedure to use for designing regular expressions from finite automata. However, since it is mechanical, it works in all cases to derive correct expressions and thus serves to establish the theorem that a regular expression can be constructed for any deterministic finite automaton.

In the larger picture, this proof completes the proof of the equivalence of regular expressions and finite automata.

Reviewing the Construction of Regular Expressions from Finite Automata

Because regular expressions are defined inductively, we need to proceed inductively in our proof. Unfortunately, finite automata are not defined inductively, nor do they offer any obvious ordering for induction. Since we are not so much interested in the automata as in the languages they accept, we can look at the set of strings accepted by a finite automaton. Every such string leads the automaton from the start state to an accepting state through a series of transitions. We could conceivably attempt an induction on the length of the strings accepted by the automaton, but this length has little relationship to either the automaton (a very short path through the automaton can easily produce an arbitrarily long string—think of a loop on the start state) or the regular expressions describing the language (a simple expression can easily denote an infinite collection of strings).

What we need is an induction that allows us to build regular expressions describing strings (i.e., sequences of transitions through the automaton) in a progressive fashion; terminates easily; and has simple base cases. The simplest sequence of transitions through an automaton is a single transition (or no transition at all). While that seems to lead us right back to induction on the number of transitions (on the length of strings), such need not be the case. We can view a single transition as one that does not pass through any other state and thus as the base case of an induction that will allow a larger and larger collection of intermediate states to be used in fabricating paths (and thus regular expressions).

Hence our preliminary idea about induction can be stated as follows: we will start with paths (strings) that allow no intermediate state, then proceed with paths that allow one intermediate state, then a set of two intermediate states, and so forth. This ordering is not yet sufficient, however: *which* intermediate state(s) should we allow? If we allow any single intermediate state, then any two, then any three, and so on, the ordering is not strict: there are many different subsets of k intermediate states out of the n states of the machine and none is comparable to any other. It would be much better to have a single subset of allowable intermediate states at each step of the induction.

We now get to our final idea about induction: we shall number the states of the finite automaton and use an induction based on that numbering. The induction will start with paths that allow no intermediate state, then proceed to paths that can pass (arbitrarily often) through state 1, then to paths that can pass through states 1 and 2, and so on. This process looks good until we remember that we want paths from the start state to an accepting state: we may not be able to find such a path that also obeys our requirements. Thus we should look not just at paths from the start state to an accepting state, but at paths from any vertex to any other. Once we have regular expressions for all source/target pairs, it will be simple enough to keep those that describe paths from the start state to an accepting state.

Now we can formalize our induction: at step k of the induction, we shall compute, for each pair (i, j) of vertices, all paths that go from vertex i through vertex j and that are allowed to pass through any of the vertices numbered from 1 to k. If the starting vertex for these paths, vertex i, is among the first k vertices, then we allow paths that loop through vertex i; otherwise we allow the path only to leave vertex i but not see it again on its way to vertex j. Similarly, if vertex j is among the first k vertices, the path may go through it any number of times; otherwise the path can only reach it and stop.

In effect, at each step of the induction, we define a new, somewhat larger finite automaton composed of the first k states of the original automaton, together with all transitions among these k states, plus any transition from state i to any of these states that is not already included, plus any transition to state j from any of these states that is not already included, plus any transition from state i to state j, if not already included. Think of these states and transitions as being highlighted in red, while the rest of the automaton is blue; we can play only with the red automaton at any step of the induction. However, from one step to the next, another blue state gets colored red along with any transitions between it and the red states and any transition to it from state i and any transition from it to state j. When the induction is complete, k equals n, the number of states of the original machine, and all states have been colored red, so we are playing with the original machine.

To describe with regular expressions what is happening, we begin by describing paths from i to j that use no intermediate state (no state numbered higher than 0). That is simple, since such transitions occur either under ε (when $i = j$) or under a single symbol, in which case we just look up the transition table of the automaton. The induction step simply colors one more blue node in red. Hence we can add to all existing paths from i to j those paths that now go through the new node; these paths can go through the new node several times (they can include a loop that takes them back to the new node over and over again) before reaching node j. Since only the portion that touches the new node is new, we simply break any such paths into segments, each of which leaves or enters the new node but does not pass through it. Every such segment goes through only old red nodes and so can be described recursively, completing the induction.

3.4 The Pumping Lemma and Closure Properties

3.4.1 The Pumping Lemma

We saw earlier that a language is regular if we can construct a finite automaton that accepts all strings in that language or a regular expression that represents that language. However, so far we have no tool to prove that a language is not regular.

The pumping lemma is such a tool. It establishes a necessary (but not sufficient) condition for a language to be regular. We cannot use the pumping lemma to establish that a language is regular, but we can use it to prove that a language is not regular, by showing that the language does not obey the lemma.

The pumping lemma is based on the idea that all regular languages must exhibit some form of regularity (pun intended—that is the origin of the name "regular languages"). Put differently, all strings of arbitrary length (i.e., all "sufficiently long" strings) belonging to a regular language must have some repeating pattern(s). (The short strings can each be accepted in a unique way, each through its own unique path through the machine. In particular, any finite language has no string of arbitrary length and so has only "short" strings and need not exhibit any regularity.)

Consider a finite automaton with n states, and let z be a string of length at least n that is accepted by this automaton. In order to accept z, the automaton makes a transition for each input symbol and thus moves through at least $n + 1$ states, one more than exist in the automaton. Therefore the automaton will go through at least one loop in accepting the string. Let the string be $z = x_1 x_2 x_3 \ldots x_{|z|}$; then Figure 3.19 illustrates the accepting path for z. In view of our preceding remarks, we can divide the

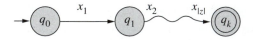

Figure 3.19   An accepting path for z.

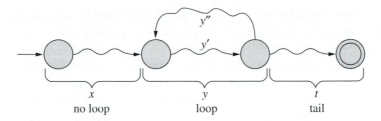

Figure 3.20 The three parts of an accepting path, showing potential looping.

path through the automaton into three parts: an initial part that does not contain any loop, the first loop encountered, and a final part that may or may not contain additional loops. Figure 3.20 illustrates this partition. We used x, y, and t to denote the three parts and further broke the loop into two parts, y' and y'', writing $y = y'y''y'$, so that the entire string becomes $xy'y''y't$. Now we can go through the loop as often as we want, from zero times (yielding $xy't$) to twice (yielding $xy'y''y'y''y't$) to any number of times (yielding a string of the form $xy'(y''y')^*t$); all of these strings must be in the language. This is the spirit of the pumping lemma: you can "pump" some string of unknown, but nonzero length, here $y''y'$, as many times as you want and always obtain another string in the language—no matter what the starting string z was (as long, that is, as it was long enough). In our case the string can be viewed as being of the form uvw, where we have $u = xy'$, $v = y''y'$, and $w = t$. We are then saying that any string of the form uv^*w is also in the language. We have (somewhat informally) proved the *pumping lemma* for regular languages.

Theorem 3.4 For every regular language L, there exists some constant n (the size of the smallest automaton that accepts L) such that, for every string $z \in L$ with $|z| \geq n$, there exist u, v, $w \in \Sigma^*$ with $z = uvw$, $|v| \geq 1$, $|uv| \leq n$, and, for all $i \in \mathbb{N}$, $uv^iw \in L$. $\square$

Writing this statement succinctly, we obtain

$$L \text{ is regular } \Rightarrow (\exists n \forall z, \ |z| \geq n, \ \exists u, v, w, \ |uv| \leq n, \ |v| \geq 1, \ \forall i, \ uv^iw \in L)$$

so that the contrapositive is

$$(\forall n \exists z, \ |z| \geq n, \ \forall u, v, w, \ |uv| \leq n, \ |v| \geq 1, \ \exists i, \ uv^iw \notin L)$$
$$\Rightarrow L \text{ is not regular}$$

Thus to show that a language is not regular, all we need to do is find a string z that contradicts the lemma. We can think of playing the adversary in a game where our opponent is attempting to convince us that the language is regular and where we are intent on providing a counterexample. If our opponent claims that the language is regular, then he must be able to provide a finite automaton for the language. Yet no matter what that automaton is, our counterexample must work, so we cannot pick n, the number of states of the claimed automaton, but must keep it as a parameter in order for our construction to work for any number of states. On the other hand, we get to choose a specific string, z, in the language and give it to our opponent. Our opponent, who (claims that he) knows a finite automaton for the language, then tells us where the first loop used by his machine lies and how long it is (something we have no way of knowing since we do not have the automaton). Thus we cannot choose the decomposition of z into u, v, and w, but, on the contrary, must be prepared for any decomposition given to us by our opponent. Thus for each possible decomposition into u, v, and w (that obeys the constraints), we must prepare our counterexample, that is, a pumping number i (which can vary from decomposition to decomposition) such that the string uv^iw is not in the language.

To summarize, the steps needed to prove that a language is not regular are:

1. Assume that the language is regular.
2. Let some parameter n be the constant of the pumping lemma.
3. Pick a "suitable" string z with $|z| \geqslant n$.
4. Show that, for every legal decomposition of z into uvw (i.e., obeying $|v| \geqslant 1$ and $|uv| \leqslant n$), there exists $i \geqslant 0$ such that uv^iw does not belong to L.
5. Conclude that assumption (1) was false.

Failure to proceed through these steps invalidates the potential proof that L is not regular but does not prove that L is regular! If the language is finite, the pumping lemma is useless, as it has to be, since all finite languages are regular: in a finite language, the automaton's accepting paths all have length less than the number of states in the machine, so that the pumping lemma holds vacuously.

Consider the language $L_1 = \{0^i 1^i \mid i \geqslant 0\}$. Let n be the constant of the pumping lemma (that is, n is the number of states in the corresponding deterministic finite automaton, should one exist). Pick the string $z = 0^n 1^n$; it satisfies $|z| \geqslant n$. Figure 3.21 shows how we might decompose $z = uvw$ to ensure $|uv| \leqslant n$ and $|v| \geqslant 1$. The uv must be a string of 0s, so pumping v

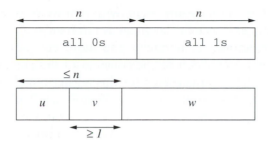

Figure 3.21 Decomposing the string z into possible choices for u, v, and w.

will give more 0s than 1s. It follows that the pumped string is not in L_1, which would contradict the pumping lemma if the language were regular. Therefore the language is not regular.

As another example, let L_2 be the set of all strings, the length of which is a perfect square. (The alphabet does not matter.) Let n be the constant of the lemma. Choose any z of length n^2 and write $z = uvw$ with $|v| \geq 1$ and $|uv| \leq n$; in particular, we have $1 \leq |v| \leq n$. It follows from the pumping lemma that, if the language is regular, then the string $z' = uv^2w$ must be in the language. But we have $|z'| = |z| + |v| = n^2 + |v|$ and, since we assumed $1 \leq |v| \leq n$, we conclude $n^2 < n^2 + 1 \leq n^2 + |v| \leq n^2 + n < (n+1)^2$, or $n^2 < |z'| < (n+1)^2$, so that $|z'|$ is not a perfect square and thus z' is not in the language. Hence the language is not regular.

As a third example, consider the language $L_3 = \{a^i b^j c^k \mid 0 \leq i < j < k\}$. Let n be the constant of the pumping lemma. Pick $z = a^n b^{n+1} c^{n+2}$, which clearly obeys $|z| \geq n$ as well as the inequalities on the exponents—but is as close to failing these last as possible. Write $z = uvw$, with $|uv| \leq n$ and $|v| \geq 1$. Then uv is a string of a's, so that $z' = uv^2w$ is the string $a^{n+|v|} b^{n+1} c^{n+2}$; since we assumed $|v| \geq 1$, the number of a's is now at least equal to the number of b's, not less, so that z' is not in the language. Hence L is not regular.

As a fourth example, consider the set L_4 of all strings x over $\{0, 1\}^*$ such that, in at least one prefix of x, there are four more 1s than 0s. Let n be the constant of the pumping lemma and choose $z = 0^n 1^{n+4}$; z is in the language, because z itself has four more 1s than 0s (although no other prefix of z does: once again, our string z is on the edge of failing membership). Let $z = uvw$; since we assumed $|uv| \leq n$, it follows that uv is a string of 0s and that, in particular, v is a string of one or more 0s. Hence the string $z' = uv^2w$, which must be in the language if the language is regular, is of the form $0^{n+|v|} 1^{n+4}$;

but this string does not have any prefix with four more 1s than 0s and so is not in the language. Hence the language is not regular.

As a final example, let us tackle the more complex language $L_5 = \{a^i b^j c^k \mid i \neq j \text{ or } j \neq k\}$. Let n be the constant of the pumping lemma and choose $z = a^n b^{n!+n} c^{n!+n}$—the reason for this mysterious choice will become clear in a few lines. (Part of the choice is the now familiar "edge" position: this string already has the second and third groups of equal size, so it suffices to bring the first group to the same size to cause it to fail entirely.) Let $z = uvw$; since we assumed $|uv| \leq n$, we see that uv is a string of a's and thus, in particular, v is a string of one or more a's. Thus the string $z' = uv^i w$, which must be in the language for all values of $i \geq 0$ if the language is regular, is of the form $a^{n+(i-1)|v|} b^{n!+n} c^{n!+n}$. Choose i to be $(n!/|v|) + 1$; this value is a natural number, because $|v|$ is between 1 and n, and because $n!$ is divisible by any number between 1 and n (this is why we chose this particular value $n! + n$). Then we get the string $a^{n!+n} b^{n!+n} c^{n!+n}$, which is not in the language. Hence the language is not regular.

Consider applying the pumping lemma to the language $L_6 = \{a^i b^j c^k \mid i > j > k \geq 0\}$. L_6 is extremely similar to L_3, yet the same application of the pumping lemma used for L_3 fails for L_6: it is no use to pump more a's, since that will not contradict the inequality, but reinforce it. In a similar vein, consider the language $L_7 = \{0^i 1^j 0^j \mid i, j > 0\}$; this language is similar to the language L_1, which we already proved not regular through a straightforward application of the pumping lemma. Yet the same technique will fail with L_7, because we cannot ensure that we are not just pumping initial 0s—something that would not prevent membership in L_7.

In the first case, there is a simple way out: instead of pumping up, pump down by one. From uvw, we obtain uw, which must also be in the language if the language is regular. If we choose for L_6 the string $z = a^{n+2} b^{n+1}$, then uv is a string of a's and pumping down will remove at least one a, thereby invalidating the inequality. We can do a detailed case analysis for L_7, which will work. Pick $z = 01^n 0^n$; then uv is 01^k for some $k \geq 0$. If k equals 0, then uv is just 0, so u is ε and v is 0, and pumping down once creates the string $1^n 0^n$, which is not in the language, as desired. If k is at least 1, then either u is ε, in which case pumping up once produces the string $01^k 01^n 0^n$, which is not in the language; or u has length at least 1, in which case v is a string of 1s and pumping up once produces the string $01^{n+|v|} 0^n$, which is not in the language either. Thus in all three cases we can pump the string so as to produce another string not in the language, showing that the language is not regular. But contrast this laborious procedure with the proof obtained from the extended pumping lemma described below.

What we really need is a way to shift the position of the uv substring within the entire string; having it restricted to the front of z is too limiting. Fortunately our statement (and proof) of the pumping lemma does not really depend on the location of the n characters within the string. We started at the beginning because that was the simplest approach and we used n (the number of states in the smallest automaton accepting the language) rather than some larger constant because we could capture in that manner the first loop along an accepting path. However, there may be many different loops along any given path. Indeed, in any stretch of n characters, $n + 1$ states are visited and so, by the pigeonhole principle, a loop must occur. These observations allow us to rephrase the pumping lemma slightly.

Lemma 3.1 For any regular language L there exists some constant $n > 0$ such that, for any three strings z_1, z_2, and z_3 with $z = z_1 z_2 z_3 \in L$ and $|z_2| = n$, there exists strings $u, v, w \in \Sigma^*$ with $z_2 = uvw$, $|v| \geq 1$, and, for all $i \in \mathbb{N}$, $z_1 u v^i w z_3 \in L$. $\qquad\square$

This restatement does not alter any of the conditions of the original pumping lemma (note that $|z_2| = n$ implies $|uv| \leq n$, which is why the latter inequality was not stated explicitly); however, it does allow us to move our focus of attention anywhere within a long string. For instance, consider again the language L_7: we shall pick $z_1 = 0^n$, $z_2 = 1^n$, and $z_3 = 0^n$; clearly, $z = z_1 z_2 z_3 = 0^n 1^n 0^n$ is in L_7. Since z_2 consists only of 1s, so does v; therefore the string $z_1 u v^2 w z_3$ is $0^n 1^{n+|v|} 0^n$ and is not in L_7, so that L_7 is not regular. The new statement of the pumping lemma allowed us to move our focus of attention to the 1s in the middle of the string, making for an easy proof. Although L_2 does not need it, the same technique is also advantageously applied: if n is the constant of the pumping lemma, pick $z_1 = a^{n+1}$, $z_2 = b^n$, and $z_3 = \varepsilon$. Now write $z_2 = uvw$: it follows that v is a string of one or more b's, so that the string $z_1 u v^2 w z_3$ is $a^{n+1} b^{n+|v|}$, which is not in the language, since we have $n + |v| \geq n + 1$. Table 3.1 summarizes the use of (our extended version of) the pumping lemma.

Exercise 3.2 Develop a pumping lemma for strings that are *not* in the language. In a deterministic finite automaton where all transitions are specified, arbitrary long strings that get rejected must be rejected through a path that includes one or more loops, so that a lemma similar to the pumping lemma can be proved. What do you think the use of such a lemma would be? $\qquad\square$

Table 3.1 How to use the pumping lemma to prove nonregularity.

- Assume that the language is regular.
- Let n be the constant of the pumping lemma; it will be used to parameterize the construction.
- Pick a suitable string z in the language that has length at least n. (In many cases, pick z "at the edge" of membership—that is, as close as possible to failing some membership criterion.)
- Decompose z into three substrings, $z = z_1 z_2 z_3$, such that z_2 has length exactly n. You can pick the boundaries as you please.
- Write z_2 as the concatenation of three strings, $z_2 = uvw$; note that the boundaries delimiting u, v, and w are not known—all that can be assumed is that v has nonzero length.
- Verify that, for any choice of boundaries, i.e., any choice of u, v, and w with $z_2 = uvw$ and where v has nonzero length, there exists an index i such that the string $z_1 u v^i w z_3$ is not in the language.
- Conclude that the language is not regular.

3.4.2 Closure Properties of Regular Languages

By now we have established the existence of an interesting family of sets, the regular sets. We know how to prove that a set is regular (exhibit a suitable finite automaton or regular expression) and how to prove that a set is not regular (use the pumping lemma). At this point, we should ask ourselves what other properties these regular sets may possess; in particular, how do they behave under certain basic operations? The simplest question about any operator applied to elements of a set is "Is it closed?" or, put negatively, "Can an expression in terms of elements of the set evaluate to an element not in the set?" For instance, the natural numbers are closed under addition and multiplication but not under division—the result is a rational number; the reals are closed under the four operations (excluding division by 0) but not under square root—the square root of a negative number is not a real number; and the complex numbers are closed under the four operations and under any polynomial root-finding.

From our earlier work, we know that the regular sets must be closed under concatenation, union, and Kleene closure, since these three operations were defined on regular expressions (regular sets) and produce more regular expressions. We alluded briefly to the fact that they must be closed under intersection and complement, but let us revisit these two results.

The complement of a language $L \subseteq \Sigma^*$ is the language $\overline{L} = \Sigma^* - L$. Given a deterministic finite automaton for L in which every transition is defined (if some transitions are not specified, add a new rejecting trap state and define every undefined transition to move to the new trap state), we can build a deterministic finite automaton for $\overline{L}$ by the simple expedient of turning every rejecting state into an accepting state and vice versa. Since regular languages are closed under union and complementation, they are also closed under intersection by DeMorgan's law. To see directly that intersection is closed, consider regular languages L_1 and L_2 with associated automata M_1 and M_2. We construct the new machine M for the language $L_1 \cap L_2$ as follows. The set of states of M is the Cartesian product of the sets of states of M_1 and M_2; if M_1 has transition $\delta'(q'_i, a) = q'_j$ and M_2 has transition $\delta''(q''_k, a) = q''_l$, then M has transition $\delta((q'_i, q''_k), a) = (q'_j, q''_l)$; finally, (q', q'') is an accepting state of M if q' is an accepting state of M_1 and q'' is an accepting state of M_2.

Closure under various operations can simplify proofs. For instance, consider the language $L_8 = \{a^i b^j \mid i \neq j\}$; this language is closely related to our standard language $\{a^i b^i \mid i \in \mathbb{N}\}$ and is clearly not regular. However, a direct proof through the pumping lemma is somewhat challenging; a much simpler proof can be obtained through closure. Since regular sets are closed under complement and intersection and since the set $a^* b^*$ is regular (denoted by a regular expression), then, if L_8 is regular, so must be the language $\overline{L_8} \cap a^* b^*$. However, the latter is our familiar language $\{a^i b^i \mid i \in \mathbb{N}\}$ and so is not regular, showing that L_8 is not regular either.

A much more impressive closure is closure under *substitution*. A substitution from alphabet Σ to alphabet Δ (not necessarily distinct) is a mapping from Σ to $2^{\Delta^*} - \{\emptyset\}$ that maps each character of Σ onto a (nonempty) regular language over Δ. The substitution is extended from a character to a string by using concatenation as in a regular expression: if we have the string ab over Σ, then its image is $f(ab)$, the language over Δ composed of all strings constructed of a first part chosen from the set $f(a)$ concatenated with a second part chosen from the set $f(b)$. Formally, if w is ax, then $f(w)$ is $f(a)f(x)$, the concatenation of the two sets. Finally the substitution is extended to a language in the obvious way:

$$f(L) = \bigcup_{w \in L} f(w)$$

To see that regular sets are closed under this operation, we shall use regular expressions. Since each regular set can be written as a regular expression, each of the $f(a)$ for $a \in \Sigma$ can be written as a regular expression. The language L is regular and so has a regular expression E. Simply substitute for each character $a \in \Sigma$ appearing in E the regular (sub)expression for $f(a)$; the result is clearly a (typically much larger) regular expression. (The alternate mechanism, which uses our extension to strings and then to languages, would require a new result. Clearly, concatenation of sets corresponds exactly to concatenation of regular expressions and union of sets corresponds exactly to union of regular expressions. However, $f(L) = \bigcup_{w \in L} f(w)$ involves a countably infinite union, not just a finite one, and we do not yet know whether or not regular expressions are closed under infinite union.)

A special case of substitution is *homomorphism*. A homomorphism from a language L over alphabet Σ to a new language $f(L)$ over alphabet Δ is defined by a mapping $f \colon \Sigma \to \Delta^*$; in words, the basic function maps each symbol of the original alphabet to a single string over the new alphabet. This is clearly a special case of substitution, one where the regular languages to which each symbol can be mapped consist of exactly one string each.

Substitution and even homomorphism can alter a language significantly. Consider, for instance, the language $L = (a + b)^*$ over the alphabet $\{a, b\}$—this is just the language of all possible strings over this alphabet. Now consider the very simple homomorphism from $\{a, b\}$ to subsets of $\{0, 1\}^*$ defined by $f(a) = 01$ and $f(b) = 1$; then $f(L) = (01 + 1)^*$ is the language of all strings over $\{0, 1\}$ that do not contain a pair of 0s and (if not equal to ε) end with a 1—a rather different beast. This ability to modify languages considerably without affecting their regularity makes substitution a powerful tool in proving languages to be regular or not regular.

To prove a new language L regular, start with a known regular language L_0 and define a substitution that maps L_0 to L. To prove a new language L not regular, define a substitution that maps L to a new language L_1 known not to be regular. Formally speaking, these techniques are known as *reductions*; we shall revisit reductions in detail throughout the remaining chapters of this book.

We add one more operation to our list: the *quotient* of two languages. Given languages L_1 and L_2, the quotient of L_1 by L_2, denoted L_1/L_2, is the language $\{x \mid \exists y \in L_2, \ xy \in L_1\}$.

Theorem 3.5 If R is regular, then so is R/L for any language L.   □

The proof is interesting because it is nonconstructive, unlike all other proofs we have used so far with regular languages and finite automata. (It has to be nonconstructive, since we know nothing whatsoever about L; in particular, it is possible that no procedure exists to decide membership in L or to enumerate the members of L.)

Proof. Let M be a finite automaton for R. We define the new finite automaton M' to accept R/L as follows. M' is an exact copy of M, with one exception: we define the accepting states of M' differently—thus M' has the same states, transitions, and start state as M, but possibly different accepting states. A state q of M is an accepting state of M' if and only if there exists a string y in L that takes M from state q to one of its accepting states.   *Q.E.D.*

M', including its accepting states, is well defined; however, we may be unable to construct M', because the definition of accepting state may not be computable if we have no easy way of listing the strings of L. (Naturally, if L is also regular, we can turn the existence proof into a constructive proof.)

Example 3.3 We list some quotients of regular expressions:

$$0^*10^*/0^* = 0^*10^* \quad 0^*10^*/10^* = 0^*$$
$$0^*10^*/0^*1 = 0^* \quad 0^*10^+/0^*1 = \emptyset$$
$$101/101 = \varepsilon \quad (1^* + 10^+)/(0^+ + 11) = 1^* + 10^* \qquad \square$$

Exercise 3.3 Prove the following closure properties of the quotient:

- If L_2 includes ε, then, for any language L, L/L_2 includes all of L.
- If L is not empty, then we have $\Sigma^*/L = \Sigma^*$.
- The quotient of any language L by Σ^* is the language composed of all prefixes of strings in L. $\square$

If L_1 is not regular, then we cannot say much about the quotient L_1/L_2, even when L_2 is regular. For instance, let $L_1 = \{0^n 1^n \mid n \in \mathbb{N}\}$, which we know is not regular. Now contrast these two quotients:

- $L_1/1^+ = \{0^n 1^m \mid n > m \in \mathbb{N}\}$, which is not regular, and
- $L_1/0^+1^+ = 0^*$, which is regular.

Table 3.2 summarizes the main closure properties of regular languages.

Table 3.2   Closure properties of regular languages.

- concatenation and Kleene closure
- complementation, union, and intersection
- homomorphism and substitution
- quotient by any language

3.4.3 *Ad Hoc* Closure Properties

In addition to the operators just shown, numerous other operators are closed on the regular languages. Proofs of closure for these are often *ad hoc*, constructing a (typically nondeterministic) finite automaton for the new language from the existing automata for the argument languages. We now give several examples, in increasing order of difficulty.

Example 3.4 Define the language swap(L) to be

$$\{a_2a_1 \ldots a_{2n}a_{2n-1} \mid a_1a_2 \ldots a_{2n-1}a_{2n} \in L\}$$

We claim that swap(L) is regular if L is regular.

Let M be a deterministic finite automaton for L. We construct a (deterministic) automaton M' for swap(L) that mimics what M does when it reads pairs of symbols in reverse. Since an automaton cannot read a pair of symbols at once, our new machine, in some state corresponding to a state of M (call it q), will read the odd-indexed symbol (call it a) and "memorize" it—that is, use a new state (call it $[q, a]$) to denote what it has read. It then reads the even-indexed symbol (call it b), at which point it has available a pair of symbols and makes a transition to whatever state machine M would move to from q on having read the symbols b and a in that order.

As a specific example, consider the automaton of Figure 3.22(a). After grouping the symbols in pairs, we obtain the automaton of Figure 3.22(b).

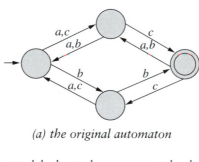

(a) the original automaton

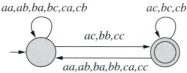

(b) the automaton after grouping symbols in pairs

Figure 3.22   A finite automaton used for the swap language.

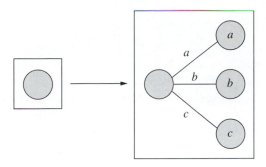

Figure 3.23   The substitute block of states for the swap language.

Our automaton for swap(L) will have a four-state block for each state of the pair-grouped automaton for L, as illustrated in Figure 3.23. We can formalize this construction as follows—albeit at some additional cost in the number of states of the resulting machine. Our new machine M' has state set $Q \cup (Q \times \Sigma)$, where Q is the state set of M; it has transitions of the type $\delta'(q, a) = [q, a]$ for all $q \in Q$ and $a \in \Sigma$ and transitions of the type $\delta'([q, a], b) = \delta(\delta(q, b), a)$ for all $q \in Q$ and $a, b \in \Sigma$; its start state is q_0, the start state of M; and its accepting states are the accepting states of M. $\square$

Example 3.5   The approach used in the previous example works when trying to build a machine that reads strings of the same length as those read by M; however, when building a machine that reads strings shorter than those read by M, nondeterministic ε transitions must be used to *guess* the "missing" symbols.

Define the language odd(L) to be

$$\{a_1 a_3 a_5 \ldots a_{2n-1} \mid \exists a_2, a_4, \ldots, a_{2n}, a_1 a_2 \ldots a_{2n-1} a_{2n} \in L\}$$

When machine M' for odd(L) attempts to simulate what M would do, it gets only the odd-indexed symbols and so must guess which even-indexed symbols would cause M to accept the full string. So M' in some state q corresponding to a state of M reads a symbol a and moves to some new state not in M (call it $[q, a]$); then M' makes an ε transition that amounts to guessing what the even-indexed symbol could be. The replacement block of states that results from this construction is illustrated in Figure 3.24. Thus we have $q' \in \delta'([q, a], \varepsilon)$ for all states q' with $q' = \delta(\delta(q, a), b)$ for any choice of b; formally, we write

$$\delta'([q, a], \varepsilon) = \{\delta(\delta(q, a), b) \mid b \in \Sigma\}$$

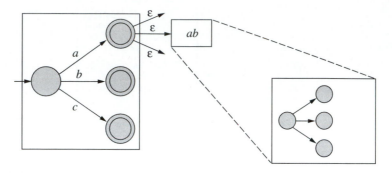

Figure 3.24   The substitute block of states for the odd language.

In this way, M' makes two transitions for each symbol read, enabling it to simulate the action of M on the twice-longer string that M needs to verify acceptance.

As a specific example, consider the language $L = (00 + 11)^*$, recognized by the automaton of Figure 3.25(a). For this choice of L, odd(L) is just Σ^*. After grouping the input symbols in pairs, we get the automaton of Figure 3.25(b). Now our new nondeterministic automaton has a block of three states for each state of the pair-grouped automaton and so six states in all, as shown in Figure 3.26. Our automaton moves from the start state to one of the two accepting states while reading a character from the

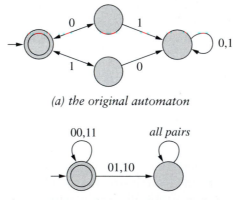

(a) the original automaton

(b) the automaton after grouping symbols in pairs

Figure 3.25   The automaton used in the odd language.

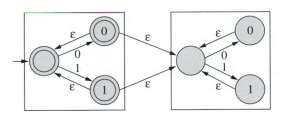

Figure 3.26   The nondeterministic automaton for the odd language.

input—corresponding to an odd-indexed character in the string accepted by M—and makes an ε transition on the next move, effectively guessing the even-indexed symbol in the string accepted by M. If the guess is good (corresponding to a 0 following a 0 or to a 1 following a 1), our automaton returns to the start state to read the next character; if the guess is bad, it moves to a rejecting trap state (a block of three states). As must be the case, our automaton accepts Σ^*—albeit in an unnecessarily complicated way.   □

Example 3.6 As a final example, let us consider the language

$$\{x \mid \exists u, v, w \in \Sigma^*, \ |u| = |v| = |w| = |x| \text{ and } uvxw \in L\}$$

In other words, given L, our new language is composed of the third quarter of each string of L that has length a multiple of 4. Let M be a (deterministic) finite automaton for L with state set Q, start state q_0, accepting states F, and transition function δ. As in the odd language, we have to guess a large number of absent inputs to feed to M. Since the input is the string x, the processing of the guessed strings u, v, and w must take place while we process x itself. Thus our machine for the new language will be composed, in effect, of four separate machines, each a copy of M; each copy will process its quarter of $uvxw$, with three copies processing guesses and one copy processing the real input. The key to a solution is tying together these four machines: for instance, the machine processing x should start from the state reached by the machine processing v once v has been completely processed.

This problem at first appears daunting—not only is v guessed, but it is not even processed when the processing of x starts. The answer is to use yet more nondeterminism and to *guess* what should be the starting state of each component machine. Since we have four of them, we need a guess for the starting states of the second, third, and fourth machines (the first naturally starts in state q_0). Then we need to verify these guesses by checking, when the input has been processed, that the first machine has reached the state guessed as the start of the second, that the second machine has reached the state guessed as the start of the third, and the the third machine has reached the state guessed as the start of the fourth. In addition, of course, we must also check that the fourth machine ended in some state in F. In order to check initial guesses, these initial guesses must be retained; but each machine will move from its starting state, so that we must encode in the state of our new machine both the current state of each machine and the initial guess about its starting state.

This chain of reasoning leads us to define a state of the new machine as a seven-tuple, say $(q_i, q_j, q_k, q_l, q_m, q_n, q_o)$, where q_i is the current state of the first machine (no guess is needed for this machine), q_j is the guessed starting state for the second machine and q_k its current state, q_l is the guessed starting state for the third machine and q_m its current state, and q_n is the guessed starting state for the fourth machine and q_o its current state; and where all q_x are states of M.

The initial state of each machine is the same as the guess, that is, our new machine can start from any state of the form $(q_0, q_j, q_j, q_l, q_l, q_n, q_n)$, for any choice of j, l, and n. In order to make it possible, we add one more state to our new machine (call it S'), designate it as the unique starting state, and add ε transitions from it to the $|Q|^3$ states of the form $(q_0, q_j, q_j, q_l, q_l, q_n, q_n)$. When the input has been processed, it will be accepted if the state reached by each machine matches the start state used by the next machine and if the state reached by the fourth machine is a state in F, that is, if the state of our new machine is of the form $(q_j, q_j, q_l, q_l, q_n, q_n, q_f)$, with $q_f \in F$ and for any choices of j, l, and n.

Finally, from some state $(q_i, q_j, q_k, q_l, q_m, q_n, q_o)$, our new machine can move to a new state $(q_{i'}, q_j, q_{k'}, q_l, q_{m'}, q_n, q_{o'})$ when reading character c from the input string x whenever the following four conditions are met:

- there exists $a \in \Sigma$ with $\delta(q_i, a) = q_{i'}$
- there exists $a \in \Sigma$ with $\delta(q_k, a) = q_{k'}$
- $\delta(q_m, c) = q_{m'}$
- there exists $a \in \Sigma$ with $\delta(q_o, a) = q_{o'}$

Overall, our new machine, which is highly nondeterministic, has $|Q|^7 + 1$ states. While the machine is large, its construction is rather straightforward; indeed, the principle generalizes easily to more complex situations, as explored in Exercises 3.31 and 3.32.   □

These examples illustrate the conceptual power of viewing a state of the new machine as a tuple, where, typically, members of the tuple are states from the known machine or alphabet characters. State transitions of the new machine are then defined on the tuples by defining their effect on each member of tuple, where the state transitions of the known machine can be used to good effect. When the new language includes various substrings of the known regular language, the tuple notation can be used to record starting and current states in the exploration of each substring. Initial state(s) and accepting states can then be set up so as to ensure that the substrings, which are processed sequentially in the known machine but concurrently in the new machine, have to match in the new machine as they automatically did in the known machine.

3.5   Conclusion

Finite automata and regular languages (and regular grammars, an equivalent mechanism based on generation that we did not discuss, but that is similar in spirit to the grammars used in describing legal syntax in programming languages) present an interesting model, with enough structure to possess nontrivial properties, yet simple enough that most questions about them are decidable. (We shall soon see that most questions about universal models of computation are undecidable.) Finite automata find most of their applications in the design of logical circuits (by definition, any "chip" is a finite-state machine, the difference from our model being simply that, whereas our finite-state automata have no output function, finite-state machines do), but computer scientists see them most often in parsers for regular expressions. For instance, the expression language used to specify search strings in Unix is a type of regular expression, so that the Unix tools built for searching and matching are essentially finite-state automata. As another example, tokens in programming languages (reserved words, variables names, etc.) can easily be described by regular expressions and so their parsing reduces to running a simple finite-state automaton (e.g., lex).

However, finite automata cannot be used for problem-solving; as we have seen, they cannot even count, much less search for optimal solutions. Thus if we want to study what can be computed, we need a much more powerful model; such a model forms the topic of Chapter 4.

3.6   Exercises

Exercise 3.4 Give deterministic finite automata accepting the following languages over the alphabet $\Sigma = \{0, 1\}$:

1. The set of all strings that contain the substring 010.
2. The set of all strings that do not contain the substring 000.
3. The set of all strings such that every substring of length 4 contains at least three 1s.
4. The set of all strings that contain either an even number of 0s or at most three 0s (that is, if the number of 0s is even, the string is in the language, but if the number of 0s is odd, then the string is in the language only if that number does not exceed 3).
5. The set of all strings such that every other symbol is a 1 (starting at the first symbol for odd-length string and at the second for even-length strings; for instance, both 10111 and 0101 are in the language).

   This last problem is harder than the previous four since this automaton has no way to tell in advance whether the input string has odd or even length. Design a solution that keeps track of everything needed for *both* cases until it reaches the end of the string.

Exercise 3.5 Design finite automata for the following languages over $\{0, 1\}$:

1. The set of all strings where no pair of adjacent 0s appears in the last four characters.
2. The set of all strings where pairs of adjacent 0s must be separated by at least one 1, except in the last four characters.

Exercise 3.6 In less than 10 seconds for each part, verify that each of the following languages is regular:

1. The set of all C programs written in North America in 1997.
2. The set of all first names given to children born in New Zealand in 1996.
3. The set of numbers that can be displayed on your hand-held calculator.

Exercise 3.7 Describe in English the languages (over $\{0, 1\}$) accepted by the following deterministic finite automata. (The initial state is identified by a short unlabeled arrow; the final state—these deterministic finite automata have only one final state each—is identified by a double circle.)

1.

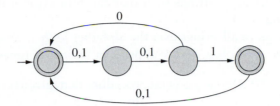

2.

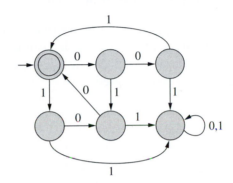

3.

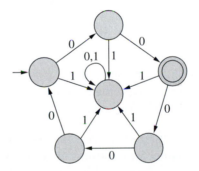

Exercise 3.8 Prove or disprove each of the following assertions:

1. Every nonempty language contains a nonempty regular language.
2. Every language with nonempty complement is contained in a regular language with nonempty complement.

Exercise 3.9 Give both deterministic and nondeterministic finite automata accepting the following languages over the alphabet $\Sigma = \{0, 1\}$; then prove lower bounds on the size of any deterministic finite automaton for each language:

1. The set of all strings such that, at some place in the string, there are two 0s separated by an even number of symbols.

2. The set of all strings such that the fifth symbol from the end of the string is a 1.
3. The set of all strings over the alphabet $\{a, b, c, d\}$ such that one of the three symbols a, b, or c appears at least four times in all.

Exercise 3.10 Devise a general procedure that, given some finite automaton M, produces the new finite automaton M' such that M' rejects ε, but otherwise accepts all strings that M accepts.

Exercise 3.11 Devise a general procedure that, given a deterministic finite automaton M, produces an equivalent deterministic finite automaton M' (i.e., an automaton that defines the same language as M) in which the start state, once left, cannot be re-entered.

Exercise 3.12* Give a nondeterministic finite automaton to recognize the set of all strings over the alphabet $\{a, b, c\}$ such that the string, interpreted as an expression to be evaluated, evaluates to the same value left-to-right as it does right-to-left, under the following nonassociative operation:

	a	b	c
a	a	b	b
b	b	c	a
c	c	a	b

Then give a deterministic finite automaton for the same language and attempt to prove a nontrivial lower bound on the size of any deterministic finite automaton for this problem.

Exercise 3.13 Prove that every regular language is accepted by a *planar* nondeterministic finite automaton. A finite automaton is planar if its transition diagram can be embedded in the plane without any crossings.

Exercise 3.14* In contrast to the previous exercise, prove that there exist regular languages that cannot be accepted by any planar deterministic finite automaton. (Hint: Exercise 2.21 indicates that the average degree of a node in a planar graph is always less than six, so that every planar graph must have at least one vertex of degree less than six. Thus a planar finite automaton must have at least one state with no more than five transitions leading into or out of that state.)

Exercise 3.15 Write regular expressions for the following languages over $\{0, 1\}$:

1. The language of Exercise 3.5(1).

2. The language of Exercise 3.5(2).
3. The set of all strings with at most one triple of adjacent 0s.
4. The set of all strings not containing the substring 110.
5. The set of all strings with at most one pair of consecutive 0s and at most one pair of consecutive 1s.
6. The set of all strings in which every pair of adjacent 0s appears before any pair of adjacent 1s.

Exercise 3.16 Let P and Q be regular expressions. Which of the following equalities is true? For those that are true, prove it by induction; for the others, give a counterexample.

1. $(P^*)^* = P^*$
2. $(P + Q)^* = (P^*Q^*)^*$
3. $(P + Q)^* = P^* + Q^*$

Exercise 3.17 For each of the following languages, give a proof that it is or is not regular.

1. $\{x \in \{0, 1\}^* \mid x \neq x^R\}$
2. $\{x \in \{0, 1, 2\}^* \mid x = w2w, \text{ with } w \in \{0, 1\}^*\}$
3. $\{x \in \{0, 1\}^* \mid x = w^R wy, \text{ with } w, y \in \{0, 1\}^+\}$
4. $\{x \in \{0, 1\}^* \mid x \notin \{01, 10\}^*\}$
5. The set of all strings (over $\{0, 1\}$) that have equal numbers of 0s and 1s and such that the number of 0s and the number of 1s in any prefix of the string never differ by more than two.
6. $\{0^l 1^m 0^n \mid n \geq l \text{ or } n \geq m, \; l, m, n \in \mathbb{N}\}$
7. $\{0^{\lfloor \sqrt{n} \rfloor} \mid n \in \mathbb{N}\}$
8. The set of all strings x (over $\{0, 1\}$) such that, in at least one substring of x, there are four more 1s than 0s.
9. The set of all strings over $\{0, 1\}^*$ that have the same number of occurrences of the substring 01 as of the substring 10. (For instance, we have $101 \in L$ and $1010 \notin L$.)
10. $\{0^i 1^j \mid gcd(i, j) = 1\}$ (that is, i and j are relatively prime)

Exercise 3.18 Let L be $\{0^n 1^n \mid n \in \mathbb{N}\}$, our familiar nonregular language. Give two different proofs that the complement of L (with respect to $\{0, 1\}^*$) is not regular.

Exercise 3.19 Let Σ be composed of all two-component vectors with entries of 0 and 1; that is, Σ has four characters in it: $\binom{0}{0}$, $\binom{0}{1}$, $\binom{1}{0}$, and $\binom{1}{1}$. Decide whether each of the following languages over Σ^* is regular:

1. The set of all strings such that the "top row" is the reverse of the "bottom row." For instance, we have $\binom{0}{0}\binom{1}{0}\binom{0}{1}\binom{0}{0} \in L$ and $\binom{0}{0}\binom{1}{1}\binom{0}{1}\binom{0}{0} \notin L$.
2. The set of all strings such that the "top row" is the complement of the "bottom row" (that is, where the top row has a 1, the bottom row has a 0 and vice versa).
3. The set of all strings such that the "top row" has the same number of 1s as the "bottom row."

Exercise 3.20 Let Σ be composed of all three-component vectors with entries of 0 and 1; thus Σ has eight characters in it. Decide whether each of the following languages over Σ^* is regular:

1. The set of all strings such that the sum of the "first row" and "second row" equals the "third row," where each row is read left-to-right as an unsigned binary integer.
2. The set of all strings such that the product of the "first row" and "second row" equals the "third row," where each row is read left-to-right as an unsigned binary integer.

Exercise 3.21 Recall that Roman numerals are written by stringing together symbols from the alphabet $\Sigma = \{I, V, X, L, C, D, M\}$, always using the largest symbol that will fit next, with one exception: the last "digit" is obtained by subtraction from the previous one, so that 4 is IV, 9 is IX, 40 is XL, 90 is XC, 400 is CD, and 900 is CM. For example, the number 4999 is written $MMMMCMXCIX$ while the number 1678 is written $MDCLXXVIII$. Is the set of Roman numerals regular?

Exercise 3.22* Let L be the language over $\{0, 1, +, \cdot\}$ that consists of all legal (nonempty) regular expressions written without parentheses and without Kleene closure (the symbol $\cdot$ stands for concatenation). Is L regular?

Exercise 3.23* Given a string x over the alphabet $\{a, b, c\}$, define $||x||$ to be the value of string according to the evaluation procedure defined in Exercise 3.12. Is the language $\{xy \mid ||x|| = ||y||\}$ regular?

Exercise 3.24 A *unitary* language is a nonempty regular language that is accepted by a deterministic finite automaton with a single accepting state. Prove that, if L is a regular language, then it is unitary if and only if, whenever strings u, uv, and w belong to L, then so does string wv.

Exercise 3.25 Prove or disprove each of the following assertions.

1. If L^* is regular, then L is regular.
2. If $L = L_1 L_2$ is regular and L_2 is finite, then L_1 is regular.

3. If $L = L_1 + L_2$ is regular and L_2 is finite, then L_1 is regular.
4. If $L = L_1/L_2$ is regular and L_2 is regular, then L_1 is regular.

Exercise 3.26 Let L be a language and define the language $\text{SUB}(L) = \{x \mid \exists w \in L,\ x$ is a subsequence of $w\}$. In words, $\text{SUB}(L)$ is the set of all subsequences of strings of L. Prove that, if L is regular, then so is $\text{SUB}(L)$.

Exercise 3.27 Let L be a language and define the language $\text{CIRC}(L) = \{w \mid w = xy$ and $yx \in L\}$. If L is regular, does it follow that $\text{CIRC}(L)$ is also regular?

Exercise 3.28 Let L be a language and define the language $\text{NPR}(L) = \{x \in L \mid x = yz$ and $z \neq \varepsilon \Rightarrow y \notin L\}$; that is, $\text{NPR}(L)$ is composed of exactly those strings of L that are prefix-free (the proper prefixes of which are not also in L). Prove that, if L is regular, then so is $\text{NPR}(L)$.

Exercise 3.29 Let L be a language and define the language $\text{PAL}(L) = \{x \mid xx^R \in L\}$, where x^R is the reverse of string x; that is, L is composed of the first half of whatever palindromes happen to belong to L. Prove that, if L is regular, then so is $\text{PAL}(L)$.

Exercise 3.30* Let L be any regular language and define the language $\text{FL}(L) = \{xz \mid \exists y,\ |x| = |y| = |z|$ and $xyz \in L\}$; that is, $\text{FL}(L)$ is composed of the first and last thirds of strings of L that happen to have length $3k$ for some k. Is $\text{FL}(L)$ always regular?

Exercise 3.31* Let L be a language and define the language $\text{FRAC}(i, j)(L)$ to be the set of strings x such that there exist strings $x_1, \ldots, x_{i-1}, x_{i+1}, \ldots, x_j$ with $x_1 \ldots x_{i-1} x x_{i+1} \ldots x_j \in L$ and $|x_1| = \ldots = |x_{i-1}| = |x_{i+1}| = \ldots = |x_j| = |x|$. That is, $\text{FRAC}(i, j)(L)$ is composed of the ith of j pieces of equal length of strings of L that happen to have length divisible by j. In particular, $\text{FRAC}(1, 2)(L)$ is made of the first halves of even-length strings of L and $\text{FRAC}(3, 4)(L)$ is the language used in Example 3.6. Prove that, if L is regular, then so is $\text{FRAC}(i, j)(L)$.

Exercise 3.32* Let L be a language and define the language $f(L) = \{x \mid \exists y, z,\ |y| = 2|x| = 4|z|$ and $xyxz \in L\}$. Prove that, if L is regular, then so is $f(L)$.

Exercise 3.33** Prove that the language $\text{SUB}(L)$ (see Exercise 3.26) is regular for *any* choice of language L—in particular, L need not be regular.

Hint: observe that the set of subsequences of a fixed string is finite and thus regular, so that the set of subsequences of a finite collection of strings is also finite and regular. Let S be any set of strings. We say that a string x

is a minimal element of S if x has no proper subsequence in S. Let $M(L)$ be the set of minimal elements of the complement of SUB(L). Prove that $M(L)$ is finite by showing that no element of $M(L)$ is a subsequence of any other element of $M(L)$ and that any set of strings with that property must be finite. Conclude that the complement of SUB(L) is finite.

3.7   Bibliography

The first published discussion of finite-state machines was that of McCulloch and Pitts [1943], who presented a version of neural nets. Kleene [1956] formalized the notion of a finite automaton and also introduced regular expressions, proving the equivalence of the two models (Theorem 3.3 and Section 3.3.3). At about the same time, three independent authors, Huffman [1954], Mealy [1955], and Moore [1956], also discussed the finite-state model at some length, all from an applied point of view—all were working on the problem of designing switching circuits with feedback loops, or sequential machines, and proposed various design and minimization methods. The nondeterministic finite automaton was introduced by Rabin and Scott [1959], who proved its equivalence to the deterministic version (Theorem 3.1). Regular expressions were further developed by Brzozowski [1962, 1964]. The pumping lemma (Theorem 3.4) is due to Bar-Hillel *et al.* [1961], who also investigated several closure operations for regular languages. Closure under quotient (Theorem 3.5) was shown by Ginsburg and Spanier [1963]. Several of these results use a grammatical formalism instead of regular expressions or automata; this formalism was created in a celebrated paper by Chomsky [1956]. Exercises 3.31 and 3.32 are examples of proportional removal operations; Seiferas and McNaughton [1976] characterized which operations of this type preserve regularity. The interested reader should consult the classic text of Hopcroft and Ullman [1979] for a lucid and detailed presentation of formal languages and their relation to automata; the texts of Harrison [1978] and Salomaa [1973] provide additional coverage.

CHAPTER 4

Universal Models of Computation

Now that we have familiarized ourselves with a simple model of computation and, in particular, with the type of questions that typically arise with such models as well as with the methodologies that we use to answer such questions, we can move on to the main topic of this text: models of computation that have power equivalent to that of an idealized general-purpose computer or, equivalently, models of computation that can be used to characterize problem-solving by humans and machines.

Since we shall use these models to determine what can and cannot be computed in both the absence and the presence of resource bounds (such as bounds on the running time of a computation), we need to establish more than just the model itself; we also need a reasonable charging policy for it. When analyzing an algorithm, we typically assume some vague model of computing related to a general-purpose computer in which most simple operations take constant time, even though many of these operations would, in fact, require more than constant time when given arbitrary large operands. Implicit in the analysis (in spite of the fact that this analysis is normally carried out in asymptotic terms) is the assumption that every quantity fits within one word of memory and that all data fit within the addressable memory. While somewhat sloppy, this style of analysis is well suited to its purpose, since, with a few exceptions (such as public-key cryptography, where very large numbers are commonplace), the implicit assumption holds in most practical applications. It also has the advantage of providing results that remain independent of the specific environment under which the algorithm is to be run. The vague model of computation assumed by the analysis fits any modern computer and fails to fit[1] only very unusual machines or hardware, such as massively parallel machines, quantum computers, optical computers, and DNA computers (the last three of which remain for now in the laboratory or on the drawing board).

When laying the foundations of a theory, however, it pays to be more careful, if for no other purpose than to justify our claims that the exact choice of computational model is mostly irrelevant. In discussing the choice of computational model, we have to address three separate questions: (i) How is the input (and output) represented? (ii) How does the computational model compute? and (iii) What is the cost (in time and space) of a computation in the model? We take up each of these questions in turn.

4.1   Encoding Instances

Any instance of a problem can be described by a string of characters over some finite alphabet. As an example, consider the satisfiability problem. Recall that an instance of this problem is a Boolean expression consisting of k clauses over n variables, written in conjunctive normal form. Such an instance can be encoded clause by clause by listing, for each clause, which literals appear in it. The literals themselves can be encoded by assigning each variable a distinct number from 0 to $n - 1$ and by preceding that number by a bit indicating whether the variable is complemented or not. Different literals can thus have codes of different lengths, so that we need a symbol to separate literals within a clause (say a comma). Similarly, we need a symbol to separate clauses in our encoding (say a number sign). For example, the instance

$$(x_0 \vee \overline{x}_2) \wedge (\overline{x}_1 \vee x_2 \vee x_3) \wedge (\overline{x}_0 \vee \overline{x}_3)$$

would be encoded as

$$00, 110\#11, 010, 011\#10, 111$$

Alternately, we can eliminate the need for separators between literals by using a fixed-length code for the variables (of length $\lceil \log_2 n \rceil$ bits), still

---

[1]In fact, the model does not really fail to fit; rather, it needs simple and fairly obvious adaptations—for instance, parallel and optical computers have several computing units rather than one and quantum computers work with quantum bits, each of which can store more than one bit of information. Indeed, all analyses done to date for these unusual machines have been done using the conventional model of computation, with the required alterations.

preceded by a bit indicating complementation. Now, however, we need to know the code length for each variable or, equivalently, the number of variables; we can write this as the first item in the code, followed by a separator, then followed by the clauses. Our sample instance would then yield the code

$$100\#000110\#101010011\#100111$$

The lengths of the first and of the second encodings must remain within a ratio of $\lceil \log_2 n \rceil$ of each other; in particular, one encoding can be converted to the other in time polynomial in the length of the code. We could go one more step and make the encoding of each clause be of fixed length: simply let each clause be represented by a string of n symbols, where each symbol can take one of of three values, indicating that the corresponding variable does not appear in the clause, appears uncomplemented, or appears complemented. With a binary alphabet, we use two bits per symbol: "00" for an absent variable, "01" for an uncomplemented variable, and "10" for a complemented one. We now need to know either how many variables or how many clauses are present (the other quantity can easily be computed from the length of the input). Again we write this number first, separating it from the description of the clauses by some other symbol. Our sample instance (in which each clause uses $4 \cdot 2 = 8$ bits) is then encoded as

$$100\#0100100000100101110000010$$

This encoding always has length $\Theta(kn)$. When each clause includes almost every variable, it is more concise than the first two encodings, which then have length $\Theta(kn \log n)$, but the lengths of all three remain polynomially related. On the other hand, when each clause includes only a constant number of variables, the first two encodings have length $O(k \log n)$, so that the length of our last encoding need no longer be polynomially related to the length of the first two. Of the three encodings, the first two are reasonable, but the third is not, as it can become exponentially longer than the first two. We shall require of all our encodings that they be reasonable in that sense.

Of course, we really should compare encodings on the same alphabet, without using some arbitrary number of separators. Let us restrict ourselves to a binary alphabet, so that everything becomes a string of bits. Since our first representation uses four symbols and our third uses three, we shall use two bits per symbol in either case. Using our first representation and encoding "0" as "00," "1" as "11," the comma as "01," and the number sign as "10," our sample instance becomes

$$00000111000010111101\ldots11$$
$$0\ 0\ ,\ 1\ 0\ 0\ \#\ 1\ 1\ ,\ldots\ 1$$

The length of the encoding grew by a factor of two, the length of the codes chosen for the symbols. In general, the choice of any fixed alphabet to represent instances does not affect the length of the encoding by more than a constant factor, as long as the alphabet has at least two symbols.

More difficult issues are raised when encoding complex structures, such as a graph. Given an undirected graph, $G = (E, V)$, we face an enormous choice of possible encodings, with potentially very different lengths. Consider encoding the graph as an adjacency matrix: we need to indicate the number of vertices (using $\Theta(\log |V|)$ bits) and then, for each vertex, write a list of the matrix entries. Since each matrix entry is simply a bit, the total length of the encoding is always $\Theta(|V|^2)$.

Now consider encoding the graph by using adjacency lists. Once again, we need to indicate the number of vertices; then, for each vertex, we list the vertices (if any) present in the adjacency lists, separating adjacency lists by some special symbol. The overall encoding looks very much like that used for satisfiability; its length is $\Theta(|V| + |E| \log |V|)$.

Finally, consider encoding the graph as a list of edges. Using a fixed-length code for each vertex (so that the code must begin by an indication of the number of vertices), we simply write a collection of pairs, without any separator. Such a code uses $\Theta(|E| \log |V|)$ bits.

While the lengths of the first two encodings (adjacency matrix and adjacency lists) are polynomially related, the last encoding could be far more concise on an extremely sparse graph. For instance, if the graph has only a constant number of edges, then the last encoding has length $\Theta(\log |V|)$, while the second has length $\Theta(|V|)$, which is exponentially larger. Fortunately, the anomaly arises only for uninteresting graphs (graphs that have far fewer than $|V|$ edges). Moreover, we can encode any graph by breaking the list of vertices into two sublists, one containing all isolated vertices and the other containing all vertices of degree one or higher. The list of isolated vertices is given by a single number (its size), while the connected vertices are identified individually. The result is an encoding that mixes the two styles just discussed and remains reasonable under all graph densities.

Finally, depending on the problem and the chosen encodings, not every bit string represents a valid instance of the problem. While an encoding in which every string is meaningful might be more elegant, it is certainly not required. All that we need is the ability to differentiate (as efficiently as possible) between a string encoding a valid instance and a meaningless string. For instance, in our first and second encodings for Boolean formulae in conjunctive normal form, only strings of a certain form encode instances—in our first encoding, a comma and a number sign cannot be adjacent, while in our second encoding, the number of bits between any two number signs must be a multiple of a given constant. With almost any encoding, making this distinction is easy. In fact, the problem of distinguishing valid instances from meaningless input resides, not in the encoding, but in the assumptions made about valid instances. For instance, a graph problem, all instances of which are planar graphs and are encoded according to one of the schemes discussed earlier, requires us to differentiate efficiently between planar graphs (valid instances) and nonplanar graphs (meaningless inputs); as mentioned in Section 2.4, this decision can be made in linear time and thus efficiently. On the other hand, a graph problem, all instances of which are Hamiltonian graphs given in the same format, requires us to distinguish between Hamiltonian graphs and other graphs, something for which only exponential-time algorithms have been developed to date. Yet the same graphs, if given in a format where the vertices are listed in the order in which they appear in a Hamiltonian circuit, make for a reasonable input description because we can reject any input graph not given in this specific format, whether or not the graph is actually Hamiltonian.

4.2   Choosing a Model of Computation

Of significantly greater concern to us than the encoding is the choice of a model of computation. In this section, we discuss two models of computation, establish that they have equivalent power in terms of absolute computability (without resource bounds), and finally show that, as for encodings, they are polynomially related in terms of their effect on running time and space, so that the choice of a model (as long as it is reasonable) is immaterial while we are concerned with the boundary between tractable and intractable problems. We shall examine only two models, but our development is applicable to any other reasonable model.

4.2.1   Issues of Computability

Before we can ask questions of complexity, such as "Can the same problem be solved in polynomial time on all reasonable models of computation?" we

```
procedure Q (x: bitstring);
  function P (x,y: bitstring): boolean;
    begin
      ...
    end;
  begin
    if not P(x,x) then goto 99;
1:  goto 1;
99:
  end;
```

Figure 4.1   The unsolvability of the halting problem.

must briefly address the more fundamental question of computability, to wit "What kind of problem can be solved on a given model of computation?" We have seen that most problems are unsolvable, so it should not come as a surprise that among these are some truly basic and superficially simple problems. The classical example of an unsolvable problem is the *Halting Problem*: "Does there exist an algorithm which, given two bit strings, the first representing a program and the second representing data, determines whether or not the program run on the data will stop?" This is obviously the most fundamental problem in computer science: it is a simplification of "Does the program return the correct answer?" Yet a very simple contradiction argument shows that no such algorithm can exist. Suppose that we had such an algorithm and let P be a program for it (P itself is, of course, just a string of bits); P returns as answer either `true` (the argument program does stop when run on the argument data) or `false` (the argument program does not stop when run on the argument data). Then consider Figure 4.1. Procedure Q takes a single bit string as argument. If the program represented by this bit string stops when run on itself (i.e., with its own description as input), then Q enters an infinite loop; otherwise Q stops. Now consider what happens when we run Q on itself: Q stops if and only if $P(Q, Q)$ returns `false`, which happens if and only if Q does not stop when run on itself—a contradiction. Similarly, Q enters an infinite loop if and only if $P(Q, Q)$ returns `true`, which happens if and only if Q stops when run on itself—also a contradiction. Since our construction from the hypotheses is perfectly legitimate, our assumption that P exists must be false. Hence the halting problem is unsolvable (in our world of programs and bit strings; however, the same argument carries over to any other general model of computation).

Exercise 4.1 This proof of the unsolvability of the halting problem is really a proof by diagonalization, based on the fact that we can encode and thus enumerate all programs. Recast the proof so as to bring the diagonalization to the surface. □

The existence of unsolvable problems in certain models of computation (or logic or mathematics) led in the 1930s to a very careful study of computability, starting with the design of *universal* models of computation. Not, of course, that there is any way to prove that a model of computation is universal (just defining the word "universal" in this context is a major challenge): what logicians meant by this was a model capable of carrying out any algorithmic process. Over a dozen very different such models were designed, some taking inspiration from mathematics, some from logic, some from psychology; more have been added since, in particular many inspired from computer science. The key result is that all such models have been proved equivalent from a computability standpoint: what one can compute, all others can. In that sense, these models are truly universal.

4.2.2 The Turing Machine

Perhaps the most convincing model, and the standard model in computer science, is the *Turing machine*. The British logician Alan Turing designed it to mimic the problem-solving mechanism of a scientist. The idealized scientist sits at a desk with an unbounded supply of paper, pencils, and erasers and thinks; in the process of thinking the scientist will jot down some notes, look up some previous notes, possibly altering some entries. Decisions are made on the basis of the material present in the notes (but only a fixed portion of it—say a page—since no more can be confined to the scientist's fixed-size memory) and of the scientist's current mental state. Since the brain encloses a finite volume and thought processes are ultimately discrete, there are only a finite number of distinct mental states. A Turing machine (see Figure 4.2) is composed of: (i) an unbounded tape (say magnetic tape) divided into squares, each of which can store one symbol from a fixed tape alphabet—this mimics the supply of paper; (ii) a read/write head that scans one square at a time and is moved left or right by one square at each step—this mimics the pencils and erasers and the consulting, altering, and writing of notes; and (iii) a finite-state control—this mimics the brain. The machine is started in a fixed initial state with the head on the first square of the input string and the rest of the tape blank: the scientist is getting ready to read the description of the problem. The machine stops on entering a final state with the head on the first square of the output string and the rest of the tape blank: the scientist has solved the

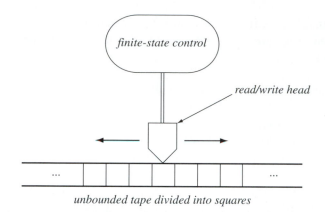

unbounded tape divided into squares

Figure 4.2   The organization of a Turing machine.

problem, discarded any notes made in the process, and kept only the sheets describing the solution. At any given step, the finite-state control, on the basis of the current state and the current contents of the tape square under the head, decides which symbol to write on that square, in which direction to move the head, and which state to enter next.

Thus a Turing machine is much like a finite automaton equipped with a tape. An instruction in the finite-state control is a five-tuple

$$\delta(q_i, a) = (q_j, b, L/R)$$

Like the state transition of a finite automaton, the choice of transition is dictated by the current state q_i and the current input symbol a (but now the current input symbol is the symbol stored on the tape square under the head). Part of the transition is to move to a new state q_j, but, in addition to a new state, the instruction also specifies the symbol b to be written in the tape square under the head and whether the head is to move left (L) or right (R) by one square. A Turing machine program is a set of such instructions; the instructions of a Turing machine are not written in a sequence, since the next instruction to follow is determined entirely by the current state and the symbol under the head. Thus a Turing machine program is much like a program in a logic language such as Prolog. There is no sequence inherent in the list of instructions; pattern-matching is used instead to determine which instruction is to be executed next. Like a finite automaton, a Turing machine may be deterministic (for each combination of current state and current input symbol, there is at most one applicable five-tuple) or nondeterministic, with the same convention: a nondeterministic machine accepts its input if there is any way for it to do so. In the rest of this section, we shall deal with the deterministic variety and thus shall take "Turing machine" to mean "deterministic Turing machine." We shall return to the nondeterministic version when considering Turing machines for decision problems and shall show that it can be simulated by a deterministic version, so that, with Turing machines as with finite automata, nondeterminism does not add any computational power.

The Turing machine model makes perfect sense but hardly resembles a modern computer. Yet writing programs (i.e., designing the finite-state control) for Turing machines is not as hard as it seems. Consider the problem of incrementing an unsigned integer in binary representation: the machine is started in its initial state, with its head immediately to the left of the number on the tape; it must stop in the final state with its head immediately to the left of the incremented number on the tape. (In order to distinguish data from blank tape, we must assume the existence of a third symbol, the blank symbol, ␣.) The machine first scans the input to the right until it encounters a blank—at which time its head is sitting at the right of the number. Then it moves to the left, changing the tape as necessary; it keeps track of whether or not there is a running carry in its finite state (two possibilities, necessitating two states). Each bit seen will be changed according to the current state and will also dictate the next state to enter. The resulting program is shown in both diagrammatic and tabular form in Figure 4.3. In the diagram, each state is represented as a circle and each step as an arrow labeled by the current symbol, the new symbol, and the direction of head movement. For instance, an arc from state i to state j labeled $x/y, L$ indicates that the machine, when in state i and reading symbol x, must change x to y, move its head one square to the left, and enter state j.

Exercise 4.2 Design Turing machines for the following problems:

1. Decrementing an unsigned integer (decrementing zero leaves zero; verify that your machine does not leave a leading zero on the tape).
2. Multiplying an unsigned integer by three (you may want to use an additional symbol during the computation).
3. Adding two unsigned integers (assume that the two integers are written consecutively, separated only by an additional symbol)—this last task requires a much larger control than the first two.   □

The great advantage of the Turing machine is its simplicity and uniformity. Since there is only one type of instruction, there is no question as to appropriate choices for time and space complexity measures: the time taken

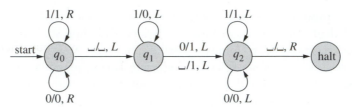

$$1/1, R \qquad 1/0, L \qquad 1/1, L$$

start q_0 — $\_/\_, L$ — q_1 — $0/1, L$ / $\_/1, L$ — q_2 — $\_/\_, R$ — halt

$0/0, R$ $\qquad\qquad\qquad\qquad 0/0, L$

(a) in diagrammatic form

Current State	Symbol Read	Next State	Symbol Written	Head Motion	Comments
q_0	1	q_0	1	R	Scan past right end of integer
q_0	0	q_0	0	R	
q_0	␣	q_1	␣	L	Place head over rightmost bit
q_1	1	q_1	0	L	Propagate carry left
q_1	0	q_2	1	L	End of carry propagation
q_1	␣	q_2	1	L	
q_2	1	q_2	1	L	Scan past left end of integer
q_2	0	q_2	0	L	
q_2	␣	halt	␣	R	Place head over leftmost bit

(b) in tabular form

Figure 4.3   A Turing machine for incrementing an unsigned integer.

by a Turing machine is simply the number of steps taken by the computation and the space used by a Turing machine is simply the total number of distinct tape squares scanned during the computation. The great disadvantage of the Turing machine, of course, is that it requires much time to carry out elementary operations that a modern computer can execute in one instruction. Elementary arithmetic, simple tests (e.g., for parity), and especially access to a stored quantity all require large amounts of time on a Turing machine. These are really problems of scale: while incrementing a number on a Turing machine requires, as Figure 4.3 illustrates, time proportional to the length of the number's binary representation, the same is true of a modern computer when working with very large numbers: we would need an unbounded-precision arithmetic package. Similarly, whereas accessing an arbitrary stored quantity cannot be done in constant time with a Turing machine, the same is again true of a modern computer: only those locations within the machine's address space can be accessed in (essentially) constant time.

4.2.3   Multitape Turing Machines

The abstraction of the Turing machine is appealing, but there is no compelling choice for the details of its specification. In particular, there is no reason why the machine should be equipped with a single tape. Even the most disorganized mathematician is likely to keep drafts, reprints, and various notes, if not in neatly organized files, at least in separate piles on the floor. In order to endow our Turing machine model with multiple tapes, it is enough to replicate the tape and head structure of our one-tape model. A k-tape Turing machine will be equipped with k read/write heads, one per tape, and will have transitions given by $(3k + 2)$-tuples of the form

$$\delta(q_i, a_1, a_2, \ldots, a_k) = (q_j, b_1, L/R, b_2 L/R, \ldots, b_k, L/R)$$

where the a_is are the characters read (one per tape, under that tape's head), the b_is are the characters written (again one per tape), and the L/R entries tell the machine how to move (independently) each of its heads. Clearly, a k-tape machine is as powerful as our standard model—just set k to 1 (or just use one of the tapes and ignore the others). The question is whether adding $k - 1$ tapes adds any power to the model—or at least enables it to solve certain problems more efficiently. The answer to the former is no, as we shall shortly prove, while the answer to the latter is yes, as the reader is invited to verify.

Exercise 4.3 Verify that a two-tape Turing machine can recognize the language of palindromes over $\{0, 1\}$ in time linear in the size of the input, while a one-tape Turing machine appears to require time quadratic in the size of the input. ☐

In fact, the quadratic increase in time evidenced in the example of the language of palindromes is a worst-case increase.

Theorem 4.1 A k-tape Turing machine can be simulated by a standard one-tape machine at a cost of (at most) a quadratic increase in running time. ☐

The basic idea is the use of the alphabet symbols of the one-tape machine to encode a "vertical slice" through the k tapes of the k-tape machine, that is, to encode the contents of tape square i on each of the k tapes into a single character. However, that idea alone does not suffice: we also need to encode the positions of the k heads, since they move independently and thus need not all be at the same tape index. We can do this by adding a single bit to the description of the content of each tape square on each of the k tapes: the bit is set to 1 if the head sits on this tape square and to 0 otherwise. The

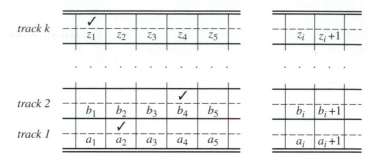

Figure 4.4   Simulating k tapes with a single k-track tape.

concept of encoding a vertical slice through the k tapes still works—we just
have a somewhat larger set of possibilities: $(\Sigma \cup \{0, 1\})^k$ instead of just Σ^k.
In effect, we have replaced a multitape machine by a one-tape, "multitrack"
machine. Figure 4.4 illustrates the idea. There remains one last problem:
in order to "collect" the k characters under the k heads of the multitape
machine, the one-tape machine will have to scan several of its own squares;
we need to know where to scan and when to stop scanning in order to
retain some reasonable efficiency. Thus our one-tape machine will have to
maintain some basic information to help it make this scan. Perhaps the
simplest form is an indication of how many of the k heads being simulated
are to the right of the current position of the head of the one-tape machine,
an indication that can be encoded into the finite state of the simulating
machine (thereby increasing the number of states of the one-tape machine
by a factor of k).

Proof. Let M_k, for some k larger than 1, be a k-tape Turing machine;
we design a one-tape Turing machine M that simulates M_k. As discussed
earlier, the alphabet of M is large enough to encode in a single character the
k characters under the k heads of M_k as well as each of the k bits denoting,
for each of the k tapes, whether or not a head of M_k sits on the current
square. The finite control of M stores the current state of M_k along with
the number of heads of M_k sitting to the right of the current position of the
head of M; it also stores the characters under the heads of M_k as it collects
them. Thus if M_k has q states and a tape alphabet of s characters, M has
$q \cdot k \cdot (s + 1)^k$ states—the $(s + 1)$ term accounts for tape symbols not yet
collected—and a tape alphabet of $(2s)^k$ characters—the $(2s)$ term accounts
for the extra marker needed at each square to denote the positions of the k
heads.

To simulate one move of M_k, our new machine M makes a left-to-right sweep of its tape, from the leftmost head position of M_k to its rightmost head position, followed by a right-to-left sweep. On the left-to-right sweep, M records in its finite control the content of each tape square of M_k under a head of M_k, updating the record every time it scans a vertical slice with one or more head markers and decreasing its count (also stored in its finite control) of markers to the right of the current position. When this count reaches zero, M resets it to k and starts a right-to-left scan. Since it has recorded the k characters under the heads of M_k as well as the state of M_k, M can now simulate the correctly chosen transition of M_k. Thus in its right-to-left sweep, M updates each character under a head of M_k and "moves" that head (that is, it changes that square's marker bit to 0 while setting the marker bit of the correct adjacent square to 1), again counting down from k the number of markers to the left of the current position. When the count reaches 0, M resets it to k and reverses direction, now ready to simulate the next transition of M_k.

Since M_k starts its computation with all of its heads aligned at index 1, the distance (in tape squares) from its leftmost head to its rightmost head after i steps is at most $2i$ (with one head moving left at each step and one moving right at each step). Thus simulating step i of M_k is going to cost M on the order of $4i$ steps ($2i$ steps per sweep), so that, if M_k runs for a total of n steps, then M takes on the order of $\sum_{i=1}^{n} 4i = O(n^2)$ steps.　　*Q.E.D.*

In contrast to the time increase, note that M uses exactly the same number of tape squares as M_k. However, its alphabet is significantly larger. Instead of s symbols, it uses $(2s)^k$ symbols; in terms of bits, each character uses $k(1 + \log s)$ bits instead of $\log s$ bits—a constant-factor increase for each fixed value of k.

To summarize, we have shown that one-tape and multitape Turing machines have equivalent computational power and, moreover, that a multitape Turing machine can be simulated by a one-tape Turing machine with at most a quadratic time penalty and constant-factor space penalty.

4.2.4　The Register Machine

The standard model of computation designed to mimic modern computers is the family of *RAM* (register machine) models. One of the many varieties of such machines is composed of a central processor and an unbounded number of registers; the processor carries out instructions (from a limited repertoire) on the registers, each of which can store an arbitrarily large integer. As is the case with the Turing machine, the program is not stored in

```
        ; adds R0 and R1 and returns result in R0
        ; loop invariant: R0 + R1 is constant
loop: JumpOnZero R1,done  ; R0 + R1 in R0, 0 in R1
        Dec R1
        Inc R0
        JumpOnZero R2,loop   ; unconditional branch (R2 = 0)
done: Halt
```

Figure 4.5   A RAM program to add two unsigned integers.

the memory that holds the data. An immediate consequence is that a RAM program cannot be self-modifying; another consequence is that any given RAM program can refer only to a fixed number of registers. The machine is started at the beginning of its program with the input data preloaded in its first few registers and all other registers set to zero; it stops upon reaching the halt instruction, with the answer stored in its first few registers. The simplest such machine includes only four instructions: increment, decrement, jump on zero (to some label), and halt. In this model, the program to increment an unsigned integer has two instructions—an increment and a halt—and takes two steps to execute, in marked contrast to the Turing machine designed for the same task. Figure 4.5 solves the third part of Exercise 4.2 for the RAM model. Again, compare its relative simplicity (five instructions—a constant-time loop executed m times, where m is the number stored in register R1) with a Turing machine design for the same task. Of course, we should not hasten to conclude that RAMs are inherently more efficient than Turing machines. The mechanism of the Turing machine is simply better suited for certain string-oriented tasks than that of the RAM. Consider for instance the problem of concatenating two input words over $\{0, 1\}$: the Turing machine requires only one pass over the input to carry out the concatenation, but the RAM (on which a concatenation is basically a shift followed by an addition) requires a complex series of arithmetic operations.

To bring the RAM model closer to a typical computer, we might want to include integer addition, subtraction, multiplication, and division, as well as register transfer operations. (In the end, we shall add addition, subtraction, and register transfer to our chosen model.) The question now is how to charge for time and space. Space is not too difficult. We can either charge for the maximum number of bits used among all registers during the computation or charge for the maximum number of bits used in any register during the computation—the two can differ only by a constant ratio, since the number of registers is fixed for any program. In general, we want the space measure not to exceed the time measure (to within a constant factor), since a program cannot use arbitrarily large amounts of space in one unit of time. (Such a relationship clearly holds for the Turing machine: in one step, the machine can use at most one new tape square.) In this light, it is instructive to examine briefly the consequences of possible charging policies. Assume that we assign unit cost to the first four instructions mentioned—even though this allows incrementing an arbitrarily large number in constant time. Since the increment instruction is the only one which may result in increasing space consumption and since it never increases space consumption by more than one bit, the space used by a RAM program grows no faster than the time used by it plus the size of the input:

$$\text{SPACE} = \text{O}(Input\ size + \text{TIME})$$

Let us now add register transfers at unit cost; this allows copying an arbitrary amount of data in constant time. A register copy may increase space consumption much faster than an increment instruction, but it cannot increase any number—at most, it can copy the largest number into every named register. Since the number of registers is fixed for a given program, register transfers do not contribute to the asymptotic increase in space consumption. Consequently, space consumption remains asymptotically bounded by time consumption. We now proceed to include addition and subtraction, once again at unit cost. Since the result of an addition is at most one bit longer than the longer of the two summands, any addition operation asymptotically increases storage consumption by one bit (asymptotic behavior is again invoked, since the first few additions may behave like register transfers). Once more the relationship between space and time is preserved.

Our machine is by now fairly realistic for numbers of moderate size—though impossibly efficient in dealing with arbitrarily large numbers. What happens if we now introduce unit cost multiplication and division? A product requires about as many bits as needed by the two multiplicands; in other words, by multiplying a number by itself, the storage requirements can double. This behavior leads to an exponential growth in storage requirements. (Think of a program that uses just two registers and squares whatever is in the first register as many times as indicated by the second. When started with n in the first register and m in the second, this program stops with n^{2^m} in the first register and 0 in the second. The time used is m, but the storage is $2^m \log n$—assuming that all numbers are unsigned binary numbers.) Such behavior is very unrealistic in any model; rather than design some suitable charge for the operation, we shall simply use a RAM model without multiplication.

Our model remains unrealistic in one respect: its way of referencing storage. A RAM in which each register must be explicitly named has neither indexing capability nor indirection—two staples of modern computer architectures. In fact, incrementation of arbitrary integers in unit time and indirect references are compatible in the sense that the space used remains bounded by the sum of the input size and the time taken. However, the reader can verify (see Exercise 4.11) that the combination of register transfer, addition, and indirect reference allows the space used by a RAM program to grow quadratically with time:

$$\text{Space} = O(\text{Time}^2)$$

At this point, we can go with the model described earlier or we can accept indexing but adopt a charging policy under which the time for a register transfer or an addition is proportional to the number of bits in the source operands. We choose to continue with our first model.

4.2.5   Translation Between Models

We are now ready to tackle the main question of this section: how does the choice of a model (and associated space and time measures) influence our assessment of problems? We need to show that each model can compute whatever function can be computed by the other, and then decide how, if at all, the complexity of a problem is affected by the choice of model. We prove below that our two models are equivalent in terms of computability and that the choice of model causes only a polynomial change in complexity measures. The proof consists simply of simulating one machine by the other (and vice versa) and noting the time and space requirements of the simulation. (The same construction, of course, establishes the equivalence of the two models from the point of view of computability.) While the proof is quite simple, it is also quite long; therefore, we sketch its general lines and illustrate only a few simulations in full detail.

In order to simulate a RAM on a Turing machine, some conventions must be established regarding the representation of the RAM's registers. A satisfactory solution uses an additional tape symbol (say a colon) as a separator and has the tape contain all registers at all times, ordered as a sequential list. In order to avoid ambiguities, let us assume that each integer in a RAM register is stored in binary representation without leading zeros; if the integer is, in fact, zero, then nothing at all is stored, as signaled by two consecutive colons on the tape. The RAM program itself is translated into the finite-state control of the Turing machine. Thus each RAM instruction becomes a block of Turing machine states with appropriate transitions while the program becomes a collection of connected blocks. In order to allow blocks to be connected and to use only standard blocks, the position of the head must be an invariant at entrance to and exit from a block. In Figure 4.6, which depicts the blocks corresponding to the "jump on zero," the "increment," and the "decrement," the head sits on the leftmost nonblank square on the tape when a block is entered and when it is left.[2]

Consider the instruction JumpOnZero Ri, *label* (starting the numbering of the registers from R1). First the Turing machine scans over $(i - 1)$ registers, using $(i - 1)$ states to do so. After moving its head to the right of the colon separating the $(i - 1)$st register from the ith, the Turing machine can encounter a colon or a blank—in which case Ri contains zero—or a one—in which case Ri contains a strictly positive integer. In either case, the Turing machine repositions the head over the leftmost bit of R1 and makes a transition to the block of states that simulate the (properly chosen) instruction to execute. The simulation of the instruction Inc is somewhat more complicated. Again the Turing machine scans right, this time until it finds the rightmost bit of the ith register. It now increments the value of this register using the algorithm of Figure 4.3. However, if the propagation of the carry leads to an additional bit in the representation of the number and if the ith register is not the first, then the Turing machine uses three states to shift the contents of the first through $(i - 1)$st registers left by one position. The block for the instruction Dec is similar; notice, however, that a right shift is somewhat more complex than a left shift, due to the necessity of looking ahead one tape square.

Exercise 4.4 Design a Turing machine block to simulate the register transfer instruction. □

From the figures as well as from the description, it should be clear that the block for an instruction dealing with register i differs from the block for an instruction dealing with register j, $j \neq i$. Thus the number of different blocks used depends on the number of registers named in the RAM program: with k registers, we need up to $3k + 1$ different Turing machine blocks.

---

[2] For the sake of convenience in the figure, we have adopted an additional convention regarding state transitions: a transition labeled with only a direction indicates that, on all symbols not already included in another transition from the same state, the machine merely moves its head in the direction indicated, recopying whatever symbol was read without change.

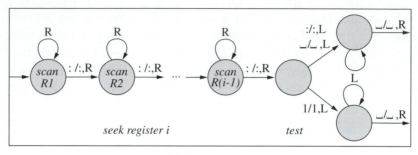

(a) jump on zero

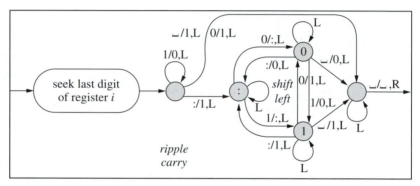

(b) increment

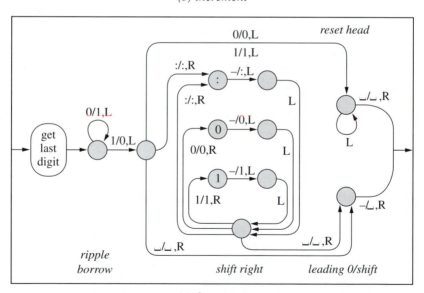

(c) decrement

Figure 4.6   Turing machine blocks simulating RAM instructions.

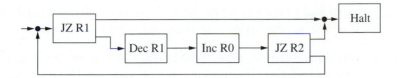

Figure 4.7 The Turing machine program produced from the RAM program of Figure 4.5.

An important point to keep in mind is that blocks are not reused but copied as needed (they are not so much subroutines as in-line macros): each instruction in the RAM program gets translated into its own block. For example, the RAM program for addition illustrated in Figure 4.5 becomes the collection of blocks depicted in Figure 4.7. The reason for avoiding reuse is that each Turing machine block is used, not as a subroutine, but as a macro. In effect, we replace each instruction of the RAM program by a Turing machine block (a macro expansion) and the connectivity among the blocks describes the flow of the program.

Our simulation is efficient in terms of space: the space used by the Turing machine is at most a constant multiple of the space used by the RAM, or

$$\text{SPACE}_{TM} = \Theta(\text{SPACE}_{RAM})$$

In contrast, much time is spent in seeking the proper register on which to carry out the operation, in shifting blocks of tape up or down to keep all registers in a sequential list, and in returning the head to the left of the data at the end of a block. Nevertheless, the time spent by the Turing machine in simulating the jump and increment instructions does not exceed a constant multiple of the total amount of space used on the tape—that is, a constant multiple of the space used by the RAM program. Thus our most basic RAM model can be simulated on a Turing machine at a cost increase in time proportional to the space used by the RAM, or

$$\text{TIME}_{TM} = O(\text{TIME}_{RAM} \cdot \text{SPACE}_{RAM})$$

Similarly, the time spent in simulating the register transfer instruction does not exceed a constant multiple of the square of the total amount of space used on the tape and uses no extra space.

Exercise 4.5 Design a block simulating RAM addition (assuming that such an instruction takes three register names, all three of which could refer to the same register). Verify that the time required for the simulation is, at worst, proportional to the square of the total amount of space used on the tape, which in turn is proportional to the space used by the registers.   □

By the previous exercise, then, RAM addition can be simulated on a Turing machine using space proportional to the space used by the RAM and time proportional to the square of the space used by the RAM. Subtraction is similar to addition, decrementing is similar to incrementing. Since the space used by a RAM is itself bounded by a constant multiple of the time used by the RAM program, it follows that any RAM program can be simulated on a Turing machine with at most a quadratic increase in time and a linear increase in space.

Simulating a Turing machine with a RAM requires representing the state of the machine as well as its tape contents and head position using only registers. The combination of the control state, the head position, and the tape contents completely describes the Turing machine at some step of execution; this snapshot of the machine is called an *instantaneous description*, or ID. A standard technique is to divide the tape into three parts: the square under the head, those to the left of the head, and those to the right. As the left and right portions of the tape are subject to the same handling, they must be encoded in the same way, with the result that we read the squares to the left of the head from left to right, but those to the right of the head from right to left. If the Turing machine has an alphabet of d characters, we use base d numbers to encode the tape pieces. Because blanks on either side of the tape in use could otherwise create problems, we assign the value of zero to the blank character. Now each of the three parts of the tape is encoded into a finite number and stored in a register, as illustrated in Figure 4.8. Each Turing machine state is translated to a group of one or more RAM instructions, with state changes corresponding to unconditional jumps (which can be accomplished with a conditional jump by testing an extra register set to zero for the specific purpose of forcing transfers). Moving from one transition to another of the Turing machine requires testing the register that stores the code of the symbol under the head, through repeated decrements and a jump on zero. Moving the head

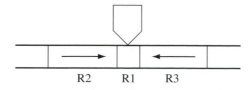

R2   R1   R3

Figure 4.8   Encoding the tape contents into registers.

is simulated in the RAM by altering the contents of the three registers maintaining the tape contents; this operation, thanks to our encoding, reduces to dividing one register by d (to drop its last digit), multiplying another by d and adding the code of the symbol rewritten, and setting a third (the square under the head) to the digit dropped from the first register. Formally, in order to simulate the transition $\delta(q, a) = (q', b, L)$, we execute

$$R1 \leftarrow b$$
$$R3 \leftarrow d \cdot R3 + R1$$
$$R1 \leftarrow R2 \bmod d$$
$$R2 \leftarrow R2 \div d$$

and, in order to simulate the transition $\delta(q, a) = (q', b, R)$, we execute

$$R1 \leftarrow b$$
$$R2 \leftarrow d \cdot R2 + R1$$
$$R1 \leftarrow R3 \bmod d$$
$$R3 \leftarrow R3 \div d$$

where $a \bmod b$ is the integer remainder of a by b, and $a \div b$ is the integer quotient of a by b. Except for the division, all operations can be carried out in constant time by our RAM model (the multiplication by d can be done with a constant number of additions). The division itself requires more time, but can be accomplished (by building the quotient digit by digit) in time proportional to the number of digits of the operand—or equivalently in time proportional to the space used by the Turing machine. Thus we can write, much as before,

$$\text{SPACE}_{RAM} = \Theta(\text{SPACE}_{TM})$$
$$\text{TIME}_{RAM} = O(\text{TIME}_{TM} \cdot \text{SPACE}_{TM})$$

and so conclude that any Turing machine can be simulated on a RAM with at most a quadratic increase in time and a linear increase in space.

We have thus added an element of support for the celebrated *Church-Turing thesis*: the Turing machine and the RAM (as well as any of a number of other models such as lambda calculus or partial recursive functions) are universal models of computation.

4.3 Model Independence

Many variations of the RAM have been proposed: charged RAMs, where the cost of an operation is proportional to the length of its operands; bounded RAMS, where the size of numbers stored in any register is bounded by a constant; and, as discussed earlier, indexed RAMs, where a fixed number of CPU registers can also be used as index registers for memory addressing. Similarly, many variations of the Turing machine have been proposed, such as random-access Turing machines, which can access an arbitrary stored quantity in constant time, and multitape Turing machines, equipped with several tapes and heads (some of which may be read-only or write-only). Several variants are explored in the exercises at the end of this chapter. An important variation is the *off-line Turing machine*, used mainly in connection with space complexity. This machine uses three tapes, each equipped with its own head. One tape is the input tape, equipped with a read-only head; another is the output tape, equipped with a write-only head that can move only to the right; the third tape is the work (or scratch) tape, equipped with a normal read/write head. Space consumption is measured on the work tape only, thereby allowing sublinear space measures by charging neither for input space nor for output space. Yet the complexity of programs run on any one of these machines is still polynomially related to that of the same program simulated on any other. This *polynomial relatedness* justifies our earlier contention that the exact choice of model is irrelevant with respect to intractability: choosing a different model will not render an intractable problem tractable nor will it achieve the converse. In the following, we use Turing machines when we need a formal model, but otherwise we continue our earlier practice of using an ill-defined model similar to a modern computer.

In any reasonable model of computation, space requirements cannot grow asymptotically faster than time requirements, i.e.,

$$\textsc{Space} = \textsc{O}(\textsc{Time}) \tag{4.1}$$

Moreover, given fixed space bounds, no model can expend arbitrary amounts of time in computation and still halt. This is easiest to see in a Turing machine. During the computation, our machine never found itself twice in exactly the same instantaneous description (same tape contents, same head position, and same state), or else it would have entered an infinite loop. Assume that, on an input of size n, our Turing machine, with an alphabet of d symbols and a finite control of s states, uses $f(n)$ tape squares. Then there are $d^{f(n)}$ possible tape contents, $f(n)$ possible head positions, and s possible states, so that the total number of configurations is $s \cdot f(n) \cdot d^{f(n)}$, which is $\textsc{O}(c^{f(n)})$ for a suitable choice of c. Thus the following relation holds for Turing machines (and for all other reasonable models of computation, due to polynomial relatedness):

$$\textsc{Time} = \textsc{O}(c^{\textsc{Space}}), \quad \text{for some constant } c \tag{4.2}$$

4.4 Turing Machines as Acceptors and Enumerators

We presented Turing machines as general computing engines. In order to view them as language acceptors (like our finite automata), we need to adopt some additional conventions. We shall assume that the string to be tested is on the tape and that the Turing machine accepts the string (decides it is in the language) if it stops with just a "yes" (some preagreed symbol) on the tape and rejects the string if it stops with just a "no" on the tape. Of course, a Turing machine might not always stop; as a language acceptor, though, it must stop on every string, since we do not get a decision otherwise. However, a lesser level of information can be obtained if we consider a machine that can list all strings in the language but cannot always decide membership. Such a machine is able to answer "yes": if it can list all strings in the language, it can just watch its own output and stop with "yes" as soon as the desired string appears in the list. However, it is not always able to answer "no": while it never gives a wrong answer, it might fail to stop when fed a string not in the language. Of course, failure to stop is not a condition we can detect, since we never know if the machine might not stop in just one more step. Thus an enumerating Turing machine, informally, is one that lists all strings in the language. Note that the listing is generally in arbitrary order—if it were in some total ordering, we would then be able to verify that a string does not belong to the language by observing the output and waiting until either the desired string is produced or some string that follows the desired string in the total ordering is produced.

While nondeterminism in general Turing machines is difficult to use (if the different decisions can lead to a large collection of different outputs, what has the machine computed?), nondeterminism in machines limited to function as language acceptors can be defined just as for finite automata: if there is any way for the Turing machine to accept its input, it will do so. All happens as if the nondeterministic machine, whenever faced with a choice, automatically (and at no cost) chose the correct next step—indeed, this is an alternate way of defining nondeterminism. As the choice cannot in practice be made without a great deal of additional information concerning the alternatives, another model of nondeterminism uses the "rabbit" analogy, in which a nondeterministic Turing machine is viewed as a purely deterministic machine that is also a prolific breeder. Whenever faced with a choice for the next step, the machine creates one replica of itself for each possible choice and sends the replicas to explore the choices. As soon as one of its progeny identifies the instance as a "yes" instance, the whole machine stops and accepts the instance. On the other hand, the machine cannot answer "no" until all of its descendants have answered "no"—a determination that requires counting. The asymmetry here resides in the ability of the machine to perform a very large logical "or" at no cost, since a logical "or" necessitates only the detection of a single "yes" answer, whereas a similar logical "and" appears to require a very large amount of time due to the need for an exhaustive assessment of the situation.

In fact, whatever language can be decided by a nondeterministic Turing machine can also be accepted by a deterministic Turing machine.

Theorem 4.2 Any language accepted by a nondeterministic Turing machine can be accepted by a deterministic Turing machine.   □

The proof is simply a simulation of the nondeterministic machine. Since the machine to be simulated need not always halt, we must ensure that the simulation halts whenever the machine to be simulated halts, including cases when the nondeterministic machine has an accepting path in a tree of computations that includes nonterminating paths. We do this by conducting a breadth-first search of the tree of possible computations of the nondeterministic machine.

Proof. We can simplify the construction by using a three-tape deterministic Turing machine; we know that such a machine can be simulated with a one-tape machine. Let M_n be the nondeterministic machine and M_d be the new three-tape deterministic machine. At each step, M_n has at most some number k of possible choices, since its finite-state control contains only a finite number of five-tuples. Thus, as M_n goes through its computation, each step it takes can be represented by a number between 1 and k. A sequence of such numbers defines a computation of M_n. (Strictly speaking, not all such sequences define a valid computation of M_n, but we can easily check whether or not a sequence does define one and restrict our attention to those sequences that do.) Naturally, we do not know how long the accepting sequence is, but we do know that one exists for each string in the language.

Our new machine M_d will use the second tape to enumerate all possible sequences of moves for M_n, beginning with the short sequences and increasing the length of the sequences after exhausting all shorter ones. Using the sequence on the second tape as a guide, M_d will now proceed to simulate M_n on the third tape, using the first tape for the input. If the simulation results in M_n's entering an accepting configuration (halting state and proper contents of tape), then our machine M_d accepts its input; otherwise it moves on to the next sequence of digits. It is clear from this description that M_d will accept exactly what M_n accepts. If M_d finds that all sequences of digits of some given length are illegal sequences for M_n, then it halts and rejects its input. Again, it is clear that whatever is rejected by M_d would have been rejected by M_n. If M_n halts and rejects, then every one of its computation paths halts and rejects, so that M_n has some longest halting path, say of length n, and thus has no legal move beyond the nth step on any path. Under the same input, M_d must also halt and reject after examining all computations of up to n steps, so that M_d rejects exactly the same strings as M_n.   Q.E.D.

4.5   Exercises

Exercise 4.6 Prove that allowing a Turing machine to leave its head stationary during some transitions does not increase its computational power.

Exercise 4.7 Prove that, for each Turing machine that halts under all inputs, there is an equivalent Turing machine (that computes the same function) that never moves it head more than one character to the left of its starting position.

Exercise 4.8 In contrast to the previous two exercises, verify that a Turing machine that, at each transition, can move its head to the right or leave it in place but cannot move it to the left, is *not* equivalent to our standard model. Is it equivalent to our finite automaton model, or is it more powerful?

Exercise 4.9* Prove that a Turing machine that can write each tape square at most once during its computation is equivalent to our standard version. (Hint: this new model will use far more space than the standard model.)

Exercise 4.10 A two-dimensional Turing machine is equipped with a two-dimensional tape rather than a one-dimensional tape. The two-dimensional tape is an unbounded grid of tape squares over which the machine's head can move in four directions: left, right, up, and down. Define such a machine formally, and then show how to simulate it on a conventional Turing machine.

Exercise 4.11 Verify that a RAM that includes addition and register transfer in its basic instruction set and that can reference arbitrary registers through indirection on named registers can use space at a rate that is quadratic in the running time.

Exercise 4.12 Devise a charging policy for the RAM described in the previous exercise that will prevent the consumption of space at a rate higher than the consumption of time.

Exercise 4.13 Verify that a RAM need not have an unbounded number of registers. Use prime encoding to show that a three-register RAM can simulate a k-register RAM for any fixed $k > 3$.

Exercise 4.14 Define a RAM model where registers store values in unary code; then show how to simulate the conventional RAM on such a model.

Exercise 4.15 Use the results of the previous two exercises to show that a two-register RAM where all numbers are written in unary can simulate an arbitrary RAM.

Exercise 4.16* Define a new Turing machine model as follows. The machine is equipped with three tapes: a read-only input tape (with a head that can be moved left or right or left in place at will), a write-only output tape (where the head only moves right or stays in place), and a work tape. The work tape differs from the usual version (of an off-line Turing machine) in that the machine cannot write on it but can only place "pebbles" (identical markers) on it, up to three at any given time. On reading a square of the work tape, the machine can distinguish between an empty square and one with a pebble, and can remove the pebble or leave it in place. A move of this machine is similar to a move of the conventional off-line Turing machine. It is of the form $\delta(q, a, b) = (q', L/R/-, c, L/R/-, d/-, R/-)$, where a is the character under the head on the input tape; b and c are the contents (before and after the move, respectively) of the work tape square under the head (either nothing or a pebble); and d is the character written on the output tape (which may be absent, as the machine need not write something at each move), while the three $L/R/-$ (only $R/-$ in the case of the output tape) denote the movements for the three heads.

Show that this machine model is universal. Perhaps the simplest way to do so is to use the result of Exercise 4.15 and show that the three-pebble machine can simulate the two-register RAM. An alternative is to begin by using a five-pebble machine (otherwise identical to the model described here), show how to use it to simulate a conventional off-line Turing machine, then complete the proof by simulating the five-pebble machine on the three-pebble machine by using prime encoding.

Exercise 4.17 Consider enhancing the finite automaton model with a form of storage. Specifically, we shall add a queue and allow the finite automaton to remove and read the character at the head of the queue as well as to add a character to the tail of the queue. The character read or added can be chosen from the queue alphabet (which would typically include the input alphabet and some additional symbols) or it can be the empty string (if the queue is empty or if we do not want to add a character to the queue). Thus the transition function of our enhanced finite automaton now maps a triple (state, input character, queue character) to a pair (state, queue character).

Show that this machine model is universal.

Exercise 4.18 Repeat the previous exercise, but now add two stacks rather than one queue; thus the transition function now maps a quadruple (state, input character, first stack character, second stack character) to a triple (state, first stack character, second stack character).

Exercise 4.19 (Refer to the previous two exercises.) Devise suitable measures of time and space for the enhanced finite-automaton models (with a queue and with two stacks). Verify that your measures respect the basic relationships between time and space and that the translation costs obey the quadratic (for time) and linear (for space) relationships discussed in the text.

Exercise 4.20 A *Post system* is a collection of rules for manipulating natural numbers, together with a set of conventions on how this collection is to be used. Each rule is an equation of the form

$$ax + b \rightarrow cx + d$$

where a, b, c, and d are natural numbers (possibly 0) and x is a variable over the natural numbers. Given a natural number n, a rule $ax + b \rightarrow cx + d$ can be applied to n if we have $n = ax_0 + b$ for some x_0, in which case applying the rule yields the new natural number $cx_0 + d$. For instance, the rule $2x + 5 \rightarrow x + 9$ can be applied to 11, since 11 can be written as $2 \cdot 3 + 5$; applying the rule yields the new number $3 + 9 = 12$.

Since a Post system contains some arbitrary number of rules, it may well be that several rules can apply to the same natural number, yielding a set of new natural numbers. In turn, these numbers can be transformed through rules to yield more numbers, and so on. Thus a Post system can be viewed as computing a map $f: \mathbb{N} \rightarrow 2^{\mathbb{N}}$, where the subset produced contains all natural numbers that can be derived from the given argument by using zero or more applications of the rules.

To view a Post system as a computing engine for partial functions mapping $\mathbb{N}$ to $\mathbb{N}$, we need to impose additional conventions. While any number of conventions will work, perhaps the simplest is to order the rules and require that the first applicable rule be used. In that way, the starting number is transformed in just one new number, which, in turn, is transformed into just one new number, and so on. Some combinations of rules and initial numbers will then give rise to infinite series of applications of rules (some rule or other always applies to the current number), while others will terminate. At termination, the current number (to which no rule applies) is taken to be the output of the computation. Under this convention, the Post system computes a partial function.

1. Give a type of rule that, once used, will always remain applicable.
2. Give a system that always stops, yet does something useful.
3. Give a system that will transform $2^n 3^m$ into 2^{m+n} and stop (although it may not stop on inputs of different form), thereby implementing addition through prime encoding.
4. Give a system that will transform $2^n 3^m$ into 2^{mn} and stop (although it may not stop on inputs of different form), thereby implementing multiplication through prime encoding.

Exercise 4.21* (Refer to the previous exercise.) Use the idea of prime encoding to prove that our version of Post systems is a universal model of computation. The crux of the problem is how to handle tests for zero: this is where the additive term in the rules comes into play. You may want to use the two-register RAM of Exercise 4.15.

4.6   Bibliography

Models of computation were first proposed in the 1930s in the context of computability theory—see Machtey and Young [1978] and Hopcroft and Ullman [1979]. More recent proposals include a variety of RAM models; most interesting are those of Aho, Hopcroft, and Ullman [1974] and Schonhage [1980]. Our RAM model is a simplified version derived from the computability model of Shepherdson and Sturgis [1963]. A thorough discussion of machine models and their simulation is given by van Emde Boas [1990]; the reader will note that, although more efficient simulations than ours have been developed, all existing simulations between reasonable models still require a supralinear increase in time complexity, so that our development of model-independent classes remains unaffected. Time and space as complexity measures were established early; the aforementioned references all discuss such measures and how the choice of a model affects them.

CHAPTER 5

Computability Theory

Computability can be studied with any of the many universal models of computation. However, it is best studied with mathematical tools and thus best based on the most mathematical of the universal models of computation, the *partial recursive functions*. We introduce partial recursive functions by starting with the simpler primitive recursive functions. We then build up to the partial recursive functions and recursively enumerable (r.e.) sets and make the connection between r.e. sets and Turing machines. Finally, we use partial recursive functions to prove two of the fundamental results in computability theory: Rice's theorem and the recursion (or fixed-point) theorem.

Throughout this chapter, we limit our alphabet to one character, a; thus any string we consider is from $\{a\}^*$. Working with some richer alphabet would not gain us any further insight, yet would involve more details and cases. Working with a one-symbol alphabet is equivalent to working with natural numbers represented in base 1. Thus, in the following, instead of using the strings $\varepsilon, a, aa, \ldots, a^k$, we often use the numbers $0, 1, 2, \ldots, k$; similarly, instead of writing ya for inductions, we often write $n + 1$, where we have $n = |y|$.

One difficulty that we encounter in studying computability theory is the tangled relationship between mathematical functions that are computable and the programs that compute them. A partial recursive function is a computing tool and thus a form of program. However, we identify partial recursive functions with the mathematical (partial) functions that they embody and thus also speak of a partial recursive function as a mathematical function that can be computed through a partial recursive implementation. Of course, such a mathematical function can then be computed through an infinite number of different partial recursive functions (a behavior we would certainly expect in any programming language, since we can always pad an existing program with useless statements that do not affect the result of the computation), so that the correspondence is not one-to-one. Moving back and forth between the two universes is often the key to proving results in computability theory—we must continuously be aware of the type of "function" under discussion.

5.1   Primitive Recursive Functions

Primitive recursive functions are built from a small collection of base functions through two simple mechanisms: one a type of generalized function composition and the other a "primitive recursion," that is, a limited type of recursive (inductive) definition. In spite of the limited scope of primitive recursive functions, most of the functions that we normally encounter are, in fact, primitive recursive; indeed, it is not easy to define a total function that is not primitive recursive.

5.1.1   Defining Primitive Recursive Functions

We define primitive recursive functions in a constructive manner, by giving base functions and construction schemes that can produce new functions from known ones.

Definition 5.1 The following functions, called the *base functions*, are primitive recursive:

- Zero: $\mathbb{N} \to \mathbb{N}$ always returns zero, regardless of the value of its argument.
- Succ: $\mathbb{N} \to \mathbb{N}$ adds 1 to the value of its argument.
- $P_i^k \colon \mathbb{N}^k \to \mathbb{N}$ returns the ith of its k arguments; this is really a countably infinite family of functions, one for each pair $1 \le i \le k \in \mathbb{N}$.   □

(Note that $P_1^1(x)$ is just the identity function.) We call these functions primitive recursive simply because we have no doubt of their being easily computable. The functions we have thus defined are formal mathematical functions. We claim that each can easily be computed through a program; therefore we shall identify them with their implementations. Hence the term "primitive recursive function" can denote either a mathematical function or a program for that function. We may think of our base functions as the fundamental statements in a functional programming language and thus think of them as unique. Semantically, we interpret P_i^k to return its ith argument without having evaluated the other $k - 1$ arguments at all—a convention that will turn out to be very useful.

Our choice of base functions is naturally somewhat arbitrary, but it is motivated by two factors: the need for basic arithmetic and the need to handle functions with several arguments. Our first two base functions give us a foundation for natural numbers—all we now need to create arbitrary natural numbers is some way to compose the functions. However, we want to go beyond simple composition and we need some type of logical test. Thus we define two mechanisms through which we can combine primitive recursive functions to produce more primitive recursive functions: a type of generalized composition and a type of recursion. The need for the former is evident. The latter gives us a testing capability (base case vs. recursive case) as well as a standard programming tool. However, we severely limit the form that this type of recursion can take to ensure that the result is easily computable.

Definition 5.2 The following construction schemes are primitive recursive:

- *Substitution*: Let g be a function of m arguments and $h_1, h_2, \ldots, h_m$ be functions of n arguments each; then the function f of n arguments is obtained from g and the h_is by substitution as follows:

$$f(x_1, \ldots, x_n) = g(h_1(x_1, \ldots, x_n), \ldots, h_m(x_1, \ldots, x_n))$$

- *Primitive Recursion*: Let g be a function of $n - 1$ arguments and h a function of $n + 1$ arguments; then the function of f of n arguments is obtained from g and h by primitive recursion as follows:

$$\begin{cases} f(0, x_2, \ldots, x_n) = g(x_2, \ldots, x_n) \\ f(i + 1, x_2, \ldots, x_n) = h(i, f(i, x_2, \ldots, x_n), x_2, \ldots, x_n) \end{cases} \qquad \square$$

(We used 0 and $i + 1$ rather than Zero and Succ(i): the 0 and the $i + 1$ denote a pattern-matching process in the use of the rules, not applications of the base functions Zero and Succ.) This definition of primitive recursion makes sense only for $n > 1$. If we have $n = 1$, then g is a function of zero arguments, in other words a constant, and the definition then becomes:

- Let x be a constant and h a function of two arguments; then the function of f of one argument is obtained from x and h by primitive recursion as follows: $f(0) = x$ and $f(i + 1) = h(i, f(i))$.

```
(defun f (g &rest fns)
   "Defines f from g and the h's (grouped into the list fns)
      through substitution"
   #'(lambda (&rest args)
        (apply g (map (lambda (h)
                         (apply h args))
                      fns))))
```

(a) the Lisp code for substitution

```
(defun f (g h)
   "Defines f from the base case g and the recursive step h
      through primitive recursion"
   #'(lambda (&rest args)
        if (zerop (car args))
           (apply g (cdr args))
           (apply h ((-1 (car args))
                     (apply f ((-1 (car args)) (cdr args)))
                     (cdr args)))))
```

(b) the Lisp code for primitive recursion

Figure 5.1   A programming framework for the primitive recursive construction schemes.

Note again that, if a function is derived from easily computable functions
by substitution or primitive recursion, it is itself easily computable: it is
an easy matter in most programming languages to write code modules
that take functions as arguments and return a new function, obtained
through substitution or primitive recursion. Figure 5.1 gives a programming
framework (in Lisp) for each of these two constructions.

   We are now in a position to define formally a primitive recursive
function; we do this for the programming object before commenting on
the difference between it and the mathematical object.

Definition 5.3 A function (program) is *primitive recursive* if it is one of
the base functions or can be obtained from these base functions through a
finite number of applications of substitution and primitive recursion.   □

The definition reflects the syntactic view of the primitive recursive definition
mechanism. A mathematical primitive recursive function is then simply a
function that can be implemented with a primitive recursive program; of
course, it may also be implemented with a program that uses more powerful
construction schemes.

Definition 5.4 A (mathematical) function is *primitive recursive* if it can be defined through a primitive recursive construction.   □

Equivalently, we can define the (mathematical) primitive recursive functions to be the smallest family of functions that includes the base functions and is closed under substitution and primitive recursion.

Let us begin our study of primitive recursive functions by showing that the simple function of one argument, dec, which subtracts 1 from its argument (unless, of course, the argument is already 0, in which case it is returned unchanged), is primitive recursive. We define it as

$$\begin{cases} \text{dec}(0) = 0 \\ \text{dec}(i + 1) = P_1^2(i, \text{dec}(i)) \end{cases}$$

Note the syntax of the inductive step: we did not just use $\text{dec}(i + 1) = i$ but formally listed all arguments and picked the desired one. This definition is a program for the mathematical function dec in the computing model of primitive recursive functions.

Let us now prove that the concatenation functions are primitive recursive. For that purpose we return to our interpretation of arguments as strings over $\{a\}^*$. The concatenation functions simply take their arguments and concatenate them into a single string; symbolically, we want

$$\text{con}_n(x_1, x_2, \ldots, x_n) = x_1 x_2 \ldots x_n$$

If we know that both con_2 and con_n are primitive recursive, we can then define the new function con_{n+1} in a primitive recursive manner as follows:

$$\begin{aligned} \text{con}_{n+1}(x_1, \ldots, x_{n+1}) = \\ \text{con}_2\big(\text{con}_n(P_1^{n+1}(x_1, \ldots, x_{n+1}), \ldots, P_n^{n+1}(x_1, \ldots, x_{n+1})), \\ P_{n+1}^{n+1}(x_1, \ldots, x_{n+1})\big) \end{aligned}$$

Proving that con_2 is primitive recursive is a bit harder because it would seem that the primitive recursion takes place on the "wrong" argument— we need recursion on the second argument, not the first. We get around this problem by first defining the new function $\text{con}'(x_1, x_2) = x_2 x_1$, and then using it to define con_2. We define con' as follows:

$$\begin{cases} \text{con}'(\varepsilon, x) = P_1^1(x) \\ \text{con}'(ya, x) = \text{Succ}(P_2^3(y, \text{con}'(y, x), x)) \end{cases}$$

Now we can use substitution to define $\text{con}_2(x, y) = \text{con}'(P_2^2(x, y), P_1^2(x, y))$.

Defining addition is simpler, since we can take immediate advantage of the known properties of addition to shift the recursion onto the first argument and write

$$\begin{cases} \text{add}(0, x) = P_1^1(x) \\ \text{add}(i + 1, x) = \text{Succ}(P_2^3(i, \text{add}(i, x), x)) \end{cases}$$

These very formal definitions are useful to reassure ourselves that the functions are indeed primitive recursive. For the most part, however, we tend to avoid the pedantic use of the P_i^j functions. For instance, we would generally write

$$\text{con}'(i + 1, x) = \text{Succ}(\text{con}'(i, x))$$

rather than the formally correct

$$\text{con}'(i + 1, x) = \text{Succ}(P_2^3(i, \text{con}'(i, x), x))$$

Exercise 5.1 Before you allow yourself the same liberties, write completely formal definitions of the following functions:

1. the level function $\text{lev}(x)$, which returns 0 if x equals 0 and returns 1 otherwise;
2. its complement is_zero(x);
3. the function of two arguments minus(x, y), which returns $x - y$ (or 0 whenever $y \geqslant x$);
4. the function of two arguments mult(x, y), which returns the product of x and y; and,
5. the "guard" function $x \# y$, which returns 0 if x equals 0 and returns y otherwise (verify that it can be defined so as to avoid evaluating y whenever x equals 0). □

Equipped with these new functions, we are now able to verify that a given (mathematical) primitive recursive function can be implemented with a large variety of primitive recursive programs. Take, for instance, the simplest primitive recursive function, Zero. The following are just a few (relatively speaking: there is already an infinity of different programs in these few lines) simple primitive recursive programs that all implement this same function:

- Zero(x)
- minus(x, x)

- dec(Succ(Zero(x))), which can be expanded to use k consecutive Succ preceded by k consecutive dec, for any $k > 0$
- for any primitive recursive function f of one argument, Zero($f(x)$)
- for any primitive recursive function f of one argument, dec(lev($f(x)$))

The reader can easily add a dozen other programs or families of programs that all return zero on any argument and verify that the same can be done for the other base functions. Thus any built-up function has an infinite number of different programs, simply because we can replace any use of the base functions by any one of the equivalent programs that implement these base functions.

Our trick with the permutation of arguments in defining con_2 from con' shows that we can move the recursion from the first argument to any chosen argument without affecting closure within the primitive recursive functions. However, it does not yet allow us to do more complex recursion, such as the "course of values" recursion suggested by the definition

$$\begin{cases} f(0, x) = g(x) \\ f(i + 1, x) = h(i, x, \langle i + 1, f(i, x), f(i - 1, x), \ldots, f(0, x) \rangle_{i+2}) \end{cases} \quad (5.1)$$

Yet, if the functions g and h are primitive recursive, then f as just defined is also primitive recursive (although the definition we gave is not, of course, entirely primitive recursive). What we need is to show that

$$p(i, x) = \langle i + 1, f(i, x), f(i - 1, x), \ldots, f(0, x) \rangle_{i+2}$$

is primitive recursive whenever g and h are primitive recursive, since the rest of the construction is primitive recursive. Now $p(0, x)$ is just $\langle 1, g(x) \rangle$, which is primitive recursive, since g and pairing are both primitive recursive. The recursive step is a bit longer:

$$\begin{aligned}
p(i + 1, x) &= \langle i + 2, f(i + 1, x), f(i, x), \ldots, f(0, x) \rangle_{i+3} \\
&= \langle i + 2, \\
&\quad h(i, x, \langle i + 1, f(i, x), f(i - 1, x), \ldots, f(0, x) \rangle_{i+2}), \\
&\quad f(i, x), \ldots, f(0, x) \rangle_{i+3} \\
&= \langle i + 2, h(i, x, p(i, x)), f(i, x), \ldots, f(0, x) \rangle_{i+3} \\
&= \langle i + 2, \langle h(i, x, p(i, x)), f(i, x), \ldots, f(0, x) \rangle_{i+2} \rangle \\
&= \langle i + 2, \langle h(i, x, p(i, x)), \langle f(i, x), \ldots, f(0, x) \rangle_{i+1} \rangle \rangle \\
&= \langle i + 2, \langle h(i, x, p(i, x)), \Pi_2(p(i, x)) \rangle \rangle
\end{aligned}$$

and now we are done, since this last definition is a valid use of primitive recursion.

Exercise 5.2 Present a completely formal primitive recursive definition of f, using projection functions as necessary.   □

We need to establish some other definitional mechanisms in order to make it easier to "program" with primitive recursive functions. For instance, it would be helpful to have a way to define functions by cases. For that, we first need to define an "if ... then ... else ..." construction, for which, in turn, we need the notion of a *predicate*. In mathematics, a predicate on some universe S is simply a subset of S (the predicate is true on the members of the subset, false elsewhere). To identify membership in such a subset, mathematics uses a *characteristic function*, which takes the value 1 on the members of the subset, 0 elsewhere. In our universe, if given some predicate P of n variables, we define its characteristic function as follows:

$$c_P(x_1, \ldots, x_n) = \begin{cases} 1 & \text{if } (x_1, \ldots, x_n) \in P \\ 0 & \text{if } (x_1, \ldots, x_n) \notin P \end{cases}$$

We say that a predicate is primitive recursive if and only if its characteristic function can be defined in a primitive recursive manner.

Lemma 5.1 If P and Q are primitive recursive predicates, so are their negation, logical *or*, and logical *and*.   □

   Proof.
$$c_{not\,P}(x_1, \ldots, x_n) = \text{is\_zero}(c_P(x_1, \ldots, x_n))$$
$$c_{P\,or\,Q}(x_1, \ldots, x_n) = \text{lev}(\text{con}_2(c_P(x_1, \ldots, x_n), c_Q(x_1, \ldots, x_n)))$$
$$c_{P\,and\,Q}(x_1, \ldots, x_n) = \text{dec}(\text{con}_2(c_P(x_1, \ldots, x_n), c_Q(x_1, \ldots, x_n))) \qquad \text{Q.E.D.}$$

Exercise 5.3 Verify that definition by cases is primitive recursive. That is, given primitive recursive functions g and h and primitive recursive predicate P, the new function f defined by

$$f(x_1, \ldots, x_n) = \begin{cases} g(x_1, \ldots, x_n) & \text{if } P(x_1, \ldots, x_n) \\ h(x_1, \ldots, x_n) & \text{otherwise} \end{cases}$$

is also primitive recursive. (We can easily generalize this definition to multiple disjoint predicates defining multiple cases.) Further verify that this definition can be made so as to avoid evaluation of the function(s) specified for the case(s) ruled out by the predicate.   □

Somewhat more interesting is to show that, if P is a primitive recursive predicate, so are the two bounded quantifiers

$$\exists y \leqslant x \, [P(y, z_1, \ldots, z_n)]$$

which is true if and only if there exists some number $y \leqslant x$ such that $P(y, z_1, \ldots, z_n)$ is true, and

$$\forall y \leqslant x \, [P(y, z_1, \ldots, z_n)]$$

which is true if and only if $P(y, z_1, \ldots, z_n)$ holds for all initial values $y \leqslant x$.

Exercise 5.4 Verify that the primitive recursive functions are closed under the bounded quantifiers. Use primitive recursion to sweep all values $y \leqslant x$ and logical connectives to construct the answer. □

Equipped with these construction mechanisms, we can develop our inventory of primitive recursive functions; indeed, most functions with which we are familiar are primitive recursive.

Exercise 5.5 Using the various constructors of the last few exercises, prove that the following predicates and functions are primitive recursive:

- $f(x, z_1, \ldots, z_n) = \min y \leqslant x \, [P(y, z_1, \ldots, z_n)]$ returns the smallest y no larger than x such that the predicate P is true; if no such y exists, the function returns $x + 1$.
- $x \leqslant y$, true if and only if x is no larger than y.
- $x \mid y$, true if and only if x divides y exactly.
- is_prime(x), true if and only if x is prime.
- prime(x) returns the xth prime. □

We should by now have justified our claim that most familiar functions are primitive recursive. Indeed, we have not yet seen any function that is *not* primitive recursive, although the existence of such functions can be easily established by using diagonalization, as we now proceed to do.

Our definition scheme for the primitive recursive functions (viewed as programs) shows that they can be enumerated: we can easily enumerate the base functions and all other programs are built through some finite number of applications of the construction schemes, so that we can enumerate them all.

Exercise 5.6 Verify this assertion. Use pairing functions and assign a unique code to each type of base function and each construction scheme. For instance, we can assign the code 0 to the base function Zero, the code 1 to the base function Succ, and the code 2 to the family $\{P_i^j\}$, encoding a specific function P_i^j as $\langle 2, i, j \rangle_3$. Then we can assign code 3 to substitution and code 4 to primitive recursion and thus encode a specific application of substitution

$$f(x_1, \ldots, x_n) = g(h_1(x_1, \ldots, x_n), \ldots, h_m(x_1, \ldots, x_n))$$

where function g has code c_g and function h_i has code c_i for each i, by

$$\langle 3, m, c_g, c_1, \ldots, c_m \rangle_{m+3}$$

Encoding a specific application of primitive recursion is done in a similar way.

When getting a code c, we can start taking it apart. We first look at $\Pi_1(c)$, which must be a number between 0 and 4 in order for c to be the code of a primitive recursive function; if it is between 0 and 2, we have a base function, otherwise we have a construction scheme. If $\Pi_1(c)$ equals 3, we know that the outermost construction is a substitution and can obtain the number of arguments (m in our definition) as $\Pi_1(\Pi_2(c))$, the code for the composing function (g in our definition) as $\Pi_1(\Pi_2(\Pi_2(c)))$, and so forth. Further decoding thus recovers the complete definition of the function encoded by c whenever c is a valid code. Now we can enumerate all (definitions of) primitive recursive functions by looking at each successive natural number, deciding whether or not it is a valid code, and, if so, printing the definition of the corresponding primitive recursive function. This enumeration lists all possible definitions of primitive recursive functions, so that the same mathematical function will appear infinitely often in the enumeration (as we saw for the mathematical function that returns zero for any value of its argument).   □

Thus we can enumerate the (programs implementing the) primitive recursive functions. We now use diagonalization to construct a new function that cannot be in the enumeration (and thus cannot be primitive recursive) but is easily computable because it is defined through a program. Let the primitive recursive functions in our enumeration be named f_0, f_1, f_2, etc.; we define the new function g with $g(k) = \text{Succ}(f_k(k))$. This function provides effective diagonalization since it differs from f_k at least in the value it returns on argument k; thus g is clearly not primitive recursive. However, it is also clear that g is easily computable once the enumeration scheme is known, since each of the f_is is itself easily computable. We conclude that there exist computable functions that are not primitive recursive.

5.1.2 Ackermann's Function and the Grzegorczyk[1] Hierarchy

It remains to identify a *specific* computable function that is not primitive recursive—something that diagonalization cannot do. We now proceed to define such a function and prove that it *grows too fast* to be primitive recursive. Let us define the following family of functions:

- the first function iterates the successor:

$$\begin{cases} f_1(0, x) = x \\ f_1(i + 1, x) = \text{Succ}(f_1(i, x)) \end{cases}$$

- in general, the $n + 1$st function (for $n \geqslant 1$) is defined in terms of the nth function:

$$\begin{cases} f_{n+1}(0, x) = f_n(x, x) \\ f_{n+1}(i + 1, x) = f_n(f_{n+1}(i, x), x) \end{cases}$$

In essence, Succ acts like a one-argument f_0 and forms the basis for this family. Thus $f_0(x)$ is just $x + 1$; $f_1(x, y)$ is just $x + y$; $f_2(x, y)$ is just $(x + 2) \cdot y$; and $f_3(x, y)$, although rather complex, grows as y^{x+3}.

Exercise 5.7 Verify that each f_i is a primitive recursive function. □

Consider the new function $F(x) = f_x(x, x)$, with $F(0) = 1$. It is perfectly well defined and easily computable through a simple (if highly recursive) program, but we claim that it cannot be primitive recursive. To prove this claim, we proceed in two steps: we prove first that every primitive recursive function is bounded by some f_i, and then that F grows faster than any f_i. (We ignore the "details" of the number of arguments of each function. We could fake the number of arguments by adding dummy ones that get ignored or by repeating the same argument as needed or by pairing all arguments into a single argument.) The second part is essentially trivial, since F has been built for that purpose: it is enough to observe that f_{i+1} grows faster than f_i. The first part is more challenging; we use induction on the number of applications of construction schemes (composition or primitive recursion) used in the definition of primitive recursive functions. The base case requires a proof that f_1 grows as fast as any of the base functions (Zero, Succ, and P_i^j). The inductive step requires a proof that, if h is defined through one application of either substitution or primitive recursion from

---

[1] Grzegorczyk is pronounced (approximately) g'zhuh-gore-chick.

some other primitive recursive functions g_is, each of which is bounded by f_k, then h is itself bounded by some f_l, $l \geqslant k$. Basically, the f_i functions have that bounding property because f_{i+1} is defined from f_i by primitive recursion without "wasting any power" in the definition, i.e., without losing any opportunity to make f_{i+1} grow. To define $f_{n+1}(i + 1, x)$, we used the two arguments allowable in the recursion, namely, x and the recursive call $f_{n+1}(i, x)$, and we fed these two arguments to what we knew by inductive hypothesis to be the fastest-growing primitive recursive function defined so far, namely f_n. The details of the proof are now mechanical. F is one of the many ways of defining *Ackermann's function* (also called Péter's or Ackermann-Péter's function). We can also give a single recursive definition of a similar version of Ackermann's function if we allow multiple, rather than primitive recursion:

$$\begin{cases} A(0, n) = \mathrm{Succ}(n) \\ A(m + 1, 0) = A(m, 1) \\ A(m + 1, n + 1) = A(m, A(\mathrm{Succ}(m), n)) \end{cases}$$

Then $A(n, n)$ behaves much as our $F(n)$ (although its exact values differ, its growth rate is the same).

The third statement (the general case) uses double, nested recursion; from our previous results, we conclude that primitive recursive functions are not closed under this type of construction scheme. An interesting aspect of the difference between primitive and generalized recursion can be brought to light graphically: consider defining a function of two arguments $f(i, j)$ through recursion and mentally prepare a table of all values of $f(i, j)$—one row for each value of i and one column for each value of j. In computing the value of $f(i, j)$, a primitive recursive scheme allows only the use of previous rows, but there is no reason why we should not also be able to use previous columns in the current row. Moreover, the primitive recursive scheme forces the use of values on previous rows in a monotonic order: the computation must proceed from one row to the previous and cannot later use a value from an "out-of-order" row. Again, there is no reason why we should not be able to use previously computed values (prior rows and columns) in any order, something that nested recursion does.

Thus not every function is primitive recursive; moreover, primitive recursive functions can grow only so fast. Our family of functions f_i includes functions that grow extremely fast (basically, f_1 acts much like addition, f_2 like multiplication, f_3 like exponentiation, f_4 like a tower of exponents, and so on), yet not fast enough, since F grows much faster yet. Note also that we have claimed that primitive recursive functions are very easy to compute, which may be doubtful in the case of, say, $f_{1000}(x)$. Yet again, $F(x)$ would be much harder to compute, even though we can certainly write a very concise program to compute it.

As we defined it, Ackermann's function is an example of a *completion*. We have an infinite family of functions $\{f_i \mid i \in \mathbb{N}\}$ and we "cap" it (complete it, but "capping" also connotes the fact that the completion grows faster than any function in the family) by Ackermann's function, which behaves on each successive argument like the next larger function in the family.

An amusing exercise is to resume the process of construction once we have Ackermann's function, F. That is, we proceed to define a new family of functions $\{g_i\}$ exactly as we defined the family $\{f_i\}$, except that, where we used Succ as our base function before, we now use F:

- $g_1(0, x) = x$ and $g_1(i + 1, x) = F(g_1(i, x))$;
- in general, $g_{n+1}(0, x) = g_n(x, x)$ and $g_{n+1}(i + 1, x) = g_n(g_{n+1}(i, x), x)$.

Now F acts like a one-argument g_0; all successive g_is grow increasingly faster, of course. We can once again repeat our capping definition and define $G(x) = g_x(x, x)$, with $G(0) = 1$. The new function G is now a type of super-Ackermann's function—it is to Ackermann's function what Ackermann's function is to the Succ function and thus grows mind-bogglingly fast! Yet we can repeat the process and define a new family $\{h_i\}$ based on the function G, and then cap it with a new function H; indeed, we can repeat this process *ad infinitum* to obtain an infinite collection of infinite families of functions, each capped with its own one-argument function. Now we can consider the family of functions $\{\text{Succ}, F, G, H, \ldots\}$—call them $\{\phi_0, \phi_1, \phi_2, \phi_3, \ldots\}$—and cap *that* family by $\Phi(x) = \phi_x(x)$. Thus $\Phi(0)$ is just $\text{Succ}(0) = 1$, while $\Phi(1)$ is $F(1) = f_1(1, 1) = 2$, and $\Phi(2)$ is $G(2)$, which entirely defies description. . . . You can verify quickly that $G(2)$ is $g_1(g_1(g_1(2, 2), 2), 2) = g_1(g_1(F(8), 2), 2)$, which is $g_1(F(F(F(\ldots F(F(2)) \ldots))), 2)$ with $F(8)$ nestings (and then the last call to g_1 iterates F again for a number of nestings equal to the value of $F(F(F(\ldots F(F(2)) \ldots)))$ with $F(8)$ nestings)!

If you are not yet tired and still believe that such incredibly fast-growing functions and incredibly large numbers can exist, we can continue: make Φ the basis for a whole new process of generation, as Succ was first used. After generating again an infinite family of infinite families, we can again cap the whole construction with, say, Ψ. Then, of course, we can repeat the process, obtaining another two levels of families capped with, say, Ξ. But observe that we are now in the process of generating a brand new infinite family at a brand new level, namely the family $\{\Phi, \Psi, \Xi, \ldots\}$, so we can cap *that* family in turn and. . . . Well, you get the idea; this process can continue forever and create higher and higher levels of completion. The resulting rich hierarchy is known as the *Grzegorczyk hierarchy*. Note that, no matter how fast any of these functions grows, it is always computable—at least in theory. Certainly, we can write a fairly concise but very highly recursive computer program that will compute the value of any of these functions on any argument. (For any but the most trivial functions in this hierarchy, it will take all the semiconductor memory ever produced and several trillions of years just to compute the value on argument 2, but it is theoretically doable.) Rather astoundingly, after this dazzling hierarchy, we shall see in Section 5.6 that there exist functions (the so-called "busy beaver" functions) that grow *very much* faster than *any* function in the Grzegorczyk hierarchy—so fast, in fact, that they are provably uncomputable . . . food for thought.

5.2   Partial Recursive Functions

Since we are interested in characterizing computable functions (those that can be computed by, say, a Turing machine) and since primitive recursive functions, although computable, do not account for all computable functions, we may be tempted to add some new scheme for constructing functions and thus enlarge our set of functions beyond the primitive recursive ones. However, we would do well to consider what we have so far learned and done.

As we have seen, as soon as we enumerate total functions (be they primitive recursive or of some other type), we can use this enumeration to build a new function by diagonalization; this function will be total and computable but, by construction, will not appear in the enumeration. It follows that, in order to account for all computable functions, we must make room for *partial* functions, that is, functions that are not defined for every input argument. This makes sense in terms of computing as well: not all programs terminate under all inputs—under certain inputs they may enter an infinite loop and thus never return a value. Yet, of course, whatever a program computes is, by definition, computable!

When working with partial functions, we need to be careful about what we mean by using various construction schemes (such as substitution, primitive recursion, definition by cases, etc.) and predicates (such as equality). We say that two partial functions are equal whenever they are defined on exactly the same arguments and, for those arguments, return the same values. When a new partial function is built from existing partial functions, the new function will be defined only on arguments on which all functions used in the construction are defined. In particular, if some partial function ϕ is defined by recursion and *diverges* (is undefined) at $(y, x_1, \ldots, x_n)$, then it also diverges at $(z, x_1, \ldots, x_n)$ for all $z \geqslant y$. If $\phi(x)$ converges, we write $\phi(x) \downarrow$; if it diverges, we write $\phi(x) \uparrow$.

We are now ready to introduce our third formal scheme for constructing computable functions. Unlike our previous two schemes, this one can construct partial functions even out of total ones. This new scheme is most often called μ-recursion, although it is defined formally as an unbounded search for a minimum. That is, the new function is defined as the smallest value for some argument of a given function to cause that given function to return 0. (The choice of a test for zero is arbitrary: any other recursive predicate on the value returned by the function would do equally well. Indeed, converting from one recursive predicate to another is no problem.)

Definition 5.5 The following construction scheme is partial recursive:

- *Minimization* or *μ-Recursion*: If ψ is some (partial) function of $n + 1$ arguments, then ϕ, a (partial) function of n arguments, is obtained from ψ by minimization if

  - $\phi(x_1, \ldots, x_n)$ is defined if and only if there exists some $m \in \mathbb{N}$ such that, for all p, $0 \leqslant p \leqslant m$, $\psi(p, x_1, \ldots, x_n)$ is defined and $\psi(m, x_1, \ldots, x_n)$ equals 0; and,
  - whenever $\phi(x_1, \ldots, x_n)$ is defined, i.e., whenever such an m exists, then $\phi(x_1, \ldots, x_n)$ equals q, where q is the least such m.

  We then write $\phi(x_1, \ldots, x_n) = \mu y[\psi(y, x_1, \ldots, x_n) = 0]$.

  $\square$

Like our previous construction schemes, this one is easily computable: there is no difficulty in writing a short program that will cycle through increasingly larger values of y and evaluate ψ for each, looking for a value of 0. Figure 5.2 gives a programming framework (in Lisp) for this construction. Unlike our previous schemes, however, this one, even when

```
(defun phi (psi)
    "Defines phi from psi through mu-recursion"
    #'(lambda f (0 &rest args)
        (defun f
            #'(lambda (i &rest args)
                if (zerop (apply psi (i args)))
                i
                (apply f ((+1 i) args))))))
```

Figure 5.2 A programming framework for μ-recursion.

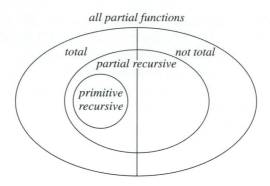

Figure 5.3   Relationships among classes of functions.

started with a total ψ, may not define values of ϕ for each combination of arguments. Whenever an m does not exist, the value of ϕ is undefined, and, fittingly, our simple program diverges: it loops through increasingly large ys and never stops.

Definition 5.6 A *partial recursive function* is either one of the three base functions (Zero, Succ, or $\{P_i^j\}$) or a function constructed from these base functions through a finite number of applications of substitution, primitive recursion, and μ-recursion. ☐

In consequence, partial recursive functions are enumerable: we can extend the encoding scheme of Exercise 5.6 to include μ-recursion. If the function also happens to be total, we shall call it a *total recursive function* or simply a *recursive function*. Figure 5.3 illustrates the relationships among the various classes of functions (from $\mathbb{N}$ to $\mathbb{N}$) discussed so far—from the uncountable set of all partial functions down to the enumerable set of primitive recursive functions. Unlike partial recursive functions, total recursive functions cannot be enumerated. We shall see a proof later in this chapter but for now content ourselves with remarking that such an enumeration would apparently require the ability to decide whether or not an arbitrary partial recursive function is total—that is, whether or not the program halts under all inputs, something we have noted cannot be done.

Exercise 5.8 We remarked earlier that any attempted enumeration of total functions, say $\{f_1, f_2, \dots\}$, is subject to diagonalization and thus incomplete, since we can always define the new total function $g(n) = f_n(n) + 1$ that does not appear in the enumeration. Thus the total functions cannot be enumerated. Why does this line of reasoning not apply directly to the recursive functions? ☐

5.3   Arithmetization: Encoding a Turing Machine

We claim that partial recursive functions characterize exactly the same set of computable functions as do Turing machine or RAM computations. The proof is not particularly hard. Basically, as in our simulation of RAMs by Turing machines and of Turing machines by RAMS, we need to "simulate" a Turing machine or RAM with a partial recursive function. The other direction is trivial and already informally proved by our observation that each construction scheme is easily computable. However, our simulation this time introduces a new element: whereas we had simulated a Turing machine by constructing an equivalent RAM and thus had established a correspondence between the set of all Turing machines and the set of all RAMs, we shall now demonstrate that any Turing machine can be simulated by a *single* partial recursive function. This function takes as arguments a description of the Turing machine and of the arguments that would be fed to the machine; it returns the value that the Turing machine would return for these arguments. Thus one result of this endeavor will be the production of a code for the Turing machine or RAM at hand. This encoding in many ways resembles the codes for primitive recursive functions of Exercise 5.6, although it goes beyond a static description of a function to a complete description of the functioning of a Turing machine. This encoding is often called *arithmetization* or *Gödel numbering*, since Gödel first demonstrated the uses of such encodings in his work on the completeness and consistency of logical systems. A more important result is the construction of a *universal function*: the one partial recursive function we shall build can simulate any Turing machine and thus can carry out any computation whatsoever. Whereas our models to date have all been turnkey machines built to compute just one function, this function is the equivalent of a stored-program computer.

   We choose to encode a Turing machine; encoding a RAM is similar, with a few more details since the RAM model is somewhat more complex than the Turing machine model. Since we know that deterministic Turing machines and nondeterministic Turing machines are equivalent, we choose the simplest version of deterministic Turing machines to encode. We consider only deterministic Turing machines with a unique halt state (a state with no transition out of it) and with fully specified transitions out of all other states; furthermore, our deterministic Turing machines will have a tape alphabet of one character plus the blank, $\Sigma = \{c, \_\}$. Again, the choice of a one-character alphabet does not limit what the machine can compute, although, of course, it may make the computation extremely inefficient.

Since we are concerned for now with computability, not complexity, a one-character alphabet is perfectly suitable. We number the states so that the start state comes first and the halt state last. We assume that our deterministic Turing machine is started in state 1, with its head positioned on the first square of the input. When it reaches the halt state, the output is the string that starts at the square under the tape and continues to the first blank on the right.

In order to encode a Turing machine, we need to describe its finite-state control. (Its current tape contents, head position, and control state are not part of the description of the Turing machine itself but are part of the description of a step in the computation carried out by the Turing machine on a particular argument.) Since every state except the halt state has fully specified transitions, there will be two transitions for each state: one for c and one for $\_$. If the Turing machine has the two entries $\delta(q_i, c) = (q_j, c', L/R)$ and $\delta(q_i, \_) = (q_k, c'', L/R)$, where c' and c'' are alphabet characters, we code this pair of transitions as

$$D_i = \langle \langle j, c', L/R \rangle_3, \langle k, c'', L/R \rangle_3 \rangle$$

In order to use the pairing functions, we assign numerical codes to the alphabet characters, say 0 to $\_$ and 1 to c, as well as to the L/R directions, say 0 to L and 1 to R. Now we encode the entire transition table for a machine of $n + 1$ states (where the $(n + 1)$st state is the halt state) as

$$D = \langle n, \langle D_1, \ldots, D_n \rangle_n \rangle$$

Naturally, this encoding, while injective, is not surjective: most natural numbers are not valid codes. This is not a problem: we simply consider every natural number that is not a valid code as corresponding to the totally undefined function (e.g., a Turing machine that loops forever in a couple of states). However, we do need a predicate to recognize a valid code; in order to build such a predicate, we define a series of useful primitive recursive predicates and functions, beginning with self-explanatory decoding functions:

- nbr_states$(x) = \text{Succ}(\Pi_1(x))$
- table$(x) = \Pi_2(x)$
- trans$(x, i) = \Pi_i^{\Pi_1(x)}(\text{table}(x))$
- $\begin{cases} \text{triple}(x, i, 1) = \Pi_1(\text{trans}(x, i)) \\ \text{triple}(x, i, 0) = \Pi_2(\text{trans}(x, i)) \end{cases}$

All are clearly primitive recursive. In view of our definitions of the Π functions, these various functions are well defined for any x, although what they recover from values of x that do not correspond to encodings cannot be characterized. Our predicates will thus define expectations for valid encodings in terms of these various decoding functions. Define the helper predicates is_move$(x) = [x = 0] \vee [x = 1]$, is_char$(x) = [x = 0] \vee [x = 1]$, and is_bounded$(i, n) = [1 \leq i \leq n]$, all clearly primitive recursive. Now define the predicate

is_triple$(z, n) =$
$$\text{is\_bounded}(\Pi_1^3(z), \text{Succ}(n)) \wedge \text{is\_char}(\Pi_2^3(z)) \wedge \text{is\_move}(\Pi_3^3(z))$$

which checks that an argument z represents a valid triple in a machine with $n + 1$ states by verifying that the next state, new character, and head move are all well defined. Using this predicate, we can build one that checks that a state is well defined, i.e., that a member of the pairing in the second part of D encodes valid transitions, as follows:

$$\text{is\_trans}(z, n) = \text{is\_triple}(\Pi_1(z), n) \wedge \text{is\_triple}(\Pi_2(z), n)$$

Now we need to check that the entire transition table is properly encoded; we do this with a recursive definition that allows us to sweep through the table:

$$\begin{cases} \text{is\_table}(y, 0, n) = 1 \\ \text{is\_table}(y, i + 1, n) = \text{is\_trans}(\Pi_1(y), n) \wedge \text{is\_table}(\Pi_2(y), i, n) \end{cases}$$

This predicate needs to be called with the proper initial values, so we finally define the main predicate, which tests whether or not some number x is a valid encoding of a Turing machine, as follows:

$$\text{is\_TM}(x) = \text{is\_table}(\text{table}(x), \Pi_1(x), \text{nbr\_states}(x))$$

Now, in order to "execute" a Turing machine program on some input, we need to describe the tape contents, the head position, and the current control state. We can encode the tape contents and head position together by dividing the tape into three sections: from the leftmost nonblank character to just before the head position, the square under the head position, and from just after the head position to the rightmost nonblank character.

Unfortunately, we run into a nasty technical problem at this juncture: the alphabet we are using for the partial recursive functions has only one symbol (a), so that numbers are written in unary, but the alphabet used on the tape of the Turing machine has two symbols ($\sqcup$ and c), so that the code for the left- or right-hand side of the tape is a binary code. (Even though both the input and the output written on the Turing machine tape are expressed in unary—just a string of cs—a configuration of the tape during execution is a mixed string of blanks and cs and thus must be encoded as a binary string.) We need conversions in both directions in order to move between the coded representation of the tape used in the simulation and the single characters manipulated by the Turing machine. Thus we make a quick digression to define conversion functions. (Technically, we would also need to redefine partial recursive functions from scratch to work on an alphabet of several characters. However, only Succ and primitive recursion need to be redefined—Succ becomes an Append that can append any of the characters to its argument string and the recursive step in primitive recursion now depends on the last character in the string. Since these redefinitions are self-explanatory, we use them below without further comments.) If we are given a string of n cs (as might be left on the tape as the output of the Turing machine), its value considered as a binary number is easily computed as follows (using string representation for the binary number, but integer representation for the unary number):

$$\begin{cases} b\_to\_u(\varepsilon) = 0 \\ b\_to\_u(x\_) = \text{Succ}(\text{double}(b\_to\_u(x))) \\ b\_to\_u(xc) = \text{Succ}(\text{double}(b\_to\_u(x))) \end{cases}$$

where $\text{double}(x)$ is defined as $\text{mult}(x, 2)$. (Only the length of the input string is considered: blanks in the input string are treated just like cs. Since we need only use the function when given strings without blanks, this treatment causes no problem.) The converse is harder: given a number n in unary, we must produce the string of cs and blanks that will denote the same number encoded in binary—a function we need to translate back and forth between codes and strings during the simulation. We again use number representation for the unary number and string representation for the binary number:

$$\begin{cases} u\_to\_b(0) = \varepsilon \\ u\_to\_b(n + 1) = \text{ripple}(u\_to\_b(n)) \end{cases}$$

where the function ripple adds a carry to a binary-coded number, rippling the carry through the number as necessary:

$$\begin{cases} \text{ripple}(\varepsilon) = c \\ \text{ripple}(x\_) = \text{con}_2(x, c) \\ \text{ripple}(xc) = \text{con}_2(\text{ripple}(x), \_) \end{cases}$$

Now we can return to the question of encoding the tape contents. If we denote the three parts just mentioned (left of the head, under the head, and right of the head) with u, v, and w, we encode the tape and head position as

$$\langle \mathsf{b\_to\_u}(u),\ v,\ \mathsf{b\_to\_u}(w^R) \rangle_3$$

Thus the left- and right-hand side portions are considered as numbers written in binary, with the right-hand side read right-to-left, so that both parts always have c as their most significant digit; the symbol under the head is simply given its coded value (0 for blank and 1 for c). Initially, if the input to the partial function is the number n, then the tape contents will be encoded as

$$\mathsf{tape}(n) = \langle 0,\ \mathsf{lev}(n),\ \mathsf{b\_to\_u}(\mathsf{dec}(n)) \rangle_3$$

where we used lev for the value of the symbol under the head in order to give it value 0 if the symbol is a blank (the input value is 0 or the empty string) and a value of 1 otherwise.

Let us now define functions that allow us to describe one transition of the Turing machine. Call them $\mathsf{next\_state}(x, t, q)$ and $\mathsf{next\_tape}(x, t, q)$, where x is the Turing machine code, t the tape code, and q the current state. The next state is easy to specify:

$$\mathsf{next\_state}(x, t, q) = \begin{cases} \Pi_1^3(\mathsf{triple}(x, q, \Pi_2^3(t))) & 1 \leqslant q < \mathsf{nbr\_states}(x) \\ q & \text{otherwise} \end{cases}$$

The function for the next tape contents is similar but must take into account the head motion; thus, if q is well defined and not the halt state, and if its head motion at this step, $\Pi_3^3(\mathsf{triple}(x, q, \Pi_2^3(t)))$, equals L, then we set

$$\mathsf{next\_tape}(x, t, q) = \langle \mathsf{div2}(\Pi_1^3(t)),\ \mathsf{odd}(\Pi_1^3(t)),$$
$$\mathsf{add}(\mathsf{double}(\Pi_3^3(t)),\ \Pi_2^3(\mathsf{triple}(x, q, \Pi_2^3(t)))) \rangle_3$$

and if $\Pi_3^3(\mathsf{triple}(x, q, \Pi_2^3(t)))$ equals R, then we set

$$\mathsf{next\_tape}(x, t, q) = \langle \mathsf{add}(\mathsf{double}(\Pi_1^3(t)),\ \Pi_2^3(\mathsf{triple}(x, q, \Pi_2^3(t)))),$$
$$\mathsf{odd}(\Pi_3^3(t)),\ \mathsf{div2}(\Pi_3^3(t)) \rangle_3$$

and finally, if q is the halt state or is not well defined, we simply set

$$\mathsf{next\_tape}(x, t, q) = t$$

These definitions made use of rather self-explanatory helper functions; we define them here for completeness:

- $\text{odd}(0) = 0$ and $\text{odd}(n + 1) = \text{is\_zero}(\text{odd}(n))$,
- $\text{div2}(0) = 0$ and $\text{div2}(n + 1) = \begin{cases} \text{Succ}(\text{div2}(n)) & \text{odd}(n) \\ \text{div2}(n) & \text{otherwise} \end{cases}$

Now we are ready to consider the execution of one complete step of a Turing machine:

$$\text{next\_id}(\langle x, t, q \rangle_3) = \langle x, \text{next\_tape}(x, t, q), \text{next\_state}(x, t, q) \rangle_3$$

and generalize this process to i steps:

$$\begin{cases} \text{step}(\langle x, t, q \rangle_3, 0) = \langle x, t, q \rangle_3 \\ \text{step}(\langle x, t, q \rangle_3, i + 1) = \text{next\_id}(\text{step}(\langle x, t, q \rangle_3, i)) \end{cases}$$

All of these functions are primitive recursive. Now we define the crucial function, which is not primitive recursive—indeed, not even total:

$$\text{stop}(\langle x, y \rangle) = \mu i [\Pi_3^3(\text{step}(\langle x, \text{tape}(y), 1 \rangle_3, i)) = \text{nbr\_states}(x)]$$

This function simply seeks the smallest number of steps that the Turing machine coded by x, started in state 1 (the start state) with y as argument, needs to reach the halting state (indexed $\text{nbr\_states}(x)$). If the Turing machine coded by x halts on input $t = \text{tape}(y)$, then the function stop returns a value. If the Turing machine coded by x does not halt on input t, then $\text{stop}(\langle x, y \rangle)$ is not defined. Finally, if x does not code a Turing machine, there is not much we can say about stop.

Now consider running our Turing machine x on input y for $\text{stop}(\langle x, y \rangle)$ steps and returning the result; we get the function

$$\theta(x, y) = \Pi_2^3(\text{step}(\langle x, \text{tape}(y), 1 \rangle_3, \text{stop}(\langle x, y \rangle)))$$

As defined, $\theta(x, y)$ is the paired triple describing the tape contents (or is undefined if the machine does not stop). But we have stated that the output of the Turing machine is considered to be the string starting at the position under the head and stopping before the first blank. Thus we write

$$\text{out}(x, y) = \begin{cases} 0 & \text{if } \Pi_2^3(\theta(x, y)) = 0 \\ \text{add}(\text{double}(\text{b\_to\_u}(\text{strip}(\text{u\_to\_b}(\Pi_2^3(\theta(x, y)))))), \Pi_3^3(\theta(x, y))) \end{cases}$$

where the auxiliary function strip changes the value of the current string on the right of the head to include only the first contiguous block of cs and is defined as

$$\begin{cases} \text{strip}(\varepsilon) = \varepsilon \\ \text{strip}(\_x) = \varepsilon \\ \text{strip}(cx) = \text{con}_2(c, \text{strip}(x)) \end{cases}$$

Our only remaining problem is that, if x does not code a Turing machine, the result of out(x, y) is unpredictable and meaningless. Let x_0 be the index of a simple two-state Turing machine that loops in the start state for any input and never enters the halt state. We define

$$\phi_{\text{univ}}(x, y) = \begin{cases} \text{out}(x, y) & \text{is\_TM}(x) \\ \text{out}(x_0, y) & \text{otherwise} \end{cases}$$

so that, if x does not code a Turing machine, the function is completely undefined. (An interesting side effect of this definition is that every code is now considered legal: basically, we have chosen to decode indices that do not meet our encoding format by producing for them a Turing machine that implements the totally undefined function.) The property of our definition by cases (that the function given for the case ruled out is not evaluated) now assumes critical importance—otherwise our new function would *always* be undefined!

This function ϕ_{univ} is quite remarkable. Notice first that it is defined with a single use of μ-recursion; everything else in its definition is primitive recursive. Yet $\phi_{\text{univ}}(x, y)$ returns the output of the Turing machine coded by x when run on input y; that is, it is a *universal* function. Since it is partial recursive, it is computable and there is a *universal Turing machine* that actually computes it. In other words, there is a single code i such that $\phi_i(x, y)$ computes $\phi_x(y)$, the output of the Turing machine coded by x when run on input y. Since this machine is universal, asking a question about it is as hard as asking a question about all of the Turing machines; for instance, deciding whether this specific machine halts under some input is as hard as deciding whether any arbitrary Turing machine halts under some input.

Universal Turing machines are fundamental in that they answer what could have been a devastating criticism of our theory of computability so far. Up to now, every Turing machine or RAM we saw was a "special-purpose" machine—it computed only the function for which it was programmed. The universal Turing machine, on the other hand, is a general-purpose computer: it takes as input a program (the code of a Turing machine) and data (the argument) and proceeds to execute the program on the data. Every reasonable model of computation that claims to be as powerful as Turing machines or RAMs must have a specific machine with that property.

Finally, note that we can easily compose two Turing machine programs; that is, we can feed the output of one machine to the next machine and regard the entire two-phase computation as a single computation. To do so, we simply take the codes for the two machines, say

$$\begin{cases} x = \langle m, \langle D_1, \ldots, D_m \rangle_m \rangle \\ y = \langle n, \langle E_1, \ldots, E_n \rangle_n \rangle \end{cases}$$

and produce the new code

$$z = \langle \mathrm{add}(m, n), \langle D_1, \ldots, D_m, E_1', \ldots, E_n' \rangle_{m+n} \rangle$$

where, if we start with

$$E_i = \langle \langle j, c, L/R \rangle_3, \langle k, d, L/R \rangle_3 \rangle$$

we then obtain

$$E_i' = \langle \langle \mathrm{add}(j, m), c, L/R \rangle_3, \langle \mathrm{add}(k, m), d, L/R \rangle_3 \rangle$$

The new machine is legal; it has $m + n + 1$ states, one less than the number of states of the two machines taken separately, because we have effectively merged the halt state of the first machine with the start state of the second. Thus if neither individual machine halts, the compound machine does not halt either. If the first machine halts, what it leaves on the tape is used by the second machine as its input, so that the compound machine correctly computes the composition of the functions computed by the two machines. This composition function, moreover, is primitive recursive!

Exercise 5.9 Verify this last claim. □

5.4   Programming Systems

In this section, we abstract and formalize the lessons learned in the arithmetization of Turing machines. A *programming system*, $\{\phi_i \mid i \in \mathbb{N}\}$, is an enumeration of all partial recursive functions; it is another synonym for a Gödel numbering. We can let the index set range over all of $\mathbb{N}$, even though we have discussed earlier the fact that most encoding schemes are not surjective (that is, they leave room for values that do not correspond to valid encodings), precisely because we can tell the difference between a legal encoding and an illegal one (through our is_TM predicate in the Turing machine model, for example). As we have seen, we can decide to "decode" an illegal code into a program that computes the totally undefined function; alternately, we could use the legality-checking predicate to re-index an enumeration and thus enumerate only legal codes, indexed directly by $\mathbb{N}$.

We say that a programming system is *universal* if it includes a universal function, that is, if there is an index i such that, for all x and y, we have $\phi_i(\langle x, y \rangle) = \phi_x(y)$. We write ϕ_{univ} for this ϕ_i. We say that a programming system is *acceptable* if it is universal and also includes a total recursive function $c()$ that effects the composition of functions, i.e., that yields $\phi_{c(\langle x,y \rangle)} = \phi_x \cdot \phi_y$. We saw in the previous section that our arithmetization of Turing machines produced an acceptable programming system. A programming system can be viewed as an indexed collection of all programs writable in a given programming language; thus the system $\{\phi_i\}$ could correspond to all Lisp programs and the system $\{\psi_j\}$ to all C programs. (Since the Lisp programs can be indexed in different ways, we would have several different programming systems for the set of all Lisp programs.) Any reasonable programming language (that allows us to enumerate all possible programs) is an acceptable programming system, because we can use it to write an interpreter for the language itself.

In programming we can easily take an already defined function (subroutine) of several arguments and hold some of its arguments to fixed constants to define a new function of fewer arguments. We prove that this capability is a characteristic of any acceptable programming system and ask you to show that it can be regarded as a *defining* characteristic of acceptable programming systems.

Theorem 5.1 Let $\{\phi_i \mid i \in \mathbb{N}\}$ be an acceptable programming system. Then there is a total recursive function s such that, for all i, all $m \geq 1$, all $n \geq 1$, and all $x_1, \ldots, x_m, y_1, \ldots, y_n$, we have

$$\phi_{s(i,m,x_1,\ldots,x_m)}(y_1, \ldots, y_n) = \phi_i(x_1, \ldots, x_m, y_1, \ldots, y_n) \qquad \square$$

This theorem is generally called the s-m-n theorem and s is called an s-m-n function. After looking at the proof, you may want to try to prove the converse (an easier task), namely that a programming system with a total recursive s-m-n function (s-1-1 suffices) is acceptable. The proof of our theorem is surprisingly tricky.

Proof. Since we have defined our programming systems to be listings of functions of just one argument, we should really have written

$$\phi_{s(\langle i, m, \langle x_1, \ldots, x_m \rangle_m \rangle_3)}(\langle y_1, \ldots, y_n \rangle_n) = \phi_i(\langle x_1, \ldots, x_m, y_1, \ldots, y_n \rangle_{m+n})$$

Write $\overline{x} = \langle x_1, \ldots, x_m \rangle_m$ and $\overline{y} = \langle y_1, \ldots, y_n \rangle_n$. Now note that the following function is primitive recursive (an easy exercise):

$$\text{Con}(\langle m, \langle x_1, \ldots, x_m \rangle_m, \langle y_1, \ldots, y_n \rangle_n \rangle_3) = \langle x_1, \ldots, x_m, y_1, \ldots, y_n \rangle_{m+n}$$

Since Con is primitive recursive, there is some index k with $\phi_k = \text{Con}$. The desired s-m-n function can be implicitly defined by

$$\phi_{s(\langle i, m, \overline{x} \rangle_3)}(\overline{y}) = \phi_i(\text{Con}(\langle m, \overline{x}, \overline{y} \rangle_3))$$

Now we need to show how to get a construction for s, that is, how to bring it out of the subscript. We use our composition function c (there is one in any acceptable programming system) and define functions that manipulate indices so as to produce pairing functions. Define $f(y) = \langle \varepsilon, y \rangle$ and $g(\langle x, y \rangle) = \langle \text{Succ}(x), y \rangle$, and let i_f be an index with $\phi_{i_f} = f$ and i_g an index with $\phi_{i_g} = g$. Now define $h(\varepsilon) = i_f$ and $h(xa) = c(i_g, h(x))$ for all x. Use induction to verify that we have $\phi_{h(x)}(y) = \langle x, y \rangle$. Thus we can write

$$\phi_{h(x)} \cdot \phi_{h(y)}(z) = \phi_{h(x)}(\langle y, z \rangle) = \langle x, \langle y, z \rangle \rangle = \langle x, y, z \rangle_3$$

We are finally ready to define s as

$$s(\langle i, m, x \rangle_3) = c(\langle i, c(\langle k, c(\langle h(m), h(x) \rangle) \rangle) \rangle)$$

We now have

$$\phi_{s(\langle i, m, x \rangle_3)}(y) = \phi_i \cdot \phi_k \cdot \phi_{h(m)} \cdot \phi_{h(x)}(y)$$
$$= \phi_i \cdot \phi_k(\langle m, x, y \rangle_3)$$
$$= \phi_i(\text{Con}(\langle m, x, y \rangle_3)) = \phi_i(\langle x, y \rangle)$$

as desired.   Q.E.D.

(We shall omit the use of pairing from now on in order to simplify notation.) If c is primitive recursive (which is not necessary in an arbitrary acceptable programming system but was true for the one we derived for Turing machines), then s is primitive recursive as well.

As a simple example of the use of s-m-n functions (we shall see many more in the next section), let us prove this important theorem:

Theorem 5.2 If $\{\phi_i\}$ is a universal programming system and $\{\psi_j\}$ is a programming system with a recursive s-1-1 function, then there is a recursive function t that translates the $\{\phi_i\}$ system into the $\{\psi_j\}$ system, i.e., that ensures $\phi_i = \psi_{t(i)}$ for all i.   ☐

Proof. Let ϕ_{univ} be the universal function for the $\{\phi_i\}$ system. Since the $\{\psi_j\}$ system contains all partial recursive functions, it contains ϕ_{univ}; thus there is some k with $\psi_k = \phi_{univ}$. (But note that ψ_k is not necessarily universal for the $\{\psi_j\}$ system!) Define $t(i) = s(k, i)$; then we have

$$\psi_{t(i)}(x) = \psi_{s(k,i)}(x) = \psi_k(i, x) = \phi_{univ}(i, x) = \phi_i(x)$$

as desired.   *Q.E.D.*

In particular, any two acceptable programming systems can be translated into each other. By using a stronger result (Theorem 5.7, the recursion theorem), we could show that any two acceptable programming systems are in fact isomorphic—that is, there exists a total recursive bijection between the two. In effect, there is only one acceptable programming system! It is worth noting, however, that these translations ensure only that the input/output behavior of any program in the $\{\phi_i\}$ system can be reproduced by a program in the $\{\psi_j\}$ system; individual characteristics of programs, such as length, running time, and so on, are not preserved by the translation. In effect the translations are between the mathematical functions implemented by the programs of the respective programming systems, not between the programs themselves.

Exercise 5.10* Prove that, in any acceptable programming system $\{\phi_i\}$, there is a total recursive function step such that, for all x and i:

- there is an m_x such that step$(i, x, m) \neq 0$ holds for all $m \geqslant m_x$ if and only if $\phi_i(x)$ converges; and,
- if step(i, x, m) does not equal 0, then we have step$(i, x, m) =$ Succ$(\phi_i(x))$.

(The successor function is used to shift all results up by one in order to avoid a result of 0, which we use as a flag to denote failure.) The step function that we constructed in the arithmetization of Turing machines is a version of this function; our new formulation is a little less awkward, as it avoids tape encoding and decoding. (Hint: the simplest solution is to translate the step function used in the arithmetization of Turing machines; since both systems are acceptable, we have translations back and forth between the two.)   ☐

5.5   Recursive and R.E. Sets

We define notions of recursive and recursively enumerable (r.e.) sets. Intuitively, a set is recursive if it can be decided and r.e. if it can be enumerated.

Definition 5.7 A set is *recursive* if its characteristic function is a recursive function; a set is *r.e.* if it is the empty set or the range of a recursive function.   □

The recursive function (call it f) that defines the r.e. set, is an enumerator for the r.e. set, since the list $\{f(0), f(1), f(2), \ldots\}$ contains all elements of the set and no other elements.

We make some elementary observations about recursive and r.e. sets.

Proposition 5.1

1. If a set is recursive, so is its complement.
2. If a set is recursive, it is also r.e.
3. If a set and its complement are both r.e., then they are both recursive.

    □

Proof.

1. Clearly, if c_S is the characteristic function of S and is recursive, then is_zero(c_S) is the characteristic function of $\overline{S}$ and is also recursive.

2. Given the recursive characteristic function c_S of a nonempty recursive set (the empty set is r.e. by definition), we construct a new total recursive function f whose range is S. Let y be some arbitrary element of S and define

$$f(x) = \begin{cases} x & c_S(x) = 1 \\ y & \text{otherwise} \end{cases}$$

3. If either the set or its complement is empty, they are clearly both recursive. Otherwise, let f be a function whose range is S and g be a function whose range is the complement of S. If asked whether some string x belongs to S, we simply enumerate both S and its complement, looking for x. As soon as x turns up in one of the two enumerations (and it must eventually, within finite time, since the two enumerations together enumerate all of Σ^*), we are done. Formally, we write

$$c_S(x) = \begin{cases} 1 & f(\mu y[f(y) = x \text{ or } g(y) = x]) = x \\ 0 & \text{otherwise} \end{cases}$$

Q.E.D.

The following result is less intuitive and harder to prove but very useful.

Theorem 5.3 A set is r.e. if and only if it is the range of a partial recursive function and if and only if it is the domain of a partial recursive function.   □

Proof. The theorem really states that three definitions of r.e. sets are equivalent: our original definition and the two definitions given here. The simplest way to prove such an equivalence is to prove a circular chain of implications: we shall prove that (i) an r.e. set (as originally defined) is the range of a partial recursive function; (ii) the range of a partial recursive function is the domain of some (other) partial recursive function; and, (iii) the domain of a partial recursive function is either empty or the range of some (other) total recursive function.

By definition, every nonempty r.e. set is the range of a total and thus also of a partial, recursive function. The empty set itself is the range of the totally undefined function. Thus our first implication is proved.

For the second part, we use the step function defined in Exercise 5.10 to define the partial recursive function:

$$\theta(x, y) = \mu z[\text{step}(x, \Pi_1(z), \Pi_2(z)) = \text{Succ}(y)]$$

This definition uses dovetailing: θ computes ϕ_x on all possible arguments $\Pi_1(z)$ for all possible numbers of steps $\Pi_2(z)$ until the result is y. Effectively, our θ function converges whenever y is in the range of ϕ_x and diverges otherwise. Since θ is partial recursive, there is some index k with $\phi_k = \theta$; now define $g(x) = s(k, x)$ by using an s-m-n construction. Observe that $\phi_{g(x)}(y) = \theta(x, y)$ converges if and only if y is in the range of ϕ_x, so that the range of ϕ_x equals the domain of $\phi_{g(x)}$.

For the third part, we use a similar but slightly more complex construction. We need to ensure that the function we construct is total and enumerates the (nonempty) domain of the given function ϕ_x. In order to meet these requirements, we define a new function through primitive recursion. The base case of the function will return some arbitrary element of the domain of ϕ_x, while the recursive step will either return a newly discovered element of the domain or return again what was last returned. The basis is defined as follows:

$$f(x, 0) = \Pi_1(\mu z[\text{step}(x, \Pi_1(z), \Pi_2(z)) \neq 0])$$

This construction dovetails ϕ_x on all possible arguments $\Pi_1(z)$ for all possible steps $\Pi_2(z)$ until an argument is found on which ϕ_x converges, at which point it returns that argument. It must terminate because we know that ϕ_x has nonempty domain. This is the base case—the first argument found by dovetailing on which ϕ_x converges. Now define the recursive step as follows:

$$f(x, y+1) = \begin{cases} f(x, y) & \text{step}(x, \Pi_1(\text{Succ}(y)), \Pi_2(\text{Succ}(y))) = 0 \\ \Pi_1(\text{Succ}(y)) & \text{step}(x, \Pi_1(\text{Succ}(y)), \Pi_2(\text{Succ}(y))) \neq 0 \end{cases}$$

On larger second arguments y, f either recurses with a smaller second argument or finds a value $\Pi_1(\text{Succ}(y))$ on which ϕ_x converges in at most $\Pi_2(\text{Succ}(y))$ steps. Thus the recursion serves to extend the dovetailing to larger and larger possible arguments and larger and larger numbers of steps beyond those used in the base case. In consequence every element in the domain of ϕ_x is produced by f at some point. Since f is recursive, there exists some index j with $\phi_j = f$; use the s-m-n construction to define $h(x) = s(j, x)$. Now $\phi_{h(x)}(y) = f(x, y)$ is an enumeration function for the domain of ϕ_x.   Q.E.D.

Of particular interest to us is the *halting set* (sometimes called the diagonal set),

$$K = \{x \mid \phi_x(x) \downarrow\}$$

that is the set of functions that are defined "on the diagonal." K is the canonical nonrecursive r.e. set. That it is r.e. is easily seen, since we can just run (using dovetailing between the number of steps and the value of x) each ϕ_x and print the values of x for which we have found a value for $\phi_x(x)$. That it is nonrecursive is an immediate consequence of the unsolvability of the halting problem. We can also recouch the argument in recursion-theoretic notation as follows. Assume that K is recursive and let c_K be its characteristic function. Define the new function

$$g(x) = \begin{cases} 0 & c_K(x) = 0 \\ \text{undefined} & c_K(x) = 1 \end{cases}$$

We claim that $g(x)$ cannot be partial recursive; otherwise there would be some index i with $g = \phi_i$, and we would have $\phi_i(i) = g(i) = 0$ if and only if $g(i) = c_K(i) = 0$ if and only if $\phi_i(i) \uparrow$, a contradiction. Thus c_K is not partial recursive and K is not a recursive set. From earlier results, it follows that $\overline{K} = \Sigma^* - K$ is not even r.e., since otherwise both it and K would be r.e. and thus both would be recursive. In proving results about sets, we often use *reductions* from K.

Example 5.1 Consider the set $T = \{x \mid \phi_x \text{ is total}\}$. To prove that T is not recursive, it suffices to show that, if it were recursive, then so would K. Consider some arbitrary x and define the function $\theta(x, y) = y + \text{Zero}(\phi_{\text{univ}}(x, x))$. Since this function is partial recursive, there must be some index i with $\phi_i(x, y) = \theta(x, y)$. Now use the s-m-n theorem (in its s-1-1 version) to get the new index $j = s(i, x)$ and consider the function $\phi_j(y)$. If x is in K, then $\phi_j(y)$ is the identity function $\phi_j(y) = y$, and thus total, so that j is in T. On the other hand, if x is not in K, then ϕ_j is the totally undefined function and thus j is not in T. Hence membership of x in K is equivalent to membership of j in T. Since K is not recursive, neither is T. (In fact, T is not even r.e.—something we shall shortly prove.)   □

Definition 5.8 A *reduction* from set A to set B is a recursive function f such that x belongs to A if and only if $f(x)$ belongs to B.   □

(This particular type of reduction is called a *many-one reduction*, to emphasize the fact that it is carried out by a function and that this function need not be injective or bijective.) The purpose of a reduction from A to B is to show that B is at least as hard to solve or decide as A. In effect, what a reduction shows is that, if we knew how to solve B, we could use that knowledge to solve A, as is illustrated in Figure 5.4. If we have a "magic blackbox" to solve B—say, to decide membership in B—then the figure illustrates how we could construct a new blackbox to solve A. The new box simply transforms its input, x, into one that will be correctly interpreted by the blackbox for B, namely $f(x)$, and then asks the blackbox for B to solve the instance $f(x)$, using its answer as is.

Example 5.2 Consider the set $S(y, z) = \{x \mid \phi_x(y) = z\}$. To prove that $S(y, z)$ is not recursive, we again use a reduction from K. We define the new partial recursive function $\theta(x, y) = z + \text{Zero}(\phi_{\text{univ}}(x, x))$; since this is a valid partial recursive function, it has an index, say $\theta = \phi_i$. Now we use the s-m-n theorem to obtain $j = s(i, x)$. Observe that, if x is in K, then $\phi_j(y)$ is the

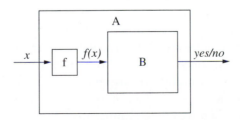

Figure 5.4   A many-one reduction from A to B.

constant function z, and thus, in particular, j is in $S(y, z)$. On the other hand, if x is not in K, then ϕ_j is the totally undefined function, and thus j is not in $S(y, z)$. Hence we have $x \in K \Leftrightarrow j \in S(y, z)$, the desired reduction. Unlike T, $S(y, z)$ is clearly r.e.: to enumerate it, we can use dovetailing, on all x and number of steps, to compute $\phi_x(y)$ and check whether the result (if any) equals z, printing all x for which the computation terminated and returned a z. ☐

These two examples of reductions of K to nonrecursive sets share one obvious feature and one subtle feature. The obvious feature is that both use a function that carries out the computation of $\text{Zero}(\phi_x(x))$ in order to force the function to be totally undefined whenever x is not in K and to ignore the effect of this computation (by reducing it to 0) when x is in K. The more subtle feature is that the sets to which K is reduced do not contain the totally undefined function. This feature is critical, since the totally undefined function is precisely what the reduction produces whenever x is not in K and so must not be in the target set in order for the reduction to work. Suppose now that we have to reduce K to a set that does contain the totally undefined function, such as the set $NT = \{x \mid \exists y, \phi_x(y) \uparrow\}$ of nontotal functions. Instead of reducing K to NT, we can reduce K to $\overline{NT}$, which does not contain the totally undefined function, with the same effect, since the complement of a nonrecursive set must be nonrecursive. Thus proofs of nonrecursiveness by reduction from K can always be made to a set that does not include the totally undefined function. This being the case, all such reductions, say from K to a set S, look much the same: all define a new function $\theta(x, y)$ that includes within it $\text{Zero}(\phi_{\text{univ}}(x, x))$—which ensures that, if x_0 is not in K, $\phi(y) = \theta(x_0, y)$ will be totally undefined and thus not in S, giving us half of the reduction. In addition, $\theta(x, y)$ is defined so that, whenever x_0 is in K (and the term $\text{Zero}(\phi_{\text{univ}}(x, x))$ disappears entirely), the function $\phi(y) = \theta(x_0, y)$ is in S, generally in the simplest possible way. (For instance, with no additional terms, our θ would already be in a set of total functions, or in a set of constant functions, or in a set of functions that return 0 for at least one argument, and so on.)

So how do we prove that a set is not even r.e.? Let us return to the set T of the total functions. We have claimed that this set is not r.e. (Intuitively, although we can enumerate the partial recursive functions, we cannot verify that a function is total, since that would require verifying that the function is defined on each of an infinity of arguments.) We know of at least one non-r.e. set, namely $\overline{K}$. So we reduce $\overline{K}$ to T, that is, we show that, if we could enumerate T, then we could enumerate $\overline{K}$.

Example 5.3 Earlier we used a simple reduction from K to T, that is, we produced a total recursive function f with $x \in K \Leftrightarrow f(x) \in T$. What we need now is another total recursive function g with $x \in \overline{K} \Leftrightarrow g(x) \in T$, or, equivalently, $x \in K \Leftrightarrow g(x) \notin T$. Unfortunately, we cannot just complement our definition; we *cannot* just define

$$
\theta(x, y) = \begin{cases} 1 & x \notin K \\ \text{undefined} & \text{otherwise} \end{cases}
$$

because $x \notin K$ can be "discovered" only by leaving the computation undefined. However, recalling the step function of Exercise 5.10, we *can* define

$$
\theta(x, y) = \begin{cases} 1 & \text{step}(x, x, y) = 0 \\ \text{undefined} & \text{otherwise} \end{cases}
$$

and this is a perfectly fine partial function. As such, there is an index i with $\phi_i = \theta$; by using the s-m-n theorem, we conclude that there is a total recursive function g with $\phi_{g(x)}(y) = \theta(x, y)$. Now note that, if x is not in K, then $\phi_{g(x)}$ is just the constant function 1, since $\phi_x(x)$ never converges for any y steps; in particular, $\phi_{g(x)}$ is total and thus $g(x)$ is in T. Conversely, if x is in K, then $\phi_x(x)$ converges and thus must converge after some number y_0 of steps; but then $\phi_{g(x)}(y)$ is undefined for y_0 and for all larger arguments and thus is not total—that is, $g(x)$ is not in T. Putting both parts together, we conclude that our total recursive function has the property $x \in K \Leftrightarrow g(x) \notin T$, as desired. Since $\overline{K}$ is not r.e., neither is T; otherwise, we could enumerate members of $\overline{K}$ by first computing $g(x)$ and then asking whether $g(x)$ is in T. □

Again, such reductions, say from $\overline{K}$ to some set S, are entirely stereotyped; all feature a definition of the type

$$
\theta(x, y) = \begin{cases} f(y) & \text{step}(x, x, y) = 0 \\ g(y) & \text{otherwise} \end{cases}
$$

Typically, $g(y)$ is the totally undefined function and $f(y)$ is of the type that belongs to S. Then, if x_0 is not in K, the function $\theta(x_0, y)$ is exactly $f(y)$ and thus of the type characterized by S; whereas, if x_0 is in K, the function $\theta(x_0, y)$ is undefined for almost all values of y, which typically will ensure that it does not belong to S. (If, in fact, S contains functions that are mostly or totally undefined, then we can use the simpler reduction featuring $\phi_{\text{univ}}(x, x)$.)

Table 5.1   The standard reductions from K and from $\overline{K}$.

- If S does not contain the totally undefined function, then let

$$\theta(x, y) = \phi(y) + \text{Zero}(\phi_{\text{univ}}(x, x))$$

where $\phi(y)$ is chosen to belong to S.
- If S does contain the totally undefined function, then reduce to $\overline{S}$ instead.

(a) reductions from K to S

- If S does not contain the totally undefined function, then let

$$\theta(x, y) = \begin{cases} \phi(y) & \text{step}(x, x, y) = 0 \\ \psi(y) & \text{otherwise} \end{cases}$$

where $\phi(y)$ is chosen to belong to S and $\psi(y)$ is chosen to complement $\phi(y)$ so as to form a function that does not belong to S—$\psi(y)$ can often be chosen to be the totally undefined function.
- If S does contain the totally undefined function, then let

$$\theta(x, y) = \phi(y) + \text{Zero}(\phi_{\text{univ}}(x, x))$$

where $\phi(y)$ is chosen *not* to belong to S.

(b) reductions from $\overline{K}$ to S

Table 5.1 summarizes the four reduction styles (two each from K and from $\overline{K}$). These are the "standard" reductions; certain sets may require somewhat more complex constructions or a bit more ingenuity.

Example 5.4 Consider the set $S = \{x \mid \exists y \, [\phi_x(y) \downarrow \wedge \forall z, \; \phi_x(z) \neq 2 \cdot \phi_x(y)]\}$; in words, this is the set of all functions that cannot everywhere double whatever output they can produce. This set is clearly not recursive; we prove that it is not even r.e. by reducing $\overline{K}$ to it. Since S does not contain the totally undefined function (any function in it must produce at least one value that it cannot double), our suggested reduction is

$$\theta(x, y) = \begin{cases} \phi(y) & \text{step}(x, x, y) > 0 \\ \psi(y) & \text{otherwise} \end{cases}$$

where ϕ is chosen to belong to S and ψ is chosen to complement ϕ so as to form a function that does not belong to S. We can choose the constant function 1 for ϕ: since this function can produce only 1, it cannot double it and thus belongs to S. But then our function ψ must produce all powers of two, since, whenever x is in K, our θ function will produce 1 for all $y \leqslant y_0$. It takes a bit of thought to realize that we can set $\psi(y) = \Pi_1(y)$ to solve this problem. $\square$

5.6   Rice's Theorem and the Recursion Theorem

In our various reductions from K, we have used much the same mechanism every time; this similarity points to the fact that a much more general result should obtain—something that captures the fairly universal nature of the reductions. A crucial factor in all of these reductions is the fact that the sets are defined by a mathematical property, not a property of programs. In other words, if some partial recursive function ϕ_i belongs to the set and some other partial recursive function ϕ_j has the same input/output behavior (that is, the two functions are defined on the same arguments and return the same values whenever defined), then this other function ϕ_j is also in the set. This factor is crucial because all of our reductions work by constructing a new partial recursive function that (typically) either is totally undefined (and thus not in the set) or has the same input/output behavior as some function known to be in the set (and thus is assumed to be in the set). Formalizing this insight leads to the fundamental result known as Rice's theorem:

Theorem 5.4 Let $\mathscr{C}$ be any class of partial recursive functions defined by their input/output behavior; then the set $P_{\mathscr{C}} = \{x \mid \phi_x \in \mathscr{C}\}$ is recursive if and only if it is trivial—that is, if and only if it is either the empty set or its complement. $\square$

In other words, *any* nontrivial input/output property of programs is undecidable! In spite of its sweeping scope, this result should not be too surprising: if we cannot even decide whether or not a program halts, we are in a bad position to decide whether or not it exhibits a certain input/output behavior. The proof makes it clear that failure to decide halting implies failure to decide anything else about input/output behavior.

Proof. The empty set and its complement are trivially recursive. So now let us assume that $P_{\mathscr{C}}$ is neither the empty set nor its complement. In particular, $\mathscr{C}$ itself contains at least one partial recursive function (call it ψ) and yet does not contain all partial recursive functions. Without loss of generality, let us assume that $\mathscr{C}$ does not contain the totally undefined function. Define the function $\theta(x, y) = \psi(y) + \text{Zero}(\phi_{\text{univ}}(x, x))$; since this is a primitive recursive definition, there is an index i with $\phi_i(x, y) = \theta(x, y)$. We use the s-m-n theorem to obtain $j = s(i, x)$, so that we get the partial recursive function $\phi_j(y) = \psi(y) + \text{Zero}(\phi_{\text{univ}}(x, x))$. Note that, if x is in K, then ϕ_j equals ψ and thus j is in $P_{\mathscr{C}}$, whereas, if x is not in K, then ϕ_j is the totally undefined function and thus j is not in $P_{\mathscr{C}}$. Hence we have $j \in P_{\mathscr{C}} \Leftrightarrow x \in K$, the desired reduction. Therefore $P_{\mathscr{C}}$ is not recursive.   Q.E.D.

Note again that Rice's theorem is limited to input/output behavior—it is about classes of mathematical functions, not about classes of programs. In examining the proof, we note that our conclusion relies on the statement that, since ϕ_j equals ψ when x is in K, ϕ_j belongs to the same class as ψ. That is, because the two partial recursive functions ϕ_j and ψ implement the same input/output mapping (the same mathematical function), they must share the property defining the class. In contrast, if the class were defined by some program-specific predicate, such as limited length of code, then we could not conclude that ϕ_j must belong to the same class as ψ: the code for ϕ_j is longer than the code for ψ (since it includes the code for ψ as well as the code for ϕ_{univ}) and thus could exceed the length limit which ψ meets. Thus any time we ask a question about programs such that two programs that have identical input/output behavior may nevertheless give rise to different answers to our question, Rice's theorem becomes inapplicable. Of course, many such questions remain undecidable, but their undecidability has to be proved by other means.

Following are some examples of sets that fall under Rice's theorem:

- The set of all programs that halt under infinitely many inputs.
- The set of all programs that never halt under any input.
- The set of all pairs of programs such that the two programs in a pair compute the same function.

In contrast, the set $\{x \mid x$ is the shortest code for the function $\phi_x\}$ distinguishes between programs that have identical input/output behavior and thus does not fall under Rice's theorem. Yet this set is also nonrecursive, which we now proceed to prove for a somewhat restricted subset.

Theorem 5.5 The length of the shortest program that prints n and halts is not computable.   □

Proof. Our proof proceeds by contradiction. Assume there is a function, call it f, that can compute this length; that is, $f(n)$ returns the length of the shortest program that prints n and halts. Then, for fixed m, define the new, constant-valued function $g(x)$ as follows:

$$g(x) = \mu i \, [f(i) \geq m]$$

If f is recursive, then so is g, because there are infinitely many programs that print n and then halt (just pad the program with useless instructions) and so the minimization must terminate. Now $g(x)$, in English, returns a natural number i such that no program of length less than m prints i and halts. What can we say about the length of a program for g? If we code m in binary (different from what we have done for a while, but not affecting computability), then we can state that the length of a program for g need not exceed some constant plus $\log_2 m$. The constant takes into account the fixed-length code for f (which does not depend on m) and the fixed-length code for the minimization loop. The $\log_2 m$ takes into account the fact that g must test the value of $f(i)$ against m, which requires that information about m be hard-coded into the program. Thus for large m, the length of g is certainly less than m; let m_0 be such a value of m. But then, for this m_0, g prints the smallest integer i such that no program of length less than m_0 can print i, yet g has length less than m_0 itself—a contradiction. Hence f cannot be recursive.   Q.E.D.

Our g is a formalization of the famous *Berry's paradox*, which can be phrased as: "Let k be the least natural number that cannot be denoted in English with fewer than a thousand characters." This statement has fewer than a thousand characters and denotes k. Berry's paradox provides the basis for the theory of *Algorithmic Information Theory*, built by Gregory Chaitin. Because it includes both self-reference and an explicit resource bound (length), Berry's paradox is stronger than the equally famous *liar's paradox*, which can be phrased as: "This sentence is false"[2] and which can be seen as equivalent to the halting problem and thus the basis for the theory of computability.

We can turn the argument upside down and conclude that we cannot decide, for each fixed n, what is the largest value that can be printed by a program of length n that starts with an empty tape and halts after printing that value. This problem is a variation of the famous *busy beaver* problem, which asks how many steps a program of length n with no input can

---

[2] The liar's paradox is attributed to the Cretan Epimenides, who is reported to have said, "All Cretans are liars." This original version of the liar's paradox is not a true paradox, since it is consistent with the explanation that there is a Cretan (not Epimenides, who also reported that he had slept for 40 years...) who is not a liar. For a true paradox, Epimenides should have simply said "I always lie." The version we use, a true paradox, is attributed to Eubulides (6th century B.C.), a student of Euclid.

run before halting. Our busy beaver problem should be compared to the Grzegorczyk hierarchy of Section 5.1: the busy beaver function (for each n, print the largest number that a program of length n can compute on an empty input) grows so fast that it is uncomputable!

There exists a version of Rice's theorem for r.e. sets, that is, an exact characterization of r.e. sets that can be used to prove that some sets are r.e. and others are not. Unfortunately, this characterization (known as the Rice-Shapiro theorem) is rather complex, especially when compared to the extremely simple characterization of Rice's theorem. In consequence, we do not state it here but leave the reader to explore it in Exercise 5.25.

We conclude with a quick look at the recursion theorem, a fundamental result used in establishing the correctness of definitions based on general recursion, as well as those based on fixed points (such as denotational semantics for programming languages). Recall that no set of total functions can be immune to diagonalization, but that we defined the partial recursive functions specifically to overcome the self-reference problem. Because partial recursive functions are immune to the dangers of self-reference, we can use self-reference to build new results. Thus the recursion theorem can be viewed as a very general mechanism for defining functions in terms of themselves.

Theorem 5.6 For every total recursive function f, there is an index i (depending on f) with $\phi_i = \phi_{f(i)}$.   □

In other words, i is a *fixed point* for f within the given programming system. Superficially, this result is counterintuitive: among other things, it states that we cannot write a program that consistently alters any given program so as to change its input/output behavior.

Proof. The basic idea in the proof is to run $\phi_x(x)$ and use its result (if any) as an index within the programming system to define a new function. Thus we define the function $\theta(x, y) = \phi_{\mathrm{univ}}(\phi_{\mathrm{univ}}(x, x), y)$. Since this is a partial recursive function, we can use the standard s-m-n construction to conclude that there is a total recursive function g with $\phi_{g(x)}(y) = \theta(x, y)$. Now consider the total recursive function $f \cdot g$. There is some index m with $\phi_m = f \cdot g$; set $i = g(m)$. Now, since ϕ_m is total, we have $\phi_m(m) \downarrow$ and also

$$\phi_i(y) = \phi_{g(m)}(y) = \theta(m, y) = \phi_{\phi_m(m)}(y) = \phi_{f(g(m))}(y) = \phi_{f(i)}(y)$$

as desired.   *Q.E.D.*

A simple application of the recursion theorem is to show that there exists a program that, under any input, outputs exactly itself; in our terms, there is an index n with $\phi_n(x) = n$ for all x. Define the function $\phi(x, y) = x$, then use the s-m-n construction to get a function f with $\phi_{f(x)}(y) = x$ for all x. Now apply the recursion theorem to obtain n, the fixed point of f. (You might want to write such a program in Lisp.) Another simple application is a different proof of Rice's theorem. Let $\mathscr{C}$ be a nontrivial class of partial recursive functions, and let $j \in P_{\mathscr{C}}$ and $k \notin P_{\mathscr{C}}$. Define the function

$$f(x) = \begin{cases} k & x \in P_{\mathscr{C}} \\ j & x \notin P_{\mathscr{C}} \end{cases}$$

Thus f transforms the index of any program in $P_{\mathscr{C}}$ into k, the index of a program not in $P_{\mathscr{C}}$, and, conversely, transforms the index of any program not in $P_{\mathscr{C}}$ into j, the index of a program in $P_{\mathscr{C}}$. If $P_{\mathscr{C}}$ were recursive, then f would be a total recursive function; but f cannot have a fixed point i with $\phi_{f(i)} = \phi_i$ (because, by construction, one of i and $f(i)$ is inside $P_{\mathscr{C}}$ and the other outside, so that ϕ_i and $\phi_{f(i)}$ cannot be equal), thus contradicting the recursion theorem. Hence $P_{\mathscr{C}}$ is not recursive.

The only problem with the recursion theorem is that it is nonconstructive: it tells us that f has a fixed point, but not how to compute that fixed point. However, this can easily be fixed by a few changes in the proof, so that we get the stronger version of the recursion theorem.

Theorem 5.7 There is a total recursive function h such that, for all x, if ϕ_x is total, then we have $\phi_{h(x)} = \phi_{\phi_x(h(x))}$. □

This time, the fixed point is computable for any given total function $f = \phi_x$ through the single function h.

Proof. Let j be the index of a program computing the function g defined in the proof of the recursion theorem. Let c be the total recursive function for composition and define $h(x) = g(c(x, j))$. Straightforward substitution verifies that this h works as desired.   *Q.E.D.*

5.7   Degrees of Unsolvability

The many-one reductions used in proving sets to be nonrecursive or non-r.e. have interesting properties in their own right. Clearly, any set reduces to itself (through the identity function). Since, in an acceptable programming system, we have an effective composition function c, if set A reduces to set B through f and set B reduces to set C through g, then set A reduces to set C through $c(f, g)$. Thus reductions are reflexive and transitive and can be used to define an equivalence relation by symmetry: we say that sets A and B are equivalent if they reduce to each other. The classes of equivalence defined by this equivalence relation are known as *many-one degrees of unsolvability*, or just *m-degrees*.

Proposition 5.2 There is a unique m-degree that contains exactly the (nontrivial) recursive sets. □

Proof. If set A is recursive and set B reduces to A through f, then set B is recursive, with characteristic function $c_B = c_A \cdot f$. Hence an m-degree that contains some recursive set S must contain only recursive sets, since all sets in the degree must reduce to S and thus are recursive. Finally, if A and B are two nontrivial recursive sets, we can always reduce one to the other. Pick two elements, $x \in B$ and $y \notin B$, then define f to map any element of A to x and any element of $\overline{A}$ to y. This function f is recursive, since A is recursive, so that A reduces to B through f. *Q.E.D.*

The two trivial recursive sets are somewhat different: we cannot reduce a nontrivial recursive set to either $\mathbb{N}$ or the empty set, nor can we reduce one trivial set to the other. Indeed no other set can be reduced to the empty set and no other set can be reduced to $\mathbb{N}$, so that each of the two forms its own separate m-degree of unsolvability.

Proposition 5.3 An m-degree of unsolvability that contains an r.e. set contains only r.e. sets. □

Proof. If A is r.e. and B reduces to A through f, then, as we have seen before, B is r.e. with domain function $\phi_B = \phi_A \cdot f$. *Q.E.D.*

We have seen that the diagonal set K is in some sense characteristic of the nonrecursive sets; we formalize this intuition through the concept of completeness.

Definition 5.9 Let $\mathscr{C}$ be a collection of sets and A some set in $\mathscr{C}$. We say that A is *many-one complete* for $\mathscr{C}$ if every set in $\mathscr{C}$ many-one reduces to A. □

Theorem 5.8 The diagonal set K is many-one complete for the class of r.e. sets. □

Proof. Let A be any r.e. set with domain function ϕ_A. Using standard s-m-n techniques, we can construct a recursive function f obeying

$$\phi_{f(x)}(y) = y + \mathrm{Zero}(\phi_A(x)) = \begin{cases} y & x \in A \\ \text{undefined} & \text{otherwise} \end{cases}$$

Then x belongs to A if and only if $f(x)$ belongs to K, as desired. *Q.E.D.*

We can recast our earlier observation about nontrivial recursive sets in terms of completeness.

Proposition 5.4 Any nontrivial recursive set is many-one complete for the class of recursive sets.   □

Since the class of nontrivial recursive sets is closed under complementation, any nontrivial recursive set many-one reduces to its complement. However, the same is not true of r.e. sets: for instance, $\overline{K}$ does not reduce to its complement—otherwise $\overline{K}$ would be r.e.

In terms of m-degrees, then, we see that we have three distinct m-degrees for the recursive sets: the degree containing the empty set, the degree containing $\mathbb{N}$, and the degree containing all other recursive sets. Whenever a set in an m-degree reduces to a set in a second m-degree, we say that the first m-degree reduces to the second. This extension of the terminology is justified by the fact that each degree is an equivalence class under reduction. Thus we say that both our trivial recursive m-degrees reduce to the m-degree of nontrivial recursive sets. Figure 5.5 illustrates the simple lattice of the recursive m-degrees. What can we say about the nonrecursive r.e. degrees? We know that all reduce to the degree of K, because K is many-one complete for the r.e. sets. However, we shall prove that not all nonrecursive r.e. sets belong to the degree of K, a result due to Post. We begin with two definitions.

Definition 5.10 A set A is *productive* if there exists a total function f such that, for each i with $dom\phi_i \subseteq A$, we have $f(i) \in A - dom\phi_i$.   □

Thus $f(i)$ is a witness to the fact that A is not r.e., since, for each candidate partial recursive function ϕ_i, it shows that A is not the domain of ϕ_i. The set $\overline{K}$ is productive, with the trivial function $f_K(i) = i$, because, if we have some function ϕ_i with $dom\phi_i \subseteq \overline{K}$, then, by definition, $\phi_i(i)$ diverges and thus we have both $i \notin dom\phi_i$ and $i \in \overline{K}$.

Definition 5.11 A set is *creative* if it is r.e. and its complement is productive.   □

nontrivial
recursive sets

$\{\emptyset\}$ $\{\mathbb{N}\}$

Figure 5.5   The lattice of the recursive m-degrees.

For instance, K is creative. Notice that an r.e. set is recursive if and only if its complement is r.e.; but if the complement is productive, then we have witnesses against its being r.e. and thus witnesses against the original set's being recursive.

Theorem 5.9 An r.e. set is many-one complete for the class of r.e. sets if and only if it is creative.   □

Proof. We begin with the "only if" part: assume the C is many-one complete for r.e. sets. We need to show that C is creative or, equivalently, that $\overline{C}$ is productive. Since C is complete, K reduces to C through some function $f = \phi_m$. Now define the new function

$$\psi(x, y, z) = \phi_{\text{univ}}(x, \phi_{\text{univ}}(y, z)) = \phi_x(\phi_y(z))$$

By the s-m-n theorem, there exists a recursive function $g(x, y)$ with $\phi_{g(x,y)}(z) = \psi(z)$. We claim that the recursive function $h(x) = f(g(x, m))$ is a productive function for $\overline{C}$. Assume then that we have some function ϕ_i with $dom\phi_i \subseteq \overline{C}$ and consider $h(i) = f(g(i, m))$; we want to show that $h(i)$ belongs to $\overline{C} - dom\phi_i$. We have

$$f(g(i, m)) \in \overline{C} \Leftrightarrow g(i, m) \in \overline{K}$$
$$\Leftrightarrow \phi_{g(i,m)}(g(i, m)) \uparrow$$
$$\Leftrightarrow \phi_i(\phi_m(g(i, m))) \uparrow$$
$$\Leftrightarrow \phi_i(f(g(i, m))) \uparrow$$

It thus remains only to verify that $f(g(i, m))$ does not belong to C. But, if $f(g(i, m))$ were to belong to C, then (from the above) $\phi_i(f(g(i, m)))$ would converge and $f(g(i, m))$ would belong to $dom\phi_i$, so that we would have $dom\phi_i \not\subseteq \overline{C}$, a contradiction.

Now for the "if" part: let C be a creative r.e. set with productive function f, and let B be an r.e. set with domain function ϕ_B. We need to show that B many-one reduces to C. Define the new function $\psi(x, y, z)$ to be totally undefined if y is not in B (by invoking $\text{Zero}(\phi_B(y))$) and to be otherwise defined only for $z = f(x)$. By the s-m-n theorem, there exists a recursive function $g(x, y)$ with $\psi(x, y, z) = \phi_{g(x,y)}(z)$ and, by the recursion theorem, there exists a fixed point x_y with $\phi_{x_y}(z) = \phi_{g(x_y,y)}(z)$. By the extended recursion theorem, this fixed point can be computed for each y by some recursive function $e(y) = x_y$. Thus we have

$$dom\phi_{e(y)} = dom\phi_{g(e(y),y)} = \begin{cases} \{f(e(y))\} & y \in B \\ \varnothing & \text{otherwise} \end{cases}$$

But $\overline{C}$ is productive, so that $dom\phi_{e(y)} \subseteq \overline{C}$ implies $f(e(y)) \in \overline{C} - dom\phi_{e(y)}$. Hence, if y belongs to B, then the domain of $\phi_{e(y)}$ is $\{f(e(y))\}$, in which case $f(e(y))$ cannot be a member of $\overline{C} - dom\phi_{e(y)}$, so that $dom\phi_{e(y)}$ is not a subset of $\overline{C}$ and $f(e(y))$ must be a member of C. Conversely, if y does not belong to B, then $dom\phi_{e(y)}$ is empty and thus a subset of $\overline{C}$, so that $f(e(y))$ belongs to $\overline{C}$. Hence we have reduced B to C through $f \cdot e$. Q.E.D.

Therefore, in order to show that there exist r.e. sets of different m-degrees, we need only show that there exists noncreative r.e. sets.

Definition 5.12 A *simple* set is an r.e. set such that its complement is infinite but does not contain any infinite r.e. subset. □

By Exercise 5.28, a simple set cannot be creative.

Theorem 5.10 There exists a simple set. □

Proof. We want a set S which, for each x such that ϕ_x has infinite domain, contains an element of that domain, thereby preventing it from being a subset of $\overline{S}$. We also want to ensure that $\overline{S}$ is infinite by "leaving out" of S enough elements. Define the partial recursive function ψ as follows:

$$\psi(x) = \Pi_1(\mu y[\Pi_1(y) > 2x \text{ and } step(x, \Pi_1(y), \Pi_2(y)) \neq 0])$$

Now let S be the range of ψ; we claim that S is simple. It is clearly r.e., since it is the range of a partial recursive function. When $\psi(x)$ converges, it is larger than $2x$ by definition, so that S contains at most half of the members of any initial interval of $\mathbb{N}$; thus $\overline{S}$ is infinite. Now let $dom\phi_x$ be any infinite r.e. set; because the domain is infinite, there is a smallest y such that we have $\Pi_1(y) > 2x$, $\Pi_1(y) \in dom\phi_x$, and $step(x, \Pi_1(y), \Pi_2(y)) \neq 0$. Then $\psi(x)$ is $\Pi_1(y)$ for that value of y, so that $\Pi_1(y)$ belongs to S and the domain of ϕ_x is not a subset of $\overline{S}$. Q.E.D.

Since a simple set is not creative, it cannot be many-one complete for the r.e. sets. Since K is many-one complete for the r.e. sets, it cannot be many-one reduced to a simple set and thus cannot belong to the same m-degree. Hence there are at least two different m-degrees among the nonrecursive r.e. sets. In fact, there are infinitely many m-degrees between the degree of nontrivial recursive sets and the degree of K, with infinitely many pairs of incomparable degrees—but the proofs of such results lie beyond the scope of this text. We content ourselves with observing that our *Infinite Hotel* story provides us with an easy proof of the following result.

Theorem 5.11 Any two m-degrees have a least upper-bound. □

In other words, given two *m*-degrees $\mathcal{A}$ and $\mathcal{B}$, there exists an *m*-degree $\mathcal{C}$ such that (i) $\mathcal{A}$ and $\mathcal{B}$ both reduce to $\mathcal{C}$ and (ii) if $\mathcal{A}$ and $\mathcal{B}$ both reduce to any other *m*-degree $\mathcal{D}$, then $\mathcal{C}$ reduces to $\mathcal{D}$.

Proof. Let $\mathcal{A}$ and $\mathcal{B}$ be our two *m*-degrees, and pick $A \in \mathcal{A}$ and $B \in \mathcal{B}$. Define the set C by $C = \{2x \mid x \in A\} \cup \{2x + 1 \mid x \in B\}$—the trick used in the *Infinite Hotel*. Clearly both A and B many-one reduce to C. Thus both $\mathcal{A}$ and $\mathcal{B}$ reduce to $\mathcal{C}$, the *m*-degree containing, and defined by, C. Let $\mathcal{D}$ be some *m*-degree to which both $\mathcal{A}$ and $\mathcal{B}$ reduce. Pick some set $D \in \mathcal{D}$, and let f be the reduction from A to D and g be the reduction from B to D. We reduce C to D by the simple mapping

$$h(x) = \begin{cases} f(\frac{x}{2}) & x \text{ is even} \\ g(\frac{(x-1)}{2}) & x \text{ is odd} \end{cases}$$

Hence $\mathcal{C}$ reduces to $\mathcal{D}$.   Q.E.D.

The *m*-degrees of unsolvability of the r.e. sets form an *upper semilattice*.

5.8   Exercises

Exercise 5.11 Prove that the following functions are primitive recursive by giving a formal construction.

1. The function $\exp(n, m)$ is the exponent of the the *m*th prime in the prime power decomposition of n, where we consider the 0th prime to be 2. (For instance, we have $\exp(1960, 2) = 1$ because 1960 has a single factor of 5.)
2. The function $\max y \leqslant x[g(y, z_1, \ldots, z_n)]$, where g is primitive recursive, returns the largest value in $\{g(0, \ldots), g(1, \ldots), \ldots, g(x, \ldots)\}$.
3. The Fibonacci function $F(n)$ is defined by $F(0) = F(1) = 1$ and $F(n) = F(n - 1) + F(n - 2)$. (Hint: use the course-of-values recursion defined in Equation 5.1.)

Exercise 5.12 Verify that *iteration* is primitive recursive. A function f is constructed from a function g by iteration if we have $f(x, y) = g^x(y)$, where we assume $g^0(y) = y$.

Exercise 5.13 Verify that the function f defined as follows:

$$\begin{cases} f(0, x) = g(x) \\ f(i + 1, x) = f(i, h(x)) \end{cases}$$

is primitive recursive whenever g and h are.

Exercise 5.14 Write a program (in the language of your choice) to compute the values of Ackermann's function and tabulate the first few values—but be careful not to launch into a computation that will not terminate in your lifetime! Then write a program that could theoretically compute the values of a function at a much higher level in the Grzegorczyk hierarchy.

Exercise 5.15 Prove that the following three sets are not recursive by explicit reduction from the set K—do not use Rice's theorem.

1. $\{x \mid \phi_x$ is a constant function$\}$
2. $\{x \mid \phi_x$ is not the totally undefined function$\}$
3. $\{x \mid$ there is y with $\phi_x(y) \downarrow$ and such that ϕ_y is total$\}$

Exercise 5.16 For each of the following sets and its complement, classify them as recursive, nonrecursive but r.e., or non-r.e. You may use Rice's theorem to prove that a set is not recursive. To prove that a set is r.e., show that it is the range or domain of a partial recursive function. For the rest, use closure results or reductions.

1. $S(y) = \{x \mid y$ is in the range of $\phi_x\}$.
2. $\{x \mid \phi_x$ is injective$\}$.
3. The set of all primitive recursive programs.
4. The set of all (mathematical) primitive recursive functions.
5. The set of all partial recursive functions that grow at least as fast as n^2.
6. The set of all r.e. sets that contain at least three elements.
7. The set of all partial recursive functions with finite domain.
8. The three sets of Exercise 5.15.

Exercise 5.17 Prove formally that the *Busy Beaver* problem is undecidable. The busy beaver problem can be formalized as follows: compute, for each fixed n, the largest value that can be printed by a program of length n (that halts after printing that value). This question is intuitively the converse of Theorem 5.5.

Exercise 5.18 Let S be an r.e. set; prove that the sets $D = \bigcup_{x \in S} dom\phi_x$ and $R = \bigcup_{x \in S} ran\phi_x$ are both r.e.

Exercise 5.19 Let K_t be the set $\{x \mid \exists y \leqslant t,\ step(x, x, y) > 0\}$; that is, K_t is the set of functions that converge on the diagonal in at most t steps.

1. Prove that, for each fixed t, K_t is recursive, and verify the equality $\bigcup_{t \in \mathbb{N}} K_t = K$.
2. Conclude that, if S is an r.e. set, the set $\bigcap_{x \in S} dom\phi_x$ need not be r.e.

Exercise 5.20 Prove that every infinite r.e. set has an injective enumerating function (that is, one that does not repeat any element).

Exercise 5.21 Prove that an infinite r.e. set is recursive if and only if it has an injective, monotonically increasing enumerating function.

Exercise 5.22 Let $S = \{\{i, j\} \mid \phi_i \text{ and } \phi_j \text{ compute the same function}\}$. Is S recursive, nonrecursive but r.e., or non-r.e.?

Exercise 5.23 Define the following two disjoint sets: $A = \{x \mid \phi_x(x) = 0\}$ and $B = \{x \mid \phi_x(x) = 1\}$. Prove that both sets are nonrecursive but r.e. (the same proof naturally works for both) and that they are *recursively inseparable*, i.e., that there is no recursive set C with $A \subseteq C$ and $B \subseteq \overline{C}$. Such a set would recursively separate A and B in the sense that it would draw a recursive boundary dividing the elements of A from those of B. (Hint: use the characteristic function of the putative C to derive a contradiction.)

Exercise 5.24 This exercise explores ways of defining partial functions that map finite subsets of $\mathbb{N}$ to $\mathbb{N}$. Define the primitive recursive function

$$f(i, x) = \Pi_{\text{Succ}(x)}^{\text{Succ}(\Pi_1(i))}(\Pi_2(i))$$

1. Define the sequence of partial recursive functions $\{\psi_i\}$ by

$$\psi_i(x) = \begin{cases} f(i, x) & x < \text{Succ}(\Pi_1(i)) \\ \text{undefined} & \text{otherwise} \end{cases}$$

   Verify that this sequence includes every function that maps a nonempty finite initial subset of $\mathbb{N}$ (i.e., some set $\{0, 1, \ldots, k\}$) to $\mathbb{N}$.
2. Define the sequence of partial recursive functions $\{\pi_i\}$ by

$$\pi_i(x) = \begin{cases} \text{dec}(f(i, x)) & x < \text{Succ}(\Pi_1(i)) \text{ and } f(i, x) > 0 \\ \text{undefined} & \text{otherwise} \end{cases}$$

   Verify that this sequence includes every function that maps a finite subset of $\mathbb{N}$ to $\mathbb{N}$.

Exercise 5.25* This exercise develops the Rice-Shapiro theorem, which characterizes r.e. sets in much the same way as Rice's theorem characterizes recursive sets. The key to extending Rice's theorem resides in finite input/output behaviors, each of which defines a recursive set. In essence, a class of partial recursive functions is r.e. if and only if each partial recursive function in the class is the extension of some finite input/output behavior in an r.e. set of such behaviors. Exercise 5.24 showed that the sequence $\{\pi_i\}$ captures all possible finite input/output behaviors; our formulation of the Rice-Shapiro theorem uses this sequence.

Let $\mathscr{C}$ be any class of (mathematical) partial recursive functions. Then the set $\{x \mid \phi_x \in \mathscr{C}\}$ is r.e. if and only if there exists an r.e. set I with

$$\phi_x \in \mathscr{C} \Leftrightarrow \exists i \in I, \ \pi_i \subseteq \phi_x$$

(where $\pi_i \subseteq \phi_x$ indicates that ϕ_x behaves exactly like π_i on all arguments on which π_i is defined—and may behave in any way whatsoever on all other arguments).

Exercise 5.26 Use the recursion theorem to decide whether there are indices with the following properties:

1. The domain of ϕ_n is $\{n^2\}$.
2. The domain of ϕ_n is $\mathbb{N} - \{n\}$.
3. The domain of ϕ_n is K and also contains n.

Exercise 5.27 Prove that the set $S(c) = \{x \mid c \notin dom\phi_x\}$, where c is an arbitrary constant, is productive.

Exercise 5.28 Prove that every productive set has an infinite r.e. subset.

Exercise 5.29 Let S be a set; the *cylindrification* of S is the set $S \times \mathbb{N}$. Prove the following results about cylinders:

1. A set and its cylindrification belong to the same m-degree.
2. If a set is simple, its cylindrification is not creative.

Exercise 5.30* Instead of using many-one reductions, we could have used one-one reductions, that is, reductions effected by an injective function. One-one reductions define one-degrees rather than m-degrees. Revisit all of our results concerning m-degrees and rephrase them for one-degrees. Recursive sets now get partitioned into finite sets of each size, infinite sets with finite complements, and infinite sets with infinite complements. Note also that our basic theorem about creative sets remains unchanged: an r.e. set is one-complete for the r.e. sets exactly when it is complete. Do a set and its cylindrification (see previous exercise) belong to the same one-degree?

5.9 Bibliography

Primitive recursive functions were defined in 1888 by the German mathematician Julius Wilhelm Richard Dedekind (1831–1916) in his attempt to provide a constructive definition of the real numbers. Working along the same lines, Ackermann [1928] defined the function that bears his name. Gödel [1931] and Kleene [1936] used primitive recursive functions again, giving them a modern formalism. The course-of-values mechanism (Equation 5.1) was shown to be closed within the primitive recursive functions by Péter [1967], who used prime power encoding rather than pairing in her proof; she also showed (as did Grzegorczyk [1953]) that the bounded quantifiers and the bounded search scheme share the same property.

Almost all of the results in this chapter were proved by Kleene [1952]. The first text on computability to pull together all of the threads developed in the first half of the twentieth century was that of Davis [1958]. Rogers [1967] wrote the classic, comprehensive text on the topic, now reissued by MIT Press in paperback format. A more modern treatment with much the same coverage is offered by Tourlakis [1984]. An encyclopedic treatment can be found in the two-volume work of Odifreddi [1989], while the text of Pippenger [1997] offers an advanced treatment. Readers looking for a strong introductory text should consult Cutland [1980], whose short paperback covers the same material as our chapter, but in more detail. In much of our treatment, we followed the concise approach of Machtey and Young [1978], whose perspective on computability, like ours, was strongly influenced by modern results in complexity.

The text of Epstein and Carnielli [1989] relates computability theory to the foundations of mathematics and, through excerpts from the original articles of Hilbert, Gödel, Kleene, Post, Turing, and others, mixed with critical discussions, offers much insight into the development of the field of computability. Davis [1965] edited an entire volume of selected reprints from the pioneers of the 1930s—from Hilbert to Gödel, Church, Kleene, Turing, Post, and others. These articles are as relevant today as they were then and exemplify a clarity of thought and writing that has become too rare.

Berry's paradox has been used by Chaitin [1990a,1990b] in building his theory of algorithmic information theory, which grew from an original solution to the question of "what is a truly random string"—to which he and the Russian mathematician Kolmogorov answered "any string which is its own shortest description." Chaitin maintains, at URL `http://www.cs.auckland.ac.nz/CDMTCS/chaitin/`, a Web site with much of his work on-line, along with tools useful in exploring some of the consequences of his results.

CHAPTER 6

Complexity Theory: Foundations

Problem-solving is generally focused on algorithms: given a problem and a general methodology, how can we best apply the methodology to solve the problem and what can we say about the resulting algorithm? We analyze each algorithm's space and time requirements; in the case of approximation algorithms, we also attempt to determine how close the solution produced is to the optimal solution. While this approach is certainly appropriate from a practical standpoint, it does not enable us to conclude that a given algorithm is "best"—or even that it is "good"—as we lack any reference point. In order to draw such conclusions, we need results about the complexity of the problem, not just about the complexity of a particular algorithm that solves it. The objective of complexity theory is to establish bounds on the behavior of the best possible algorithms for solving a given problem—whether or not such algorithms are known.

Viewed from another angle, complexity theory is the natural extension of computability theory: now that we know what can and what cannot be computed in absolute terms, we move to ask what can and what cannot be computed within reasonable resource bounds (particularly time and space).

Characterizing the complexity of a problem appears to be a formidable task: since we cannot list all possible algorithms for solving a problem—much less analyze them—how can we derive a bound on the behavior of the best algorithm? This task has indeed proved to be so difficult that precise complexity bounds are known for only a few problems. Sorting is the best known example—any sorting algorithm that sorts N items by successive comparisons must perform at least $\lceil \log_2 N! \rceil \approx N \log_2 N$ comparisons in the worst case. Sorting algorithms that approach this bound exist: two such are heapsort and mergesort, both of which require at most $O(n \log n)$ comparisons and thus are (within a constant factor) optimal in this respect. Hence the lower bound for sorting is very tight. However, note that even here the bound is not on the cost of any sorting algorithm but only on the cost of any comparison-based algorithm. Indeed, by using bit manipulations and address computations, it is possible to sort in $o(n \log n)$ time.

In contrast, the best algorithms known for many of the problems in this book require exponential time in the worst case, yet current lower bounds for these problems are generally only linear—and thus trivial, since this is no more than the time required to read the input. Consequently, even such an apparently modest goal as the characterization of problems as tractable (solvable in polynomial time) or intractable (requiring exponential time) is beyond the reach of current methodologies. While characterization of the absolute complexity of problems has proved difficult, characterization of their relative complexity has proved much more successful. In this approach, we attempt to show that one problem is harder than another, meaning that the best possible algorithm for solving the former requires more time, space, or other resources than the best possible algorithm for solving the latter, or that all members of a class of problems are of equal difficulty, at least with regard to their asymptotic behavior. We illustrate the basic idea informally in the next section, and then develop most of the fundamental results of the theory in the ensuing sections.

6.1   Reductions

6.1.1   Reducibility Among Problems

As we have seen in Chapter 5, reductions among sets provide an effective tool for studying computability. To study complexity, we need to define reductions among problems and to assess or bound the cost of each reduction. For example, we can solve the marriage problem by transforming it into a special instance of a network flow problem and solving that instance. Another example is the convex hull problem: a fairly simple transformation shows that we can reduce sorting to the computation of two-dimensional convex hulls in linear time. In this case, we can also devise a linear-time reduction in the other direction, from the convex hull problem to sorting—through the Graham scan algorithm—thereby enabling us to conclude that sorting a set of numbers and finding the convex hull of a set of points in two dimensions are computationally equivalent to within a linear-time additive term.

```
function Hamiltonian(G: graph; var circuit: list_of_edges):
  boolean;
  (* Returns a Hamiltonian circuit for G if one exists. *)
  var G': graph;
  function TSP(G: graph; var tour: list_of_edges): integer;
    (* Function returning an optimal tour and its length *)
    ...
  begin
    let N be the number of vertices in G;
    define G' to be K_N with edge costs given by
```

$$
c_{ij} = \begin{cases} 1 & (v_i, v_j) \in G \\ 2 & (v_i, v_j) \notin G \end{cases}
$$

```
    if TSP(G', circuit) = N
      then Hamiltonian := true
      else Hamiltonian := false
  end;
```

Figure 6.1   Reduction of Hamiltonian circuit to traveling salesman.

As a more detailed example, consider the two problems *Traveling Salesman* and *Hamiltonian Circuit*. No solution that is guaranteed to run in polynomial time is known for either problem. However, were we to discover a polynomial-time solution for the traveling salesman problem, we could immediately construct a polynomial-time solution for the Hamiltonian circuit problem, as described in Figure 6.1. Given a particular graph of N vertices, we first transform this instance of the Hamiltonian circuit problem into an instance of the traveling salesman problem by associating each vertex of the graph with a city and by setting the distance between two cities to one if the corresponding vertices are connected by an edge in the original graph and to two otherwise. If our subroutine for *Traveling Salesman* returns an optimal tour of length N, then this tour uses only connections of unit length and thus corresponds to a Hamiltonian circuit. If the length of the optimal tour exceeds N, then no Hamiltonian circuit exists. Since the transformation can be done in $O(N^2)$ time, the overall running time of this algorithm for the Hamiltonian circuit problem is determined by the running time of our subroutine for the traveling salesman problem. We say that we have *reduced* the Hamiltonian circuit problem to the traveling salesman problem because the problem of determining a Hamiltonian circuit has been "reduced" to that of finding a suitably short tour.

The terminology is somewhat unfortunate: reduction connotes diminution and thus it would seem that, by "reducing" a problem to another, the amount of work would be lessened. This is true only in the sense that a reduction enables us to solve a new problem with the same algorithm used for another problem.[1] The original problem has not really been simplified. In fact, the correct conclusion to draw from such a reduction is that the original problem is, if anything, easier than the one to which it is reduced. There might exist some entirely different solution method for the original problem, one which uses less time than the sum of the times taken to transform the problem, to run the subroutine, and to reinterpret the results. In our example, we may well believe that the Hamiltonian circuit problem is easier than the traveling salesman problem, since instances of the latter produced by our transformation have a very special form. We can conclude from this discussion that, if the traveling salesman problem is tractable, so is the Hamiltonian circuit problem and that, conversely, if the Hamiltonian circuit problem is intractable, then so is the traveling salesman problem.

Informally, then, a problem A *reduces* to another problem B, written as $A \leqslant_t B$ (the t to be explained shortly), if a solution for B can be used to construct a solution for A. Our earlier example used a rather restricted form of reduction, as the subroutine was called only once and its answer was adopted with only minor modification. Indeed, had we stated both problems as decision problems, with the calling sequence of TSP consisting of a graph, G, and a bound, k, on the length of the desired tour, and with only a boolean value returned, then Hamiltonian could adopt the result returned by TSP without any modification whatsoever.

A more complex reduction may make several calls to the subroutine with varied parameter values. We present a simple example of such a reduction. An instance of the *Partition* problem is given by a set of objects and an integer-valued size associated with each object. The question is: "Can the set be partitioned into two subsets, such that the sum of the sizes of the elements in one subset is equal to the sum of the sizes of the elements in the other subset?" (As phrased, *Partition* is a decision problem.) An instance of the *Smallest Subsets* problem also comprises a set of objects with associated sizes; in addition, it includes a positive size bound B. The question is: "How many different subsets are there such that the sum of the elements of each

---

[1]Reductions are common in mathematics. A mathematician was led into a room containing a table, a sink, and an empty bucket on the floor. He was asked to put a full bucket of water on the table. He quickly picked up the bucket, filled it with water, and placed it on the table. Some time later he was led into a room similarly equipped, except that this time the bucket was already full of water. When asked to perform the same task, he pondered the situation for a time, then carefully emptied the bucket in the sink, put it back on the floor, and announced, "I've reduced the task to an earlier problem."

subset is no larger than B?" (As phrased, *Smallest Subsets* is an enumeration problem.) We reduce the partition problem to the smallest subsets problem. Obviously, an instance of the partition problem admits a solution only if the sum of all the sizes is an even number. Thus we start by computing this sum. If it is odd, we immediately answer "no" and stop; otherwise, we use the procedure for solving *Smallest Subsets* with the same set of elements and the same sizes as in the partition problem. Let T denote half the sum of all the sizes. On the first call, we set $B = T$; the procedure returns some number. We then call the procedure again, using a bound of $B = T - 1$. The difference between the two answers is the number of subsets with the property that the sum of the sizes of the elements in the subsets equals T. If this difference is zero, we answer "no"; otherwise, we answer "yes."

Exercise 6.1 Reduce *Exact Cover by Two-Sets* to the general matching problem. An instance of the first problem is composed of a set containing an even number of elements, say $2N$, and a collection of subsets of the set, each of which contains exactly two elements. The question is: "Does there exist a subcollection of N subsets that covers the set?" An instance of general matching is an undirected graph and the objective is to select the largest subset of edges such that no two selected edges share a vertex. Since the general matching problem is solvable in polynomial time and since your reduction should run in very low polynomial time, it follows that *Exact Cover by Two-Sets* is also solvable in polynomial time.   □

Exercise 6.2 The decision version of the smallest subsets problem, known as *K-th Largest Subset*, is: "Given a set of objects with associated sizes and given integers B and K, are there at least K distinct subsets for which the sum of the sizes of the elements is less than or equal to B?" Show how to reduce the partition problem to *K-th Largest Subset*. Excluding the work done inside the procedure that solves instances of the K-th largest subset problem, how much work is done by your reduction? (This is a reduction that requires a large number of subroutine calls: use binary search to determine the number of subsets for which the sum of the sizes of the elements is less than or equal to half the total sum.)   □

If we have both $A \leqslant_t B$ and $B \leqslant_t A$, then, to within the coarseness dictated by the type of the reduction, the two problems may be considered to be of equivalent complexity, which we denote by $A \equiv_t B$. The $\leqslant_t$ relation is automatically reflexive and it is only reasonable, in view of our aims, to require it to be transitive—i.e., to choose only reductions with that property. Thus we can treat $\leqslant_t$ as a partial order and compare problems in terms of their complexity. However, this tool is entirely one-sided: in order to show that problem A is strictly more difficult than problem B, we need to prove that, while problem B reduces to problem A, problem A cannot be reduced to problem B—a type of proof that is likely to require other results.

Which reduction to use depends on the type of comparison that we intend to make: the finer the comparison, the more restricted the reduction. We can restrict the resources available to the reduction. For instance, if we wish only to distinguish tractable from intractable, we want $A \leqslant_t B$ to imply that A is tractable if B is. Thus the only restriction that need be placed on the reduction t is that it require no more than polynomial time. In particular, since polynomials are closed under composition (that is, given polynomials $p(\ )$ and $q(\ )$, there exists a polynomial $r(\ )$ satisfying $p(q(x)) = r(x)$ for all x), the new procedure for A can call upon the procedure for B a polynomial number of times. On the other hand, if we wish to distinguish between problems requiring cubic time and those requiring only quadratic time, then we want $A \leqslant_t B$ to imply that A is solvable in quadratic time if B is. The reduction t must then run in quadratic time overall so that, in particular, it can make only a constant number of calls to the procedure for B. Thus the resources allotted to the reduction depend directly on the complexity classes to be compared.

We can also choose a specific type of reduction: the chosen type establishes a minimum degree of similarity between the two problems. For instance, our first example of reduction implies a strong similarity between the Hamiltonian circuit problem and a restricted class of traveling salesman problems, particularly when both are viewed as decision problems, whereas our second example indicates only a much looser connection between the partition problem and a restricted class of smallest subsets problems.

While a very large number of reduction types have been proposed, we shall distinguish only two types of reductions: (i) *Turing* (or *algorithmic*) *reductions*, which apply to any type of problem; and (ii) *many-one reductions* (also called *transformations*), which apply only to decision problems. These are the same many-one reductions that we used among sets in computability: we can use them for decision problems because a decision problem may be viewed as a set—the set of all "yes" instances of the problem.

Definition 6.1

- A problem A *Turing reduces* to a problem B, denoted $A \leqslant_T B$, if there exists an algorithm for solving A that uses an *oracle* (i.e., a putative solution algorithm) for B.
- A decision problem A *many-one reduces* to a decision problem B, denoted $A \leqslant_m B$, if there exists a mapping, $f: \Sigma^* \rightarrow \Sigma^*$, such that

"yes" instances of A are mapped onto "yes" instances of B and "no" instances of A, as well as meaningless strings, are mapped onto "no" instances of B. □

Turing reductions embody the "subroutine" scheme in its full generality, while many-one reductions are much stricter and apply only to decision problems. Viewing the mapping f in terms of a program, we note that f may not call on B in performing the translation. All it can do is transform the instance of A into an instance of B, make one call to the oracle for B, and adopt the oracle's answer for its own—it cannot even complement that answer. The principle of a many-one reduction is illustrated in Figure 6.2. The term "many-one" comes from the fact that the function f is not necessarily injective and thus may map many instances of A onto one instance of B. If the map is injective, then we speak of a *one reduction*; if the map is also surjective, then the two problems are *isomorphic* under the chosen reduction.

Exercise 6.3 Verify that $A \leqslant_m B$ implies $A \leqslant_T B$; also verify that both Turing and many-one reductions (in the absence of resource bounds) are transitive. □

We shall further qualify the reduction by the allowable amount of resources used in the reduction; thus we speak of a "polynomial-time transformation" or of a "logarithmic-space Turing reduction." Our reduction from the Hamiltonian circuit problem to the traveling salesman problem in its decision version is a polynomial-time transformation, whereas our reduction from the partition problem to the smallest subsets problem is a polynomial-time Turing reduction.

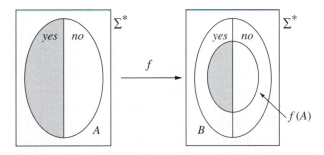

Figure 6.2   A many-one reduction from problem A to problem B.

6.1.2   Reductions and Complexity Classes

Complexity classes are characterized simply by one or more resource bounds: informally, a *complexity class* for some model of computation is the set of all decision problems solvable on this model under some given resource bounds. (We shall formally define a number of complexity classes in Section 6.2.) Each complexity class thus includes all classes of strictly smaller complexity; for instance, the class of intractable problems contains the class of tractable problems. A complexity class, therefore, differs from an equivalence class in that it includes problems of widely varying difficulty, whereas all problems in an equivalence class are of similar difficulty. This distinction is very similar to that made in Section 2.3 between the O( ) and Θ( ) notations. For instance, searching an ordered array can be done in logarithmic time on a RAM, but we can also assert that it is solvable in polynomial time or even in exponential time; thus the class of problems solvable in exponential time on a RAM includes searching an ordered array along with *much* harder problems, such as deciding whether an arbitrarily quantified Boolean formula is a tautology. In order to characterize the hardest problems in a class, we return to the notion of complete problems, first introduced in Definition 5.9.

Definition 6.2 Given a class of problems, $\mathscr{C}$, and a type of reduction, t, a problem A is *complete* for $\mathscr{C}$ (or simply $\mathscr{C}$-complete) under t if: (i) A belongs to $\mathscr{C}$, and (ii) every problem in $\mathscr{C}$ reduces to A under t. $\square$

Writing the second condition formally, we obtain $\forall B \in \mathscr{C},\ B \leq_t A$, which shows graphically that, in some sense, A is the *hardest* problem in $\mathscr{C}$. Any complete problem must reduce to any other. Thus the set of all complete problems for $\mathscr{C}$ forms an equivalence class under t—which is intuitively satisfying, since each complete problem is supposed to be the hardest in $\mathscr{C}$ and thus no particular complete problem could be harder than any other. Requiring a problem to be complete for a class is typically a very stringent condition, so we do not expect every class to have complete problems; yet, as we shall see in this chapter and the next chapter, complete problems for certain classes are surprisingly common.

   If complete problems exist for a complexity class under a suitable type of reduction (one that uses fewer resources than are available in the class), then they characterize the boundaries of a complexity class in the following ways: (i) if any one of the complete problems can be solved efficiently, then all of the problems in the class can be solved efficiently; and (ii) if a new problem can be shown to be strictly more difficult than some complete problem, then the new problem cannot be a member of the complexity class. We formalize these ideas by introducing additional terminology.

Definition 6.3 Given a class of problems, $\mathscr{C}$, a reduction, t, and a problem, A, complete for $\mathscr{C}$ under t, a problem B_1 is *hard* for $\mathscr{C}$ (or $\mathscr{C}$-hard) under t if we have $A \leqslant_t B_1$; and a problem B_2 is *easy* for $\mathscr{C}$ (or $\mathscr{C}$-easy) under t if we have $B_2 \leqslant_t A$. A problem that is both $\mathscr{C}$-hard and $\mathscr{C}$-easy is termed $\mathscr{C}$-*equivalent*.   ☐

Exercise 6.4 Any problem complete for $\mathscr{C}$ under some reduction t is thus automatically $\mathscr{C}$-equivalent. However, the converse need not be true: explain why.   ☐

In consequence, completeness can be used to characterize a problem's complexity. Completeness in some classes is strong evidence of a problem's difficulty; in other classes, it is a proof of the problem's intractability. For instance, consider the class of all problems solvable in polynomial space. (The chosen model is irrelevant, since we have seen that translations among models cause only constant-factor increases in space, which cannot affect the polynomial bound.) This class includes many problems (traveling salesman, satisfiability, partition, etc.) for which the current best solutions require exponential time—i.e., currently intractable problems. It has not been shown that any of the problems in the class truly requires exponential time; however, completeness in this class (with respect to polynomial-time reductions) may safely be taken as strong *evidence* of intractability. Now consider the class of all problems solvable in exponential time. (Again the model is irrelevant: translations among models cause at most quadratic increases in time, which cannot affect the exponential bound.) This class is known to contain provably intractable problems, that is, problems that cannot be solved in polynomial time. Thus completeness in this class (with respect to polynomial-time reductions again) constitutes a *proof* of intractability: if any complete problem were solvable efficiently, then all problems in the class would also be solvable efficiently, contradicting the existence of provably intractable problems.

All of these considerations demonstrate the importance of reductions in the analysis of problem complexity. In the following sections, we set up an appropriate formalism for the definition of complexity classes, consider the very important complexity class known as NP, and explore various ramifications and consequences of the theory. To know in advance that the problem at hand is probably or provably intractable will not obviate the need for solving the problem, but it will indicate which approaches are likely to fail (seeking optimal solutions) and which are likely to succeed (seeking approximate solutions). Even when we have lowered our sights (from finding optimal solutions to finding approximate solutions), the theory may make some important contributions. As we shall see in Chapter 8, it is sometimes possible to show that "good" approximations are just as hard to find as optimal solutions.

6.2   Classes of Complexity

Now that we have established models of computation as well as time and space complexity measures on these models, we can turn our attention to complexity classes. We defined such classes informally in the previous section: given some fixed model of computation and some positive-valued function $f(n)$, we associate with it a family of problems, namely all of the problems that can be solved on the given computational model in time (or space) bounded by $f(n)$.[2] We need to formalize this definition in a useful way. To this end, we need to identify and remedy the shortcomings of the definition, as well as to develop tools that will allow us to distinguish among various classes. We already have one tool that will enable us to set up a partial order of complexity classes, namely the time and space relationships described by Equations 4.1 and 4.2. We also need a tool that can separate complexity classes—a tool with which we can prove that some problem is strictly harder than some other. This tool takes the form of hierarchy theorems and translational lemmata. Complexity theory is built from these two tools; as a result, a typical situation in complexity theory is a pair of relations of the type $\mathcal{A} \subseteq \mathcal{B} \subseteq \mathcal{C}$ and $\mathcal{A} \subset \mathcal{C}$. The first relations can be compared to springs and the second to a rigid rod, as illustrated in Figure 6.3. Classes $\mathcal{A}$ and $\mathcal{C}$ are securely separated by the rod, while class $\mathcal{B}$ is suspended between the two on springs and thus can sit anywhere between the two, not excluding equality with one or the other (by flattening the corresponding spring).

In Section 6.2.1, we use as our model of computation a deterministic Turing machine with a single read/write tape; we do add a read-only input tape and a write-only output tape to obtain the standard off-line model (see Section 4.3) as needed when considering sublinear space bounds. The results we obtain are thus particular to one model of computation, although

---

[2]More general definitions exist. Abstract complexity theory is based on the partial recursive functions of Chapter 5 and on measures of resource use, called complexity functions, that are defined on all convergent computations. Even with such a minimal structure, it becomes possible to prove versions of the hierarchy theorems and translational lemmata given in this section.

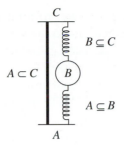

Figure 6.3 A typical situation in complexity theory.

it will be easily seen that identical results can be proved for any reasonable model. In Section 6.2.2, we discuss how we can define classes of complexity that remain unaffected by the choice of model or by any (finite) number of translations between models.

6.2.1 Hierarchy Theorems

We can list at least four objections to our informal definition of complexity classes:

1. Since no requirement whatsoever is placed on the resource bound, $f(n)$, it allows the definition of absurd families (such as the set of all problems solvable in $O(e^{-n}n)$ time or $O(n|\sin n|)$ space).
2. Since there are uncountably many possible resource bounds, we get a correspondingly uncountable number of classes—far more than we can possibly be interested in, as we have only a countable number of solvable problems.
3. Since two resource bounds may differ only infinitesimally (say by 10^{-10} and only for one value of n), in which case they probably define the same family of problems, our definition is likely to be ill-formed.
4. Model-independence, which adds an uncertainty factor (linear for space, quadratic for time), is certain to erase any distinction among many possible families.

A final source of complication is that the size of the output itself may dictate the complexity of a problem—a common occurrence in enumeration problems.

In part because of this last problem, but mainly because of convenience, most of complexity theory is built around (though not limited to) decision problems. Decision problems, as we have seen, may be viewed as sets of "yes" instances; asking for an answer to an instance is then equivalent to asking whether the instance belongs to the set. In the next few sections, we shall limit our discussion to decision problems and thus now offer some justification for this choice.

First, decision problems are often important problems in their own right. Examples include the satisfiability of Boolean formulae, the truth of logic propositions, the membership of strings in a language, the planarity of graphs, or the existence of safe schedules for resource allocation. Secondly, any optimization problem can be turned into a decision problem through the simple expedient of setting a bound upon the value of the objective function. In such a case, the optimization problem is surely no easier than the decision problem. In fact, a solution to the optimization problem provides an immediate solution to the decision problem—it is enough to compare the value of the objective function for the optimal solution with the prescribed bound. In other words, the decision version reduces to the original optimization problem.[3] Hence, any intractability results that we derive about decision versions of optimization problems immediately carry over to the original optimization versions, yet we may hope that decision versions are more easily analyzed and reduced to each other. Finally, we shall see later that optimization problems typically reduce to their decision versions, so that optimization and decision versions are of equivalent complexity.

Let us now return to our task of defining complexity classes. The hierarchy theorems that establish the existence of distinct classes of complexity are classic applications of diagonal construction. However, the fact that we are dealing with resource bounds introduces a number of minor complications, many of which must be handled through small technical results. We begin by restricting the possible resource bounds to those that can be computed with reasonable effort.

Definition 6.4 A function, $f(n)$, is *time-constructible* if there exists a Turing machine[4] such that (i) when started with any string of length n on its tape, it runs for at most $f(n)$ steps before stopping; and (ii) for each value of n, there exists at least one string of length n which causes the machine to run for exactly $f(n)$ steps. If, in addition, the machine runs

---

[3]In fact, it is conceivable that the decision version would not reduce to the original optimization version. For instance, if the objective function were exceedingly difficult to compute and the optimal solution might be recognized by purely structural features (independent from the objective function), then the optimization version could avoid computing the objective function altogether while the decision version would require such computation. However, we know of no natural problem of that type.

[4]The choice of a Turing machine, rather than a RAM or other model, is for convenience only; it does not otherwise affect the definition.

for exactly $f(n)$ steps on every string of length n, then $f(n)$ is said to be *fully time-constructible*. *Space-constructible* and *fully space-constructible* functions are similarly defined, using an off-line Turing machine. □

Any constant, polynomial, or exponential function is both time- and space-constructible (see Exercise 6.15); the functions $\lceil \log n \rceil$ and $\lceil {}^k\sqrt{n} \rceil$ are fully space-constructible, but clearly not time-constructible.

Exercise 6.5 Prove that any space-constructible function that is nowhere smaller than n is also fully space-constructible. □

Obviously, there exist at most countably many fully time- or space-constructible functions, so that limiting ourselves to such resource bounds answers our second objection. Our first objection also disappears, for the most part, since nontrivial time-constructible functions must be $\Omega(n)$ and since corresponding space-constructible functions are characterized as follows.

Theorem 6.1 If $f(n)$ is space-constructible and nonconstant, then it is $\Omega(\log \log n)$. □

Our third objection, concerning infinitesimally close resource bounds, must be addressed by considering the most fundamental question: given resource bounds $f(n)$ and $g(n)$, with $g(n) \geq f(n)$ for all n—so that any problem solvable within bound $f(n)$ is also solvable within bound $g(n)$—under which conditions will there exist a problem solvable within bound $g(n)$ but not within bound $f(n)$? We can begin to answer by noting that, whenever f is $\Theta(g)$, the two functions must denote the same class—a result known as *linear speed-up*.

Lemma 6.1 Let f and g be two functions from $\mathbb{N}$ to $\mathbb{N}$ such that $f(n)$ is $\Theta(g(n))$. Then any problem solvable in $g(n)$ time (respectively space) is also solvable in $f(n)$ time (respectively space). □

In both cases the proof consists of a simple simulation based upon a change in alphabet. By encoding suitably large (but finite) groups of symbols into a single character drawn from a larger alphabet, we can reduce the storage as well as the running time by any given constant factor. Hence given two resource bounds, one dominated by the other, the two corresponding classes can be distinct only if one bound grows asymptotically faster than the other. However, the reader would be justified in questioning this result. The change in alphabet works for Turing machines and for some other models of computation but is hardly fair (surely the cost of a single step on a Turing machine should increase with the size of the alphabet, since each step requires a matching on the character stored in a tape square) and does not carry over to all models of computation. Fortunately for us, model-independence will make the whole point moot—by forcing us to ignore not just constant factors but any polynomial factors. Therefore, we use the speed-up theorem to help us in proving the hierarchy theorems (its use simplifies the proofs), but we do not claim it to be a characteristic of computing models.

In summary, we have restricted resource bounds to be time- or space-constructible and will further require minimal gaps between the resource bounds in order to preserve model-independence; together, these considerations answer all four of our objections. Before we can prove the hierarchy theorems, we need to clear up one last, small technical problem. We shall look at all Turing machines and focus on those that run within some time or space bound. However, among Turing machines that run within a certain space bound, there exist machines that may never terminate on some inputs (a simple infinite loop uses constant space and runs forever).

Lemma 6.2 If M is a Turing machine that runs within space bound $f(n)$ (where $f(n)$ is everywhere as large as $\lceil \log n \rceil$), then there exists a Turing machine M' that obeys the same space (but not necessarily time) bound, accepts the same strings, and halts under all inputs. □

In order to see that this lemma holds, it is enough to recall Equation 4.2: a machine running in $f(n)$ space cannot run for more than $c^{f(n)}$ steps (for some constant $c > 1$) without entering an infinite loop. Thus we can run a simulation of M that halts when M halts or when $c^{f(n)}$ steps have been taken, whichever comes first. The counter takes $\Theta(f(n))$ space in addition to the space required by the simulated machine, so that the total space needed is $\Theta(f(n))$; by Lemma 6.1, this bound can be taken to be exactly $f(n)$.

Theorem 6.2 [Hierarchy Theorem for Deterministic Space] Let $f(n)$ and $g(n)$ be fully space-constructible functions as large as $\lceil \log n \rceil$ everywhere. If we have

$$\lim_{n \to \infty} \inf \frac{f(n)}{g(n)} = 0$$

then there exists a function computable in space bounded by $g(n)$ but not in space bounded by $f(n)$. □

The notation inf stands for the *infimum*, which is the largest lower bound on the ratio; formally, we have $\inf h(n) = \min\{h(i) \mid i = n, n + 1, n + 2, \dots\}$. In the theorem, it is used only as protection against ratios that may not converge at infinity.

   The proof, like our proof of the unsolvability of the halting problem, uses diagonalization; however, we now use diagonalization purely constructively, to build a new function with certain properties. Basically, what the construction does is to (attempt to) simulate in turn each Turing machine on the diagonal, using at most $g(n)$ space in the process. Of these Turing machines, only a few are of real interest: those that run in $f(n)$ space. Ideally, we would like to enumerate only those Turing machines, simulate them on the diagonal, obtain a result, and alter it, thereby defining, in proper diagonalizing manner, a new function (not a Turing machine, this time, but a list of input/output pairs, i.e., a mathematical function) that could not be in the list and thus would take more than $f(n)$ space to compute—and yet that could be computed by our own diagonalizing simulation, which is guaranteed to run in $g(n)$ space. Since we cannot recursively distinguish Turing machines that run in $f(n)$ space from those that require more space, we (attempt to) simulate *every* machine and otherwise proceed as outlined earlier. Clearly, altering diagonal elements corresponding to machines that take more than $f(n)$ space to run does not affect our construction. Figure 6.4(a) illustrates the process. However, we cannot guarantee that our simulation will succeed on every diagonal element for every program that runs in $f(n)$ space; failure may occur for one of three reasons:

- Our simulation incurs some space overhead (typically a multiplicative constant), which may cause it to run out of space—for small values of n, $c \cdot f(n)$ could exceed $g(n)$.
- Our guarantee about $f(n)$ and $g(n)$ is only asymptotic—for a finite range (up to some unknown constant N), $f(n)$ may exceed $g(n)$, so that our simulation will run out of space and fail.
- The Turing machine we simulate does not converge on the diagonal—even if we can simulate this machine in $g(n)$ space, our simulation cannot return a value.

The first two cases are clearly two instances of the same problem; both are cured asymptotically. If we fail to simulate machine M_i, we know that there exists some other machine, say M_j, that has exactly the same behavior but can be chosen with an arbitrarily larger index (we can pad M_i with as many unreachable control states as necessary) and thus can be chosen to exceed the unknown constant N, so that our simulation of $M_j(j)$ will not run out of space. If $M_j(j)$ stops, then our simulation returns a value that can be altered, thereby ensuring that we define a mathematical function different from that implemented by M_j (and thus also different from that implemented by M_i). Figure 6.4(b) illustrates these points. Three $f(n)$ machines (joined on the left) compute the same function; the simulation of the first on its diagonal argument fails to converge, the simulation of the second on its

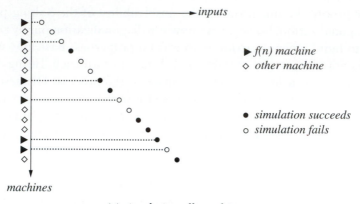

(a) simulating all machines

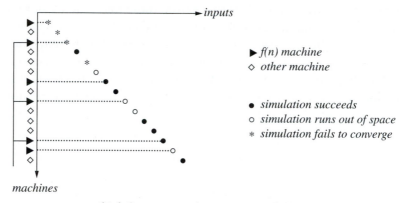

(b) failing to complete some simulations

Figure 6.4   A graphical view of the proof of the hierarchy theorems.

(different) diagonal argument runs out of space, but the simulation of the third succeeds and enables us to ensure that our new mathematical function is distinct from that implemented by these three machines. The third case has entirely distinct causes and remedies. It is resolved by appealing to Lemma 6.2: if $M_i(i)$ is undefined, then there exists some other machine M_k which always stops and which agrees with M_i wherever the latter stops. Again, if the index k is not large enough, we can increase it to arbitrarily large values by padding.

Proof. We construct an off-line Turing machine $\hat{M}$ that runs in space bounded by g and always differs in at least one input from any machine that runs in space f. Given input x, $\hat{M}$ first marks $g(|x|)$ squares on its work tape, which it can do since g is fully space-constructible. The marks will enable the machine to use exactly $g(n)$ space on an input of size n. Now, given input x, $\hat{M}$ attempts to simulate M_x run on input x; if machine M_x runs within space $f(|x|)$, then machine $\hat{M}$ will run in space at most $\alpha \cdot f(|x|)$ for some constant α. (The details of the simulation are left to the reader.) If $\hat{M}$ encounters an unmarked square during the simulation, it immediately quits and prints 0; if $\hat{M}$ successfully completes the simulation, it adds 1 to the value produced by M_x. Of course, $\hat{M}$ may fail to stop, because M_x fails to stop when run on input x.

Now let M_i be a machine that runs in space bounded by $f(n)$. Then there exists a functionally equivalent Turing machine with an encoding, say j, large enough that we have $\alpha \cdot f(|j|) < g(|j|)$. This encoding always exists because, by hypothesis, $g(n)$ grows asymptotically faster than $f(n)$. Moreover, we can assume that M_i halts under all inputs (if not, then we can apply Lemma 6.2 to obtain such a machine and again increase the index as needed). Then $\hat{M}$ has enough space to simulate M_j, so that, on input j, $\hat{M}$ produces an output different from that produced by M_j—and thus also by M_i. Hence the function computed by $\hat{M}$ within space $g(n)$ is not computable by any machine within space $f(n)$, from which our conclusion follows. *Q.E.D.*

The diagonalization is very similar to that used in the classical argument of Cantor. Indices in one dimension represent machines while indices in the other represent inputs; we look along the diagonal, where we determine whether the xth machine halts when run on the xth input, and produce a new machine $\hat{M}$ that differs from each of the enumerated machines along the diagonal. The only subtle point is that we cannot do that everywhere along the diagonal, because the simulation may run out of space or fail to converge. This problem is of no consequence, however, since, for each Turing machine, there are an infinity of Turing machines with larger codes that have the same behavior. Thus, if $\hat{M}$ fails to output something different from what M_i would output under the same input (because neither machine stops or because $\hat{M}$ cannot complete its simulation and thus outputs 0, which just happens to be what M_i produces under the same input), then there exists an M_j equivalent to M_i such that $\hat{M}$ successfully simulates $M_j(j)$. Thus, on input j, $\hat{M}$ outputs something different from what M_j, and thus also M_i, outputs.

The situation is somewhat more complex for time bounds, simply because ensuring that our Turing machine simulation does not exceed given time bounds requires significant additional work. However, the difference between the space and the time results may reflect only our inability to prove a stronger result for time rather than some fundamental difference in resolution between space and time hierarchies.

Theorem 6.3 [Hierarchy Theorem for Deterministic Time] Let $f(n)$ and $g(n)$ be fully time-constructible functions. If we have

$$\liminf_{n \to \infty} \frac{f(n)}{g(n)} = 0$$

then there exists a function computable in time bounded by $g(n)\lceil \log g(n) \rceil$ but not in time bounded by $f(n)$. $\square$

Our formulation of the hierarchy theorem for deterministic space is slightly different from the original version, which was phrased for multitape Turing machines. That formulation placed the logarithmic factor in the ratio rather than the class definition, stating that, if the ratio $\frac{f \log f}{g}$ goes to zero in the limit, then there exists a function computable in $g(n)$ time but not in $f(n)$ time. Either formulation suffices for our purposes of establishing machine-independent classes of complexity, but ours is slightly easier to prove in the context of single-tape Turing machines.

   Proof. The proof follows closely that of the hierarchy theorem for space, although our machines are now one-tape Turing machines. While our construction proceeds as if we wanted to prove that the constructed function is computable in time bounded by $g(n)$, the overhead associated with the bookkeeping forces the larger bound. We construct a Turing machine that carries out two separate tasks (on separate pieces of the tape) in an interleaved manner: (i) a simulation identical in spirit to that used in the previous proof and (ii) a counting task that checks that the first task has not used more than $g(n)$ steps. The second task uses the Turing machine implicit in the full time-constructibility of $g(n)$ and just runs it (simulates it) until it stops. Each task run separately takes only $g(n)$ steps (the first only if stopped when needed), but the interleaving of the two adds a factor of $\log g(n)$: we intercalate the portion of the tape devoted to counting immediately to the left of the current head position in the simulation, thereby allowing us to carry out the counting (decrementing the counter by one for each simulated step) without alteration and the simulation with only the penalty of shifting the tape portion devoted to counting by one position for each change of head position in the simulation. Since the counting task uses at most $\log g(n)$ tape squares, the penalty for the interleaving is exactly $\log g(n)$ steps for each step in the simulation, up to the cut-off of $g(n)$ simulation steps. An initialization step sets up a counter with value $g(n)$.   *Q.E.D.*

These two hierarchy theorems tell us that a rich complexity hierarchy exists for each model of computation and each charging policy. Further structure is implied by the following *translational lemma*, given here for space, but equally valid (with the obvious changes) for time.

Lemma 6.3 Let $f(n)$, $g_1(n)$, and $g_2(n)$ be fully space-constructible functions, with $g_2(n)$ everywhere larger than $\log n$ and $f(n)$ everywhere larger than n. If every function computable in $g_1(n)$ space is computable in $g_2(n)$ space, then every function computable in $g_1(f(n))$ space is computable in $g_2(f(n))$ space.   □

6.2.2 Model-Independent Complexity Classes

We have achieved our goal of defining valid complexity classes on a fixed model of computation; the result is a very rich hierarchy indeed, as each model of computation induces an infinite time hierarchy and a yet finer space hierarchy. We can now return to our fourth objection: since we do not want to be tied to a specific model of computation, how can we make our time and space classes model-independent? The answer is very simple but has drastic consequences: since a change in computational model can cause a polynomial change in time complexity, the bounds used for defining classes of time complexity should be invariant under polynomial mappings. (Strictly speaking, this statement applies only to time bounds: space bounds need only be invariant under multiplication by arbitrary constants. However, we often adopt the same convention for space classes for the sake of simplicity and uniformity.) In consequence, classes that are distinct on a fixed model of computation will be merged in our model-independent theory. For instance, the time bounds n^k and n^{k+1} define distinct classes on a fixed model of computation, according to Theorem 6.3. However, the quadratic increase in time observed in our translations between Turing machines and RAMs means that the bounds n^k and n^{2k} are indistinguishable in a model-independent theory. We now briefly present some of the main model-independent classes of time and space complexity, verifying only that the definition of each is well-founded but not discussing the relationships among these classes.

Deterministic Complexity Classes

Almost every nontrivial problem requires at least linear time, since the input must be read; hence the lowest class of time complexity of any interest includes all sets recognizable in linear time. Model-independence now dictates that such sets be grouped with all other sets recognizable in polynomial time. We need all of these sets because the quadratic cost of translation from one model to another can transform linear time into quadratic time or, in general, a polynomial of degree k into one of degree $2k$. We need no more sets because, as defined, our class is invariant under polynomial translation costs (since the polynomial of a polynomial is just another polynomial). Thus the lowest model-independent class of time complexity is the class of all sets recognizable in polynomial time, which we denote P; it is also the class of tractable (decision) problems. The next higher complexity class will include problems of superpolynomial complexity and thus include intractable problems. While the hierarchy theorems allow us to define a large number of such classes, we mention only two of them—the classes of all sets recognizable in two varieties of exponential time, which we denote E and Exp.

Definition 6.5

1. P is the class of all sets recognizable in polynomial time. Formally, a set S is in P if and only if there exists a Turing machine M such that M, run on x, stops after $O(|x|^{O(1)})$ steps and returns "yes" if x belongs to S, "no" otherwise.

2. E is the class of all sets recognizable in simple exponential time. Formally, a set S is in E if and only if there exists a Turing machine M such that M, run on x, stops after $O(2^{O(|x|)})$ steps and returns "yes" if x belongs to S, "no" otherwise.

3. Exp is the class of all sets recognizable in exponential time. Formally, a set S is in Exp if and only if there exists a Turing machine M such that M, run on x, stops after $O(2^{|x|^{O(1)}})$ steps and returns "yes" if x belongs to S, "no" otherwise.   □

The difference between our two exponential classes is substantial; yet, from our point of view, both classes contain problems that take far too much time to solve and so both characterize sets that include problems beyond practical applications. Although E is a fairly natural class to define, it presents some difficulties—in particular, it is not closed under polynomial transformations, which will be our main tool in classifying problems. Thus we use mostly Exp rather than E.

Exercise 6.6 Verify that P and Exp are closed under polynomial-time transformations and that E is not.   □

Our hierarchy theorem for time implies that P is a proper subset of E and that E is a proper subset of Exp. Most of us have seen a large number of problems (search and optimization problems, for the most part) solvable in polynomial time; the decision versions of these problems thus belong to P.

Since our translations among models incur only a linear penalty in storage, we could define a very complex hierarchy of model-independent space complexity classes. However, as we shall see, we lack the proper tools for classifying a set within a rich hierarchy; moreover, our main interest is in time complexity, where the hierarchy is relatively coarse due to the constraint of model-independence. Thus we content ourselves with space classes similar to the time classes; by analogy with P and Exp, we define the space complexity classes PSpace and ExpSpace. Again our hierarchy theorem for space implies that PSpace is a proper subset of ExpSpace. As we have required our models of computation not to consume space faster than time (Equation 4.1), we immediately have $P \subseteq PSpace$ and $Exp \subseteq ExpSpace$. Moreover, since we have seen that an algorithm running in $f(n)$ space can take at most $c^{f(n)}$ steps (Equation 4.2), we also have $PSpace \subseteq Exp$.

Most of the game problems discussed earlier in this text are solvable in polynomial space (and thus exponential time) through backtracking, since each game lasts only a polynomial number of moves. To find in ExpSpace a problem that does not appear to be in Exp, we have to define a very complex problem indeed. A suitable candidate is a version of the game of *Peek*. *Peek* is a two-person game played by sliding perforated plates into one of two positions within a rack until one player succeeds in aligning a column of perforations so that one can "peek" through the entire stack of plates. Figure 6.5 illustrates this idea. In its standard version, each player can move only certain plates but can see the position of the plates manipulated by the other player. This game is clearly in Exp because a standard game-graph search will solve it.

In our modified version, the players cannot see each other's moves, so that a player's strategy no longer depends on the opponent's moves but consists simply in a predetermined sequence of moves. As a result, instead of checking at each node of the game graph that, for each move of the second player, the first player has a winning choice, we must now check that the same fixed choice for the ith move of the first player is a winning move regardless of the moves made so far by the second player. In terms of algorithms, it appears that we have to check, for every possible sequence of moves for the first player, whether that sequence is a winning strategy, by checking every possible corresponding path in the game graph. We can certainly do that in exponential space by generating and storing the game graph and then repeatedly traversing it, for each possible strategy of the first player, along all possible paths dictated by that strategy and by the possible moves of the second player. However, this approach takes doubly

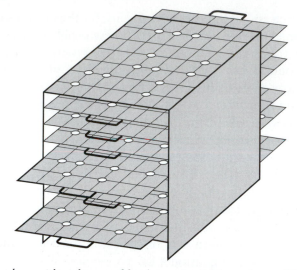

(a) a box with eight movable plates, six slid in and two slid out

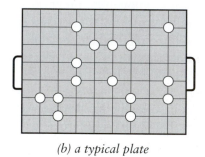

(b) a typical plate

Figure 6.5   A sample configuration of the game of Peek.

exponential time, and it is not clear that (simply) exponential time can suffice.

We also know of many problems that can be solved in sublinear space; hence we should also pay attention to possible space complexity classes below these already defined. While we often speak of algorithms running in constant additional storage (such as search in an array), all of these actually use at least logarithmic storage in our theoretical model. For instance, binary search maintains three indices into the input array; in order to address any of the n array positions, each index must have at least $\lceil \log_2 n \rceil$ bits. Thus we can begin our definition of sublinear space classes with the class of all sets recognizable in logarithmic space, which we denote by L. Using the same reasoning as for other classes, we see that L is a proper subset of PSPACE and also that it is a (not necessarily proper) subset of P. From $O(\log n)$, we can increase the space resources to $O(\log^2 n)$. Theorem 6.2 tells us that the resulting class, call it L^2, is a proper superset of L but remains a proper subset of PSPACE. Since translation among models increases space only by a constant factor, both L and this new class are model-independent. On the other hand, our relation between time and space allows an algorithm using $O(\log^2 n)$ space to run for $O(c^{\log^2 n}) = O(n^{\alpha \log n})$ steps (for some constant $\alpha > 0$), which is not polynomial in n, since the exponent of the logarithm can be increased indefinitely. Thus we cannot assert that L^2 is a subset of P; indeed, the nature of the relationship between L^2 and P remains unknown. A similar derivation shows that each higher exponent, $k \geqslant 2$, defines a new, distinct class, L^k. Since each class is characterized by a polynomial function of $\log n$, it is natural to define a new class, POLYL, as the class of all sets recognizable in space bounded by some polynomial function of $\log n$; the hierarchy theorem for space implies POLYL $\subset$ PSPACE.

Definition 6.6

1. L is the class of all sets recognizable in logarithmic space. Formally, a set S is in L if and only if there exists an off-line Turing machine M such that M, run on x, stops having used $O(\log |x|)$ squares on its work tape and returns "yes" if x belongs to S, "no" otherwise. L^i is defined similarly, by replacing $\log n$ with $\log^i n$.

2. POLYL is the class of all sets recognizable in space bounded by some polynomial function of $\log n$. Formally, a set S is in POLYL if and only if there exists an off-line Turing machine M such that M, run on x, stops having used $O(\log^{O(1)} |x|)$ squares on its work tape and returns "yes" if x belongs to S, "no" otherwise.   □

The reader will have no trouble identifying a number of problems solvable in logarithmic or polylogarithmic space. In order to identify tractable problems that do not appear to be thus solvable, we must identify problems for which all of our solutions require a linear or polynomial amount of extra storage. Examples of such include strong connectivity and biconnectivity as well as the matching problem: all are solvable in polynomial time, but all appear to require linear extra space.

Exercise 6.7 Verify that POLYL is closed under logarithmic-space transformations. To verify that the same is true of each L^i, refer to Exercise 6.11.   □

We now have a hierarchy of well-defined, model-independent time and space complexity classes, which form the partial order described in Figure 6.6. Since each class in the hierarchy contains all lower classes, classifying a problem means finding the lowest class that contains the

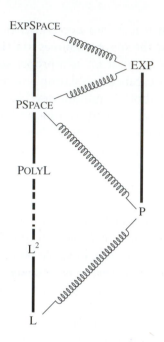

Figure 6.6   A hierarchy of space and time complexity classes.

problem—which, unless the problem belongs to L, also involves proving that the problem does not belong to a lower class. Unfortunately, the latter task appears very difficult indeed, even when restricted to the question of tractability. For most of the problems that we have seen so far, no polynomial time algorithms are known, nor do we have proofs that they require superpolynomial time. In this respect, the decision versions seem no easier to deal with than the optimization versions.

However, the decision versions of a large fraction of our difficult problems share one interesting property: if an instance of the problem has answer "yes," then, given a solution structure—an example of a *certificate*—the correctness of the answer is easily verified in (low) polynomial time. For instance, verifying that a formula in conjunctive normal form is indeed satisfiable is easily done in linear time given the satisfying truth assignment. Similarly, verifying that an instance of the traveling salesman problem admits a tour no longer than a given bound is easily done in linear time given the order in which the cities are to be visited. Answering a decision problem in the affirmative is most likely done constructively, i.e., by identifying a solution structure; for the problems in question, then, we can easily verify that the answer is correct.

Not all hard problems share this property. For instance, an answer of "yes" to the game of *Peek* (meaning that the first player has a winning strategy), while conceptually easy to verify (all we need is the game tree with the winning move identified on each branch at each level), is very expensive to verify—after all, the winning strategy presumably does not admit a succinct description and thus requires exponential time just to read, let alone verify. Other problems do not appear to have any useful certificate at all. For instance, the problem "Is the largest clique present in the input graph of size k?" has a "yes" answer only if a clique of size k is present in the input graph and no larger clique can be found—a certificate can be useful for the first part (by obviating the need for a search) but not, it would seem, for the second. The lack of symmetry between "yes" and "no" answers may at first be troubling, but the reader should keep in mind that the notion of a certificate is certainly not an algorithmic one. A certificate is something that we chance upon or are given by an oracle—it exists but may not be derivable efficiently. Hence the asymmetry is simply that of chance: in order to answer "yes," it suffices to be lucky (to find one satisfactory solution), but in order to answer "no," we must be thorough and check all possible structures for failure.

Certificates and Nondeterminism

Classes of complexity based on the use of certificates, that is, defined by a bound placed on the time or space required to verify a given certificate, correspond to nondeterministic classes. Before explaining why certificates and nondeterminism are equivalent, let us briefly define some classes of complexity by using the certificate paradigm.

Succinct and easily verifiable certificates of correctness for "yes" in-stances are characteristic of the class of decision problems known as NP.

Definition 6.7 A decision problem belongs to NP if there exists a Turing machine T and a polynomial $p(\ )$ such that an instance x of the problem is a "yes" instance if and only if there exists a string c_x (the certificate) of length not exceeding $p(|x|)$ such that T, run with x and c_x as inputs, returns "yes" in no more than $p(|x|)$ steps. □

(For convenience, we shall assume that the certificate is written to the left of the initial head position.) The certificate is succinct, since its length is polynomially bounded, and easily verified, since this can be done in polynomial time. (The requirement that the certificate be succinct is, strictly speaking, redundant: since the Turing machine runs for at most $p(|x|)$ steps, it can look at no more than $p(|x|)$ tape squares, so that at most $p(|x|)$ characters of the certificate are meaningful in the computation.) While each distinct "yes" instance may well have a distinct certificate, the certificate-checking Turing machine T and its polynomial time bound $p(\,)$ are unique for the problem. Thus a "no" instance of a problem in NP simply does not have a certificate easily verifiable by any Turing machine that meets the requirements for the "yes" instances; in contrast, for a problem not in NP, there does not even exist such a Turing machine.

Exercise 6.8 Verify that NP is closed under polynomial-time transformations.   □

It is easily seen that P is a subset of NP. For any problem in P, there exists a Turing machine which, when started with x as input, returns "yes" or "no" within polynomial time. In particular, this Turing machine, when given a "yes" instance and an arbitrary (since it will not be used) certificate, returns "yes" within polynomial time. A somewhat more elaborate result is the following.

Theorem 6.4 NP is a subset of Exp.   □

Proof. Exponential time allows a solution by exhaustive search of any problem in NP as follows. Given a problem in NP—that is, given a problem, its certificate-checking Turing machine, and its polynomial bound—we enumerate all possible certificates, feeding each in turn to the certificate-checking Turing machine, until either the machine answers "yes" or we have exhausted all possible certificates. The key to the proof is that all possible certificates are succinct, so that they exist "only" in exponential number. Specifically, if the tape alphabet of the Turing machine has d symbols (including the blank) and the polynomial bound is described by $p(\,)$, then an instance x has a total of $d^{p(|x|)}$ distinct certificates, each of length $p(|x|)$. Generating them all requires time proportional to $p(|x|) \cdot d^{p(|x|)}$, as does checking them all (since each can be checked in no more than $p(|x|)$ time). Since $p(|x|) \cdot d^{p(|x|)}$ is bounded by $2^{q(|x|)}$ for a suitable choice of polynomial q, any problem in NP has a solution algorithm requiring at most exponential time.   Q.E.D.

Each potential certificate defines a separate computation of the underlying deterministic machine; the power of the NP machine lies in being able to guess which computation path to choose.

Thus we have $P \subseteq NP \subseteq Exp$, where at least one of the two containments is proper, since we have $P \subset Exp$; both containments are conjectured to be proper, although no one has been able to prove or disprove this conjecture. While proving that NP is contained in Exp was simple, no equivalent result is known for E. We know that E and NP are distinct classes, simply because the latter is closed under polynomial transformations while the former is not. However, the two classes could be incomparable or one could be contained in the other—and any of these three outcomes is consistent with our state of knowledge.

The class NP is particularly important in complexity theory. The main reason is simply that almost all of the hard, yet "reasonable," problems encountered in practice fall (when in their decision version) in this class. By "reasonable" we mean that, although hard to solve, these problems admit concise solutions (the certificate is essentially a solution to the search version), solutions which, moreover, are easy to verify—a concise solution would not be very useful if we could not verify it in less than exponential time.[5] Another reason, of more importance to theoreticians than to practitioners, is that it embodies an older and still unresolved question about the power of nondeterminism.

The acronym NP stands for "nondeterministic polynomial (time)"; the class was first characterized in terms of nondeterministic machines—rather than in terms of certificates. In that context, a decision problem is deemed to belong to NP if there exists a nondeterministic Turing machine that recognizes the "yes" instances of the problem in polynomial time. Thus we use the convention that the charges in time and space (or any other resource) incurred by a nondeterministic machine are just those charges that a deterministic machine would have incurred along the least expensive accepting path.

This definition is equivalent to ours. First, let us verify that any problem, the "yes" instances of which have succinct certificates, also has a nondeterministic recognizer. Whenever our machine reads a tape square where the certificate has been stored, the nondeterministic machine is faced with a choice of steps—one for each possible character on the tape—and chooses the proper one—effectively guessing the corresponding character of the certificate. Otherwise, the two machines are identical. Since our certificate-checking machine takes polynomial time to verify the certificate, the nondeterministic machine also requires no more than polynomial time to accept the instance. (This idea of guessing the certificate is yet another possible characterization of nondeterminism.) Conversely, if a decision problem is recognized in polynomial time by a nondeterministic machine, then it has a certificate-checking machine and each of its "yes" instances

---

[5]A dozen years ago, a chess magazine ran a small article about some unnamed group at M.I.T. that had allegedly run a chess-solving routine on some machine for several years and finally obtained the solution: White has a forced win (not unexpected), and the opening move should be Pawn to Queen's Rook Four (a never-used opening that any chess player would scorn, it had just the right touch of bizarreness). The article was a hoax, of course. Yet, even if it had been true, who would have trusted it?

has a succinct certificate. The certificate is just the sequence of moves made by the nondeterministic Turing machine in its accepting computation (a sequence that we know to be bounded in length by a polynomial function of the size of the instance) and the certificate-checking machine just verifies that such sequences are legal for the given nondeterministic machine. In the light of this equivalence, the proof of Theorem 6.4 takes on a new meaning: the exponential-time solution is just an exhaustive exploration of all the computation paths of the nondeterministic machine. In a sense, nondeterminism appears as an artifact to deal with existential quantifiers at no cost to the algorithm; in turn, the source of asymmetry is the lack of a similar artifact[6] to deal with universal quantifiers.

Nondeterminism is a general tool: we have already applied it to finite automata as well as to Turing machines and we just applied it to resource-bounded computation. Thus we can consider nondeterministic versions of the complexity classes defined earlier; in fact, hierarchy theorems similar to Theorems 6.2 and 6.3 hold for the nondeterministic classes. (Their proofs, however, are rather more technical, which is why we shall omit them.) Moreover, the search technique used in the proof of Theorem 6.4 can be used for any nondeterministic time class, so that we have

$$\text{DTIME}(f(n)) \subseteq \text{NTIME}(f(n)) \subseteq \text{DTIME}(c^{f(n)})$$

where we added a one-letter prefix to reinforce the distinction between deterministic and nondeterministic classes.

Nondeterministic space classes can also be defined similarly. However, of the two relations for time, one translates without change,

$$\text{DSPACE}(f(n)) \subseteq \text{NSPACE}(f(n))$$

whereas the other can be tightened considerably: going from a nondeterministic machine to a deterministic one, instead of causing an exponential increase (as for time), causes only a quadratic one.

Theorem 6.5 [Savitch] Let $f(n)$ be any fully space-constructible bound at least as large as $\log n$ everywhere; then we have $\text{NSPACE}(f) \subseteq \text{DSPACE}(f^2)$.

□

Proof. What makes this result nonobvious is the fact that a machine running in $\text{NSPACE}(f)$ could run for $O(2^f)$ steps, making choices all along

---

[6]Naturally, such an artifact has been defined: an *alternating* Turing machine has both "or" and "and" states in which existential and universal quantifiers are handled at no cost.

the way, which appears to leave room for a superexponential number of possible configurations. In fact, the number of possible configurations for such a machine is limited to $O(2^f)$, since it cannot exceed the total number of tape configurations times a constant factor.

We show that a deterministic Turing machine running in $DSPACE(f^2(n))$ can simulate a nondeterministic Turing machine running in $NSPACE(f(n))$. The simulation involves verifying, for each accepting configuration, whether this configuration can be reached from the initial one. Each configuration requires $O(f(n))$ storage space and only one accepting configuration need be kept on tape at any given time, although all $O(2^{f(n)})$ potential accepting configurations may have to be checked eventually. We can generate successive accepting configurations, for example, by generating all possible configurations at the final time step and eliminating those that do not meet the conditions for acceptance.

If accepting configuration I_a can be reached from initial configuration I_0, it can be reached in at most $O(2^{f(n)})$ steps. This number may seem too large to check, but we can use a divide-and-conquer technique to bring it under control. To check whether I_a can be reached from I_0 in at most 2^k steps, we check whether there exists some intermediate configuration I_i such that I_i can be reached from I_0 in at most 2^{k-1} steps and I_a can be reached from I_i in at most 2^{k-1} steps. Figure 6.7 illustrates this idea. The effective result, for each accepting configuration, is a tree of configurations with $O(2^{f(n)})$ leaves and height equal to $f(n)$. Intermediate configurations (such as I_i) must be generated and remembered, but, with a depth-first traversal of the tree, we need only store $\Theta(f(n))$ of them—one for every node (at every level) along the current exploration path from the root. Thus the total space required for checking one tree is $\Theta(f^2(n))$. Each accepting configuration is checked in turn, so we need only store the previous accepting configuration as we move from one tree search to the next; hence the space needed for the entire procedure is $\Theta(f^2(n))$. By Lemma 6.1, we can reduce $O(f^2(n))$ to a strict bound of $f^2(n)$, thereby proving our theorem.   Q.E.D.

The simulation used in the proof is clearly extremely inefficient in terms of time: it will run the same reachability computations over and over, whereas a time-efficient algorithm would store the result of each and look them up rather than recompute them. But avoiding any storage (so as to save on space) is precisely the goal in this simulation, whereas time is of no import.

Savitch's theorem implies $NPSPACE = PSPACE$ (and also $NEXPSPACE = EXPSPACE$), an encouragingly simple situation after the complex hierarchies of time complexity classes. On the other hand, while we have $L \subseteq NL \subseteq L^2$, both inclusions are conjectured to be proper; in fact, the polylogarithmic space hierarchy is defined by the four relationships:

$$L^k \subset L^{k+1}$$
$$NL^k \subset NL^{k+1}$$
$$L^k \subseteq NL^k$$
$$NL^k \subseteq L^{2k}$$

Fortunately, Savitch's theorem has the same consequence for PolyL as it does for PSpace and for higher space complexity classes: none of these classes differs from its nondeterministic counterpart. These results offer a particularly simple way of proving membership of a problem in PSpace or PolyL, as we need only prove that a certificate for a "yes" instance can be checked in that much space—a much simpler task than designing a deterministic algorithm that solves the problem.

Example 6.1 Consider the problem of *Function Generation*. Given a finite set S, a collection of functions, $\{f_1, f_2, \ldots, f_n\}$, from S to S, and a target function g, can g be expressed as a composition of the functions in the collection? To prove that this problem belongs to PSpace, we prove that it belongs to NPSpace. If g can be generated through composition, it can be

```
for each accepting ID I_a do
   if reachable(I_0,I_a,f(n))
     then print "yes" and stop
print "no"

function reachable(I_1,I_2,k)
   /* returns true whenever if ID I_2 is reachable
      from ID I_1 in at most 2^k steps */
   reachable = false
   if k = 0
     then reachable = transition(I_1,I_2)
     else for all ID I while not reachable do
             if reachable(I_1,I,k-1)
               then if reachable(I,I_2,k-1)
                      then reachable = true

function transition(I_1,I_2)
   /* returns true whenever ID I_2 is reachable
      from ID I_1 in at most one step */
```

Figure 6.7 The divide-and-conquer construction used in the proof of Savitch's theorem.

generated through a composition of the form

$$g = f_{i_1} \cdot f_{i_2} \cdot \ldots \cdot f_{i_k}$$

for some value of k. We can require that each successively generated function, that is, each function g_j defined by

$$g_j = f_{i_1} \cdot f_{i_2} \cdot \ldots \cdot f_{i_j}$$

for $j < k$, be distinct from all previously generated functions. (If there was a repetition, we could omit all intermediate compositions and obtain a shorter derivation for g.) There are at most $|S|^{|S|}$ distinct functions from S to S, which sets a bound on the length k of the certificate (this is obviously not a succinct certificate!); we can count to this value in polynomial space. Now our machine checks the certificate by constructing each intermediate composition g_j in turn and comparing it to the target function g. Only the previous function g_{j-1} is retained in storage, so that the extra storage is simply the room needed to store the description of three functions (the target function, the last function generated, and the newly generated function) and is thus polynomial. At the same time, the machine maintains a counter to count the number of intermediate compositions; if the counter exceeds $|S|^{|S|}$ before g has been generated, the machine rejects the input. Hence the problem belongs to NPSPACE and thus, by Savitch's theorem, to PSPACE. Devising a deterministic algorithm for the problem that runs in polynomial space would be much more difficult.   □

We now have a rather large number of time and space complexity classes. Figure 6.8 illustrates them and those interrelationships that we have established or can easily derive—such as NP ⊆ NPSPACE = PSPACE (following P ⊆ PSPACE). The one exception is the relationship NL ⊆ P; while we clearly have NL ⊆ NP (for the same reasons that we have L ⊆ P), proving NL ⊆ P is somewhat more difficult; we content ourselves for now with using the result.[7] The reader should beware of the temptation to conclude that problems in NL are solvable in polynomial time *and* $O(\log^2 n)$ space: our results imply only that they are solvable in polynomial time *or* $O(\log^2 n)$ space. In other words, given such a problem, there exists an algorithm that solves it in polynomial time (but may require polynomial space) and there exists another algorithm that solves it in $O(\log^2 n)$ space (but may not run in polynomial time).

---

[7]A simple way to prove this result is to use the completeness of *Digraph Reachability* for NL; since the problem of reachability in a directed graph is easily solved in linear time and space, the result follows. Since we have not defined NL-completeness nor proved this particular result, the reader may simply want to keep this approach in mind and use it after reading the next section and solving Exercise 7.37.

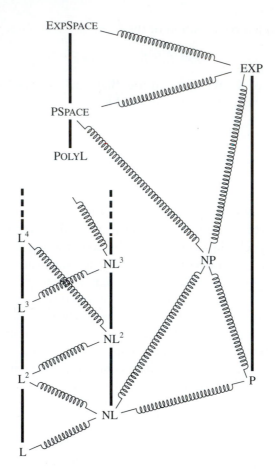

Figure 6.8   A hierarchy of space and time complexity classes.

6.3   Complete Problems

Placing a problem at an appropriate level within the hierarchy cannot be done with the same tools that we used for building the hierarchy. In order to find the appropriate class, we must establish that the problem belongs to the class and that it does not belong to any lower class. The first part is usually done by devising an algorithm that solves the problem within the resource bounds characteristic of the class or, for nondeterministic classes, by demonstrating that "yes" instances possess certificates verifiable within these bounds. The second part needs a different methodology. The hierarchy theorems cannot be used: although they separate classes by establishing the existence of problems that do not belong to a given class, they do not apply to a specific problem.

Fortunately, we already have a suitable tool: completeness and hardness. Consider for instance a problem that we have proved to belong to Exp, but for which we have been unable to devise any polynomial-time algorithm. In order to show that this problem does not belong to P, it suffices to show that it is complete for Exp under polynomial-time (Turing or many-one) reductions. Similarly, if we assume $P \neq NP$, we can show that a problem in NP does not also belong to P by proving that it is complete for NP under polynomial-time (Turing or many-one) reductions. In general, if we have two classes of complexity $\mathcal{C}_1$ and $\mathcal{C}_2$ with $\mathcal{C}_1 \subset \mathcal{C}_2$ and we want to show that some problem in $\mathcal{C}_2$ does not also belong to $\mathcal{C}_1$, it suffices to show that the problem is $\mathcal{C}_2$-complete under a reduction that leaves $\mathcal{C}_1$ unchanged (i.e., that does not enable us to solve problems outside of $\mathcal{C}_1$ within the resource bounds of $\mathcal{C}_1$). Given the same two classes and given a problem not known to belong to $\mathcal{C}_2$, we can prove that this problem does not belong to $\mathcal{C}_1$ by proving that it is $\mathcal{C}_2$-hard under the same reduction.

Exercise 6.9 Prove these two assertions. □

Thus completeness and hardness offer simple mechanisms for proving that a problem does not belong to a class.

Not every class has complete problems under a given reduction. Our first step, then, is to establish the existence of complete problems for classes of interest under suitable reductions. In proving any problem to be complete for a class, we must begin by establishing that the problem does belong to the class. The second part of the proof will depend on our state of knowledge. In proving our first problem to be complete, we must show that every problem in the class reduces to the target problem, in what is often called a *generic* reduction. In proving a succeeding problem complete, we need only show that some known complete problem reduces to it: transitivity of reductions then implies that any problem in the class reduces to our problem, by combining the implicit reduction to the known complete problem and the reduction given in our proof. This difference is illustrated in Figure 6.9. Specific reductions are often much simpler than generic ones. Moreover, as we increase our catalog of known complete problems for a class, we increase our flexibility in developing new reductions: the more complete problems we know, the more likely we are to find one that is quite close to a new problem to be proved complete, thereby facilitating the development of a reduction.

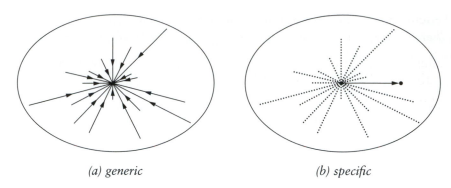

(a) generic   (b) specific

Figure 6.9   Generic versus specific reductions.

In the rest of this section, we establish a first complete problem for a number of classes of interest, beginning with NP, the most useful of these classes; in Chapter 7 we develop a catalog of useful NP-complete problems.

6.3.1   NP-Completeness: Cook's Theorem

In our hierarchy of space and time classes, the class immediately below NP is P. In order to distinguish between the two classes, we must use a reduction that requires no more than polynomial time. Since decision problems all have the same simple answer set, requiring the reductions to be many-one (rather than Turing) is not likely to impose a great burden and promises a finer discrimination. Moreover, both P and NP are clearly closed under polynomial-time many-one reductions, whereas, because of the apparent asymmetry of NP, only P is as clearly closed under the Turing version. Thus we define NP-completeness through polynomial-time transformations. (Historically, polynomial-time Turing reductions were the first used—in Cook's seminal paper; Karp then used polynomial-time transformations in the paper that really put the meaning of NP-completeness in perspective.[8] Since then, polynomial-time transformations have been most common, although logarithmic-space transformations—a further restriction—have also been used.) Cook proved in 1971 that *Satisfiability* is NP-complete. An instance of the problem is given by a collection of clauses; the question is whether these clauses can all be satisfied by a truth assignment, i.e., an assignment of the logical values *true* or *false*

---

[8]This historical sequence explains why polynomial-time many-one and Turing reductions are sometimes called Karp and Cook reductions, respectively.

to each variable. A *clause* is a logical disjunction (logical "or") of literals; a *literal* is either a variable or the logical complement of a variable.

Example 6.2 Here is a "yes" instance of *Satisfiability*: it is composed of five variables—a, b, c, d, and e—and four clauses—$\{a, c, \overline{e}\}, \{\overline{b}\}, \{b, c, d, e\}$, and $\{\overline{d}, e\}$. Using Boolean connectives, we can write it as the Boolean formula

$$(a \vee c \vee \overline{e}) \wedge (\overline{b}) \wedge (b \vee c \vee d \vee e) \wedge (\overline{d} \vee e)$$

That it is a "yes" instance can be verified by evaluating the formula for the (satisfying) truth assignment

$$a \leftarrow \text{false} \quad b \leftarrow \text{false} \quad c \leftarrow \text{true} \quad d \leftarrow \text{false} \quad e \leftarrow \text{false}$$

In contrast, here are a couple of "no" instances of *Satisfiability*. The first has one variable, a, and one clause, the empty clause; it clearly cannot be satisfied by any truth assignment to the variable a. The second has three variables—a, b, and c—and four clauses—$\{a\}, \{\overline{a}, b\}, \{\overline{a}, \overline{c}\}$, and $\{\overline{b}, c\}$. Satisfying the first clause requires that the variable a be set to "true"; satisfying the second and third clauses then requires that b be set to "true" and c be set to "false." But then the fourth clause is not satisfied, so that there is no way to satisfy all four clauses at once. ☐

Theorem 6.6 [Cook] *Satisfiability* is NP-complete. ☐

Proof. The proof is long, but not complicated; moreover, it is quite instructive. Since there is clearly no hope of reducing all problems one by one, the proof proceeds by simulating the certificate-checking Turing machine associated with each problem in NP. Specifically, we show that, given an instance of a problem in NP—as represented by the instance x and the certificate-checking Turing machine T and associated polynomial bound $p(\ )$—an instance of *Satisfiability* can be produced in polynomial time, which is satisfiable (a "yes" instance) if and only if the original instance is a "yes" instance. Since the instance is part of the certificate-checking Turing machine in its initial configuration (the instance is part of the input and thus written on the tape), it suffices to simulate a Turing machine through a series of clauses. The certificate itself is unknown: all that need be shown is that it exists; hence it need not be specified in the simulation of the initial configuration. As seen previously, simulating a Turing machine involves: (i) representing each of its configurations, as characterized by the contents of the tape, the position of the head, and the current state of the finite control—what is known as an *instantaneous description* (ID); and

(ii) ensuring that all transitions between configurations are legal. All of this must be done with the sole means of Boolean variables and clauses.

Let us first address the description of the machine at a given stage of computation. Since the machine runs for at most $p(|x|)$ steps, all variables describing the machine will exist in $p(|x|) + 1$ copies. At step i, we need a variable describing the current control state; however, the Turing machine has, say, s control states which cannot be accounted for by a single Boolean variable. Thus we set up a total of $s \cdot (p(|x|) + 1)$ state variables, $q(i, j)$, $0 \leqslant i \leqslant p(|x|)$, $1 \leqslant j \leqslant s$. If $q(i, j)$ is true, then T is in state j at step i. Of course, for each i, exactly one of the $q(i, j)$ must be true. The following clauses ensure that T is in at least some state at each step:

$$\{q(i, 1), q(i, 2), \ldots, q(i, s)\}, \quad 0 \leqslant i \leqslant p(|x|)$$

Now, at each step, and for each pair of states (k, l), $1 \leqslant k < l \leqslant s$, if T is in state k, then it cannot be in state l. This requirement can be translated as $q(i, k) \Rightarrow \overline{q(i, l)}$. Since $a \Rightarrow b$ is logically equivalent to $\bar{a} \vee b$, the following clauses will ensure that T is in a unique state at each step:

$$\{\overline{q(i, k)}, \overline{q(i, l)}\}, \quad 0 \leqslant i \leqslant p(|x|), \quad 1 \leqslant k < l \leqslant s$$

Now we need to describe the tape contents and head position. Since the machine starts with its head on square 1 (arbitrarily numbered) and runs for at most $p(|x|)$ steps, it cannot scan any square to the left of $-p(|x|) + 1$ or to the right of $p(|x|) + 1$. Hence we need only consider the squares between $-p(|x|) + 1$ and $p(|x|) + 1$ when describing the tape contents and head position. For each step and each such square, then, we set up a variable describing the head position, $h(i, j)$. If $h(i, j)$ is true, then the head is on square j at step i. As for the control state, we need clauses to ensure that the head scans some square at each step,

$$\{h(i, -p(|x|) + 1), \ldots, h(i, 0), \ldots, h(i, p(|x|) + 1)\}, \quad 0 \leqslant i \leqslant p(|x|)$$

and that it scans at most one square at each step,

$$\{\overline{h(i, k)}, \overline{h(i, l)}\}, \quad 0 \leqslant i \leqslant p(|x|), \quad -p(|x|) + 1 \leqslant k < l \leqslant p(|x|) + 1$$

The same principle applies for describing the tape contents, except that each square contains one of d tape alphabet symbols, thereby necessitating d variables for each possible square at each possible step. Hence we set up a total of $d \cdot (2p(|x|) + 1) \cdot (p(|x|) + 1)$ variables, $t(i, j, k)$, $0 \leqslant i \leqslant p(|x|)$, $-p(|x|) + 1 \leqslant j \leqslant p(|x|) + 1$, $1 \leqslant k \leqslant d$. Each square, at each step, must contain at least one symbol, which is ensured by the following clauses:

$$\{t(i, j, 1), t(i, j, 2), \ldots, t(i, j, d)\},$$
$$0 \leqslant i \leqslant p(|x|), \; -p(|x|) + 1 \leqslant j \leqslant p(|x|) + 1$$

Each tape square, at each step, may contain at most one symbol, which is in turn ensured by the following clauses:

$$\{\overline{t(i, j, k)}, \overline{t(i, j, l)}\},$$
$$0 \leqslant i \leqslant p(|x|), \; -p(|x|) + 1 \leqslant j \leqslant p(|x|) + 1, \; 1 \leqslant k < l \leqslant d$$

The group of clauses so far is satisfiable if and only if the machine is in a unique, well-defined configuration at each step. Now we must describe the machine's initial and final configurations, and then enforce its transitions. Let 1 be the start state and s the halt state; also let the first tape symbol be the blank and the last be a separator. In the initial configuration, squares $-p(|x|) + 1$ through -1 contain the certificate, square 0 contains the separator, squares 1 through $|x|$ contain the description of the instance, and squares $|x| + 1$ through $p(|x|) + 1$ are blank. The following clauses accomplish this initialization:

$$\{h(0, 1)\}, \; \{q(0, 1)\},$$
$$\{t(0, 0, d)\},$$
$$\{t(0, 1, x_1)\}, \{t(0, 2, x_2)\}, \ldots, \{t(0, |x|, x_{|x|})\},$$
$$\{t(0, j, 1)\}, \; |x| + 1 \leqslant j \leqslant p(|x|) + 1,$$

where x_i is the index of the ith symbol of string x. The halt state must be entered by the end of the computation (it could be entered earlier, but the machine can be artificially "padded" so as always to require exactly $p(|x|)$ time). At this time also, the tape must contain the code for yes, say symbol 2 in square 1, with the head on that square. These conditions are ensured by the following clauses:

$$\{h(p(|x|), 1)\}, \; \{q(p(|x|), s)\}, \; \{t(p(|x|), 1, 2)\},$$
$$\{t(p(|x|), j, 1)\}, \; -p(|x|) + 1 \leqslant j \leqslant p(|x|) + 1, \; j \neq 1$$

Now it just remains to ensure that transitions are legal. All that need be done is to set up a large number of logical implications, one for each possible transition, of the form "if T is in state q with head reading symbol t in square j at step i, then T will be in state q' at step $i + 1$, with the only tape square changed being square j." First, the following clauses ensure that, if T is not scanning square j at step i, then the contents of square j will remain unchanged at step $i + 1$ (note that the implication $(\overline{a} \wedge b) \Rightarrow c$ is translated into the disjunction $a \vee \overline{b} \vee c$):

$$\{h(i, j), \overline{t(i, j, k)}, t(i + 1, j, k)\},$$
$$0 \leqslant i < p(|x|), \; -p(|x|) + 1 \leqslant j \leqslant p(|x|) + 1, \; 1 \leqslant k \leqslant d$$

Secondly, the result of each transition (new state, new head position, and new tape symbol) is described by three clauses. These clauses are

$$\{\overline{h(i, j)}, \overline{q(i, l)}, \overline{t(i, j, k)}, q(i + 1, l')\},$$
$$\{\overline{h(i, j)}, \overline{q(i, l)}, \overline{t(i, j, k)}, h(i + 1, j')\},$$
$$\{\overline{h(i, j)}, \overline{q(i, l)}, \overline{t(i, j, k)}, t(i + 1, j, k')\},$$

for each quadruple (i, j, k, l), $0 \leqslant i < p(|x|)$, $-p(|x|) + 1 \leqslant j \leqslant p(|x|) + 1$, $1 \leqslant l \leqslant s$, and $1 \leqslant k \leqslant d$, such that T, when in state l with its head on square j reading symbol k, writes symbol k' on square j, moves its head to adjacent square j' (either $j + 1$ or $j - 1$), and enters state l'. (Note that the implication $(a \wedge b \wedge c) \Rightarrow d$ is translated into the disjunction $\overline{a} \vee \overline{b} \vee \overline{c} \vee d$.)

Table 6.1 summarizes the variables and clauses used in the complete construction. The length of each clause—with the single exception of clauses of the third type—is bounded by a constant (i.e., by a quantity that does not depend on x), while the total number of clauses produced is $O(p^3(|x|))$.

For each "yes" instance x, there exists a certificate c_x such that T, started with x and c_x on its tape, stops after $p(|x|)$ steps, leaving symbol 2 ("yes") on its tape if and only if the collection of clauses produced by our generic transformation for this instance of the problem is satisfiable. The existence of a certificate for x thus corresponds to the existence of a valid truth assignment for the variables describing the tape contents to the left of the head at step 0, such that this truth assignment is part of a satisfying truth assignment for the entire collection of clauses. Just as the certificate, c_x, is the only piece of information that the checker needs in order to answer the question deterministically in polynomial time, the contents of the tape to the left of the head is the only piece of information needed to reconstruct the complete truth assignment to all of our variables in deterministic polynomial time.

Our transformation mapped a string x and a Turing machine T with polynomial time bound $p(\ )$ to a collection of $O(p^3(|x|))$ clauses, each of constant (or polynomial) length, over $O(p^2(|x|))$ variables. Hence the size of the instance of *Satisfiability* constructed by the transformation is a polynomial function of the size of the original instance, $|x|$; it is easily verified that the construction can be carried out in polynomial time.   Q.E.D.

Thus NP-complete problems exist. (We could have established this existence somewhat more simply by solving Exercise 6.25 for NP, but the "standard" complete problem described there—a bounded version of the halting problem—is not nearly as useful as *Satisfiability*.) Assuming P $\neq$ NP, no

Table 6.1 Summary of the construction used in Cook's proof.

Variables

Name	Number	Meaning
$q(i, j)$	$s \cdot \beta$	The Turing machine is in state j at time i
$h(i, j)$	$\beta \cdot \gamma$	The head is on square j at time i
$t(i, j, k)$	$d \cdot \beta \cdot \gamma$	Tape square j contains symbol k at time i

Clauses

Clause	Number	Meaning
$\{q(i, 1), q(i, 2), \ldots, q(i, s)\}$	β	The Turing machine is in at least one state at time i
$\{\overline{q(i, k)}, \overline{q(i, l)}\}$	$\beta \cdot \dfrac{s(s-1)}{2}$	The Turing machine is in at most one state at time i
$\{h(i, -\alpha), \ldots, h(i, 0), \ldots, h(i, \alpha)\}$	β	The head sits on at least one tape square at time i
$\{\overline{h(i, k)}, \overline{h(i, l)}\}$	$\alpha \cdot \beta \cdot \gamma$	The head sits on at most one tape square at time i
$\{t(i, j, 1), t(i, j, 2), \ldots, t(i, j, d)\}$	$\beta \cdot \gamma$	Every tape square contains at least one symbol at time i
$\{\overline{t(i, j, k)}, \overline{t(i, j, l)}\}$	$\beta \cdot \gamma \cdot \dfrac{d(d-1)}{2}$	Every tape square contains at most one symbol at time i
$\{h(0, 0)\}$	1	Initial head position
$\{q(0, 1)\}$	1	Initial state
$\{t(0, 0, d)\}$ $\{t(0, 1, x_1)\}, \ldots, \{t(0, |x|, x_{|x|})\},$ $\{t(0, |x| + 1, 1)\}, \ldots, \{t(0, \beta, 1)\}$	$\beta + 1$	Initial tape contents
$\{h(\alpha, 1)\}$	1	Final head position
$\{q(\alpha, s)\}$	1	Final state
$\{t(\alpha, -\alpha, 1)\}, \ldots, \{t(\alpha, 0, 1)\},$ $\{t(\alpha, 1, 2)\},$ $\{t(\alpha, 2, 1)\}, \ldots, \{t(\alpha, \alpha, 1)\}$	γ	Final tape contents
$\{h(i, j), \overline{t(i, j, k)}, t(i + 1, j, k)\}$	$d \cdot \alpha \cdot \gamma$	From time i to time $i + 1$ no change to tape squares not under the head
$\{\overline{h(i, j)}, \overline{q(i, l)}, \overline{t(i, j, k)}, q(i + 1, l')\}$	$s \cdot d \cdot \alpha \cdot \gamma$	Next state
$\{\overline{h(i, j)}, \overline{q(i, l)}, \overline{t(i, j, k)}, h(i + 1, j')\}$	$s \cdot d \cdot \alpha \cdot \gamma$	Next head position
$\{\overline{h(i, j)}, \overline{q(i, l)}, \overline{t(i, j, k)}, t(i + 1, j, k')\}$	$s \cdot d \cdot \alpha \cdot \gamma$	Next character in tape square

with $\alpha = p(|x|)$, $\beta = p(|x|) + 1$, and $\gamma = 2p(|x|) + 1$

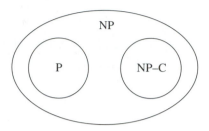

Figure 6.10   The world of NP.

NP-complete problem may belong to P (recall that if one NP-complete problem is solvable in polynomial time, then so are all problems in NP, implying P = NP), so that the picture of NP and its neighborhood is as described in Figure 6.10. Are all problems in NP either tractable (solvable in polynomial time) or NP-complete? The question is obviously trivial if P equals NP, but it is of great interest otherwise, because a negative answer implies the existence of intractable problems that are not complete for NP and thus cannot be proved hard through reduction. Unfortunately, the answer is no: unless P equals NP, there must exist problems in NP − P that are not NP-complete (a result that we shall not prove). Candidates for membership in this intermediate category include *Graph Isomorphism*, which asks whether two given graphs are isomorphic, and *Primality*, which asks whether a given natural number is prime.

Now that we have an NP-complete problem, further NP-completeness proofs will be composed of two steps: (i) a proof of membership in NP— usually a trivial task, and (ii) a polynomial-time transformation from a known NP-complete problem. Cook first proved that *Satisfiability* and *Subgraph Isomorphism* (in which the question is whether a given graph contains a subgraph isomorphic to another given graph) are NP-complete. Karp then proved that another 21 problems of diverse nature (including such common problems as *Hamiltonian Circuit*, *Set Cover*, and *Knapsack*) are also NP-complete. By now, the list of NP-complete problems has grown to thousands, taken from all areas of computer science as well as some apparently unrelated areas (such as metallurgy, chemistry, physics, biology, finance, etc.). Among those problems are several of great importance to the business community, such as *Integer Programming* and its special cases, which have been studied for many years by researchers and practitioners in mathematics, operations research, and computer science. The fact that no polynomial-time algorithm has yet been designed for any of them, coupled with the sheer size and diversity of the equivalence class of NP-complete problems, is considered strong evidence of the intractability of NP-complete problems. In other words, it is conjectured that P is a proper subset of NP, although this conjecture has resisted the most determined attempts at proof or disproof for the last twenty-five years.

If we assume P ≠ NP, a proof of NP-completeness is effectively a proof of intractability—by which, as the reader will recall, we mean worst-case complexity larger than polynomial. (Many NP-complete problems have relatively few hard cases and large numbers of easy cases. For instance, a randomly generated graph almost certainly has a Hamiltonian circuit, even though, as we shall prove in Section 7.1, deciding whether an arbitrary graph has such a circuit is NP-complete. Similarly, a randomly generated graph is almost certainly not three-colorable, even though deciding whether an arbitrary graph is three-colorable is NP-complete.) Moreover, since the decision version of a problem Turing reduces to its optimization version and (obviously) to its complement (there is no asymmetry between "yes" and "no" instances under Turing reductions: we need only complement the answer), a single proof of NP-completeness immediately yields proofs of intractability for the various versions of the problem. These considerations explain why the question "Is P equal to NP?" is the most important open problem in theoretical computer science: on its outcome depends the "fate" of a very large family of problems of considerable practical importance. A positive answer, however unlikely, would send all algorithm designers back to the drawing board; a negative answer would turn the thousands of proofs of NP-completeness into proofs of intractability, showing that, in fact, complexity theory has been remarkably successful at identifying intractable problems.

6.3.2 Space Completeness

The practical importance of the space complexity classes resides mostly in (i) the large number of PSPACE-hard problems and (ii) the difference between PolyL and P and its effect on the parallel complexity of problems. (Any problem within PolyL requires relatively little space to solve; if the problem is also tractable (in P), then it becomes a good candidate for the application of parallelism. Thus the class P ∩ PolyL is of particular interest in the study of parallel algorithms. We shall return to this topic in Section 9.4.)

Polynomial Space

With very few exceptions (see Section 6.3.3), all problems of any interest are solvable in polynomial space; yet we do not even know whether there are problems solvable in polynomial space that are not solvable in polynomial time. The conjecture, of course, is P ≠ PSPACE, since, among other things, this inequality would follow immediately from a proof of P ≠ NP. If in fact the containments described by Figure 6.8 are all strict, as is conjectured, then a proof of PSPACE-hardness is the strongest evidence of intractability we can obtain, short of a direct proof of intractability. (Even if we had P = NP, we could still have P ≠ PSPACE, so that, while NP-complete problems would become tractable, PSPACE-complete problems would remain intractable.) Indeed, PSPACE-hard problems are not "reasonable" problems in terms of our earlier definition: their solutions are not easily verifiable. The interest of the class PSPACE thus derives from the potential it offers for strong evidence of intractability. Since a large number of problems, including a majority of two-person game problems, can be proved PSPACE-hard, this interest is justified. A further reason for studying PSPACE is that it also describes exactly the class of problems solvable in polynomial time through an interactive protocol between an all-powerful prover and a deterministic checker—an interaction in which the checker seeks to verify the truth of some statement with the help of questions that it can pose to the prover. We shall return to such protocols in Section 9.5.

A study of PSPACE must proceed much like a study of NP, that is, through the characterization of complete problems. Since we cannot separate P from PSPACE, the reductions used must be of the same type as those used within NP, using at most polynomial time. As in our study of NP, we must start by identifying a basic PSPACE-complete problem. A convenient problem, known as *Quantified Boolean Formula* (or *QBF* for short), is essentially an arbitrarily quantified version of *SAT*, our basic NP-complete problem. An instance of *QBF* is given by a well-formed Boolean formula where each variable is quantified, either universally or existentially; the question is whether the resulting proposition is true. (Note the difference between a predicate and a fully quantified Boolean formula: the predicate has unbound variables and so may be true for some variable values and false for others, whereas the fully quantified formula has no unbound variables and so has a unique truth value.)

Example 6.3 In its most general form, an instance of *QBF* can make use of any of the Boolean connectives and so can be quite complex. A fairly simple example of such instances is

$$\forall a \exists b \big((\overline{a} \wedge (\forall c(b \wedge c))) \vee (\exists d \forall e(\overline{d} \Rightarrow (a \vee e))) \big)$$

You may want to spend some time convincing yourself that this is a "yes" instance—this is due to the second term in the disjunction, since we can choose to set c to "true," thereby satisfying the implication by default. More typically, instances of *QBF* take some more restricted form where the quantifiers alone are responsible for the complexity. One such form is *QSAT*, the arbitrarily quantified version of *Satisfiability*, where the quantifiers are all up front and the quantified formula is in the form prescribed for *Satisfiability*. An instance of *QSAT* is

$$\forall a \exists b \forall c \exists d \big((a \vee \overline{b}) \wedge (a \vee c) \wedge (b \vee c \vee \overline{d})\big)$$

This instance is a "no" instance: since both a and c are universally quantified, the expression should evaluate to "true" for any assignment of values to the two variables, yet it evaluates to "false" (due to the second conjunct) when both are set to "false."   □

Theorem 6.7 *QBF* is PSPACE-complete.   □

Proof. That *QBF* is in PSPACE is easily seen: we can just cycle through all possible truth assignments, verifying the truth value of the formula for each assignment. Only one truth assignment need be stored at any step, together with a counter of the number of assignments checked so far; this requires only polynomial space. Evaluating the formula for a given truth assignment is easily done in polynomial space. Thus the problem can be solved in polynomial space (albeit in exponential time). The generic reduction from any problem in PSPACE to *QBF* is done through the simulation by a suitable instance of *QBF* of the given space-bounded Turing machine, used in exactly the same manner as in the proof of Cook's theorem. Let M be a polynomial space-bounded deterministic Turing machine that decides a problem in PSPACE; let $p()$ be its polynomial bound, d its number of alphabet symbols, and s its number of states. We encode each instantaneous description of M with $d \cdot s \cdot p^2(n)$ variables: one variable for each combination of current state (s choices), current head position ($p(n)$ choices), and current tape contents ($d \cdot p(n)$ choices). For some constant c, M may make up to $c^{p(n)}$ moves on inputs of size n. Since the number of moves is potentially exponential, we use our divide-and-conquer technique. We encode the transitions in exponential intervals. For each $j, 0 \leqslant j \leqslant p(n) \cdot \log c$, we write a quantified Boolean formula $F_j(I_1, I_2)$ (where I_1 and I_2 are distinct sets of variables) that is true if and only if I_1 and I_2 represent valid instantaneous descriptions (IDs) of M and M can go in no more than 2^j steps from the ID described by I_1 to that described by I_2. Now, for input string x of length n, our quantified formula becomes

$$Q_x = \exists I_0 \exists I_f \big[INITIAL(I_0) \wedge FINAL(I_f) \wedge F_{p(n) \cdot \log c}(I_0, I_f)\big]$$

where I_0 and I_f are sets of existentially quantified variables, $INITIAL(I_0)$ asserts that I_0 represents the initial ID of M under input x, and $FINAL(I_f)$ asserts that I_f represents an accepting ID of M. This formula obviously has the desired property that it is true if and only if M accepts x. Thus it remains to show how to construct the $F_j(I_1, I_2)$ for each j, which is easily done by recursion. When j equals 0, we assert that I_1 and I_2 represent valid IDs of M and that either they are the same ID (zero step) or M can go from the first to the second in one step; these assertions are encoded with the same technique as used for Cook's proof. The obvious induction step is

$$F_j(I_1, I_2) = \exists I \big[F_{j-1}(I_1, I) \wedge F_{j-1}(I, I_2) \big]$$

but that doubles the length of the formula at each step, thereby using more than polynomial space. (Used in this way, the divide-and-conquer approach does not help since all of the steps end up being coded anyhow.) An ingenious trick allows us to use only one copy of F_{j-1}, contriving to write it as a single "subroutine" in the formula. With two auxiliary collections of variables J and K, we set up a formula which asserts that $F_{j-1}(J, K)$ must be true when we have either $J = I_1$ and $K = I$ or $J = I$ and $K = I_2$:

$$F_j(I_1, I_2) = \exists I \, \exists J \, \exists K \big[((J = I_1 \wedge K = I) \vee (J = I \wedge K = I_2)) \Rightarrow F_{j-1}(J, K) \big]$$

We can code a variable in F_j in time $O(j \cdot p(n) \cdot (\log j + \log p(n)))$, since each variable takes $O(\log j + \log p(n))$ space. Set $j = \log c \cdot p(n)$; then Q_x can be written in $O(p^2(n) \cdot \log n)$ time, so that we have a polynomial-time reduction.   Q.E.D.

As noted in Example 6.3, we can restrict QBF to Boolean formulae consisting of a conjunction of disjuncts—the arbitrarily quantified version of *Satisfiability*. An instance of this simplified problem, $QSAT$, can be written

$$\forall x_1, x_2, \ldots, x_n, \; \exists y_1, y_2, \ldots, y_n, \; \cdots, \; \forall z_1, z_2, \ldots, z_n,$$
$$P(x_1, x_2, \ldots, x_n, y_1, y_2, \ldots, y_n, \ldots, z_1, z_2, \ldots, z_n),$$

where $P()$ is a collection of clauses. The key in the formulation of this problem is the arbitrary alternation of quantifiers because, whenever two identical quantifiers occur in a row, we can simply remove the second; in particular, when all quantifiers are existential, $QSAT$ becomes our old acquaintance *Satisfiability* and thus belongs to NP.

Exercise 6.10 The proof of completeness for QBF uses only existential quantifiers; how then do the arbitrary quantifiers of $QSAT$ arise?   □

Many other PSPACE-complete problems have been identified, including problems from logic, formal languages, and automata theory and, more interestingly for us, from the area of two-person games. Asking whether the first player in a game has a winning strategy is tantamount to asking a question of the form "Is it true that there is a move for Player 1 such that, for any move of Player 2, there is a move for Player 1 such that, for any move of Player 2, ... , such that for any move of Player 2, the resulting position is a win for Player 1?" This question is in the form of a quantified Boolean formula, where each variable is quantified and the quantifiers alternate. It comes as no surprise, then, that deciding whether the first player has a winning strategy is PSPACE-hard for many games. Examples include generalizations (to arbitrarily large boards or arbitrary graphs) of Hex, Checkers, Chess, Gomoku, and Go. To be PSPACE-complete, the problem must also be in PSPACE, which puts a basic requirement on the game: it cannot last for more than a polynomial number of moves. Thus, while generalized Hex, Gomoku, and Instant Insanity are PSPACE-complete, generalized Chess, Checkers, and Go are not, unless special termination rules are adopted to ensure games of polynomial length. (In fact, without the special termination rules, all three of these games have been proved EXP-complete, that is, intractable.)

Polylogarithmic Space

The classes of logarithmic space complexity are of great theoretical interest, but our reason for discussing them is their importance in the study of parallelism. We have seen that both L and NL are subsets of P, but it is believed that L^2 and all larger classes up to and including POLYL are incomparable with P and with NP. One of the most interesting questions is whether, in fact, L equals P—the equivalent, one level lower in the complexity hierarchy, of the question "Is P equal to PSPACE?" Since the two classes cannot be separated, we resort to our familiar method of identifying complete problems within the larger class; thus we seek P-complete problems. However, since L is such a restricted class, we need a reduction with tighter resource bounds, so as to be closed within L. The solution is a *logspace* transformation: a many-one reduction that uses only logarithmic space on the off-line Turing machine model. Despite their very restricted nature, logspace transformations have the crucial property of reductions: they are transitive.

Exercise 6.11* Verify that logspace transformations are transitive. (The difficulty is that the output produced by the first machine cannot be considered to be part of the work tape of the compound machine, since that might require more than logarithmic space. The way to get around this difficulty is to trade time for space, effectively recomputing as needed to obtain small pieces of the output.) Further show that, if set A belongs to any of the complexity classes mentioned so far and set B (logspace) reduces to set A, then set B also belongs to that complexity class.   □

An immediate consequence of these properties is that, if a problem is P-complete and also belongs to L^k, then P is a subset of L^k—and thus of PolyL. In particular, if a P-complete problem belongs to L, then we have $L = P$.[9] Notice that most of our proofs of NP-completeness, including the proof of Cook's theorem, involve logspace reductions; we never stored any part of the output under construction, only a constant number of counters and indices. An interesting consequence is that, if any logspace-complete problem for NP belongs to L^k, then NP itself is a subset of L^k—a situation judged very unlikely.

The first P-complete problem, *Path System Accessibility* (PSA), was identified by Cook. An instance of *PSA* is composed of a finite set, V, of vertices, a subset $S \subseteq V$ of starting vertices, a subset $T \subseteq V$ of terminal vertices, and a relation $R \subseteq V \times V \times V$. A vertex $v \in V$ is deemed accessible if it belongs to S or if there exist accessible vertices x and y such that $(x, y, v) \in R$. The question is whether T contains any accessible vertices.

Example 6.4 Here is a simple "yes" instance of *PSA*: $V = \{a, b, c, d, e\}$, $S = \{a\}$, $T = \{e\}$, and $R = \{(a, a, b), (a, b, c), (a, b, d), (c, d, e)\}$. By applying the first triple and noting that a is accessible, we conclude that b is also accessible; by using the second and third triples with our newly acquired knowledge that both a and b are accessible, we conclude that c and d are also accessible; and by using the fourth triple, we now conclude that e, a member of the target set, is accessible.

Another "yes" instance is given by $V = \{a, b, c, d, e, f, g, h\}$, $S = \{a, b\}$, $T = \{g, h\}$, and $R = \{(a, b, c), (a, b, f), (c, c, d), (d, e, f), (d, e, g), (d, f, g), (e, f, h)\}$. Note that not every triple is involved in a successful derivation of accessibility for a target element and that some elements (including some target elements) may remain inaccessible (here e and h).   □

Theorem 6.8 *PSA is P-complete.*   □

Proof. That *PSA* is in P is obvious: a simple iterative algorithm (cycle through all possible triples to identify newly accessible vertices, adding

---

[9]The same tool could be, and is, used for attempting to separate NL from L by identifying NL-complete problems. For practical purposes, though, whether a problem belongs to L or to NL makes little difference: in either case, the problem is tractable and requires very little space. Thus we concentrate on the distinction between P and the logarithmic space classes.

them to the set when they are found, until a complete pass through all currently accessible vertices fails to produce any addition) constructs the set of all accessible vertices in polynomial time. Given an arbitrary problem in P, we must reduce it in deterministic logspace to a *PSA* problem. Let M be a deterministic Turing machine that solves our arbitrary problem in time bounded by some polynomial $p(\ )$. If M terminates in less than $p(|x|)$ time on input X, we allow the final configuration to repeat, so that all computations take exactly $p(|x|)$ steps, going through $p(|x|) + 1$ IDs. We can count to $p(|x|)$ in logarithmic space, since $\log p(|x|)$ is $O(\log |x|)$.

We shall construct V to include all possible IDs of M in a $p(|x|)$-time computation. However, we cannot provide complete instantaneous descriptions, because there is an exponential number of them. Instead the vertices of V will correspond to five-tuples, (t, i, c, h, s), which describe a step number, t; the contents of a tape square at that step, (i, c)—where i designates the square and c the character stored there; the head position at that step, h; and the control state at that step, s. We call these abbreviated instantaneous descriptions, of which there are $O(p^3(|x|))$, *short IDs*.

The initial state is described by $2p(|x|) + 1$ short IDs, one for each tape square:

$$(0, i, 1, 1, 1), \text{ for } -p(|x|) + 1 \leq i \leq 0,$$
$$(0, 1, x_1, 1, 1), (0, 2, x_2, 1, 1), \ldots , (0, |x|, x_{|x|}, 1, 1),$$
$$(0, i, 1, 1, 1), \text{ for } |x| + 1 \leq i \leq p(|x|) + 1,$$

using the same conventions as in our proof of Cook's theorem. These $2p(|x|) + 1$ IDs together form subset S, while further IDs can be made accessible through the relation. If the machine, when in state s and reading symbol c, moves to state s', replacing symbol c with symbol c' and moving its head to the right, then our relation includes, for each value of t, $0 \leq t < p(|x|)$, and for each head position, $-p(|x|) \leq h \leq p(|x|)$, the following triples of short IDs:

$$((t, h, c, h, s), (t, h, c, h, s), (t + 1, h, c', h + 1, s'))$$

indicating the changed contents of the tape square under the head at step t; and

$$((t, h, c, h, s), (t, i, j, h, s), (t + 1, i, j, h + 1, s'))$$

for each possible combination of tape square, $i \neq h$, and tape symbol, j, indicating that the contents of tape squares not under the head at step t remain unchanged at step $t + 1$.

In an accepting computation, the machine, after exactly $p(|x|)$ steps, is in its halt state, with the head on tape square 1, and with the tape empty except for square 1, which contains symbol 2. In the *PSA* problem, we shall require that *all* of the corresponding $2p(|x|) + 1$ five-tuples be accessible. Since the problem asks only that *some* vertex in T be accessible, we cannot simply place these five-tuples in T. Instead, we set up a fixed collection of additional five-tuples, which we organize, through the relation R, as a binary tree with the $2p(|x|) + 1$ five-tuples as leaves. The root of this tree is the single element of T; it becomes accessible if and only if every one of the $2p(|x|) + 1$ five-tuples describing the final accepting configuration are accessible. (This last construction is dictated by our convention of acceptance by the Turing machine. Had we instead defined acceptance as reaching a distinct accepting state at step $p(|x|)$, regardless of tape contents, this part of the construction could have been avoided.)

The key behind our entire construction is that the relation R exactly mimics the deterministic machine: for each step that the machine takes, the relation allows us to make another $2p(|x|) + 1$ five-tuples accessible, which together describe the new configuration. Since we can count to $p(|x|)$ in logarithmic space, the entire construction can be done in logarithmic space (through multiply nested loops, one for all steps, one for all tape squares, one for all head positions, one for all alphabet symbols, and one for all control states).   Q.E.D.

Our proof shows that *PSA* remains P-complete even when the set T of target elements contains a single element. Similarly, we can restrict the set S of initially accessible elements to contain exactly one vertex. Given an arbitrary instance V, $R \subseteq V \times V \times V$, $S \subseteq V$, and $T \subseteq V$ of PSA, we add one new element α to the set; add one triple (α, α, v) to R for each element $v \in S$; and make the new set of initially accessible elements consist of the single element α. Thus we can state that *PSA* remains P-complete even when restricted to a single starting element and a single target element.

Rather than set up a class of P-complete problems, we could also attempt to separate P from PolyL by setting up a class of problems logspace-complete for PolyL. However, such problems do not exist for PolyL! This rather shocking result, coming as it does after a string of complete problems for various classes, is very easy to verify. Any problem complete for PolyL would have to belong to L^k for some k. Since the problem is complete, all problems in PolyL reduce to it in logarithmic space. It then follows from Exercise 6.11 that L^k equals PolyL, which contradicts our result that L^k is a proper subset of L^{k+1}. An immediate consequence of this result is that

PolyL is distinct from P and NP: both P and NP contain logspace-complete problems, while PolyL does not.

Exercise 6.12 We can view P as the infinite union $P = \bigcup_{k \in \mathbb{N}} \text{Time}(n^k)$. Why then does the argument that we used for PolyL not apply to P? We can make a similar remark about PSpace and ask the same question.   □

6.3.3 Provably Intractable Problems

As the preceding sections evidence abundantly, very few problems have been proved intractable. In good part, this is due to the fact that all proofs of intractability to date rely on the following simple result.

Theorem 6.9 If a complexity class $\mathscr{C}$ contains intractable problems and problem A is $\mathscr{C}$-hard, then A is intractable.   □

Exercise 6.13 Prove this result.   □

What complexity classes contain intractable problems? We have argued, without proof, that Exp and ExpSpace are two such classes. If such is indeed the case, then a problem can be proved intractable by proving that it is hard for Exp or for ExpSpace.

Exercise 6.14 Use the hierarchy theorems to prove that both Exp and ExpSpace contain intractable problems.   □

The specific result obtained (i.e., the exact "flavor" of intractability that is proved) is that, given any algorithm solving the problem, there are infinitely many instances on which the running time of the algorithm is bounded below by an exponential function of the instance size. The trouble is that, under our usual assumptions regarding the time and space complexity hierarchies, this style of proof cannot lead to a proof of intractability of problems in NP or in PSpace. For instance, proving that a problem in NP is hard for Exp would imply NP = PSpace = Exp, which would be a big surprise. Even more strongly, a problem in PSpace cannot be hard for ExpSpace, since this would imply PSpace = ExpSpace, thereby contradicting Theorem 6.2.

Proving hardness for Exp or ExpSpace is done in the usual way, using polynomial-time transformations. However, exponential time or space allow such a variety of problems to be solved that there is no all-purpose, basic complete problem for either class. Many of the published intractability proofs use a generic transformation rather than a reduction from a known hard problem; many of these generic transformations, while not particularly difficult, are fairly intricate. In consequence, we do not present any proof but content ourselves with a few observations.

The first "natural" problems (as opposed to the artificial problems that the proofs of the hierarchy theorems construct by diagonalization) to be proved intractable came from formal language theory; these were quickly followed by problems in logic and algebra. Not all of these intractable problems belong to EXP or even to EXPSPACE; in fact, a famous problem due to Meyer (decidability of a logic theory called "weak monadic second-order theory of successor") is so complex that it is not even *elementary*, that is, it cannot be solved by any algorithm running in time bounded by

$$2^{2^{\cdot^{\cdot^{\cdot^{n}}}}}$$

for any fixed stack of 2s in the exponent! (Which goes to show that even intractability is a relative concept!) Many two-person games have been proved intractable (usually EXP-complete), including generalizations to arbitrary large boards of familiar games such as Chess, Checkers, and Go (without rules to prevent cycling, since such rules, as mentioned earlier, cause these problems to fall within PSPACE), as well as somewhat *ad hoc* games such as *Peek*, described in the previous section. Stockmeyer and Chandra proposed *Peek* as a basic EXP-complete game, which could be reduced to a number of other games without too much difficulty. *Peek* is nothing but a disguised version of a game on Boolean formulae: the players take turns modifying truth assignments according to certain rules until one succeeds in producing a satisfying truth assignment. Such "satisfiability" games are the natural extension to games of our two basic complete problems, *SAT* and *QSAT*. Proving that such games are EXP-complete remains a daunting task, however; since each proof is still pretty much *ad hoc*, we shall not present any.

The complexity of *Peek* derives mostly from the fact that it permits exponentially long games. Indeed, if a polynomial-time bound is placed on all plays (declaring all cut-off games to be draws), then the decision problem becomes PSPACE-complete—not much of a gain from a practical perspective, of course. (This apparent need for more than polynomial space is characteristic of all provably intractable problems; were it otherwise, the problems would be in PSPACE and thus not provably intractable—at least, not at this time.)

To a large extent, we can view most EXP-complete and NEXP-complete problems as P-complete or NP-complete problems, the instances of which are specified in an exceptionally concise manner; that is, in a sense, EXP is "succinct" P and NEXP is succinct NP. A simple example is the question of inequivalence of regular expressions: given regular expressions E_1 and

E_2, is it true that they denote different regular languages? This problem is in NP if the regular expressions cannot use Kleene closure (the so-called *star-free* regular expressions).

Proposition 6.1 *Star-Free Regular Expression Inequivalence* is in NP.   □

Proof. The checker is given a guess of a string that is denoted by the first expression but not by the second. It constructs in linear time an expression tree for each regular expression (internal nodes denote unions or concatenations, while leaves are labeled with $\emptyset$, ε, or alphabet symbols as needed). It then traverses each tree in postorder and records which prefixes of the guessed string (if any) can be represented by each subtree. When done, it has either found a way to represent the entire string or verified that such cannot be done. If the guessed string has length n, it has $n + 1$ prefixes (counting itself), so that the time needed is $O(n \cdot \max\{|E_1|, |E_2|\})$, where $|E_i|$ denotes the length of expression E_i. Now note that a regular expression that does not use Kleene closure cannot denote strings longer than itself. Indeed, the basic expressions all denote strings of length 1 or less; union does not increase the length of strings; and concatenation only sums lengths at the price of an extra symbol. Thus n cannot exceed $\max\{|E_1|, |E_2|\}$ and the verification takes polynomial time.   *Q.E.D.*

In fact, as we shall see in Section 7.1, the problem is NP-complete. Now, however, consider the same problem when Kleene closure is allowed. The closure allows us to denote arbitrarily long strings with one expression; thus it is now possible that the shortest string that is denoted by the first expression but not by the second has superpolynomial length. If such is the case, our checking mechanism will take superpolynomial time; indeed, the problem is then PSPACE-complete, even if one of the two expressions is simply Σ^*. In fact, if we allow both Kleene closure and intersection, then the inequivalence problem is complete (with respect to polynomial-time reductions) for Exp; and if we allow both Kleene closure and exponential notation (that is, we allow ourselves to write E^k for $E \cdot E \cdot \ldots \cdot E$ with k terms), then it is complete for ExpSpace.

6.4   Exercises

Exercise 6.15 Verify that constant, polynomial, and exponential functions are all time- and space-constructible.

Exercise 6.16 Prove Lemma 6.3. Pad the input so that every set recognizable in $g_1(f(n))$ space becomes, in its padded version, recognizable in $g_1(n)$

space and thus also in $g_2(n)$ space; then construct a machine to recognize the original set in $g_2(f(n))$ space by simulating the machine that recognizes the padded version in $g_2(n)$ space.

Exercise 6.17* Use the translational lemma, the hierarchy theorem for space, and Savitch's theorem to build as detailed a hierarchy as possible for nondeterministic space.

Exercise 6.18* Use the hierarchy theorems and what you know of the space and time hierarchies to prove $P \neq \text{DSPACE}(n)$. ($\text{DSPACE}(n)$ is the class of sets recognizable in linear space, a machine-independent class. This result has no bearing on whether P is a proper subset of PSPACE, since $\text{DSPACE}(n)$ is itself a proper subset of PSPACE.)

Exercise 6.19* A function f is *honest* if and only if, for every value y in the range of f, there exists some x in the domain of f with $f(x) = y$ and $|x| \leq p(|y|)$ for some fixed polynomial $p(\ )$. A function f is *polynomially computable* if and only if there exists a deterministic Turing machine M and a polynomial $p(\ )$ such that, for all x in the domain of f, M, started with x on its tape, halts after at most $p(|x|)$ steps and returns $f(x)$.
   Prove that a set is in NP if and only if it is the range of an honest, polynomially computable function. (Hint: you will need to use dovetailing in one proof. Also note that an honest function is allowed to produce arbitrarily small output on some inputs, as long as that same output is produced "honestly" for at least one input.)

Exercise 6.20* Prove that $P = NP$ implies $\text{EXP} = \text{NEXP}$. (Hint: this statement can be viewed as a special case of a translational lemma for time; thus use the same technique as in proving the translational lemma—see Exercise 6.16.)

Exercise 6.21 Verify that the reduction used in the proof of Cook's theorem can be altered (if needed) so as to use only logarithmic space, thereby proving that *Satisfiability* is NP-complete with respect to logspace reductions.

Exercise 6.22 (Refer to the previous exercise.) Most NP-complete problems can be shown to be NP-complete under logspace reductions. Suppose that someone proved that some NP-complete problem cannot be logspace-complete for NP. What would be the consequences of such a result?

Exercise 6.23 Devise a deterministic algorithm to solve the *Digraph Reachability* problem (see Exercise 7.37) in $O(\log^2 n)$ space. (Hint: trade time for space by resorting to recomputing values rather than storing them.)

Exercise 6.24* A function, $f: \mathbb{N} \to \mathbb{N}$, is said to be *subexponential* if, for any positive constant ϵ, f is $O(2^{n^{\epsilon}})$, but $2^{n^{\epsilon}}$ is not $O(f)$. Define the complexity class SUBEXP by

$$\text{SUBEXP} = \cup \{\text{TIME}(f) \mid f \text{ is subexponential}\}$$

(This definition is applicable both to deterministic and nondeterministic time.) Investigate the class SUBEXP: Can you separate it from P, NP, or EXP? How does it relate to POLYL and PSPACE? What would the properties of SUBEXP-complete problems be? What if a problem complete for some other class of interest is shown to belong to SUBEXP?

Exercise 6.25 Let $\mathscr{C}$ denote a complexity class and M a Turing machine within the class (i.e., a machine running within the resource bounds of the class). Prove that, under the obvious reduction(s), the set $\{(M, x) \mid M \in \mathscr{C} \text{ and } M \text{ accepts } x\}$ (a bounded version of the halting problem) is complete for the class $\mathscr{C}$, where $\mathscr{C}$ can be any of NL, P, NP, or PSPACE.

We saw that the halting set is complete for the recursive sets; it is intuitively satisfying to observe that the appropriately bounded version of the same problem is also complete for the corresponding subset of the recursive sets. Classes with this property are called *syntactic* classes of complexity. (Contrast with the result of Exercise 7.51.)

Exercise 6.26 The following are flawed proofs purporting to settle the issue of P versus NP. Point out the flaw in each proof.

First Proof. We prove P = NP nonconstructively by showing that, for each polynomial-time nondeterministic Turing machine, there must exist an equivalent polynomial-time deterministic Turing machine. By definition, the nondeterministic machine applies a choice function at each step in order to determine which of several possible next moves it will make. If there is a suitable move, it will choose; otherwise the choice is irrelevant. In the latter case, the deterministic machine can simulate the nondeterministic machine by using any arbitrary move from the nondeterministic machine's choice of moves. In the former case, although we do not know which is the correct next move, this move does exist; thus there exists a deterministic machine that correctly simulates the nondeterministic machine at this step. By merging these steps, we get a deterministic machine that correctly simulates the nondeterministic machine—although we do not know how to construct it.

Second Proof. We prove P $\neq$ NP by showing that any two NP-complete problems are isomorphic. (The next paragraph is perfectly correct; it gives some necessary background.)

It is easy to see that, if all NP-complete problems are isomorphic, then we must have P $\neq$ NP. (Recall that two problems are isomorphic if there exists a bijective polynomial-time transformation from one problem to the other.) Such is the case because P contains finite sets, which cannot be isomorphic to the infinite sets which make up NP-complete problems. Yet, if P were equal to NP, then all problems in NP would be NP-complete (because all problems in P are trivially P-complete under polynomial-time reductions) and hence isomorphic, a contradiction. We shall appeal to a standard result from algebra, known as the Schroeder-Bernstein theorem: given two infinite sets A and B with injective (one-to-one) functions $f: A \rightarrow B$ and $g: B \rightarrow A$, there exists a bijection (one-to-one correspondence) between A and B.

From the Schroeder-Bernstein theorem, we need only demonstrate that, given any two NP-complete problems, there exists a one-to-one (as opposed to many-one) mapping from one to the other. We know that there exists a many-one mapping from one to the other, by definition of completeness; we need only make this mapping one-to-one. This we do simply by padding: as we enumerate the instances of the first problem, we transform them according to our reduction scheme but follow the binary string describing the transformed instance by a separator and by a binary string describing the "instance number"—i.e., the sequence number of the original instance in the enumeration. This padding ensures that no two instances of the first problem get mapped to the same instance of the second problem and thus yields the desired injective map.

Third Proof. We prove $P \neq NP$ by contradiction. Assume $P = NP$. Then *Satisfiability* is in P and thus, for some k, is in $\text{TIME}(n^k)$. But every problem in NP reduces to *Satisfiability* in polynomial time, so that every problem in NP is also in $\text{TIME}(n^k)$. Therefore NP is a subset of $\text{TIME}(n^k)$ and hence so is P. But the hierarchy theorem for time tells us that there exists a problem in $\text{TIME}(n^{k+1})$ (and thus also in P) that is not in $\text{TIME}(n^k)$, a contradiction.

Exercise 6.27 We do not know whether, for decision problems within NP, Turing reductions are more powerful than many-one reductions, although such is the case for decision problems in some larger classes. Verify that a proof that Turing reductions are more powerful than many-one reductions within NP implies that P is a proper subset of NP.

Exercise 6.28 Define a *truth-table reduction* to be a Turing reduction in which (i) the oracle is limited to answering "yes" or "no" and (ii) every call to the oracle is completely specified before the first call is made (so that the calls do not depend on the result of previous calls). A *conjunctive polynomial-time reduction* between decision problems is a truth-table reduction that runs in polynomial time and that produces a "yes" instance exactly when the oracle has answered "yes" to every query. Prove that NP is closed under conjunctive polynomial-time reductions.

6.5   Bibliography

The Turing award lecture of Stephen Cook [1983] provides an excellent overview of the development and substance of complexity theory. The texts of Machtey and Young [1978] and Hopcroft and Ullman [1979] cover the fundamentals of computability theory as well as of abstract complexity theory. Papadimitriou and Steiglitz [1982] and Sommerhalder and van Westrhenen [1988] each devote several chapters to models of computation, complexity measures, and NP-completeness, while Hopcroft and Ullman [1979] provide a more detailed treatment of the theoretical foundations. Garey and Johnson [1979] wrote the classic text on NP-completeness and related subjects; in addition to a lucid presentation of the topics, their text contains a categorized and annotated list of over 300 known NP-hard problems. New developments are covered regularly by D.S. Johnson in "The NP-Completeness Column: An Ongoing Guide," which appears in the *Journal of Algorithms* and is written in the same style as the text of Garey and Johnson. The more recent text of Papadimitriou [1994] offers a modern and somewhat more advanced perspective on the field; it is the ideal text to pursue a study of complexity theory beyond the coverage offered here. In a more theoretical flavor, the conference notes of Hartmanis [1978] provide a good introduction to some of the issues surrounding the question of P vs. NP. Stockmeyer [1987] gives a thorough survey of computational complexity, while Shmoys and Tardos [1995] present a more recent survey from the perspective of discrete mathematics. The monograph of Wagner and Wechsung [1986] provides, in a very terse manner, a wealth of results in computability and complexity theory. The two-volume monograph of Balcázar, Diaz, and Gabarró [1988, 1990] offers a self-contained and comprehensive discussion of the more theoretical aspects of complexity theory. Johnson [1990] discusses the current state of knowledge regarding all of the complexity classes defined here and many, many more, while Seiferas [1990] presents a review of machine-independent complexity theory.

Time and space as complexity measures were established early; the aforementioned references all discuss such measures and how the choice of a model affects them. The notion of abstract complexity measures is due to Blum [1967]. The concept of reducibility has long been established in computability theory; Garey and Johnson mention early uses of reductions in the context of algorithms. The seminal article in complexity theory is that of Hartmanis and Stearns [1965], in which Theorem 6.2 appears; Theorem 6.3 is due to Hartmanis [1968]; Theorem 6.1 was proved by Hartmanis, Lewis, and Stearns [1965]; and Lemma 6.3 was proved by Ruby and Fischer [1965]. The analogs of Theorems 6.2 and 6.3 for

nondeterministic machines were proved by Cook [1973] and Seiferas *et al.*
[1973], then further refined, for which see Seiferas [1977] and Seiferas *et
al.* [1978]. That POLYL cannot have complete problems was first observed
by Book [1976]. The fundamental result about nondeterministic space,
Theorem 6.5, appears in Savitch [1970]. The proof that NL is a subset of
P is due to Cook [1974].

Cook's theorem (and the first definition of the class NP) appears in
Cook [1971a]; soon thereafter, Karp [1972] published the paper that really put NP-completeness in perspective, with a list of over 20 important
NP-complete problems. The idea of NP and of NP-complete problems had
been "in the air": Edmonds [1963] and Cobham [1965] had proposed very
similar concepts, while Levin [1973] independently derived Cook's result.
We follow Garey and Johnson's lead in our presentation of Cook's theorem,
although our definition of NP owes more to Papadimitriou and Steiglitz.
(The *k-th Heaviest Subset* problem used as an example for Turing reductions is adapted from their text.) The first P-complete problem, *PSA*, was
given by Cook [1970]; Jones and Laaser [1976] present a large number of
P-complete problems, while Jones [1975] and Jones *et al.* [1976] do the
same for NL-complete problems. An exhaustive reference on the subject
of P-complete problems is the text of Greenlaw *et al.* [1995]. Stockmeyer
and Meyer [1973] prove that *QBF* is PSPACE-complete; in the same paper, they also provide EXP-complete problems. The proof of intractability
of the weak monadic second order theory of successor is due to Meyer
[1975]. Stockmeyer and Chandra [1979] investigate two-person games and
provide a family of basic EXP-complete games, including the game of *Peek*.
Intractable problems in formal languages, logic, and algebra are discussed in
the texts of Hopcroft and Ullman and of Garey and Johnson. Viewing problems complete for higher complexity classes as succinct versions of problems
at lower levels of the hierarchy was proposed by, among others, Galperin
and Widgerson [1983] and studied in detail by Balcázar *et al.* [1992].

CHAPTER 7

Proving Problems Hard

In this chapter, we address the question of how to prove problems hard. As the reader should expect by now, too many of the problems we face in computing are in fact hard—when they are solvable at all. While proving a problem to be hard will not make it disappear, it will prevent us from wasting time in searching for an exact algorithm. Moreover, the same techniques can then be applied again to investigate the hardness of approximation, a task we take up in the next chapter.

We begin by completeness proofs under many-one reductions. While such tight reductions are not necessary (the more general Turing reductions would suffice to prove hardness), they provide the most information and are rarely harder to derive than Turing reductions. In Section 7.1, we present a dozen detailed proofs of NP-completeness. Such proofs are the most useful for the reader: optimization problems appear in most application settings, from planning truck routes for a chain of stores or reducing bottlenecks in a local network to controlling a robot or placing explosives and seismographs to maximize the information gathered for mineral exploration. We continue in Section 7.2 with four proofs of P-completeness. These results apply only to the setting of massively parallel computing (spectacular speed-ups are very unlikely for P-hard problems); but parallelism is growing more commonplace and the reductions themselves are of independent interest, due to the stronger resource restrictions. In Section 7.3, we show how completeness results translate to hardness and easiness results for the optimization and search versions of the same problems, touch upon the use of Turing reductions in place of many-one reductions, and explore briefly the consequences of the collapse that a proof of P = NP would cause.

7.1   Some Important NP-Complete Problems

We have repeatedly stated that the importance of the class NP is due to the large number of common problems that belong to it and, in particular, to the large number of NP-complete problems. In this section, we give a sampling of such problems, both as an initial catalog and as examples of specific reductions.

The very reason for which *Satisfiability* was chosen as the target of our generic transformation—its great flexibility—proves somewhat of a liability in specific reductions, which work in the other direction. Indeed, the more restricted a problem (the more rigid its structure and that of its solutions), the easier it is to reduce it to another problem: we do not have to worry about the effect of the chosen transformation on complex, unforeseen structures. Thus we start by proving that a severely restricted form of the problem, known as *Three-Satisfiability* (*3SAT* for short), is also NP-complete. In reading the proof, recall that a proof of NP-completeness by specific reduction is composed of two parts: (i) a proof of membership in NP and (ii) a polynomial-time transformation from the known NP-complete problem to the problem at hand, such that the transformed instance admits a solution if and only if the original instance does.

Theorem 7.1 *3SAT* is NP-complete. (*3SAT* has the same description as the original satisfiability problem, except that each clause is restricted to exactly three literals, no two of which are derived from the same variable.)   □

Proof. That *3SAT* is in NP is an immediate consequence of the membership of *SAT* in NP, since the additional check on the form of the input is easily carried out in polynomial time. Thus we need only exhibit a polynomial-time transformation from *SAT* to *3SAT* in order to complete our proof.

We set up one or more clauses in the *3SAT* problem for each clause in the *SAT* problem; similarly, for each variable in the *SAT* problem, we set up a corresponding variable in the *3SAT* problem. For convenience and as a reminder of the correspondence, we name these variables of *3SAT* by the same names used in the *SAT* instance; thus we use x, y, z, and so forth, in both the original and the transformed instances. The reader should keep in mind, however, that the variables of *3SAT*, in spite of their names, are completely different from the variables of *SAT*. We *intend* a correspondence but cannot assume it; we have to *verify* that such a correspondence indeed exists.

Consider an arbitrary clause in *SAT*: three cases can arise. In the first case, the clause has exactly three literals, derived from three different variables, in which case an identical clause is used in the *3SAT* problem. In the second case, the clause has two or fewer literals. Such a clause can be "padded" by introducing new, redundant variables and transforming the one clause into two or four new clauses as follows. If clause c has only one variable, say $c = \{\hat{x}\}$ (where the symbol $\hat{}$ indicates that the variable may or may not be complemented), we introduce two new variables, call them z_{c1} and z_{c2}, and transform c into four clauses:

$$\{\hat{x}, z_{c1}, z_{c2}\} \quad \{\hat{x}, \bar{z}_{c1}, z_{c2}\} \quad \{\hat{x}, z_{c1}, \bar{z}_{c2}\} \quad \{\hat{x}, \bar{z}_{c1}, \bar{z}_{c2}\}$$

(If the clause has only two literals, we introduce only one new variable and transform the one clause into two clauses in the obvious manner.) The new variables are clearly redundant, that is, their truth value in no way affects the satisfiability of the new clauses.

In the third case, the clause has more than three literals. Such a clause must be partitioned into a number of clauses of three literals each. The idea here is to place each literal in a separate clause and "link" all clauses by means of additional variables. (The first two and the last two literals are kept together to form the first and the last links in the chain.) Let clause c have k literals, say $\{\hat{x}_1, \ldots, \hat{x}_k\}$. Then we introduce $(k - 3)$ new variables, $z_{c1}, \ldots, z_{c(k-3)}$, and transform c into $(k - 2)$ clauses:

$$\{\hat{x}_1, \hat{x}_2, z_{c1}\} \quad \{\bar{z}_{c1}, \hat{x}_3, z_{c2}\} \quad \{\bar{z}_{c2}, \hat{x}_4, z_{c3}\} \quad \cdots \quad \{\bar{z}_{c(k-3)}, \hat{x}_{k-1}, \hat{x}_k\}$$

This collection of new clauses is equivalent to the single original clause. To see this, first note that a satisfying truth assignment for the original clause (i.e., one that sets at least one of the literals $\hat{x}_i$ to true) can be extended to a satisfying truth assignment for the collection of transformed clauses by a suitable choice of truth values for the extra variables. Specifically, assume that $\hat{x}_i$ was set to true; then we set all z_{cj}, $j \geq i - 1$, to false and all z_{cl}, $l < i - 1$, to true. Then each of the transformed clauses has a true $\hat{z}$ literal in it, except the clause that has the literal $\hat{x}_i$; thus all transformed clauses are satisfied. Conversely, assume that all literals in the original clause are set to false; then the collection of transformed clauses reduces to

$$\{z_{c1}\} \quad \{\bar{z}_{c1}, z_{c2}\} \quad \{\bar{z}_{c2}, z_{c3}\} \quad \cdots \quad \{\bar{z}_{c(k-4)}, z_{c(k-3)}\} \quad \{\bar{z}_{c(k-3)}\}$$

But this collection is a falsehood, as no truth assignment to the z variables can satisfy it. (Each two-literal clause is an implication; together these implications form a chain that resolves to the single implication $z_{c1} \Rightarrow z_{c(k-3)}$. Combining this implication with the first clause by using *modus ponens*, we are left with two clauses, $\{z_{c(k-3)}\}$ and $\{\bar{z}_{c(k-3)}\}$, a contradiction.)

Table 7.1   The structure of a proof of NP-completeness.

- *Part 1*: Prove that the problem at hand is in NP.
- *Part 2*: Reduce a known NP-complete problem to the problem at hand.
  - Define the reduction: how is a typical instance of the known NP-complete problem mapped to an instance of the problem at hand?
  - Prove that the reduction maps a "yes" instance of the NP-complete problem to a "yes" instance of the problem at hand.
  - Prove that the reduction maps a "no" instance of the NP-complete problem to a "no" instance of the problem at hand. This part is normally done through the contrapositive: given a transformed instance that is a "yes" instance of the problem at hand, prove that it had to be mapped from a "yes" instance of the NP-complete problem.
  - Verify that the reduction can be carried out in polynomial time.

Hence the instance of the *3SAT* problem resulting from our transformation admits a solution if and only if the original instance of the *SAT* problem did. It remains only to verify that the transformation can be done in polynomial time. In fact, it can be done in linear time, scanning clauses one by one, removing duplicate literals, and either dropping, copying, or transforming each clause as appropriate (transforming a clause produces a collection of clauses, the total size of which is bounded by a constant multiple of the size of the original clause).   *Q.E.D.*

In light of this proof, we can refine our description of a typical proof of NP-completeness, obtaining the structure described in Table 7.1.

3SAT is quite possibly the most important NP-complete problem from a theoretical standpoint, since far more published reductions start from *3SAT* than from any other NP-complete problem. However, we are not quite satisfied yet: *3SAT* is ill-suited for reduction to problems presenting either inherent symmetry (there is no symmetry in *3SAT*) or an extremely rigid solution structure (*3SAT* admits solutions that satisfy one, two, or three literals per clause—quite a lot of variability). Hence we proceed by proving that two even more restricted versions of *Satisfiability* are also NP-complete:

- *One-in-Three-3SAT (1in3SAT)* has the same description as *3SAT*, except that a satisfying truth assignment must set exactly one literal to true in each clause.
- *Not-All-Equal 3SAT (NAE3SAT)* has the same description as *3SAT*, except that a satisfying truth assignment may not set all three literals

of any clause to true. This constraint results in a symmetric problem: the complement of a satisfying truth assignment is a satisfying truth assignment.

A further restriction of these two problems leads to their *positive* versions: a positive instance of a problem in the *Satisfiability* family is one in which no variable appears in complemented form. While *Positive 3SAT* is a trivial problem to solve, we shall prove that both *Positive 1in3SAT* and *Positive NAESAT* are NP-complete. With these two problems as our departure points, we shall then prove that the following eight problems, each selected for its importance as a problem or for a particular feature demonstrated in the reduction, are NP-complete:

- *Maximum Cut (MxC)*: Given an undirected graph and a positive integer bound, can the vertices be partitioned into two subsets such that the number of edges with endpoints in both subsets is no smaller than the given bound?
- *Graph Three-Colorability (G3C)*: Given an undirected graph, can it be colored with three colors?
- *Partition*: Given a set of elements, each with a positive integer size, and such that the sum of all element sizes is an even number, can the set be partitioned into two subsets such that the sum of the sizes of the elements of one subset is equal to that of the other subset?
- *Hamiltonian Circuit (HC)*: Given an undirected graph, does it have a Hamiltonian circuit?
- *Exact Cover by Three-Sets (X3C)*: Given a set with $3n$ elements for some natural number n and a collection of subsets of the set, each of which contains exactly three elements, do there exist in the collection n subsets that together cover the set?
- *Vertex Cover (VC)*: Given an undirected graph of n vertices and a positive integer bound k, is there a subset of at most k vertices that covers all edges (i.e., such that each edge has at least one endpoint in the chosen subset)?
- *Star-Free Regular Expression Inequivalence (SF-REI)*: Given two regular expressions, neither one of which uses Kleene closure, is it the case that they denote different languages? (Put differently, does there exist a string x that belongs to the language denoted by one expression but not to the language denoted by the other?)
- *Art Gallery (AG)*: Given a simple polygon, P, of n vertices and a positive integer bound, $B \leq n$, can at most B "guards" be placed at vertices of the polygon in such a way that every point in the interior of the polygon is visible to at least one guard? (A simple polygon is

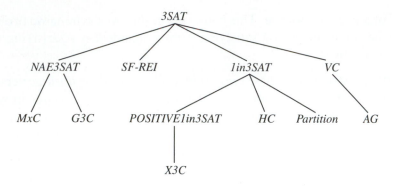

Figure 7.1   The scheme of reductions for our basic proofs of NP-completeness.

one with a well-defined interior; a point is visible to a guard if and only if the line segment joining the two does not intersect any edge of the polygon.)

Notice that *MxC*, *G3C*, and *Partition* are symmetric in nature (the three colors or the two subsets can be relabeled at will), while *HC* and *X3C* are quite rigid (the number of edges or subsets in the solution is fixed, and so is their relationship), and *VC*, *SF-REI*, and *AG* are neither (in the case of *VC*, for instance, the covering subset is distinguished from its complement—hence no symmetry—and each edge can be covered by one or two vertices—hence no rigidity). These observations suggest reducing *NAE3SAT* to the first three problems, *1in3SAT* to the next two, and *3SAT* to the last three. In fact, with the exception of *Partition*, we proceed exactly in this fashion. Our scheme of reductions is illustrated in Figure 7.1.

Theorem 7.2   *One-in-Three 3SAT is NP-complete.*   □

Proof. Since *3SAT* is in NP, so is *1in3SAT*: we need to make only one additional check per clause, to verify that exactly one literal is set to true.

Our transformation takes a *3SAT* instance and adds variables to give more flexibility in interpreting assignments. Specifically, for each original clause, say $\{\hat{x}_{i1}, \hat{x}_{i2}, \hat{x}_{i3}\}$, we introduce four new variables, a_i, b_i, c_i, and d_i, and produce three clauses:

$$\{\overline{\hat{x}}_{i1}, a_i, b_i\} \quad \{b_i, \hat{x}_{i2}, c_i\} \quad \{c_i, d_i, \overline{\hat{x}}_{i3}\}$$

Hence our transformation takes an instance with n variables and k clauses and produces an instance with $n + 4k$ variables and $3k$ clauses; it is easily carried out in polynomial time.

We claim that the transformed instance admits a solution if and only if the original instance does. Assume that the transformed instance admits a solution—in which exactly one literal per clause is set to true. Observe that such a solution cannot exist if all three original literals are set to false. (The first and last literal are complemented and hence true in the transformed instance, forcing the remaining literals in their clauses to false. However, this sets all four additional variables to false, so that the middle clause is not satisfied.) Hence at least one of the original literals must be true and thus any solution to the transformed instance corresponds to a solution to the original instance.

Conversely, assume that the original instance admits a solution. If the middle literal is set to true in such a solution, then we set b_i and c_i to false in the transformed instance and let $a_i = \hat{x}_{i1}$ and $d_i = \hat{x}_{i3}$. If the middle literal is false but the other two are true, we may set a_i and c_i to true and b_i and d_i to false. Finally, if only the first literal is true (the case for the last literal is symmetric), we set b_i to true and a_i, c_i, and d_i to false. In all cases, a solution for the original instance implies the existence of a solution for the transformed instance. *Q.E.D.*

Theorem 7.3 *Not-All-Equal 3SAT* is NP-complete. □

Proof. Since *3SAT* is in NP, so is *NAE3SAT*: we need to make only one additional check per clause, to verify that at least one literal was set to false.

Since the complement of a satisfying truth assignment is also a satisfying truth assignment, we cannot distinguish true from false for each variable; in effect, a solution to *NAE3SAT* is not so much a truth assignment as it is a partition of the variables. Yet we must make a distinction between true and false in the original problem, *3SAT*; this requirement leads us to encode truth values. Specifically, for each variable, x, in *3SAT*, we set up two variables in *NAE3SAT*, say x' and x''; assigning a value of true to x will correspond to assigning different truth values to the two variables x' and x''. Now we just write a Boolean formula that describes, in terms of the new variables, the conditions under which each original clause is satisfied. For example, the clause $\{x, \overline{y}, z\}$ gives rise to the formula

$$(x' \wedge \overline{x}'') \vee (\overline{x}' \wedge x'') \vee (y' \wedge y'') \vee (\overline{y}' \wedge \overline{y}'') \vee (z' \wedge \overline{z}'') \vee (\overline{z}' \wedge z'')$$

Since we need a formula in conjunctive form, we use distributivity and expand the disjunctive form given above; in doing so, a number of terms cancel out (because they include the disjunction of a variable and its complement) and we are left with the eight clauses

$\{x', x'', y', \overline{y}'', z', z''\} \{x', x'', y', \overline{y}'', \overline{z}', \overline{z}''\} \{x', x'', \overline{y}', y'', z', z''\} \{x', x'', \overline{y}', y'', \overline{z}', \overline{z}''\}$
$\{\overline{x}', \overline{x}'', y', \overline{y}'', z', z''\} \{\overline{x}', \overline{x}'', y', \overline{y}'', \overline{z}', \overline{z}''\} \{\overline{x}', \overline{x}'', \overline{y}', y'', z', z''\} \{\overline{x}', \overline{x}'', \overline{y}', y'', \overline{z}', \overline{z}''\}$

It only remains to transform these six-literal clauses into three-literal clauses, using the same mechanism as in Theorem 7.1. The eight clauses of six literals become transformed into thirty-two clauses of three literals; three additional variables are needed for each of the eight clauses, so that a total of twenty-four additional variables are required for each original clause. This completes the transformation. An instance of *3SAT* with n variables and k clauses gives rise to an instance of *NAE3SAT* with $32k$ clauses and $2n + 24k$ variables. The transformation is easily accomplished in polynomial time.

The construction guarantees that a solution to the transformed instance implies the existence of a solution to the original instance. An exhaustive examination of the seven possible satisfying assignments for an original clause shows that there always exists an assignment for the additional variables in the transformed clauses that ensures that each transformed clause has one true and one false literals.   *Q.E.D.*

NAE3SAT may be viewed as a partition problem. Given n variables and a collection of clauses over these variables, how can the variables be partitioned into two sets so that each clause includes a variable assigned to each set? In this view, it becomes clear that a satisfying truth assignment for the problem is one which, in each clause, assigns "true" to one literal, "false" to another, and "don't care" to a third.

Now we have three varieties of *3SAT* for use in reductions. Three more are the subject of the following exercise.

Exercise 7.1

1. Prove that *Positive 1in3SAT* is NP-complete (use a transformation from *1in3SAT*).
2. Repeat for *Positive NAE3SAT*.
3. Prove that *Monotone 3SAT* is NP-complete; an instance of this problem is similar to one of *3SAT*, except that the three literals in a clause must be all complemented or all uncomplemented.
4. Prove that *Maximum Two-Satisfiability (Max2SAT)* is NP-complete. An instance of *Max2SAT* is composed of a collection of clauses with two literals each and a positive integer bound k no larger than the number of clauses. The question is "Does there exist a truth assignment such that at least k of the clauses are satisfied?"   □

While many reductions start with a problem "similar" to the target problem, the satisfiability problems provide convenient, all-purpose starting points. In other words, our advice to the reader is: first attempt to identify a close cousin of your problem (using your knowledge and reference lists such as those appearing in the text of Garey and Johnson or in Johnson's

Table 7.2 The three steps in proving membership in NP.

- Assess the size of the input instance in terms of natural parameters.
- Define a certificate and the checking procedure for it.
- Analyze the running time of the checking procedure, using the same natural parameters, then verify that this time is polynomial in the input size.

column in the *Journal of Algorithms*), but do not spend excessive time in your search—if your search fails, use one of the six versions of *3SAT* described earlier. Of course, you must start by establishing that the problem does belong to NP; such proofs of membership can be divided into three steps, as summarized in Table 7.2.

The following proofs will show some of the approaches to transforming satisfiability problems into graph and set problems.

Theorem 7.4 *Maximum Cut* is NP-complete. □

Proof. Membership in NP is easily established. Given a candidate partition, we can examine each edge in turn and determine whether it is cut; keeping a running count of the number of cut edges, we finish by comparing this count with the given bound. The size of the input is the size of the graph, $O(|E| \log |V|)$, plus the bound, $O(\log B)$; scanning the edges, determining whether each is cut, and counting the cut ones takes $O(|E|)$ time, which is clearly polynomial in the input size.

We transform *NAE3SAT* into *MxC*. Since the vertices must be partitioned into two subsets, we can use the partitioning for ensuring a legal truth assignment. This suggests using one edge connecting two vertices (the "true" and the "false" vertices) for each variable; we shall ensure that any solution cuts each such edge. Of the three literals in each clause, we want one or two to be set to true and the other(s) to false; this suggests using a triangle for each clause, since a triangle can only be cut with two vertices on one side and one on the other—provided, of course, that we ensure that each triangle be cut.

Unfortunately, we cannot simply set up a pair of vertices for each variable, connect each pair (to ensure a legal truth assignment), and connect in a triangle the vertices corresponding to literals appearing together in a clause (to ensure a satisfying truth assignment), because the result is generally not a graph due to the creation of multiple edges between the same two vertices. The problem is due to the interaction of the triangles corresponding to clauses. Another aspect of the same problem is that

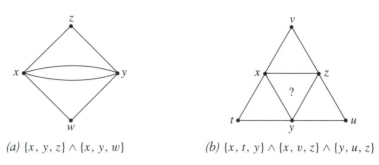

(a) $\{x, y, z\} \wedge \{x, y, w\}$ (b) $\{x, t, y\} \wedge \{x, v, z\} \wedge \{y, u, z\}$

Figure 7.2   Problems with the naïve transformation for MxC.

triangles that do not correspond to any clause but are formed by edges derived from three "legitimate" triangles may appear in the graph. Each aspect is illustrated in Figure 7.2.

The obvious solution is to keep these triangles separate from each other and thus also from the single edges that connect each uncomplemented literal to its complement. Such separation, however, leads to a new problem: consistency. Since we now have a number of vertices corresponding to the same literal (if a literal appears in k clauses, we have $k + 1$ vertices corresponding to it), we need to ensure that all of these vertices end up on the same side of the partition together. To this end, we must connect all of these vertices in some suitable manner. The resulting construction is thus comprised of three parts, which are characteristic of transformations derived from a satisfiability problem: a part to ensure that the solution corresponds to a legal truth assignment; a part to ensure that the solution corresponds to a satisfying truth assignment; and a part to ensure such consistency in the solution as will match consistency in the assignment of truth values.

Specifically, given an instance of $NAE3SAT$ with n variables and k clauses, we transform it in polynomial time into an instance of MxC with $2n + 3k$ vertices and $n + 6k$ edges as follows. For each variable, we set up two vertices (corresponding to the complemented and uncomplemented literals) connected by an edge. For each clause, we set up a triangle, where each vertex of the triangle is connected by an edge to the complement of the corresponding "literal vertex." Finally, we set the minimum number of edges to be cut to $n + 5k$. This transformation is clearly feasible in polynomial time. Figure 7.3 shows the result of the transformation applied to a simple instance of $NAE3SAT$.

Given a satisfying truth assignment for the instance of $NAE3SAT$, we put all vertices corresponding to true literals on one side of the partition and

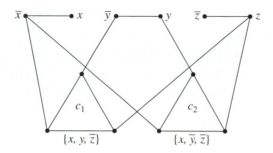

Figure 7.3   The construction used in Theorem 7.4.

all others on the other side. Since the truth assignment is valid, each edge between a literal and its complement is cut, thereby contributing a total of n to the cut sum. Since the truth assignment is a solution, each triangle is cut (not all three vertices may be on the same side, as this would correspond to a clause with three false or three true literals), thereby contributing a total of $5k$ to the cut sum. Hence we have a solution to MxC.

Conversely, observe that $n + 5k$ is the maximum attainable cut sum: we cannot do better than cut each clause triangle and each segment between complementary literals. Moreover, the cut sum of $n + 5k$ can be reached only by cutting all triangles and segments. (If all three vertices of a clause triangle are placed on the same side of the partition, at most three of the six edges associated with the clause can be cut.) Hence a solution to MxC yields a solution to $NAE3SAT$: cutting each segment ensures a valid truth assignment and cutting each triangle ensures a satisfying truth assignment.   *Q.E.D.*

It is worth repeating that instances produced by a many-one reduction need not be representative of the target problem. As we saw with *Satisfiability* and as Figure 7.3 makes it clear for *Maximum Cut*, the instances produced are often highly specialized. Referring back to Figure 6.2, we observe that the subset $f(A)$ of instances produced through the transformation, while infinite, may be a very small and atypical sample of the set B of all instances of the target problem. In effect, the transformation f identifies a collection $f(A)$ of hard instances of problem B; these hard instances suffice to make problem B hard, but we have gained no information about the instances in $B - f(A)$.

Setting up triangles corresponding to clauses is a common approach when transforming satisfiability problems to graph problems. The next proof uses the same technique.

Theorem 7.5 *Graph Three-Colorability* is NP-complete.   □

Proof. Membership in NP is easily established. Given a coloring, we need only verify that at most three colors are used, then look at each edge in turn, verifying that its endpoints are colored differently. Since the input (the graph) has size $O(|E| \log |V|)$ and since the verification of a certificate takes $O(|V| + |E|)$ time, the checker runs in polynomial time.

Transforming a satisfiability problem into *G3C* presents a small puzzle: from a truth assignment, which "paints" each variable in one of two "colors," how do we go to a coloring using *three* colors? (This assumes that we intend to make vertices correspond to variables and a coloring to a truth assignment, which is surely not the only way to proceed but has the virtue of simplicity.) One solution is to let two of the colors correspond to truth values and use the third for other purposes—or for a "third" truth value, namely the "don't care" encountered in *NAE3SAT*.

Starting from an instance of *NAE3SAT*, we set up a triangle for each variable and one for each clause. All triangles corresponding to variables have a common vertex, which preempts one color, so that the other two vertices of each such triangle, corresponding to the complemented and uncomplemented literals, must be assigned two different colors chosen from a set of two. Assigning these two colors corresponds to a legal truth assignment. To ensure that the only colorings possible correspond to satisfying truth assignments, we connect each vertex of a clause triangle to the corresponding (in this case, the complement) literal vertex. Each such edge forces its two endpoints to use different colors. The reader can easily verify that a clause triangle can be colored if and only if not all three of its corresponding literal vertices have been given the same color, that is, if and only if not all three literals in the clause have been assigned the same truth value. Thus the transformed instance admits a solution if and only if the original instance does.

The transformation takes an instance with n variables and k clauses and produces a graph with $2n + 3k + 1$ vertices and $3(n + 2k)$ edges; it is easily done in polynomial time. A sample transformation is illustrated in Figure 7.4.   *Q.E.D.*

Theorem 7.6 *Vertex Cover* is NP-complete.   □

Exercise 7.2 Prove this theorem by reducing *3SAT* to *VC*, using a construction similar to one of those used above.   □

Not all proofs of NP-completeness involving graphs are as simple as the previous three. We now present a graph-oriented proof of medium difficulty that requires the design of a graph fragment with special properties. Such

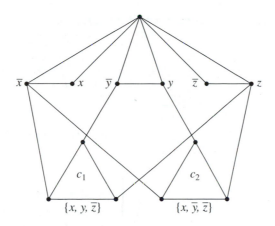

Figure 7.4   The construction used in Theorem 7.5.

fragments, called *gadgets*, are typical of many proofs of NP-completeness for graph problems. How to design a gadget remains quite definitely an art. Ours is a rather simple piece; more complex gadgets have been used for problems where the graph is restricted to be planar or to have a bounded degree; Section 8.1 presents several such gadgets.

Theorem 7.7 *Hamiltonian Circuit* is NP-complete.   □

Proof. Membership in NP is easily established. Given a guess at the circuit (that is, a permutation of the vertices), it suffices to scan each vertex in turn, verifying that an edge exists between the current vertex and the previous one (and verifying that an edge exists between the last vertex and the first).

In order to transform a problem involving truth assignments to one involving permutation of vertices, we need to look at our problem in a different light. Instead of requiring the selection of a permutation of vertices, we can look at it as requiring the selection of certain edges. Then a truth assignment can be regarded as the selection of one of two edges; similarly, setting exactly one out of three literals to true can be regarded as selecting one out of three edges. Forcing a selection in the *HC* problem can then be done by placing all of these selection pieces within a simple loop, adding vertices of degree 2 to force any solution circuit to travel along the loop, as illustrated in Figure 7.5.

It remains somehow to tie up edges representing clause literals and edges representing truth assignments. Ideal for this purpose would be a gadget that acts as a logical *exclusive-OR* (XOR) between edges. With such a tool, we could then set up a graph where the use of one truth value for a variable

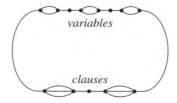

Figure 7.5   The key idea for the Hamiltonian circuit problem.

(i.e., the use of one of the two edges associated with the variable) prevents the use of any edge associated with the complementary literal (since this literal is false, it cannot be used to satisfy any clause). Hence the specific construction we need is one which, given one "edge" (a pair of vertices, say $\{a, b\}$) and a collection of other "edges" (pairs of vertices, say $\{x_1, y_1\}$, ... ,$\{x_k, y_k\}$), is such that any Hamiltonian path from a to b either does not use any edge of the gadget, in which case any path from x_i to y_i each must use only edges from the gadget, or uses only edges from the gadget, in which case no path from x_i to y_i may use any edge of the gadget. The graph fragment shown in Figure 7.6 fulfills those conditions.

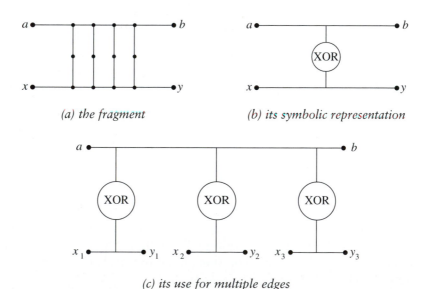

(a) the fragment   (b) its symbolic representation

(c) its use for multiple edges

Figure 7.6   The graph fragment used as exclusive OR and its symbolic representation.

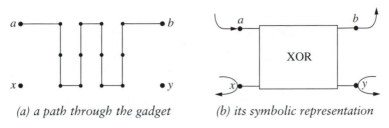

(a) a path through the gadget   (b) its symbolic representation

Figure 7.7 How the XOR gadget works.

Notice that the "edge" from a to b or from x_i to y_i is not really an edge but a chain of edges. This property allows us to set up two or three such "edges" between two vertices without violating the structure of a graph (in which there can be at most one edge between any two vertices). To verify that our gadget works as advertised, first note that all middle vertices (those between the "edge" from a to b and the other "edges") have degree 2, so that all edges drawn vertically in the figure must be part of any Hamiltonian circuit. Hence only alternate horizontal edges can be selected, with the alternation reversed between the "edge" from a to b and the other "edges," as illustrated in Figure 7.7, which shows one of the two paths through the gadget. It follows that a Hamiltonian path from a to b using at least one edge from the fragment must visit all internal vertices of the fragment, so that any path from x_i to y_i must use only edges external to the fragment. The converse follows from the same reasoning, so that the fragment of Figure 7.6 indeed fulfills our claim. In the remainder of the construction, we use the graphical symbolism illustrated in the second part of Figure 7.6 to represent our gadget.

Now the construction is simple: for each clause we set up two vertices connected by three "edges" and for each variable appearing in at least one clause we set up two vertices connected by two "edges." We then connect all of these components in series into a single loop, adding one intermediate vertex between any two successive components. Finally we tie variables and clauses pieces together with our XOR connections. (If a variable appears only in complemented or only in uncomplemented form, then one of the two "edges" in its truth-setting component is a real edge, since it is not part of any XOR construct. Since we constructed truth-setting components only for those variables that appear at least once in a clause, there is no risk of creating duplicate edges.) This construction is illustrated in Figure 7.8; it takes an instance with n variables and k clauses and produces a graph with $3n + 39k$ vertices and $4n + 53k$ edges and can be done in polynomial time.

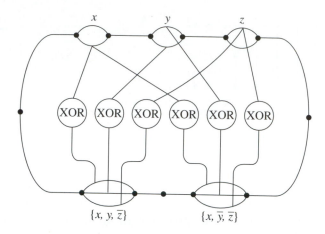

Figure 7.8   The entire construction for the Hamiltonian circuit problem.

Any Hamiltonian circuit must traverse exactly one "edge" in each component. This ensures a legal truth assignment by selecting one of two "edges" in each truth-setting component and also a satisfying truth assignment by selecting exactly one "edge" in each clause component. (The actual truth assignment sets to *false* each literal corresponding to the edge traversed in the truth-setting component, because of the effect of the XOR.) Conversely, given a satisfying truth assignment, we obtain a Hamiltonian circuit by traversing the "edge" corresponding to the true literal in each clause and the edge corresponding to the value *false* in each truth-setting component. Hence the transformed instance admits a solution if and only if the original one does.   *Q.E.D.*

Exercise 7.3 Prove that *Hamiltonian Path* is NP-complete. An instance of the problem is a graph and the question asks whether or not the graph has a Hamiltonian path, i.e., a simple path that includes all vertices.   □

Set cover problems provide very useful starting points for many transformations. However, devising a first transformation to a set cover problem calls for techniques somewhat different from those used heretofore.

Theorem 7.8 *Exact Cover by Three-Sets* is NP-complete.   □

Proof. Membership in NP is obvious. Given the guessed cover, we need only verify, by scanning each subset in the cover in turn, that all set elements are covered. We want to reduce *Positive 1in3SAT* to X3C. The first question to address is the representation of a truth assignment; one possible solution is to set up two three-sets for each variable and to ensure that exactly one of the two three-sets is selected in any solution. The latter can be achieved by taking advantage of the requirement that the cover be exact: once a three-set is picked, any other three-set that overlaps with it is automatically excluded. Since a variable may occur in several clauses of the *1in3SAT* problem and since each element of the *X3C* problem may be covered only once, we need several copies of the construct corresponding to a variable (to provide an "attaching point" for each literal). This in turn raises the issue of consistency: all copies must be "set" to the same value.

Let an instance of *Positive 1in3SAT* have n variables and k clauses. For each clause, $c = \{x, y, z\}$, we set up six elements, x_c, y_c, z_c, t_c, f'_c, and f''_c. The first three will represent the three literals, while the other three will distinguish the true literal from the two false literals. For each variable, we construct a component with two attaching points (one corresponding to true, the other to false) for each of its occurrences, as illustrated in Figure 7.9 and described below. Let variable x occur n_x times (we assume that each variable considered occurs at least once). We set up $4n_x$ elements, of which $2n_x$ will be used as attaching points while the others will ensure consistency. Call the attaching points X^t_i and X^f_i, for $1 \le i \le n_x$; call the other points p^i_x, for $1 \le i \le 2n_x$. Now we construct three-sets. The component associated with variable x has $2n_x$ sets:

- $\{p^{2i-1}_x, p^{2i}_x, X^t_i\}$ for $1 \le i \le n_x$,
- $\{p^{2i}_x, p^{2i+1}_x, X^f_i\}$ for $1 \le i < n_x$, and
- $\{p^{2n_x}_x, p^1_x, X^f_{n_x}\}$.

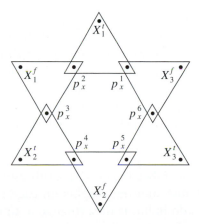

a variable with three occurrences

Figure 7.9   The component used in Theorem 7.8.

Each clause $c = \{x, y, z\}$ gives rise to nine three-sets, three for each literal. The first of these sets, if picked for the cover, indicates that the associated literal is the one set to true in the clause; for literal x in clause c, this set is $\{x_c, t_c, X_i^t\}$ for some attaching point i. If one of the other two is picked, the associated literal is set to false; for our literal, these sets are $\{x_c, f_c', X_i^f\}$ and $\{x_c, f_c'', X_i^f\}$. Overall, our transformation produces an instance of X3C with $18k$ elements and $15k$ three-sets and is easily carried out in polynomial time.

Now notice that, for each variable x, the element p_x^1 can be covered only by one of two sets: $\{p_x^1, p_x^2, X_1^t\}$ or $\{p_x^{2n_x}, p_x^1, X_{n_x}^f\}$. If the first is chosen, then the second cannot be chosen too, so that the element $p_x^{2n_x}$ must be covered by the only other three-set in which it appears, namely $\{p_x^{2n_x-1}, p_x^{2n_x}, X_{n_x}^t\}$. Continuing this chain of reasoning, we see that the choice of cover for p_x^1 entirely determines the cover for all p_x^i, in the process covering either (i) all of the X_i^f and none of the X_i^t or (ii) the converse. Thus a covering of the components associated with variables corresponds to a legal truth assignment, where the uncovered elements correspond to literal values. Turning to the components associated with the clauses, notice that exactly three of the nine sets must be selected for the cover. Whichever set is selected to cover the element t_c must include a true literal, thereby ensuring that at least one literal per clause is true. The other two sets chosen cover f_c' and f_c'' and thus must contain one false literal each, ensuring that at most one literal per clause is true. Our conclusion follows.   Q.E.D.

From this reduction and the preceding ones, we see that a typical reduction from a satisfiability problem to another problem uses a construction with three distinct components, as summarized in Table 7.3.

We often transform an asymmetric satisfiability problem into a symmetric problem in order to take advantage of the rigidity of *1in3SAT*. In such cases, we must provide an indication of which part of the solution is meant to represent true and which false. This is often done by means of *enforcers* (in the terminology of Garey and Johnson). The following proof presents a simple example of the use of enforcers; it also illustrates another important technique: creating exponentially large numbers out of sets.

Theorem 7.9 *Partition* is NP-complete.   □

Proof. Once again, membership in NP is easily established. Given a guess for the partition, we just sum the weights on each side and compare the results, which we can do in linear time (that is, in time proportional to the length of the words representing the weights—*not* in time proportional to the weights themselves).

Table 7.3 The components used in reductions from satisfiability problems.

- *Truth Assignment*: This component corresponds to the variables of the satisfiability instance; typically, there is one piece for each variable. The role of this component is to ensure that any solution to the transformed instance must include elements that correspond to a legal truth assignment to the variables of the satisfiability instance. (By legal, we mean that each variable is assigned one and only one truth value.)
- *Satisfiability Checking*: This component corresponds to the clauses of the satisfiability instance; typically, there is one piece for each clause. The role of this component is to ensure that any solution to the transformed instance must include elements that correspond to a satisfying truth assignment—typically, each piece ensures that its corresponding clause has to be satisfied.
- *Consistency*: This component typically connects clause (satisfiability checking) components to variable (truth assignment) components. The role of this component is to ensure that any solution to the transformed instance must include elements that force consistency among all parts corresponding to the same literal in the satisfiability instance. (It prevents using one truth value in one clause and a different one in another clause for the same variable.)

Since we intend to reduce *1in3SAT*, a problem without numbers, to *Partition*, the key to the transformation resides in the construction of the weights. In addition, our construction must provide means of distinguishing one side of the partition from the other—assuming that the transformation follows the obvious intent of regarding one side of the partition as corresponding to true values and the other as corresponding to false values. The easiest way to produce numbers is to set up a string of digits in some base, where each digit corresponds to some feature of the original instance. A critical point is to prevent any carry or borrow in the arithmetic operations applied to these numbers—as long as no carry or borrow arises, each digit can be considered separately, so that we are back to individual features of the original instance. With these observations we can proceed with our construction.

We want a literal and its complement to end up on opposite sides of the partition (thereby ensuring a legal truth assignment); also, for each clause, we want two of its literals on one side of the partition and the remaining literal on the other side. These observations suggest setting up two elements per variable (one for the uncomplemented literal and one for the complemented literal), each assigned a weight of $k + n$ digits (where n is the number of variables and k the number of clauses). The last n digits are used to identify each variable: in the weights of the two elements corresponding to the ith variable, all such digits are set to 0, except for the ith, which is set to 1. The first k digits characterize membership in each clause; the jth of these digits is set to 1 in the weight of a literal if this literal appears in the jth clause, otherwise it is set to 0. Thus, for instance, if variable x_2 (out of four variables) appears uncomplemented in the first clause and complemented in the second (out of three clauses), then the weight of the element corresponding to the literal x_2 will be 1000100 and that of the element corresponding to $\bar{x}_2$ will be 0100100. The two weights have the same last four digits, 0100, identifying them as belonging to elements corresponding to the second of four variables.

Observe that the sum of all $2n$ weights is a number, the first k digits of which are all equal to 3, and the last n digits of which are all equal to 2—a number which, while a multiple of 2, is not divisible by 2 without carry operations. It remains to identify each side of the partition; we do this by adding an enforcer, in the form of an element with a uniquely identifiable weight—which also ensures that the total sum becomes divisible by 2 on a digit by digit basis. A suitable choice of weight for the enforcer sets the last n digits to 0 (which makes this weight uniquely identifiable, since all other weights have one of these digits set to 1) and the first k digits to 1. Now the overall sum is a number, the first k digits of which are all equal to 4, and the last n digits of which are all equal to 2 (which indicates that considering these numbers to be written in base 5 or higher will prevent any carry); this number is divisible by 2 without borrowing. Figure 7.10 shows a sample encoding. The side of true literals will be flagged by the presence of the enforcer. The complete construction takes an instance of $1in3SAT$

	c_1	c_2	c_3	x	y	z	w
x	1	1	0	1	0	0	0
$\bar{x}$	0	0	1	1	0	0	0
y	1	0	0	0	1	0	0
$\bar{y}$	0	1	1	0	1	0	0
z	0	1	0	0	0	1	0
$\bar{z}$	1	0	0	0	0	1	0
w	0	0	1	0	0	0	1
$\bar{w}$	0	0	0	0	0	0	1
enforcer	1	1	1	0	0	0	0

Figure 7.10   The encoding for *Partition* of the *1in3SAT* instance given by $c_1 = \{x, y, \bar{z}\}$, $c_2 = \{x, \bar{y}, z\}$, and $c_3 = \{\bar{x}, \bar{y}, w\}$.

with n variables and k clauses and produces (in no more than quadratic time) an instance of *Partition* with $2n + 1$ elements, each with a weight of $n + k$ digits.

In our example, the instance produced by the transformation has 9 elements with decimal weights 1,110,000; 1,101,000; 1,000,100; 1,000,010; 110,100; 100,010; 11,000; 10,001; and 1—for a total weight of 4,444,222. A solution groups the elements with weights 1,110,000; 1,000,100; 100,010; 11,000; and 1 on one side—corresponding to the assignment $x \leftarrow$ false, $y \leftarrow$ true, $z \leftarrow$ true, and $w \leftarrow$ false. Note that, with just four variables and three clauses, the largest weights produced already exceed a million.

We claim that the transformed instance admits a solution if and only if the original does. Assume then that the transformed instance admits a solution. Since the sum of all weights on either side must be $22\ldots211\ldots1$, each side must include exactly one literal for each variable, which ensures a legal truth assignment. Since the enforcer contributes a 1 in each of the first k positions, the "true" side must include exactly one literal per clause, which ensures a satisfying truth assignment. Conversely, assume that the instance of *1in3SAT* admits a satisfying truth assignment. We place all elements corresponding to true literals on one side of the partition together with the enforcer and all other elements on the other side. Thus each side has one element for each variable, so that the last n digits of the sum of all weights on either side are all equal to 1. Since each clause has exactly one true literal and two false ones, the "true" side includes exactly one element per clause and the "false" side includes exactly two elements per clause; in addition, the "true" side also includes the enforcer, which contributes a 1 in each of the first k positions. Thus the first k digits of the sum of weights on each side are all equal to 2. Hence the sum of the weights on each side is equal to $22\ldots211\ldots1$ and our proof is complete.   Q.E.D.

Notice that exponentially large numbers must be created, because any instance of *Partition* with small numbers is solvable in polynomial time using dynamic programming. The dynamic program is based upon the recurrence

$$\begin{cases} f(i, M) = \max(f(i-1, M),\, f(i-1, M-s_i)) \\ f(0, j) = 0 \;\; \text{for } j \neq 0 \\ f(0, 0) = 1 \end{cases}$$

where $f(i, M)$ equals 1 or 0, indicating whether there exists a subset of the first i elements that sums to M. Given an instance of *Partition* with n elements and a total sum of N, this program produces an answer in $O(n \cdot N^2)$ time. Since the size of the input is $O(n \log N)$, this is not a polynomial-time algorithm; however, it behaves as one whenever N is a polynomial function of n. Thus the instances of *Partition* produced by our transformation must involve numbers of size $\Omega(2^n)$ so as not to be trivially tractable. (The reader will note that producing such numbers does not force our transformation to take exponential time, since n bits are sufficient to describe a number of size 2^n.) *Partition* is interesting in that its complexity depends intimately on two factors: the subset selection (as always) and the large numbers involved. The dynamic programming algorithm provides an algorithm that is linear in n, the number of elements involved, but exponential in $\log N$, the values described, while a simple backtracking search provides an algorithm that is linear in $\log N$ but exponential in n.

The interest of our next problem lies in its proof. It uses the freedom inherent in having two separate structures, constructing one to reflect the details of the instance and the other as a uniform "backdrop" (reflecting only the size of the instance) against which to set off the first.

Theorem 7.10 *Star-Free Regular Expression Inequivalence (SF-REI)* is NP-complete. □

Proof. We have seen in Proposition 6.1 that this problem is in NP. We prove it NP-complete by transforming *3SAT* to it. Given an instance of *3SAT* with variables $V = \{x_1, \ldots, x_n\}$ and clauses $C = \{\{\hat{x}_i, \hat{y}_i, \hat{z}_i\}, 1 \leq i \leq r\}$, we construct an instance Σ, E_1, E_2 of SF-REI as follows. The alphabet Σ has two characters, say $\{T, F\}$. One of the regular expressions will denote all possible strings of n variables, where each variable may appear complemented or not, and where the variables appear in order, 1 through n. There are 2^n such strings, which can be denoted by a regular expression with n terms:

$$E_1 = (T + F) \cdot (T + F) \cdot \ldots \cdot (T + F)$$

The intent of this expression is to describe all possible truth assignments. The second expression is derived from the clauses; each clause will give rise to a subexpression and the final expression will be the union of all such subexpressions. The intent of this expression is to describe all truth assignments that make the collection of clauses evaluate to false; each subexpression will describe all truth assignments that make its corresponding clause evaluate to false. In order to avoid problems of permutations, we also require that variables appear in order 1 through n. Each subexpression is very similar to the one expression above; the difference is that, for the literals mentioned in the corresponding clause, only the false truth value appears in a term, instead of the union of both truth values. For instance, the clause

$\{\overline{x}_1, x_2, \overline{x}_4\}$ gives rise to the subexpression:

$$T \cdot F \cdot (T + F) \cdot T \cdot (T + F) \cdot \ldots \cdot (T + F)$$

This construction clearly takes polynomial time.

Now suppose there is a satisfying truth assignment for the variables; then this assignment makes all clauses evaluate to true, so that the corresponding string is not in the language denoted by E_2 (although it, like all other strings corresponding to legal truth assignments, is in the language denoted by E_1). Conversely, if a string denoted by E_1 is not denoted by E_2, then the corresponding truth assignment must be a satisfying truth assignment; if it were not, then at least one clause would not be satisfied and our string would appear in E_2 by its association with that clause, contradicting our hypothesis.   Q.E.D.

Finally, we turn to a geometric construction. Such constructions are often difficult for two reasons: first, we need to design an appropriate collection of geometric gadgets and secondly, we need to ensure that all coordinates are computable (and representable) in time and space polynomial in the input size.

Theorem 7.11 *Art Gallery* is NP-complete.   □

Proof. A well-known algorithm in computational geometry decomposes a simple polygon into triangles, each vertex of which is a vertex of the polygon, in low polynomial time. The planar dual of this decomposition (obtained by placing one vertex in each triangle and connecting vertices corresponding to triangles that share an edge) is a tree. A certificate for our problem will consist of a triangulation of the polygon and its dual tree, a placement of the guards, and for each guard a description of the area under its control, given in terms of the dual tree and the triangulation. This last includes bounding segments as needed to partition a triangle as well as the identity of each guard whose responsibility includes each adjacent piece of the partitioned triangle. In polynomial time, we can then verify that the triangulation and its dual tree are valid and that all triangles of the triangulation of the simple polygon are covered by at least one guard. (The certificate does not describe all of the area covered by each guard; instead, it arbitrarily assigns multiply-covered areas to some of its guards so as to generate a partition of the interior of the simple polygon.) Finally, we verify in polynomial time that each piece (triangle or fraction thereof) is indeed visible in its entirety by its assigned guard. We do not go into details

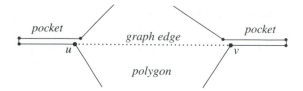

Figure 7.11   The two pockets corresponding to the graph edge $\{u, v\}$.

here but refer the reader to one of the standard texts on computational geometry[1] for a description of the algorithms involved.

To prove that the problem is NP-complete, we reduce the known NP-complete problem *Vertex Cover* to it. An instance of *Vertex Cover* is given by a graph, $G = (V, E)$, and a bound B. Let the graph have n vertices, $n = |V|$. Our basic idea is to produce a convex polygon of n vertices, then to augment it (and make it nonconvex) with constructs that reflect the edges. A single guard suffices for a convex art gallery: by definition of convexity, any point in a convex polygon can see any other point inside the polygon. Thus our additional constructs will attach to the basic convex polygon pieces that cannot be seen from everywhere—indeed, that can be seen in their entirety only from the vertices corresponding to the two endpoints of an edge. We shall place two additional constructs for each graph edge; these constructs will be deep and narrow "pockets" (as close as possible to segments) aligned with the (embedding of the corresponding) graph edge and projecting from the polygon at each end of the edge. Figure 7.11 illustrates the concept of pocket for one edge of the graph.

Now we need to demonstrate that the vertices on the perimeter of the resulting polygon can be produced (including their coordinates) in perimeter order in polynomial time. We begin with the vertices of the polygon before adding the pockets. Given a graph of n vertices, we create n points $p_0, \ldots, p_{n-1}$; we place point p_0 at the origin and point p_i, for $1 \leqslant i \leqslant n - 1$, at coordinates $(ni(i - 1), 2ni)$. The resulting polygon, illustrated in Figure 7.12(a), is convex: the slope from p_i to p_{i+1} (for $i \geqslant 1$) is $\frac{1}{i}$, which decreases as i increases. In general, the slope between p_i and p_j (for $j > i \geqslant 1$) is $\frac{2}{j+i-1}$; these slopes determine the sides of the pockets. Thus all quantities are polynomial in the input size. In order to specify the pockets for a single vertex, we need to construct the union of the pockets that were set up for each edge incident upon this vertex and thus need to

---

[1] For instance, see *Computational Geometry* by F. Preparata and I. Shamos.

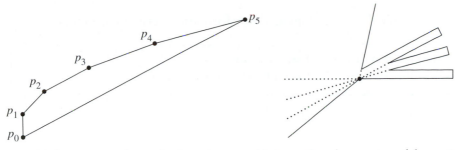

(a) the convex polygon for 6 vertices   (b) the pockets for a vertex of degree 3

Figure 7.12   The construction for the *Art Gallery* problem.

compute the intersection of successive pockets. Figure 7.12(b) illustrates the result: if a vertex has degree d in the graph, it has d associated pockets in the corresponding instance of AG, with $3d$ vertices in addition to the original. In all, we construct from a graph $G = (V, E)$ a simple polygon with $|V| + 6|E|$ vertices. Each intersection is easily computed from the slopes and positions of the lines involved and the resulting coordinates remain polynomial in the input size. Pockets of depth n and width 1 (roughly, that is: we set the depth and width by using the floor of square roots rather than their exact values in order to retain rational values) are deep and narrow enough to ensure that only two vertices of the original convex polygon can view either pocket in its entirety—namely the two vertices corresponding to the edge for which the pockets were built.

Now it is easy to see that a solution to the instance of VC immediately yields a solution to the transformed instance; we just place guards at the vertices (of the original convex polygon) corresponding to the vertices in the cover. The converse is somewhat obscured by the fact that guards could be placed at some of the additional $6|E|$ vertices defining the pockets, vertices that have no immediate counterpart in the original graph instance. However, note that we can always move a guard from one of the additional vertices to the corresponding vertex of the original convex polygon without decreasing coverage of the polygon (if two guards had been placed along the pockets of a single original vertex, then we can even save a guard in the process). The result is a solution to the instance of AG that has a direct counterpart as a solution to the original instance of VC. Our conclusion follows.   Q.E.D.

In all of the reductions used so far, including this latest reduction from a problem other than satisfiability, we established an explicit and

Table 7.4   Developing a transformation between instances.

- List the characteristics of each instance.
- List the characteristics of a certificate for each instance.
- Use the characteristics of the certificates to develop a conceptual correspondence between the two problems, then develop it into a correspondence between the elements of the two instances.
- Where gadgets are needed, carefully list their requisite attributes before setting out to design them.

---

direct correspondence between certificates for "yes" instances of the two problems. We summarize this principle as the last of our various guidelines for NP-completeness proofs in Table 7.4.

From these basic problems, we can very easily prove that several other problems are also NP-complete (when phrased as decision problems, of course). The proof technique in the six cases of Theorem 7.12 is *restriction*, by far the simplest method available. Restriction is a simplified reduction where the transformation used is just the identity, but we may choose to look at it the other way. The problem to be proved NP-complete is shown to restrict to a known NP-complete problem; in other words, it is shown to contain all instances of this NP-complete problem as a special case. The following theorem demonstrates the simplicity of restriction proofs.

Theorem 7.12 The following problems are NP-complete:

1. *Chromatic Number*: Given a graph and a positive integer bound, can the graph be colored with no more colors than the given bound?
2. *Set Cover*: Given a set, a collection of subsets of the set, and a positive integer bound, can a subcollection including no more subsets than the given bound be found which covers the set?
3. *Knapsack*: Given a set of elements, a positive integer "size" for each element, a positive integer "value" for each element, a positive integer size bound, and a positive integer value bound, can a subset of elements be found such that the sum of the sizes of its elements is no larger than the size bound and the sum of the values of its elements is no smaller than the value bound?
4. *Subset Sum*: Given a set of elements, a positive integer size for each element, and a positive integer goal, can a subset of elements be found such that the sum of the size of its elements is exactly equal to the goal?

5. *Binpacking*: Given a set of elements, a positive integer size for each element, a positive integer "bin size," and a positive integer bound, can the elements be partitioned into no more subsets than the given bound and so that the sum of the sizes of the elements of any subset is no larger than the bin size?

6. *0-1 Integer Programming*: Given a set of pairs $(\mathbf{x}, b)$, where each $\mathbf{x}$ is an m-tuple of integers and b an integer, and given an m-tuple of integers $\mathbf{c}$ and an integer B, does there exist an m-tuple of integers $\mathbf{y}$, each component of which is either 0 or 1, with $(\mathbf{x}, \mathbf{y}) \leq b$ for each pair $(\mathbf{x}, b)$ and with $(\mathbf{c}, \mathbf{y}) \geq B$? Here $(\mathbf{a}, \mathbf{b})$ denotes the scalar product of $\mathbf{a}$ and $\mathbf{b}$. □

Proof. All proofs are by restriction. We indicate only the necessary constraints, leaving the reader to verify that the proofs thus sketched are indeed correct. Membership in NP is trivial for all six problems.

1. We restrict *Chromatic Number* to *G3C* by allowing only instances with a bound of 3.

2. We restrict *Set Cover* to *X3C* by allowing only instances where the set has a number of elements equal to some multiple of 3, where all subsets have exactly three elements, and where the bound is equal to a third of the size of the set.

3. We restrict *Knapsack* to *Partition* by allowing only instances where the size of each element is equal to its value, where the sum of all sizes is a multiple of 2, and where the size bound and the value bound are both equal to half the sum of all sizes.

4. We restrict *Subset Sum* to *Partition* by allowing only instances where the sum of all sizes is a multiple of 2 and where the goal is equal to half the sum of all sizes.

5. We restrict *Binpacking* to *Partition* by allowing only instances where the sum of all sizes is a multiple of 2, where the bin size is equal to half the sum of all sizes, and where the bound on the number of bins is 2.

6. We restrict *0-1 Integer Programming* to *Knapsack* by allowing only instances with a single $(\mathbf{x}, b)$ pair and where all values are natural numbers. Then $\mathbf{x}$ denotes the sizes, b the size bound, $\mathbf{c}$ the values, and B the value bound of an instance of *Knapsack*. *Q.E.D.*

A restriction proof works by placing restrictions on the type of *instance* allowed, not on the type of *solution*. For instance, we could not "restrict" *Set Cover* to *Minimum Disjoint Cover* (a version of *Set Cover* where all subsets in the cover must be disjoint) by requiring that any solution be composed only of disjoint sets. Such a requirement would change the question and hence the problem itself, whereas a restriction only narrows down the collection of possible instances.

The idea of restriction can be used for apparently unrelated problems. For instance, our earlier reduction from *Traveling Salesman* to *HC* (in their decision versions) can be viewed as a restriction of *TSP* to those instances where all intercity distances have values of 1 or 2; this subproblem is then seen to be identical (isomorphic) to *HC*. The following theorems provide two more examples.

Theorem 7.13 *Clique* is NP-complete. An instance of the problem is given by a graph, G, and a bound, k; the question is "Does G contain a clique (a complete subgraph) of size k or larger?"   □

Proof. Our restriction here is trivial—no change—because the problem as stated is already isomorphic to *Vertex Cover*. Vertices correspond to vertices; wherever the instance of *Clique* has an edge, the corresponding instance of *VC* has none and vice versa; and the bound for *VC* equals the number of vertices minus the bound for *Clique*.   *Q.E.D.*

We leave a proof of the next theorem to the reader.

Exercise 7.4 Prove that *Subgraph Isomorphism* is NP-complete by restricting it to *Clique*. An instance of the problem is given by two graphs, G and H, where the first graph has as many vertices and as many edges as the second; the question is "Does G contain a subgraph isomorphic to H?"   □

As a last example, we consider a slightly more complex use of restriction; note, however, that this proof remains much simpler than any of our reductions from the *3SAT* problems, confirming our earlier advice.

Theorem 7.14 *k-Clustering* is NP-complete. An instance of the problem is given by a set of elements, a positive integer measure of "dissimilitude" between pairs of elements, a natural number k no larger than the cardinality of the set, and a positive integer bound. The question is "Can the set be partitioned into k nonempty subsets such that the sum over all subsets of the sums of the dissimilitudes between pairs of elements within the same subset does not exceed the given bound?"   □

Proof. Membership in NP is obvious. We restrict the problem to instances where k equals 2 and all measures of dissimilitude have value 0 or 1. The resulting problem is isomorphic to *Maximum Cut*, where each vertex corresponds to an element, where there exists an edge between two vertices exactly when the dissimilitude between the corresponding vertices equals 1, and where the bound of *MxC* equals the sum of all dissimilitudes minus the bound of *k-Clustering*.   *Q.E.D.*

At this point, the reader will undoubtedly have noticed several characteristics of NP-complete problems. Perhaps the most salient characteristic is that the problem statement must allow some freedom in the choice of the solution structure. When this bit of leeway is absent, a problem, even when suspected not to be in P, may not be NP-complete. A good example is the graph isomorphism problem: while subgraph isomorphism is NP-complete, graph isomorphism (is a given graph isomorphic to another one) is not known—and not believed—to be so. Many of the NP-complete problems discussed so far involve the selection of a loosely structured subset, by which we mean a subset such that the inclusion of an element does not lead directly to the inclusion of another. The difficulty of the problem resides in the subset search. The property obeyed by the subset need not be difficult to verify; indeed the definition of NP guarantees that such a property is easily verifiable. Another striking aspect of NP-complete problems is the distinction between the numbers 2 and 3: *3SAT* is NP-complete, but *2SAT* is solvable in linear time; *G3C* is NP-complete, but *G2C*, which just asks whether a graph is bipartite, is solvable in linear time; *X3C* is NP-complete, but *X2C* is in P; three-dimensional matching is NP-complete (see Exercise 7.20), but two-dimensional matching is just "normal" matching and is in P. (At times, there also appears to be a difference between 1 and 2—such as scheduling tasks on 1 or 2 processors. This apparent difference is just an aspect of subset search, however: while scheduling tasks on one processor is just a permutation problem, scheduling them on two processors requires selecting which tasks to run on which machine.) This difference appears mostly due to the effectiveness of matching techniques on many problems characterized by pairs. (The boundary may be higher: *G3C* is NP-complete for all graphs of bounded degree when the bound is no smaller than 4, but it is solvable in polynomial time for graphs of degree 3.) Such characteristics may help in identifying potential NP-complete problems.

7.2   Some P-Completeness Proofs

P-complete problems derive their significance mostly from the need to distinguish between P and L or between P and the class of problems that are profitably parallelizable, a class that (as we shall see in Section 9.4) is a subset of P ∩ POLYL. That distinction alone might not justify the inclusion of proofs of P-completeness here; however, the constraints imposed by the resource bound used in the transformation (logarithmic space) lead to an interesting style of transformation—basically functions implemented by a few nested loops. The difference between polynomial time and logarithmic space not being well understood (obviously, since we do not know whether L is a proper subset of P), any illustration of potential differences is useful. In this spirit, we present proofs of P-completeness, two of them through reductions from *PSA*, for three different problems:

- *Unit Resolution*: Given a collection of clauses (disjuncts), can the empty clause be derived by unit resolution, that is, by resolving a one-literal clause with another clause that contains the literal's complement; for instance, $\{x\}$ and $\{\overline{x}, \hat{y}_1, \ldots, \hat{y}_n\}$ yield $\{\hat{y}_1, \ldots, \hat{y}_n\}$ by unit resolution.
- *Circuit Value (CV)*: A circuit (a combinational logic circuit realizing some Boolean function) is represented by a sequence $a_1, \ldots, a_n$, where each a_i is one of three entities: (i) a logic value (true or false); (ii) an AND gate, with the indices of its two inputs (both of them less than i); or (iii) an OR gate, with the indices of its two inputs (both of them less than i). The output of the circuit is the output of the last gate, a_n. The question is simply "Is the output of the circuit true?"
- *Depth-First Search*: Given a rooted graph (directed or not) and two distinguished vertices of the graph, u and v, will u be visited before or after v in a recursive depth-first search of the graph?

Theorem 7.15 *Unit Resolution* is P-complete.   □

Proof. The problem is in P. Each application of unit resolution decreases the total number of literals involved. An exhaustive search algorithm uses each single literal clause in turn and attempts to resolve it against every other clause, storing the result; the single-literal clause is then discarded. The resolution process will typically create some new single-literal clauses, which get used in the same fashion. Eventually, either all single-literal clauses (including newly generated ones) are used or the empty clause is derived. This process works in polynomial time because, with n variables and m initial clauses, at most $2mn$ resolutions can ever be made. Intuitively, the problem is P-complete because we need to store newly generated clauses.

We prove the problem P-complete by transforming *PSA* to it. Essentially, each initially reachable, as well as each terminal, element in *PSA* becomes a one-literal clause in our problem, while the triples of *PSA* become clauses of three elements in our problem. Specifically, the elements of *PSA* become variables in our problem; for each initially reachable element x, we set a one-literal clause $\{x\}$; for each terminal element y, we set a one-literal clause $\{\bar{y}\}$; and for each triple in the relation (x, y, z), we set a three-literal clause $\{\bar{x}, \bar{y}, z\}$, which is logically equivalent to the implication $x \wedge y \Rightarrow z$. We can carry out this transformation on a strictly local basis because all we need store is the current element or triple being transformed; thus our transformation runs in logarithmic space. We claim that, at any point in the resolution process, there is a clause $\{x\}$ only if x is accessible; moreover, if x is accessible, the clause $\{x\}$ can be derived. This claim is easy to prove by induction and the conclusion follows.   Q.E.D.

This negative result affects the interpretation of logic languages based on unification (such as Prolog). Since unit resolution is an extremely simplified form of unification, we can conclude that unification-based languages cannot be executed at great speeds on parallel machines.

Theorem 7.16 *Circuit Value* is P-complete.   □

Actually, our construction uses only AND and OR gates, so we are proving the stronger statement that *Monotone Circuit Value* is P-complete.

Proof. That the problem is in P is clear. We can propagate the logic values from the input to each gate in turn until the output value has been computed. Intuitively, what makes the problem P-complete is the need to store intermediate computations.

We prove that CV is P-complete by a reduction from *PSA*. We use the version of *PSA* produced in our original proof of P-completeness (Theorem 6.8), which has a single element in its target set. The basic idea is to convert a triple (x, y, z) of *PSA* into an AND gate with inputs x and y and output z, since this mimics exactly what takes place in *PSA*. The circuit will have all elements of *PSA* as inputs, with those inputs that correspond to elements of the initial set of *PSA* set to true and all other inputs set to false.

The real problem is to propagate logical values for each of the inputs. In *PSA*, elements can become accessible through the application of the proper sequence of triples; in our circuit, this corresponds to transforming certain inputs from false to true because of the true output of an AND gate. Thus what we need is to propagate truth values from the inputs to the current stage and eventually to the output, which is simply the final value of one of the elements; each step in the propagation corresponds to the application of one triple from *PSA*. A step in the propagation may not yield anything new. Indeed, the output of the AND gate could be false, even though the value that we are propagating is in fact already true—that is, although accessibility is never lost once gained, truth values could fluctuate.

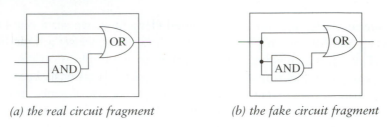

(a) the real circuit fragment   (b) the fake circuit fragment

Figure 7.13   The real and "fake" circuit fragments.

We should therefore combine the "previous" truth value for our element and the output of the AND gate through an OR gate to obtain the new truth value for the element.

Thus for each element z of *PSA*, we will set up a "propagation line" from input to output. This line is initialized to a truth value (true for elements of the initial set, false otherwise) and is updated at each "step," i.e., for each triple of *PSA* that has z as its third element. The update is accomplished by a circuit fragment made of an AND gate feeding into an OR gate: the AND gate implements the triple while the OR gate combines the potential new information gained through the triple with the existing information. Figure 7.13(a) illustrates the circuit fragment corresponding to the triple (x, y, z). When all propagation is complete, the "line" that corresponds to the element in the target set of *PSA* is the output of the circuit.

The remaining problem is that we have no idea of the order in which we should process the triples. The order could be crucial, since, if we use a triple too early, it may not produce anything new because one of the first two elements is not yet accessible, whereas, if applied later, it could produce a new accessible element. We have to live with some fixed ordering, yet this ordering could be so bad as to produce only one new accessible element. Thus we have to repeat the process, each time with the same ordering. How many times do we need to repeat it? Since, in order to make a difference, each pass through the ordering must produce at least one newly accessible element, $n - 1$ stages (where n is the total number of elements) always suffice. (Actually, we can use just $n - k - l + 1$ stages, where k is the number of initially accessible elements and l is the size of the target set; however, $n - 1$ is no larger asymptotically and extra stages cannot hurt.)

From an instance of *PSA* with n elements and m triples, we produce a circuit with n "propagation lines," each with a total of $m \cdot (n - 1)$ propagation steps grouped into $n - 1$ stages. We can view this circuit more or less as a matrix of n rows and $m \cdot (n - 1)$ columns, in which the values

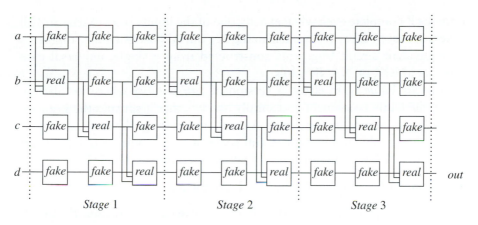

Figure 7.14   The complete construction for a small instance of *PSA*.

of the $i + 1$st column are derived from those of the ith column by keeping
$n - 1$ values unchanged and by using the AND-OR circuit fragment on
the one row affected by the triple considered at the $i + 1$st propagation
stage. If this triple is (x, y, z), then the circuit fragment implements the
logical function $z(i + 1) = z(i) \lor (x(i) \land y(i))$. In order to make index
computations perfectly uniform, it is helpful to place a circuit fragment
at each row, not just at the affected row; the other $n - 1$ circuit fragments
have exactly the same size but do not affect the new value. For instance,
they can implement the logical function $z(i + 1) = z(i) \lor (z(i) \land z(i))$, as
illustrated in Figure 7.13(b). Figure 7.14 illustrates the entire construction
for a very small instance of *PSA*, given by $X = \{a, b, c, d\}$, $S = \{a\}$, $T = \{d\}$,
and $R = \{(a, a, b), (a, b, c), (b, b, d)\}$.

Now the entire transformation can be implemented with nested loops:

```
for i=1 to n-1 do      (* n-1 stages for n elements *)
   for j=1 to m do     (* one pass through all m triples *)
   (current triple is, say, (x,y,z) )
      for k=1 to n do   (* update column values *)
      if k=z then place the real AND-OR circuit fragment
             else place the fake AND-OR circuit fragment
```

Indices of gates are simple products of the three indices and of the constant
size of the AND-OR circuit fragment and so can be computed on the fly in
the inner loop. Thus the transformation takes only logarithmic space (for
the three loop indices and the current triple).   *Q.E.D.*

Our special version of *PSA* with a single element forming the entire initially
accessible set can be used for the reduction, showing that *Monotone CV*

remains P-complete even when exactly one of the inputs is set to true and all others are set to false. We could also replace our AND-OR circuit fragments by equivalent circuit fragments constructed from a single, universal gate type, i.e., NOR or NAND gates.

Circuit Value is, in effect, a version of *Satisfiability* where we already know the truth assignment and simply ask whether it satisfies the Boolean formula represented by the circuit. As such, it is perhaps the most important P-complete problem, giving us a full scale of satisfiability problems from P-complete (*CV*) all the way up to ExpSpace-complete (blind *Peek*).

Theorem 7.17 *Depth-First Search* is P-complete.   □

Proof. The problem is clearly in P, since we need only traverse the graph in depth-first order (a linear-time process), noting which of u or v is first visited. Intuitively, the problem is P-complete because we need to mark visited vertices in order to avoid infinite loops.

We prove this problem P-complete by transforming *CV* to it. (This problem is surprisingly difficult to show complete; the transformation is rather atypical for a P-complete problem, in being at least as complex as a fairly difficult NP-hardness proof.) To simplify the construction, we use the version of *CV* described earlier in our remarks: the circuit has a single input set to true, has a single output, and is composed entirely of NOR gates.

We create a gadget that we shall use for each gate. This graph fragment has two vertices to connect it to the inputs of the gate and as many vertices as needed for the fan-out of the gate. Specifically, if gate i has inputs $In(i, 1)$ and $In(i, 2)$, and output $Out(i)$, which is used as inputs to m further gates, with indices $j_1, \ldots, j_m$, we set up a gadget with $m + 6$ vertices. These vertices are: an entrance vertex $E(i)$ and an exit vertex $X(i)$, which we shall use to connect gadgets in a chain; two vertices $In(i, 1)$ and $In(i, 2)$ that correspond to the inputs of the gate; two vertices $S(i)$ and $T(i)$ that serve as beginning and end of an up-and-down chain of m vertices that connect to the outputs of the gate. The gadget is illustrated in Figure 7.15.

We can verify that there are two ways of traversing this gadget from the entrance to the exit vertex. One way is to proceed from $E(i)$ through $In(i, 1)$ and $In(i, 2)$ to $S(i)$, then down the chain by picking up all vertices (in other gadgets) that are outputs of this gate, ending at $T(i)$, then moving to $X(i)$. This traversal visits all of the vertices in the gadget, plus all of the vertices in other gadgets (vertices labeled $In(j_x, y)$, where y is 1 or 2 and $1 \leq x \leq m$) that correspond to the fan-out of the gate. The other way moves from $E(i)$ to $T(i)$, ascends that chain of m vertices without visiting any of the input vertices in other gadgets, reaches $S(i)$, and from there moves to

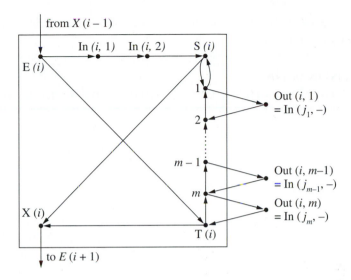

Figure 7.15   The gadget for depth-first search.

X(i). This traversal does not visit any vertex corresponding to inputs, not even the two, In(i, 1) and In(i, 2), that belong to the gadget itself. The two traversals visit S(i) and T(i) in opposite order.

We chain all gadgets together by connecting X(i) to E($i + 1$) (of course, the gadgets are already connected through their input/output vertices). The complete construction is easily accomplished in logarithmic space, as it is very uniform—a simple indexing scheme allows us to use a few nested loops to generate the digraph.

We claim that the output of the last gate, gate n, is true if and only if the depth-first search visits S(n) before T(n). The proof is an easy induction: the output of the NOR gate is true if and only if both of its inputs are false, so that, by induction, the vertices In(n, 1) and In(n, 2) of the last gate have not been visited in the traversal of the previous gadgets and thus must be visited in the traversal of the last gadget, which can be done only by using the first of the two possible traversals, which visits S(n) before T(n). The converse is similarly established.   *Q.E.D.*

Since depth-first search is perhaps the most fundamental algorithm for state-space exploration, whether in simple tasks, such as connectivity of graphs, or in complex ones, such as game tree search, this result shows that parallelism is unlikely to lead to major successes in a very large range of endeavors.

7.3   From Decision to Optimization and Enumeration

With the large existing catalog of NP-complete problems and with the rich hierarchy of complexity classes that surrounds NP, complexity theory has been very successful (assuming that all of the standard conjectures hold true) at characterizing difficult decision problems. But what about search, optimization, and enumeration problems? We deliberately restricted our scope to decision problems at the beginning of this chapter; our purpose was to simplify our study, while we claimed that generality remained unharmed, as all of our work on decision problems would extend to optimization problems. We now examine how this generalization works.

7.3.1   Turing Reductions and Search Problems

As part of our restriction to decision problems, we also chose to restrict ourselves to many-one reductions. Our reasons were: (i) complexity classes are generally closed under many-one reductions, while the use of Turing reductions enlarges the scope to search and optimization problems—problems for which no completeness results could otherwise be obtained, since they do not belong to complexity classes as we have defined them; and (ii) the less powerful many-one reductions could lead to finer discrimination. In considering optimization problems, we use the first argument in reverse, taking advantage of the fact that search and optimization problems can be reduced to decision problems.

We begin by extending the terminology of Definition 6.3; there we defined hard, easy, and equivalent problems in terms of complete problems, using the same type of reduction for all four. Since our present intent is to address search and optimization problems, we generalize the concepts of hard, easy, and equivalent problems to search and optimization versions by using Turing reductions from these versions to decision problems. We give the definition only for NP, the class of most interest to us, but obvious analogs exist for any complexity class. In particular, note that our generalization does not make use of complete problems, so that it is applicable to classes such as PolyL, which do not have such problems.

Definition 7.1 A problem is NP-*hard* if every problem in NP Turing reduces to it in polynomial time; it is NP-*easy* if it Turing reduces to some problem in NP in polynomial time; and it is NP-*equivalent* if it is both NP-hard and NP-easy.   □

The characteristics of hard problems are respected with this generalization; in particular, an NP-hard problem is solvable in polynomial time only if P equals NP, in which case all NP-easy problems are tractable. Since many-one reductions may be viewed as (special cases of) Turing reductions, any NP-complete problem is automatically NP-equivalent; in fact, NP-equivalence is the generalization through Turing reductions of NP-completeness.[2] In particular, an NP-equivalent problem is tractable if and only if P equals NP. Since L, P, Exp, and other such classes are restricted to decision problems, we shall prefix the class name with an F to denote the class of all functions computable within the resource bounds associated with the class; hence FL denotes the class of all functions computable in logarithmic space, FP the class of all functions computable in polynomial time, and so forth. We use this notation only with deterministic classes, since we have not defined nondeterminism beyond Boolean-valued functions.

Exercise 7.5   Prove that FP is exactly the class of P-easy problems.   □

We argued in a previous section that the decision version of an optimization problem always reduces to the optimization version. Hence any optimization problem, the decision version of which is NP-complete, is itself NP-hard. For instance, *Traveling Salesman*, *Maximum Cut*, *k-Clustering*, and *Set Cover* are all NP-hard—in decision, search, and optimization versions. Can the search and optimization versions of these problems be reduced to their decision versions? For all of the problems that we have seen, the answer is yes. The technique of reduction is always the same: first we find the optimal value of the objective function by a process of binary search (a step that is necessary only for optimization versions); then we build the optimal solution structure piece by piece, verifying each choice through calls to the oracle for the decision version. The following reduction from the optimization version of *Knapsack* to its decision version illustrates the two phases.

Theorem 7.18   *Knapsack* is NP-easy.   □

Proof.   Let an instance of *Knapsack* have n objects, integer-valued weight function w, integer-valued value function v, and weight bound B. Such an instance is described by an input string of size $O(n \log w_{max} + n \log v_{max})$,

---

[2] Whether Turing reductions are more powerful than many-one reductions within NP itself is not known; however, Turing reductions are known to be more powerful than many-one reductions within Exp.

where w_{max} is the weight of the heaviest object and v_{max} is the value of the most valuable object. First note that the value of the optimal solution is larger than zero and no larger than $n \cdot v_{max}$; while this range is exponential in the input size, it can be searched with a polynomial number of comparisons using binary search. We use this idea to determine the value of the optimal solution. Our algorithm issues $\log n + \log v_{max}$ queries to the decision oracle; the value bound is initially set at $\lfloor n \cdot v_{max}/2 \rfloor$ and then modified according to the progress of the search. At the outcome of the search, the value of the optimal solution is known; call it V_{opt}.

Now we need to ascertain the composition of an optimal solution. We proceed one object at a time: for each object in turn, we determine whether it may be included in an optimal solution. Initially, the partial solution under construction includes no objects. To pick the first object, we try each in turn: when trying object i, we ask the oracle whether there exists a solution to the new knapsack problem formed of $(n-1)$ objects (all but the ith), with weight bound set to $B - w(i)$ and value bound set to $V_{opt} - v(i)$. If the answer is "no," we try with the next object; eventually the answer must be "yes," since a solution with value V_{opt} is known to exist, and the corresponding object, say j, is included in the partial solution. The weight bound is then updated to $W - w(j)$ and the value bound to $V_{opt} - v(j)$, and the process is repeated until the updated value bound reaches zero. At worst, for a solution including k objects, we shall have examined $n - k + 1$ objects—and thus called the decision routine $n - k + 1$ times—for our first choice, $n - k$ for our second, and so on, for a total of $\frac{kn - 3k(k-1)}{2}$ calls. Hence the construction phase requires only a polynomial number of calls to the oracle.

The complete procedure is given in Figure 7.16; it calls upon the oracle a polynomial number of times (at most $(\log v_{max} + \log n + n(n+1)/2)$ times) and does only a polynomial amount of additional work in between the calls, so that the complete reduction runs in polynomial time. Hence the optimization version of *Knapsack* Turing reduces to its decision version in polynomial time.   Q.E.D.

(We made our reduction unnecessarily complex by overlooking the fact that objects eliminated in the choice of the next object to include need not be considered again. Obviously, this fact is of paramount importance in a search algorithm that attempts to solve the problem, but it makes no difference to the correctness of the proof.) While all reductions follow this model, not all are as obvious; we often have to rephrase the problem to make it amenable to reduction.

```
Procedure Knapsack(1,n,limit: integer; weight,value: intarray;
                var solution: boolarray);
  (* 1--n is the range of objects to choose from;
     limit is the weight limit on any packing;
     value, weight are arrays of natural numbers of size n;
     solution is a boolean array of size n: true means that
     the corresponding element is part of the optimal solution *)
  begin
    (* The sum of all values is a safe upper bound. *)
    sum := 0;
    for i:=1 to n do sum := sum+value[i];

    (* Use binary search to determine the optimal value.
         The oracle for the decision version takes one more
         parameter, the target value, and returns true if
         the target value can be reached or exceeded. *)
    low := 0; high := sum
    while low < high do
      begin
        mid := (low+high) div 2;
        if oracle(1,n,limit,value,weight,mid)
          then high := mid
          else low := mid
      end;
    optimal := low;

    (* Build the optimal knapsack one object at a time.
         currentvalue is the sum of the values of the objects
         included so far; currentweight plays the same role
         for weights; index points to the next candidate
         element for inclusion. *)
    for i:=1 to n do solution[i] := false;
    currentvalue := 0; currentweight := 0;
    index := 0;
    repeat (* Find next element that can be added *)
      index := index+1;
      if oracle(index,n,limit-currentweight,value,weight,
                optimal-currentvalue)
        then begin
                solution[index] := true;
                currentvalue := currentvalue+value[index];
                currentweight := currentweight+weight[index]
             end
    until currentvalue = optimal
  end; (* Knapsack *)
```

Figure 7.16 Turing reduction from optimization to decision version of *Knapsack.*

Exercise 7.6 Prove that *Minimum Test Set* (see Exercise 2.10) is NP-easy. (Hint: a direct approach at first appears to fail, because there is no way to set up new instances with partial knowledge when tests are given as subsets of classes. However, recasting the problem in terms of pairs separated so far and of pairs separated by each test allows an easy reduction.)   □

The two key points in the proof are: (i) the range of values of the objective function grows at most exponentially with the size of the instance, thereby allowing a binary search to run in polynomial time; and (ii) the *completion* problem (given a piece of the solution structure, can the piece be completed into a full structure of appropriate value) has the same structure as the optimization problem itself, thereby allowing it to reduce easily to the decision problem. A search or optimization problem is termed *self-reducible* whenever it reduces to its own decision version. Of course, self-reducibility is not even necessary. In order for the problem to be NP-easy, it is sufficient that it reduces to some NP-complete decision problem—in fact, to some collection of NP-complete problems, as a result of the following lemma, the proof of which we leave to the reader.

Lemma 7.1 Let Π be some NP-complete problem; then an oracle for any problem in NP, or for any finite collection of problems in NP, can be replaced by the oracle for Π with at most a polynomial change in the running time and number of oracle calls.   □

For instance, *Traveling Salesman* is NP-easy, although completing a partially built tour differs considerably from building a tour from scratch—in completing a tour, what is needed is a simple path between two distinct cities that includes all remaining cities, not a cycle including all remaining cities.

Exercise 7.7 Prove that *Traveling Salesman* is NP-easy. (Hint: it is possible to set up a configuration in which obtaining an optimal tour is equivalent to completing a partial tour in the original problem, so that a direct self-reduction works. However, it may be simpler to show that completing a partial tour is itself NP-complete and to reduce the original problem to both its decision version and the completion problem.)   □

In fact, all NP-complete decision problems discussed in the previous sections are easily seen to have NP-equivalent search or optimization versions— versions that are all self-reducible. Table 7.5 summarizes the steps in a typical Turing reduction from a search or optimization problem to its decision version.

While we have not presented any example of hardness or equivalence proofs for problems, the decision versions of which are in classes other than

Table 7.5 The structure of a typical proof of NP-easiness.

- If dealing with an optimization problem, establish lower and upper bounds for the value of the objective function at an optimal solution; then use binary search with the decision problem oracle to determine the value of the optimal solution.
- Determine what changes (beyond the obvious) need to be made to an instance when a first element of the solution has been chosen. This step may require considerable ingenuity.
- Build up the solution, one element at a time, from the empty set. In order to determine which element to place in the solution next, try all remaining elements, reflect the changes, and then interrogate the oracle on the existence of an optimal solution to the instance formed by the remaining pieces changed as needed.

NP, similar techniques apply. Hence Turing reductions allow us to extend our classification of decision problems to their search or optimization versions with little apparent difficulty. It should be noted, however, that Turing reductions, being extremely powerful, mask a large amount of structure. In the following sections, we examine in more detail the structure of NP-easy decision problems and related questions; researchers have also used special reductions among optimization problems to study the fine structure of NP-easy optimization problems (see the bibliography).

7.3.2 The Polynomial Hierarchy

One of the distinctions (among decision problems) that Turing reductions blur is that between a problem and its complement. As previously mentioned, it does not appear that the complement of a problem in NP is necessarily also in NP (unless, of course, the problem is also in P), since negative answers to problems in NP need not have concise certificates—but rather may require an exhaustive elimination of all possible solution structures. Since each problem in NP has a natural complement, we shall set up a new class to characterize these problems.

Definition 7.2 The class coNP is composed of the complements of the problems in NP. □

Thus for each problem in NP, we have a corresponding problem in coNP, with the same set of valid instances, but with "yes" and "no" instances reversed by negating the question. For instance, *Unsatisfiability* is in coNP as is *Non-Three-Colorability*. As usual, it is conjectured that the new class, coNP, is distinct from the old, NP; this is a stronger conjecture than P ≠ NP,

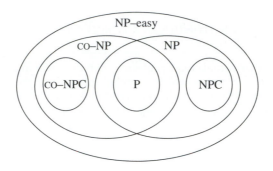

Figure 7.17   The world of decision problems around NP.

since $NP \neq coNP$ implies $P \neq NP$, while we could have $NP = coNP$ and yet $P \neq NP$.

Exercise 7.8   Prove that $NP \neq coNP$ implies $P \neq NP$.   □

It is easily seen that, given any problem complete for NP, this problem's complement is complete for coNP; moreover, in view of the properties of complete problems, no NP-complete problem can be in coNP (and vice versa) if the conjecture holds.

Exercise 7.9   Prove that, if an NP-complete problem belongs to coNP, then NP equals coNP.   □

The world of decision problems, under our new conjecture, is pictured in Figure 7.17.

The definition of coNP from NP can be generalized to any nondeterministic class to yield a corresponding co-nondeterministic class. This introduction of co-nondeterminism restores the asymmetry that we have often noted. For instance, while nondeterministic machines, in the rabbit analogy, can carry out an arbitrarily large logical "OR" at no cost, co-nondeterministic machines can do the same for a logical "AND." As another example, problems in nondeterministic classes have concise certificates for their "yes' instances, while those in co-nondeterministic classes have them for their "no" instances. While it is conjectured that NP differs from coNP and that NExp differs from coNExp, it turns out, somewhat surprisingly, that NL equals coNL and, in general, that NL^k equals $coNL^k$—a result known as the Immerman-Szelepcsényi theorem (see Exercise 7.56).

The introduction of co-nondeterministic classes, in particular coNP, prompts several questions. The first is suggested by Figure 7.17: What are the classes $NP \cap coNP$ and $NP \cup coNP$? Is $NP \cap coNP$ equal to P?

The second question is of importance because it is easier to determine membership in NP ∩ coNP than in P—the latter requires the design of an algorithm, but the former needs only verification that both "yes" and "no" instances admit succinct certificates. Unfortunately, this is yet another open question, although, as usual in such cases, the standard conjecture is that the two classes differ, with P ⊂ NP ∩ coNP. However, to date, membership in NP ∩ coNP appears to be an indication that the problem may, in fact, belong to P. Two early candidates for membership in (NP ∩ coNP) − P were linear programming and primality testing. Duality of linear programs ensures that linear programming is in both NP and coNP; however, linear programming is in P, as shown by Khachian [1979] with the ellipsoid algorithm. Compositeness, the complement of primality, is clearly in NP: a single nontrivial divisor constitutes a succinct certificate. Surprisingly, primality is also in NP—that is, every prime number has a succinct certificate—so that primality testing is in NP ∩ coNP. But, while this has not yet been proved, it is strongly suspected that primality is in P. Indeed, if the extended Riemann hypothesis of number theory is true, then primality is definitely in P. Even without this hypothesis, current primality testing algorithms run in time proportional to $n^{\log \log n}$ for an input of size n, which is hardly worse than polynomial. Such excellent behavior is taken as evidence that a polynomial-time algorithm is "just around the corner."

The similar question, "Is NP ∪ coNP equal to the set of all NP-easy decision problems?" has a more definite answer: the answer is "no" under the standard conjecture. In fact, we can even build a potentially infinite hierarchy between the two classes, using the number of calls to the decision oracle as the resource bound! Consider, for example, the following problems:

- *Optimal Vertex Cover*: Given a graph and a natural number K, does the minimum cover for the graph have size K?
- *Minimal Unsatisfiability*: Given an instance of *SAT*, is it the case that it is unsatisfiable, but that removing any one clause makes it satisfiable?
- *Unique Satisfiability*: Given an instance of *SAT*, is it satisfiable by exactly one truth assignment?
- *Traveling Salesman Factor*: Given an instance of *TSP* and a natural number i, is the length of the optimal tour a multiple of i?

(Incidentally, notice the large variety of decision problems that can be constructed from a basic optimization problem.)

Exercise 7.10 Prove that these problems are NP-equivalent; pay particular attention to the number of oracle calls used in each Turing reduction.   □

Exercise 7.11 Let us relax *Minimal Unsatisfiability* by not requiring that the original instance be unsatisfiable; prove that the resulting problem is simply NP-complete.   □

For each of the first three problems, the set of "yes" instances can be obtained as the intersection of two sets of "yes" instances, one of a problem in NP and the other of a problem in coNP. Such problems are common enough (it is clear that each of these three problems is representative of a large class—"exact answer" for the first, "criticality" for the second, and "uniqueness" for the third) that a special class has been defined for them.

Definition 7.3 The class D^p is the class of all sets, Z, that can be written as $Z = X \cap Y$, for $X \in$ NP and $Y \in$ coNP.   □

From its definition, we conclude that D^p contains both NP and coNP; in fact, it is conjectured to be a proper superset of NP $\cup$ coNP, as we can show that $D^p =$ NP $\cup$ coNP holds if and only if NP $=$ coNP does (see Exercise 7.41). The separation between these classes can be studied through complete problems: the first two problems are many-one complete for D^p while the fourth is many-one complete for the class of NP-easy decision problems. (The exact situation of *Unique Satisfiability* is unknown: along with most uniqueness versions of NP-complete problems, it is in D^p, cannot be in NP unless NP equals coNP, yet is not known to be D^p-complete.)

The basic D^p-complete problem is, of course, a satisfiability problem—namely, the *SAT-UNSAT* problem. An instance of this problem is given by two sets of clauses on two disjoint sets of variables and the question asks whether or not the first set is satisfiable and the second unsatisfiable.

Theorem 7.19 *SAT-UNSAT* is D^p-complete.   □

Proof. We need to show that *SAT-UNSAT* is in D^p and that any problem in D^p many-one reduces to it in polynomial time. The first part is easy: *SAT-UNSAT* is the intersection of a version of *SAT* (where the question is "Is the collection of clauses represented by the first half of the input satisfiable?") and a version of *UNSAT* (where the question is "Is the collection of clauses represented by the second half of the input unsatisfiable?").

The second part comes down to figuring out how to use the knowledge that (i) any problem $X \in D^p$ can be written as the intersection $X = Y_1 \cap Y_2$ of a problem $Y_1 \in$ NP and a problem $Y_2 \in$ coNP and (ii) *SAT* is NP-complete while *UNSAT* is coNP-complete, so that we have $Y_1 \leqslant_m^p$ *SAT* and $Y_2 \leqslant_m^p$ *UNSAT*. We can easily reduce *SAT* to *SAT-UNSAT* by the simple device of tacking onto the *SAT* instance a known unsatisfiable set of clauses on a different set of variables; similarly, we can easily reduce *UNSAT* to

SAT-UNSAT. It is equally easy to reduce *SAT* and *UNSAT* *simultaneously* to *SAT-UNSAT*: just tack the *UNSAT* instance onto the *SAT* one; the resulting transformed instance is a "yes" instance if and only if both original instances are "yes" instances.

Now our reduction is very simple: given an instance of problem X, say x, we know that it is also an instance of problems Y_1 and Y_2. So we apply to x the known many-one reductions from Y_1 to *SAT*, yielding instance x_1, and from Y_2 to *UNSAT*, yielding instance x_2. We then concatenate these two instances into the new instance $z = x_1 \# x_2$ of *SAT-UNSAT*. The reduction from x to z is a many-one polynomial time reduction with the desired properties.   *Q.E.D.*

Another question raised by Figure 7.17 is whether NP-easy problems constitute the set of all problems solvable in polynomial time if P equals NP. As long as the latter equality remains possible, characterizing the set of all problems that would thereby be tractable is of clear interest. Any class with this property, i.e., any class (such as NP, coNP, and D^p) that collapses into P if P equals NP, exists as a separate entity only under our standard assumption. In fact, there is a potentially infinite hierarchy of such classes, known as the *polynomial hierarchy*. In order to understand the mechanism for its construction, consider the class of all NP-easy decision problems: it is the class of all decision problems solvable in polynomial time with the help of an oracle for some suitable NP-complete problem. With an oracle for *one* NP-complete problem, we can solve in polynomial time *any* problem in NP, since all can be transformed into the given NP-complete problem; hence an oracle for some NP-complete problem may be considered as an oracle for all problems in NP. (This is the substance of Lemma 7.1.) Thus the class of NP-easy decision problems is the class of problems solvable in polynomial time with the help of an oracle for the class NP; we denote this symbolically by P^{NP}, using a superscript for the oracle.

If P were equal to NP, an oracle for NP would just be an oracle for P, which adds no power whatsoever, since we can always solve problems in P in polynomial time; hence we would have $P^{NP} = P^P = P$, as expected. Assuming that P and NP differ, we can combine nondeterminism, co-nondeterminism, and the oracle mechanism to define further classes. To begin with, rather than using a deterministic polynomial-time Turing machine with our oracle for NP, what if we used a nondeterministic one? The resulting class would be denoted by NP^{NP}. As with P^{NP}, this class depends on our standard conjectures for its existence: if P were equal to NP, we would have $NP^{NP} = NP^P = NP = P$. Conversely, since we have $NP \subseteq NP^{NP}$ (because an oracle can only add power), if problems in NP^{NP} were solvable in polynomial time, then so would problems in NP, so that we must then have $P = NP$. In other words, problems in NP^{NP} are solvable in polynomial time if and only if P equals NP—just like the NP-easy problems! Yet we do not know that such problems are NP-easy, so that NP^{NP} may be a new complexity class.

Exercise 7.12 Present candidates for membership in $NP^{NP} - P^{NP}$; such candidates must be solvable with the help of a guess, a polynomial amount of work, and a polynomial number of calls to oracles for NP.   □

We can now define the class consisting of the complements of problems in NP^{NP}, a class which we denote by $coNP^{NP}$. These two classes are similar to NP and coNP but are one level higher in the hierarchy. Pursuing the similarity, we can define a higher-level version of NP-easy problems, the NP^{NP}-easy problems. Another level can now be defined on the basis of these NP^{NP}-easy problems, so that a potentially infinite hierarchy can be erected. Problems at any level of the hierarchy have the property that they can be solved in polynomial time if and only if P equals NP—hence the name of the hierarchy. To simplify notation, the three types of classes in the hierarchy are referred to by Greek letters indexed by the level of the class in the hierarchy. The deterministic classes are denoted by Δ, the nondeterministic ones by Σ, and the co-nondeterministic ones by Π. Since these are the names used for the classes in Kleene's arithmetic hierarchy (which is indeed similar), a superscript p is added to remind us that these classes are defined with respect to polynomial time bounds. Thus P, at the bottom, is Δ_1^p (and also, because an oracle for P is no better than no oracle at all, Δ_0^p, Σ_0^p, and Π_0^p), while NP is Σ_1^p and coNP is Π_1^p. At the next level, the class of NP-easy decision problems, P^{NP}, is Δ_2^p, while NP^{NP} is Σ_2^p and $coNP^{NP}$ is Π_2^p.

Definition 7.4 The *polynomial hierarchy* is formed of three types of classes, each defined recursively: the deterministic classes Δ_k^p, the nondeterministic classes Σ_k^p, and the co-nondeterministic classes Π_k^p. These classes are defined recursively as:

$$\begin{cases} \Delta_0^p = \Sigma_0^p = \Pi_0^p = P \\ \Delta_{k+1}^p = P^{\Sigma_k^p} \\ \Sigma_{k+1}^p = NP^{\Sigma_k^p} \\ \Pi_{k+1}^p = co\text{-}\Sigma_{k+1}^p \end{cases}$$

The infinite union of these classes is denoted PH.   □

The situation at a given level of the hierarchy is illustrated in Figure 7.18; compare this figure with Figure 7.17.

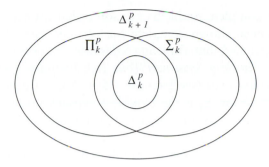

Figure 7.18   The polynomial hierarchy: one level.

An alternate characterization of problems within the polynomial hierarchy can be based on certificates. For instance, a problem A is in Σ_2^p if there exist a deterministic Turing machine M and a polynomial $p(\ )$ such that, for each yes instance x of A, there exist a concise certificate c_x and an exponential family of concise certificates F_x such that M accepts each triple of inputs (x, c_x, z), for any string $z \in F_x$, in time bounded by $p(|x|)$. The c_x certificate gives the values of the existentially quantified variables of x and the family F_x describes all possible truth assignments for the universally quantified variables. Similar characterizations obtain for all nondeterministic and co-nondeterministic classes within PH.

Complete problems are known at each level of the hierarchy—although, if the hierarchy is infinite, no complete problem can exist for PH itself (as is easily verified using the same reasoning as for PolyL). Complete problems for the Σ_k^p and Π_k^p classes are just *SAT* problems with a suitable alternation of existential and universal quantifiers. For instance, the following problem is complete for Σ_2^p. An instance is given by a Boolean formula in the variables $x_1, x_2, \ldots, x_n$ and $y_1, y_2, \ldots, y_n$; the question is "Does there exist a truth assignment for the x_i variables such that, for any truth assignment for the y_i variables, the formula evaluates to true?" In general, a complete problem for Σ_k^p has k alternating quantifiers, with the outermost existential, while a complete problem for Π_k^p is similar but has a universal outermost quantifier. A proof of completeness is not very difficult but is rather long and not particularly enlightening, for which reasons we omit it. Note the close connection between these complete problems and *QSAT*: the only difference is in the pattern of alternation of quantifiers, which is fixed for each complete problem within the polynomial hierarchy but unrestricted for *QSAT*—another way of verifying that PH is contained within PSpace.

While these complete problems are somewhat artificial, more natural problems have been shown complete for various classes within PH. We had already mentioned that *Traveling Salesman Factor* is complete for Δ_2^p; so are *Unique Traveling Salesman Tour* (see Exercise 7.48) and *Integer Expression Inequivalence* (see Exercise 7.50). A natural problem that can be shown complete for Δ_3^p is the *Double Knapsack* problem. An instance of this problem is given by an n-tuple of natural numbers $x_1, x_2, \ldots, x_n$, an m-tuple of natural numbers $y_1, y_2, \ldots, y_m$, and natural numbers N and k; the question is "Does there exist a natural number M—to be defined—with a 1 as its kth bit?" To define the number M, we let S be the set of natural numbers such that, for each $s \in S$, there exists a subset $I_s \subseteq \{1, 2, \ldots, m\}$ with $\sum_{i \in I_s} x_i = s$ and there does not exist any subset $J_s \subseteq \{1, 2, \ldots, n\}$ with $\sum_{j \in J_s} y_j = s$. M is then the largest number in S that does not exceed N—or 0 if S is empty.[3]

However, it is not known (obviously, since such knowledge would solve the question P vs. NP) whether the hierarchy is truly infinite or collapses into some Σ_k^p. In particular, we could have P $\neq$ NP but NP $=$ coNP, with the result that the whole hierarchy would collapse into NP. Overall, the polynomial hierarchy is an intriguing theoretical construct and illustrates the complexity of the issues surrounding our fundamental question of the relationship between P and NP. As we shall see in Chapter 8, several questions of practical importance are equivalent to questions concerning the polynomial hierarchy. The hierarchy also answers the question that we asked earlier: "What are the problems solvable in polynomial time if P equals NP?" Any problem that is Turing-reducible to some problem in PH (we could call such problem PH-easy) possesses this property, so that, if the hierarchy does not collapse, such problems form a proper superset of the NP-easy problems.

7.3.3   Enumeration Problems

There remains one type of problem to consider: enumeration problems. Every problem that we have seen, whether decision, search, or optimization, has an enumeration version, asking how many (optimal or feasible) solutions exist for a given instance. While decision problems may be regarded as computing the Boolean-valued characteristic function of a set, enumeration problems include all integer-valued functions. There is no doubt that

---

[3]The problem might more naturally be called *Double Subset Sum*; however, cryptographers, who devised the problem to avoid some of the weaknesses of *Subset Sum* as a basis for encryption, generally refer to the encryption schemes based on *Subset Sum* as knapsack schemes.

enumeration versions are as hard as decision versions—knowing how many solutions exist, we need only check whether the number is zero in order to solve the decision version. In most cases, we would consider enumeration versions to be significantly harder than decision, search, or optimization versions; after all, knowing how to find, say, one Hamiltonian circuit for a graph does not appear to help very much in determining how many distinct Hamiltonian circuits there are in all, especially since there may be an exponential number of them. Moreover, enumeration problems appear difficult even when the corresponding decision problems are simple: counting the number of different perfect matchings or of different cycles or of different spanning trees in a graph seems distinctly more complex than the simple task of finding one such perfect matching or cycle or spanning tree. However, some enumeration tasks can be solved in polynomial time; counting the number of spanning trees of a graph and counting the number of Eulerian paths of a graph are two nontrivial examples. Simpler examples include all problems, the optimization version of which can be solved in polynomial time using dynamic programming techniques.

Exercise 7.13 Use dynamic programming to devise a polynomial-time algorithm that counts the number of distinct optimal solutions to the matrix chain product problem. □

Definition 7.5 An integer-valued function f belongs to #P (read "number P" or "sharp P") if there exist a deterministic Turing machine T and a polynomial $p(\ )$ such that, for each input string x, the value of the function, $f(x)$, is exactly equal to the number of distinct concise certificates for x (that is, strings c_x such that T, started with x and c_x on its tape, stops and accepts x after at most $p(|x|)$ steps). □

In other words, there exists a nondeterministic polynomial-time Turing machine that can accept x in exactly $f(x)$ different ways. By definition, the enumeration version of any problem in NP is in #P.

Completeness for #P is defined in terms of polynomial-time Turing reductions rather than in terms of polynomial transformations, since the problems are not decision problems. However, polynomial transformations may still be used if they preserve the number of solutions, that is, if the number of solutions to the original instance equals the number of solutions of the transformed instance. Such transformations are called *parsimonious*. Due to its properties, a parsimonious transformation not only is a polynomial transformation between two decision problems, but also automatically induces a Turing reduction between the associated enumeration problems. Hence parsimonious transformations are the tool of choice in proving #P-completeness results for NP-hard problems. In fact, restricting ourselves to parsimonious transformations for this purpose is unnecessary; it is enough that the transformation be *weakly parsimonious*, allowing the number of solutions to the original problem to be computed in polynomial time from the number of solutions to the transformed problem.

Most proofs of NP-completeness, including Cook's proof, can be modified so as to make the transformation weakly parsimonious. That the generic transformation used in the proof of Cook's theorem can be made such is particularly important, as it gives us our first #P-complete problem: counting the number of satisfying truth assignments for a collection of clauses. Observe that the transformations we used in Section 7.1 in the proofs of NP-completeness of *MxC*, *HC*, and *Partition* are already parsimonious; moreover, all restriction proofs use an identity transformation, which is strictly parsimonious. The remaining transformations involved can be made weakly parsimonious, so that all NP-complete problems of Section 7.1 have #P-complete enumeration versions. Indeed, the same statement can be made about all known NP-complete problems. In consequence, were #P-complete problems limited to the enumeration versions of NP-complete problems, they would be of very little interest. However, some enumeration problems associated with decision problems in P are nevertheless #P-complete.

One such problem is counting the number of perfect matchings in a bipartite graph. We know that finding one such matching (or determining that none exists) is solvable in low polynomial time, yet counting them is #P-complete. A closely related problem is computing the *permanent* of a square matrix. Recall that the permanent of an $n \times n$ matrix $\mathbf{A} = (a_{ij})$ is the number $\sum_{\pi} \prod_{i=1}^{n} a_{i\pi(i)}$, where the sum is taken over all permutations π of the indices. If the matrix is the adjacency matrix of a graph, then all of its entries are either 0 or 1, so that each product term in the definition of the permanent equals either 0 or 1. Hence computing the permanent of a 0/1 matrix may be viewed as counting the number of nonzero product terms. In the adjacency matrix of a bipartite graph, each product term equals 1 if and only if the corresponding permutation of indices denotes a perfect matching; hence counting the number of perfect matchings in a bipartite graph is equivalent to computing the permanent of the adjacency matrix of that graph. Although the permanent of a matrix is defined in a manner similar to the determinant (in fact, in the definition in terms of cofactors, the only difference derives from the lack of alternation of signs in the definition of the permanent), mathematicians have long known how to compute the determinant in low polynomial time, while they have so far been unable to devise any polynomial algorithm to compute the permanent. The proof that computing the permanent is a #P-complete problem provides the first evidence that no such algorithm may exist.

How do #P-complete problems compare with other hard problems? Since they are all NP-hard (because the decision version of an NP-complete problem Turing reduces to its #P-complete enumeration version), they cannot be solved in polynomial time unless P equals NP. However, even if P equals NP, #P-complete problems may remain intractable. In other words, #P-hardness appears to be very strong evidence of intractability. While it is difficult to compare #P, a class a functions, with our other complexity classes, which are classes of sets, we can use #P-easy decision problems, the class $P^{\#P}$ in our oracle-based notation, instead. It is easy to see that this class is contained in PSPACE; it contains PH, a result that we shall not prove.

It should be pointed out that many counting problems, while in #P and apparently hard, do not seem to be #P-complete. Some are NP-easy (such as counting the number of distinct isomorphisms between two graphs, which is no harder than deciding whether the two graphs are isomorphic—see Exercise 7.54). Others are too restricted (such as counting how many graphs of n vertices possess a certain property, problems that have only one instance for each value of n—see Exercise 7.55).

7.4 Exercises

Exercise 7.14* Prove that these two variants of *3SAT* are both in P.

- *Strong 3SAT* requires that at least two literals be set to true in each clause.
- *Odd 3SAT* requires that an odd number of literals be set to true in each clause.

Exercise 7.15* Does *Vertex Cover* remain NP-complete when we also require that each edge be covered by exactly one vertex? (Clearly, not all graphs have such covers, regardless of the value of the bound; for instance, a single triangle cannot be covered in this manner.)

Exercise 7.16 Consider a slight generalization of *Maximum Cut*, in which each edge has a positive integer weight and the bound is on the sum of the weights of the cut edges. Will the naïve transformation first attempted in our proof for *MxC* work in this case, with the following change: whenever multiple edges between a pair of vertices arise, say k in number, replace them with a single edge of weight k.

Exercise 7.17 What is wrong with this reduction from *G3C* to *Minimum Vertex-Deletion Bipartite Subgraph* (delete at most K vertices such that the resulting graph is bipartite)?

- Given an instance $G = (V, E)$ of G3C, just let the instance of *MVDBS* be G itself, with bound $K = \lfloor |V|/3 \rfloor$.

Identify what makes the transformation fail and provide a specific instance of *G3C* that gets transformed into an instance with opposite answer.

Exercise 7.18 Prove that *Exact Cover by Four-Sets* is NP-complete. An instance of the problem is given by a set S of size $4k$ for some positive integer k and by a collection of subsets of S, each of size 4; the question is "Do there exist k subsets in the collection that together form a partition of S?" (Hint: use a transformation from X3C.)

Exercise 7.19 Prove that *Cut into Acyclic Subgraphs* is NP-complete. An instance of the problem is given by a directed graph; the question is "Can the set of vertices be partitioned into two subsets such that each subset induces an acyclic subgraph?" (Hint: transform one of the satisfiability problems.)

Exercise 7.20 Prove that *Three-Dimensional Matching* is NP-complete. An instance of the problem is given by three sets of equal cardinality and a set of triples such that the ith element of each triple is an element of the ith set, $1 \leqslant i \leqslant 3$; the question is "Does there exist a subset of triples such that each set element appears exactly once in one of the triples?" Such a solution describes a perfect matching of all set elements into triples. (Hint: this problem is very similar to X3C.)

Exercise 7.21 Prove that both *Vertex-* and *Edge-Dominating Set* are NP-complete. An instance of the problem is given by an undirected graph $G = (V, E)$ and a natural number B; the question is "Does there exist a subset of vertices $V' \subseteq V$ of size at most B such that every vertex (respectively, edge) of the graph is dominated by at least one vertex in V'?" We say that a vertex *dominates* another if there exists an edge between the two and we say that a vertex dominates an edge if there exist two edges that complete the triangle (from the vertex to the two endpoints of the edge). (Hint: use a transformation from VC; the same construction should work for both problems.)

Exercise 7.22 (Refer to the previous exercise.) Let us further restrict *Vertex-Dominating Set* by requiring that (i) the dominating set, V', is an independent set (no edges between any two of its members) and (ii) each vertex in $V - V'$ is dominated by at most one vertex in V'. Prove that the resulting problem remains NP-complete. (Hint: use a transformation from *Positive 1in3SAT*.)

Exercise 7.23 Prove that *Longest Common Subsequence* is NP-complete. An instance of this problem is given by an alphabet Σ, a finite set of strings on the alphabet $R \subseteq \Sigma^*$, and a natural number K. The question is "Does there exist a string, $w \in \Sigma^*$, of length at least K, that is a subsequence of each string in R?" (Hint: use a transformation from VC.)

Exercise 7.24 Prove that the decision version of *Optimal Identification Tree* is NP-complete. An instance of the optimization problem is given by a collection of m categories $\{O_1, O_2, \ldots, O_m\}$ and a collection of n dichotomous tests $\{T_1, T_2, \ldots, T_n\}$, each of which is specified by an $m \times 1$ binary vector of outcomes. The optimization problem is to construct a decision tree with minimal average path length:

$$\sum_{i=1}^{m} (\text{depth}(O_i) - 1)$$

where $\text{depth}(O_i) - 1$ is the number of tests that must be performed to identify an object in category O_i. The tree has exactly one leaf for each category; each interior node corresponds to a test. While the same test cannot occur twice on the same path in an optimal tree, it certainly can occur several times in the tree. (Hint: use a transformation from X3C.)

Exercise 7.25 Prove that the decision version of *Minimum Test Set* (see Exercises 2.10 and 7.6) is NP-complete. (Hint: use a transformation from X3C.)

Exercise 7.26 Prove that *Steiner Tree in Graphs* is NP-complete. An instance of the problem is given by a graph with a distinguished subset of vertices; each edge has a positive integer length and there is a positive integer bound. The question is "Does there exist a tree that spans all of the vertices in the distinguished subset—and possibly more—such that the sum of the lengths of all the edges in the tree does not exceed the given bound?" (Hint: use a transformation from X3C.)

Exercise 7.27 Although finding a minimum spanning tree is a well-solved problem, finding a spanning tree that meets an added or different constraint is almost always NP-complete. Prove that the following problems (in their decision version, of course) are NP-complete. (Hint: four of them can be restricted to *Hamiltonian Path*; use a transformation from X3C for the other two.)

1. *Bounded-Diameter Spanning Tree*: Given a graph with positive integer edge lengths, given a positive integer bound D, no larger than the number of vertices in the graph, and given a positive integer bound K, does there exist a spanning tree for the graph with diameter (the number of edges on the longest simple path in the tree) no larger than D and such that the sum of the lengths of all edges in the tree does not exceed K?

2. *Bounded-Degree Spanning Tree*: This problem has the same statement as *Bounded-Diameter Spanning Tree*, except that the diameter bound is replaced by a degree bound (that is, no vertex in the tree may have a degree larger than D).

3. *Maximum-Leaves Spanning Tree*: Given a graph and an integer bound no larger than the number of vertices, does the graph have a spanning tree with no fewer leaves (nodes of degree 1 in the tree) than the given bound?

4. *Minimum-Leaves Spanning Tree*: This problem has the same statement as *Maximum-Leaves Spanning Tree* but asks for a tree with no more leaves than the given bound.

5. *Spanning Tree with Specified Leaves*: Given a graph and a distinguished subset of vertices, does the graph have a spanning tree, the leaves of which form the given subset?

6. *Isomorphic Spanning Tree*: Given a graph and a tree, does the graph have a spanning tree isomorphic to the given tree?

Exercise 7.28 Like spanning trees, two-colorings are easy to obtain when not otherwise restricted. The following two versions of the problem, however, are NP-complete. Both have the same instances, composed of a graph and a positive integer bound K.

- *Minimum Vertex-Deletion Bipartite Subgraph* asks whether or not the graph can be made bipartite by deleting at most K vertices.
- *Minimum Edge-Deletion Bipartite Subgraph* asks whether or not the graph can be made bipartite by deleting at most K edges.

(Hint: use a transformation from *Vertex Cover* for the first version and one from *MxC* for the second.)

Exercise 7.29 Prove that *Monochromatic Vertex Triangle* is NP-complete. An instance of the problem is given by a graph; the question is "Can the graph be partitioned into two vertex sets such that neither induced subgraph contains a triangle?" The partition can be viewed as a two-coloring of the vertices; in this view, forbidden triangles are those with all three vertices of the same color. (Hint: use a transformation from *Positive NAE3SAT*; you must design a small gadget that ensures that its two end vertices always end up on the same side of the partition.)

Exercise 7.30* Repeat the previous exercise, but for *Monochromatic Edge Triangle*, where the partition is into two edge sets. The same starting problem and general idea for the transformation will work, but the gadget must be considerably more complex, as it must ensure that its two end edges always end up on the same side of the partition. (The author's gadget uses only three extra vertices but a large number of edges.)

Exercise 7.31 Prove that *Consecutive Ones Submatrix* is NP-complete. An instance of the problem is given by an $m \times n$ matrix with entries drawn from $\{0, 1\}$ and a positive integer bound K; the question is "Does the matrix contains an $m \times K$ submatrix that has the "consecutive ones" property?" A matrix has that property whenever its columns can be permuted so that, in each row, all the 1s occur consecutively. (Hint: use a transformation from *Hamiltonian Path*.)

Exercise 7.32* Prove that *Comparative Containment* is NP-complete. An instance of the problem is given by a set, S, and two collections of subsets of S, say $B \subseteq 2^S$ and $C \subseteq 2^S$; the question is "Does there exist a subset, $X \subseteq S$, obeying

$$|\{b \in B | X \subseteq b\}| \geq |\{c \in C | X \subseteq c\}|$$

that is, such that X is contained (as a set) in at least as many subsets in the collection B as in subsets in the collection C?"

   Use a transformation from *Vertex Cover*. In developing the transformation, you must face two difficulties typical of a large number of reductions. One difficulty is that the original problem contains a parameter—the bound on the cover size—that has no corresponding part in the target problem; the other difficulty is the reverse—the target problem has two collections of subsets, whereas the original problem only has one. The first difficulty is overcome by using the bound as part of the transformation, for instance by using it to control the number of elements, of subsets, of copies, or of similar constructs; the second is overcome much as was done in our reduction to *SF-REI*, by making one collection reflect the structure of the instance and making the other be more general to serve as a foil.

Exercise 7.33* Prove that *Betweenness* is NP-complete. An instance of this problem is given by a set, S, and a collection of ordered triples from the set, $C \subseteq S \times S \times S$; the question is "Does there exist an indexing of S, $i: S \to \{1, 2, \ldots, |S|\}$, such that, for each triple, $(a, b, c) \in C$, we have either $i(a) < i(b) < i(c)$ or $i(c) < i(b) < i(a)$?" (Hint: there is a deceptively simple—two triples per clause—transformation from *Positive NAE3SAT*.)

Exercise 7.34* Given some NP-complete problem by its certificate-checking machine M, define the following language:

$$L = \{(M, p(\ ), y) \mid \exists x \text{ such that } M \text{ accepts } (x, y) \text{ in } p(|x|) \text{ time}\}$$

In other words, L is the set of all machine/certificate pairs such that the certificate leads the machine to accept some input string or other. What can you say about the complexity of membership in L?

Exercise 7.35 Prove that *Element Generation* is P-complete. An instance of the problem consists of a finite set S, a binary operation on S denoted $\odot: S \times S \rightarrow S$, a subset $G \subseteq S$ of generators, and a target element $t \in S$. The question is "Can the target element be produced from the generators through the binary operation?" In other words, does there exist some parenthesized expression involving only the generators and the binary operation that evaluates to the target element? (Hint: the binary operation $\odot$ is not associative; if it were, the problem would become simply NL-complete, for which see Exercise 7.38.)

Exercise 7.36 Prove that *CV* (but not *Monotone CV*!) remains P-complete even when the circuit is planar.

Exercise 7.37 Prove that *Digraph Reachability* is (logspace) complete for NL (you must use a generic transformation, since this is our first NL-complete problem). An instance of the problem is given by a directed graph (a list of vertices and list of arcs); the question is "Can vertex n (the last in the list) be reached from vertex 1?"

Exercise 7.38 Using the result of the previous exercise, prove that *Associative Generation* is NL-complete. This problem is identical to *Element Generation* (see Exercise 7.35), except that the operation is associative.

Exercise 7.39 Prove that *Two-Unsatisfiability* is NL-complete. An instance of this problem is an instance of *2SAT*; the question is whether or not the collection of clauses is unsatisfiable.

Exercise 7.40 Prove that *Optimal Identification Tree* (see Exercise 7.24 above) is NP-equivalent.

Exercise 7.41* Prove that the following three statements are equivalent:

- $\Delta_2^p = \text{NP} \cup \text{coNP}$

- $D^p = \text{NP} \cup \text{coNP}$
- $\text{NP} = \text{coNP}$

The only nontrivial implication is from the second to the third statement. Use a *nondeterministic* polynomial-time many-one reduction from the known D^p-complete problem *SAT-UNSAT* to a known coNP-complete problem. Since the reduction clearly leaves NP unchanged, it shows that *SAT-UNSAT* belongs to NP only if $\text{NP} = \text{coNP}$. Now define a mirror image that reduces *SAT-UNSAT* to a known NP-complete problem.

Exercise 7.42 Prove that, if we had a solution algorithm that ran in $O(n^{\log n})$ time for some NP-complete problem, then we could solve any problem in PH in $O(n^{\log^k n})$ time, for suitable k (which depends on the level of the problem within PH).

Exercise 7.43 Prove that the enumeration version of *SAT* is #P-complete (that is, show that the generic transformation used in the proof of Cook's theorem can be made weakly parsimonious).

Exercise 7.44 Consider the following three decision problems, all variations on *SAT*; an instance of any of these problems is simply an instance of *SAT*.

- Does the instance have at least three satisfying truth assignments?
- Does the instance have at most three satisfying truth assignments?
- Does the instance have exactly three satisfying truth assignments?

Characterize as precisely as possible (using completeness proofs where possible) the complexity of each version.

Exercise 7.45* Prove that *Unique Satisfiability* (described in Section 7.3.2) cannot be in NP unless NP equals coNP.

Exercise 7.46* Prove that *Minimal Unsatisfiability* (described in Section 7.3.2) is D^p-complete. (Hint: Develop separate transformations to this problem from *SAT* and from *UNSAT*; then show that you can reduce two instances of this problem to a single one. The combined reduction is then a valid reduction from *SAT-UNSAT*. A reduction from either *SAT* or *UNSAT* can be developed by adding a large collection of new variables and clauses so that specific "regions" of the space of all possible truth assignments are covered by a unique clause.)

Exercise 7.47** Prove that *Optimal Vertex Cover* (described in Section 7.3.2) is D^p-complete. (Hint: develop separate transformations from *SAT* and *UNSAT* and combine them into a single reduction from *SAT-UNSAT*.)

Exercise 7.48[**] Prove that *Unique Traveling Salesman Tour* is complete for Δ_2^p. An instance of this problem is given by a list of cities and a (symmetric) matrix of intercity distances; the question is whether or not the optimal tour is unique. (Hint: a problem cannot be complete for Δ_2^p unless solving it requires a supralogarithmic number of calls to the decision oracle. Since solving this problem can be done by finding the value of the optimal solution and then making two oracle calls, the search must take a supralogarithmic number of steps. Thus the distances produced in your reduction must be exponentially large.)

Exercise 7.49 Prove that *Minimal Boolean Expression* is in Π_2^p. An instance of the problem is given by a Boolean formula and the question is "Is this formula the shortest among all equivalent Boolean formulae?" Does the result still hold if we also require that the minimal formula be unique?

Exercise 7.50[**] Prove that *Integer Expression Inequivalence* is complete for Δ_2^p. This problem is similar to *SF-REI* but is given in terms of arithmetic rather than regular expression. An instance of the problem is given by two integer expressions. An integer expression is defined inductively as follows. The binary representation of an integer n is the integer expression denoting the set $\{n\}$; if e and f are two integer expressions denoting the sets E and F, then $e \cup f$ is an integer expression denoting the set $E \cup F$ and $e + f$ is an integer expression denoting the set $\{i + j \mid i \in E$ and $j \in F\}$. The question is "Do the two given expressions denote different sets?" (In contrast, note that *Boolean Expression Inequivalence* is in NP.)

Exercise 7.51[*] Let $\mathscr{C}$ denote a complexity class and M a Turing machine in that class. Prove that the set $\{(M, x) \mid M \in \mathscr{C}$ and M accepts $x\}$ is undecidable for $\mathscr{C} = $ NP $\cap$ coNP. Contrast this result with that of Exercise 6.25; classes of complexity for which this set is undecidable are often called *semantic* classes.

Exercise 7.52 Refer to Exercises 6.25 and 7.51, although you need not have solved them in order to solve this exercise. If the bounded halting problem for NP is NP-complete but that for NP $\cap$ coNP is undecidable, why can we not conclude immediately that NP differs from NP $\cap$ coNP and thus, in particular, that P is unequal to NP?

Exercise 7.53[*] Show that the number of distinct Eulerian circuits of a graph can be computed in polynomial time.

Exercise 7.54[*] Verify that computing the number of distinct isomorphisms between two graphs is no harder than deciding whether or not the two graphs are in fact isomorphic.

Exercise 7.55* A *tally language* is a language in which every string uses only one symbol from the alphabet; if we denote this symbol by *a*, then every tally language is a subset of $\{a\}^*$. In particular, a tally language has at most one string of each length. Show that a tally language cannot be NP-complete unless P equals NP.

Exercise 7.56* Develop the proof of the Immerman-Szelepscényi theorem as follows. To prove the main result, NL = coNL, we first show that a nondeterministic Turing machine running in logarithmic space can compute the number of vertices reachable from vertex 1 in a digraph—a counting version of the NL-complete problem *Digraph Reachability*. Verify that the following program either quits or returns the right answer and that there is always a sequence of guesses that enables it to return the right answer.

```
|S(0)| = 1;
for i=1 to |V|-1 do (* compute |S(i)| from |S(i-1)| *)
  size_Si = 0;
  for j=1 to |V| do (* increment size_Si if j is in S(i) *)
    (* j is in S(i) if it is 0 or 1 step away
       from a vertex of S(i-1) *)
    in_Si = false;
    size_Si_1 = 0; (* recompute as a consistency check *)
    for k=1 to |V| while not in_Si do
        (* consider only those vertices k in S(i-1) *)
        (* k is in S(i-1) if we can guess a path of
           i-1 vertices from 1 to k *)
        guess i-1 vertices;
        if (guessed vertices form a path from 1 to k)
          then size_Si_1 = size_Si_1 + 1; (* k is in S(i-1) *)
               if j=k or {j,k} in E
                  then in_Si = true (* j is in S(i) *)
          (* implicit else: bad guess or k not in S(i-1) *)
  if in_Si
    then size_Si = size_Si + 1
    else if size_Si_1 <> |S(i-1)| then quit;
        (* inconsistency flags a bad guess of i-1 vertices
           when testing vertices for membership in S(i-1) *)
  |S(i)| = size_Si
```

Now the main result follows easily: given a nondeterministic Turing machine for a problem in NL, we construct another nondeterministic Turing machine that also runs in logarithmic space and solves the complement of the problem. The new machine with input *x* runs the code just given on the digraph formed by the IDs of the first machine run on *x*. If it ever encounters an accepting ID, it rejects the input; if it computes $|S(|V| - 1)|$ without having found an accepting ID, it accepts the input. Verify that this new machine works as claimed.   □

7.5   Bibliography

Garey and Johnson [1979] wrote the standard text on NP-completeness and related subjects; in addition to a lucid presentation of the topics, their text contains a categorized and annotated list of over 300 known NP-hard problems. New developments are covered by D.S. Johnson in "The NP-Completeness Column: An Ongoing Guide," which appears irregularly in the *Journal of Algorithms* and is written in the same style as the Garey and Johnson text. Papadimitriou [1994] wrote the standard text on complexity theory; it extends our coverage to other classes not mentioned here as well as to more theoretical topics.

Our proofs of NP-completeness are, for the most part, original (or at least independently derived), compiled from the material of classes taught by the author and from Moret and Shapiro [1985]. The XOR construct used in the proof of NP-completeness of *HC* comes from Garey, Johnson, and Tarjan [1976]. An exhaustive reference on the subject of P-complete problems is the text of Greenlaw *et al.* [1994].

Among studies of optimization problems based on reductions finer than the Turing reduction, the work of Krentel [1988a] is of particular interest; the query hierarchy that we mentioned briefly (based on the number of oracle calls) has been studied by, among others, Wagner [1988]. The proof that co-nondeterminism is equivalent to nondeterminism in space complexity is due independently to Immerman [1988] and to Szelepcsényi [1987]. Miller [1976] proved that *Primality* is in P if the extended Riemann hypothesis holds, while Pratt [1975] showed that every prime has a concise certificate. Leggett and Moore [1981] pioneered the study of Δ_2^p in relation with NP and coNP and proved that many optimality problems ("Does the optimal solution have value K?") are not in NP $\cup$ coNP unless NP equals coNP; Exercise 7.50 is taken from their work. The class D^p was introduced by Papadimitriou and Yannakakis [1984], from which Exercise 7.47 is taken, and further studied by Papadimitriou and Wolfe [1988], where the solution of Exercise 7.46 can be found; *Unique Satisfiability* is the subject of Blass and Gurevich [1982]. *Unique Traveling Salesman Tour* was proved to be Δ_2^p-complete (Exercise 7.48) by Papadimitriou [1984], while the *Double Knapsack* problem was shown Δ_3^p-complete by Krentel [1988b]. The polynomial hierarchy is due to Stockmeyer [1976].

The class #P was introduced by Valiant [1979a], who gave several #P-complete counting problems. Valiant [1979b] proved that the permanent is #P-complete; further #P-hard problems can be found in Provan [1986]. Simon [1977] had introduced parsimonious transformations in a similar context.

CHAPTER 8

Complexity Theory in Practice

Knowing that a problem is NP-hard or worse does not make the problem disappear; some solution algorithm must still be designed. All that has been learned is that no practical algorithm that always returns the optimal solution can be designed. Many options remain open. We may hope that real-world instances will present enough structure that an optimal algorithm (using backtracking or branch-and-bound techniques) will run quickly; that is, we may hope that all of the difficult instances are purely theoretical constructs, unlikely to arise in practice. We may decide to restrict our attention to special cases of the problem, hoping that some of the special cases are tractable, while remaining relevant to the application at hand. We may rely on an approximation algorithm that runs quickly and returns good, albeit suboptimal, results. We may opt for a probabilistic approach, using efficient algorithms that return optimal results in most cases, but may fail miserably—possibly to the point of returning altogether erroneous answers—on some instances. The algorithmic issues are not our current subject; let us just note that very little can be said beforehand as to the applicability of a specific technique to a specific problem. However, guidance of a more general type can be sought from complexity theory once again, since the applicability of a technique depends on the nature of the problem. This chapter describes some of the ways in which complexity theory may help the algorithm designer in assessing hard problems. Some of the issues just raised, such as the possibility that real-world instances have sufficient added constraints to allow a search for optimal solutions, cannot at present be addressed within the framework of complexity theory, as we know of no mechanism with which to characterize the structure of instances. Others, however, fall within the purview of current methodologies, such as the analysis of subproblems, the value of approximation methods, and the power of probabilistic approaches; these form the topics of this chapter.

8.1   Circumscribing Hard Problems

The reader will recall from Chapter 4 that many problems, when taken in their full generality, are undecidable. Indeed, such fundamental questions as whether a program is correct or whether it halts under certain inputs are undecidable. Yet all instructors in programming classes routinely decide whether student programs are correct. The moral is that, although such problems are undecidable in their full generality, most of their instances are quite easily handled. We may hope that the same principle applies to (provably or probably—we shall use the term without qualifiers) intractable problems and that most instances are in fact easily solvable. From a practical standpoint, easily solvable just means that our solution algorithm runs quickly on most or all instances to which it is applied. In this context, some means of predicting the running time would be very welcome, enabling us to use our algorithm judiciously. From a theoretical standpoint, however, we cannot measure the time required by an algorithm on a single instance in our usual terms (polynomial or exponential), since these terms are defined only for infinite classes of instances. Consequently, we are led to consider restricted versions of our hard problems and to examine their complexity. Since possible restrictions are infinitely varied, we must be content here with presenting some typical restrictions for our most important problems in order to illustrate the methodology.

8.1.1   Restrictions of Hard Problems

We have already done quite a bit of work in this direction for the satisfiability problem. We know that the general *SAT* problem is NP-complete and that it remains so even if it is restricted to instances where each clause contains exactly three literals. We also know that the problem becomes tractable when restricted to instances where each clause contains at most two literals. In terms of the number of literals per clause, then, we have completely classified all variants of the problem. However, there are other "dimensions" along which we can vary the requirements placed on instances: for instance, we could consider the number of times that a variable may appear among all clauses. Call a satisfiability problem *k,l-SAT* if it is restricted to instances where each clause contains k literals and each variable appears at most l times among all clauses; in that notation, our familiar *3SAT* problem becomes *3,l-SAT*. We know that *2,l-SAT* is solvable in polynomial time for any l; a rather different approach yields a polynomial-time algorithm that solves *k,2-SAT*.

Exercise 8.1 Prove that *k,2-SAT* is solvable in polynomial time for any k.

□

Consider now the *k,k-SAT* problem. It is also solvable in polynomial time; in fact, it is a trivial problem because all of its instances are satisfiable! We derive this rather surprising result by reducing *k,l-SAT* to a bipartite matching problem. Notice that a satisfying assignment in effect singles out one literal per clause and sets it to true; what happens to the other literals in the clause is quite irrelevant, as long as it does not involve a contradiction. Thus an instance of *k,l-SAT* may be considered as a system of m (the number of clauses) sets of k elements each (the variables of the clause); a solution is then a selection of n elements (the true literals) such that each of the m sets contains at least one variable corresponding to a selected element. In other words, a satisfying assignment is a set of not necessarily distinct representatives, with the constraint that the selection of one element always prohibits the selection of another (the complement of the literal selected). Thus the *k,l-SAT* problem reduces to a much generalized version of the *Set of Distinct Representatives* problem. In a *k,k-SAT* problem, however, none of the k variables contained in a clause is contained in more than k clauses in all, so that any i clauses taken together always contain at least i distinct variables. This condition fulfills the hypothesis of Hall's theorem (see Exercise 2.27), so that the transformed problem always admits a set of distinct representatives. In terms of the satisfiability problem, there exists an injection from the set of clauses to the set of variables such that each clause contains the variable to which it is mapped. Given this map, it is easy to construct a satisfying truth assignment: just set each variable to the truth value that satisfies the corresponding clause—since all representative variables are distinct, there can be no conflict.

How many occurrences of a literal may be allowed before a satisfiability problem becomes NP-complete? The following theorem shows that allowing three occurrences is sufficient to make the general *SAT* problem NP-complete, while four are needed to make *3SAT* NP-complete—thereby completing our classification of *3,l-SAT* problems, since we have just shown that *3,3-SAT* is trivial.

Theorem 8.1 *3,4-SAT* is NP-complete.   □

Proof. We first provide a simple reduction from *3SAT* to a relaxed version of *3,3-SAT* where clauses are allowed to have either two or three literals each. This proves that three occurrences of each variable are enough to make *SAT* NP-complete; we then finish the transformation to *3,4-SAT*.

Let an instance of *3SAT* be given. If no variable appears more than three times, we are done. If variable x appears k times (in complemented or uncomplemented form), with $k > 3$, we replace it by k variables, $x_1, \ldots, x_k$, and replace its ith occurrence, say $\hat{x}$, by $\hat{x}_i$. To ensure that all x_i variables be given the same truth value, we write a circular list of implications:

$$x_1 \Rightarrow x_2, \; x_2 \Rightarrow x_3, \; \ldots, \; x_{k-1} \Rightarrow x_k, \; x_k \Rightarrow x_1$$

which we can rewrite as a collection of clauses of two literals each:

$$\{\overline{x_1}, x_2\}, \; \{\overline{x_2}, x_3\}, \; \ldots, \; \{\overline{x_{k-1}}, x_k\}, \; \{\overline{x_k}, x_1\}$$

The resulting collection of clauses includes clauses of two literals and clauses of three literals, has no variable occurring more than three times, and can easily be produced from the original instance in polynomial time. Hence *SAT* is NP-complete even when restricted to instances where no clause has more than three literals and where no variable appears more than three times.

Now we could use the padding technique of Theorem 7.1 to turn the two-literal clauses into three-literal clauses. The padding would duplicate all our "implication" clauses, thereby causing the substitute variables x_i to appear five times. The result is a transformation into instances of *3,5-SAT*, showing that the latter is NP-complete. A transformation to *3,4-SAT* requires a more complex padding technique, which we elaborate below. For each two-literal clause, say $c = \{\hat{x}, \hat{y}\}$, we use four additional variables, $f_c, p_c, q_c,$ and r_c. Variable f_c is added to the two-literal clause and we write five other clauses to force it to assume the truth value "false." These clauses are:

$$\{\overline{p_c}, q_c, \overline{f_c}\}, \{\overline{q_c}, r_c, \overline{f_c}\}, \{\overline{r_c}, p_c, \overline{f_c}\} \{p_c, q_c, r_c\}, \{\overline{p_c}, \overline{q_c}, \overline{r_c}\}$$

The first three clauses are equivalent to the implications:

$$p_c \vee \overline{q_c} \Rightarrow \overline{f_c} \qquad q_c \vee \overline{r_c} \Rightarrow \overline{f_c} \qquad r_c \vee \overline{p_c} \Rightarrow \overline{f_c}$$

The last two clauses assert that one or more of the preconditions are met:

$$(p_c \vee \overline{q_c}) \wedge (q_c \vee \overline{r_c}) \wedge (r_c \vee \overline{p_c})$$

Hence the five clauses taken together force f_c to be set to false, so that its addition to the original two-literal clause does not affect the logical value of the clause. Each of the additional variables appears exactly four times and no other variable appears more than three times, so that the resulting instance has no variable appearing more than four times. We have just described a transformation into instances of *3,4-SAT*. This transformation is easily accomplished in polynomial time, which completes our proof.   *Q.E.D.*

Many otherwise hard problems may become tractable when restricted to special instances; we give just one more example here, but the reader will find more examples in the exercises and references, as well as in the next section.

Example 8.1 Consider the *Binpacking* problem. Recall that an instance of this problem is given by a set, S, of elements, each with a size, $s: S \rightarrow \mathbb{N}$, and by a bin size, B. The goal is to pack all of the elements into the smallest number of bins. Now let us restrict this problem to instances where all elements are large, specifically, where all elements have sizes at least equal to a third of the bin size. We claim that, in that case, the problem is solvable in polynomial time. A bin will contain one, two, or three elements; the case of three elements is uniquely identifiable, since every element involved must have size equal to $B/3$. Thus we can begin by checking whether B is divisible by three. If it is, we collect all elements of size $B/3$ and group them by threes, with each such group filling one bin; leftover elements of size $B/3$ are placed back with the other elements. This preprocessing phase takes at most linear time. Now we identify all possible pairs of elements that can fit together in a bin, a step that takes at most quadratic time. (Elements too large to fit with any other in a bin will occupy their own bin.) Now we need only select the largest subset of pairs that do not share any element— that is, we need to solve a maximum matching problem, a problem for which many polynomial-time solutions exist. Once a maximum matching has been identified, any elements not in the matching are assigned their own bin. Overall, the running time of this algorithm is dominated by the running time of the matching algorithm, which is a low polynomial. A simple case analysis shows that the algorithm is optimal.   □

We might embark upon an exhaustive program of classification for reasonable[1] variants of a given hard problem. The richest field by far has proved

---

[1] By "reasonable" we do not mean only plausible, but also easily verifiable. Recall that we must be able to distinguish erroneous input from correct input in polynomial time. Thus a reasonable variant is one that is characterized by easily verifiable features.

to be that of graph problems: the enormous variety of named "species" of graphs provides a wealth of ready-made subproblems for any graph problem. We refer the reader to the current literature for results in this area and present only a short discussion of the graph coloring and Hamiltonian circuit problems.

We know that deciding whether an arbitrary graph is three-colorable is NP-complete: this is the *G3C* problem of the previous chapter. In fact, the problem is NP-complete for any fixed number of colors larger than two; it is easily solvable in linear time for two colors, a problem equivalent to asking whether the graph is bipartite. What about the restriction of the problem to planar graphs—corresponding, more or less, to the problem of coloring maps? Since planarity can be tested in linear time, such a restriction is reasonable. The celebrated four-color theorem states that any planar graph can be colored with four colors; thus graph coloring for planar graphs is trivial for any fixed number of colors larger than or equal to four.[2] The following theorem shows that *G3C* remains hard when restricted to planar graphs.

Theorem 8.2 *Planar G3C is NP-complete.*   □

Proof. This proof is an example of the type discussed in Section 7.1, as it requires the design of a gadget. We reduce *G3C* to its planar version by providing a "crossover" gadget to be used whenever the embedding of the graph in the plane produces crossing edges. With all crossings removed from the embedding, the result is a planar graph; if we can ensure that it is three-colorable if and only if the original graph is, we will have proved our result.

Two crossing edges cannot share an endpoint; hence they are independent of each other from the point of view of coloring. Thus a crossing gadget must replace the two edges in such a way that: (i) the gadget is planar and three-colorable (of course); (ii) the coloring of the endpoints of one original edge in no way affects the coloring of the endpoints of the other; and (iii) the two endpoints of an original edge cannot be given the same color. We design a planar, three-colorable gadget with four endpoints, x, x', y, and y', which can be colored only by assigning the same color to x and x' and, independently, the same color to y and y'. The reader can verify that the graph fragment illustrated in the first part of Figure 8.1 fulfills these requirements. The second part of the figure shows how to use this gadget to remove crossings from some edge $\{a, b\}$. One endpoint of

---

[2]The problem is trivial only as a decision problem. Finding a coloring is a very different story. Although the proof of the four-color theorem is in effect a polynomial-time coloring algorithm, its running time and overhead are such that it cannot be applied to graphs of any significant size, leaving one to rely upon heuristics and search methods.

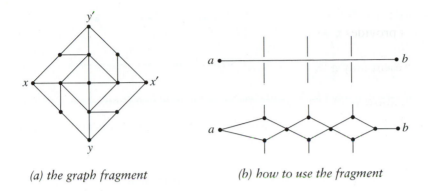

(a) the graph fragment   (b) how to use the fragment

Figure 8.1   The gadget used to replace edge crossings in graph colorability.

the edge (here a) is part of the leftmost gadget, while the other endpoint remains distinct and connected to the rightmost gadget by an edge that acts exactly like the original edge. Embedding an arbitrary graph in the plane, detecting all edge crossings, and replacing each crossing with our gadget are all easily done in polynomial time.   *Q.E.D.*

Planarity is not the only reasonable parameter involved in the graph colorability problem. Another important parameter in a graph is the maximum degree of its vertices. A theorem due to Brooks [1941] (that we shall not prove here) states that the chromatic number of a connected graph never exceeds the maximum vertex degree of the graph by more than one; moreover, the bound is reached if and only if the graph is a complete graph or an odd circuit. In particular, a graph having no vertex degree larger than three is three-colorable if and only if it is not the complete graph on four vertices, a condition that can easily be checked in linear time. Thus *G3C* restricted to graphs of degree three is in P. However, as vertices are allowed to have a degree equal to four, an abrupt transition takes place.

Theorem 8.3 *G3C* is NP-complete even when restricted to instances where no vertex degree may exceed four.   ☐

Proof. This time we need to replace any vertex of degree larger than four with a gadget such that: (i) the gadget is three-colorable and contains no vertex with degree larger than four (obviously); (ii) there is one "attaching point" for each vertex to which the original vertex was connected; and (iii) all attaching points must be colored identically. A building block for our gadget that possesses all of these properties is shown in Figure 8.2(a); this building block provides three attaching points (the three "corners" of

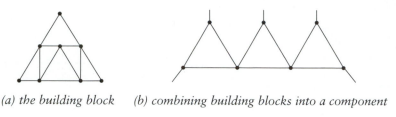

(a) the building block   (b) combining building blocks into a component

Figure 8.2   The gadget used to reduce vertex degree for graph colorability.

the "triangle"). More attaching points are provided by stringing together several such blocks as shown in Figure 8.2(b). A new block is attached to the existing component by sharing one attaching point, with a net gain of one attaching point, so that a string of k building blocks provides $k + 2$ attaching points. The transformation preserves colorability and is easily carried out in polynomial time. *Q.E.D.*

The reader will have observed that the component used in the proof is planar, so that the transformations used in Theorems 8.2 and 8.3 may be combined (in that order) to show that G3C is NP-complete even when restricted to planar graphs where no vertex degree exceeds four.

A similar analysis can be performed for the Hamiltonian circuit problem. We know from Section 7.1 that deciding whether an arbitrary graph has a Hamiltonian circuit is NP-complete. Observe that our proof of this result produces graphs where no vertex degree exceeds four and that can be embedded in the plane in such a way that the only crossings involve XOR components. Thus we can show that the Hamiltonian circuit problem remains NP-complete when restricted to planar graphs of degree not exceeding three by producing: (i) a degree-reducing gadget to substitute for each vertex of degree 4; (ii) a crossing gadget to replace two XOR components that cross each other in an embedding; and (iii) a clause gadget to prevent crossings between XOR components and clause pieces.

Theorem 8.4 *HC is NP-complete even when restricted to planar graphs where no vertex degree exceeds three.*   □

Proof. The degree-reducing gadget must allow a single path to enter from any connecting edge and exit through any other connecting edge while visiting every vertex in the component; at the same time, the gadget must not allow two separate paths to pass through while visiting all vertices. The reader can verify that the component illustrated in Figure 8.3(a) has the required properties; moreover, the gadget itself is planar, so that we can combine it with the planar reduction that we now describe.

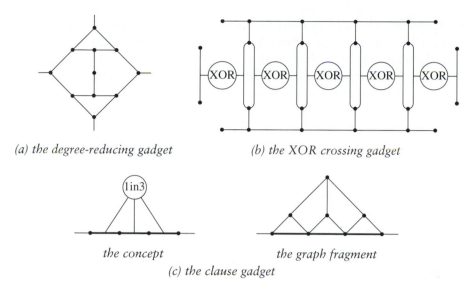

(a) the degree-reducing gadget   *(b) the XOR crossing gadget*

the concept   *the graph fragment*

(c) the clause gadget

Figure 8.3   The gadgets for the Hamiltonian circuit problem.

We must design a planar gadget that can be substituted for the crossing of two independent XOR components. We can achieve this goal by combining XOR components themselves with the idea underlying their design; the result is illustrated in Figure 8.3(b). Observe that the XOR components combine transitively (because the gadget includes an odd number of them) to produce an effective XOR between the vertical edges. The XOR between the horizontal edges is obtained in exactly the same fashion as in the original XOR component, by setting up four segments— each of which must be traversed—that connect enlarged versions of the horizontal edges. The reader may easily verify that the resulting graph piece effects the desired crossing.

Finally, we must also remove a crossing between an XOR piece and a "segment" corresponding to a literal in a clause piece or in a variable piece. We can trivially avoid crossings with variable pieces by considering instances derived from *Positive 1in3SAT* rather than from the general *1in3SAT*; in such instances, XOR components touch only one of the two segments and so all crossings can be avoided. However, crossings with the segments of the clause pieces remain, so that we must design a new gadget that will replace the triple edges of each clause. We propose to place the three edges (from which any valid circuit must choose only one) in series rather than in parallel as in our original construction; by placing them in series and facing the inside of the constructed loop, we avoid any crossings with XOR components. Our gadget must then ensure that any path through it uses exactly one of the three series edges. Figure 8.3(c) illustrates the concept and shows a graph fragment with the desired properties. The reader may verify by exhaustion that any path through the gadget that visits every vertex must cross exactly one of the three critical edges.   Q.E.D.

With the methodology used so far, every hard special case needs its own reduction; in the case of graph problems, each reduction requires its own gadgets. We should be able to use more general techniques in order to prove that entire classes of restrictions remain NP-complete with just one or two reductions and a few gadgets. Indeed, we can use our results on (3,4)-SAT to derive completeness results for graph problems with limited degree. In most transformations from SAT, the degree of the resulting graph is determined by the number of appearances of a literal in the collection of clauses, because each appearance must be connected by a consistency component to the truth-setting component. Such is the case for Vertex Cover: all clause vertices have degree 3, but the truth-setting vertices have degree equal to $m + 1$, where m is the number of appearances of the corresponding literal. Since we can limit this number to 4 through Theorem 8.1, we can ensure that the graph produced by the transformation has no vertex of degree exceeding 5.

Proposition 8.1 *Vertex Cover* remains NP-complete when limited to graphs of degree 5.   □

In fact, we can design a gadget to reduce the degree down to 3 (Exercise 8.10).

A common restriction among graph problems is the restriction to planar graphs. Let us examine that restriction in some detail. For many graph problems, we have a proof of NP-completeness for the general version of the problem, typically done by reduction from one of the versions of 3SAT. In order to show that the planar versions of these graph problems remain NP-complete, we could, as we did so far, proceed problem by problem, developing a separate reduction with its associated crossing gadgets for each problem. Alternately, we could design special "planar" versions of the standard 3SAT problems, such that the graphs produced by the existing reduction from the standard 3SAT version to the general graph version produce only planar graphs when applied to our "planar" 3SAT version and thus can be viewed as a reduction to the planar version of the problem, thereby proving that version to be NP-complete. In order for this scheme to work, the planar 3SAT version must, of course, be NP-complete itself and must combine with the general reduction so as to produce only planar graphs. As we have observed (see Table 7.3), most constructions from *3SAT* are made of three parts: (i) a part (one fragment per variable) that ensures legal truth assignments; (ii) a part (one fragment per clause) that ensures satisfying truth assignments; and (iii) a part that ensures consistency of truth assignments among clauses and variables. In transforming to a graph problem, planarity is typically lost in the third part. Hence we seek a version of *3SAT* that leads to planar connection patterns between clause fragments and variable fragments.

Definition 8.1 The *Planar Satisfiability* problem is the *Satisfiability* problem restricted to "planar" instances. An instance of *SAT* is deemed planar if its graph representation (to be defined) is planar. □

The simplest way to define a graph representation for an instance of *Satisfiability* is to set up a vertex for each variable, a vertex for each clause, and an edge between a variable vertex and a clause vertex whenever the variable appears in the clause—thereby mimicking the skeleton of a typical transformation from *SAT* to a graph problem. However, some additional structure may be desirable—the more we can add, the better. Many graph constructions from *SAT* connect the truth assignments fragments together (as in our construction for *G3C*); others connect the satisfaction fragments together; still others do both (as in our construction for *HC*). Another constraint to consider is the introduction of polarity: with a single vertex per variable and a single vertex per clause, no difference is made between complemented and uncomplemented literals, whereas using an edge between two vertices for each variable would provide such a distinction (and would more closely mimic our general reductions). Let us define two versions:

- *Polar representation*: Each variable gives rise to two vertices connected by an edge, each clause gives rise to a single vertex, and edges connect clauses to all vertices corresponding to literals that appear within the clause.
- *Nonpolar representation*: Variables and clauses give rise to a single vertex each, edges connect clauses to all vertices corresponding to variables that appear within the clause, and all variable vertices are connected together in a circular chain.

Theorem 8.5 With the representations defined above, the polar and nonpolar versions of *Planar Three-Satisfiability* are NP-complete. □

For a proof, see Exercise 8.8.

Corollary 8.1 *Planar Vertex Cover* is NP-complete. □

Proof. It suffices to observe that our reduction from *3SAT* uses only local replacement, uses a clause piece (a triangle) that can be assimilated to a single vertex in terms of planarity, and does not connect clause pieces. The conclusion follows immediately from the NP-completeness of the polar version of *Planar 3SAT*.   Q.E.D.

The reader should not conclude from Proposition 8.1 and Corollary 8.1 that *Vertex Cover* remains NP-complete when restricted to planar graphs of degree 5: the two reductions cannot be combined, since they do not start from the same problem. We would need a planar version of *(3,4)-SAT* in order to draw this conclusion.

Further work shows that *Planar 1in3SAT* is also NP-complete; surprisingly, however, *Planar NAE3SAT* is in P, in both polar and nonpolar versions.

Exercise 8.2 Use the result of Exercise 8.11 and our reduction from *NAE3SAT* to *MxC* (Theorem 7.4) to show that the polar version of *Planar NAE3SAT* is in P. To prove that the nonpolar version of *Planar NAE3SAT* is also in P, modify the reduction.   □

This somewhat surprising result leaves open the possibility that graph problems proved complete by transformation from *NAE3SAT* may become tractable when restricted to planar instances. (Given the direction of the reduction, this is the strongest statement we can make.) Indeed, such is the case for at least one of these problems, *Maximum Cut*, as discussed in Exercise 8.11.

The use of these planar versions remains somewhat limited. For instance, even though we reduced *1in3SAT* to *HC*, our reduction connected both the variable pieces and the clause pieces and also involved pieces that cannot be assimilated to single vertices in terms of planarity (because of the crossings between XOR components and variable or clause edges). The second problem can be disposed of by using *Positive 1in3SAT* (which then has to be proved NP-complete in its planar version) and by using the clause gadget of Figure 8.3(c). The first problem, however, forces the definition of a new graph representation for satisfiability problems. Thus in order to be truly effective, this technique requires us to prove that a large number of planar variants of *Satisfiability* remain NP-complete; the savings over an *ad hoc*, problem-by-problem approach are present but not enormous. Table 8.1 summarizes our two approaches to proving that special cases remain NP-complete.

The most comprehensive attempt at classifying the variants of a problem is the effort of a group of researchers at the Mathematisch Centrum in Amsterdam who endeavored to classify thousands of deterministic scheduling

Table 8.1   How to Prove the NP-Completeness of Special Cases

- *The (semi)generic approach*: Consider the reduction used in proving the general version to be NP-hard; the problem used in that reduction may have a known NP-complete special case that, when used in the reduction, produces only the type of instance you need.
- *The* ad hoc *approach*: Use a reduction from the general version of the problem to its special case; this reduction will typically require one or more specific gadgets. You may want to combine this approach with the generic approach, in case the generic approach restricted the instances to a subset of the general problem but a superset of your problem.

problems. When faced with these many different cases, one cannot tackle each case individually. The Centrum group started by systematizing the scheduling problems and unifying them all into a single problem with a large number of parameters. Each assignment of values to the parameters defines a specific type of scheduling problem, such as "scheduling unit-length tasks on two identical machines under general precedence constraints and with release times and completion deadlines in order to minimize overall tardiness." Thus the parameters include, but are not limited to, the type of tasks, the type of precedence order, the number and type of machines, additional relevant constraints (such as the existence of deadlines or the permissibility of preemption), and the function to be optimized. In a recent study by the Centrum group, the parameters included allowed for the description of 4,536 different types of scheduling problems.

The parameterization of a problem induces an obvious partial order on the variants of the problem: variant B is no harder than variant A if variant A is a generalization of variant B. For instance, scheduling tasks under the constraint of precedence relations (which determine a partial order) is a generalization of the problem of scheduling independent tasks; similarly, scheduling tasks of arbitrary lengths is a generalization of the problem of scheduling tasks of unit length. Notice that, if variant B is a generalization of variant A, then variant A reduces to variant B in polynomial time by simple restriction, as used in Section 7.1. Recall that, if A reduces to B and B is tractable, then A is tractable and that, conversely, if A reduces to B and A is intractable, then B is intractable. Thus the partial order becomes a powerful tool for the classification of parameterized problems. The Centrum group wrote a simple program that takes all known results (hardness and tractability) about the variants of a parameterized problem and uses the partial order to classify as many more variants as possible. From the partial order, it is also possible to compute maximal tractable problems (the most general versions that are still solvable in polynomial time) as well as minimal hard problems (the most restricted versions that are still NP-hard). Furthermore, the program can also find extremal unclassified problems, that is, the easiest and hardest of unclassified problems. Such problems are of interest since a proof of hardness for the easiest problems (or a proof of tractability for the hardest problems) would allow an immediate classification of all remaining unclassified problems. With respect to the 4,536 scheduling problems examined by the Centrum group, the distribution in 1982 was 3,730 hard variants, 416 tractable variants, and 390 unclassified variants, the latter with 67 extremal problems.

The results of such an analysis can be used to determine the course of future complexity research in the area. In order to complete the classification of all variants as tractable or hard, all we need to do is to identify a minimal subset of the extremal unclassified problems that, when classified, automatically leads to the classification of all remaining unclassified problems. The trouble is that this problem is itself NP-complete!

Theorem 8.6 The *Minimal Research Program* problem is NP-complete. An instance of this problem is given by a set of (unclassified) problems S, a partial order on S denoted $<$, and a bound B. The question is whether or not there exists a subset $S' \subseteq S$, with $|S| \leq B$, and a complexity classification function $c\colon S' \to \{\text{hard, easy}\}$ such that c can be extended to a total function on S by applying the two rules: (i) $x < y$ and $c(y) = \text{easy}$ implies $c(x) = \text{easy}$; and (ii) $x < y$ and $c(x) = \text{hard}$ implies $c(y) = \text{hard}$. $\square$

For a proof, see Exercise 8.12.

8.1.2   Promise Problems

All of the restrictions that we have considered so far have been reasonable restrictions, characterized by easily verifiable features. Only such restrictions fit within the framework developed in the previous chapters: since illegal instances must be detected and rejected, checking whether an instance obeys the stated restriction cannot be allowed to dominate the execution time. In particular, restrictions of NP-complete problems must be verifiable in polynomial time. Yet this feature may prove unrealistic: it is quite conceivable that all of the instances generated in an application must, due to the nature of the process, obey certain conditions that cannot easily be verified. Given such a collection of instances, we might be able to devise an algorithm that works correctly and efficiently only when applied to the instances of the collection. As a result, we should observe an apparent contradiction: the restricted problem would remain hard from the point of view of complexity theory, yet it would be well solved in practice.

An important example of such an "unreasonable"[3] restriction is the restriction of graph problems to *perfect* graphs. One of many definitions of perfect graphs states that a graph is perfect if and only if the chromatic number of every subgraph equals the size of the largest clique of the subgraph. Deciding whether or not an arbitrary graph is perfect is NP-easy (we can guess a subgraph with a chromatic number larger than the size of its largest clique and obtain both the chromatic number and the size of the largest clique through oracle calls) but not known (nor expected) to be in P, making the restriction difficult to verify. Several problems that are NP-hard on general graphs are solvable in polynomial time on perfect graphs; examples are *Chromatic Number*, *Independent Set*, and *Clique*. That we cannot verify in polynomial time whether a particular instance obeys the restriction is irrelevant if the application otherwise ensures that all instances will be perfect graphs. Moreover, even if we do not have this guarantee, there are many classes of perfect graphs that are recognizable in polynomial time (such as chordal graphs, interval graphs, and permutation graphs). Knowing the result about perfect graphs avoids a lengthy reconstruction of the algorithms for each special case.

We can bring complexity theory to bear upon such problems by introducing the notion of a *promise problem*. Formally, a promise problem is stated as a regular problem, with the addition of a predicate defined on instances—the promise. An algorithm solves a promise problem if it returns the correct solution within the prescribed resource bounds for any instance that fulfills the promise. No condition whatsoever is placed on the behavior of the algorithm when run on instances that do not fulfill the promise: the algorithm could return the correct result, return an erroneous result, exceed the resource bounds, or even fail to terminate. There is still much latitude in these definitions as the type of promise can make an enormous difference on the complexity of the task.

Exercise 8.3 Verify that there exist promises (not altogether silly, but plainly unreasonable) that turn some undecidable problems into decidable ones and others that turn some intractable problems into tractable ones. □

---

[3]By "unreasonable" we simply mean hard to verify; we do not intend it to cover altogether silly restrictions, such as restricting the Hamiltonian circuit problem to instances that have a Hamiltonian circuit.

The next step is to define some type(s) of promise; once that is done, then we can look at the classes of complexity arising from our definition. An intriguing and important type of promise is that of *uniqueness*; that is, the promise is that each valid instance admits at most one solution. Such a promise arises naturally in applications to cryptology: whatever cipher is chosen, it must be uniquely decodable—if, that is, the string under consideration is indeed the product of encryption. Thus in cryptology, there is no need to verify the validity of the promise of uniqueness. How does such a promise affect our NP-hard and #P-hard problems? Some are immediately trivialized. For instance, any symmetric problem (such as *NAE3SAT*) becomes solvable in constant time: since it always has an even number of solutions, the promise of uniqueness is tantamount to a promise of nonexistence. Such an outcome is somewhat artificial, however: if the statement of *NAE3SAT* asked for a partition of the variables rather than for a truth assignment, the problem would be unchanged and yet the promise of uniqueness would not trivialize it. As another example of trivialization, the #P-complete problem of counting perfect matchings becomes, with a promise of uniqueness, a simple decision problem, which we know how to solve in polynomial time. Other problems become tractable in a more interesting manner. For instance, the *Chromatic Index* problem (dual of the chromatic number, in that it considers edge rather than vertex coloring) is solvable in polynomial time with a promise of uniqueness, as a direct consequence of a theorem of Thomason's [1978] stating that the only graph that has a unique edge-coloring requiring k colors, with $k \geq 4$, is the k-star.

Finally, some problems apparently remain hard—but how do we go about proving that? Since we cannot very well deal with promise problems, we introduce the notion of a problem's completion. Formally, a "normal" problem is the *completion* of a promise problem if the two problems have the same answers for all instances that fulfill the promise. Thus a completion problem is an extension of a promise problem, with answers defined arbitrarily for all instances not fulfilling the promise. Completion is the reverse of restriction: we can view the promise problem as a restriction of the normal problem to those instances that obey the promise. The complexity of a promise problem is then precisely the complexity of the *easiest* of its completions—which returns us to the world of normal problems. Proving that a promise problem is hard then reduces to proving that none of its completions is in P—or rather, since we cannot prove any such thing for most interesting problems, proving that none of its completions is in P unless some widely believed conjecture is false. The conjecture that we have used most often so far is $P \neq NP$; in this case, however, it appears that a stronger conjecture is needed. In Section 8.4 we introduce several classes of randomized complexity, including the class RP, which lies between P and

NP; as always, the inclusions are believed to be proper. Thus the conjecture RP $\neq$ NP implies P $\neq$ NP. The following theorem is quoted without proof (the proof involves a suitable, i.e., randomized, reduction from the promise version of *SAT* to *SAT* itself).

Theorem 8.7 *Uniquely Promised SAT* (*SAT* with a promise of uniqueness) cannot be solved in polynomial time unless RP equals NP. □

From this hard promise problem, other problems with a promise of uniqueness can be proved hard by the simple means of a parsimonious transformation. Since a parsimonious transformation preserves the number of solutions, it preserves uniqueness as a special case and thus preserves the partition of instances into those fulfilling the promise and those not fulfilling it. (The transformation must be strictly parsimonious; the weak version of parsimony where the number of solutions to one instance is easily related to the number of solutions to the transformed instance is insufficient here.) An immediate consequence of our work with strictly parsimonious transformations in Section 7.3.3 is that a promise of uniqueness does not make the following problems tractable: *3SAT*, *Hamiltonian Circuit*, *Traveling Salesman*, *Maximum Cut*, *Partition*, *Subset Sum*, *Binpacking*, *Knapsack*, and *0-1 Integer Programming*. The fact that *Subset Sum* remains hard under a promise of uniqueness is of particular interest in cryptology, as this problem forms the basis for the family of knapsack ciphers (even though the knapsack ciphers are generally considered insecure due to other characteristics).

Verifying the promise of uniqueness is generally hard for hard problems. Compare for instance *Uniquely Promised SAT*, a promise problem, with *Unique Satisfiability*, which effectively asks to verify the promise of uniqueness; the first is in NP and not believed to be NP-complete, whereas the second is in $\Delta_2^p - (\text{NP} \cup \text{coNP})$. As mentioned earlier, deciding the question of uniqueness appears to be in $\Delta_2^p - (\text{NP} \cup \text{coNP})$ for most NP-complete problems. There are exceptions, such as *Chromatic Index*. However, *Chromatic Index* is an unusual problem in many respects: among other things, its search version is the same as its decision version, as a consequence of a theorem of Vizing's (see Exercise 8.14), which states that the chromatic index of a graph either equals the maximum degree of the graph or is one larger.

8.2 Strong NP-Completeness

We noted in Section 7.1 that the *Partition* problem was somehow different from our other basic NP-complete problems in that it required the presence of large numbers in the description of its instances in order for it to be NP-hard. Viewed in a more positive light, *Partition* is tractable when restricted to instances with (polynomially) small element values. This characteristic is in fact common to a class of problems, which we now proceed to study.

Let us begin by reviewing our knowledge of the *Partition* problem. An instance of it is given by a set of elements, $\{x_1, x_2, \ldots, x_n\}$, where each element x_i has size s_i, and the question is "Can this set be partitioned into two subsets in such a way that the sum of the sizes of the elements in one subset equals the sum of the sizes of the elements in the other subset?" We can assume that the sum of all the sizes is some even integer N. This problem can be solved by dynamic programming, using the recurrence

$$\begin{cases} f(0, 0) = 1 \\ f(0, j) = 0 \text{ for } j \neq 0 \\ f(i, M) = \max(f(i - 1, M), f(i - 1, M - s_i)) \end{cases}$$

where $f(i, M)$ equals 1 or 0, indicating whether or not there exists a subset of the first i elements that sums to M; this algorithm runs in $O(n \cdot N^2)$ time. As we observed before, the running time is not polynomial in the input size, since the latter is $O(n \log N)$. However, this conclusion relies on our convention about reasonable encodings. If, instead of using binary notation for the s_i values, we had used unary notation, then the input size would have been $O(n \cdot N)$ and the dynamic programming algorithm would have run in quadratic time.

This abrupt change in behavior between unary and binary notation is not characteristic of all NP-complete problems. For instance, the *Maximum Cut* problem, where an instance is given by a graph, $G = (V, E)$, and a bound, $B \leq |E|$, remains NP-hard even when encoded in unary. In binary, we can encode the bound with $\log B = O(\log |E|)$ bits and the graph with $O(|E| \log |V| + |V|)$ bits, as discussed in Chapter 4. In unary, the bound B now requires $B = O(|E|)$ symbols and the graph requires $O(|E| \cdot |V| + |V|)$ symbols. While the unary encoding is not as succinct as the binary encoding, it is in fact hardly longer and is bounded by a polynomial function in the length of the binary encoding, so that it is also a reasonable encoding. It immediately follows that the problem remains NP-complete when coded in unary. In order to capture this essential difference between *Partition* and *Maximum Cut*, we define a special version of polynomial time, measured in terms of unary inputs.

Definition 8.2 An algorithm runs in *pseudo-polynomial time* on some problem if it runs in time polynomial in the length of the input encoded in unary. □

For convenience, we shall denote the length of a reasonable binary encoding of instance I by $len(I)$ and the length of a unary encoding of I by $max(I)$. Since unary encodings are always at least as long as binary encodings, it follows that any polynomial-time algorithm is also a pseudo-polynomial time algorithm. The dynamic programming algorithm for *Partition* provides an example of a pseudo-polynomial time algorithm that is not also a polynomial-time one.

A pseudo-polynomial time solution may in fact prove very useful in practice, since its running time may remain quite small for practical instances. Moreover, the existence of such a solution also helps us circumscribe the problem (the goal of our first section in this chapter), as it implies the existence of a subproblem in P: simply restrict the problem to those instances I where $len(I)$ and $max(I)$ remain polynomially related. Hence a study of pseudo-polynomial time appears quite worthwhile.

Under our standard assumption of $P \neq NP$, no NP-complete problem can be solved by a polynomial-time algorithm. However, *Partition*, at least, can be solved by a pseudo-polynomial time algorithm; further examples include the problems *Subset Sum*, *Knapsack*, *Binpacking into Two Bins*, and some scheduling problems that we have not mentioned. On the other hand, since unary and binary encodings remain polynomially related for all instances of the *Maximum Cut* problem, it follows that any pseudo-polynomial time algorithm for this problem would also be a polynomial-time algorithm; hence, under our standard assumption, there cannot exist a pseudo-polynomial time algorithm for *Maximum Cut*.

Definition 8.3 An NP-complete problem is *strongly* NP-*complete* if it cannot be solved in pseudo-polynomial time unless P equals NP. □

The same reasoning applies to any problem that does not include arbitrarily large numbers in the description of its instances, since all such problems have reasonable unary encodings; hence problems such as *Satisfiability*, *Graph Three-Colorability*, *Vertex Cover*, *Hamiltonian Circuit*, *Set Cover*, and *Betweenness* are all strongly NP-complete problems. Such results are rather trivial; the real interest lies in problems that cannot be reasonably encoded in unary, that is, where $max(I)$ cannot be bounded by a polynomial in $len(I)$. Beside *Partition*, *Knapsack*, and the other problems mentioned earlier, a list of such problems includes *Traveling Salesman*, *k-Clustering*, *Steiner Tree in Graphs*, *Bounded Diameter Spanning Tree*, and many others.

Our transformation between *Hamiltonian Circuit* and *Traveling Salesman* produced instances of the latter where all distances equal 1 or 2 and where the bound equals the number of cities. This restricted version of

TSP is itself NP-complete but, quite clearly, can be encoded reasonably in unary—it does not include arbitrarily large numbers in its description. Hence this special version of *TSP*, and by implication the general *Traveling Salesman* problem, is a strongly NP-complete problem. Thus we find another large class of strongly NP-complete problems: all those problems that remain hard when their "numbers" are restricted into a small range. Indeed, this latter characterization is equivalent to our definition.

Proposition 8.2 A problem $\Pi \in$ NP is strongly NP-complete if and only if there exists some polynomial $p(\ )$ such that the restriction of Π to those instances with $max(I) \leq p(len(I))$ is itself NP-complete. $\square$

(We leave the easy proof to the reader.) This equivalent characterization shows that the concept of strong NP-completeness stratifies problems according to the values contained in their instances; if the set of instances containing only polynomially "small" numbers is itself NP-complete, then the problem is strongly NP-complete.

Hence the best way to show that a problem is strongly NP-complete is to construct a transformation that produces only small numbers; in such a manner, we can show that *k-Clustering*, *Steiner Tree in Graphs*, and the various versions of spanning tree problems are all strongly NP-complete problems. More interestingly, we can define problems that are strongly NP-complete yet do not derive directly from a "numberless" problem.

Theorem 8.8 *Subset Product* is strongly NP-complete. An instance of this problem is given by a finite set S, a size function $s: S \rightarrow \mathbb{N}$, and a bound B. The question is "Does there exist a subset S' of S such that the product of the sizes of the elements of S' is equal to B?" $\square$

Proof. Membership in NP is obvious. We transform $X3C$ to our problem using prime encoding. Given an instance of $X3C$, say $T = \{x_1, \ldots, x_{3n}\}$ and $C \subseteq 2^T$ (with $c \in C \Rightarrow |c| = 3$), let the first $3n$ primes be denoted by $p_1, \ldots, p_{3n}$. We set up an instance of *Subset Product* with set $S = C$, size function $s: \{x_i, x_j, x_k\} \rightarrow p_i p_j p_k$, and bound $B = \prod_{i=1}^{3n} p_i$. Observe that B (the largest number involved) can be computed in time $O(n \log p_{3n})$ given the first $3n$ primes; finding the ith prime itself need not take longer than $O(p_i)$ divisions (by the brute-force method of successive divisions). We now appeal to a result from number theory that we shall not prove: p_i is $O(i^2)$. Using this information, we conclude that the complete transformation runs in polynomial time. That the transformation is a valid many-one reduction is an obvious consequence of the unique factorization theorem. Hence the problem is NP-complete. Finally, since the numbers produced by the transformation are only polynomially large, it follows that the problem is in fact strongly NP-complete. *Q.E.D.*

While *Subset Product* has a more "genuine" flavor than *Traveling Salesman*, it nevertheless is not a particularly useful strongly NP-complete problem.

Theorem 8.9 For each fixed $k \geq 3$, *k-Partition* is strongly NP-complete. An instance of this problem (for $k \geq 3$) is given by a set of kn elements, each with a positive integer size; the sum of all the sizes is a multiple of n, say Bn, and the size $s(x)$ of each element x obeys the inequality $B/(k+1) < s(x) < B/(k-1)$. The question is "Can the set be partitioned into n subsets such that the sum of the sizes of the elements in each subset equals B?" □

(The size restrictions amount to forcing each subset to contain exactly k elements, hence the name *k-Partition*.) This problem has no clear relative among the "numberless" problems; in fact, its closest relative appears to be our standard *Partition*. The proof, while conceptually simple, involves very detailed assignments of sizes and lengthy arguments about modulo arithmetic; the interested reader will find references in the bibliography.

Corollary 8.2 *Binpacking* is strongly NP-complete. □

The proof merely consists in noting that an instance of *k-Partition* with kn elements and total size Bn may also be regarded as an instance of *Binpacking* with bin capacity B and number of bins bounded by n.

While these two problems are strongly NP-complete in their general formulation, they are both solvable in pseudo-polynomial time for each fixed value of n. That is, *Binpacking into k Bins* and *Partition into k Subsets* are solvable in pseudo-polynomial time for each fixed k.

An additional interest of strongly NP-complete problems is that we may use them as starting points in reductions that can safely ignore the difference between the value of a number and the length of its representation. Consider reducing the standard *Partition* problem to some problem Π and let x_i be the size of the ith element in an instance of the standard *Partition* problem. Creating a total of x_i pieces in an instance of Π to correspond in some way to the ith element of *Partition* cannot be allowed, as such a construction could take more than polynomial time (because x_i need not be polynomial in the size of the input). However, the same technique is perfectly safe when reducing *k-Partition* to Π or to some other problem.

Definition 8.4 A many-one reduction, f, from problem Π to problem Π' is a *pseudo-polynomial transformation* if there exist polynomials $p(\,,\,)$, $q_1(\,)$, and $q_2(\,,\,)$, such that, for an arbitrary instance I of Π:

1. $f(I)$ can be computed in $p(len(I), max(I))$ time;
2. $len(I) \leq q_1(len'(f(I)))$; and
3. $max'(f(I)) \leq q_2(len(I), max(I))$. □

The differences between a polynomial transformation and a pseudo-polynomial one are concentrated in the first condition: the latter can take time polynomial in both $len(I)$ and $max(I)$, not just in $len(I)$ like the former. In some cases, this looser requirement may allow a pseudo-polynomial transformation to run in exponential time on a subset of instances! The other two conditions are technicalities: the second forbids very unusual transformations that would shrink the instance too much; and the third prevents us from creating exponentially large numbers during a pseudo-polynomial transformation in the same way that we did, for instance, in our reduction from $1in3SAT$ to *Partition*.

In terms of such a transformation, our observation can be rephrased as follows.

Proposition 8.3 If Π is strongly NP-complete, Π' belongs to NP, and Π reduces to Π' through a pseudo-polynomial transformation, then Π' is strongly NP-complete. $\square$

Proof. We appeal to our equivalent characterization of strongly NP-complete problems. Since Π is strongly NP-complete, there exists some polynomial $r()$ such that Π restricted to instances I with $max(I) \leq r(len(I))$ is NP-complete; denote by Π_r this restricted version of Π. Now consider the effect of f on Π_r: it runs in time polynomial in $len(I)$—in at most $p(len(I), r(len(I)))$ time, to be exact; and it creates instances I' of Π' that all obey the inequality $max(I') \leq q_2(r(q_1(len'(I'))), q_1(len'(I')))$. Thus it is a polynomial-time transformation between Π_r and $\Pi'_{r'}$, where $r'(x)$ is the polynomial $q_2(r(q_1(x)), q_1(x))$. Hence $\Pi'_{r'}$ is NP-complete, so that Π' is strongly NP-complete.   *Q.E.D.*

The greater freedom inherent in pseudo-polynomial transformations can be very useful, not just in proving other problems to be strongly NP-complete, but also in proving NP-complete some problems that lack arbitrarily large numbers or in simple proofs of NP-completeness. We begin with a proof of strong NP-completeness.

Theorem 8.10 *Minimum Sum of Squares* is strongly NP-complete. An instance of this problem is given by a set, S, of elements, a size for each element, $s: S \rightarrow \mathbb{N}$, and positive integer bounds $N < |S|$ and J. The question is "Can S be partitioned into N disjoint subsets (call them S_i, $1 \leq i \leq N$) such that the sum over all N subsets of $(\sum_{x \in S_i} s(x))^2$ does not exceed J?" $\square$

Proof. For convenience in notation, set $B = \sum_x s(x)$. That the problem is NP-complete in the usual sense is obvious, as it restricts to *Partition* by setting $N = 2$ and $J = \frac{1}{2}B^2$. We can also restrict our problem to k-*Partition*, thereby proving our problem to be strongly NP-complete, as follows. We restrict our problem to those instances where $|S|$ is a multiple of k, with $N = S/k$ and $J = B^2/N$. Both restrictions rely on the fact that the minimal sum of squares is obtained when all subsets have the same total size, as is easily verified through elementary algebra.   *Q.E.D.*

The transformation used in reducing *k-Partition* to *Minimum Sum of Squares* did not make use of the freedom inherent in pseudo-polynomial transformations; in fact, the transformation is a plain polynomial-time transformation. The following reduction shows how the much relaxed constraint on time can be put to good use.

Theorem 8.11 *Edge Embedding on a Grid* is strongly NP-complete. An instance of this problem is given by a graph, $G = (V, E)$, and two natural numbers, M and N. The question is "Can the vertices of G be embedded in an $M \times N$ grid?" In other words, does there exist an injection $f : V \to \{1, 2, \ldots, M\} \times \{1, 2, \ldots, N\}$ such that each edge of G gives rise to a vertical or horizontal segment in the grid? (Formally, given edge $\{u, v\} \in E$ and letting $f(u) = (u_x, u_y)$ and $f(v) = (v_x, v_y)$, we must have either $u_x = v_x$ or $u_y = v_y$.)   □

Proof. The problem is clearly in NP. We reduce *Three-Partition* to it with a pseudo-polynomial time transformation as follows. Let an instance of *Three-Partition* be given by a set S, with $|S| = 3n$, and size function $s : S \to \mathbb{N}$, with $\sum_{x \in S} s(x) = nB$. We shall assume that each element of S has size at least as large as $\max\{3, n + 1\}$; if such were not the case, we could simply multiply all sizes by that value. For each element $x \in S$, we set up a distinct subgraph of G; this subgraph is simply the complete graph on $s(x)$ vertices, $K_{s(x)}$. The total graph G is thus made of $3n$ separate complete graphs of varying sizes. Finally, we set $M = B$ and $N = n$; call the M dimension horizontal and the N dimension vertical.

The number of grid points is nB, which is exactly the number of vertices of G. Since each subgraph has at least three vertices, it can be embedded on a grid in only one way: with all of its vertices on the same horizontal or vertical—otherwise, at least one of the edge embeddings would be neither vertical nor horizontal. Since subgraphs have at least $n + 1$ vertices and the grid has height n, subgraphs can be embedded only horizontally. Finally, since the horizontal dimension is precisely B, the problem as posed reduces to one of grouping the subgraphs of G into n subsets such that each subset contains exactly B vertices in all—which is exactly equivalent to *Three-Partition*.

The time taken by the transformation is polynomial in nB but not in $n \log B$; the former is $max(I)$, while the latter is $len(I)$. Thus the transformation runs in pseudo-polynomial time, but not in polynomial time. Since the transformed instance has size $O(B^2)$—because each complete subgraph on $s(x)$ vertices has $O(s^2(x))$ edges—and since its largest number is $M = B$, which is basically the same as the largest number in an instance of k-*Partition*, our transformation is a valid pseudo-polynomial time transformation, from which our conclusion follows.   Q.E.D.

We should thus modify our description of the structure of a typical proof of NP-completeness (Table 7.1, page 228): if the known NP-complete problem is in fact strongly NP-complete, then the last step, "verify that the reduction can be carried out in polynomial time," should be amended by replacing "polynomial time" with "pseudo-polynomial time."

8.3   The Complexity of Approximation

Having done our best to circumscribe our problem, we may remain faced with an NP-complete problem. What strategy should we now adopt? Once again, we can turn to complexity theory for guidance and ask about the complexity of certain types of approximation for our problem. Some approximations may rely on the probability distribution of the solutions. For instance, given a fixed number of colors, a randomly chosen graph has a vanishingly small probability of being colorable with this many colors; a randomly chosen dense graph is almost certain to include a Hamiltonian circuit; and so on. Other approximations (heuristics) do well in practice but have so far defied formal analysis, both in terms of performance and in terms of running time. However, some approximations provide certain guarantees, either deterministic or probabilistic. We take up approximations with deterministic guarantees in this section and those with probabilistic guarantees in Section 8.4.

8.3.1   Definitions

If our problem is a decision problem, only probabilistic approaches can succeed—after all, "yes" is a very poor approximation for "no." Let us then assume that we are dealing with an optimization problem. Recall that an optimization problem is given by a collection of instances, a collection of (feasible) solutions, and an objective function defined over the solutions; the goal is to return the solution with the best objective value. Since this definition includes any type of optimization problem and we want to focus on those optimization problems that correspond to decision problems in NP, we formalize and narrow our definition.

Definition 8.5 An NP-*optimization* (NPO) problem is given by:

- a collection of instances recognizable in polynomial time;
- a polynomial p and, for each instance x, a collection of feasible solutions, $S(x)$, such that each feasible solution $y \in S(x)$ has length bounded by $p(|x|)$ and such that membership in $S(x)$ of strings of polynomially bounded length is decidable in polynomial time; and,
- an objective function defined on the space of all feasible solutions and computable in polynomial time.

The class NPO is the set of all NPO problems.   □

The goal for an instance of an NPO problem is to find a feasible solution that optimizes (maximizes or minimizes, depending on the problem) the value of the objective function. Our definition of NPO problems ensures that all such problems have concise and easily recognizable feasible solutions, just as decision problems in NP have concise and easily checkable certificates. Our definition also ensures that the value of a feasible solution is computable in polynomial time. An immediate consequence of our definition is that the decision version of an NPO problem (does the instance admit a solution at least as good as some bound B?) is solvable in polynomial time whenever the NPO problem itself is. Therefore if the decision version of an NPO problem is NP-complete, the NPO problem itself cannot be solved in polynomial time unless P equals NP—hence our interest in approximations for NPO problems. We can similarly define the class PO of optimization problems solvable in polynomial time.

Exercise 8.4 Verify that P equals NP if and only if PO equals NPO.   □

Let us assume that, while the optimal solution to instance I has value $f(I)$, our approximation algorithm returns a solution with value $\hat{f}(I)$. To gauge the worth of our algorithm, we can look at the difference between the values of the two solutions, $|f(I) - \hat{f}(I)|$, or at the ratio of that difference to the value of the (optimal or approximate) solution. The difference measure is of interest only when it can be bounded over all possible instances by a constant; otherwise the ratio measure is preferable. (The reader will encounter ratio measures defined without recourse to differences. In such measures, the ratio for a minimization problem is that of the value of the optimal solution to the value of the approximate solution, with the fraction reversed for maximization problems.) The ratio measure can be defined over all instances or only in asymptotic terms—the rationale for the latter being that sophisticated approximation methods may need large instances to show their worth, just like sophisticated algorithms often show their fast running times only on large instances. Finally, any of these three measures (difference, ratio, and asymptotic ratio) can be defined as a worst-case measure or an average-case measure. In practice, as for time and space complexity measures, it is very difficult to define average-case behavior of approximation methods. Hence we consider three measures of the quality of an approximation method.

Definition 8.6 Let Π be an optimization problem, let $\mathcal{A}$ be an approximation algorithm for Π, and, for an arbitrary instance I of Π, let $f(I)$ be the value of the optimal solution to I and $\hat{f}(I)$ the value of the solution returned by $\mathcal{A}$. Define the approximation ratio for $\mathcal{A}$ on instance I of a maximization problem to be $R_{\mathcal{A}}(I) = \frac{|f(I) - \hat{f}(I)|}{f(I)}$ and that of a minimization problem to be $R_{\mathcal{A}}(I) = \frac{|f(I) - \hat{f}(I)|}{\hat{f}(I)}$.

- The *absolute distance* of $\mathcal{A}$ is $D_{\mathcal{A}} = \sup_{I \in \Pi}\{|f(I) - \hat{f}(I)|\}$.
- The *absolute ratio* of $\mathcal{A}$ is $R_{\mathcal{A}} = \inf_{I \in \Pi}\{r \geq 0 \mid R_{\mathcal{A}}(I) \leq r\}$.
- The *asymptotic ratio* of $\mathcal{A}$ is $R_{\mathcal{A}}^{\infty} = \inf_{I \in S}\{r \geq 0 \mid R_{\mathcal{A}}(I) \leq r\}$, where S is any set of instances of Π for which there exists some positive integer bound N such that $f(I) \geq N$ holds for all I in S.   □

Under these definitions, an exact algorithm has $D_{\mathcal{A}} = R_{\mathcal{A}} = 0$, while approximation algorithms have ratios between 0 and 1. A ratio of $1/2$, for instance, denotes an algorithm that cannot err by more than 100%. A ratio of 1 denotes an algorithm that can return arbitrarily bad solutions.

Yet another variation on these measures is one that measures the ratio of the error introduced by the approximation to the maximum error possible for the instance, that is, one that measures the ratio of the difference between the approximate and optimal solutions to the difference between the pessimal and optimal solutions. Since the pessimal value for many maximization problems is zero, the two measures often coincide.

Determining the quality of an approximation belongs to the domain of algorithm analysis. Our concern here is to determine the complexity of approximation guarantees for NP-hard optimization problems. We want to know whether such problems can be approximated in polynomial time to within a constant distance or ratio or whether such guarantees make the approximation as hard to obtain as the optimal solution. Our main difficulty stems from the fact that many-one polynomial-time reductions, which served us so well in analyzing the complexity of exact problems, are much less useful in analyzing the complexity of approximations, because they do not preserve the quality of approximations. We know of NP-equivalent optimization problems for which the optimal solution can be approached within one unit and of others where obtaining an approximation within any constant ratio is NP-hard.

Example 8.2 Consider the twin problems of *Vertex Cover* and *Independent Set*. We have seen that, given a graph $G = (V, E)$, the subset of vertices V' is a minimum vertex cover for G if and only if the subset $V - V'$ is a maximum independent set of G. Hence a reduction between the two decision problems consists of copying the graph unchanged and complementing the bound, from B in VC to $|V| - B$ in *Independent Set*. The reduction is an isomorphism and thus about as simple a reduction as possible. Yet, while there exists a simple approximation for *VC* that never returns a cover of size larger than twice that of the minimal cover (simply do the following until all edges have been removed: select a remaining edge at random, place both its endpoints in the cover, and remove it and all edges adjacent to its two endpoints—see Exercise 8.23), we do not know of an approximation algorithm for *Independent Set* that would provide a ratio guarantee. That we cannot use the *VC* approximation and transform the solution through our reduction is easily seen. If we have, say, $2n$ vertices and a minimum cover of $n - 1$ vertices and thus a maximum independent set of $n + 1$ vertices, then our *VC* approximation would always return a cover of no more than $2n - 2$ vertices, corresponding to an independent set of at least two vertices. For the *VC* approximation, we have $R_\mathcal{A} = 1/2$, but for the corresponding *Independent Set*, we get $R_\mathcal{A} = {}^{n-1}/_{n+1}$, which grows arbitrarily close to 1 (and thus arbitrarily bad) for large values of n. □

In the following pages, we begin by examining the complexity of certain guarantees; we then ascertain what, if anything, is preserved by reductions among NP-complete problems; finally, we develop new polynomial-time reductions that preserve approximation guarantees and use them in erecting a primitive hierarchy of approximation problems.

8.3.2 Constant-Distance Approximations

We begin with the strictest of performance guarantees: that the approximation remains within constant distance of the optimal solution. Under such circumstances, the absolute ratio is bounded by a constant. That ensuring such a guarantee can be any easier than finding the optimal solution appears nearly impossible at first sight. A little thought eventually reveals some completely trivial examples, in which the value of the optimal solution never exceeds some constant—almost any such problem has an easy

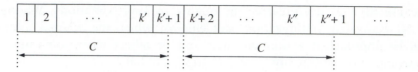

Figure 8.4   The simple distance-one approximation for *Maximum Two-Binpacking*.

approximation to within a constant distance. *Chromatic Number of Planar Graphs* is a good example, since all planar graphs are four-colorable, any planar graph can be colored with five colors in low polynomial time, yet deciding three-colorability (the *G3C* problem) is NP-complete. Almost as trivial is the *Chromatic Index* problem, which asks how many colors are needed for a valid edge-coloring of a graph; the decision version is known to be NP-complete. As mentioned earlier, Vizing's theorem (Exercise 8.14) states that the chromatic index of a graph equals either its maximum degree or its maximum degree plus one. Moreover the constructive proof of the theorem provides a $O(|E| \cdot |V|)$ algorithm that colors the edges with $d_{\max} + 1$ colors.

Our first nontrivial problem is a variation on *Partition*.

Definition 8.7   An instance of *Maximum Two-Binpacking* is given by a set S, a size function $s: S \to \mathbb{N}$, a bin capacity C, and a positive integer bound k. The question is "Does there exist a subset of S with at least k elements that can be partitioned into two subsets, each of which has total size not exceeding C?"   □

This problem is obviously NP-complete, since it suffices to set $k = |S|$ and $l = \frac{1}{2}(\sum_{x \in S} s(x))$ in order to restrict it to the *Partition* problem. Consider the following simple solution. Let k' be the largest index such that the sum of the k' smallest elements does not exceed C and let k'' be the largest index such that the sum of the k'' smallest elements does not exceed $2C$. We can pack the k' smallest elements in one bin, ignore the $(k' + 1)$st smallest element, and pack the next $k'' - k' - 1$ smallest elements in the second bin, thereby packing a total of $k'' - 1$ elements in all. However, the optimal solution cannot exceed k'', so that our approximation is at most one element away from it. Figure 8.4 illustrates the idea. The same idea can clearly be extended to the *Maximum k-Binpacking* problem, but now the deviation from the optimal may be as large as $k - 1$ (which remains a constant for any fixed k).

Our second problem is more complex.

Definition 8.8 An instance of *Safe Deposit Boxes* is given by a collection of deposit boxes $\{B_1, B_2, \ldots, B_n\}$, each containing a certain amount $s_{i,j}$, $1 \leqslant i \leqslant m$ and $1 \leqslant j \leqslant n$, of each of m currencies and by target currency amounts $\mathbf{b} = (b_i)$, $0 \leqslant i \leqslant m$, and a target bound $k > 0$. The question is "Does there exist a subcollection of at most k safe deposit boxes that among themselves contain sufficient currency to meet target $\mathbf{b}$?" □

(The goal, then, is to break open the smallest number of safe deposit boxes in order to collect sufficient amounts of each of the currencies.) This problem arises in resource allocation in operating systems, where each process requires a certain amount of each of a number of different resources in order to complete its execution and release these resources. Should a deadlock arise (where the processes all hold some amount of resources and all need more resources than remain available in order to proceed), we may want to break it by killing a subset of processes that among themselves hold sufficient resources to allow one of the remaining processes to complete. What makes the problem difficult is that the currencies (resources) are not interchangeable. This problem is NP-complete for each fixed number of currencies larger than one (see Exercise 8.17) but admits a constant-distance approximation (see Exercise 8.18).

Our third problem is a variant on a theme explored in Exercise 7.27, in which we asked the reader to verify that the *Bounded-Degree Spanning Tree* problem is NP-complete. If we ignore the total length of the tree and focus instead on minimizing the degree of the tree, we obtain the *Minimum-Degree Spanning Tree* problem, which is also NP-complete.

Theorem 8.12 The *Minimum-Degree Spanning Tree* problem can be approximated to within one from the minimum degree. □

The approximation algorithm proceeds through successive iterations from an arbitrary initial spanning tree; see Exercise 8.19.

In general, however, NP-hard optimization problems cannot be approximated to within a constant distance unless P equals NP. We give one example of the reduction technique used in all such cases.

Theorem 8.13 Unless P equals NP, no polynomial-time algorithm can find a vertex cover that never exceeds the size of the optimal cover by more than some fixed constant. □

Proof. We shall reduce the optimization version of the *Vertex Cover* problem to its approximation version by taking advantage of the fact that the value of the solution is an integer. Let the constant of the theorem be k. Let $G = (E, V)$ be an instance of *Vertex Cover* and assume that an optimal vertex cover for G contains m vertices. We produce the new graph G_{k+1} by making $(k+1)$ distinct copies of G, so that G_{k+1} has $(k+1)|V|$ vertices and $(k+1)|E|$ edges; more interestingly, an optimal vertex cover for G_{k+1} has $(k+1)m$ vertices. We now run the approximation algorithm on G_{k+1}: the result is a cover for G_{k+1} with at most $(k+1)m+k$ vertices. The vertices of this collection are distributed among the $(k+1)$ copies of G; moreover, the vertices present in any copy of G form a cover of G, so that, in particular, at least m vertices of the collection must appear in any given copy. Thus at least $(k+1)m$ of the vertices are accounted for, leaving only k vertices; but these k vertices are distributed among $(k+1)$ copies, so that one copy did not receive any additional vertex. For that copy of G, the supposed approximation algorithm actually found a solution with m vertices, that is, an optimal solution. Identifying that copy is merely a matter of scanning all copies and retaining that copy with the minimum number of vertices in its cover. Hence the optimization problem reduces in polynomial time to its constant-distance approximation version.   Q.E.D.

The same technique of "multiplication" works for almost every NP-hard optimization problem, although not always through simple replication. For instance, in applying the technique to the *Knapsack* problem, we keep the same collection of objects, the same object sizes, and the same bag capacity, but we multiply the value of each object by $(k+1)$. Exercises at the end of the chapter pursue some other, more specialized "multiplication" methods; Table 8.2 summarizes the key features of these methods.

8.3.3   Approximation Schemes

We now turn to ratio approximations. The ratio guarantee is only one part of the characterization of an approximation algorithm: we can also ask whether the approximation algorithm can provide only some fixed ratio guarantee or, for a price, any nonzero ratio guarantee—and if so, at what price. We define three corresponding classes of approximation problems.

Definition 8.9

- An optimization problem Π belongs to the class APX if there exists a precision requirement, ε, and an approximation algorithm, $\mathcal{A}$, such that $\mathcal{A}$ takes as input an instance I of Π, runs in time polynomial in $|I|$, and obeys $R_\mathcal{A} \leqslant \varepsilon$.
- An optimization problem Π belongs to the class PTAS (and is said to be *p-approximable*) if there exists a *polynomial-time approximation scheme*, that is, a family of approximation algorithms, $\{\mathcal{A}_i\}$, such that,

Table 8.2   How to Prove the NP-Hardness of Constant-Distance Approximations.

- Assume that a constant-distance approximation with distance k exists.
- Transform an instance x of the problem into a new instance $f(x)$ of the same problem through a type of "multiplication" by $(k + 1)$; specifically, the transformation must ensure that
  - any solution for x can be transformed easily to a solution for $f(x)$, the value of which is $(k + 1)$ times the value of the solution for x;
  - the transformed version of an optimal solution for x is an optimal solution for $f(x)$; and
  - a solution for x can be recovered from a solution for $f(x)$.
- Verify that one of the solutions for x recovered from a distance-k approximation for $f(x)$ is an optimal solution for x.
- Conclude that no such constant-distance approximation can exist unless P equals NP.

---

for each fixed precision requirement $\varepsilon > 0$, there exists an algorithm in the family, say $\mathcal{A}_j$, that takes as input an instance I of Π, runs in time polynomial in $|I|$, and obeys $R_{\mathcal{A}_j} \leq \varepsilon$.
- An optimization problem Π belongs to the class FPTAS (and is said to be *fully p-approximable*) if there exists a *fully polynomial-time approximation scheme*, that is, a single approximation algorithm, $\mathcal{A}$, that takes as input both an instance I of Π and a precision requirement ε, runs in time polynomial in $|I|$ and $1/\varepsilon$, and obeys $R_{\mathcal{A}} \leq \varepsilon$. □

From the definition, we clearly have PO $\subseteq$ FPTAS $\subseteq$ PTAS $\subseteq$ Apx $\subseteq$ NPO. The definition for FPTAS is a uniform definition, in the sense that a single algorithm serves for all possible precision requirements and its running time is polynomial in the precision requirement. The definition for PTAS does not preclude the existence of a single algorithm but allows its running time to grow arbitrarily with the precision requirement—or simply allows entirely distinct algorithms to be used for different precision requirements.

Very few problems are known to be in FPTAS. None of the strongly NP-complete problems can have optimization versions in FPTAS—a result that ties together approximation and strong NP-completeness in an intriguing way.

Theorem 8.14 Let Π be an optimization problem; if its decision version is strongly NP-complete, then Π is not fully *p*-approximable. □

Proof. Let Π_d denote the decision version of Π. Since the bound, B, introduced in Π to turn it into the decision problem Π_d, ranges up to (for a maximization problem) the value of the optimal solution and since, by definition, we have $B \leq max(I)$, it follows that the value of the optimal solution cannot exceed $max(I)$. Now set $\varepsilon = \frac{1}{(max(I)+1)}$, so that an ε-approximate solution must be an exact solution. If Π were fully p-approximable, then there would exist an ε-approximation algorithm $\mathcal{A}$ running in time polynomial in (among other things) $1/\varepsilon$. However, time polynomial in $1/\varepsilon$ is time polynomial in $max(I)$, which is pseudo-polynomial time. Hence, if Π were fully p-approximable, there would exist a pseudo-polynomial time algorithm solving it, and thus also Π_d, exactly, which would contradict the strong NP-completeness of Π_d.   Q.E.D.

This result leaves little room in FPTAS for the optimization versions of NP-complete problems, since most NP-complete problems are strongly NP-complete. It does, however, leave room for the optimization versions of problems that do not appear to be in P and yet are not known to be NP-complete.

The reader is familiar with at least one fully p-approximable problem: *Knapsack*. The simple greedy heuristic based on value density, with a small modification (pick the single item of largest value if it gives a better packing than the greedy packing), guarantees a packing of value at least half that of the optimal packing (an easy proof). We can modify this algorithm by doing some look-ahead: try all possible subsets of k or fewer items, complete each subset by the greedy heuristic, and then keep the best of the completed solutions. While this improved heuristic is expensive, since it takes time $\Omega(n^k)$, it does run in polynomial time for each fixed k; moreover its approximation guarantee is $R_{\mathcal{A}} = 1/k$ (see Exercise 8.25), which can be made arbitrarily good. Indeed, this family of algorithms shows that *Knapsack* is p-approximable. However, the running time of an algorithm in this family is proportional to $n^{1/\varepsilon}$ and thus not a polynomial function of the precision requirement. In order to show that *Knapsack* is fully p-approximable, we must make real use of the fact that *Knapsack* is solvable in pseudo-polynomial time.

Given an instance with n items where the item of largest value has value V and the item of largest size has size S, the dynamic programming solution runs in $O(n^2 V \log(nSV))$ time. Since the input size is $O(n \log(SV))$, only one term in the running time, the linear term V, is not actually polynomial. If we were to scale all item values down by some factor F, the new running time would be $O(n^2 \frac{V}{F} \log(nS\frac{V}{F}))$; with the right choice for F, we can make this expression polynomial in the input size. The value of the optimal solution to the scaled instance, call it $f_F(I_F)$, can be easily related to the value of the optimal solution to the original instance, $f(I)$, as well as to the value in unscaled terms of the optimal solution to the scaled version, $f(I_F)$:

$$f(I_F) \geqslant F \cdot f_F(I_F) \geqslant f(I) - nF$$

How do we select F? In order to ensure a polynomial running time, F should be of the form $\frac{V}{x}$ for some parameter x; in order to ensure an approximation independent of n, F should be of the form $\frac{y}{n}$ for some parameter y (since then the value $f(I_F)$ is within y of the optimal solution). Let us simply set $F = \frac{V}{kn}$, for some natural number k. The dynamic programming solution now runs on the scaled instance in $O(kn^3 \log(kn^2 S))$ time, which is polynomial in the size of the input, and the solution returned is at least as large as $f(I) - \frac{V}{k}$. Since we could always place in the knapsack the one item of largest value, thereby obtaining a solution of value V, we have $f(I) \geqslant V$; hence the ratio guarantee of our algorithm is

$$R_{\mathcal{A}} = \frac{f(I) - f(I_F)}{f(I)} \leqslant \frac{V/k}{V} = \frac{1}{k}$$

In other words, we can obtain the precision requirement $\varepsilon = 1/k$ with an approximation algorithm running in $O(1/\varepsilon n^3 \log(1/\varepsilon n^2 S))$ time, which is polynomial in the input size and in the precision requirement. Hence we have derived a fully polynomial-time approximation scheme for the *Knapsack* problem.

In fact, the scaling mechanism can be used with a variety of problems solvable in pseudo-polynomial time, as the following theorem states.

Theorem 8.15 Let Π be an optimization problem with the following properties:

1. $f(I)$ and $max(I)$ are polynomially related through $len(I)$; that is, there exist bivariate polynomials p and q such that we have both $f(I) \leqslant p(len(I), max(I))$ and $max(I) \leqslant q(len(I), f(I))$;
2. the objective value of any feasible solution varies linearly with the parameters of the instance; and,
3. Π can be solved in pseudo-polynomial time.

Then Π is fully p-approximable. $\qquad \square$

(For a proof, see Exercise 8.27.) This theorem gives us a limited converse of Theorem 8.14 but basically mimics the structure of the *Knapsack* problem. Other than *Knapsack* and its close relatives, very few NPO problems that have an NP-complete decision version are known to be in FPTAS.

An alternate characterization of problems that belong to PTAS or FPTAS can be derived by stratifying problems on the basis of the size of the solution rather than the size of the instance.

Definition 8.10 An optimization problem is *simple* if, for each fixed B, the set of instances with optimal values not exceeding B is decidable in polynomial time. It is *p-simple* if there exists a fixed bivariate polynomial, q, such that the set of instances I with optimal values not exceeding B is decidable in $q(|I|, B)$ time.   □

For instance, *Chromatic Number* is not simple, since it remains NP-complete for planar graphs, in which the optimal value is bounded by 4. On the other hand, *Clique*, *Vertex Cover*, and *Set Cover* are simple, since, for each fixed B, the set of instances with optimal values bounded by B can be solved in polynomial time by exhaustive search of all $\binom{n}{B}$ collections of B items (vertices or subsets). *Partition* is *p*-simple by virtue of its dynamic programming solution. Our definition of simplicity moves from simple problems to *p*-simple problems by adding a uniformity condition, much like our change from *p*-approximable to fully *p*-approximable. Simplicity is a necessary but, alas, not sufficient condition for membership in PTAS(for instance, *Clique*, while simple, cannot be in PTAS unless P equals NP, as we shall shortly see).

Theorem 8.16 Let Π be an optimization problem.

- If Π is *p*-approximable ($\Pi \in$ PTAS), then it is simple.
- If Π is fully *p*-approximable ($\Pi \in$ FPTAS), then it is *p*-simple.   □

Proof. We give the proof for a maximization problem; the same line of reasoning, with the obvious changes, proves the result for minimization problems. The approximation scheme can meet any precision requirement $\varepsilon = \frac{1}{B+2}$ in time polynomial in the size of the input instance I. (Our choice of $B + 2$ instead of B is to take care of boundary conditions.) Thus we have

$$\frac{f(I) - \hat{f}(I)}{f(I)} \leqslant \frac{1}{B+2}$$

or

$$\frac{\hat{f}(I)}{f(I)} \geqslant \frac{B+1}{B+2}$$

Hence we can have $\hat{f}(I) \leqslant B$ only when we also have $f(I) \leqslant B$. But $f(I)$ is the value of the optimal solution, so we obviously can only have $\hat{f}(I) \geqslant B$

when we also have $f(I) \geq B$. Hence we conclude

$$\hat{f}(I) \leq B \Leftrightarrow f(I) \leq B$$

and, since the first inequality is decidable in polynomial time, so is the second. Since the set of instances I that have optimal values not exceeding B is thus decidable in polynomial time, the problem is simple. Adding uniformity to the running time of the approximation algorithm adds uniformity to the decision procedure for the instances with optimal values not exceeding B and thus proves the second statement of our theorem. *Q.E.D.*

We can further tie together our results with the following observation.

Theorem 8.17 If Π is an NPO problem with an NP-complete decision version and, for each instance I of Π, $f(I)$ and $max(I)$ are polynomially related through $len(I)$, then Π is p-simple if and only if it can be solved in pseudo-polynomial time. □

(For a proof, see Exercise 8.28.)

The class PTAS is much richer than the class FPTAS. Our first attempt at providing an approximation scheme for *Knapsack*, through an exhaustive search of all $\binom{n}{k}$ subsets and their greedy completions (Exercise 8.25), provides a general technique for building approximations schemes for a class of NPO problems.

Definition 8.11 An instance of a *maximum independent subset* problem is given by a collection of items, each with a value. The feasible solutions of the instance form an independence system; that is, every subset of a feasible solution is also a feasible solution. The goal is to maximize the sum of the values of the items included in the solution. □

Now we want to define a well-behaved completion algorithm, that is, one that can ensure the desired approximation by not "losing too much" as it fills in the rest of the feasible solution. Let f be the objective function of our maximum independent subset problem; we write $f(S)$ for the value of a subset and $f(x)$ for the value of a single element. Further let I^* be an optimal solution, let J be a feasible solution of size k, and let J^* be the best possible feasible superset of J, i.e., the best possible completion of J. We want our algorithm, running on J, to return some completion $\hat{J}$ obeying

$$f(\hat{J}) \geq \frac{k-1}{k} f(J^*) - \frac{1}{k} f(I^*) - \max_{x \in J^*-J} f(x)$$

and running in polynomial time. Now, if the algorithm is given a feasible solution of size less than k, it leaves it untouched; if it is not given a feasible solution, its output is not defined. We call such an algorithm a polynomial-time k-completion algorithm.

We claim that such a completion algorithm will guarantee a ratio of $3/k$. If the optimal solution has k or fewer elements, then the algorithm will find it directly; otherwise, let J_0 be the subset of I^* of size k that contains the k largest elements of I^*. The best possible completion of J_0 is I^* itself—that is, we have $J_0^* = I^*$. Now we must have

$$f(\hat{J}_0) \geq \frac{k-1}{k} f(J_0^*) - \frac{1}{k} f(I^*) - \max_{x \in J_0^* - J_0} f(x) \geq \frac{k-3}{k} f(J_0^*) = \frac{k-3}{k} f(I^*)$$

because we have

$$\max_{x \in J_0^* - J_0} f(x) \geq \frac{1}{k+1} f(J_0^*)$$

since the optimal completion has at least $k + 1$ elements. Since all subsets of size k are tested, the subset J_0 will be tested and the completion algorithm will return a solution at least as good as $\hat{J}_0$. We have just proved the simpler half of the following characterization theorem.

Theorem 8.18 A maximum independent subset problem is in PTAS if and only if, for any k, it admits a polynomial-time k-completion algorithm.   ☐

The other half of the characterization is the source of the specific subtractive terms in the required lower bound.

The problem with this technique lies in proving that the completion algorithm is indeed well behaved. The key aspect of the technique is its examination of a large, yet polynomial, number of different solutions. Applying the same principle to other problems, we can derive a somewhat more useful technique for building approximation schemes—the *shifting* technique. Basically, the shifting technique decomposes a problem into suitably sized "adjacent" subpieces and then creates subproblems by grouping a number of adjacent subpieces. We can think of a linear array of some kl subpieces in which the subpieces end up in l groups of k consecutive subpieces each. The grouping process has no predetermined boundaries and so we have k distinct choices obtained by shifting (hence the name) the boundaries between the groups. For each of the k choices, the approximation algorithm solves each subproblem (each group) and merges the solutions to the subproblems into an approximate solution to the entire problem; it then chooses the best of the k approximate solutions

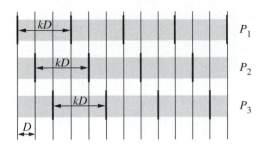

Figure 8.5   The partitions created by shifting.

thus obtained. In effect, this technique is a compromise between a dynamic programming approach, which would examine *all* possible groupings of subpieces, and a divide-and-conquer approach, which would examine a single grouping. One example must suffice here; exercises at the end of the chapter explore some other examples.

Consider then the *Disk Covering* problem: given n points in the plane and disks of fixed diameter D, cover all points with the smallest number of disks. (Such a problem can model the location of emergency facilities such that no point is farther away than $1/2 D$ from a facility.) Our approximation algorithm divides the area in which the n points reside (from minimum to maximum abscissa and from minimum to maximum ordinate) into vertical strips of width D—we ignore the fact that the last strip may be somewhat narrower. For some natural number k, we can group k consecutive strips into a single strip of width kD and thus partition the area into vertical strips of width kD. By shifting the boundaries of the partition by D, we obtain a new partition; this step can be repeated $k-1$ times to obtain a total of k distinct partitions (call them $P_1, P_2, \ldots, P_k$) into vertical strips of width kD. (Again, we ignore the fact that the strips at either end may be somewhat narrower.) Figure 8.5 illustrates the concept. Suppose we have an algorithm $\mathcal{A}$ that finds good approximate solutions within strips of width at most kD; we can apply this algorithm to each strip in partition P_i and take the union of the disks returned for each strip to obtain an approximate solution for the complete problem. We can repeat the process k times, once for each partition, and choose the best of the k approximate solutions thus obtained.

Theorem 8.19 If algorithm $\mathcal{A}$ has absolute approximation ratio $R_\mathcal{A}$, then the shifting algorithm has absolute approximation ratio $\frac{kR_\mathcal{A}+1}{k+1}$. $\square$

Proof. Denote by N the number of disks in some optimal solution. Since $\mathcal{A}$ yields $R_\mathcal{A}$-approximations, the number of disks returned by our algorithm

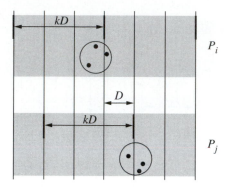

Figure 8.6 Why disks cannot cover points from adjacent strips in two distinct partitions.

for partition P_i is bounded by $\frac{1}{R_{si}} \sum_{j \in P_i} N_j$, where N_j is the optimal number of disks needed to cover the points in vertical strip j in partition P_i and where j ranges over all such strips. By construction, a disk cannot cover points in two elementary strips (the narrow strips of width D) that are not adjacent, since the distance between nonadjacent elementary strips exceeds the diameter of a disk. Thus if we could obtain locally optimal solutions within each strip (i.e., solutions of value N_j for strip j), taking their union would yield a solution that exceeds N by at most the number of disks that, in a globally optimal solution, cover points in two adjacent strips. Denote this last quantity by O_i; that is, O_i is the number of disks in the optimal solution that cover points in two adjacent strips of partition P_i. Our observation can be rewritten as $\sum_{j \in P_i} N_j \leq N + O_i$. Because each partition has a different set of adjacent strips and because each partition is shifted from the previous one by a full disk diameter, none of the disks that cover points in adjacent strips of P_i can cover points in adjacent strips of P_j, for $i \neq j$, as illustrated in Figure 8.6. Thus the total number of disks that can cover points in adjacent strips in *any* partition is at most N—the total number of disks in an optimal solution. Hence we can write $\sum_{i=1}^{k} O_i \leq N$. By summing our first inequality over all k partitions and substituting our second inequality, we obtain

$$\sum_{i=1}^{k} \sum_{j \in P_i} N_j \leq (k+1) \cdot N$$

and thus we can write

$$\min_{i=1,\ldots,k} \sum_{j \in P_i} N_j \leq \frac{1}{k} \sum_{i=1}^{k} \sum_{j \in P_i} N_j \leq \frac{k+1}{k} N$$

Using now our first bound for our shifting algorithm, we conclude that its approximation is bounded by $\frac{1}{1-R_{sl}} \cdot \frac{k+1}{k} \cdot N$ and thus has an absolute approximation ratio of $\frac{kR_{sl}+1}{k+1}$, as desired.   *Q.E.D.*

This result generalizes easily to coverage by uniform convex shapes other than disks, with suitable modifications regarding the effective diameter of the shape. It gives us a mechanism by which to extend the use of an expensive approximation algorithm to much larger instances; effectively, it allows us to use a divide-and-conquer strategy and limit the divergence from optimality. However, it presupposes the existence of a good, if expensive, approximation algorithm.

In the case of *Disk Covering*, we do not have any algorithm yet for covering the points in a vertical strip. Fortunately, what works once can be made to work again. Our new problem is to minimize the number of disks of diameter D needed cover a collection of points placed in a vertical strip of width kD, for some natural number k. With no restriction on the height of the strip, deriving an optimal solution by exhaustive search could take exponential time. However, we can repeat the divide-and-conquer strategy: we now divide each vertical strip into elementary rectangles of height D and then group k adjacent rectangles into a single square of side kD (again, the end pieces may fall short). The result is k distinct partitions of the vertical strip into a collection of squares of side kD. Theorem 8.19 applies again, so that we need only devise a good approximation algorithm for placing disks to cover the points within a square—a problem for which we can actually afford to compute the *optimal* solution as follows. We begin by noting that a square of size kD can easily be covered completely by $(k+1)^2 + k^2 = O(k^2)$ disks of diameter D, as shown in Figure 8.7.[4] Since $(k+1)^2 + k^2$ is a constant for any constant k, we need only consider a constant number of disks for covering a square. Moreover, any disk that covers at least two points can always be assumed to have these two points on its periphery; since there are two possible circles of diameter D that pass through a pair of points, we have to consider at most $2\binom{n_i}{2}$ disk positions for the n_i points present within some square i. Hence we need only consider $O(n_i^{O(k^2)})$ distinct arrangements of disks in square i; each arrangement can be checked in $O(n_i k^2)$ time, since we need only check that each point resides

---

[4]This covering pattern is known in quilt making as the double wedding ring; it is not quite optimal, but its leading term, $2k^2$, is the same as that of the optimal covering.

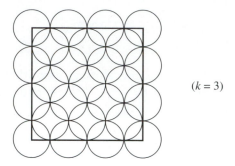

$(k = 3)$

Figure 8.7   How to cover a square of side kD with $(k + 1)^2 + k^2$ disks of diameter D.

within one of the disks. Overall, we see that an optimal disk covering can be obtained for each square in time polynomial in the number of points present within the square.

Putting all of the preceding findings together, we obtain a polynomial-time approximation scheme for *Disk Covering*.

Theorem 8.20   There is an approximation scheme for *Disk Covering* such that, for every natural number k, the scheme provides an absolute approximation ratio of $\frac{2k+1}{(k+1)^2}$ and runs in $O(k^4 n^{O(k^2)})$ time.   □

8.3.4   Fixed-Ratio Approximations

In the previous sections, we established some necessary conditions for membership in PTAS as well as some techniques for constructing approximation schemes for several classes of problems. However, there remains a very large number of problems that have some fixed-ratio approximation and thus belong to Apx but do not appear to belong to PTAS, although they obey the necessary condition of simplicity. Examples include *Vertex Cover* (see Exercise 8.23), *Maximum Cut* (see Exercise 8.24), and the most basic problem of all, namely *Maximum 3SAT (Max3SAT)*, the optimization version of *3SAT*. An instance of this problem is given by a collection of clauses of three literals each, and the goal is to return a truth assignment that maximizes the number of satisfied clauses. Because this problem is the optimization version of our most fundamental NP-complete problem, it is natural to regard it as the key problem in Apx. Membership of *Max3SAT* or *MaxkSAT* (for any fixed k) in Apx is easy to establish.

Theorem 8.21   *MaxkSAT* has a 2^{-k}-approximation.   □

Proof. Consider the following simple algorithm.

- Assign to each remaining clause c_i weight $2^{-|c_i|}$; thus every unassigned literal left in a clause halves the weight of that clause. (Intuitively, the weight of a clause is inversely proportional to the number of ways in which that clause could be satisfied.)
- Pick any variable x that appears in some remaining clause. Set x to true if the sum of the weights of the clauses in which x appears as an uncomplemented literal exceeds the sum of the clauses in which it appears as a complemented literal; set it to false otherwise.
- Update the clauses and their weights and repeat until all clauses have been satisfied or reduced to a falsehood.

We claim that this algorithm will leave at most $m2^{-k}$ unsatisfied clauses (where m is the number of clauses in the instance); since the best that any algorithm could do would be to satisfy all m clauses, our conclusion follows. Note that $m2^{-k}$ is exactly the total weight of the m clauses of length k in the original instance; thus our claim is that the number of clauses left unsatisfied by the algorithm is bounded by $\sum_{i=1}^{m} 2^{-|c_i|}$, the total weight of the clauses in the instance—a somewhat more general claim, since it applies to instances with clauses of variable length.

To prove our claim, we use induction on the number of clauses. With a single clause, the algorithm clearly returns a satisfying truth assignment and thus meets the bound. Assume then that the algorithm meets the bound on all instances of m or fewer clauses. Let x be the first variable set by the algorithm and denote by m_t the number of clauses satisfied by the assignment, m_f the number of clauses losing a literal as a result of the assignment, and $m_u = m + 1 - m_t - m_f$ the number of clauses unaffected by the assignment. Also let w_{m+1} denote the total weight of all the clauses in the original instance, w_t the total weight of the clauses satisfied by the assignment, w_u the total weight of the unaffected clauses, and w_f the total weight of the clauses losing a literal *before* the loss of that literal; thus we can write $w_{m+1} = w_t + w_u + w_f$. Because we must have had $w_t \geqslant w_f$ in order to assign x as we did, we can write $w_{m+1} = w_t + w_u + w_f \geqslant w_u + 2w_f$. The remaining $m - m_t = m_u + m_f$ clauses now have a total weight of $w_u + 2w_f$, because the weight of every clause that loses a literal doubles. By inductive hypothesis, our algorithm will leave at most $w_u + 2w_f$ clauses unsatisfied among these clauses and thus also in the original problem; since we have, as noted above, $w_{m+1} \geqslant w_u + 2w_f$, our claim is proved.   *Q.E.D.*

How are we going to classify problems within the classes NPO, Apx, and PTAS? By using reductions, naturally. However, the type of reduction

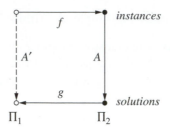

Figure 8.8   The requisite style of reduction between approximation problems.

we now need is quite a bit more complex than the many-one reduction used in completeness proofs for decision problems. We need to establish a correspondence between solutions as well as between instances; moreover, the correspondence between solutions must preserve approximation ratios. The reason for these requirements is that we need to be able to retrieve a good approximation for problem Π_1 from a reduction to a problem Π_2 for which we already have an approximate solution algorithm with certain guarantees. Figure 8.8 illustrates the scheme of the reduction. By using map f between instances and map g between solutions, along with known algorithm $\mathcal{A}$, we can obtain a good approximate solution for our original problem. In fact, by calling in succession the routines implementing the map f, the approximation algorithm $\mathcal{A}$ for Π_2, and the map g, we are effectively defining the new approximation algorithm $\mathcal{A}'$ for problem Π_1 (in mathematical terms, we are making the diagram commute). Of course, we may want to use different reductions depending on the classes we want to separate: as we noted in Chapter 6, the tool must be adapted to the task. Since all of our classes reside between PO and NPO, all of our reductions should run in polynomial time; thus both the f map between instances and the g map between solutions must be computable in polynomial time. Differences among possible reductions thus come from the requirements they place on the handling of the precision requirement. We choose a definition that gives us sufficient generality to prove results regarding the separation of NPO, APX, and PTAS; we achieve the generality by introducing a third function that maps precision requirements for Π_1 onto precision requirements for Π_2.

Definition 8.12 Let Π_1 and Π_2 be two problems in NPO. We say that Π_1 *PTAS-reduces* to Π_2 if there exist three functions, f, g, and h, such that

- for any instance x of Π_1, $f(x)$ is an instance of Π_2 and is computable in time polynomial in $|x|$;
- for any instance x of Π_1, any solution y for instance $f(x)$ of Π_2, and any rational precision requirement ε (expressed as a fraction), $g(x, y, \varepsilon)$ is a solution for x and is computable in time polynomial in $|x|$ and $|y|$;
- h is a computable injective function on the set of rationals in the interval $[0, 1)$;
- for any instance x of Π_1, any solution y for instance $f(x)$ of Π_2, and any precision requirement ε (expressed as a fraction), if the value of y obeys precision requirement $h(\varepsilon)$, then the value of $g(x, y, \varepsilon)$ obeys the precision requirement ε. □

This reduction has all of the characteristics we have come to associate with reductions in complexity theory.

Proposition 8.4

- PTAS-reductions are reflexive and transitive.
- If Π_1 PTAS-reduces to Π_2 and Π_2 belongs to Apx (respectively, PTAS), then Π_1 belongs to Apx (respectively, PTAS). □

Exercise 8.5 Prove these statements. □

We say that an optimization problem is *complete* for NPO (respectively, Apx), if it belongs to NPO (respectively, Apx) and every problem in NPO (respectively, Apx) PTAS-reduces to it. Furthermore, we define one last class of optimization problems to reflect our sense that *Max3SAT* is a key problem.

Definition 8.13 The class OptNP is exactly the class of problems that PTAS-reduce to *Max3SAT*. □

We define OptNP-completeness as we did for NPO- and Apx-completeness. In view of Theorem 8.21 and Proposition 8.4, we have OptNP $\subseteq$ Apx. We introduce OptNP because we have not yet seen natural problems that are complete for NPO or Apx, whereas OptNP, by its very definition, has at least one, *Max3SAT* itself. The standard complete problems for NPO and Apx are, in fact, generalizations of *Max3SAT*.

Theorem 8.22 The *Maximum Weighted Satisfiability* (*MaxWSAT*) problem has the same instances as *Satisfiability*, with the addition of a weight function mapping each variable to a natural number. The objective is to find a satisfying truth assignment that maximizes the total weight of the true variables. An instance of the *Maximum Bounded Weighted Satisfiability* problem is an instance of *MaxWSAT* with a bound W such that the sum of the weights of all variables in the instance must lie in the interval $[W, 2W]$.

- *Maximum Weighted Satisfiability* is NPO-complete.
- *Maximum Bounded Weighted Satisfiability* is Apx-complete.   □

Proof. We prove only the first result; the second requires a different technique, which is explored in Exercise 8.33.

That *MaxWSAT* is in NPO is easily verified. Let Π be a problem in NPO and let M be a nondeterministic machine that, for each instance of Π, guesses a solution, checks that it is feasible, and computes its value. If the guess fails, then M halts with a 0 on the tape; otherwise it halts with the value of the solution, written in binary and "in reverse," with its least significant bit on square 1 and increasing bits to the right of that position. By definition of NPO, M runs in polynomial time. For M and any instance x, the construction used in the proof of Cook's theorem yields a Boolean formula of polynomial size that describes exactly those computation paths of M on input x and guess y that lead to a nonzero answer. (That is, the Boolean formula yields a bijection between satisfying truth assignments and accepting paths.) We assign a weight of 0 to all variables used in the construction, except for those that denote that a tape square contains the character 1 at the end of computation—and that only for squares to the right of position 0. That is, only the tape squares that contain a 1 in the binary representation of the value of the solution for x will count toward the weight of the *MaxWSAT* solution. Using the notation of Table 6.1, we assign weight 2^{i-1} to variable $t(p(|x|), i, 1)$, for each i from 1 to $p(|x|)$, so that the weight of the *MaxWSAT* solution equals the value of the solution computed by M.

This transformation between instances can easily be carried out in polynomial time; a solution for the original problem can be recovered by looking at the assignment of the variables describing the initial guess (to the left of square 0 at time 1); and the precision-mapping function h is just the identity.   Q.E.D.

Strictly speaking, our proof showed only that any maximization problem in NPO PTAS-reduces to *MaxWSAT*; to finish the proof, we would need to show that any minimization problem in NPO also PTAS-reduces to *MaxWSAT* (see Exercise 8.31).

Unless P equals NP, no NPO-complete problem can be in Apx and no Apx-complete problem can be in PTAS. OptNP-complete problems interest us because, in addition to *Max3SAT*, they include many natural problems: *Bounded-Degree Vertex Cover, Bounded-Degree Independent Set, Maximum Cut,* and many others. In addition, we can use PTAS-reductions from *Max3SAT*, many of them similar (with respect to instances) to the reductions used in proofs of NP-completeness, to show that a number of optimization problems are OptNP-hard, including *Vertex Cover, Traveling Salesman with Triangle Inequality, Clique*, and many others. Such results are useful because OptNP-hard problems cannot be in PTAS unless P equals NP, as we now proceed to establish.

Proving that an NPO problem does not belong to PTAS (unless, of course, P equals NP) is based on the use of *gap-preserving reductions*. In its strongest and simplest form, a gap-preserving reduction actually *creates* a gap: it maps a decision problem onto an optimization problem and ensures that all "yes" instances map onto instances with optimal values on one side of the gap and that all "no" instances map onto instances with optimal values on the other side of the gap. Our NP-completeness proofs provide several examples of such gap-creating reductions. For instance, our reduction from *NAE3SAT* to *G3C* was such that all satisfiable instances were mapped onto three-colorable graphs, whereas all unsatisfiable instances were mapped onto graphs requiring at least four colors. It follows immediately that no polynomial-time algorithm can approximate *G3C* with an absolute ratio better than $3/4$, since such an algorithm could then be used to solve *NAE3SAT*. We conclude that, unless P equals NP, *G3C* cannot be in PTAS.

In defining the reduction, we need only specify the mapping between instances and some condition on the behavior of optimal solutions. (For simplicity, we give the definition for a reduction between two maximization problems; obvious modifications make it applicable to reductions between two minimization problems or between a minimization problem and a maximization problem.)

Definition 8.14 Let Π_1 and Π_2 be two maximization problems; denote the value of an optimal solution for an instance x by $opt(x)$. A *gap-preserving reduction* from Π_1 to Π_2 is a polynomial-time map from instances of Π_1 to instances of Π_2, together with two pairs of functions, (c_1, r_1) and (c_2, r_2), such that r_1 and r_2 return values no smaller than 1 and the following implications hold:

$$opt(x) \geq c_1(x) \Rightarrow opt(f(x)) \geq c_2(f(x))$$

$$opt(x) \leq \frac{c_1(x)}{r_1(x)} \Rightarrow opt(f(x)) \leq \frac{c_2(f(x))}{r_2(f(x))} \qquad \Box$$

Observe that the definition imposes no condition on the behavior of the transformation for instances with optimal values that lie within the gap.

The typical use of a gap-preserving reduction is to combine it with a gap-creating reduction such as the one described for *G3C*. We just saw that the reduction *g* used in the proof of NP-completeness of *G3C* gave rise to the implications

$$x \text{ satisfiable} \Rightarrow opt(g(x)) = 3$$
$$x \text{ not satisfiable} \Rightarrow opt(g(x)) \geqslant 4$$

Assume that we have a gap-preserving reduction f, with pairs $(3, {}^{3}\!/\!_{4})$ and (c', r') from *G3C* to some minimization problem Π'. We can combine g and f to obtain

$$x \text{ satisfiable} \Rightarrow opt(h(g(x))) \leqslant c'(h(g(x)))$$
$$x \text{ not satisfiable} \Rightarrow opt(h(g(x))) \geqslant \frac{c'(h(g(x)))}{r'(h(g(x)))}$$

so that the gap created in the optimal solutions of *G3C* by g is translated into another gap in the optimal solutions of Π'—the gap is preserved (although it can be enlarged or shrunk). The consequence is that approximating Π' with an absolute ratio greater than r' is NP-hard.

Up until 1991, gap-preserving reductions were of limited interest, because the problems for which we had a gap-creating reduction were relatively few and had not been used much in further transformations. In particular, nothing was known about OptNP-complete problems or even about several important OptNP-hard problems such as *Clique*. Through a novel characterization of NP in terms of probabilistic proof checking (covered in Section 9.5), it has become possible to prove that *Max3SAT*—and thus any of the OptNP-hard problems—cannot be in PTAS unless P equals NP.

Theorem 8.23 For each problem Π in NP, there is a polynomial-time map f from instances of Π to instances of *Max3SAT* and a fixed $\varepsilon > 0$ such that, for any instance x of Π, the following implications hold:

$$x \text{ is a "yes" instance} \Rightarrow opt(f(x)) = |f(x)|$$
$$x \text{ is a "no" instance} \Rightarrow opt(f(x)) < (1 - \varepsilon)|f(x)|$$

where $|f(x)|$ denotes the number of clauses in $f(x)$. □

In other words, f is a gap-creating reduction to *Max3SAT*.

Proof. We need to say a few words about the alternate characterization of NP. The gist of this characterization is that a "yes" instance of a problem in NP has a certificate that can be verified probabilistically in polynomial time by inspecting only a constant number of bits of the certificate, chosen with the help of a logarithmic number of random bits. If x is a "yes" instance, then the verifier will accept it with probability 1 (that is, it will accept no matter what the random bits are); otherwise, the verifier will reject it with probability at least $1/2$ (that is, at least half of the random bit sequences will lead to rejection).

Since Π is in NP, a "yes" instance of size n has a certificate that can be verified in polynomial time with the help of at most $c_1 \log n$ random bits and by reading at most c_2 bits from the certificate. Consider any fixed sequence of random bits—there are $2^{c_1 \log n} = n^{c_1}$ such sequences in all. For a fixed sequence, the computation of the verifier depends on c_2 bits from the certificate and is otherwise a straightforward deterministic polynomial-time computation. We can examine all 2^{c_2} possible outcomes that can result from looking up these c_2 bits. Each outcome determines a computation path; some paths lead to acceptance and some to rejection, each in at most a polynomial number of steps. Because there is a constant number of paths and each path is of polynomial length, we can examine all of these paths, determine which are accepting and which rejecting, and write a formula of constant size that describes the accepting paths in terms of the bits of the certificate read during the computation. This formula is a disjunction of at most 2^{c_2} conjuncts, where each conjunct describes one path and thus has at most c_2 literals. Each such formula is satisfiable if and only if the c_2 bits of the certificate examined under the chosen sequence of random bits can assume values that lead the verifier to accept its input. We can then take all n^{c_1} such formulae, one for each sequence of random bits, and place them into a single large conjunction. The resulting large conjunction is satisfiable if and only if there exists a certificate such that, for each choice of $c_1 \log n$ random bits (i.e., for each choice of the c_2 certificate bits to be read), the verifier accepts its input.

The formula, unfortunately, is not in *3SAT* form: it is a conjunction of n^{c_1} disjunctions, each composed of conjuncts of literals. However, we can rewrite each disjunction as a conjunction of disjuncts, each with at most 2^{c_2} literals, then use our standard trick to cut the disjuncts into a larger collection of disjuncts with three literals each. Since all manipulations involve only constant-sized entities (depending solely on c_2), the number of clauses in the final formula is a constant times n^{c_1}, say kn^{c_1}.

If the verifier rejects its input, then it does so for at least one half of the possible choices of random bits. Therefore, at least one half of the constant-size formulae are unsatisfiable. But then at least one out of every k clauses must be false for these $\frac{1}{2}n^{c_1}$ formulae, so that we must have at

Table 8.3   The NP-Hardness of Approximation Schemes.

- If the problem is not p-simple or if its decision version is strongly NP-complete, then it is not in FPTAS unless P equals NP.
- If the problem is not simple or if it is OptNP-hard, then it is not in PTAS unless P equals NP.

---

least $\frac{1}{2k}n^{c_1}$ unsatisfied clauses in any assignment. Thus if the verifier accepts its input, then all kn^{c_1} clauses are satisfied, whereas, if it rejects its input, then at most $(k - \frac{1}{2k})n^{c_1} = (1 - \frac{1}{2k^2})kn^{c_1}$ clauses can be satisfied. Since k is a fixed constant, we have obtained the desired gap, with $\varepsilon = \frac{1}{2k^2}$.   Q.E.D.

Corollary 8.3 No OptNP-hard problem can be in PTAS unless P equals NP.   □

We defined OptNP to capture the complexity of approximating our basic NP-complete problem, *3SAT*; this definition proved extremely useful in that it allowed us to obtain a number of natural complete problems and, more importantly, to prove that PTAS is a proper subset of OptNP unless P equals NP. However, we have not characterized the relationship between OptNP and Apx—at least not beyond the simple observation that the first is contained in the second. As it turns out, the choice of *Max3SAT* was justified even beyond the results already derived, as the following theorem (which we shall not prove) indicates.

Theorem 8.24 *Maximum Bounded Weighted Satisfiability* PTAS-reduces to *Max3SAT*.   □

In view of Theorem 8.22, we can immediately conclude that *Max3SAT* is Apx-complete! This result immediately settles the relationship between OptNP and Apx.

Corollary 8.4 OptNP equals Apx.   □

Thus Apx does have a large number of natural complete problems—all of the OptNP-complete problems discussed earlier. Table 8.3 summarizes what we have learned about the hardness of polynomial-time approximation schemes.

8.3.5   No Guarantee Unless P Equals NP

Superficially, it would appear that Theorem 8.23 is limited to ruling out membership in PTAS and that we need other tools to rule out membership in Apx. Yet we can still use the same principle; we just need bigger gaps or some gap-amplifying mechanism. We give just two examples, one in which we can directly produce enormous gaps and another in which a modest gap is amplified until it is large enough to use in ruling out membership in Apx.

Theorem 8.25 Approximating the optimal solution to *Traveling Salesman* within any constant ratio is NP-hard.   □

Proof. We proceed by contradiction. Assume that we have an approximation algorithm $\mathcal{A}$ with absolute ratio $R_{\mathcal{A}} = \varepsilon$. We reuse our transformation from HC, but now we produce large numbers tailored to the assumed ratio. Given an instance of HC with n vertices, we produce an instance of TSP with one city for each vertex and where the distance between two cities is 1 when there exists an edge between the two corresponding vertices and $\lceil n/\varepsilon \rceil$ otherwise. This reduction produces an enormous gap. If an instance x of HC admits a solution, then the corresponding optimal tour uses only graph edges and thus has total length n. However, if x has no solution, then the very best tour must move at least once between two cities not connected by an edge and thus has total length at least $n - 1 + \lceil n/\varepsilon \rceil$. The resulting gap exceeds the ratio ε, a contradiction. (Put differently, we could use $\mathcal{A}$ to decide any instance x of HC in polynomial time by testing whether the length of the approximate tour $\mathcal{A}(x)$ exceeds n/ε.)   Q.E.D.

Thus the general version of *TSP* is not in Apx, unlike its restriction to instances obeying the triangle inequality, for which a $2/3$-approximation is known.

Theorem 8.26 Approximating the optimal solution to *Clique* within any constant ratio is NP-hard.   □

Proof. We develop a gap-amplifying procedure, show that it turns any constant-ratio approximation into an approximation scheme, then appeal to Theorem 8.23 to conclude that no constant-ratio approximation can exist.

Let G be any graph on n vertices. Consider the new graph G^2 on n^2 vertices, where each vertex of G has been replaced by a copy of G itself, and vertices in two copies corresponding to two vertices joined by an edge in the original are connected with all possible n^2 edges connecting a vertex in one copy to a vertex in the other. Figure 8.9 illustrates the construction for a small graph. We claim that G has a clique of size k if and only if G^2 has a clique of size k^2. The "only if" part is trivial: the k copies of the clique of G corresponding to the k clique vertices in G form a clique of size k^2 in G^2. The "if" part is slightly harder, since we have no *a priori* constraint

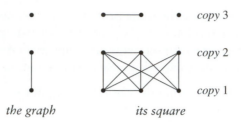

copy 3

copy 2

copy 1

the graph   *its square*

Figure 8.9 Squaring a graph.

on the composition of the clique in G^2. However, two copies of G in the larger graph are either fully connected to each other or not at all. Thus if two vertices in different copies belong to the large clique, then the two copies must be fully connected and an edge exists in G between the vertices corresponding to the copies. On the other hand, if two vertices in the same copy belong to the large clique, then these two vertices are connected by an edge in G. Thus every edge used in the large clique corresponds to an edge in G. Therefore, if the large clique has vertices in k or more distinct copies, then G has a clique of size k or more and we are done. If the large clique has vertices in at most k distinct copies, then it must include at least k vertices from some copy (because it has k^2 vertices in all) and thus G has a clique of size at least k. Given a clique of size k^2 in G^2, this line of reasoning shows not only the existence of a clique of size k in G, but also how to recover it from the large clique in G^2 in polynomial time.

Now assume that we have an approximation algorithm $\mathcal{A}$ for *Clique* with absolute ratio ε. Then, given some graph G with a largest clique of size k, we compute G^2; run $\mathcal{A}$ on G^2, yielding a clique of size at least εk^2; and then recover from this clique one of size at least $\sqrt{\varepsilon k^2} = k\sqrt{\varepsilon}$. This new procedure, call it $\mathcal{A}'$, runs in polynomial time if $\mathcal{A}$ does and has ratio $R_{\mathcal{A}'} = \sqrt{R_{\mathcal{A}}}$. But we can use the same idea again to derive procedure $\mathcal{A}''$ with ratio $R_{\mathcal{A}''} = \sqrt{R_{\mathcal{A}'}} = \sqrt[4]{R_{\mathcal{A}}}$. More generally, i applications of this scheme yield procedure $\mathcal{A}^i$ with absolute ratio $\sqrt[i]{R_{\mathcal{A}}}$. Given any desired approximation ratio ε, we can apply the scheme $\lceil \frac{\log \varepsilon}{\log R_{\mathcal{A}}} \rceil$ times to obtain a procedure with the desired ratio. Since $\lceil \frac{\log \varepsilon}{\log R_{\mathcal{A}}} \rceil$ is a constant and since each application of the scheme runs in polynomial time, we have derived a polynomial-time approximation scheme for *Clique*. But *Clique* is OptNP-hard and thus, according to Theorem 8.23, cannot be in PTAS, the desired contradiction.   *Q.E.D.*

Exercise 8.6 Verify that, as a direct consequence of our various results in the preceding sections, the sequence of inclusions, PO ⊆ FPTAS ⊆ PTAS ⊆ OptNP = Apx ⊆ NPO, is proper (at every step) if and only if P does not equal NP.   □

8.4   The Power of Randomization

A randomized algorithm uses a certain number of random bits during its execution. Thus its behavior is unpredictable for a single execution, but we can often obtain a probabilistic characterization of its behavior over a number of runs—typically of the type "the algorithm returns a correct answer with a probability of at least c." While the behavior of a randomized algorithm must be analyzed with probabilistic techniques, many of them similar to the techniques used in analyzing the average-case behavior of a deterministic algorithm, there is a fundamental distinction between the two. With randomized algorithms, the behavior depends only on the algorithm, not on the data; whereas, when analyzing the average-case behavior of a deterministic algorithm, the behavior depends on the data as well as on the algorithm—it is the data that induces a probability distribution. Indeed, one of the benefits of randomization is that it typically suppresses data dependencies. As a simple example of the difference, consider the familiar sorting algorithm `quicksort`. If we run `quicksort` with the partitioning element chosen as the first element of the interval, we have a deterministic algorithm. Its worst-case running time is quadratic and its average-case running time is $O(n \log n)$ under the assumption that all input permutations are equally likely—a data-dependent distribution. On the other hand, if we choose the partitioning element at random within the interval (with the help of $O(\log n)$ random bits), then the input permutation no longer matters—the expectation is now taken with respect to our random bits. The worst-case remains quadratic, but it can no longer be triggered repeatedly by the same data sets—no adversary can cause our algorithm to perform really poorly.

Randomized algorithms have been used very successfully to speed up existing solutions to tractable problems and also to provide approximate solutions for hard problems. Indeed, no other algorithm seems suitable for the approximate solution of a decision problem: after all, "no" is a very poor approximation for "yes." A randomized algorithm applied to a decision problem returns "yes" or "no" with a probabilistic guarantee as to the correctness of the answer; if statistically independent executions of the algorithm can be used, this probability can be improved to any level desired by the user. Now that we have learned about nondeterminism, we can put randomized algorithms in another perspective: while a nondeterministic algorithm always makes the correct decision whenever faced with a choice, a randomized algorithm approximates a nondeterministic one by making a random decision. Thus if we view the process of solving an instance of the problem as a computation tree, with a branch at each decision point, a nondeterministic algorithm unerringly follows a path to an accepting leaf, if any, while a randomized algorithm follows a random path to some leaf.

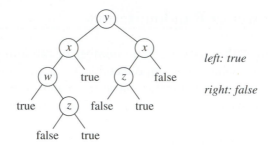

Figure 8.10   A binary decision tree for the function $\overline{x}y + x\overline{z} + yw$.

As usual, we shall focus on decision problems. Randomized algorithms are also used to provide approximate solutions for optimization problems, but that topic is outside the scope of this text.

A *Monte Carlo* algorithm runs a polynomial time but may err with probability less than some constant (say $1/2$); a one-sided Monte Carlo decision algorithm never errs when it returns one type of answer, say "no," and errs with probability less than some constant (say $1/2$) when it returns the other, say "yes." Thus, given a "no" instance, all of the leaves of the computation tree are "no" leaves and, given a "yes" instance, at least half of the leaves of the computation tree are "yes" leaves. We give just one example of a one-sided Monte Carlo algorithm.

Example 8.3 Given a Boolean function, we can construct for it a *binary decision tree*. In a binary decision tree, each internal node represents a variable of the function and has two children, one corresponding to setting that variable to "true" and the other corresponding to setting that variable to "false." Each leaf is labeled "true" or "false" and represents the value of the function for the (partial) truth assignment represented by the path from the root to the leaf. Figure 8.10 illustrates the concept for a simple Boolean function. Naturally a very large number of binary decision trees represent the same Boolean function. Because binary decision trees offer concise representations of Boolean functions and lead to a natural and efficient evaluation of the function they represent, manipulating such trees is of interest in a number of areas, including compiling and circuit design.

One fundamental question that arises is whether or not two trees represent the same Boolean function. This problem is clearly in coNP: if the two trees represent distinct functions, then there is at least one truth assignment under which the two functions return different values, so that we can guess this truth assignment and verify that the two binary decision trees return distinct values. To date, however, no deterministic polynomial-time algorithm has been found for this problem, nor has anyone been able to prove it CONP-complete. Instead of guessing a truth assignment to the n variables and computing a Boolean value, thereby condensing a lot of computations into a single bit of output and losing discriminations made along the way, we shall use a random assignment of integers in the range $S = [0, 2n - 1]$, and compute (modulo p, where p is a prime at least as large as $|S|$) an integer as characteristic of the entire tree under this assignment. If variable x is assigned value i, then we assign value $1 - i$ (modulo p) to its complement, so that the sum of the value of x and of $\bar{x}$ is 1. For each leaf of the tree labeled "true," we compute (modulo p) the product of the the values of the variables encountered along the path; we then sum (modulo p) all of these values. The two resulting numbers (one per tree) are compared. If they differ, our algorithm concludes that the trees represent different functions, otherwise it concludes that they represent the same function. The algorithm clearly gives the correct answer whenever the two values differ but may err when the two values are equal. We claim that at least $(|S| - 1)^n$ of the possible $(|S|)^n$ assignments of values to the n variables will yield distinct values when the two functions are distinct; this claim immediately implies that the probability of error is bounded by

$$\frac{(|S| - 1)^n}{|S|^n} = \left(\frac{2n - 1}{2n}\right)^n > \frac{1}{2}$$

and that we have a one-sided Monte Carlo algorithm for the problem.

The claim trivially holds for functions of one variable; let us then assume that it holds for functions of n or fewer variables and consider two distinct functions, f and g, of $n + 1$ variables. Consider the two functions of n variables obtained from f by fixing some variable x; denote them $f_{x=0}$ and $f_{x=1}$, so that we can write $f = \bar{x} f_{x=0} + x f_{x=1}$. If f and g differ, then $f_{x=0}$ and $g_{x=0}$ differ, or $f_{x=1}$ and $g_{x=1}$ differ, or both. In order to have the value computed for f equal that computed for g, we must have

$$(1 - |x|)|f_{x=0}| + |x||f_{x=1}| = (1 - |x|)|g_{x=0}| + |x||g_{x=1}|$$

(where we denote the value assigned to x by $|x|$ and the value computed for f by $|f|$). But if $|f_{x=0}|$ and $|g_{x=0}|$ differ, we can write

$$|x|(|f_{x=1}| - |f_{x=0}| - |g_{x=1}| + |g_{x=0}|) = |f_{x=0}| - |g_{x=0}|$$

which has at most one solution for $|x|$ since the right-hand side is nonzero. Thus we have at least $(|S| - 1)$ assignments to x that maintain the difference in values for f and g given a difference in values for $|f_{x=0}|$ and $|g_{x=0}|$; since, by inductive hypothesis, the latter can be obtained with at least $(|S| - 1)^n$ assignments, we conclude that at least $(|S| - 1)^{n+1}$ assignments will result in different values whenever f and g differ, the desired result.   □

A *Las Vegas* algorithm never errs but may not run in polynomial time on all instances. Instead, it runs in polynomial time on average—that is, assuming that all instances of size n are equally likely and that the running time on instance x is $f(x)$, the expression $\sum_x 2^{-n} f(x)$, where the sum is taken over all instances x of size n, is bounded by a polynomial in n. Las Vegas algorithms remain rare; perhaps the best known is an algorithm for primality testing.

Compare these situations with that holding for a nondeterministic algorithm. Here, given a "no" instance, the computation tree has only "no" leaves, while, given a "yes" instance, it has at least one "yes" leaf. We could attempt to solve a problem in NP by using a randomized method: produce a random certificate (say encoded in binary) and verify it. What guarantee would we obtain? If the answer returned by the algorithm is "yes," then the probability of error is 0, as only "yes" instances have "yes" leaves in their computation tree. If the answer is "no," on the other hand, then the probability of error remains large. Specifically, since there are $2^{|x|}$ possible certificates and since only one of them may lead to acceptance, the probability of error is bounded by $(1 - 2^{-|x|})$ times the probability that instance x is a "yes" instance. Since the bound depends on the input size, we cannot achieve a fixed probability of error by using a fixed number of trials—quite unlike Monte Carlo algorithms. In a very strong sense, a nondeterministic algorithm is a generalization of a Monte Carlo algorithm (in particular, both are one-sided), with the latter itself a generalization of a Las Vegas algorithm.

These considerations justify a study of the classes of (decision) problems solvable by randomized methods. Our model of computation is that briefly suggested earlier, a *random Turing machine*. This machine is similar to a nondeterministic machine in that it has a choice of (two) moves at each step and thus must make decisions, but unlike its nondeterministic cousin, it does so by tossing a fair coin. Thus a random Turing machine defines a binary computation tree where a node at depth k is reached with probability 2^{-k}. A random Turing machine operates in polynomial time if the height of its computation tree is bounded by a polynomial function of the instance size. Since aborting the computation after a polynomial number of moves may prevent the machine from reaching a conclusion, leaves of a polynomially bounded computation tree are marked by one of "yes," "no," or "don't know." Without loss of generality, we shall assume that all leaves are at the same level, say $p(|x|)$ for instance x. Then the probability that the machine answers yes is simply equal to $N_y 2^{-p(|x|)}$, where N_y is the number of "yes" leaves; similar results hold for the other two answers. We define the following classes.

Definition 8.15

- PP is the class of all decision problems for which there exists a polynomial-time random Turing machine such that, for any instance x of Π:
    - if x is a "yes" instance, then the machine accepts x with probability larger than $1/2$;
    - if x is a "no" instance, then the machine rejects x with probability larger than $1/2$.

- BPP is the class of all decision problems for which there exists a polynomial-time random Turing machine and a positive constant $\varepsilon \leqslant 1/2$ (but see also Exercise 8.34) such that, for any instance x of Π:
    - if x is a "yes" instance, then the machine accepts x with probability no less than $1/2 + \varepsilon$;
    - if x is a "no" instance, then the machine rejects x with probability no less than $1/2 + \varepsilon$.

    (The "B" indicates that the probability is bounded away from $1/2$.)
- RP is the class of all decision problems for which there exists a polynomial-time random Turing machine and a positive constant $\varepsilon \leqslant 1$ such that, for any instance x of Π:
    - if x is a "yes" instance, then the machine accepts x with probability no less than ε;
    - if x is a "no" instance, then the machine always rejects x. □

Since RP is a one-sided class, we define its complementary class, coRP, in the obvious fashion. The class RP ∪ coRP embodies our notion of problems for which (one-sided) Monte Carlo algorithms exist, while RP ∩ coRP corresponds to problems for which Las Vegas algorithms exist. This last class is important, as it can also be viewed as the class of problems for which there exist probabilistic algorithms that never err.

Lemma 8.1 A problem Π belongs to RP ∩ coRP if and only if there exists a polynomial-time random Turing machine and a positive constant $\varepsilon \leqslant 1$ such that

- the machine accepts or rejects an arbitrary instance with probability no less than ε;
- the machine accepts only "yes" instances and rejects only "no" instances.   □

We leave the proof of this result to the reader. This new definition is almost the same as the definition of NP ∩ coNP: the only change needed is to make ε dependent upon the instance rather than only upon the problem. This same change turns the definition of RP into the definition of NP, the definition of coRP into that of coNP, and the definition of BPP into that of PP.

Exercise 8.7 Verify this statement.   □

We can immediately conclude that RP ∩ coRP is a subset of NP ∩ coNP, RP is a subset of NP, coRP is a subset of coNP, and BPP is a subset of PP. Moreover, since all computation trees are limited to polynomial height, it is obvious that all of these classes are contained within PSPACE. Finally, since no computation tree is required to have all of its leaves labeled "yes" for a "yes" instance and labeled "no" for a "no" instance, we also conclude that P is contained within all of these classes.

Continuing our examination of relationships among these classes, we notice that the ε value given in the definition of RP could as easily have been specified larger than $1/2$. Given a machine M with some ε no larger than $1/2$, we can construct a machine M' with an ε larger than $1/2$ by making M' iterate M for a number of trials sufficient to bring up ε. (This is just the main feature of Monte Carlo algorithms: their probability of error can be decreased to any fixed value by running a fixed number of trials.) Hence the definition of RP and coRP is just a strengthened (on one side only) version of the definition of BPP, so that both RP and coRP are within BPP. We complete this classification by proving the following result.

Theorem 8.27 NP (and hence also coNP) is a subset of PP.   □

Proof. As mentioned earlier, we can use a random Turing machine to approximate the nondeterministic machine for a problem in NP. Comparing definitions for NP and PP, we see that we need only show how to take the nondeterministic machine M for our problem and turn it into a suitable random machine M'. As noted, M accepts a "yes" instance with probability larger than zero but not larger than any fixed constant (if only one leaf in the computation tree is labeled "yes," the instance is a "yes" instance, but the probability of acceptance is only $2^{-p(|x|)}$). We need to make this probability larger than $1/2$. We can do this through the simple expedient of tossing

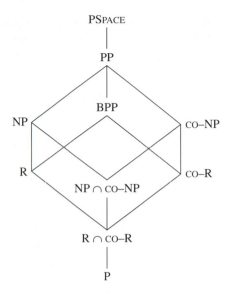

Figure 8.11   The hierarchy of randomized complexity classes.

one coin before starting any computation and accepting the instance *a priori* if the toss produces, say heads. This procedure introduces an *a priori*
probability of acceptance, call it p_a, of $1/2$; thus the probability of accep-
tance of "yes" instance x is now at least $1/2 + 2^{-p(|x|)}$. We are not quite done,
however, because the probability of rejection of a "no" instance, which was
exactly 1 without the coin toss, is now $1 - p_a = 1/2$. The solution is quite
simple: it is enough to make p_a less than $1/2$, while still large enough so that
$p_a + 2^{-p(|x|)} > 1/2$. Tossing an additional $p(|x|)$ coins will suffice: M' accepts
a priori exactly when the first toss returns heads and the next $p(|x|)$ tosses
do not all return tails, so that $p_a = 1/2 - 2^{-p(|x|)-1}$. Hence a "yes" instance is
accepted with probability $p_a + 2^{-p(|x|)} = 1/2 + 2^{-p(|x|)-1}$ and a "no" instance
is rejected with probability $1 - p_a = 1/2 + 2^{-p(|x|)-1}$. Since M' runs in poly-
nomial time if and only if M does, our conclusion follows.   *Q.E.D.*

The resulting hierarchy of randomized classes and its relation to P, NP, and
PSPACE is shown in Figure 8.11.

Before we proceed with our analysis of these classes, let us consider one
more class of complexity, corresponding to the Las Vegas algorithms, that
is, corresponding to algorithms that always return the correct answer but
have a random execution time, the expectation of which is polynomial. The
class of decision problems solvable with this type of algorithms is denoted

by ZPP (where the "Z" stands for zero error probability). As it turns out, we already know about this class, as it is no other than RP ∩ coRP.

Theorem 8.28 ZPP equals RP ∩ coRP.   □

Proof. We prove containment in each direction.

(ZPP ⊆ RP ∩ coRP)   Given a machine M for a problem in ZPP, we construct a machine M' that answers the conditions for RP ∩ coRP by simply cutting the execution of M after a polynomial amount of time. This prevents M from returning a result so that the resulting machine M', while running in polynomial time and never returning a wrong answer, has a small probability of not returning any answer. It remains only to show that this probability is bounded above by some constant $\varepsilon < 1$. Let $q()$ be the polynomial bound on the expected running time of M. We define M' by stopping M on all paths exceeding some polynomial bound $r()$, where we choose polynomials $r()$ and $r'()$ such that $r(n) + r'(n) = q(n)$ and such that $r()$ provides the desired ε (we shall shortly see how to do that). Without loss of generality, we assume that all computations paths that lead to a leaf within the bound $r()$ do so in exactly $r(n)$ steps. Denote by p_x the probability that M' does not give an answer. On an instance of size n, the expected running time of M is given by $(1 - p_x) \cdot r(n) + p_x \cdot t_{\max}(n)$, where $t_{\max}(n)$ is the average number of steps on the paths that require more than polynomial time. By hypothesis, this expression is bounded by $q(n) = r(n) + r'(n)$. Solving for p_x, we obtain

$$p_x \leq \frac{r'(n)}{t_{\max}(n) - r(n)}$$

This quantity is always less than 1, as the difference $t_{\max}(n) - r(n)$ is superpolynomial by assumption. Since we can pick $r()$ and $r'()$, we can make p_x smaller than any given $\varepsilon > 0$.

(RP ∩ coRP ⊆ ZPP)   Given a machine M for a problem in RP ∩ coRP, we construct a machine M' that answers the conditions for ZPP. Let $1/k$ (for some rational number $k > 1$) be the bound on the probability that M does not return an answer, let $r()$ be the polynomial bound on the running time of M, and let $k^{q(n)}$ be a bound on the time required to solve an instance of size n deterministically. (We know that this last bound is correct as we know that the problem, being in RP ∩ coRP, is in NP.) On an instance of size n, M' simply runs M for up to $q(n)$ trials. As soon as M returns an answer, M' returns the same answer and stops; on the other hand, if none of the $q(n)$ successive runs of M returns an answer, then M' solves the instance deterministically. Since the probability that M does not return any answer in $q(n)$ trials is $k^{-q(n)}$, the expected running time of M' is bounded by $(1 - k^{-q(n)}) \cdot r(n) + k^{-q(n)} \cdot k^{q(n)} = 1 + (1 - k^{-q(n)}) \cdot r(n)$. Hence the expected running time of M' is bounded by a polynomial in n.

Q.E.D.

Since all known randomized algorithms are Monte Carlo algorithms, Las Vegas algorithms, or ZPP algorithms, the problems that we can now address with randomized algorithms appear to be confined to a subset of RP ∪ coRP. Moreover, as the membership of an NP-complete problem in RP would imply NP = RP, an outcome considered unlikely (see Exercise 8.39 for a reason), it follows that this subset of RP ∪ coRP does not include any NP-complete or coNP-complete problem. Hence randomization, in its current state of development, is far from being a panacea for hard problems.

What of the other two classes of randomized complexity? Membership in BPP indicates the existence of randomized algorithms that run in polynomial time with an arbitrarily small, fixed probability of error.

Theorem 8.29 Let Π be a problem in BPP. Then, for any $\delta > 0$, there exists a polynomial-time randomized algorithm that accepts "yes" instances and rejects "no" instances of Π with probability at least $1 - \delta$. ☐

Proof. Since Π is in BPP, it has a polynomial-time randomized algorithm $\mathcal{A}$ that accepts "yes" instances and rejects "no" instances of Π with probability at least $1/2 + \varepsilon$, for some constant $\varepsilon > 0$. Consider the following new algorithm, where k is an odd integer to be defined shortly.

```
yes_count := 0;
for i := 1 to k do
   if A(x) accepts
      then yes_count := yes_count+1
if yes_count > k div 2
   then accept
   else reject
```

If x is a "yes" instance of Π, then $\mathcal{A}(x)$ accepts with probability at least $1/2 + \varepsilon$; thus the probability of observing exactly j acceptances (and thus $k - j$ rejections) in the k runs of $\mathcal{A}(x)$ is at least

$$\binom{k}{j} (1/2 + \varepsilon)^j (1/2 - \varepsilon)^{k-j}$$

We can derive a simplified bound for this value when j does not exceed $k/2$ by equalizing the two powers to $k/2$:

$$\binom{k}{j}(1/2 + \varepsilon)^j (1/2 - \varepsilon)^{k-j} \leq \binom{k}{j}(1/4 - \varepsilon^2)^{k/2}$$

Summing these probabilities for values of j not exceeding $k/2$, we obtain the probability that our new algorithm will reject a "yes" instance:

$$\sum_{j=0}^{k/2} \binom{k}{j}(1/2 + \varepsilon)^j (1/2 - \varepsilon)^{k-j} \leq (1/4 - \varepsilon^2)^{k/2} \sum_{j=0}^{k/2} \binom{k}{j} \leq (1 - 4\varepsilon^2)^{k/2}$$

Now we choose k so as to ensure $(1 - 4\varepsilon^2)^{k/2} \leq \delta$ which gives us the condition

$$k \geq \frac{2 \log \delta}{\log(1 - 4\varepsilon^2)}$$

so that k is a constant depending only on the input constant δ.   Q.E.D.

Thus BPP *is the correct generalization of* P *through randomization*; stated differently, *the class of tractable decision problems is* BPP. Since BPP includes both RP and coRP, we may hope that it will contain new and interesting problems and take us closer to the solution of NP-complete problems. However, few, if any, algorithms for natural problems use the full power implicit in the definition of BPP. Moreover, BPP does not appear to include many of the common hard problems; the following theorem (which we shall not prove) shows that it sits fairly low in the hierarchy.

Theorem 8.30 BPP is a subset of $\Sigma_2^p \cap \Pi_2^p$ (where these two classes are the nondeterministic and co-nondeterministic classes at the second level of the polynomial hierarchy discussed in Section 7.3.2).   □

If NP is not equal to coNP, then neither NP nor coNP is closed under complementation, whereas BPP clearly is; thus under our standard conjecture, BPP cannot equal NP or coNP. A result that we shall not prove states that adding to a machine for the class BPP an oracle that solves any problem in BPP itself does not increase the power of the machine; in our notation, BPP^{BPP} equals BPP. By comparison, the same result holds trivially for the class P (reinforcing the similarity between P and BPP), while it does not appear to hold for NP, since we believe that NP^{NP} is a proper superset of NP. An immediate consequence of this result and of Theorem 8.30 is that, if we had NP $\subseteq$ BPP, then the entire polynomial hierarchy would collapse into BPP—something that would be very surprising. Hence BPP does not appear to contain any NP-complete problem, so that the scope of randomized algorithms is indeed fairly restricted.

What then of the largest class, PP? Membership in PP is not likely to be of much help, as the probabilistic guarantee on the error bound is very poor. The amount by which the probability exceeds the bound of $1/2$ may depend on the instance size; for a problem in NP, we have seen that this quantity is only $2^{-p(n)}$ for an instance of size n. Reducing the probability of error to a small fixed value for such a problem requires an *exponential* number of trials. PP is very closely related to #P, the class of enumeration problems corresponding to decision problems in NP. We know that a complete problem (under Turing reductions) for #P is "How many satisfying truth assignments are there for a given *3SAT* instance?" The very similar problem "Do more than half of the possible truth assignments satisfy a given *3SAT* instance?" is complete for PP (Exercise 8.36). In a sense, PP contains the decision version of the problems in #P—instead of asking for the number of certificates, the problems ask whether the number of certificates meets a certain bound. As a result, an oracle for PP is as good as an oracle for #P, that is, P^{PP} is equal to $P^{\#P}$.

In conclusion, randomized algorithms have the potential for providing efficient and elegant solutions for many problems, as long as said problems are not too hard. Whether or not a randomized algorithm indeed makes a difference remains unknown; the hierarchy of classes described earlier is not firm, as it rests on the usual conjecture that all containments are proper. If we had NP $\subseteq$ BPP, for instance, we would have RP = NP and BPP = PH, which would indicate that randomized algorithms have more potential than suspected. However, if we had P = ZPP = RP = coRP = BPP $\subset$ NP, then no gain at all could be achieved through the medium of randomized algorithms (except in the matter of providing faster algorithms for problems in P). Our standard study tool, namely complete problems, appears inapplicable here, since neither RP nor BPP appear to have complete problems (Exercise 8.39).

Another concern about randomized algorithms is their dependence on the random bits they use. In practice, these bits are not really random, since they are generated by a pseudorandom number generator. Indeed, the randomized algorithms that we can actually run are entirely deterministic—for a fixed choice of seed, the entire computation is completely fixed! Much work has been devoted to this issue, in particular to the minimization of the number of truly random bits required. Many *amplification* mechanisms have been developed, as well as mechanisms to remove biases from nonuniform generators. The bibliographic section offers suggestions for further exploration of these topics.

8.5   Exercises

Exercise 8.8* Prove that *Planar 3SAT* is NP-complete, in polar and non-polar versions.

Exercise 8.9* (Refer to the previous exercise.) Prove that *Planar 1in3SAT* is NP-complete, in polar and nonpolar versions.

Exercise 8.10 Prove that the following problems remain NP-complete when restricted to graphs where no vertex degree may exceed three. (Design an appropriate component to substitute for each vertex of degree larger than three.)

1. *Vertex Cover*
2. *Maximum Cut*

Exercise 8.11* Show that *Max Cut* restricted to planar graphs is solvable in polynomial time. (Hint: set it up as a matching problem between pairs of adjacent planar faces.)

Exercise 8.12* Prove Theorem 8.6. (Hint: use a transformation from *Vertex Cover*.)

Exercise 8.13* A curious fact about uniqueness is that the question "Does the problem have a unique solution?" appears to be harder for some NP-complete problems than for others. In particular, this appears to be a harder question for *TSP* than it is for *SAT* or even *HC*. We saw in the previous chapter that *Unique Traveling Salesman Tour* is complete for Δ_2^p (Exercise 7.48), while *Unique Satisfiability* is in D^p, a presumably proper subset of Δ_2^p. Can you explain that? Based on your explanation, can you propose other candidate problems for which the question should be as hard as for *TSP*? no harder than for *SAT*?

Exercise 8.14 Prove Vizing's theorem: the chromatic index of a graph either equals the maximum degree of the graph or is one larger. (Hint: use induction on the degree of the graph.)

Exercise 8.15 Prove that *Matrix Cover* is strongly NP-complete. An instance of this problem is given by an $n \times n$ matrix $A = (a_{ij})$ with nonnegative integer entries and a bound K. The question is whether there exists a function, $f : \{1, 2, \ldots, n\} \to \{-1, 1\}$, with

$$\sum_{i=1}^{n} \sum_{j=1}^{n} a_{ij} f(i) f(j) \leqslant K$$

(Hint: transform *Maximum Cut* so as to produce only instances with "small" numbers.)

Exercise 8.16* Prove that *Memory Management* is strongly NP-complete. An instance of this problem is given by a memory size M and collection of requests S, each with a size $s: S \to \mathbb{N}$, a request time $f: S \to \mathbb{N}$, and a release time $l: S \to \mathbb{N}$, where $l(x) > f(x)$ holds for each $x \in S$. The question "Does there exist a memory allocation scheme $\sigma: S \to \{1, 2, \ldots, M\}$ such that allocated intervals in memory do not overlap during their existence?" Formally, the allocation scheme must be such that $[\sigma(x), \sigma(x) + s(x) - 1] \cap [\sigma(y), \sigma(y) + s(y) - 1] \neq \emptyset$ implies that one of $l(x) \leq f(y)$ or $l(y) \leq f(x)$ holds.

Exercise 8.17 Prove that the decision version of *Safe Deposit Boxes* is NP-complete for each fixed $k \geq 2$.

Exercise 8.18* In this exercise, we develop a polynomial-time approximation algorithm for *Safe Deposit Boxes* for two currencies that returns a solution using at most one more box than the optimal solution.

As we noted in the text, the problem is hard only because we cannot convert the second currency into the first. We sketch an iterative algorithm, based in part upon the monotonicity of the problem (because all currencies have positive values and any exchange rate is also positive) and in part upon the following observation (which you should prove): if some subset of k boxes, selected in decreasing order by total value under some exchange rate, fails to meet the objective for both currencies, then the optimal solution must open at least $k + 1$ boxes. The interesting part in this result is that the exchange rate under which the k boxes fail to satisfy either currency requirement need not be the "optimal" exchange rate nor the extremal rates of $1:0$ and of $0:1$.

Set the initial currency exchange ratio to be $1:0$ and sort the boxes according to their values in the first currency, breaking any ties by their values in the second currency. Let the values in the first currency be $a_1, a_2, \ldots, a_n$ and those in the second currency $b_1, b_2, \ldots, b_n$; thus, in our ordering, we have $a_1 \geq a_2 \geq \cdots \geq a_n$. Select the first k boxes in the ordering such that the resulting collection, call it S, fulfills the requirement on the first currency. If the requirement on the second currency is also met, we have an optimal solution and stop. Otherwise we start an iterative process of corrections to the ordering (and, incidentally, the exchange rate); we know that $k = |S|$ is a lower bound on the value of the optimal solution. Our algorithm will maintain a collection, S, of boxes with known properties. At the beginning of each iteration, this collection meets the requirement on the first but not on the second currency. Define the values $\beta(i, j)$ to be the ratios

$$\beta(i, j) = \frac{a_i - a_j}{b_j - b_i}$$

Consider all $\beta(i, j)$ where we have both $a_i > a_j$ and $b_j > b_i$—i.e., with $\beta(i, j) > 0$—and sort them.

Now examine each $\beta(i, j)$ in turn. Set the exchange rate to $1 : \beta(i, j)$. If boxes i and j both belong to S or neither belongs to S, this change does not alter S. On the other hand, if box i belongs to S and box j does not, then we replace box i by box j in S, a change that increases the amount of the second currency and decreases the amount of the first currency. Four cases can arise:

1. The resulting collection now meets both requirements: we have a solution of size k and thus an optimal solution. Stop.
2. The resulting collection fails to meet the requirement on the first currency but satisfies the requirement on the second. We place box i back into the collection S; the new collection now meets both requirements with $k + 1$ boxes and thus is a distance-one approximation. Stop.
3. The resulting collection continues to meet the requirement on the first currency and continues to fail the requirement on the second—albeit by a lesser amount. Iterate.
4. The resulting collection fails to meet both requirements. From our observation, the optimal solution must contain at least $k + 1$ boxes. We place box i back into the collection S, thereby ensuring that the new S meets the requirement on the first currency, and we proceed to case 1 or 3, as appropriate.

Verify that the resulting algorithm returns a distance-one approximation to the optimal solution in $O(n^2 \log n)$ time. An interesting consequence of this algorithm is that there exists an exchange rate, specifically a rate of $1 : \beta(i, j)$ for a suitable choice of i and j, under which selecting boxes in decreasing order of total value yields a distance-one approximation.

Now use this two-currency algorithm to derive an $(m - 1)$-distance approximation algorithm for the m-currency version of the problem that runs in polynomial time for each fixed m. (A solution that runs in $O(n^{m+1})$ time is possible.)

Exercise 8.19* Consider the following algorithm for the *Minimum-Degree Spanning Tree* problem.

1. Find a spanning tree, call it T.

2. Let k be the degree of T. Mark all vertices of T of degree $k - 1$ or k; we call these vertices "bad." Remove the bad vertices from T, leaving a forest F.

3. While there exists some edge $\{u, v\}$ not in T connecting two components (which need not be trees) in F and while all vertices of degree k remain marked:

   (a) Consider the cycle created in T by $\{u, v\}$ and unmark any bad vertices in that cycle.

   (b) Combine all components of F that have a vertex in the cycle into one component.

4. If there is an unmarked vertex w of degree k, it is unmarked because we unmarked it in some cycle created by T and some edge $\{u, v\}$. Add $\{u, v\}$ to T, remove from T one of the cycle edges incident upon w, and return to Step 2. Otherwise T is the approximate solution.

Prove that this algorithm is a distance-one approximation algorithm. (Hint: prove that removing m vertices from a graph and thereby disconnecting the graph into d connected components indicates that the minimum-degree spanning tree for the graph must have degree at least $\frac{m+d-1}{m}$. Then verify that the vertices that remain marked when the algorithm terminates have the property that their removal creates a forest F in which no two trees can be connected by an edge of the graph.)

Exercise 8.20 Use the multiplication technique to show that none of the following NP-hard problems admits a constant-distance approximation unless P equals NP.

1. Finding a set cover of minimum cardinality.
2. Finding the truth assignment that satisfies the largest number of clauses in a 2SAT problem.
3. Finding a minimum subset of vertices of a graph such that the graph resulting from the removal of this subset is bipartite.

Exercise 8.21* Use the multiplication technique to show that none of the following NP-hard problems admits a constant-distance approximation unless P equals NP.

1. Finding an optimal identification tree. (Hint: to multiply the problem, introduce subclasses for each class and add perfectly splitting tests to distinguish between those subclasses.)
2. Finding a minimum spanning tree of bounded degree (contrast with Exercise 8.19).

3. Finding the chromatic number of a graph. (Hint: multiply the graph by a suitably chosen graph. To multiply graph G by graph G', make a copy of G for each node of G' and, for each edge $\{u, v\}$ of G', connect all vertices in the copy of G corresponding to u to all vertices in the copy of G corresponding to v.)

Exercise 8.22* The concept of constant-distance approximation can be extended to distances that are sublinear functions of the optimal value. Verify that, unless NP equals P, there cannot exist a polynomial-time approximation algorithm $\mathcal{A}$ for any of the problems of the previous two exercises that would produce an approximate solution $\hat{f}$ obeying $|f(I) - \hat{f}(I)| \leqslant f^{1-\epsilon}(I)$, for some constant $\epsilon > 0$.

Exercise 8.23 Verify that the following is a $1/2$-approximation algorithm for the *Vertex Cover* problem:

- While there remains an edge in the graph, select any such edge, add both of its endpoints to the cover, and remove all edges covered by these two vertices.

Exercise 8.24* Devise a $1/2$-approximation algorithm for the *Maximum Cut* problem.

Exercise 8.25* Verify that the approximation algorithm for *Knapsack* that enumerates all subsets of k objects, completing each subset with the greedy heuristic based on value density and choosing the best completion, always returns a solution of value not less than $\frac{k}{k+1}$ times the optimal value. It follows that, for each fixed k, there exists a polynomial-time approximation algorithm $\mathcal{A}_k$ for *Knapsack* with ratio $R_{\mathcal{A}_k} = 1/k$; hence *Knapsack* is in PTAS. (Hint: if the optimal solution has at most k objects in it, we are done; otherwise, consider the completion of the subset composed of the k most valuable items in the optimal solution.)

Exercise 8.26 Prove that the product version of the *Knapsack* problem, that is, the version where the value of the packing is the product of the values of the items packed rather than their sum, is also in FPTAS.

Exercise 8.27 Prove Theorem 8.15; the proof essentially constructs an abstract approximation algorithm in the same style as used in deriving the fully polynomial-time approximation scheme for *Knapsack*.

Exercise 8.28 Prove Theorem 8.17. Use binary search to find the value of the optimal solution.

Exercise 8.29* This exercise develops an analog of the shifting technique for planar graphs. A planar embedding of a (planar) graph defines *faces* in the plane: each face is a region of the plane delimited by a cycle of the graph and containing no other face. In any planar embedding of a finite graph, one of the faces is infinite. For instance, a tree defines a single face, the infinite face (because a tree has no cycle); a simple cycle defines two faces; and so on. An *outerplanar* graph is a planar graph that can be embedded so that all of its vertices are on the boundary of (or inside) the infinite face; for instance, trees and simple cycles are outerplanar. Most planar graphs are not outerplanar, but we can layer such graphs. The "outermost" layer contains the vertices on the boundary of, or inside, the infinite face; the next layer is similarly defined on the planar graph obtained by removing all vertices in the outermost layer; and so on. (If there are several disjoint cycles with their vertices on the infinite face, each cycle receives the same layer number.) Nodes in one layer are adjacent only to nodes in a layer that differs by at most one. If a graph can thus be decomposed into k layers, it is said to be k-outerplanar. It turns out that k-outerplanar graphs (for constant k) form a highly tractable subset of instances for a number of classical NP-hard problems, including *Vertex Cover, Independent Set, Dominating Set* (for both vertices and edges—see Exercise 7.21), *Partition into Triangles*, etc. In this exercise, we make use of the existence of polynomial-time exact algorithms for these problems on k-outerplanar graphs to develop approximation schemes for these problems on general planar graphs.

Since a general planar graph does not have a constant number of layers, we use a version of the shifting idea to reduce the work to certain levels only. For a precision requirement of ε, we set $k = \lceil \frac{1}{\varepsilon} \rceil$.

- For the *Independent Set* problem, we delete from the graph nodes in layers congruent to $i \bmod k$, for each $i = 1, \ldots, k$ in turn. This step disconnects the graph, breaking it into components formed of $k - 1$ consecutive layers each—i.e., breaking the graph into a collection of $(k - 1)$-outerplanar subgraphs. A maximum independent set can then be computed for each component; the union of these sets is itself an independent set in the original graph, because vertices from two component sets must be at least two layers apart and thus cannot be connected. We select the best of the k choices resulting from our k different partitions.

- For the *Vertex Cover* problem, we use a different decomposition scheme. We decompose the graph into subgraphs made up of $k + 1$ consecutive layers, with an overlap of one layer between any two subgraphs—for each $i = 1, \ldots, k$, we form the subgraph made of layers $i \bmod k$, $(i \bmod k) + 1, \ldots, (i \bmod k) + k$. Each subgraph is a $(k + 1)$-outerplanar graph, so that we can find an optimum vertex cover for it in polynomial time. The union of these covers is a cover for the original graph, since every single edge of the original graph is part of one (or two) of the subgraphs. Again, we select the best of the k choices resulting from our k different decompositions.

Prove that each of these two schemes is a valid polynomial-time approximation scheme.

Exercise 8.30* We say that an NPO problem Π satisfies the *boundedness* condition if there exists an algorithm $\mathcal{A}$, which takes as input an instance of Π and a natural number k such that

- for each instance x of Π and every natural number c, $y = \mathcal{A}(x, c)$ is a solution of Π, the value of which differs from the optimal by at most kc; and
- the running time of $\mathcal{A}(x, c)$ is a polynomial function of $|x|$, the degree of which may depend only on c and on the value of $\mathcal{A}(x, c)$.

Prove that an NPO problem is in PTAS if and only if it is simple and satisfies the boundedness condition.

An analog of this result exists for FPTAS membership: replace "simple" by "p-simple" and replace the constant k in the definition of boundedness by a polynomial in $|x|$.

Exercise 8.31 Prove that any minimization problem in NPO PTAS-reduces to *Max WSAT*.

Exercise 8.32 Prove that *Maximum Cut* is OptNP-complete.

Exercise 8.33* Prove the second part of Theorem 8.22. The main difficulty in proving hardness is that we do not know how to bound the value of solutions, a handicap that prevents us from following the proof used in the first part. One way around this difficulty is to use the characterization of Apx: a problem belongs to Apx if it belongs to NPO and has a polynomial-time approximation algorithm with some absolute ratio guarantee. This approximation algorithm can be used to focus on instances with suitably bounded solution values.

Exercise 8.34 Verify that replacing the constant ε by the quantity $\frac{1}{p(|x|)}$ in the definition of BPP does not alter the class.

Exercise 8.35* Use the idea of *a priori* probability of acceptance or rejection in an attempt to establish $\Sigma_2^p \cap \Pi_2^p \subseteq PP$ (a relationship that is not known to hold). What is the difference between this problem and proving $NP \subseteq PP$ (as done in Theorem 8.27) and what difficulties do you encounter?

Exercise 8.36 Prove that deciding whether at least half of the legal truth assignments satisfy an instance of *Satisfiability* is PP-complete. (Use Cook's construction to verify that the number of accepting paths is the number of satisfying assignments.)

Then verify that the knife-edge can be placed at any fraction, not just at one-half; that is, verify that deciding whether at least $1/\varepsilon$ of the legal truth assignments satisfy an instance of *Satisfiability* is PP-complete for any $\varepsilon > 1$.

Exercise 8.37 Give a reasonable definition for the class PPSPACE, the probabilistic version of PSPACE, and prove that the two classes are equal.

Exercise 8.38* A set is *immune* with respect to complexity class $\mathscr{C}$ ($\mathscr{C}$-immune) if and only if it is infinite and has only finite subsets in $\mathscr{C}$. A set is $\mathscr{C}$-bi-immune whenever both it and its complement are $\mathscr{C}$-immune. It is known that a set is P-bi-immune whenever it splits every infinite set in P.

A *special case solution* for a set is an algorithm that runs in polynomial time and answer one of "yes," "no," or "don't know"; answers of "yes" and "no" are correct, i.e., the algorithm only answers "yes" on yes instances and only answers "no" on no instances. (A special case solution has no guarantee on the probability with which it answers "don't know"; with a fixed bound on that probability, a special case solution would become a Las Vegas algorithm.)

Prove that a set is P-bi-immune if and only if every special case solution for it answers "don't know" almost everywhere. (In particular, a P-bi-immune set cannot have a Las Vegas algorithm.)

Exercise 8.39* Verify that RP and BPP are semantic classes (see Exercise 7.51); that is, verify that the bounded halting problem $\{(M, x) \mid M \in \mathscr{C} \text{ and } M \text{ accepts } x\}$ is undecidable for $\mathscr{C} = RP$ and $\mathscr{C} = BPP$.

8.6   Bibliography

Tovey [1984] first proved that *n,2-SAT* and *n,n-SAT* are in P and that *3,4-SAT* is NP-complete; our proofs generally follow his, albeit in simpler versions. We follow Garey and Johnson [1979] in their presentation of the completeness of graph coloring for planar graphs and graphs of degree 3; our construction for *Planar HC* is inspired from Garey, Johnson, and Tarjan [1976]. Lichtenstein [1982] proved that *Planar 3SAT* is NP-complete and presented various uses of this result in treating planar restrictions of other difficult problems. Dyer and Frieze [1986] proved that *Planar 1in3SAT* is also NP-complete, while Moret [1988] showed that *Planar NAE3SAT* is in P. The work of the Amsterdam Mathematisch Centrum group up to 1982 is briefly surveyed in the article of Lageweg *et al.* [1982], which also describes the parameterization of scheduling problems and their classification with the help of a computer program; Theorem 8.6 is from the same paper. Perfect graphs and their applications are discussed in detail by Golumbic [1980]; Groetschel *et al.* [1981] showed that several NP-hard problems are solvable in polynomial-time on perfect graphs and also proved that recognizing perfect graphs is in coNP. The idea of a promise problem is due to Even and Yacobi [1980], while Theorem 8.7 is from Valiant and Vazirani [1985]. Johnson [1985] gave a very readable survey of the results concerning uniqueness in his NP-completeness column. Thomason [1978] showed that the only graph that is uniquely edge-colorable with k colors (for $k \geq 4$) is the k-star.

The concept of strong NP-completeness is due to Garey and Johnson [1978]; they discussed various aspects of this property in their text [1979], where the reader will find the proof that k-*Partition* is strongly NP-complete. Their list of NP-complete problems includes approximately 30 nontrivial strongly NP-complete problems, as well as a number of NP-complete problems for which pseudo-polynomial time algorithms exist.

Nigmatullin [1975] proved a technical theorem that gives a sufficient set of conditions for the "multiplication" technique of reduction between an optimization problem and its constant-distance approximation version; Exercise 8.22, which generalizes constant-distance to distances that are sublinear functions of the optimal value, is also from his work. Vizing's theorem (Exercise 8.14) is from Vizing [1964], while the proof of NP-completeness for *Chromatic Index* is due to Holyer [1908]. Fürer and Raghavachari [1992,1994] gave the distance-one approximation algorithm for minimum-degree spanning trees (Exercise 8.19), then generalized it to minimum-degree Steiner trees. Exercise 8.18 is from Dinic and Karzanov [1978]; they gave the algorithm sketched in the exercise and went on to show that, through primal-dual techniques, they could reduce the running time (for two currencies) to $O(n^2)$ and extend the algorithm to return $(m-1)$-distance approximations for m currencies in $O(n^{m+1})$ time. Dinitz [1997] presents an updated version in English, including new results on a greedy approach to the problem. Jordan [1995] gave a polynomial-time approximation algorithm for the problem of augmenting a k-connected graph to make it $(k + 1)$-connected that guarantees to add at most $k - 2$ edges more than the optimal solution (and is provably optimal for $k = 1$ and $k = 2$). However, the general problem of k-connectivity augmentation, while not known to be in FP, is not known to be NP-hard.

Sahni and Gonzalez [1976] and Gens and Levner [1979] gave a number of problems that cannot have bounded-ratio approximations unless P equals NP; Sahni and Gonzalez also introduced the notions of p-approximable and fully p-approximable problems. Exercise 8.25 is from Sahni [1975]; the fully polynomial-time approximation scheme for *Knapsack* is due to Ibarra and Kim [1975], later improved by Lawler [1977], while its generalization, Theorem 8.15, is from Papadimitriou and Steiglitz [1982]. Garey and Johnson [1978,1979] studied the relation between fully p-approximable problems and pseudo-polynomial time algorithms and proved Theorem 8.14. Paz and Moran [1977] introduced the notion of simple problems; Theorem 8.16 is from their paper, as is Exercise 8.30. Ausiello *et al.* [1980] extended their work and unified strong NP-completeness with simplicity; Theorem 8.17 is from their paper. Theorem 8.18 on the use of k-completions for polynomial approximation schemes is from Korte and Schrader [1981]. The "shifting lemma" (Theorem 8.19) and its use in the *Disk Covering* problem is from Hochbaum and Maass [1985]; Baker [1994] independently derived a similar technique for planar graphs (Exercise 8.29).

The approximation algorithm for *MaxkSAT* (Theorem 8.21) is due to Lieberherr [1980], who improved on an earlier $1/2$-approximation for *Max3SAT* due to Johnson [1974]. Several attempts at characterizing approximation problems through reductions followed the work of Paz and Moran, most notably Crescenzi and Panconesi [1991]. Our definition of reduction among NPO problems (Definition 8.12) is from Ausiello *et al.* [1995], whose approach we follow through much of Section 8.3. The study of OPTNP and *Max3SAT* was initiated by Papadimitriou and Yannakakis [1988], who gave a number of OPTNP-complete problems. The alternate characterization of NP was developed through a series of papers, culminating in the results of Arora *et al.* [1992], from which Theorem 8.23 was taken. Theorem 8.24 is from Khanna *et al.* [1994]. Arora and Lund [1996] give a detailed survey of inapproximability results, including a very useful table (Table 10.2, p. 431) of known results as of 1995.

Hochbaum [1996] offers an excellent and concise survey of the complexity of approximation; a more thorough treatment can be found in the article of Ausiello *et al.* [1995]. A concise and very readable overview, with connections to structure theory (the theoretical aspects of complexity theory), can be found in the text of Bovet and Crescenzi [1994]. An exhaustive compendium of the current state of knowledge concerning NPO problems is maintained on-line by Crescenzi and Kann at URL `www.nada.kth.se/~viggo/problemlist/compendium.html`. As mentioned, Arora and Lund [1996] cover the recent results derived from the alternate characterization of NP through probabilistic proof checking; their write-up is also a guide on how to use current results to prove new inapproximability results. In Section 9 of their monograph, Wagner and Wechsung [1986] present a concise survey of many theoretical results concerning the complexity of approximation.

The random Turing machine model was introduced by Gill [1977], who also defined the classes ZPP, RP (which he called VPP), BPP, and PP; proved Theorem 8.27; and provided complete problems for PP. The Monte Carlo algorithm for the equivalence of binary decision diagrams is from Blum *et al.* [1980]. For more information on binary decision trees, consult the survey of Moret [1982]. Ko [1982] proved that the polynomial hierarchy collapses into Σ_2^p if NP is contained in BPP; Theorem 8.30 is from Lautemann [1983]. Johnson [1984] presented a synopsis of the field of random complexity theory in his NP-completeness column, while Welsh [1983] and Maffioli [1986] discussed a number of applications of randomized algorithms. Motwani, Naor, and Raghavan [1996] give a comprehensive discussion of randomized approximations in combinatorial optimization. Motwani and Raghavan [1995] wrote an outstanding text on randomized algorithms that includes chapters on randomized complexity, on the characterization of NP through probabilistic proof checking, on derandomization, and on random number generation.

CHAPTER 9

Complexity Theory: The Frontier

9.1   Introduction

In this chapter, we survey a number of areas of current research in complexity theory. Of necessity, our coverage of each area is superficial. Unlike previous chapters, this chapter has few proofs, and the reader will not be expected to master the details of any specific technique. Instead, we attempt to give the reader the flavor of each of the areas considered.

Complexity theory is the most active area of research in theoretical computer science. Over the last five years, it has witnessed a large number of important results and the creation of several new fields of enquiry. We choose to review here topics that extend the theme of the text—that is, topics that touch upon the practical uses of complexity theory. We begin by addressing two issues that, if it were not for their difficulty and relatively low level of development, would have been addressed in the previous chapter, because they directly affect what we can expect to achieve when confronting an NP-hard problem. The first such issue is simply the complexity of a single instance: in an application, we are rarely interested in solving a large range of instances—let alone an infinity of them—but instead often have just a few instances with which to work. Can we characterize the complexity of a single instance? If we are attempting to optimize a solution, we should like to hear that our instances are not hard; if we are designing an encryption scheme, we need to hear that our instances are hard. Barring such a detailed characterization, perhaps we can improve on traditional complexity theory, based on worst-case behavior, by considering average-case behavior. Hence our second issue: can we develop complexity classes and completeness results based on average cases? Knowing that a problem is hard in average instance is a much stronger result than simply knowing that it is hard in the worst case; if nothing else, such a result would go a long way towards justifying the use of the problem in encryption.

Assuming theoretical results are all negative, we might be tempted to resort to desperate measures, such as buying new hardware that promises major leaps in computational power. One type of computing devices for which such claims have been made is the parallel computer; more recently, optical computing, DNA computing, and quantum computing have all had their proponents, along with claims of surpassing the power of conventional computing devices. Since much of complexity theory is about modeling computation in order to understand it, we would naturally want to study these new devices, develop models for their mode of computation, and compare the results with current models. Parallel computing has been studied intensively, so that a fairly comprehensive theory of parallel complexity has evolved. Optical computing differs from conventional parallel computing more at the implementation level than at the logical level, so that results developed for parallel machines apply there too. DNA computing presents quite a different model, although not, to date, a well defined one; in any case, any model proposed so far leads to a fairly simple parallel machine. Quantum computing, on the other hand, appears to offer an entirely new level of parallelism, one in which the amount of available "circuitry" does not directly limit the degree of parallelism. Of all of the models, it alone has the potential for turning some difficult (apparently not P-easy) problems into tractable ones; but it does not, alas, enable us to solve NP-hard problems in polynomial time.

Perhaps the most exciting development in complexity theory has been in the area of proof theory. In our modern view of a proof as an attempt by one party to convince another of the correctness of a statement, studying proofs involves studying communication protocols. Researchers have focused on two distinct models: one where the prover and the checker interact for as many rounds as the prover needs to convince the checker and one where the prover simply writes down the argument as a single, noninteractive communication to the checker.

The first model (interactive proofs) is of particular interest in cryptology: a critical requirement in most communications is to establish a certain level of confidence in a number of basic assertions, such as the fact that the party at the other end of the line is who he says he is. The most intriguing result to come out of this line of research is that all problems in NP admit zero-knowledge proof protocols, that is, protocols that allow the prover to convince the checker that an instance of a problem in NP is, with high probability, a "yes" instance without transmitting *any* information whatsoever about the certificate! The second model is of even more general interest, as it relates directly to the nature of mathematical proofs—which are typically written arguments designed to be read without interaction between the reader and the writer. This line of research has culminated recently in the characterization of NP as the set of all problems, "yes" instances of which have proofs of membership that can be verified with high probability by consulting just a constant number of randomly chosen bits from the proof. This characterization, in turn, has led to new results about the complexity of approximations, as we saw in the previous chapter.

One major drawback of complexity theory is that, like mathematics, it is an existential theory. A problem belongs to a certain class of complexity if there *exists* an algorithm that solves the problem and runs within the resource bounds defining the class. This algorithm need not be known, although providing such an algorithm (directly or through a reduction) was until recently the universal method used in proving membership in a class. Results in the theory of graph minors have now come to challenge this model: with these results, it is possible to prove that certain problems are in FP without providing any algorithm—or indeed, any hints as to how to design such an algorithm. Worse yet, it has been shown that this theory is, at least in part, inherently existential in the sense that there must exist problems that can be shown with this theory to belong to FP, but for which a suitable algorithm cannot be designed—or, if designed "by accident," cannot be recognized for what it is. Surely, this constitutes the ultimate irony to an algorithm designer: "This problem has a polynomial-time solution algorithm, but you will never find it and would not recognize it if you stumbled upon it."

Along with what this chapter covers, we should say a few words about what it does not cover. Complexity theory has its own theoretical side—what we have presented in this text is really its applied side. The theoretical side addresses mostly internal questions, such as the question of P vs. NP, and attempts to recast difficult unsolved questions in other terms so as to bring out new facets that may offer new approaches to solutions. This theoretical side goes by the name of *Structure Theory*, since its main subject is the structural relationships among various classes of complexity. Some of what we have covered falls under the heading of structure theory: the polynomial hierarchy is an example, as is (at least for now) the complexity of specific instances. The interested reader will find many other topics in the literature, particularly discussions of oracle arguments and relativizations, density of sets, and topological properties in some unified representation space. In addition, the successes of complexity theory in characterizing hard problems have led to its use in areas that do not fit the traditional model of finite algorithms. In particular, many researchers have proposed models of computation over the real numbers and have defined corresponding classes of complexity. A somewhat more traditional use of complexity in defining the problem of learning from examples or from a teacher (i.e., from queries) has blossomed into the research area known as *Computational Learning Theory*. The research into the fine structure of NP and higher classes has also led researchers to look at the fine structure of P with some interesting results, chief among them the theory of *Fixed-Parameter Tractability*, which studies versions of NP-hard problems made tractable by fixing a key parameter (for instance, fixing the desired cover size in *Vertex Cover* to a constant k, in which case even the brute-force search algorithm that examines every subset of size k runs in polynomial time). Finally, as researchers in various applied sciences became aware of the implications of complexity theory, many have sought to extend the models from countable sets to the set of real numbers; while there is not yet an accepted model for computation over the reals, much work has been done in the area, principally by mathematicians and physicists. All of these topics are of considerable theoretical interest and many have yielded elegant results; however, most results in these areas have so far had little impact on optimization or algorithm design. The bibliographic section gives pointers to the literature for the reader interested in learning more in these areas.

9.2   The Complexity of Specific Instances

Most hard problems, even when circumscribed quite accurately, still possess a large number of easy instances. So what does a proof of hardness really have to say about a problem? And what, if anything, can be said about the complexity of individual instances of the problem? In solving a large optimization problem, we are interested in the complexity of the one or two instances at hand; in devising an encryption scheme, we want to know that every message produced is hard to decipher.

A bit of thought quickly reveals that the theory developed so far cannot be applied to single instances, nor even to finite collections of instances. As long as only a finite number of instances is involved, we can precompute the answers for all instances and store the answers in a table; then we can write a program that "solves" each instance very quickly through table lookup. The cost of precomputation is not included in the complexity measures that we have been using and the costs associated with table storage and table lookup are too small to matter. An immediate consequence is that we cannot circumscribe a problem only to "hard" instances: no matter how we narrow down the problem, it will always be possible to solve a finite number of its instances very quickly with the table method. The best we can do in this respect is to identify an infinite set of "hard" instances with a finitely changeable boundary. We capture this concept with the following informal definition: a *complexity core* for a problem is an infinite set of instances, all but a finite number of which are "hard." What is meant by hard needs to be defined; we shall look only at complexity cores with respect to P and thus consider hard anything that is not solvable in polynomial time.

Theorem 9.1 If a set S is not in P, then it possesses an infinite (and decidable) subset, $X \subseteq S$, such that any decision algorithm must take more than a polynomial number of steps almost everywhere on X (i.e., on all but a finite number of instances in X). $\qquad\square$

Proof. Our proof proceeds by diagonalization over all Turing machines. However, this proof is an example of a fairly complex diagonalization: we do not just "go down the diagonal" and construct a set but must check our work to date at every step along the diagonal. Denote the ith Turing machine in the enumeration by M_i and the output (if any) that it produces when run with input string x by $M_i(x)$. Let $\{p_i\}$ be the sequence of polynomials $p_i(x) = \sum_{j=0}^{i} x^j$; note that this sequence has the following two properties: (i) for any value of $n > 0$, $i > j \Rightarrow p_i(n) > p_j(n)$; and (ii) given any polynomial p, there exists an i such that $p_i(n) > p(n)$ holds for all $n > 0$.

We construct a sequence of elements of S such that the nth element, x_n, cannot be accepted in $p_n(|x_n|)$ time by any of the first n Turing machines in the enumeration.

Denote by χ_S the characteristic function of S; that is, we have $x \in S \Rightarrow \chi_S(x) = 1$ and $x \notin S \Rightarrow \chi_S(x) = 0$. We construct $X = \{x_1, x_2, \dots\}$ element by element as follows:

1. (Initialization.) Let string y be the empty string and let the stage number n be 1.
2. (We are at stage n, attempting to generate x_n.) For each i, $1 \leq i \leq n$, such that i is not yet cancelled (see below), run machine M_i on string y for $p_n(|y|)$ steps or until it terminates, whichever occurs first. If M_i terminates but does not solve instance y correctly, that is, if we have $M_i(y) \neq \chi_S(y)$, then cancel i: we need not consider M_i again, since it cannot decide membership in S.
3. For each i not yet cancelled, determine if it passed Step 2 because machine M_i did not stop in time. If so (if none of the uncancelled

M_is was able to process y), then let $x_n = y$ and proceed to Step 4. If not (if some M_i correctly processed y, so that y is not a candidate for membership in X), replace y by the next string in lexicographic order and return to Step 2.

4. (The current stage is completed; prepare the new stage.) Replace y by the next string in lexicographic order, increase n by 1, and return to Step 2.

We claim that, at each stage n, this procedure must terminate and produce an element x_n, so that the set X thus generated is infinite. Suppose that stage n does not terminate. Then Step 3 will continue to loop back to Step 2, producing longer and longer strings y; this can happen only if there exists some uncancelled i such that M_i, run on y, terminates in no more than $p_i(|y|)$ steps. But then we must have $M_i(y) = \chi_S(y)$ since i is not cancelled, so that machine M_i acts as a polynomial-time decision procedure for our problem on instance y. Since this is true for all sufficiently long strings and since we can set up a table for (the finite number of) all shorter strings, we have derived a polynomial-time decision procedure for our problem, which contradicts our assumption that our problem is not in P. Thus X is infinite; it is also clearly decidable, as each successive x_i is higher in the lexicographic order than the previous.

Now consider any decision procedure for our problem (that is, any machine M_i that computes the characteristic function χ_S) and any polynomial $p(\ )$. This precise value of i cannot get cancelled in our construction of X; hence for any n with $n \geqslant i$ and $p_n \geqslant p$, machine M_i, run on x_n, does not terminate within $p_n(|x_n|)$ steps. In other words, for all but a finite number of instances in X (the first $i - 1$ instances), machine M_i must run in super-polynomial time, which proves our theorem.   Q.E.D.

Thus every hard problem possesses an infinite and uniformly hard collection of instances. We call the set X of Theorem 9.1 a *complexity core* for S. Unfortunately this result does not say much about the complexity of individual instances: because of the possibility of table lookup, any finite subset of instances can be solved in polynomial time, and removing this subset from the complexity core leaves another complexity core. Moreover, the presence of a complexity core alone does not say that most instances of the problem belong to the core: our proof may create very sparse cores as well as very dense ones. Since most problems have a number of instances that grows exponentially with the size of the instances, it is important to know what proportion of these instances belongs to a complexity core. In the case of NP-complete problems, the number of instances of size n that belong to a complexity core is, as expected, quite large: under our standard assumptions, it cannot be bounded by any polynomial in n, as stated by the next theorem, which we present without proof.

Theorem 9.2 Every NP-complete problem has complexity cores of super-polynomial density. □

In order to capture the complexity of a single instance, we must find a way around the table lookup problem. In truth, the table lookup is not so much an impediment as an opportunity, as the following informal definition shows.

Definition 9.1 A hard instance is one that can be solved efficiently only through table lookup. □

For large problem instances, the table lookup method imposes large storage requirements. In other words, we can expect that the size of the program will grow with the size of the instance whenever the instance is to be solved by table lookup. Asymptotically, the size of the program will be entirely determined by the size of the instance; thus a large instance is hard if the smallest program that solves it efficiently is as large as the size of the table entry for the instance itself. Naturally the table entry need not be the instance itself: it need only be the most concise encoding of the instance. We have encountered this idea of the most concise encoding of a program (here an instance) before—recall Berry's paradox—and we noted at that time that it was an undecidable property. In spite of its undecidability, the measure has much to recommend itself. For instance, it can be used to provide an excellent definition of a random string—a string is completely random if it is its own shortest description. This idea of randomness was proposed independently by A. Kolmogorov and G. Chaitin and developed into *Algorithmic Information Theory* by the latter. For our purposes here, we use a very simple formulation of the shortest encoding of a string.

Definition 9.2 Let I_y be the set of yes instances of some problem Π, x an arbitrary instance of the problem, and $t(\ )$ some time bound (a function on the natural numbers).

- The t-bounded *instance complexity* of x with respect to Π, $IC^t(x|\Pi)$, is defined as the size of the smallest Turing machine that solves Π and runs in time bounded by $t(|x|)$ on instance x; if no such machine exists (because Π is an unsolvable problem), then the instance complexity is infinite.
- The *descriptional complexity* (also called information complexity or Kolmogorov complexity) of a string x, $K(x)$, is the size of the smallest Turing machine that produces x when started with the empty string.

We write $K^t(x)$ if we also require that the Turing machine halt in no more than $t(|x|)$ steps.   □

Both measures deal with the size of a Turing machine: they measure neither time nor space, although they may depend on a time bound $t(\ )$. We do not claim that the size of a program is an appropriate measure of the complexity of the algorithm that it embodies: we purport to use these size measures to characterize hard instances, not hard problems.

The instance complexity captures the size of the smallest program that efficiently solves the given instance; the descriptional complexity captures the size of the shortest encoding (i.e., table entry) for the instance. For large instances x, we should like to say that x is hard if its instance complexity is determined by its descriptional complexity. First, though, we must confirm our intuition that, for any problem, a single instance can always be solved by table lookup with little extra work; thus we must show that, for each instance x, the instance complexity of x is bounded above by the descriptional complexity of x.

Proposition 9.1 For every (solvable decision) problem Π, there exists a constant c_Π such that $IC^t(x|\Pi) \leq K^t(x) + c_\Pi$ holds for any time bound $t(\ )$ and instance x.   □

Exercise 9.1 Prove this statement. (Hint: combine the minimal machine generating x and some machine solving Π to produce a new machine solving Π that runs in no more than $t(|x|)$ steps on input x.)   □

Now we can formally define a hard instance.

Definition 9.3 Given constant c and time bound $t(\ )$, an instance x is (t, c)-*hard* for problem Π if $IC^t(x|\Pi) \geq K(x) - c$ holds.   □

We used $K(x)$ rather than $K^t(x)$ in the definition, which weakens it somewhat (since $K(x) \leq K^t(x)$ holds for any bound t and instance x) but makes it less model-dependent (recall our results from Section 4). Whereas the technical definition may appear complex, its essence is easily summed up: an instance is (t, c)-hard if the size of the smallest program that solves it within the time bound $t(\ )$ must grow with the size of the shortest encoding of the instance itself.

Since any problem in P has a polynomial-time solution algorithm of fixed size (i.e., of size bounded by a constant), it follows that the polynomial-bounded instance complexity of any instance of any problem in P should be a constant. Interestingly, the converse statement also holds, so that P can be characterized on an instance basis as well as on a problem basis.

Theorem 9.3 A problem Π is in P if and only if there exist a polynomial $p(\,)$ and a constant c such that $IC^p(x|\Pi) \leq c$ holds for all instances x of Π. □

Exercise 9.2 Prove this result. (Hint: there are only finitely many machines of size not exceeding c and only some of these solve Π, although not necessarily in polynomial time; combine these few machines into a single machine that solves Π and runs in polynomial time on all instances.) □

Our results on complexity cores do not allow us to expect that a similarly general result can be shown for classes of hard problems. However, since complexity cores are uniformly hard, we may expect that all but a finite number of their instances are hard instances; with this proviso, the converse result also holds.

Proposition 9.2 A set X is a complexity core for problem Π if and only if, for any constant c and polynomial $p(\,)$, $IC^p(x|\Pi) > c$ holds for almost every instance x in X. □

Proof. Let X be a complexity core; in particular, there are infinitely many instances x in X for which $IC^p(x|\Pi) \leq c$ holds for some constant c. Then there must be at least one machine M of size not exceeding c that solves Π and runs in polynomial time on infinitely many instances x in X. But a complexity core can have only a finite number of instances solvable in polynomial time, so that X cannot be a core—hence the desired contradiction.

Assume that X is not a complexity core. Then X must have an infinite number of instances solvable in polynomial time, so that there exists a machine M that solves Π and runs in polynomial time on infinitely many instances x in X. Let c be the size of M and $p(\,)$ its polynomial bound; then, for these infinitely many instances x, we have $IC^p(x|\Pi) \leq c$, which contradicts the hypothesis. *Q.E.D.*

Since all but a finite number of the (p, c)-hard instances have an instance complexity exceeding any constant (an immediate consequence of the fact that, for any constant c, there are only finitely many Turing machines of size bounded by c and thus only finitely many strings of descriptional complexity bounded by c), it follows that the set of (p, c)-hard instances of a problem either is finite or forms a complexity core for the problem. One last question remains: while we know that no problem in P has hard instances and that problems with complexity cores are exactly those with an infinity of hard instances, we have no direct characterization of problems not in P. Since they are not solvable in polynomial time, they are "hard" from a practical standpoint; intuitively then, they ought to have an infinite set of hard instances.

Theorem 9.4 Let Π be a problem not in P. Then, for any polynomial $p(\ )$, there exists a constant c such that Π has infinitely many (p, c)-hard instances. □

Exercise 9.3* Prove this result; use a construction by stages with cancellation similar to that used for building a complexity core. □

One aspect of (informally) hard instances that the reader has surely noted is that reductions never seem to transform them into easy instances; indeed, nor do reductions ever seem to transform easy instances into hard ones. In fact, polynomial transformations preserve complexity cores and individual hard instances.

Theorem 9.5 Let Π_1 and Π_2 be two problems such that Π_1 many-one reduces to Π_2 in polynomial time through mapping f; then there exist a constant c and a polynomial $q(\ )$ such that $IC^{q+p \cdot q}(x|\Pi_1) \leqslant IC^p(f(x)|\Pi_2) + c$ holds for all polynomials $p(\ )$ and instances x. □

Proof. Let M_f be the machine implementing the transformation and let $q(\ )$ be its polynomial time bound. Let $p(\ )$ be any nondecreasing polynomial. Finally, let M_x be a minimal machine that solves Π_2 and runs in no more than $p(|f(x)|)$ steps on input $f(x)$. Now define M'_x to be the machine resulting from the composition of M_f and M_x. M'_x solves Π_1 and, when fed instance x, runs in time bounded by $q(|x|) + p(|f(x)|)$, that is, bounded by $q(|x|) + p(q(|x|))$. Now we have

$$IC^{q+p \cdot q}(x|\Pi_1) \leqslant \text{size}(M'_x) \leqslant \text{size}(M_f) + \text{size}(M_x) + c'$$

But M_f is a fixed machine, so that we have

$$\text{size}(M_f) + \text{size}(M_x) + c' = \text{size}(M_x) + c = IC^p(f(x)|\Pi_2) + c$$

which completes the proof.   Q.E.D.

Hard instances are preserved in an even stronger sense: a polynomial transformation cannot map an infinite number of hard instances onto the same hard instance.

Theorem 9.6 In any polynomial transformation f from Π_1 to Π_2, for each constant c and sufficiently large polynomial $p(\ )$, only finitely many (p, c)-hard instances x of Π_1 can be mapped to a single instance $y = f(x)$ of Π_2. □

Exercise 9.4 Prove this result. (Hint: use contradiction; if infinitely many instances are mapped to the same instance, then instances of arbitrarily large descriptional complexity are mapped to an instance of fixed descriptional complexity. A construction similar to that used in the proof of the previous theorem then provides the contradiction for sufficiently large p.)   □

While these results are intuitively pleasing and confirm a number of observations, they are clearly just a beginning. They illustrate the importance of proper handling of the table lookup issue and provide a framework in which to study individual instances, but they do not allow us as yet to prove that a given instance is hard or to measure the instance complexity of individual instances.

9.3 Average-Case Complexity

If we cannot effectively assess the complexity of a single instance, can we still get a better grasp on the complexity of problems by studying their average-case complexity rather than (as done so far) their worst-case complexity? Average-case complexity is a very difficult problem, if only because, when compared to worst-case complexity, it introduces a brand-new parameter, the instance distribution. (Recall our discussion in Section 8.4, where we distinguished between the analysis of randomized algorithms and the average-case analysis of deterministic algorithms: we are now concerned with the latter and thus with the effect of instance distribution on the expected running time of an algorithm.) Yet it is worth the trouble, if only because we know of NP-hard problems that turn out to be "easy" on average under reasonable distributions, while other NP-hard problems appear to resist such an attack.

Example 9.1 Consider the graph coloring problem: a simple backtracking algorithm that attempts to color with some fixed number k of colors a graph of n vertices chosen uniformly at random among all $2^{\binom{n}{2}}$ such graphs runs in constant average time! The basic reason is that most of the graphs on n vertices are dense (there are far more choices for the selection of edges when the graph has $\Theta(n^2)$ edges than when it has only $O(n)$ edges), so that most of these graphs are in fact not k-colorable for fixed k—in other words, the backtracking algorithm runs very quickly into a clique of size $k + 1$. The computation of the constant is very complex; for $k = 3$, the size of the backtracking tree averages around 200—independently of n.   □

In the standard style of average-case analysis, as in the well-known average-case analysis of quicksort, we assume some probability distribution μ_n over all instances of size n and then proceed to bound the sum $\sum_{|x|=n} f(x)\mu_n(x)$, where $f(x)$ denotes the running time of the algorithm on instance x. (We use μ to denote a probability distribution rather than the more common p to avoid confusion with our notation for polynomials.) It is therefore tempting to define polynomial average time under μ as the set of problems for which there exists an algorithm that runs in $\sum_{|x|=n} f(x)\mu_n(x) = O(n^{O(1)})$ time. Unfortunately, this definition is not machine-independent! A simple example suffices to illustrate the problem. Assume that the algorithm runs in polynomial time on a fraction $(1 - 2^{-0.1n})$ of the 2^n instances of size n and in $2^{0.09n}$ time on the rest; then the average running time is polynomial. But now translate this algorithm from one model to another at quadratic cost: the resulting algorithm still takes polynomial time on a fraction $(1 - 2^{-0.1n})$ of the 2^n instances of size n but now takes $2^{0.18n}$ time on the rest, so that the average running time has become exponential! This example shows that a machine-independent definition must somehow balance the probability of difficult instances and their difficulty—roughly put, the longer an instance takes to solve, the rarer it should be. We can overcome this problem with a rather subtle definition.

Definition 9.4 A function f is *polynomial on μ-average* if there exists a constant $\varepsilon > 0$ such that the sum $\sum_x f^\varepsilon(x)\mu(x)/|x|$ converges.   □

In order to understand this definition, it is worth examining two equivalent formulations.

Proposition 9.3 Given a function f, the following statements are equivalent:

- There exists a positive constant ε such that the sum $\sum_x f^\varepsilon(x)\mu(x)/|x|$ converges.
- There exist positive constants c and d such that, for any positive real number r, we have $\mu[f(x) > r^d|x|^d] < c/r$.
- There exist positive constants c and ε such that we have

$$\sum_{|x| \leq n} f^\varepsilon(x)\mu_{\leq n}(x) \leq cn$$

for all n, where $\mu_{\leq n}(x)$ is the conditional probability of x, given that its length does not exceed n.   □

(We skip the rather technical and not particularly revealing proof.) The third formulation is closest to our first attempt: the main difference is that the average is taken over all instances of size not exceeding n rather than over all instances of size n. The second formulation is at the heart of the matter. It shows that the running time of the algorithm (our function f) cannot exceed a certain polynomial very often—and the larger the polynomial it exceeds, the lower the probability that it will happen. This constraint embodies our notion of balance between the difficulty of an instance (how long it takes the algorithm to solve it) and its probability.

We can easily see that any polynomial function is polynomial on average under any probability distribution. With a little more work, we can also verify that the conventional notion of average-case polynomial time (as we first defined it) also fits this definition in the sense that it implies it (but not, of course, the other way around). We can easily verify that the class of functions polynomial on μ-average is closed under addition, multiplication, and maximum. A somewhat more challenging task is to verify that our definition is properly machine-independent—in the sense that the class is closed under polynomial scaling. Since these functions are well behaved, we can now define a problem to be solvable in average polynomial time under distribution μ if it can be solved with a deterministic algorithm, the running time of which is bounded by a function polynomial on μ-average.

In this new paradigm, a problem is really a triple: the question, the set of instances with their answers, and a probability distribution—or a conventional problem plus a probability distribution, say (Π, μ). We call such a problem a *distributional problem*. We can define classes of distributional problems according to the time taken on μ-average—with the clear understanding that the same classical problem may now belong to any number of distributional classes, depending on the associated distribution. Of most interest to us, naturally, is the class of all distributional problems, (Π, μ), such that Π is solvable in polynomial time on μ-average; we call this class FAP (because it is a class of functions computable in "average polynomial" time) and denote its subclass consisting only of decision problems by AP. If we limit ourselves to decision problems, we can define a distributional version of each of P, NP, etc., by stating that a distributional NP problem is one, the classical version of which belongs to NP. A potentially annoying problem with our definition of distributional problems is the distribution itself: nothing prevents the existence of pairs (Π, μ) in, say AP, where the distribution μ is some horrendously complex function. It makes sense to limit our investigation to distributions that we can specify and compute; unfortunately, most "standard" distributions involve real values, which no finite algorithm can compute in finite time. Thus we must define a computable distribution as one that an algorithm can approximate to any degree of precision in polynomial time.

Definition 9.5 A real-valued function $f \colon \Sigma^* \to [0, 1]$ is polynomial-time computable if there exists a deterministic algorithm and a bivariate polynomial p such that, for any input string x and natural number k, the algorithm outputs in $O(p(|x|, k))$ time a finite fraction y obeying $|f(x) - y| \leqslant 2^{-k}$. □

In the average-case analysis of algorithms, the standard assumption made about distributions of instances is uniformity: all instances of size n are generally assumed to be equally likely. While such an assumption works for finite sets of instances, we cannot select uniformly at random from an infinite set. So how do we select a string from Σ^*? Consider doing the selection in two steps: first pick a natural number n, and then select uniformly at random from all strings of length n. Naturally, we cannot pick n uniformly; but we can come close by selecting n with probability $\rho(n)$ at least as large as some (fixed) inverse polynomial.

Definition 9.6 A polynomial-time computable distribution μ on Σ^* is said to be *uniform* if there exists a polynomial p and a distribution ρ on $\mathbb{N}$ such that we can write $\mu(x) = \rho(|x|)2^{-|x|}$ and we have $\rho(n) \geqslant 1/p(n)$ almost everywhere. □

The "default" choice is $\mu(x) = \frac{6}{\pi^2}|x|^{-2}2^{-|x|}$. These "uniform" distributions are in a strong sense representative of all polynomial-time computable distributions; not only can any polynomial-time computable distribution be dominated by a uniform distribution, but, under mild conditions, it can also dominate the *same* uniform distribution within a constant factor.

Theorem 9.7 Let μ be a polynomial-time computable distribution. There exists a constant $c \in \mathbb{N}$ and an injective, invertible, and polynomial-time computable function $g \colon \Sigma^* \to \Sigma^*$ such that, for all x, we have $\mu(x) \leqslant c \cdot 2^{-|g(x)|}$. If, in addition, $\mu(x)$ exceeds $2^{-p(|x|)}$ for some polynomial p and for all x, then there exists a second constant $b \in \mathbb{N}$ such that, for all x, we have $b \cdot 2^{-|g(x)|} \leqslant \mu(x) \leqslant c \cdot 2^{-|g(x)|}$. □

We define the class DISTNP to be the class of distributional NP problems (Π, μ) where μ is dominated by some polynomial-time computable distribution.

In order to study AP and DISTNP, we need reduction schemes. These schemes have to incorporate a new element to handle probability distributions, since we clearly cannot allow a mapping of the high-probability instances of Π_1 to the low-probability instances of Π_2. (This is an echo of Theorem 9.6 that showed that we could not map infinite collections of hard instances of one problem onto single instances of the other problem.) We need some preliminary definitions about distributions.

Definition 9.7 Let μ and ν be two distributions. We say that μ is *dominated* by ν if there exists a polynomial p such that, for all x, we have $\mu(x) \leqslant p(|x|)\nu(x)$. Now let (Π_1, μ) and (Π_2, ν) be two distributional problems and f a transformation from Π_1 to Π_2. We say that μ *is dominated* by ν with respect to f if there exists a distribution μ' on Π_1 such that μ is dominated by μ' and we have $\nu(y) = \sum_{f(x)=y} \mu'(x)$.   □

The set of all instances x of Π_1 that get mapped under f to the same instance y of Π_2 has probability $\sum_{f(x)=y} \mu(x)$ in the distributional problem (Π_1, μ); the corresponding single instance y has weight $\nu(y) = \sum_{f(x)=y} \mu'(x)$. But μ is dominated by μ', so that there exists some polynomial p such that, for all x, we have $\mu(x) \geqslant p(|x|)\mu'(x)$. Substituting, we obtain $\nu(y) \geqslant \sum_{f(x)=y} \mu(x)/p(|x|)$, showing that the probability of y cannot be much smaller than that of the set of instances x that map to it: the two are polynomially related.

We are now ready to define a suitable reduction between distributional problems. We begin with a reduction that runs in polynomial time in the worst case—perhaps not the most natural choice, but surely the simplest.

Definition 9.8 We say that (Π_1, μ) is *polynomial-time reducible* to (Π_2, ν) if there is a polynomial-time transformation from Π_1 to Π_2 such that μ is dominated by ν with respect to f.   □

These reductions are clearly reflexive and transitive; more importantly, AP is closed under them.

Exercise 9.5 Prove that, if (Π_1, μ) is polynomial-time reducible to (Π_2, ν) and (Π_2, ν) belongs to AP, then so does (Π_1, μ).   □

Under these reductions, in fact, DistNP has complete problems, including a version of the natural complete problem defined by bounded halting.

Definition 9.9 An instance of the *Distributional Bounded Halting* problem for AP is given by a triple, $(M, x, 1^n)$, where M is the index of a deterministic Turing machine, x is a string (the input for M), and n is a natural number. The question is "Does M, run on x, halt in at most n steps?" The distribution μ for the problem is given by $\mu(M, x, 1^n) = c \cdot n^{-2}|x|^{-2}|M|^{-2}2^{-|M|-|x|}$, where c is a normalization constant (a positive real number).   □

Theorem 9.8 *Distributional Bounded Halting* is DistNP-complete.   □

Proof. Let (Π, μ) be an arbitrary problem in DistNP; then Π belongs to NP. Let M be a nondeterministic Turing machine for Π and let g be the function of Theorem 9.7, so that we have $\mu(x) \leqslant 2^{-|g(x)|}$. We define a new machine M' as follows. On input y, if $g^{-1}(y)$ is defined, then M' simulates

M run on $g^{-1}(y)$; it rejects y otherwise. Thus M accepts x if and only if M' accepts $g(x)$; moreover, there exists some polynomial p such that M', run on $g(x)$, completes in $p(|x|)$ time for all x. Then we define our transformed instance as the triple $(M', g(x), 1^{p(|x|)})$, so that the mapping is injective and polynomial-time computable. Our conclusion follows easily.   Q.E.D.

A few other problems are known to be DistNP-complete, including a tiling problem and a number of word problems. DistNP-complete problems capture, at least in part, our intuitive notion of problems that are NP-complete in average instance.

The definitions of average complexity given here are robust enough to allow the erection of a formal hierarchy of classes through an analog of the hierarchy theorems. Moreover, average complexity can be combined with nondeterminism and with randomization to yield further classes and results. Because average complexity depends intimately on the nature of the distributions, results that we take for granted in worst-case contexts may not hold in average-case contexts. For instance, it is possible for a problem not to belong to P, yet to belong to AP under *every possible* polynomial-time computable distribution (although no natural example is known); yet, if the problem is in AP under every possible exponential-time computable distribution, then it must be in P. The reader will find pointers to further reading in the bibliography.

9.4   Parallelism and Communication

9.4.1   Parallelism

Parallelism on a large scale (several thousands of processors) has become a feasible goal in the last few years, although thus far only a few commercial architectures incorporate more than a token amount (a few dozen processors or so) of parallelism. The trade-off involved in parallelism is simple: time is gained at the expense of hardware. On problems that lend themselves to parallelism—not all do, as we shall see—an increase in the number of processors yields a corresponding decrease in execution time. Of course, even in the best of cases, the most we can expect by using, say, n processors, is a gain in execution time by a factor of n. An immediate consequence is that parallelism offers very little help in dealing with intractable problems: only with the expense of an exponential number of processors might it become possible to solve intractable problems in polynomial time, and expending an exponential number of processors is even less feasible than expending an exponential amount of time. With "reasonable" (i.e., polynomial) resource requirements, parallelism is thus essentially useless in dealing with intractable problems: since a polynomial of a polynomial is a polynomial, even polynomial speed-ups cannot take us outside of FP. Restricting our attention to tractable problems, then, we are faced with two important questions. First, do all tractable problems stand to gain from parallelism? Secondly, how much can be gained? (For instance, if some problem admits a solution algorithm that runs in $O(n^k)$ time on a sequential processor, will using $O(n^k)$ processors reduce the execution time to a constant?)

The term "parallel" is used here in its narrow technical sense, implying the existence of overall synchronization. In contrast, *concurrent* or *distributed* architectures and algorithms may operate asynchronously. While many articles have been published on the subject of concurrent algorithms, relatively little is known about the complexity of problems as measured on a distributed model of computation. We can state that concurrent execution, while potentially applicable to a larger class of problems than parallel execution, cannot possibly bring about larger gains in execution time, since it uses the same resources as parallel execution but with the added burden of explicit synchronization and message passing. In the following, we concentrate our attention on parallelism; at the end of this section, we take up the issue of communication complexity, arguably a better measure of complexity for distributed algorithms than time or space.

Since an additional resource becomes involved (hardware), the study of parallel complexity hinges on *simultaneous* resource bounds. Where sequential complexity theory defines, say, a class of problems solvable in polynomial time, parallel complexity theory defines, say, a class of problems solvable in sublinear time with a polynomial amount of hardware: both the time bound and the hardware bound must be obeyed simultaneously. The most frustrating problem in parallel complexity theory is the choice of a suitable model of (parallel) computation. Recall from Chapter 4 that the choice of a suitable model of sequential execution—one that would offer sufficient mathematical rigor yet mimic closely the capabilities of modern computers—is very difficult. Models that offer rigor and simplicity (such as Turing machines) tend to be unrealistically inefficient, while models that mimic modern computers tend to pose severe problems in the choice of complexity measures. The problem is exacerbated in the case of models of parallel computation; one result is that several dozen different models have been proposed in a period of about five years. Fortunately, all such models exhibit one common behavior—what has become known as the *parallel computation thesis*: with unlimited hardware, parallel time is equivalent (within a polynomial function) to sequential storage. This result alone motivates the study of space complexity! The parallel computation thesis has allowed the identification of model-independent classes of problems that lend themselves well to parallelism.

9.4.2 Models of Parallel Computation

As in the case of models of sequential computation, models of parallel computation can be divided roughly in two categories: (i) models that attempt to mimic modern parallel architectures (albeit on a much larger scale) and (ii) models that use more restricted primitives in order to achieve sufficient rigor and unambiguity.

The first kind of model typically includes shared memory and independent processors and is exemplified by the *PRAM* (or parallel RAM) model. A PRAM consists of an unbounded collection of global registers, each capable of holding an arbitrary integer, together with an unbounded collection of processors, each provided with its own unbounded collection of local registers. All processors are identically programmed; however, at any given step of execution, different processors may be at different locations in their program, so that the architecture is a compromise between *SIMD* (single instruction, multiple data stream) and *MIMD* (multiple instruction, multiple data stream) types. Execution begins with the input string x loaded in the first $|x|$ global registers (one bit per register) and with only one processor active. At any step, a processor may execute a normal RAM instruction or it may start up another processor to execute in parallel with the active processors. Normal RAM instructions may refer to local or to global registers; in the latter case, however, only one processor at a time is allowed to write into a given register (if two or more processors attempt a simultaneous write in the same register, the machine crashes). Given the unbounded number of processors, the set of problems that this model can solve in polynomial time is exactly the set of PSPACE-easy problems—an illustration of the parallel computation thesis. Note that PRAMs require a nonnegligible start-up time: in order to activate $f(n)$ processors, a minimum of $\log f(n)$ steps must be executed. (As a result, no matter how many processors are used, PRAMs cannot reduce the execution time of a nontrivial sequential problem to a constant.) The main problem with such models is the same problem that we encountered with RAMs: what are the primitive operations and what should be the cost of each such operation? In addition, there are the questions of addressing the global memory (should not such an access be costlier than an access to local memory) and of measuring the hardware costs (the number of processors alone is only a lower bound, as much additional hardware must be incorporated to manage the global memory). All shared memory models suffer from similar problems.

A very different type of model, and a much more satisfying one from a theoretical standpoint, is the *circuit* model. A circuit is just a combinational circuit implementing some Boolean function; in order to keep the model reasonable, we limit the fan-in to some constant.[1] We define the *size* of a circuit to be the number of its gates and its *depth* to be the number of gates on a longest path from input to output. The size of a circuit is a measure of the hardware needed for its realization and its depth is a measure of the time required for computing the function realized by the circuit. Given a (Boolean) function, g, of n variables, we define the size of g as the size of the smallest circuit that computes g; similarly, we define the depth of g as the depth of the shallowest circuit that computes g. Since each circuit computes a fixed function of a fixed number of variables, we need to consider families of circuits in order to account for inputs of arbitrary lengths. Given a set, L, of all "yes" instances (encoded as binary strings) for some problem, denote by L^n the set of strings of length n in L; L^n defines a Boolean function of n variables (the characteristic function of L^n). Then a *family* of circuits, $\{\xi_n \mid n \in \mathbb{N}\}$ (where each ξ_n is a circuit with n inputs), decides membership in L if and only if ξ_n computes the characteristic function of L^n. With these conventions, we can define classes of size and depth complexity; given some complexity measure $f(n)$, we let

$$\text{SIZE}(f(n)) = \{L \mid \exists \{\xi_n\} \colon \{\xi_n\} \text{ computes } L \text{ and size}(\xi_n) = O(f(n))\}$$
$$\text{DEPTH}(f(n)) = \{L \mid \exists \{\xi_n\} \colon \{\xi_n\} \text{ computes } L \text{ and depth}(\xi_n) = O(f(n))\}$$

These definitions are quite unusual: the sets that are "computable" within given size or depth bounds may well include undecidable sets! Indeed, basic results of circuit theory state that any function of n variables is computable by a circuit of size $O(2^n/n)$ and also by a circuit of depth $O(n)$, so that $\text{SIZE}(2^n/n)$—or $\text{DEPTH}(n)$—includes *all* Boolean functions. In particular, the language consisting of all "yes" instances of the halting problem is in $\text{SIZE}(2^n/n)$, yet we have proved in Chapter 4 that this language is undecidable. This apparently paradoxical result can be explained as follows. That there exists a circuit ξ_n for each input size n that correctly decides the halting problem Says only that each instance of the halting problem is either a "yes" instance or a "no" instance—i.e., that each

---

[1] In actual circuit design, a fan-in of n usually implies a delay of log n, which is exactly what we obtain by limiting the fan-in to a constant. We leave the fan-out unspecified, inasmuch as it makes no difference in the definition of size and depth complexity.

instance possesses a well-defined answer. It does *not* say that the problem is solvable, because we do not know how to *construct* such a circuit; all we know is that it exists. In fact, our proof of unsolvability in Chapter 4 simply implies that constructing such circuits is an unsolvable problem. Thus the difference between the existence of a family of circuits that computes a problem and an algorithm for constructing such circuits is exactly the same as the difference between the existence of answers to the instances of a problem and an algorithm for producing such answers.

Our definitions for the circuit complexity classes are thus too general: we should formulate them so that only decidable sets are included, that is, so that only algorithmically constructible families of circuits are considered. Such families of circuits are called *uniform*; their definitions vary depending on what resource bounds are imposed on the construction process.

Definition 9.10 A family $\{\xi_n\}$ of circuits is *uniform* if there exists a deterministic Turing machine which, given input 1^n (the input size in unary notation), computes the circuit ξ_n (that is, outputs a binary string that encodes ξ_n in some reasonable manner) in space $O(\log \text{size}(\xi_n))$. □

A similar definition allows $O(\text{depth}(\xi_n))$ space instead. As it turns out, which of the two definitions is adopted has no effect on the classes of size and depth complexity. We can now define uniform versions of the classes SIZE and DEPTH.

$$\text{USIZE}(f(n)) = \{L \mid \text{there exists a uniform family } \{\xi_n\}$$
$$\text{that computes } L \text{ and has size } O(f(n))\}$$
$$\text{UDEPTH}(f(n)) = \{L \mid \text{there exists a uniform family } \{\xi_n\}$$
$$\text{that computes } L \text{ and has depth } O(f(n))\}$$

Uniform circuit size directly corresponds to deterministic sequential time and uniform circuit depth directly corresponds to deterministic sequential space (yet another version of the parallel computation thesis). More precisely, we have the following theorem.

Theorem 9.9 Let $f(n)$ and $\lceil \log g(n) \rceil$ be easily computable (fully space constructible) space complexity bounds; then we have

$$\text{UDEPTH}(f^{O(1)}(n)) = \text{DSPACE}(f^{O(1)}(n))$$

$$\text{USIZE}(g^{O(1)}(n)) = \text{DTIME}(g^{O(1)}(n))$$ □

In particular, POLYL is equal to POLYLOGDEPTH and P is equal to PSIZE (polynomial size). In fact, the similarity between the circuit measures and the conventional space and time measures carries much farther. For instance, separating PolyLogDepth from PSize presents the same problems as separating PolyL from P, with the result that similar methods are employed—such as logdepth reductions to prove completeness of certain problems. (A corollary to Theorem 9.9 is that any P-complete problem is depth-complete for PSize; that much was already obvious for the circuit value problem.)

The uniform circuit model offers two significant advantages. First, its definition is not subject to interpretation (except for the exact meaning of uniformity) and it gives rise to natural, unambiguous complexity measures. Secondly, these two measures are precisely those that we identified as constituting the trade-off of parallel execution, *viz.* parallel time (depth) and hardware (size). Moreover, every computer is composed of circuits, so that the model is in fact fairly realistic. Its major drawback comes from the combinational nature of the circuits: since a combinational circuit cannot have cycles (feedback loops), it cannot reuse the same subunit at different stages of its computation but must include separate copies of that subunit. In other words, there is no equivalent in the circuit model of the concept of "subroutine"; as a result, the circuit size (but not its depth) may be larger than would be necessary on an actual machine. However, attempts to solve this problem by allowing cycles—leading to such models as conglomerates and aggregates—have so far proved rather unsatisfactory.

9.4.3 When Does Parallelism Pay?

As previously mentioned, only tractable problems may profit from the introduction of parallelism. Even then, parallel architectures may not achieve more than a constant speed-up factor—something that could also be attained by technological improvements or simply by paying more attention to coding. No parallel architecture can speed up execution by a factor larger than the number of processors used; in some sense, then, a successful application of parallelism is one in which this maximum speed-up is realized. However, the real potential of parallel architectures derives from their ability to achieve sublinear execution times—something that is forever beyond the reach of any sequential architecture—at a reasonable expense. Sublinear execution times may be characterized as $DTime(\log^k n)$ for some k—or PolyLogTime in our terminology.[2] The parallel computation

---

[2] We shall use the names of classes associated with decision problems, even though our entire development is equally applicable to general search and optimization problems. This is entirely a matter of convenience, since we already have a well-developed vocabulary for decision problems, a vocabulary that we lack for search and optimization problems.

thesis tells us that candidates for such fast parallel execution times are exactly those problems in POLYL. To keep hardware expenses within reasonable limits, we impose a polynomial bound on the amount of hardware that our problems may require. The parallel computation thesis then tells us that candidates for such reasonable hardware requirements are exactly those problems in P. We conclude that the most promising field of application for parallelism must be sought within the problems in $P \cap POLYL$. The reader may already have concluded that any problem within $P \cap POLYL$ is the desired type: a most reasonable conclusion, but one that fails to take into account the peculiarities of simultaneous resource bounds. We require that our problems be solvable jointly in polynomial time and polylogarithmic space, whereas it is conceivable that some problems in $P \cap POLYL$ are solvable in polynomial time—but then require polynomial space—or in polylogarithmic space—but then require subexponential time.

Two classes have been defined in an attempt to characterize those problems that lend themselves best to parallelism. One class, known as SC ("Steve's class," named for Stephen Cook, who defined it under another name in 1979), is defined in terms of sequential measures as the class of all problems solvable simultaneously in polynomial time and polylogarithmic space. Using the notation that has become standard for classes defined by simultaneous resource bounds:

$$SC = DTIME, \ DSPACE(n^{O(1)}, \ \log^{O(1)} n)$$

The other class, known as NC ("Nick's class," named in honor of Nicholas Pippenger, who proposed it in 1979), is defined in terms of (uniform) circuits as the class of all problems solvable simultaneously in polylogarithmic depth and polynomial size:

$$NC = USIZE, \ DEPTH(n^{O(1)}, \ \log^{O(1)} n)$$

Exercise 9.6 In this definition, uniformity is specified on only one of the resource bounds; does it matter?   □

Since POLYLOGDEPTH equals POLYL and PSIZE equals P, both classes (restricted to decision problems) are contained within $P \cap POLYL$. We might expect that the two classes are in fact equal, since their two resource bounds, taken separately, are identical. Yet classes defined by simultaneous resource bounds are such that both classes are presumably *proper* subsets of their common intersection class and presumably distinct. In particular, whereas both classes contain L (a trivial result to establish), NC also contains NL (a nondeterministic Turing machine running in logarithmic space can be

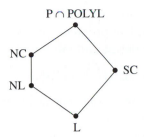

Figure 9.1   NC, SC, and related classes.

simulated by a family of circuits of polynomial size and $\log^2 n$ depth, a rather more difficult result) whereas SC is not thought to contain NL. Figure 9.1 shows the conjectured relationships among NC, SC, and related classes; as always, all containments are thought to be proper.

Both classes are remarkably robust, being essentially independent of the choice of model of computation. For SC, this is an immediate consequence of our previous developments, since the class is defined in terms of sequential models. Not only does NC not depend on the chosen definition of uniformity, it also retains its characterization under other models of parallel computation. For instance, an equivalent definition of NC is "the class of all problems solvable in polylogarithmic parallel time on PRAMs with a polynomial number of processors." Of the two classes, NC appears the more interesting and useful. It is defined directly in terms of parallel models and thus presumably provides a more accurate characterization of fast parallel execution than SC (it is quite conceivable that SC contains problems that do not lend themselves to spectacular speed-ups on parallel architectures). In spite of this, NC also appears to be the more general class. While candidates for membership in NC − SC are fairly numerous, natural (such as any NL-complete problem), and important (including matrix operations and various graph connectivity problems), it is very hard to come up with good candidates for SC − NC (all existing ones are contrived examples). Finally, even if a given parallel machine cannot achieve sublinear execution times due to hardware limitations, problems in NC still stand to profit more than any others from that architecture. Their very membership in NC suggests that they are easily decomposable and thus admit a variety of efficient parallel algorithms, some of which are bound to work well for the machine at hand.

Exactly what problems are in NC? To begin with, all problems in L are in NC (as well as in SC); they include such important tasks as integer arithmetic operations, sorting, matrix multiplication, and pattern matching. NC also includes all problems in NL, such as graph reachability and connectivity, shortest paths, and minimum spanning trees.

Exercise 9.7[*] Prove that *Digraph Reachability* is in NC.   □

Finally, NC also contains an assortment of other important problems not known to be in NL: matrix inversion, determinant, and rank; a variety of simple dynamic programming problems such as matrix chain products and optimal binary search trees; and special cases of harder problems, such as maximum flow in planar graphs and linear programming with a fixed number of variables. (Membership of these last problems in NC has been proved in a variety of ways, appealing to one or another of the equivalent characterizations of NC.) The remarkable number of simple, but common and important problems that belong to NC is not only a testimony to the importance of the class but more significantly is an indication of the potential of parallel architectures: while they may not help us with the difficult problems, they can greatly reduce the running time of day-to-day tasks that constitute the bulk of computing.

Equally important, what problems are not in NC? Since the only candidates for membership in NC are tractable problems, the question becomes "What problems are in P − NC?" (Since the only candidates are in fact problems in P ∩ POLYL, we could consider the difference between this intersection and NC. We proceed otherwise, because membership in P ∩ POLYL is not always easy to establish even for tractable problems and because it is remarkably difficult to find candidates for membership in this difference. In other words, membership in P ∩ POLYL appears to be a very good indicator of membership in NC.) In Section 7.2, we discussed a family of problems in P that are presumably not in POLYL and thus, *a fortiori*, not in NC: the P-complete problems. Thus we conclude that problems such as maximum flow on arbitrary graphs, general linear programming, circuit value, and path system accessibility are not likely to be in NC, despite their tractability.

In practice, effective applications of parallelism are not limited to problems in NC. Adding randomization (in much the same manner as done in Section 8.4) is surprisingly effective. The resulting class, denoted RNC, allows us to develop very simple parallel algorithms for many of the problems in NC and also to parallelize much harder problems, such as maximum matching. *Ad hoc* hardware can be designed to achieve sublinear parallel execution times for a wider class of problems (P-uniform NC, as opposed to the normal L-uniform NC); however, the need for special-purpose circuitry severely restricts the applications. Several efficient (in the sense that a linear increase in the number of processors affords a linear decrease in the running time) parallel algorithms have been published for some P-complete problems and even for some probably intractable problems of subexponential complexity; however, such algorithms are isolated cases. Ideally, a theory of parallel complexity would identify problems amenable to linear speed-ups through linear increases in the number of processors; however, such a class cuts across all existing complexity classes and is proving very resistant to characterization.

9.4.4 Communication and Complexity

The models of parallel computation discussed in the previous section either ignore the costs of synchronization and interprocess communication or include them directly in their time and space complexity measures. In a distributed system, the cost of communication is related only distantly to the running time of processes. For certain problems that make sense only in a distributed environment, such as voting problems, running time and space for the processes is essentially irrelevant: the real cost derives from the number and size of messages exchanged by the processes. Hence some measure of communication complexity is needed.

In order to study communication complexity, let us postulate the simplest possible model: two machines must compute some function $f(x, y)$; the first machine is given x as input and the second y, where x and y are assumed to have the same length;[3] the machines communicate by exchanging alternating messages. Each machine computes the next message to send based upon its share of the input plus the record of all the messages that it has received (and sent) so far. The question is "How many bits must be exchanged in order to allow one of the machines to output $f(x, y)$?" Clearly, an upper bound on the complexity of any function under this model is $|x|$, as the first machine can just send all of x to the second and let the second do all the computing. On the other hand, some nontrivial functions have only unit complexity: determining whether the sum of x and y (considered as integers) is odd requires a single message. For fixed x and y, then, we define the communication complexity of $f(x, y)$, call it $c(f(x, y))$, to be the minimum number of bits that must be exchanged in order for one of

---

[3] x and y can be considered as a partition of the string of bits describing a problem instance; for example, an instance of a graph problem can be split into two strings x and y by giving each string half of the bits describing the adjacency matrix.

the machines to compute f, allowing messages of arbitrary length. Let n be the length of x and y. Since the partition of the input into x and y can be achieved in many different ways, we define the *communication complexity* of f for inputs of size $2n$, $c(f_{2n})$, as the minimum of $c(f(x, y))$ over all partitions of the input into two strings, x and y, of equal length. As was the case for circuit complexity, this definition of communication complexity involves a family of functions, one for each input size.

Let us further restrict ourselves to functions f that represent decision problems, i.e., to Boolean-valued functions. Then communication complexity defines a firm hierarchy.

Theorem 9.10 Let $t(n)$ be a function with $1 < t(n) \leq n$ for all n and denote by $\text{COMM}(t(n))$ the set of decision problems f obeying $c(f_{2n}) \leq t(n)$ for all n. Then $\text{COMM}(t(n))$ is a proper superset of $\text{COMM}(t(n) - 1)$.   □

The proof is nonconstructive and relies on fairly sophisticated counting arguments to establish that a randomly chosen language has a nonzero probability (indeed an asymptotic probability of 1) of requiring n bits of communication, so that there are languages in $\text{COMM}(n) - \text{COMM}(n - 1)$. An extension of the argument from n to $t(n)$ supplies the desired proof.

Further comparisons are possible with the time hierarchy. Define the nondeterministic communication complexity in the obvious manner: a decision problem is solved nondeterministically with communication cost $t(n)$ if there exists a computation (an algorithm for communication and decision) that recognizes yes instances of size $2n$ using no more than $t(n)$ bits of communication. Does nondeterminism in this setting give rise to the same exponential gaps that are conjectured for the time hierarchy? The answer, somewhat surprisingly, is not only that it seems to create such gaps, but that the existence of such gaps can be proved! First, though, we must show that the gap is no larger than exponential.

Theorem 9.11 $\text{NCOMM}(t(n)) \subseteq \text{COMM}(2^{t(n)})$.   □

Proof. All that the second machine needs to know in order to solve the problem is the first machine's answer to any possible sequence of communications. But that is something that the first machine can provide to the second within the stated bounds. The first machine enumerates in lexicographic order all possible sequences of messages of total length not exceeding $t(n)$; with a binary alphabet, there are $2^{t(n)}$ such sequences. The first machine prepares a message of length $2^{t(n)}$, where the ith bit encodes its answer to the ith sequence of messages. Thus with a single message of length $2^{t(n)}$, the first machine communicates to the second all that the latter needs to know.   Q.E.D.

Now we get to the main result.

Theorem 9.12 There is a problem in NCOMM($\alpha \log n$) that requires $\Omega(n)$ bits of communication in any deterministic solution.   □

In order to prove this theorem, we first prove the following simple lemma.

Lemma 9.1 Let the function $f(x, y)$, where x and y are binary strings of the same length, be the logical inner product of the two strings (considered as vectors). That is, writing $x = x_1 x_2 \ldots x_n$ and $y = y_1 y_2 \ldots y_n$, we have $f(x, y) = \vee_{i=1}^{n}(x_i \wedge y_i)$. Then the (fixed-partition) communication complexity of the decision problem "Is $f(x, y)$ false?" is exactly n.   □

Proof (of lemma). For any string pair $(x, \overline{x})$ where $\overline{x}$ is the bitwise complement of x, the inner product of x and $\overline{x}$ is false. There are 2^n such pairs for strings of length n. We claim that no two such pairs can lead to the same sequence of messages; a proof of the claim immediately proves our lemma, as it implies the existence of 2^n distinct sequences of messages for strings of length n, so that at least some of these sequences must use n bits. Assume that there exist two pairs, $(x, \overline{x})$ and $(u, \overline{u})$, of complementary strings that are accepted by our two machines with the same sequence of messages. Then our two machines also accept the pairs $(x, \overline{u})$ and $(u, \overline{x})$. For instance, the pair $(x, \overline{u})$ is accepted because the same sequence of messages used for the pair $(x, \overline{x})$ "verifies" that $(x, \overline{u})$ is acceptable. The first machine starts with x and its first message is the same as for the pair $(x, \overline{x})$, then the second machine receives a message that is identical to what the first machine would have sent had its input been string u and thus answers with the same message that it would have used for the pair $(u, \overline{u})$. In that guise both machines proceed, the first as if computing $f(x, \overline{x})$ and the second as if computing $f(u, \overline{u})$. Since the two computations involve the same sequence of messages, neither machine can recognize its error and the pair $(x, \overline{u})$ is accepted. The same argument shows that the pair $(u, \overline{x})$ is also accepted. However, at least one of these two pairs has a true logical inner product and thus is not a yes instance, so that our two machines do not solve the stated decision problem, which yields the desired contradiction.   *Q.E.D.*

Proof (of theorem). Consider the question "Does a graph of $|V|$ vertices given by its adjacency matrix contain a triangle?" The problem is trivial if either side of the partition contains a triangle. If, however, the only triangles are split between the two sides, then a nondeterministic algorithm can pick three vertices for which it knows of no missing edges and send their labels to the other machine, which can then verify that it knows of no missing edges either. Since the input size is $n = |V| + |V| \cdot \frac{(|V|-1)}{2}$ and since identifying the three vertices requires $3 \log |V|$ bits, the problem is in NCOMM($\alpha \log n$) as claimed.

On the other hand, for any deterministic communication scheme, there are graphs for which the scheme can do no better than to send αn bits. We prove this assertion by an adversary argument: we construct graphs for which demonstrating the existence of a triangle is exactly equivalent to computing a logical inner product of two n-bits vectors. We start with the complete graph on $|V|$ vertices; consider it to be edge-colored with two colors, say black and white, with the first machine being given all black edges and the second machine all white edges. (Recall that the same amount of data is given to each machine: thus we consider only edge colorings that color half of the edges in white and the other half in black.) Any vertex has $|V| - 1$ edges incident to it; call the vertex "black" if more than 98% of these edges are black, "white" if more than 98% of these edges are white, and "mixed" otherwise. Thus at least 1% of the vertices must be of the mixed type. Hence we can pick a subset of 1% of the vertices such that all vertices in the subset are of mixed type; call these vertices the "top" vertices and call the other vertices "bottom" vertices. Call an edge between two bottom vertices a bottom edge; each such edge is assigned a weight, which is the number of top vertices to which its endpoints are connected by edges of different colors. (Because the graph is complete, the two endpoints of a bottom edge are connected to every top vertex.) From each top vertex there issue at least $|V|/100$ black edges and at least $|V|/100$ white edges; thus, since the graph is complete, there are at least $(|V|/100)^2$ bottom edges connected to each top vertex by edges of different colors. In particular, this implies that the total weight of all bottom edges is $\Omega(|V|^3)$.

Now we construct a subset of edges as follows. First we repeatedly select edges between bottom vertices by picking the remaining edge of largest weight and by removing it and all edges incident to its two endpoints from contention. This procedure constructs a matching on the vertices of the graph of weight $\Omega(|V|^2)$ (this last follows from our lower bound on the total weight of edges and from the fact that selecting an edge removes $O(|V|)$ adjacent edges). Now we select edges between top and bottom vertices: for each edge between bottom vertices, we select all of the white edges from one of its endpoints (which is thus "whitened") to top vertices and all of the black edges from its other endpoint (which is "blackened") to the top vertices. The resulting collection of edges defines the desired graph on n vertices.

The only possible triangles in this graph are composed of two matched bottom vertices and one top vertex; such a triangle exists if and only if the two edges between the top vertex and the bottom vertices exist—in which case these two edges are of different colors. Thus for each pair of matched (bottom) vertices, the only candidate top vertices are those that are connected to the matching edge by edges of different colors; hence the total number of candidate triangles is exactly equal to the weight of the constructed matching. Since the first machine knows only about white edges and the second only about black edges, deciding whether the graph has a triangle is exactly equivalent to computing the logical inner product of two vectors of equal length. Each vector has length equal to the weight of the matching. For each candidate triangle, the vector has a bit indicating the presence or absence of one or the other edge between a top vertex and a matched pair of vertices (the white edge for the vector of the first machine and the black edge for the vector of the second machine). Since the matching has weight $\Omega(|V|^2) = \Omega(n)$, the vectors have length $\Omega(n)$; the conclusion then follows from our lemma.   Q.E.D.

The reader should think very carefully about the sequence of constructions used in this proof, keeping in mind that the proof must establish that, for *any partition* of the input into two strings of equal length, solving the problem requires a sequence of messages with a total length linear in the size of the input. While it should be clear that the construction indeed yields a partition and a graph for which the problem of detecting triangles has linear communication complexity, it is less apparent that the construction respects the constraint "for any partition."

These results are impressive in view of the fact that communication complexity is a new concept, to which relatively little study has been devoted so far. More results are evidently needed; it is also clear that simultaneous resource bounds ought to be studied in this context. Communication complexity is not useful only in the context of distributed algorithms: it has already found applications in VLSI complexity theory. Whereas communication complexity as described here deals with deterministic or nondeterministic algorithms that collaborate in solving a problem, we can extend the model to include randomized approaches. Section 9.5 introduces the ideas behind probabilistic proof systems, which use a prover and a checker that interact in one or more exchanges.

9.5   Interactive Proofs and Probabilistic Proof Checking

We have mentioned several times the fact that a proof is more in the nature of an interaction between a prover and a checker than a monolithic, absolute composition. Indeed, the class NP is based on the idea of interaction:

to prove that an instance is a "yes" instance, a certificate must be found and then checked in polynomial time. There is a well-defined notion of checker (even if the checker remains otherwise unspecified); on the other hand, the prover is effectively the existential quantifier or the nondeterministic component of the machine. Thus NP, while capturing some aspects of the interaction between prover and checker, is both too broad—because the prover is completely unspecified and the checker only vaguely delineated—and too narrow—because membership in the class requires absolute correctness for every instance. If we view NP as the interactive equivalent of P (for a problem in P, a single machine does all of the work, whereas for a problem in NP, the work is divided between a nondeterministic prover and a deterministic checker), then we would like to investigate, at the very least, the interactive equivalent of BPP. Yet the interaction described in these cases would remain limited to just one round: the prover supplies evidence and the checker verifies it. An interaction between two scientists typically takes several rounds, with the "checker" asking questions of the "prover," questions that depend on the information accumulated so far by the checker. We study below both multi- and single-round proof systems.

9.5.1   Interactive Proofs

Meet Arthur and Merlin. You know about them already: Merlin is the powerful and subtle wizard and Arthur the honest[4] king. In our interaction, Merlin will be the prover and Arthur the checker. Arthur often asks Merlin for advice but, being a wise king, realizes that Merlin's motives may not always coincide with Arthur's own or with the kingdom's best interest. Arthur further realizes that Merlin, being a wizard, can easily dazzle him and might not always tell the truth. So whenever Merlin provides advice, Arthur will ask him to prove the correctness of the advice. However, Merlin can obtain things by magic (we would say nondeterministically!), whereas Arthur can compute only deterministically or, at best, probabilistically. Even then, Arthur cannot hide his random bits from Merlin's magic. In other words, Arthur has the power of P or, at best, BPP, whereas Merlin has (at least) the power of NP.

Definition 9.11 An *interactive proof system* is composed of a checker, which runs in probabilistic polynomial time, and a prover, which can use unbounded resources. We write such a system (P, C).

---

[4]Perhaps somewhat naïve, though. Would *you* obey a request to go in the forest, there to seek a boulder in which is embedded a sword, to retrieve said sword by slipping it out of its stone matrix, and to return it to the requester?

A problem Π admits an interactive proof if there exists a checker C and a constant $\varepsilon > 0$ such that

- there exists a prover P^* such that the interactive proof system (P^*, C) accepts every "yes" instance of Π with probability at least $1/2 + \varepsilon$; and
- for any prover P, the interactive proof system (P, C) rejects every "no" instance of Π with probability at least $1/2 + \varepsilon$. $\square$

(The reader will also see one-sided definitions where "yes" instances are always accepted. It turns out that the definitions are equivalent—in contrast to the presumed situation for randomized complexity classes, where we expect RP to be a proper subset of BPP.) This definition captures the notion of a "benevolent" prover (P^*), who collaborates with the checker and can always convince the checker of the correctness of a true statement, and of "malevolent" provers, who are prevented from doing too much harm by the second requirement. We did not place any constraint on the power of the prover, other than limiting it to computable functions, that is! As we shall see, we can then ask exactly how much power the prover needs to have in order to complete certain interactions.

Definition 9.12 The class IP(f) consists of all problems that admit an interactive proof where, for instance x, the parties exchange at most $f(|x|)$ messages. In particular, IP is the class of decision problems that admit an interactive proof involving at most a polynomial number of messages, $\text{IP} = \text{IP}(n^{O(1)})$. $\square$

This definition of interactive proofs does not exactly coincide with the definition of Arthur-Merlin games that we used as introduction. In an Arthur-Merlin game, Arthur communicates to Merlin the random bits he uses (and thus need not communicate anything else), whereas the checker in an interactive proof system uses "secret" random bits. Again, it turns out that the class IP is remarkably robust: whether or not the random bits of the checker are hidden from the prover does not alter the class.

So how is an interactive proof system developed? We give the classic example of an interactive, one-sided proof system for the problem of *Graph Nonisomorphism*: given two graphs, G_1 and G_2, are they nonisomorphic? This problem is in coNP but not believed to be in NP. One phase of our interactive proof proceeds as follows:

1. The checker chooses at random the index $i \in \{1, 2\}$ and sends to the prover a random permutation H of G_i. (Effectively, the checker is asking the prover to decide whether H is isomorphic to G_1 or to G_2.)
2. The prover tests H against G_1 and G_2 and sends back to the checker the index of the graph to which H is isomorphic.

3. The checker compares its generated index i with the index sent by the prover; if they agree, the checker accepts the instance, otherwise it rejects it.

(In this scenario, the prover needs only to be able to decide graph isomorphism and its complement; hence it is enough that it be able to solve NP-easy problems.) If G_1 and G_2 are not isomorphic, a benevolent prover can always decide correctly to which of the two H is isomorphic and send back to the checker the correct answer, so that the checker will always accept "yes" instances. On the other hand, when the two graphs are isomorphic, then the prover finds that H is isomorphic to both. Not knowing the random bit used by the checker, the prover must effectively answer at random, with a probability of $1/2$ of returning the value used by the checker and thus fooling the checker into accepting the instance. It follows that *Graph Nonisomorphism* belongs to IP; since it belongs to coNP but presumably not to NP, and since IP is easily seen to be closed under complementation, we begin to suspect that IP contains both NP and coNP. Developing an exact characterization of IP turns out to be surprisingly difficult but also surprisingly rewarding. The first surprise is the power of IP: not only can we solve NP problems with a polynomial interactive protocol, we can solve any problem in PSPACE.

Theorem 9.13 IP equals PSPACE. ☐

The second surprise comes from the techniques needed to prove this theorem. Techniques used so far in this text all have the property of *relativization*: if we equip the Turing machine models used for the various classes with an oracle for some problem, all of the results we have proved so far carry through immediately with the same proof. However, there exists an oracle A (which we shall not develop) under which the relativized version of this theorem is false, that is, under which we have $IP^A \neq PSPACE^A$, a result indicating that "normal" proof techniques cannot succeed in proving Theorem 9.13.[5] In point of fact, one part of the theorem is relatively simple: because all interactions between the prover and the checker are polynomially bounded, verifying that IP is a subset of PSPACE can be done with standard techniques.

---

[5]That IP equals PSPACE is even more surprising if we dig a little deeper. A long-standing conjecture in Complexity Theory, known as the *Random Oracle Hypothesis*, stated that any statement true with probability 1 in its relativized version with respect to a randomly chosen oracle should be true in its unrelativized version, ostensibly on the grounds that a random oracle had to be "neutral." However, after the proof of Theorem 9.13 was published, other researchers showed that, with respect to a random oracle A, IP^A *differs* from $PSPACE^A$ with probability 1, thereby disproving the random oracle hypothesis.

Exercise 9.8* Prove that IP is a subset of PSPACE. Use our results about randomized classes and the fact that PSPACE is closed under complementation and nondeterminism.   □

The key to the proof of Theorem 9.13 and a host of other recent results is the *arithmetization of Boolean formulae*, that is, the encoding of Boolean formulae into low-degree polynomials over the integers, carried out in such a way as to transform the existence of a satisfying assignment for a Boolean formula into the existence of an assignment of 0/1 values to the variables that causes the polynomial to assume a nonzero value. The arithmetization itself is a very simple idea: given a Boolean formula f in 3SAT form, we derive the polynomial function p_f from f by setting up for each Boolean variable x_i a corresponding integer variable y_i and by applying the following three rules:

1. The Boolean literal x_i corresponds to the polynomial $p_{x_i} = 1 - y_i$ and the Boolean literal $\overline{x_i}$ to the polynomial $p_{\overline{x_i}} = y_i$.
2. The Boolean clause $c = \{\hat{x}_{i_1}, \hat{x}_{i_2}, \hat{x}_{i_3}\}$ corresponds to the polynomial $p_c = 1 - p_{\hat{x}_{i_1}} p_{\hat{x}_{i_2}} p_{\hat{x}_{i_3}}$.
3. The Boolean formula over n variables $f = c_1 \wedge c_2 \wedge \cdots \wedge c_m$ (where each c_i is a clause) corresponds to the polynomial $p_f(y_1, y_2, \ldots, y_n) = p_{c_1} p_{c_2} \cdots p_{c_m}$.

The degree of the resulting polynomial p_f is at most $3m$. This arithmetization suffices for the purpose of proving the slightly less ambitious results that CONP is a subset of IP, since we can use it to encode an arbitrary instance of 3UNSAT.

Exercise 9.9 Verify that f is unsatisfiable if and only if we have

$$\sum_{y_1=0}^{1} \sum_{y_2=0}^{1} \cdots \sum_{y_n=0}^{1} p_f(y_1, y_2, \ldots, y_n) = 0$$

Define partial-sum polynomials as follows:

$$p_f^i(y_1, y_2, \ldots, y_i) = \sum_{y_{i+1}=0}^{1} \sum_{y_{i+2}=0}^{1} \cdots \sum_{y_n=0}^{1} p_f(y_1, y_2, \ldots, y_n)$$

Verify that we have both $p_f^n = p_f$ and $p_f^{i-1} = p_f^i|_{y_i=0} + p_f^i|_{y_i=1}$, so that f is unsatisfiable if and only if p_f^0 equals zero.   □

An interactive protocol for 3UNSAT then checks that p_f^0 equals zero, something that takes too long for the checker to test directly because p_f^0 has an exponential number of terms. The checker cannot just ask the prover for an evaluation since the result cannot be verified; instead, the checker will ask the prover to send (a form of) each of the partial-sum polynomials, p_f^i, in turn. What the checker will do is to choose (at random) the value of a variable, send that value to the prover, and ask the prover to return the partial-sum polynomial for that value of the variable (and past values of other variables fixed in previous exchanges). On the basis of the value it has chosen for that variable and of the partial-sum polynomial received in the previous exchange, the checker is able to predict the value of the next partial-sum polynomial and thus can check, when it receives it from the prover, whether it evaluates to the predicted value.

Overall, the protocol uses $n + 1$ rounds. In the zeroth round, the checker computes p_f and the prover sends to the checker a large prime p (of order 2^n), which the checker tests for size and for primality (we have mentioned that *Primality* belongs to ZPP); finally, the checker sets $b_0 = 0$. In each succeeding round, the checker picks a new random number r in the set $\{0, 1, \ldots, p - 1\}$, assigns it to the next variable, and computes a new value b. Thus at the beginning of round i, the numbers $r_1, \ldots, r_{i-1}$ have been chosen and the numbers $b_0, b_1, \ldots, b_{i-1}$ have been computed. In round i, then, the checker sends b_{i-1} to the prover and asks for the coefficients of the single-variable polynomial $q_i(x) = p_f^i(r_1, \ldots, r_{i-1}, x)$. On receiving the coefficients defining $q_i'(x)$ (the prime denotes that the checker does not know if the prover sent the correct coefficients), the checker evaluates $q_i'(0) + q_i'(1)$ and compares the result with b_{i-1}. If the values agree, the checker selects the next random value r_i and sets $b_i = q_i'(r_i)$. At any time, the checker stops and rejects the instance if any of its tests fails; if the end of the nth round is reached, the checker runs one last test, comparing b_n and $p_f(r_1, r_2, \ldots, r_n)$, accepting if the two are equal.

Exercise 9.10* (Requires some knowledge of probability.) Verify that the protocol described above, for a suitable choice of the prime p, establishes membership of $3UNSAT$ in IP. □

The problem with this elegant approach is that the polynomial resulting from an instance of the standard PSPACE-complete problem $Q3SAT$ will have very high degree because each universal quantifier will force us to take a product over the two values of the quantified variable. (Each existential quantifier forces us to take a sum, which does not raise the degree and so does not cause a problem.) The high resulting degree prevents the checker from evaluating the polynomial within its resource bounds. Therefore, in order to carry the technique from coNP to PSPACE, we need a way to generate a (possibly much larger) polynomial of bounded degree. To this end, we define the following operations on polynomials. If p is a polynomial and y one of its variables, we define

- $\text{and}_y(p) = p\big|_{y=0} \, p\big|_{y=1}$
- $\text{or}_y(p) = p\big|_{y=0} + p\big|_{y=1} - p\big|_{y=0} \, p\big|_{y=1}$
- $\text{reduce}_y(p) = p\big|_{y=0} + y\big(p\big|_{y=1} - p\big|_{y=0}\big)$

The first two operations will be used for universal and existential quantifiers, respectively. As its name indicates, the last operation will be used for reducing the degree of a polynomial (at the cost of increasing the number of its terms); under substitution of either $y = 0$ or $y = 1$, it is an identity. The proof of Theorem 9.13 relies on the following lemma (which we shall not prove) about these three operations.

Lemma 9.2 Let $p(y_1, y_2, \ldots, y_n)$ be a polynomial with integer coefficients and denote by $\text{test}(p)$ the problem of deciding, for given values $a_1, a_2, \ldots, a_n$, and b, whether $p(a_1, a_2, \ldots, a_n)$ equals b. If $\text{test}(p)$ belongs to IP, then so does each of $\text{test}(\text{and}_{y_i}(p))$, $\text{test}(\text{or}_{y_i}(p))$, and $\text{test}(\text{reduce}_{y_i}(p))$.   □

Now we can encode an instance of the PSPACE-complete problem Q3SAT, say $Q_1 x_1 Q_2 x_2 \ldots Q_n x_n f(x_1, x_2, \ldots, x_n)$, as follows:

1. Produce the polynomial p_f corresponding to the formula f.
2. For each $i = 1, \ldots, n$ in turn, apply reduce_{x_i}.
3. For each $i = 1, \ldots, n$ in turn, if the quantifier Q_{n+1-i} is universal, then apply $\text{and}_{x_{n+1-i}}$ else apply $\text{or}_{x_{n+1-i}}$, and (in both cases) follow by applications of reduce_{x_j} for $j = 1, \ldots, n - i$.

No polynomial produced in this process ever has degree greater than that of f—after the second step, in fact, no polynomial ever has degree greater than two. Using this low-degree polynomial, we can then proceed to devise an interactive proof protocol similar to that described for 3UNSAT, which completes (our rough sketch of) the proof.

Having characterized the power of interactive proofs, we can turn to related questions. How much power does a benevolent IP prover actually need? One problem with this question derives from the fact that restrictions on the prover can work both ways: the benevolent prover may lose some of its ability to convince the checker of the validity of a true statement, but the malevolent provers also become less able to fool the checker into accepting a false statement. A time-tested method to foil a powerful advisor who may harbor ulterior designs is to use several such advisors and keep each of them in the dark about the others (to prevent them from colluding, which would be worse than having to rely on a single advisor). The class MIP characterizes decision problems that admit polynomially-bounded interactive proofs with multiple, independent provers. Not surprisingly, this class sits much higher in the hierarchy than IP (at least under standard conjectures): it has been shown that MIP equals NExp, thereby providing a formal justification for a practice used by generations of kings and heads of state.

9.5.2   Zero-Knowledge Proofs

In cryptographic applications, there are many occasions when one party wants to convince the other party of the correctness of some statement without, however, divulging any real information. (This is a common game in international politics or, for that matter, in commerce: convince your opponents or partners that you have a certain capability without divulging anything that might enable them to acquire the same.) For instance, you might want to convince someone that a graph is three-colorable without, however, revealing anything about the three-coloring. At first, the idea seems ludicrous; certainly it does not fit well with our notion of NP, where the certificate typically *is* the solution.

However, consider the following thought experiment. Both the prover and the checker have a description of the graph with the same indexing for the vertices and have agreed to represent colors by values from $\{1, 2, 3\}$. In a given round of interaction, the prover sends to the checker n locked "boxes," one for each vertex of the graph—each box contains the color assigned to its corresponding vertex. The checker cannot look inside a box without a key; thus the checker selects at random one edge of the graph, say $\{u, v\}$, and asks the prover for the keys to the boxes for u and v. The prover sends the two keys to the checker; the checker opens the two boxes. If the colors are distinct and both in the set $\{1, 2, 3\}$, the checker accepts the claim of the prover; otherwise, it rejects the claim. If the graph is indeed three-colorable, the prover can always persuade the checker to accept—any legal coloring (randomly permuted) sent in the boxes will do. If the graph is not three-colorable, any filling of the n boxes has at least one flaw (that is, it results in at least one same-colored edge or uses at least one illegal color), which the checker discovers with probability at least $|E|^{-1}$.

With enough rounds (each round is independent of the previous ones because the prover uses new boxes with new locks and randomly permutes the three colors in the legal coloring—and, for graphs with more than one coloring, can even select different colorings in different rounds), the probability of error can be reduced to any desired constant. After k rounds, the probability of error is bounded by $(1 - |E|^{-1})^k$, so that we can guarantee a probability of error not exceeding $\frac{1}{2}$ in at most $\lceil (\log |E| - \log(|E| - 1))^{-1} \rceil$ rounds. It is instructive to contemplate what the checker learns about the coloring in one round. The checker opens two boxes that are expected to contain two distinct values chosen at random from the set $\{1, 2, 3\}$ and, assuming that the graph is indeed colorable, finds exactly that. The checker might as well have picked two colors at random from the set; the result would be indistinguishable from what has been "learned" from the prover! In other words, the correctness of the assertion has been (probabilistically) proved, but absolutely nothing has been communicated about the solution: zero knowledge has been transferred.

This experiment motivates us to define a zero-knowledge interactive proof system; we assume Definition 9.11 and simply add one more condition.

Definition 9.13 A prover strategy, P, is *perfect zero-knowledge* for problem Π if, for every probabilistic polynomial-time checker strategy, C, there exists a probabilistic polynomial-time algorithm $\mathcal{A}$ such that, for every instance x of Π, the output of the prover-checker interaction, $(P, C)(x)$, equals that of the algorithm, $\mathcal{A}(x)$. □

Thus there is nothing that the checker can compute with the help of the prover that it could not compute on its own! However, since the output of the interaction or of the algorithm is a random variable, asking for strict equality is rather demanding: when dealing with random processes, we can define equality in a number of ways, from strict equality of outcomes at each instantiation to equality of distributions to the yet weaker notion of indistinguishability of distributions. For practical purposes, the last notion suffices: we need only require that the distributions of the two variables be computationally indistinguishable in polynomial time. Formalizing this notion of indistinguishability takes some work, so we omit a formal definition but content ourselves with noting that the resulting form of zero-knowledge proof is called *computational zero-knowledge*.

Turning our thought experiment into an actual computing interaction must depend on the availability of the boxes with unbreakable locks. In practice, we want the prover to commit itself to a coloring before the checker asks to see the colors of the endpoints of a randomly chosen edge. Encryption offers an obvious solution: the prover encrypts the content of each box, using a different key for each box. With a strong encryption scheme, the checker is then unable to decipher the contents of any box if it is not given the key for that box. Unfortunately, we know of no provably hard encryption scheme that can easily be decoded with a key.

Public-key schemes such as the RSA algorithm are conjectured to be hard to decipher, but no proof is available (and schemes based on factoring are now somewhat suspect due to the quantum computing model). The dream of any cryptographer is a *one-way function*, that is, a function that is P-easy to compute but (at least) NP-hard to invert. Such functions are conjectured to exist, but their existence has not been proved.

Theorem 9.14 Assuming the existence of one-way functions, any problem in PSPACE has a computational zero-knowledge interactive proof.   □

That such is the case for any problem in NP should now be intuitively clear, since we outlined a zero-knowledge proof for the NP-complete problem *Graph Three-Colorability* which, with some care paid to technical details, can be implemented with one-way functions. That it also holds for PSPACE and thus for IP is perhaps no longer quite as surprising, yet the ability to produce zero-knowledge proofs for *any* problem at all (beyond BPP, that is) is quite astounding in itself. This ability has had profound effects on the development of cryptography.

Going beyond zero-knowledge proofs, we can start asking how much knowledge must be transferred for certain types of interactive proofs, as well as how much efficiency is to be gained by transferring more knowledge than the strict minimum required.

9.5.3   Probabilistically Checkable Proofs

Most mathematical proofs, when in final form, are static entities: they are intended as a single communication to the reader (the checker) by the writer (the prover). This limited interaction is to the advantage of the checker: the prover gets fewer opportunities to misdirect the checker. (If we return to our analogy of Arthur and Merlin, we can imagine Arthur's telling Merlin, on discovering for the nth time that Merlin has tricked him, that, henceforth, he will accept Merlin's advice only in writing, along with a one-time only argument supporting the advice.) In its simplest form, this type of interaction leads to our definition of NP: the prover runs in nondeterministic polynomial time and the checker in deterministic polynomial time. As we have seen, however, the introduction of probabilistic checking makes interactions much more interesting. So what happens when we simply require, as we did in the fully interactive setting, that the checker have a certain minimum probability of accepting true statements and rejecting false ones? Then we no longer need to see the entire proof and it becomes worthwhile to consider how much of the proof needs to be seen.

Definition 9.14 A problem Π admits a *probabilistically checkable proof* if there exists a probabilistic algorithm C (the checker) that runs in polynomial time and can query specific bits of a proof string π and a constant $\varepsilon > 0$ such that

- for every "yes" instance x of Π, there exists a proof string π such that C accepts x with probability at least $1/2 + \varepsilon$; and
- for every "no" instance x of Π and any proof string π, C rejects x with probability at least $1/2 + \varepsilon$. $\qquad\square$

(Again, the reader will also see one-sided definitions, where "no" instances are always rejected; again, it turns out that the definitions are equivalent. We used a one-sided definition in the proof of Theorem 8.23.)

Definition 9.15 The class $\mathrm{PCP}(r, q)$ consists of all problems that admit a probabilistically checkable proof where, for instance x, the checker C uses at most $r(|x|)$ random bits and queries at most $q(|x|)$ bits from the proof string. $\qquad\square$

Clearly, the proof string must assume a specific form. Consider the usual certificate for *Satisfiability*, namely a truth assignment for the n variables. It is not difficult to show that there exist Boolean functions that require the evaluation of every one of their n variables—a simple example is the parity function. No amount of randomization will enable us to determine probabilistically whether a truth assignment satisfies the parity function by checking just a few variables; in fact, even after checking $n - 1$ of the n variables, the two outcomes remain equally likely! Yet the proof string is aptly named: it is indeed an acceptable proof in the usual mathematical sense but is written down in a special way.

From our definition, we have $\mathrm{PCP}(0, 0) = \mathrm{P}$ and $\mathrm{PCP}(n^{O(1)}, 0) = \mathrm{BPP}$. A bit more work reveals that a small amount of evidence will not greatly help a deterministic checker.

Exercise 9.11 Verify that $\mathrm{PCP}(0, q)$ is the class of problems that can be decided by a deterministic algorithm running in $O(n^{O(1)} \cdot 2^{q(n)})$ time. In particular, we have $\mathrm{PCP}(0, O(\log n)) = \mathrm{P}$. $\qquad\square$

More interestingly, $\mathrm{PCP}(0, n^{O(1)})$ equals NP, since we have no randomness yet are able to inspect polynomially many bits of the proof string—that is, the entire proof string for a problem in NP. A small number of random bits does not help much when we can see the whole proof: a difficult result states that $\mathrm{PCP}(O(\log n), n^{O(1)})$ also equals NP. With sufficiently many random bits, however, the power of the system grows quickly; another result that we shall not examine further states that $\mathrm{PCP}(n^{O(1)}, n^{O(1)})$ equals NEXP.

Were these the sum of results about the PCP system, it would be regarded as a fascinating formalism to glean insight into the nature of proofs and into some of the fine structure of certain complexity classes. (Certainly anyone who has reviewed someone else's proof will recognize the notion of looking at selected excerpts of the proof and evaluating it in terms of its probability of being correct!) But, as we saw in Section 8.3, there is a deep connection between probabilistically checkable proofs and approximation, basically due to the fact that really good approximations depend in part on the existence of gap-preserving or gap-creating reductions (where the gap is based on the values of the solutions) and that good probabilistic checkers depend also on such gaps (this time measured in terms of probabilities). This connection motivated intensive research into the exact characterization of NP in terms of PCP models, culminating in this beautiful and surprising theorem.

Theorem 9.15 NP equals PCP($O(\log n)$, $O(1)$). □

In other words, every decision problem in NP has a proof that can be checked probabilistically by looking only at a constant number of bits of the proof string, using a logarithmic number of random bits. In many ways, the PCP theorem, as it is commonly known, is the next major step in the study of complexity theory after Cook's and Karp's early results. It ties together randomized approaches, proof systems, and nondeterminism—three of the great themes of complexity theory—and has already proved to be an extremely fruitful tool in the study of approximation problems.

9.6   Complexity and Constructive Mathematics

Our entire discussion so far in this text has been based on existential definitions: a problem belongs to a complexity class if there *exists* an algorithm that solves the problem and exhibits the desired characteristics. Yet, at the same time, we have implicitly assumed that placing a problem in a class is done by exhibiting such an algorithm, i.e., that it is done constructively. Until the 1980s, there was no reason to think that the gap between existential theories and constructive proofs would cause any trouble. Yet now, as a result of the work of Robertson and Seymour, the existential basis of complexity theory has come back to haunt us. Robertson and Seymour, in a long series of highly technical papers, proved that large families of problems are in P without giving actual algorithms for any of these families. Worse, their results are inherently nonconstructive: they

Figure 9.2   A nonplanar graph and its embedded homeomorphic copy of $K_{3,3}$.

cannot be turned uniformly into methods for generating algorithms. Finally, the results are nonconstructive on a second level: membership in some graph family is proved without giving any "natural" evidence that the graph at hand indeed has the required properties. Thus, as mentioned in the introduction, we are now faced with the statement that certain problems are in P, yet we will never find a polynomial-time algorithm to solve any of them, nor would we be able to recognize such an algorithm if we were staring at it. How did this happen and what might we be able to do about it?

A celebrated theorem in graph theory, known as Kuratowski's theorem (see Section 2.4), states that every nonplanar graph contains a homeomorphic copy of either the complete graph on five vertices, K_5, or the complete bipartite graph on six vertices, $K_{3,3}$. Figure 9.2 shows a nonplanar graph and its embedded $K_{3,3}$. Another family of graphs with a similar property is the family of *series-parallel* graphs.

Definition 9.16   An undirected graph G with a distinguished source vertex, s, and a distinguished (and separate) sink vertex, t, is a *series-parallel* graph, written (G, s, t), if it is one of

- the complete graph on the two vertices s and t (i.e., a single edge);
- the series composition of two series-parallel graphs (G_1, s_1, t_1) and (G_2, s_2, t_2), where the composition is obtained by taking the union of the two graphs, merging t_1 with s_2, and designating s_1 to be the source of the result and t_2 its sink; or
- the parallel composition of two series-parallel graphs (G_1, s_1, t_1) and (G_2, s_2, t_2), where the composition is obtained by taking the union of the two graphs, merging s_1 with s_2 and t_1 with t_2, and designating the merged s_1/s_2 vertex to be the source of the result and the merged t_1/t_2 its sink.   □

A fairly simple argument shows that an undirected graph with two distinct vertices designated as source and sink is series-parallel if and only if it does not contain a homeomorphic copy of the graph illustrated in Figure 9.3.

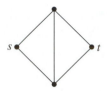

Figure 9.3   The key subgraph for series-parallel graphs.

Homeomorphism allows us to delete edges or vertices from a graph and to contract an edge (that is, to merge its two endpoints); we restate and generalize these operations in the form of a definition.

Definition 9.17 A graph H is a *minor* of a graph G if H can be obtained from G by a sequence of (edge or vertex) deletions and edge contractions.
□

(The generalization is in allowing the contraction of arbitrary edges; homeomorphism allows us to contract only an edge incident upon a vertex of degree 2.) The relation "is a minor of" is easily seen to be reflexive and transitive; in other words, it is a partial order, which justifies writing $H \leq_{minor} G$ when H is a minor of G. Planar graphs are closed under this relation, as any minor of a planar graph is easily seen to be itself planar. Kuratowski's theorem can then be restated as "A graph G is nonplanar if and only if one of the following holds: $K_5 \leq_{minor} G$ or $K_{3,3} \leq_{minor} G$." The key viewpoint on this problem is to realize that the property of planarity, a property that is closed under minor ordering, can be tested by checking whether one of a finite number of specific graphs is a minor of the graph at hand. We call this finite set of specific graphs, $\{K_5, K_{3,3}\}$ in the case of planar graphs, an *obstruction set*. The two great results of Robertson and Seymour can then be stated as follows.

Theorem 9.16

- Families of graphs closed under minor ordering have finite obstruction sets.
- Given graphs G and H, each with $O(n)$ vertices, deciding whether H is a minor of G can be done in $O(n^3)$ time.   □

The first result was conjectured by Wagner as a generalization of Kuratowski's theorem. Its proof by Robertson and Seymour required them to invent and develop an entirely new theory of graph structure; the actual proof of Wagner's conjecture is in the 15th paper in a series of about 20 papers on the topic. (Thus not only does the proof of Wagner's conjecture stand as one of the greatest achievements in mathematics, it also has the more dubious honor of being one of the most complex.) The power of the two results together is best summarized as follows.

Corollary 9.1 Membership in any family of graphs closed under minor ordering can be decided in $O(n^3)$ time.   □

Proof. Since the family of graphs is closed under minor ordering, it has a finite obstruction set, say $\{O_1, O_2, \ldots, O_k\}$. A graph G belongs to the family if and only if it does not contain as a minor any of the O_is. But we can test $O_i \leq_{\text{minor}} G$ in cubic time; after at most k such tests, where k is some fixed constant depending only on the family, we can decide membership.   *Q.E.D.*

The catch is that the Robertson-Seymour Theorem states only that a finite obstruction set *exists* for each family of graphs closed under minor ordering; it does not tell us how to find this set (nor how large it is nor how large its members are). It is thus a purely existential tool for establishing membership in P. (Another, less important, catch is that the constants involved in the cubic-time minor ordering test are gigantic—on the order of 10^{150}.)

A particularly striking example of the power of these tools is the problem known as *Three-Dimensional Knotless Embedding*. An instance of this problem is given by a graph; the question is whether this graph can be embedded in three-dimensional space so as to avoid the creation of knots. (A knot is defined much as you would expect—in particular, two interlinked cycles, as in the links of a chain, form a knot.) Clearly, removing vertices or edges of the graph can only make it easier to embed without knots; contracting an edge cannot hurt either, as a few minutes of thought will confirm. Thus the family of graphs that can be embedded without knots in three-dimensional space is closed under minor ordering—and thus there exists a cubic-time algorithm to decide whether an arbitrary graph can be so embedded. Yet we do not know of any *recursive* test for this problem! Even given a fixed embedding, we do not know how to check it for the presence of knots in polynomial time! Until the Robertson-Seymour theorem, *Three-Dimensional Knotless Embedding* could be thought of as residing in some extremely high class of complexity—if, indeed, it was even recursive. After the Robertson-Seymour theorem, we know that the problem is in P, yet *nothing else has changed*—we still have no decision algorithm for the problem.

At this point, we might simply conclude that it is only a matter of time, now that we know that the problem is solvable in polynomial time, until someone comes up with a polynomial-time algorithm for the problem. And, indeed, such has been the case for several other, less imposing, graph families closed under minor ordering. However, the Robertson-Seymour Theorem is *inherently* nonconstructive.

Theorem 9.17 There is no algorithm that, given a family of graphs closed under minor ordering, would output the obstruction set for the family.   □

Proof. Let $\{\phi_i\}$ be an acceptable programming system. Let $\{G_i\}$ be an enumeration of all graphs such that, if G_i is a minor of G_j, then G_i is enumerated before G_j. (This enumeration always exists, because minor ordering is a partial ordering: a simple topological sort produces an acceptable enumeration.) Define the auxiliary partial function

$$\theta(x) = \mu i[\text{step}(x, x, i) \neq 0]$$

Now define the function

$$f(x, t) = \begin{cases} 1 & \text{step}(x, x, t) = 0 \text{ or } (\theta(x) < t \text{ and } G_{\theta(x)} \npreceq_{\text{minor}} G_t) \\ 0 & \text{otherwise} \end{cases}$$

Observe that f is total, since we guarded the θ test with a test for convergence after t steps.

For each x, the set $S_x = \{G_t \mid f(x, t) = 1\}$ is closed under minor ordering. But now, if x belongs to K, then the set $\{G_{\theta(x)}\}$ is an obstruction set for S_x, whereas, if x does not belong to K, then the obstruction set for S_x is empty. This is a reduction from K to the problem of deciding whether the obstruction set for a family of graphs closed under minor ordering is empty, proving our theorem (since any algorithm able to output the obstruction set can surely decide whether said set is empty).   *Q.E.D.*

Exactly how disturbing is this result? Like all undecidability results, it states only that a single algorithm cannot produce obstruction sets for all graph families of interest. It does not preclude the existence of algorithms that may succeed for some families, nor does it preclude individual attacks for a particular family. Planar graphs and series-parallel graphs remind us that the minor ordering test need not even be the most efficient way of testing membership—we have linear-time algorithms with low coefficients for both problems. So we should view the Robertson-Seymour theorem more as an invitation to the development of new algorithms than as an impractical curiosity or (even worse) as a slap in the face. The undecidability result can be strengthened somewhat to show that there exists at least one fixed family of graphs closed under minor ordering for which the obstruction set is uncomputable; yet, again, this result creates a problem only for those families constructed in the proof (by diagonalization, naturally).

Robertson and Seymour went on to show that other partial orderings on graphs have finite obstruction sets. In particular, they proved the Nash-Williams conjecture: families closed under *immersion ordering* have finite obstruction sets. Immersion ordering is similar to minor ordering, but where minor ordering uses edge contraction, immersion ordering uses *edge lifting*. Given vertices u, v, and w, with edges $\{u, v\}$ and $\{v, w\}$, edge lifting removes the edges $\{u, v\}$ and $\{v, w\}$ and replaces them with the edge $\{u, w\}$. Testing for immersion ordering can also be done in polynomial time.

Corollary 9.2 Membership in a family of graphs closed under immersion ordering can be decided in polynomial time. $\qquad\square$

Indeed, we can completely turn the tables and identify P with the class of problems that have finite obstruction sets with polynomial ordering tests.

Theorem 9.18 A problem Π is in P if and only if there exists a partial ordering $\leq_\Pi$ on the instances of Π such that: (i) given two instances I_1 and I_2, testing $I_1 \leq_\Pi I_2$ can be done in polynomial time; and (ii) the set of "yes" instances of Π is closed under $\leq_\Pi$ and has a finite obstruction set. $\qquad\square$

The "if" part of the proof is trivial; it exploits the finite obstruction set in exactly the same manner as described for the Robertson-Seymour theorem. The "only if" part is harder; yet, because we can afford to define any partial order and matching obstruction set, it is not too hard. The basic idea is to define partial computations of the polynomial-time machine on the "yes" instances and use them to define the partial order.

When we turn to complexity theory, however, the inherently nonconstructive nature of the Robertson-Seymour theorem stands as an indictment of a theory based on existential arguments. While the algorithm designer can ignore the fact that some graph families closed under minors may not ever become decidable in practice, the theoretician has no such luxury. The existence of problems in P for which no algorithm can ever be found goes against the very foundations of complexity theory, which has always equated membership in P with tractability. This view was satisfactory as long as this membership was demonstrated constructively; however, the use of the existential quantifier is now "catching up" with the algorithm community. The second level of nonconstructiveness—the lack of natural evidence—is something we already discussed: how do we trust an algorithm that provides only one-bit answers? Even when the answer is uniformly "yes," natural evidence may be hard to come by. For instance, although we know that all planar graphs are four-colorable and can check planarity in linear time, we remain unable to find a four-coloring in low polynomial time. Robertson and Seymour's results further emphasize the distinction between deciding a problem and obtaining natural evidence for it.

These considerations motivate the definition of *constructive* classes of complexity. We briefly discuss one such definition, based on the relationships among the three aspects of a decision problem: evidence checking, decision, and searching (or construction). In a relational setting, all three versions of a problem admit a simple formulation; for a fixed relation $R \subseteq \Sigma^* \times \Sigma^*$, we can write:

- *Checking*: Given (x, y), does (x, y) belong to R?
- *Deciding*: Given x, does there exist a y such that (x, y) belongs to R?
- *Searching*: Given x, find a y such that (x, y) belongs to R.

The basic idea is to let each problem be equipped with its own set of *allowable* proofs; moreover, in deterministic classes, the proof itself should be constructible. As in classical complexity theory, we use checkers and evidence generators (provers), but we now give the checker as part of the problem specification rather than let it be specified as part of the solution.

Definition 9.18 A decision problem is a pair $\Pi = (I, M)$, where I is a set of instances and M is a checker. □

The checker M defines a relation between yes instances and acceptable evidence for them. Since only problems for which a checker can be specified are allowed, this definition sidesteps existence problems; it also takes us tantalizingly close to proof systems.

Solving a constructive problem entails two steps: generating suitable evidence and then checking the answer with the help of the evidence. Thus the complexity of such problems is simply the complexity of their search and checking components.

Definition 9.19 A *constructive complexity class* is a pair of classical complexity classes, $(\mathcal{C}_1, \mathcal{C}_2)$, where $\mathcal{C}_1$ denotes the resource bounds within which the evidence generator must run and $\mathcal{C}_2$ the bounds for the checker. Resource bounds are defined with respect to the classical statement of the problem, i.e., with respect to the size of the domain elements. □

For instance, we define the class P_c to be the pair (P, P), thus requiring both generator and checker to run in polynomial time; in other words, P_c is the class of all P-checkable and P-searchable relations. In contrast, we define NP_c simply as the class of all P-checkable relations, placing no constraints on the generation of evidence.

Definition 9.20 A problem (I, M) belongs to a class $(\mathcal{C}_1, \mathcal{C}_2)$ if and only if the relation defined by M on I is both $\mathcal{C}_1$-searchable and $\mathcal{C}_2$-checkable. □

These general definitions serve only as guidelines in defining interesting constructive complexity classes. Early results in the area indicate that the concept is well founded and can generate new results.

9.7 Bibliography

Complexity cores were introduced by Lynch [1975], who stated and proved Theorem 9.1; they were further studied by Orponen and Schöning [1984], who proved Theorem 9.2. Hartmanis [1983] first used descriptional complexity in the analysis of computational complexity; combining the two approaches to define the complexity of a single instance was proposed by Ko *et al.* [1986], whose article contains all of the propositions and theorems following Theorem 9.4. Chaitin [1990a,1990b] introduced and developed the theory of algorithmic information theory, based on what we termed descriptional complexity; Li and Vitányi [1993] give a thorough treatment of descriptional complexity and its various connections to complexity theory.

Our treatment of average-case complexity theory is principally inspired by Wang [1997]. The foundations of the theory, including Definitions 9.4 and 9.8, a partial version of Theorem 9.7, and a proof that a certain tiling problem is NP-complete in average instance (a much harder proof than that of Theorem 9.8), were laid by Levin [1984], in a notorious one-page paper! The term "distributional problem" and the class name DISTNP first appeared in the work of Ben-David *et al.* [1989]. That backtracking for graph coloring runs in constant average time was shown by Wilf [1984]. Blass and Gurevich [1993] used randomized reductions to prove DISTNP-completeness for a number of problems, including several problems with matrices. Wang maintains a Web page about average-case complexity theory at URL www.uncg.edu/mat/avg.html.

Cook [1981] surveyed the applications of complexity theory to parallel architectures; in particular, he discussed at some length a number of models of parallel computation, including PRAMs, circuits, conglomerates, and aggregates. The parallel computation thesis is generally attributed to Goldschlager [1982]. Kindervater and Lenstra [1986] survey parallelism as applied to combinatorial algorithms; they briefly discuss theoretical issues but concentrated on the practical implications of the theory. Karp and Ramachandran [1990] give an excellent survey of parallel algorithms and models, while Culler *et al.* [1993] present an altered version of the standard PRAM model that takes into account the cost of communication. The circuit model has a well-developed theory of its own, for which see Savage [1976]; its application to modeling parallel machines was suggested by Borodin [1977], who also discussed the role of uniformity. Theorem 9.9 is from this latter paper (and some of its references). Pippenger [1979] introduced the concept of simultaneous resource bounds. Ruzzo [1981] provided a wealth of information on the role of uniformity and the relationships among various classes defined by simultaneous resource bounds; he also gave a number of equivalent characterizations of the class NC. Cook [1985] gave a detailed survey of the class NC and presented many interesting examples. JáJá [1992] devoted a couple of chapters to parallel complexity theory, while Parberry [1987] devoted an entire textbook to it; both discuss NC and RNC. Diaz et al. [1997] study the use of parallelism in approximating P-hard problems. Allender [1986], among others, advocated the use of P-uniformity rather than L-uniformity in defining resource bounds. Our definition of communication complexity is derived from Yao [1979]; Papadimitriou and Sipser [1984] discussed the power of nondeterminism in communication as well as other issues; Theorems 9.10 through 9.12 are from their article. A thorough treatment of the area can be found in the monograph of Kushilevitz and Nisan [1996].

Interactive proofs were first suggested by Babai [1985] (who proposed Arthur-Merlin games) and Goldwasser et al. [1985], who defined the class IP. The example of graph nonisomorphism is due to Goldreich et al. [1986]. Theorem 9.13 is due to Shamir [1990], who used the arithmetization developed by Lund et al. [1992], where the proof of Lemma 9.2 can be found; our proof sketch follows the simplified proof given by Shen [1992]. The proof that IP^A differs from $PSPACE^A$ with probability 1 with respect to a random oracle A is due to Chang et al. [1994]. Zero-knowledge proofs were introduced in the same article of Goldwasser et al. [1985]; Theorem 9.14, in its version for NP, is from Goldreich et al. [1986], while the extension to PSPACE can be found in Ben-Or et al. [1990]. Goldreich and Oren [1994] give a detailed technical discussion of zero-knowledge proofs. Goldreich [1988] and Goldwasser [1989] have published surveys of the area of interactive proof systems, while Goldreich maintains pointers and several excellent overview papers at his Web site (URL theory.lcs.mit.edu/~oded/pps.html). The PCP theorem (Theorem 9.15) is from Arora et al. [1992], building on the work of Arora and Safra [1992] (who showed $NP = PCP(O(\log n), O(\log n))$ and proved several pivotal inapproximability results). Goldreich's "Taxonomy of Proof Systems" (one of the overview papers available on-line) includes a comprehensive history of the development of the PCP theorem.

The theory of graph minors has been developed in a series of over twenty highly technical papers by Robertson and Seymour, most of which have appeared in *J. Combinatorial Theory, Series B*, starting in 1983. This series surely stands as one of the greatest achievements in mathematics in the twentieth century; it will continue to influence theoretical computer science well beyond that time. Readable surveys of early results are offered by the same authors (Robertson and Seymour [1985]) and in one of Johnson's columns [1987]. Fellows and Langston [1988,1989] have pioneered the connections of graph minors to the theory of algorithms and to complexity theory; together with Abrahamson and Moret, they also proposed a framework for a constructive theory of complexity (Abrahamson *et al.* [1991]). The proof that the theory of graph minors is inherently nonconstructive is due to Friedman *et al.* [1987].

To explore some of the topics listed in the introduction to this chapter, the reader should start with the text of Papadimitriou [1994]. Structure theory is the subject of the two-volume text of Balcázar *et al.* [1988,1990]. Köbler *et al.* [1993] wrote a monograph on the complexity of the graph isomorphism problem, illustrating the type of work that can be done for problems that appear to be intractable yet easier than NP-hard problems. Downey and Fellows [1997] are completing a monograph on the topic of fixed-parameter complexity and its extension to parameterized complexity theory; an introduction appears in Downey and Fellows [1995]. Computational learning theory is best followed through the proceedings of the COLT conference; a good introduction can be found in the monograph of Kearns and Vazirani [1994]. As we have seen, complexity theory is concerned only with quantities that can be represented on a reasonable model of computation. However, many mathematicians and physicists are accustomed to manipulating real numbers and find the restriction to discrete quantities to be too much of an impediment, while appreciating the power of an approach based on resource usage. Thus many efforts have been made to develop a theory of computational complexity that would apply to the reals and not just to countable sets; interesting articles in this area include Blum *et al.* [1989] and Ko [1983].

REFERENCES

Abrahamson, K., M.R. Fellows, M.A. Langston, and B.M.E. Moret [1991], "Constructive complexity," *Discr. Appl. Math.* **34**, 3–16.

Ackermann, W. [1928], "Zum Hilbertschen Aufbau der reellen Zahlen," *Mathematische Annalen* **99**, 118–133.

Aho, A.V., J.E. Hopcroft, and J.D. Ullman [1974]. *The Design and Analysis of Algorithms.* Addison-Wesley, Reading, MA.

Allender, E. [1986], "Characterizations of PUNC and precomputation," Lecture Notes in Comput. Sci., Vol. 226, Springer Verlag, Berlin, 1–10.

Arora, S., and C. Lund [1996], "Hardness of approximation," in *Approximation Algorithms for NP-Hard Problems*, D.S. Hochbaum, ed., PWS Publishing Co., Boston, 399–446.

Arora, S., C. Lund, R. Motwani, M. Sudan, and M. Szegedy [1992], "Proof verification and hardness of approximation problems," Proc. 33rd IEEE Symp. Foundations Comput. Sci., 14–23.

Arora, S., and S. Safra [1992], "Probabilistic checkable proofs: a new characterization of NP," Proc. 33rd IEEE Symp. Foundations Comput. Sci., 1–13.

Ausiello, G., A. Marchetti-Spaccamela, and M. Protasi [1980], "Towards a unified approach for the classification of NP-complete optimization problems," *Theor. Comput. Sci.* **12**, 83–96.

Ausiello, G., P. Crescenzi, and M. Protasi [1995], "Approximate solution of NP optimization problems," *Theor. Comput. Sci.* **150**, 1–55.

Babai, L. [1985], "Trading group theory for randomness," Proc. 17th Ann. ACM Symp. Theory Comput., 411–420.

Baker, B.S. [1994], "Approximation algorithms for NP-complete problems on planar graphs," *J. ACM* **41**, 153–180.

Balcázar, J.L., J. Diaz, and J. Gabarró [1988]. *Structural Complexity I.* EATCS Monographs on Theoretical Computer Science Vol. 11, Springer Verlag, Berlin.

Balcázar, J.L., J. Diaz, and J. Gabarró [1990]. *Structural Complexity II.* EATCS Monographs on Theoretical Computer Science Vol. 22, Springer Verlag, Berlin.

Balcázar, J.L., A. Lozano, and J. Torán [1992], "The complexity of algorithmic problems in succinct instances," in *Computer Science*, R. Baeza-Yates and U. Manber, eds., Plenum Press, New York.

Bar-Hillel, Y., M. Perles, and E. Shamir [1961], "On formal properties of simple phrase structure grammars," *Z. Phonetik. Sprachwiss. Kommunikationforsch.* **14**, 143–172.

Ben-David, S., B. Chor, O. Goldreich, and M. Luby [1989], "On the theory of average case complexity," Proc. 21st Ann. ACM Symp. Theory Comput., 204–216; also in final form in *J. Comput. Syst. Sci.* **44** (1992), 193–219.

Ben-Or, M., O. Goldreich, S. Goldwasser, J. Håstad, J. Kilian, S. Micali, and P. Rogaway [1990], "Everything provable is probable in zero-knowledge," Lecture Notes in Comput. Sci., Vol. 403, Springer Verlag, Berlin, 37–56.

Blass, A., and Y. Gurevich [1982], "On the unique satisfiability problem," *Inform. and Control* **55**, 80–88.

Blass, A., and Y. Gurevich [1993], "Randomizing reductions of search problems," *SIAM J. Comput.* **22**, 949–975.

Blum, L., M. Shub, and S. Smale [1989], "On a theory of computation and complexity over the real numbers: NP-completeness, recursive functions and universal machines," *Bull. Amer. Math. Soc.* **21**, 1–46.

Blum, M. [1967], "A machine-independent theory of the complexity of recursive functions," *J. ACM* **14**, 322–336.

Blum, M., A.K. Chandra, and M.N. Wegman [1980], "Equivalence of free Boolean graphs can be decided probabilistically in polynomial time," *Inf. Proc. Lett.* **10**, 80–82.

Bondy, J.A., and U.S.R. Murty [1976]. *Graph Theory with Applications.* North-Holland, New York (1979 printing).

Book, R.V. [1976], "Translational lemmas, polynomial time, and $(\log n)^j$-space," *Theor. Comput. Sci.* **1**, 215–226.

Borodin, A. [1977], "On relating time and space to size and depth," *SIAM J. Comput.* **6**, 4, 733–744.

Bovet, D.P., and P. Crescenzi [1993]. *Introduction to the Theory of Complexity.* Prentice-Hall, Englewood Cliffs, NJ.

Brassard, G., and P. Bratley [1996]. *Fundamentals of Algorithmics.* Prentice-Hall, Englewood Cliffs, NJ.

Brooks, R.L. [1941], "On coloring the nodes of a network," *Proc. Cambridge Philos. Soc.* **37**, 194–197.

Brzozowski, J.A. [1962], "A survey of regular expressions and their applications," *IEEE Trans. on Electronic Computers* **11**, 3, 324–335.

Brzozowski, J.A. [1964], "Derivatives of regular expressions," *J. ACM* **11**, 4, 481–494.

Chaitin, G. [1990a], *Algorithmic Information Theory*. Cambridge University Press, Cambridge, UK.

Chaitin, G. [1990b], *Information, Randomness, and Incompleteness*. World Scientific Publishing, Singapore.

Chang, R., B. Chor, O. Goldreich, J. Hartmanis, J. Håstad, D. Ranjan, and P. Rohatgi [1994], "The random oracle hypothesis is false," *J. Comput. Syst. Sci.* **49**, 24–39.

Chomsky, N. [1956], "Three models for a description of a language," *IRE Trans. on Information Theory* **2**, 3, 113–124.

Cobham, A. [1965], "The intrinsic computational difficulty of functions," Proc. 1964 Int'l Congress for Logic, Methodology, and Philosophy of Science, Y. Bar-Hillel, ed., North-Holland, Amsterdam (1965), 24–30.

Cook, S.A. [1970], "Path systems and language recognition," Proc. 2nd Ann. ACM Symp. on Theory of Computing, 70–72.

Cook, S.A. [1971a], "The complexity of theorem proving procedures," Proc. 3rd Ann. ACM Symp. on Theory of Computing, 151–158.

Cook, S.A. [1971b], "Characterizations of pushdown machines in terms of time-bounded computers," *J. ACM* **18**, 4–18.

Cook, S.A. [1973], "A hierarchy for nondeterministic time complexity," *J. Comput. Syst. Sci.* **7**, 343–353.

Cook, S.A. [1974], "An observation on time-storage tradeoff," *J. Comput. Syst. Sci.* **9**, 308–316.

Cook, S.A. [1981], "Towards a complexity theory of synchronous parallel computation," *L'Enseignement Mathématique* **XXVII**, 99–124.

Cook, S.A. [1983], "An overview of computational complexity" (ACM Turing award lecture), *Commun. ACM* **26**, 400–408.

Cook, S.A. [1985], "A taxonomy of problems with fast parallel algorithms," *Inform. and Control* **64**, 2–22.

Crescenzi, P., and A. Panconesi [1991], "Completeness in approximation classes," *Inf. and Comput.* **93**, 241–262.

Culler, D., R. Karp, D. Patterson, A. Sahay, K.E. Schauser, E. Santos, R. Subramonian, and T. von Eicken [1993], "LogP: towards a realistic model of parallel computation," Proc. 4th ACM SIGPLAN Symp. on Principles and Practice of Parallel Programming.

Cutland, N.J. [1980]. *Computability: An Introduction to Recursive Function Theory*. Cambridge University Press, Cambridge, UK.

Davis, M. [1958]. *Computability and Unsolvability*. McGraw-Hill, New York; reprinted in 1982 by Dover, New York.

Davis, M. [1965], ed. *The Undecidable*. Raven Press, New York.

Diaz, J., M.J. Serna, P. Spirakis, and J. Toran [1997]. *Paradigms for Fast Parallel Approximability*. Cambridge University Press, Cambridge, UK.

Dinic, E.A., and A.V. Karzanov [1978], "A Boolean optimization problem under restrictions of one symbol," VNIISI Moskva (preprint).

Dinitz, Y. [1997], "Constant absolute error approximation algorithm for the 'safe deposit boxes' problem," Tech. Rep. CS0913, Dept. of Comput. Sci., Technion, Haifa, Israel.

Downey, R.G., and M.R. Fellows [1995], "Fixed-parameter tractability and completeness I: the basic theory," *SIAM J. Comput.* **24**, 873–921.

Downey, R.G., and M.R. Fellows [1997]. *Parameterized Complexity*. Springer Verlag, Berlin (to appear).

Dyer, M.E., and A.M. Frieze [1986], "Planar 3DM is NP-complete," *J. Algs.* **7**, 174–184.

Edmonds, J. [1965], "Paths, trees, and flowers," *Can. J. Math.* **17**, 449–467.

Epp, S.S. [1995]. *Discrete Mathematics with Applications*. PWS Publishing, Boston (2nd ed.).

Epstein, R.L., and W.A. Carnielli [1989]. *Computability: Computable Functions, Logic, and the Foundations of Mathematics*. Wadsworth and Brooks/Cole, Pacific Grove, CA.

Even, S., and Y. Yacobi [1980], "Cryptography and NP-completeness," Lecture Notes in Comput. Sci., Vol. 85, Springer Verlag, Berlin, 195–207.

Fellows, M.R., and M.A. Langston [1988], "Nonconstructive tools for proving polynomial-time decidability," *J. ACM* **35**, 727–739.

Fellows, M.R., and M.A. Langston [1989], "On search, decision, and the efficiency of polynomial-time algorithms," Proc. 21st Ann. ACM Symp. on Theory of Comp., 501–512.

Friedman H., N. Robertson, and P. Seymour [1987], "The metamathematics of the graph-minor theorem," *AMS Contemporary Math. Series* **65**, 229–261.

Fürer, M., and B. Raghavachari [1992], "Approximating the minimum-degree spanning tree to within one from the optimal degree," Proc. 3rd Ann. ACM-SIAM Symp. Discrete Algorithms, 317–324.

Fürer, M., and B. Raghavachari [1994], "Approximating the minimum-degree Steiner tree to within one of optimal," *J. Algorithms* **17**, 409–423.

Galperin, H., and A. Widgerson [1983], "Succinct representations of graphs," *Inform. and Control* **56**, 183–198.

Garey, M.R., and D.S. Johnson [1978], "Strong NP-completeness results: motivation, examples, and implications," *J. ACM* **25**, 499–508.

Garey, M.R., and D.S. Johnson [1979]. *Computers and Intractability: a Guide to the Theory of NP-Completeness*. W.H. Freeman, San Francisco.

Garey, M.R., D.S. Johnson, and R.E. Tarjan [1976], "The planar Hamilton circuit problem is NP-complete," *SIAM J. Comput.* **5**, 704–714.

Gens, G.V., and E.V. Levner [1979], "Computational complexity of approximation algorithms for combinatorial problems," Lecture Notes in Comput. Sci., Vol. 74, Springer Verlag, Berlin, 292–300.

Gersting, J.L. [1993]. *Mathematical Structures for Computer Science*. Computer Science Press, New York (3rd ed.).

Gibbons, A. [1985]. *Algorithmic Graph Theory*. Cambridge University Press, Cambridge, UK.

Gill, J. [1977], "Computational complexity of probabilistic Turing machines," *SIAM J. Comput.* **6**, 675–695.

Ginsburg, S., and E.H. Spanier [1963], "Quotients of context-free languages," *J. ACM* **10**, 4, 487–492.

Gödel, K. [1931], "Über formal unentscheidbare Sätze der Principia Mathematica und verwandter Systeme, I," *Monatshefte für Math. und Physik* **38**, 173–198.

Goldreich, O. [1988], "Randomness, interactive proofs, and zero knowledge: a survey," in *The Universal Turing Machine: A Half-Century Survey*, R. Herken, ed., Oxford University Press, Oxford, 377–405.

Goldreich, O., S. Micali, and A. Widgerson [1986], "Proofs that yield nothing but their validity or all languages in NP have zero-knowledge proof systems," Proc. 27th IEEE Symp. Foundations Comput. Sci., 174–187; also in final form in *J. ACM* **38** (1991), 691–729.

Goldreich, O., and Y. Oren [1994], "Definitions and properties of zero-knowledge proof systems," *J. Cryptology* **7**, 1–32.

Goldschlager, L.M. [1982], "A universal interconnection pattern for parallel computers," *J. ACM* **29**, 1073–1086.

Goldwasser, S. [1989], "Interactive proof systems," in *Computational Complexity Theory*, Vol. 38 in Proc. Symp. Applied Math., AMS, 108–128.

Goldwasser, S., S. Micali, and C. Rackoff [1985], "The knowledge complexity of interactive proof systems," Proc. 17th Ann. ACM Symp. on Theory of Comp., 291–304; also in final form in *SIAM J. Comput.* **18** (1989), 186–208.

Golumbic, M.C. [1980]. *Algorithmic Graph Theory and Perfect Graphs*. Academic Press, New York.

Greenlaw, R., H.J. Hoover, and W.L. Ruzzo [1995]. *Limits to Parallel Computation: P-Completeness Theory*. Oxford University Press, New York.

Grzegorczyk, A. [1953], "Some classes of recursive functions," *Rozprawy Matematyczne* **4**, 1–45.

Groetschel, M., Lovasz, L., and A. Schrijver [1981], "The ellipsoid method and its consequences in combinatorial optimization," *Combinatorica* **1**, 169–197.

Harrison, M. [1978]. *Introduction to Formal Language Theory*. Addison-Wesley, Reading, MA.

Hartmanis, J. [1968], "Computational complexity of one-tape Turing machine computations," *J. ACM* **15**, 325–339.

Hartmanis, J. [1978]. *Feasible Computations and Provable Complexity Properties*. CBMS-NSF Regional Conf. Series in Appl. Math., Vol 30, SIAM Press, Philadelphia.

Hartmanis, J. [1983], "Generalized Kolmogorov complexity and the structure of feasible computations," Proc. 24th IEEE Symp. Foundations Comput. Sci., 439–445.

Hartmanis, J., P.M. Lewis II, and R.E. Stearns [1965], "Hierarchies of memory-limited computations," Proc. 6th Ann. IEEE Symp. on Switching Circuit Theory and Logical Design, 179–190.

Hartmanis, J., and R.E. Stearns [1965], "On the computational complexity of algorithms," *Trans. AMS* **117**, 285–306.

Hochbaum, D.S., and W. Maass [1985], "Approximation schemes for covering and packing problems in image processing," *J. ACM* **32**, 130–136.

Hochbaum, D.S. [1996], "Various notions of approximations: good, better, best, and more," in *Approximation Algorithms for NP-Hard Problems*, D.S. Hochbaum, ed., PWS Publishing Co., Boston, 346–398.

Holyer, I.J. [1980], "The NP-completeness of edge colorings," *SIAM J. Comput.* **10**, 718-720.

Hopcroft, J.E., and R.E. Tarjan [1974], "Efficient planarity testing," *J. ACM* **21**, 549–568.

Hopcroft, J.E., and J.D. Ullman [1979]. *Introduction to Automata Theory, Languages, and Computations*. Addison-Wesley, Reading, MA.

Huffman, D.A. [1954], "The synthesis of sequential switching circuits," *J. Franklin Institute* **257**, 161–190 and 275–303.

Ibarra, O.H., and C.E. Kim [1975], "Fast approximation algorithms for the knapsack and sum of subsets problems," *J. ACM* **22**, 463–468.

Immerman, N. [1988], "Nondeterministic space is closed under complementation," *SIAM J. Comput.* **17**, 935–938.

JáJá, J. [1992]. *Introduction to Parallel Algorithms.* Addison-Wesley, Reading, MA.

Johnson, D.S. [1974], "Approximation algorithms for combinatorial problems," *J. Comput. Syst. Sci.* **9**, 256–278.

Johnson, D.S. [1984], "The NP-completeness column: an ongoing guide," *J. of Algorithms* **5**, 433–447.

Johnson, D.S. [1985], "The NP-completeness column: an ongoing guide," *J. of Algorithms* **6**, 291–305.

Johnson, D.S. [1987], "The NP-completeness column: an ongoing guide," *J. of Algorithms* **8**, 285–303.

Johnson, D.S. [1990], "A catalog of complexity classes," in *Handbook of Theoretical Computer Science, Volume A: Algorithms and Complexity,* van Leeuwen, J., ed., MIT Press, Cambridge, MA, 67–161.

Jones, N.D. [1975], "Space-bounded reducibility among combinatorial problems," *J. Comput. Syst. Sci.* **11**, 68–85.

Jones, N.D., and W.T. Laaser [1976], "Complete problems for deterministic polynomial time," *Theor. Comput. Sci.* **3**, 105–117.

Jones, N.D., Y.E. Lien, and W.T. Laaser [1976], "New problems complete for nondeterministic log space," *Math. Syst. Theory* **10**, 1–17.

Jordan, T. [1995], "On the optimal vertex connectivity augmentation," *J. Combin. Theory series B* **63**, 8–20.

Karp, R.M. [1972], "Reducibility among combinatorial problems," in *Complexity of Computer Computations*, R.E. Miller and J.W. Thatcher, eds., Plenum Press, New York, 85–104.

Karp, R.M., and V. Ramachandran [1990], "Parallel algorithms for shared-memory machines," in *Handbook of Theoretical Computer Science, Volume A: Algorithms and Complexity,* van Leeuwen, J., ed., MIT Press, Cambridge, MA, 869–941.

Kearns, M.J., and U.V. Vazirani [1994]. *An Introduction to Computational Learning Theory.* MIT Press, Cambridge, MA.

Khachian, L.G. [1979], "A polynomial time algorithm for linear programming," *Doklady Akad. Nauk SSSR* **244**, 1093–1096. Translated in *Soviet Math. Doklady* **20**, 191–194.

Khanna, S., R. Motwani, M. Sudan, and U. Vazirani [1994], "On syntactic versus computational views of approximability," Proc. 35th IEEE Symp. Foundations Comput. Sci., 819–836.

Kindervater, G.A.P., and J.K. Lenstra [1986], "An introduction to parallelism in combinatorial optimization," *Discrete Appl. Math.* **14**, 135–156.

Kleene, S.C. [1936], "General recursive functions of natural numbers," *Mathematische Annalen* **112**, 727–742.

Kleene, S.C. [1952]. *Introduction to Metamathematics*. North-Holland, Amsterdam.

Kleene, S.C. [1956], "Representation of events in nerve nets and finite automata," in *Automata Studies*, Princeton Univ. Press, Princeton, NJ, 3–42.

Ko, K.I. [1982], "Some observations on the probabilistic algorithms and NP-hard problems," *Inf. Proc. Letters* **14**, 39–43.

Ko, K.I. [1983], "On the definitions of some complexity classes of real numbers," *Math. Syst. Theory* **16**, 95–109.

Ko, K.I, P. Orponen, U. Schöning, and O. Watanabe [1986], "What is a hard instance of a computational problem?" Lecture Notes in Comput. Sci., Vol. 223, Springer Verlag, Berlin, 197–217.

Köbler, J, U. Schöning, and J. Torán [1993]. *The Graph Isomorphism Problem: Its Structural Complexity*. Birkäuser, Boston.

Korte, B., and R. Schrader [1981], "On the existence of fast approximation schemes," in *Nonlinear Programming*, Academic Press, New York, 353–366.

Krentel, M. [1988a], "The complexity of optimization problems," *J. Comput. Syst. Sci.* **36**, 490–509.

Krentel, M. [1988b], "Generalizations of OptP to the polynomial hierarchy," TR88-79, Dept. of Comput. Sci., Rice University, Houston.

Kuratowski, K. [1930], "Sur le problème des courbes gauches en topologie," *Fund. Math.* **15**, 271–283.

Kushilevitz, E., and N. Nisan [1996]. *Communication Complexity*. Cambridge University Press, Cambridge, UK.

Lageweg, B.J., E.L. Lawler, J.K. Lenstra, and A.H.G. Rinnooy Kan [1982], "Computer-aided complexity classification of combinatorial problems," *Commun. ACM* **25**, 817–822.

Lawler, E. [1977], "Fast approximation algorithms for knapsack problems," Proc. 18th Ann. IEEE Symp. Foundations Comput. Sci., 206–213; also in final form in *Math. Op. Res.* **4** (1979), 339–356.

Lautemann, C. [1983], "BPP and the polynomial hierarchy," *Inf. Proc. Letters* **17**, 215–217.

Leggett, E.W. Jr., and D.J. Moore [1981], "Optimization problems and the polynomial hierarchy," *Theoret. Comput. Sci.* **15**, 279–289.

Levin, L.A. [1973], "Universal sorting problems," *Prob. of Inform. Trans.* **9**, 265–266.

Levin, L.A. [1984], "Average case complete problems," Proc. 16th Ann. ACM Symp. Theory Comput., 465; also in final form in *SIAM J. Comput.* **15** (1986), 285–286.

Li, M., and P.M.B. Vitányi [1993]. *An Introduction to Kolmogorov Complexity and its Applications.* Springer Verlag, Berlin.

Lichtenstein, D. [1982], "Planar formulae and their uses," *SIAM J. Comput.* **11**, 329–343.

Lieberherr, K.J. [1980], "P-optimal heuristics," *Theor. Comput. Sci.* **10**, 123–131.

Lund, C., L. Fortnow, H. Karloff, and N. Nisan [1992], "Algebraic methods for interactive proof systems," *J. ACM* **39**, 859–868.

Lynch, N. [1975], "On reducibility to complex or sparse sets," *J. ACM* **22**, 341–345.

McCulloch, W.S., and W. Pitts [1943], "A logical calculus of the ideas immanent in nervous activity," *Bull. Math. Biophysics* **5**, 115–133.

Machtey, M., and P. Young [1978]. *An Introduction to the General Theory of Algorithms.* North Holland, Amsterdam.

Maffioli, F. [1986], "Randomized algorithms in combinatorial optimization: a survey," *Discrete Appl. Math.* **14**, 157–170.

Mealy, G.H. [1955], "A method for synthesizing sequential circuits," *Bell System Technical J.* **34**, 5, 1045–1079.

Meyer, A.R. [1975], "Weak monadic second order theory of successor is not elementary recursive," Lecture Notes in Mathematics, Vol. 453, Springer Verlag, Berlin, 132–154.

Miller, G.L. [1976], "Riemann's hypothesis and tests for primality," *J. Comput. Syst. Sci.* **13**, 300–317.

Moore, E.F. [1956], "Gedanken experiments on sequential machines," in *Automata Studies*, Princeton University Press, Princeton, NJ, 129–153.

Moret, B.M.E. [1982], "Decision trees and diagrams," *ACM Comput. Surveys* **14**, 593–623.

Moret, B.M.E. [1988], "Planar NAE3SAT is in P," *SIGACT News* **19**, 51–54.

Moret, B.M.E., and H.D. Shapiro [1985], "Using symmetry and rigidity: a simpler approach to basic NP-completeness proofs," University of New Mexico Tech. Rep. CS85-8.

Moret, B.M.E., and H.D. Shapiro [1991]. *Algorithms from P to NP. Volume I: Design and Efficiency.* Benjamin-Cummings, Redwood City, CA.

Motwani, R., J. Naor, and P. Raghavan [1996], "Randomized approximation algorithms in combinatorial optimization," in *Approximation*

Algorithms for NP-Hard Problems, D.S. Hochbaum, ed., PWS Publishing Co., Boston, 447–481.

Motwani, R., and P. Raghavan [1995]. *Randomized Algorithms*. Cambridge University Press, New York.

Nigmatullin, R.G. [1975], "Complexity of the approximate solution of combinatorial problems," *Doklady Akademii Nauk SSSR* **224**, 289–292 (in Russian).

Odifreddi, P. [1989]. *Classical Recursion Theory*. North-Holland, Amsterdam.

Orponen, P., and U. Schöning [1984], "The structure of polynomial complexity cores," Lecture Notes in Comput. Sci., Vol. 176, Springer Verlag, Berlin, 452–458.

Papadimitriou, C.H. [1984], "On the complexity of unique solutions," *J. ACM* **31**, 392–400.

Papadimitriou, C.H. [1994]. *Computational Complexity*. Addison-Wesley, Reading, MA.

Papadimitriou, C.H., and M. Sipser [1984], "Communication complexity," *J. Comput. Syst. Sci.* **28**, 260–269.

Papadimitriou, C.H., and K. Steiglitz [1982]. *Combinatorial Optimization: Algorithms and Complexity*. Prentice-Hall, Englewood Cliffs, N.J.

Papadimitriou, C.H., and D. Wolfe [1988], "The complexity of facets resolved," *J. Comput. Syst. Sci.* **37**, 2–13.

Papadimitriou, C.H., and M. Yannakakis [1984], "The complexity of facets (and some facets of complexity)," Proc. 26th Ann. IEEE Symp. Foundations Comput. Sci., 74–78; also in final form in *J. Comput. Syst. Sci.* **28** (1988), 244–259.

Papadimitriou, C.H., and M. Yannakakis [1988], "Optimization, approximation, and complexity classes," Proc. 20th Ann. ACM Symp. Theory Comput., 229–234; also in final form in *J. Comput. Syst. Sci.* **43** (1991), 425–440.

Parberry, I. [1987]. *Parallel Complexity Theory*. Pitman, London.

Paz, A., and S. Moran [1977], "Nondeterministic polynomial optimization problems and their approximation," Lecture Notes in Comput. Sci., Vol. 52, Springer Verlag, Berlin, 370–379; an expanded version appears in *Theoret. Comput. Sci.* **15** (1981), 251–277.

Péter, R. [1967]. *Recursive Functions*. Academic Press, New York.

Pippenger, N.J. [1979], "On simultaneous resource bounds," Proc. 20th Ann. IEEE Symp. Foundations Comput. Sci., 307–311.

Pippenger, N.J. [1997]. *Theories of Computability*. Cambridge University Press, Cambridge, UK.

Pratt, V. [1975], "Every prime has a succinct certificate," *SIAM J. Comput.* **4**, 214–220.

Provan, J.S. [1986], "The complexity of reliability computations in planar and acyclic graphs," *SIAM J. Comput.* **15**, 694–702.

Rabin, M.O., and D. Scott [1959], "Finite automata and their decision problems," *IBM J. Res.* **3**, 2, 115–125.

Robertson, N., and P. Seymour [1985], "Graph minors—a survey," in *Surveys in Combinatorics*, J. Anderson, ed., Cambridge University Press, Cambridge, UK, 153–171.

Rogers, H., Jr. [1987]. *Theory of Recursive Functions and Effective Computability.* MIT Press (reprint of the 1967 original), Cambridge, MA.

Rosen, K.H. [1988]. *Discrete Mathematics and Its Applications.* Random House, New York.

Ruby, S., and P.C. Fischer [1965], "Translational methods and computational complexity," Proc. 6th Ann. IEEE Symp. on Switching Circuit Theory and Logical Design, 173–178.

Ruzzo, W.L. [1981], "On uniform circuit complexity," *J. Comput. Syst. Sci.* **22**, 365–383.

Sahni, S. [1975], "Approximate algorithms for the 0/1 knapsack problem," *J. ACM* **22**, 115–124.

Sahni, S. [1981]. *Concepts in Discrete Mathematics.* Camelot Publishing Co., Fridley, MI.

Sahni, S., and T. Gonzalez [1976], "P-complete approximation problems," *J. ACM* **23**, 555–565.

Salomaa, A. [1973]. *Formal Languages.* Academic Press, New York.

Savage, J.E. [1976]. *The Complexity of Computing.* John Wiley, New York.

Savitch, W.J. [1970], "Relationship between nondeterministic and deterministic tape complexities," *J. Comput. Syst. Sci.* **4**, 177–192.

Schonhage, A. [1980], "Storage modification machines," *SIAM J. Comput.* **9**, 490–508.

Seiferas, J.I. [1977], "Techniques for separating space complexity classes," *J. Comput. Syst. Sci.* **14**, 73–99.

Seiferas, J.I. [1990], "Machine-independent complexity theory," in *Handbook of Theoretical Computer Science, Volume A: Algorithms and Complexity,* van Leeuwen, J., ed., MIT Press, Cambridge, MA, 165–186.

Seiferas, J.I., M.J. Fischer, and A.R. Meyer [1973], "Refinements of nondeterministic time and space hierarchies," Proc. 14th Ann. IEEE Symp. Switching and Automata Theory, 130–137.

Seiferas, J.I., M.J. Fischer, and A.R. Meyer [1978], "Separating nondeterministic time complexity classes," *J. ACM* **25**, 146–167.

Seiferas, J.I., and R. McNaughton [1976], "Regularity-preserving reductions," *Theoret. Comput. Sci.* **2**, 147–154.

Shamir, A. [1990], "IP=PSPACE," Proc. 31st Ann. IEEE Symp. Foundations Comput. Sci., 11–15; also in final form in *J. ACM* **39** (1992), 869–877.

Shen, A. [1992], "IP=PSPACE: simplified proof," *J. ACM* **39**, 878–880.

Shepherdson, J.C., and H.E. Sturgis [1963], "Computability of recursive functions," *J. ACM* **10**, 217–255.

Shmoys, D.B., and E. Tardos [1995], "Computational complexity," in *Handbook of Combinatorics*, R.L. Graham, M. Grötschel, and L. Lovász, eds., North-Holland, Amsterdam; Vol. II, 1599–1645.

Simon, J. [1977], "On the difference between the one and the many," Lecture Notes in Comput. Sci., Vol. 52, Springer Verlag, Berlin, 480–491.

Sommerhalder, R., and S.C. van Westrhenen [1988]. *The Theory of Computability: Programs, Machines, Effectiveness, and Feasibility.* Addison-Wesley, Wokingham, England.

Stockmeyer, L.J. [1976], "The polynomial-time hierarchy," *Theor. Comput. Sci.* **3**, 1–22.

Stockmeyer, L.J. [1987], "Classifying computational complexity of problems," *J. Symbolic Logic* **52**, 1–43.

Stockmeyer, L.J., and A.K. Chandra. [1979], "Provably difficult combinatorial games," *SIAM J. Comput.* **8**, 151–174.

Stockmeyer, L.J., and A.R. Meyer [1973], "Word problems requiring exponential time," Proc. 5th Ann. ACM Symp. on Theory of Computing, 1–9.

Szelepcsényi, R. [1987], "The method of forcing for nondeterministic automata," *Bull. of the EATCS* **33**, 96–100.

Thomason, A. [1978], "Hamiltonian cycles and uniquely edge colourable graphs," *Annals Discrete Math.* **3**, 259–268.

Tourlakis, G.J. [1984]. *Computability*. Reston Publishing Company, Reston, VA.

Tovey, C.A. [1984], "A simplified NP-complete satisfiability problem," *Discr. Appl. Math.* **8**, 85–89.

Turing, A.M. [1936], "On computable numbers, with an application to the Entscheidungsproblem," *Proc. London Mathematical Society*, Series 2, **42**, 230–265.

Valiant, L.G. [1979a], "The complexity of enumeration and reliability problems," *SIAM J. Comput.* **8**, 410–421.

Valiant, L.G. [1979b], "The complexity of computing the permanent," *Theoret. Comput. Sci.* **8**, 189–201.

Valiant, L.G., and V.V. Vazirani [1985], "NP is as easy as detecting unique solutions," Proc. 17th Ann. ACM Symp. on Theory of Computing, 458–463.

van Emde Boas, P. [1990], "Machine models and simulations," in *Handbook of Theoretical Computer Science, Volume A: Algorithms and Complexity,* van Leeuwen, J., ed., MIT Press, Cambridge, MA, 1–66.

Vizing, V.G. [1964], "On the estimate of the chromatic class of a *p*-graph," *Diskret. Analiz* **3**, 25–30.

Wagner, K.W. [1988], "Bounded query computations," Proc. 3rd Ann. IEEE Conf. on Structure in Complexity Theory, 260–277.

Wagner, K., and G. Wechsung [1986]. *Computational Complexity.* D. Reidel Publishing, Dordrecht, Germany.

Wang, J. [1997], "Average-case computational complexity theory," in *Complexity Theory Retrospective*, L. Hemaspaandra and A. Selman, eds. Springer Verlag, Berlin.

Welsh, D.J.A. [1983], "Randomized algorithms," *Discr. Appl. Math.* **5**, 133–145.

Wilf, H.S. [1984], "Backtrack: an $O(1)$ average-time algorithm for the graph coloring problem," *Inf. Proc. Letters* **18**, 119–122.

Yao, A. C.-C. [1979], "Some complexity questions related to distributive computing," Proc. 11th Ann. ACM Symp. on Theory of Computing, 209–213.

Proofs

A.1 *Quod Erat Demonstrandum*, or What Is a Proof?

Our aim in this Appendix is not to present an essay on the nature of mathematical proofs. Many of the sections in the text provide a variety of arguments that can fuel such an essay, but our aim here is simply to present examples of proofs at various levels of formality and to illustrate the main techniques, so as to give the reader some help in developing his or her own proofs.

A proof can be viewed simply as a convincing argument. In casual conversation, we may challenge someone to "prove" her assertion, be it that she memorized the *Iliad* in the original Greek or that she skied a double-diamond run. The proof presented could be her reciting *ex tempore* a sizable passage from the *Iliad* (assuming we have a copy handy and can read Greek) or a picture or video of her skiing the run. In political, economic, or social discussions, we may present a detailed argument in support of some assertion. For instance a friend may have claimed that a needle-exchange program reduces both morbidity and medical costs; when challenged, he would proceed to cite statistics, prior studies, and, on the basis of his data, construct an argument. More formally, courts of law have standards of proof that they apply in adjudicating cases, particularly in criminal law; lawyers speak of "proof beyond a reasonable doubt" (needed to convict someone of a crime) or "preponderance of evidence" (a lesser standard used in civil cases).

None of these qualifies as a mathematical proof. A mathematical proof is intended to establish the truth of a precise, formal statement and is typically couched in the same precise, formal language. In 1657, the English mathematician John Dee wrote:

> Probability and sensible proof, may well serve in things naturall and is commendable: In Mathematicall reasonings, a probably Argument, is nothing regarded: nor yet the testimony of sens, any whit credited: But onely a perfect demonstration, of truths certain, necessary, and invincible: universally and necessarily concluded is allowed as sufficient for an Argument exactly and purely Mathematicall.

One of life's great pleasures for a theoretician is writing the well-earned "q.e.d." that marks the end of a proof; it stands for the Latin *quod erat demonstrandum*, meaning literally "what was to be proved."

Our typical vision of a proof is one or more pages of formulae and text replete with appearances of "therefore," "hence," etc. Yet, when two mathematicians talk about their work, one may present a proof to the other as a brief sketch of the key ideas involved and both would agree that the sketch was a proof. In Section 7.1, we present a dozen proofs of NP-completeness for various classes of complexity in about twenty-five pages: all of these proofs and many more were given by Richard Karp in 1972 in about three pages. In Section 9.3, we discuss average-case complexity, for the most part eschewing proofs because of their complexity; yet the groundwork for the entire theory, including the basic proof of completeness, was described by Leonid Levin in 1984 in a one-page paper! (Admittedly this paper set something of a record for conciseness.) At the other extreme, several recent proofs in mathematics have taken well over a hundred pages, with at least one requiring nearly five hundred. Faced with one of these extremely long proofs, the challenge to the reader is to keep in mind all of the relevant pieces; faced with a one-page foundation for an entire area, the challenge is to fill in the steps in the (necessarily sketchy) derivations. Conversely, the challenges to the writers of these proofs were to present the very long proof in as organized and progressive a manner as possible and to present the one-page foundation without omitting any of the key ideas.

The main goal of a proof is communication: the proof is written for other people to read. In consequence, the communication must be tailored to the audience. A researcher talking to another in the same area may be able to describe a very complex result in a few minutes; when talking to a colleague in another area, he may end up lecturing for a few hours. In consequence, proofs are not completely formal: a certain amount of "handwaving" (typified by the prefatory words "it is obvious that. . .") is characteristic, because the steps in the proof are tailored to the reader.

Most mathematicians believe that every proof can be made completely formal; that is, it can be written down as a succession of elementary derivation steps from a system of axioms according to a system of rules of logical inference. Such proofs stand at one extreme of the scale: their steps are tiny. Of course, writing down any but the most trivial proofs in this completely formal style would result in extremely long and completely unintelligible proofs; on the other hand, any such proof could be verified automatically by a simple program. At the other extreme is the conversation between two researchers in the same area, where key ideas are barely sketched—the steps are huge. Thus a proof is not so much a passive object as a process: the "prover" advances arguments and the "checker" verifies them. The prover and the checker need to be working at the same level (to be comfortable with the same size of step) in order for the process to work. An interesting facet of this process is that the prover and the checker are often the same person: a proof, or an attempt at one, is often the theoretician's most reliable tool and best friend in building new theories and proposing new assertions. The attempt at proof either establishes the correctness of the assertion or points out the flaws by "stalling" at some point in the attempt. By the same token, a proof is also the designer's best friend: an attempt at proving the correctness of a design will surely uncover any remaining flaw.

In consequence, proofs cannot really be absolute; even after a proof is written, its usefulness depends on the audience. Worse yet, there is no absolute standard: just because our proof convinced us (or several people) does not make the proof correct. (Indeed, there have been several examples of proofs advanced in the last century that turned out to be flawed; perhaps the most celebrated example is the four-color theorem, which states that every planar graph can be colored with four colors. The theorem was known, as a conjecture, for several centuries and received several purported proofs in the 19th and 20th centuries, until the currently accepted proof—which fills in omissions of previous proofs, in part through an enormous, computer-driven, case analysis.) Of course, if every proof were written in completely formal style, then it could be verified mechanically. But no one would ever have the patience to write a proof in that style—this entire textbook would barely be large enough to contain one of its proofs if written in that style.

Fortunately mathematicians and other scientists have been writing and reading proofs for a long time and have evolved a certain style of communication. Most proofs are written in plain text with the help of formulae but are organized in a fairly rigid manner. The use of language is also somewhat codified—as in the frequent use of verbs such as "let" or "follow" and adverbs or conjunctions such as "therefore" or "hence." The aim is to keep the flow of a natural language but to structure the argument and reduce the ambiguity inherent in a natural language so as to make it possible to believe that the argument could be couched in a completely formal manner if one so desired (and had the leisure and patience to do it).

A.2   Proof Elements

The beginning for any proof is an *assertion*—the statement to be proved. The assertion is often in the form of an implication (if A then B), in which case we call the antecedent of the implication (A), the *hypothesis*, and its consequent (B), the *conclusion*. Of course, the assertion does not stand alone but is inspired by a rich context, so that, in addition to the stated hypothesis, all of the relevant knowledge in the field can be drawn upon.

The proof then proceeds to establish the conclusion by drawing on the hypothesis and on known results. Progress is made by using *rules of inference*. For the most part, only two rules need to be remembered, both rules with which we are familiar:

- The rule of *modus ponens*: Given that A is true and given that the implication $A \Rightarrow B$ is true, conclude that B is true:

$$A \wedge (A \Rightarrow B) \vdash B$$

- The rule of *(hypothetical) syllogism*: Given that the two implications $A \Rightarrow B$ and $B \Rightarrow C$ are true, conclude that the implication $A \Rightarrow C$ is also true:

$$(A \Rightarrow B) \wedge (B \Rightarrow C) \vdash (A \Rightarrow C)$$

For the second rule, we would simply note that implication is a transitive relation. Most other rules of inference are directly derived from these two and from basic Boolean algebra (such as de Morgan's law). For instance, the rule of *modus tollens* can be written

$$\overline{A} \wedge (B \Rightarrow A) \vdash \overline{B}$$

but is easily recognizable as *modus ponens* by replacing $(B \Rightarrow A)$ by its equivalent contrapositive $(\overline{A} \Rightarrow \overline{B})$; as another example, the rule of *disjunctive syllogism* can be written as

$$\overline{A} \wedge (A \vee B) \vdash B$$

but is recognizable as another use of *modus ponens* by remembering that $(X \Rightarrow Y)$ is equivalent to $(\overline{X} \vee Y)$ and so replacing $(A \vee B)$ by the equivalent $\overline{A} \Rightarrow B$.

A completely formal proof starts from the *axioms* of the theory. Axioms were perhaps best described by Thomas Jefferson in another context: "We hold these truths to be self-evident..." Axioms are independent of each other (one cannot be proved from the others) and together supply a sufficient basis for the theory. (A good axiomatization of a theory is an extremely difficult endeavor.) A formal proof then proceeds by applying rules of inference to the axioms until the conclusion is obtained. This is not to say that every proof is just a linear chain of inferences: most proofs build several lines of derivation that get suitably joined along the way. Of course, since implication is transitive, there is no need to go back to the axioms for every new proof: it suffices to start from previously proved results.

A mathematical proof is thus a collection of valid inferences, from known results and from the hypothesis of the theorem, that together lead to the conclusion. For convenience, we can distinguish among several proof structures: constructive proofs build up to the conclusion from the hypothesis; contradiction proofs use the law of excluded middle (a logic statement must be either true or false—there is no third choice[1]) to affirm the conclusion without deriving it from the hypothesis; induction proofs use the induction principle at the heart of counting to move from the particular to the general; and diagonalization proofs combine induction and contradiction into a very powerful tool. In the following section we take up each style in turn.

A.3 Proof Techniques

A.3.1 Construction: Linear Thinking

In its simplest form, a proof is simply a mathematical derivation, where each statement follows from the previous one by application of some elementary algebraic or logical rule. In many cases, the argument is constructive in the sense that it builds a structure, the existence of which establishes the truth of the assertion. A straight-line argument from hypothesis to conclusion typically falls in this category.

---

[1] Indeed, the scholarly name for this law is *tertium non datur*, Latin for "there is no third."

An example of a simple mathematical derivation is a proof that, if n is an odd integer, then so is n^2. Because n is an odd integer, we can write $n = 2k + 1$ for some integer k—we are using the hypothesis. We can then express n^2 as $(2k + 1)^2$. Expanding and regrouping (using known facts about arithmetic, such as associativity, distributivity, and commutativity of addition and multiplication), we get

$$n^2 = (2k + 1)^2 = 4k^2 + 4k + 1 = 2(2k^2 + 2k) + 1 = 2m + 1$$

where we have set $m = 2k^2 + 2k$, an integer. Thus n^2 is itself of the form $2m + 1$ for some integer m and hence is odd, the desired conclusion. We have constructed n^2 from an odd number n in such a way as to show conclusively that n^2 is itself odd.

Even in strict algebraic derivations, the line may not be unique or straight. A common occurrence in proofs is a *case analysis*: we break the universe of possibilities down into a few subsets and examine each in turn. As a simple example, consider proving that, if the integer n is not divisible by 3, then n^2 must be of the form $3k + 1$ for some integer k. If n is not divisible by 3, then it must be of the form $3m + 1$ or $3m + 2$ for some integer m. We consider the two cases separately. If n is of the form $3m + 1$, then we can write n^2 as $(3m + 1)^2$; expanding and regrouping, we get

$$n^2 = (3m + 1)^2 = 9m^2 + 6m + 1 = 3(3m^2 + 2m) + 1 = 3l + 1$$

where we have set $l = 3m^2 + 2m$, an integer. Thus n^2 is of the desired form in this case. If, on the other hand, n is the form $3m + 2$, then we get

$$n^2 = (3m + 2)^2 = 9m^2 + 12m + 4 = 9m^2 + 12m + 3 + 1$$
$$= 3(3m^2 + 4m + 1) + 1 = 3l' + 1$$

where we have set $l' = 3m^2 + 4m + 1$, an integer. Thus n^2 is of the desired form in this second case; overall, then, n^2 is always of the desired form and we have completed our proof.

In this text, many of our proofs have to do with sets. In particular, we often need to prove that two sets, call them S and T, with apparently quite different definitions, are in fact equal. In order to prove $S = T$, we need to show that every element of S belongs to T (i.e., we need to prove $S \subseteq T$) and, symmetrically, that every element of T belongs to S (i.e., we need to prove $T \subseteq S$). Thus a proof of set equality always has two parts. The same is true of any proof of equivalence (typically denoted by the English phrase "if and only if"): one part proves the implication in one direction (A if B, or, in logic notation, $B \Rightarrow A$) and the other part proves the implication in the other direction (A only if B or $A \Rightarrow B$). When we have to prove the equivalence of several statements, we prove a circular chain of implications instead of proving each equivalence in turn: $A \Rightarrow B \Rightarrow \cdots \Rightarrow Z \Rightarrow A$. By transitivity, every statement implies every other statement and thus all are equivalent.

We give just one small example. We prove that the following three characterizations of a finite tree are equivalent:

1. It is an acyclic and connected graph.
2. It has one more vertex than edges and is acyclic.
3. It has a unique simple path between any two vertices.

We construct three proofs. First we show that the first characterization implies the second. Both require the graph to be acyclic; assume then that the graph is also connected. In order for a graph of n vertices to be connected, it has to have at least $n - 1$ edges because every vertex must have at least one edge connecting it to the rest of the graph. But the graph cannot have more than $n - 1$ edges: adding even one more edge to the connected graph, say from vertex a to vertex b, creates a cycle, since there is already a path from a to b.

Next we show that the second characterization implies the third. Since our graph is acyclic, it will have at most one path between any two vertices. (If there were two distinct simple paths between the same two vertices, they would form a cycle from the first vertex where they diverge to the first vertex where they reconverge.) We note that an acyclic graph with any edges at all must have a vertex of degree 1—if all degrees were higher, the graph would have at least one cycle. (Vertices of degree 0 clearly do not affect this statement.) To prove that the graph is connected, we use induction, which we discuss in detail in a later section. If the graph has two vertices and one edge, it is clearly connected. Assume then that all acyclic graphs of n vertices and $n - 1$ edges, for some $n \geqslant 1$, are connected and consider an acyclic graph of $n + 1$ vertices and n edges. This graph has a vertex of degree 1; if we remove it and its associated edge, the result is an acyclic graph of n vertices and $n - 1$ edges, which is connected by the inductive hypothesis. But then the entire graph is connected, since the vertex we removed is connected to the rest of the graph by an edge.

Finally, we show that the third characterization implies the first. If there is a simple path between any two vertices, the graph is connected; if, in addition, the simple path is always unique, the graph must be acyclic (in any cycle, there are always two paths between two vertices, going around the cycle in both directions).

A.3.2   Contradiction: *Reductio ad Absurdum*

As we have stated before, many theorems take the form of implications, i.e., assertions of the form "given A, prove B." The simplest way to prove such an assertion is a straight-line proof that establishes the validity of the implication $A \Rightarrow B$, since then *modus ponens* ensures that, given A, B must also be true. An implication is equivalent to its contrapositive, that is, $A \Rightarrow B$ is equivalent to $\overline{B} \Rightarrow \overline{A}$. Now suppose that, in addition to our hypothesis A, we also assume that the conclusion is false, that is, we assume $\overline{B}$. Then, if we can establish the contrapositive, we can use *modus ponens* with it and $\overline{B}$ to obtain $\overline{A}$, which, together with our hypothesis A, yields a contradiction. This is the principle behind a proof by contradiction: it proceeds "backwards," from the negated conclusion back to a negated hypothesis and thus a contradiction. This contradiction shows that the conclusion cannot be false; by the law of excluded middle, the conclusion must then be true.

Let us prove that a chessboard of even dimensions (the standard chessboard is an 8×8 grid, but $2n \times 2n$ grids can also be considered) that is missing its leftmost top square and its rightmost bottom square (the end squares on the main diagonal) cannot be tiled with dominoes. Assume we could do it and think of each domino as painted black and white, with one white square and one black square. The situation is depicted in Figure A.1. In any tiling, we can always place the dominoes so that their black and white squares coincide with the black and white squares of the chessboard—any two adjacent squares on the board have opposite colors. Observe that all squares on a diagonal bear the same color, so that our chessboard will have unequal numbers of black and white squares—one of the numbers will exceed the other by two. However, any tiling by dominoes will have strictly equal numbers of black and white squares, a contradiction.

Figure A.1   An 8×8 chessboard with missing opposite corners and a domino tile.

Proofs by contradiction are often much easier than direct, straight-line proofs because the negated conclusion is added to the hypotheses and thus gives us one more tool in our quest. Moreover, that tool is generally directly applicable, since it is, by its very nature, intimately connected to the problem. As an example, let us look at a famous proof by contradiction known since ancient times: we prove that the square root of 2 is not a rational number. Let us then assume that it is a rational number; we can write $\sqrt{2} = a/b$, where a and b have no common factor (the fraction is irreducible). Having formulated the negated conclusion, we can now use it to good effect. We square both sides to obtain $2b^2 = a^2$, from which we conclude that a^2 must be even; then a must also be even, because it cannot be odd (we have just shown that the square of an odd number is itself odd). Therefore we write $a = 2k$ for some k. Substituting in our first relation, we obtain $2b^2 = 4k^2$, or $b^2 = 2k^2$, so that b^2, and thus also b, must be even. But then both a and b are even and the fraction a/b is not irreducible, which contradicts our hypothesis. We conclude that $\sqrt{2}$ is not a rational number. However, the proof has shown us only what $\sqrt{2}$ is not—it has not constructed a clearly irrational representation of the number, such as a decimal expansion with no repeating period.

Another equally ancient and equally famous result asserts that there is an infinity of primes. Assume that there exists only a finite number of primes; denote by n this number and denote these n primes by $p_1, \ldots, p_n$. Now consider the new number $m = 1 + (p_1 \cdot p_2 \cdot \ldots \cdot p_n)$. By construction, m is not divisible by any of the p_is. Thus either m itself is prime, or it has a prime factor other than the p_is. In either case, there exists a prime number other than the p_is, contradicting our hypothesis. Hence there is an infinity of prime numbers. Again, we have not shown how to construct a new prime beyond the collection of n primes already assumed—we have learned only that such a prime exists. (In this case, however, we have strong clues: the new number m is itself a new prime, or it has a new prime as one of its factors; thus turning the existential argument into a constructive one might not prove too hard.)

A.3.3 Induction: the Domino Principle

In logic, induction means the passage from the particular to the general. Induction enables us to prove the validity of a general result applicable to a countably infinite universe of examples. In practice, induction is based on the natural numbers. In order to show that a statement applies to all $n \in \mathbb{N}$, we prove that it applies to the first natural number—what is called the *basis* of the induction—then verify that, if it applies to any natural number, it must also apply to the next—what is called the *inductive step*. The induction principle then says that the statement must apply to all natural numbers. The induction principle can be thought of as the *domino principle*: if you set up a chain of dominoes, each upright on its edge, in such a way that the fall of domino i unavoidably causes the fall of domino $i + 1$, then it suffices to make the *first* domino fall to cause the fall of *all* dominoes. The first domino is the basis; the inductive step is the placement of the dominoes that ensures that, if a domino falls, it causes the fall of its successor in the chain. The step is only a potential: nothing happens until domino i falls. In terms of logic, the induction step is simply a generic implication: "if $P(i)$ then $P(i + 1)$"; since the implication holds for every i, we get a chain of implications,

$$\cdots \Rightarrow P(i - 1) \Rightarrow P(i) \Rightarrow P(i + 1) \Rightarrow \cdots$$

equivalent to our chain of dominoes. As in the case of our chain of dominoes, nothing happens to the chain of implications until some true statement, $P(0)$, is "fed" to the chain of implications. As soon as we know that $P(0)$ is true, we can use successive applications of *modus ponens* to propagate through the chain of implications:

$$P(0) \wedge (P(0) \Rightarrow P(1)) \vdash P(1)$$
$$P(1) \wedge (P(1) \Rightarrow P(2)) \vdash P(2)$$
$$P(2) \wedge (P(2) \Rightarrow P(3)) \vdash P(3)$$

$$\cdots$$

In our domino analogy, $P(i)$ stands for "domino i falls."

Induction is used to prove statements that are claimed to be true for an infinite, yet countable set; every time a statement uses " ... " or "and so on," you can be sure that induction is what is needed to prove it. Any object defined recursively will need induction proofs to establish its properties. We illustrate each application with one example.

Let us prove the equality

$$1^2 + 3^2 + 5^2 + \ldots + (2n - 1)^2 = n(4n^2 - 1)/3$$

The dots in the statement indicate the probable need for induction. Let us then use it for a proof. The base case is $n = 1$; in this case, the left-hand side has the single element 1^2 and indeed equals the right-hand side. Let us then assume that the relationship holds for all values of n up to some k and examine what happens with $n = k + 1$. The new left-hand side is the old left-hand side plus $(2(k+1)-1)^2 = (2k+1)^2$; the old left-hand side obeys the conditions of the inductive hypothesis and so we can write it as $k(4k^2 - 1)/3$. Hence the new left-hand side is

$$k(4k^2 - 1)/3 + (2k+1)^2 = (4k^3 - k + 12k^2 + 12k + 3)/3$$
$$= ((k+1)(4k^2 + 8k + 3))/3$$
$$= ((k+1)(4(k+1)^2 - 1))/3$$

which proves the step.

The famous Fibonacci numbers are defined recursively with a recursive step, $F(n+1) = F(n) + F(n-1)$, and with two base cases, $F(0) = 0$ and $F(1) = 1$. We want to prove the equality

$$F^2(n+2) - F^2(n+1) = F(n)F(n+3)$$

We can easily verify that the equality holds for both $n = 0$ (both sides equal 0) and $n = 1$ (both sides equal 3). We needed two bases because the recursive definition uses not just the past step, but the past two steps. Now assume that the relationship holds for all n up to some k and let us examine the situation for $n = k + 1$. We can write

$$F^2(k+3) - F^2(k+2)$$
$$= (F(k+2) + F(k+1))^2 - F^2(k+2)$$
$$= F^2(k+2) + F^2(k+1) + 2F(k+2)F(k+1) - F^2(k+2)$$
$$= F^2(k+1) + 2F(k+2)F(k+1)$$
$$= F(k+1)(F(k+1) + 2F(k+2))$$
$$= F(k+1)(F(k+1) + F(k+2) + F(k+2))$$
$$= F(k+1)(F(k+3) + F(k+2))$$
$$= F(k+1)F(k+4)$$

which proves the step.

Do not make the mistake of thinking that, just because a statement is true for a large number of values of n, it must be true for all n.[2] A famous example (attributed to Leonhard Euler) illustrating this fallacy is

_____

[2] Since engineers and natural scientists deal with measurements, they are accustomed to errors and are generally satisfied to see that most measurements fall close to the predicted values. Hence the following joke about "engineering induction." An engineer asserted that all odd numbers larger than 1 are prime. His reasoning went as follows: "3 is prime, 5 is prime, 7 is prime ... Let's see, 9 is not prime, but 11 is prime and 13 is prime; so 9 must be a measurement error and all odd numbers are indeed prime."

the polynomial $n^2 + n + 41$: if you evaluate it for $n = 0, \ldots, 39$, you will find that every value thus generated is a prime number! From observing the first 40 values, it would be very tempting to assert that $n^2 + n + 41$ is always a prime; however, evaluating this polynomial for $n = 40$ yields $1681 = 41^2$ (and it is obvious that evaluating it for $n = 41$ yields a multiple of 41). Much worse yet is the simple polynomial $991n^2 + 1$. Write a simple program to evaluate it for a range of nonzero natural numbers and verify that it never produces a perfect square. Indeed, within the range of integers that your machine can handle, it cannot produce a perfect square; however, if you use an unbounded-precision arithmetic package and spend years of computer time on the project, you may discover that, for $n = 12{,}055{,}735{,}790{,}331{,}359{,}447{,}442{,}538{,}767$, the result *is* a perfect square! In other words, you could have checked on the order of 10^{28} values before finding a counterexample!

While these examples stress the importance of proving the correctness of the induction step, the basis is equally important. The basis is the start of the induction; if it is false, then we should be able to "prove" absurd statements. A simple example is the following "proof" that every natural number is equal to its successor. We shall omit the basis and look only at the step. Assume then that the statement holds for all natural numbers up to some value k; in particular, we have $k = k + 1$. Then adding 1 to each side of the equation yields $k + 1 = k + 2$ and thus proves the step. Hence, if our assertion is valid for k, it is also valid for $k + 1$. Have we proved that every natural number is equal to its successor (and thus that all natural numbers are equal)? No, because, in order for the assertion to be valid for $k + 1$, it must first be valid for k; in order to be valid for k, it must first be valid for $k - 1$; and so forth, down to what should be the basis. But we have no basis—we have not identified some fixed value k_0 for which we can prove the assertion $k_0 = k_0 + 1$. Our dominoes are not falling because, even though we have set them up so that a fall would propagate, the first domino stands firm.

Finally, we have to be careful how we make the step. Consider the following flawed argument. We claim to show that, in any group of two or more people where at least two people are blond, everyone must be blond. Our basis is for $n = 2$: by hypothesis, any group we consider has at least two blond people in it. Since our group has exactly two people, they are both blond and we are done. Now assume that the statement holds for all groups of up to n ($n \geq 2$) people and consider a group of $n + 1$ people. This group contains at least two blond people, call them John and Mary. Remove from the group some person other than John and Mary, say Tim. The remaining group has n people in it, including two blond ones (John and Mary), and so it obeys the inductive hypothesis; hence everyone in that group is blond. The only question concerns Tim; but bring him back and now remove from the group someone else (still not John or Mary), say Jane. (We have just shown that Jane must be blond.) Again, by inductive hypothesis, the remaining group is composed entirely of blond people, so that Tim is blond and thus every one of the $n + 1$ people in the group is blond, completing our "proof" of the inductive step. So what went wrong? We can look at the flaw in one of two ways. One obvious flaw is that the argument fails for $n + 1 = 3$, since we will not find both a Tim and a Jane and thus will be unable to show that the third person in the group is blond. The underlying reason is more subtle, but fairly clear in the "proof" structure: we have used *two different* successor functions in moving from a set of size n to a set of size $n + 1$.

Induction works with natural numbers, but in fact can be used with any structures that can be linearly ordered, effectively placing them into one-to-one correspondence with the natural numbers. Let us look at two simple examples, one in geometry and the other in programming.

Assume you want to tile a kitchen with a square floor of size $2^n \times 2^n$, leaving one unit-sized untiled square in the corner for the plumbing. For decorative reasons (or because they were on sale), you want to use only L-shaped tiles, each tile covering exactly three unit squares. Figure A.2 illustrates the problem. Can it be done? Clearly, it can be done for a hamster-sized kitchen of size 2×2, since that will take exactly one tile. Thus we have proved the basis for $n = 1$. Let us then assume that all kitchens of size up to $2^n \times 2^n$ with one unit-size corner square missing can be so tiled and consider a kitchen of size $2^{n+1} \times 2^{n+1}$. We can mentally divide the kitchen into four equal parts, each a square of size $2^n \times 2^n$. Figure A.3(a) illustrates the result. One of these parts has the plumbing hole for the full kitchen

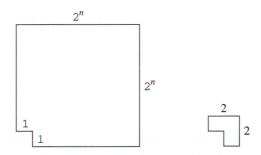

Figure A.2   The kitchen floor plan and an L-shaped tile.

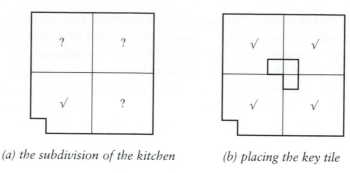

(a) the subdivision of the kitchen   (b) placing the key tile

Figure A.3   The recursive solution for tiling the kitchen.

and so obeys the inductive hypothesis; hence we can tile it. The other three, however, have no plumbing hole and must be completely tiled. How do we find a way to apply the inductive hypothesis? This is typically the crux of any proof by induction and often requires some ingenuity. Here, we place one L-shaped tile just outside the corner of the part with the plumbing hole, so that this tile has one unit-sized square in each of the other three parts, in fact at a corner of each of the other three parts, as illustrated in Figure A.3(b). Now what is left to tile in each part meets the inductive hypothesis and thus can be tiled. We have thus proved that the full original kitchen (minus its plumbing hole) can be tiled, completing the induction step. Figure A.4 shows the tilings for the smallest three kitchens. Of course, the natural numbers figure prominently in this proof—the basis was for $n = 1$ and the step moved from n to $n + 1$.

As another example, consider the programming language Lisp. Lisp is based on atoms and on the list constructor `cons` and two matching destructors `car` and `cdr`. A list is either an atom or an object built with the

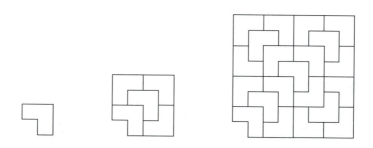

Figure A.4   Recursive tilings for the smallest three kitchens.

constructor from other lists. Assume the existence of a Boolean function
`listp` that tests whether its argument is a list or an atom (returning true
for a list) and define the new constructor `append` as follows.

```
(defn append (x y)
  (if (listp x)
    (cons (car x) (append (cdr x) y))
    y))
```

Let us prove that the function `append` is associative; that is, let us prove
the correctness of the assertion

```
(equal (append (append a b) c)
       (append a (append b c)))
```

We proceed by induction on `a`. In the base case, `a` is an atom, so that
`(listp a)` fails. The first term, `(append (append a b) c)`, becomes
`(append b c)`; and the second term, `(append a (append b c))`,
becomes `(append b c)`; hence the two are equal. Assume then that
the equality holds for all lists involving at most n uses of the constructor
and let us examine the list `a` defined by `(cons a' a")`, where both `a'`
and `a"` meet the conditions of the inductive hypothesis. The first term,
`(append (append a b) c)`, can be rewritten as

```
append (append (cons a' a") b) c
```

Applying the definition of `append`, we can rewrite this expression as

```
append (cons a' (append a" b)) c
```

A second application yields

```
cons a' (append (append a" b) c)
```

Now we can use the inductive hypothesis on the sequence of two append
operations to yield

```
cons a' (append a" (append b c))
```

The second term, `(append a (append b c))`, can be rewritten as

```
append (cons a' a") (append b c)
```

Applying the definition of `append` yields

```
cons a' (append a" (append b c))
```

which is exactly what we derived from the first term. Hence the first
and second terms are equal and we have proved the inductive step. Here
again, the natural numbers make a fairly obvious appearance, counting the
number of applications of the constructor of the abstract data type.

Induction is not limited to one process of construction: with several distinct construction mechanisms, we can still apply induction by verifying that each construction mechanism obeys the requirement. In such a case, we still have a basis but now have several steps—one for each constructor. This approach is critical in proving that abstract data types and other programming objects obey desired properties, since they often have more than one constructor.

Induction is very powerful in that it enables us to reduce the proof of some complex statement to two much smaller endeavors: the basis, which is often quite trivial, and the step, which benefits immensely from the inductive hypothesis. Thus rather than having to plot a course from the hypothesis all the way to the distant conclusion, we have to plot a course only from step n to step $n + 1$, a much easier problem. Of course, both the basis and the step need proofs; there is no reason why these proofs have to be straight-line proofs, as we have used so far. Either one may use case analysis, contradiction, or even a nested induction. We give just one simple example, where the induction step is proved by contradiction using a case analysis.

We want to prove that, in any subset of $n + 1$ numbers chosen from the set $\{1, 2, \ldots, 2n\}$, there must exist a pair of numbers such that one member of the pair divides the other. The basis, for $n = 1$ is clearly true, since the set is $\{1, 2\}$ and we must select both of its elements. Assume then that the statement holds for all n up to some k and consider the case $n = k + 1$. We shall use contradiction: thus we assume that we can find some subset S of $k + 2$ elements chosen from the set $\{1, 2, \ldots, 2k + 2\}$ such that no element of S divides any other element of S. We shall prove that we can use this set S to construct a new set S' of $k + 1$ elements chosen from $\{1, 2, \ldots, 2k\}$ such that no element of S' divides any other element of S', which contradicts the induction hypothesis and establishes our conclusion, thereby proving the induction step. We distinguish three cases: (i) S contains neither $2k + 1$ nor $2k + 2$; (ii) S contains one of these elements but not the other; and (iii) S contains both $2k + 1$ and $2k + 2$. In the first case, we remove an arbitrary element of S to form S', which thus has $k + 1$ elements, none larger than $2k$, and none dividing any other. In the second case, we remove the one element of S that exceeds $2k$ to form S', which again will have the desired properties. The third case is the interesting one: we must remove both $2k + 1$ and $2k + 2$ from S but must then add some other element (not in S) not exceeding $2k$ to obtain an S' of the correct size. Since S contains $2k + 2$, it cannot contain $k + 1$ (otherwise one element, $k + 1$, would divide another, $2k + 2$); we thus add $k + 1$ to replace the two elements $2k + 1$ and $2k + 2$ to form S'. It remains to show that no element of S' divides any other; the only candidate pairs are those involving $k + 1$, since all others were pairs in S. The element $k + 1$ cannot divide any other, since all others are too small (none exceeds $2k$). We claim that no element of S' (other than $k + 1$ itself) divides $k + 1$: any such element is also an element of S and, dividing $k + 1$, would also divide $2k + 2$ and would form with $2k + 2$ a forbidden pair in S. Thus S' has, in all three cases, the desired properties.

A.3.4   Diagonalization: Putting it all Together

Diagonalization was devised by Georg Cantor in his proof that a nonempty set cannot be placed into a one-to-one correspondence with its power set. In its most common form, diagonalization is a contradiction proof based on induction: the inductive part of the proof constructs an element, the existence of which is the desired contradiction. There is no mystery to diagonalization: instead, it is simply a matter of putting together the inductive piece and the contradiction piece. Several simple examples are given in Sections 2.8 and 2.9. We content ourselves here with giving a proof of Cantor's result. Any diagonalization proof uses the implied correspondence in order to set up an enumeration. In our case, we assume that a set S can be placed into one-to-one correspondence with its power set 2^S according to some bijection f. Thus given a set element x, we have uniquely associated with it a subset of the set, $f(x)$. Now either the subset $f(x)$ contains x or it does not; we construct a new subset of S using this information for each x. Specifically, our new subset, call it A, will contain x if and only if $f(x)$ does not contain x; given a bijection f, our new subset A is well defined. But we claim that there cannot exist a y in S such that $f(y)$ equals A. If such a y existed, then we would have $f(y) = A$ and yet, by construction, y would belong to A if and only if y did not belong to $f(y)$, a contradiction. Thus the bijection f cannot exist. More precisely, any mapping from S to 2^S cannot be surjective: there must be subsets of S, such as A, that cannot be associated with any element of S—in other words, there are "more" subsets of S than elements of S.

A.4   How to Write a Proof

Whereas developing a proof for a new theorem is a difficult and unpredictable endeavor, (re)proving a known result is often a matter of routine. The reason is that the result itself gives us guidance in how to prove it: whether to use induction, contradiction, both, or neither is often apparent from the nature of the statement to be proved. Moreover, proving a theorem is a very goal-oriented activity, with a very definite and explicit goal;

effectively, it is a path-finding problem: among all the derivations we can create from the hypotheses, which ones will lead us to the desired conclusion? This property stands in contrast to most design activities, where the target design remains ill-defined until very near the end of the process.

Of course, knowing where to go helps only if we can see a path to it; if the goal is too distant, path finding becomes difficult. A common problem that we all experience in attempting to derive a proof is getting lost on the wrong path, spending hours in fruitless derivations that do not seem to take us any closer to our goal. Such wanderings are the reason for the existence of lemmata—signposts in the wilderness. A lemma is intended as an intermediate result on the way to our main goal. (The word comes from the Greek and so has a Greek inflection for its plural; the Greek word $\lambda\varepsilon\mu\mu\alpha$ denotes what gets peeled, such as the skin of a fruit—we can see how successive lemmata peel away layers of mathematics to allow us to reach the core truth.) When faced with an apparently unreachable goal, we can formulate some intermediate, simpler, and much closer goals and call them lemmata. Not only will we gain the satisfaction of completing at least some proofs, but we will also have some advance positions from which to mount our assault on the final goal. (If these statements are reminiscent of explorations, military campaigns, or mountaineering expeditions, it is because these activities indeed resemble the derivation of proofs.) Naturally, some lemmata end up being more important than the original goal, often because the goal was very specialized, whereas the lemma provided·a broadly applicable tool.

Once we (believe that we) have a proof, we need to write it down. The first thing we should do is to write it for ourselves, to verify that we indeed have a proof. This write-up should thus be fairly formal, most likely more formal than the write-up we shall use later to communicate to colleagues; it might also be uneven in its formality, simply because there will be some points where we need to clarify our own thoughts and others where we are 100% confident. In the final write-up, however, we should avoid uneven steps in the derivation—once the complete proof is clear to us, we should be able to write it down as a smooth flow. We should, of course, avoid giant steps; in particular, we would do well to minimize the use of "it is obvious that."[3] Yet we do not want to bore the reader with

---

[3] A professor of mathematics was beginning his lecture on the proof of a somewhat tricky theorem. He wrote a statement on the board and said to the class, "It is obvious that this follows from the hypothesis." He then fell silent and stepped back looking somewhat puzzled. For the next forty minutes, he stood looking at the board, occasionally scratching his head, completely absorbed in his thoughts and ignoring the students, who fidgeted in their chairs and kept making aborted attempts to leave. Finally, just a few minutes before the end of the period, the professor smiled, lifted his head, looked at the class, said, "Yes, it is obvious," and moved on with the proof.

unnecessary, pedantic details, at least not after the first few steps. If the proof is somewhat convoluted, we should not leave it to the reader to untangle the threads of logic but should prepare a description of the main ideas and their relationships before plunging into the technical part. In particular, it is always a good idea to tell the reader if the proof will proceed by construction, by induction, by contradiction, by diagonalization, or by some combination. If the proof still looks tangled in spite of these efforts, we should consider breaking off small portions of it into supporting lemmata; typically, the more technical (and less enlightening) parts of a derivation are bundled in this manner into "technical" lemmata, so as to let the main ideas of the proof stand out. A proof is something that we probably took a long time to construct; thus it is also something that we should take the time to write as clearly and elegantly as possible.

We should note, however, that the result is what really matters: any correct proof at all, no matter how clunky, is welcome when breaking new ground. Many years often have to pass before the result can be proved by elegant and concise means. Perhaps the greatest mathematician, and certainly the greatest discrete mathematician, of the twentieth century, the Hungarian Paul Erdős (1913–1996), used to refer, only half-jokingly, to "The Book," where all great mathematical results—existing and yet to be discovered—are written with their best proofs. His own work is an eloquent testimony to the beauty of simple proofs for deep results: many of his proofs are likely to be found in The Book. As we grope for new results, our first proof rarely attains the clarity and elegance needed for inclusion into that lofty volume. However, history has shown that simple proofs often yield entirely new insights into the result itself and thus lead to new discoveries.

A.5 Practice

In this section we provide just a few examples of simple proofs to put into practice the precepts listed earlier. We keep the examples to a minimum, since the reader will find that most of the two hundred exercises in the main part of the text also ask for proofs.

Exercise A.1 *(construction)* Verify the correctness of the formula

$$(1 - x)^{-2} = 1 + 2x + 3x^2 + \dots$$

Exercise A.2 *(construction)* Prove that, for every natural number n, there exists a natural number m with at least n distinct divisors.

Exercise A.3 *(construction and case analysis)* Verify the correctness of the formula $\min(x, y) + \max(x, y) = x + y$ for any two real numbers x and y.

Exercise A.4 *(contradiction)* Prove that, if n is prime and not equal to 2, then n is odd.

Exercise A.5 *(contradiction)* Prove that $\sqrt{n}$ is irrational for any natural number n that is not a perfect square.

Exercise A.6 *(induction)* Prove that, if n is larger than 1, then n^2 is larger than n.

Exercise A.7 *(induction)* Verify the correctness of the formula

$$\sum_{i=1}^{n} i = \tfrac{1}{2}n(n+1)$$

Exercise A.8 *(induction)* Prove that $2^{2n} - 1$ is divisible by 3 for any natural number n.

Exercise A.9 *(induction)* Verify that the nth Fibonacci number can be described in closed form by

$$F_n = \frac{1}{\sqrt{5}} \left[\left(\frac{1+\sqrt{5}}{2} \right)^n - \left(\frac{1-\sqrt{5}}{2} \right)^n \right]$$

(This exercise requires some patience with algebraic manipulations.)

INDEX OF NAMED PROBLEMS

INDEX